ENCYCLOPEDIA OF
BATTLES IN NORTH AMERICA

ENCYCLOPEDIA OF
BATTLES IN
NORTH AMERICA

1517 to 1916

L. Edward Purcell and Sarah J. Purcell

Checkmark Books®
An imprint of Facts On File, Inc.

ENCYCLOPEDIA OF BATTLES IN NORTH AMERICA, 1517 to 1916

Copyright © 2000 by L. Edward Purcell and Sarah J. Purcell
Maps copyright © 2000 by Facts On File

Checkmark Books
An imprint of Facts On File, Inc.
11 Penn Plaza
New York NY 10001

Library of Congress Cataloging-in-Publication Data
Purcell, L. Edward
    Encyclopedia of battles in North America, 1517 to 1916 / L. Edward Purcell and Sarah J. Purcell.
    p. cm.
    Includes bibliographical references and index
    ISBN 0-8160-3350-1 (hardcover) ISBN 0-8160-4402-3 (pbk)
1. North America—History, Military Encyclopedias. 2. Battles—North America—History Encyclopedias.
I. Purcell, Sarah J. II. Title.
E446.5.P87 2000
970—dc221   99-3864

You can find Facts On File on the World Wide Web at http://www.factsonfile.com

Text and cover design by Cathy Rincon
Maps by Jeremy Eagle and Dale Williams

Printed in the United States of America

VB Scribe 10 9 8 7 6 5 4 3 2
   (pbk) 10 9 8 7 6 5 4 3 2 1

This book is printed on acid-free paper

ENCYCLOPEDIA OF
BATTLES IN
NORTH AMERICA

1517 to 1916

L. Edward Purcell and Sarah J. Purcell

An imprint of Facts On File, Inc.

ENCYCLOPEDIA OF BATTLES IN NORTH AMERICA, 1517 to 1916

Checkmark Books
An imprint of Facts On File, Inc.
11 Penn Plaza
New York NY 10001

Library of Congress Cataloging-in-Publication Data
Purcell, L. Edward
    Encyclopedia of battles in North America, 1517 to 1916 / L. Edward Purcell and Sarah J. Purcell.
        p.   cm.
    Includes bibliographical references and index
    ISBN 0-8160-3350-1 (hardcover)   ISBN 0-8160-4402-3 (pbk)
1. North America—History, Military Encyclopedias. 2. Battles—North America—History Encyclopedias.
I. Purcell, Sarah J. II. Title.
E446.5.P87   2000
970—dc221   99-3864

Checkmark Books are available at special discounts when purchased in bulk quantities for businesses, associations, institutions or sales promotions. Please call our Special Sales Department in New York at (212) 967-8800 or (800) 322-8755.

You can find Facts On File on the World Wide Web at http://www.factsonfile.com

Text and cover design by Cathy Rincon
Maps by Jeremy Eagle and Dale Williams

Printed in the United States of America

VB Scribe 10 9 8 7 6 5 4 3 2
    (pbk) 10 9 8 7 6 5 4 3 2 1

This book is printed on acid-free paper

DEDICATED TO THE MEN OF THE 33RD IOWA INFANTRY

MAP SYMBOLS

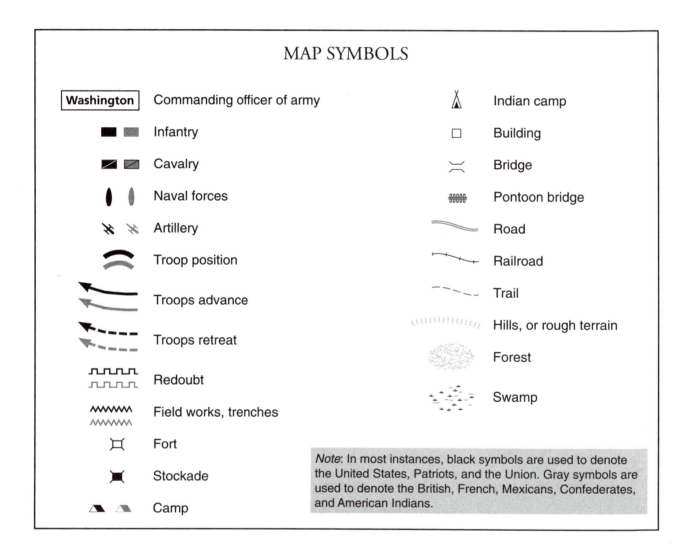

Washington	Commanding officer of army
■ ▨	Infantry
◩ ◩	Cavalry
● ◗	Naval forces
✸ ✸	Artillery
◠	Troop position
◀─	Troops advance
◀--	Troops retreat
⊓⊔⊓⊔	Redoubt
∿∿∿	Field works, trenches
⊐⊏	Fort
◆	Stockade
▲ ◣	Camp

⩓	Indian camp
□	Building
⌣⌣	Bridge
⊞⊞⊞	Pontoon bridge
〰	Road
┼┼┼	Railroad
– – –	Trail
⑊⑊⑊⑊	Hills, or rough terrain
❀	Forest
⌇	Swamp

Note: In most instances, black symbols are used to denote the United States, Patriots, and the Union. Gray symbols are used to denote the British, French, Mexicans, Confederates, and American Indians.

CONTENTS

Preface   xv

A TO Z ENTRIES   1

Adobe Walls   3

Agua Prieta   4

Alamance   4

Alamo   5

U.S.S. *Alfred* v. H.M.S. *Glasgow*   6

Allatoona Pass   6

Annapolis Royal (Port Royal)   6

Antietam (Sharpsburg)   7

Ash Hollow (Blue Lake)   10

Atlanta   10

Augusta (1780)   12

Augusta (1781)   12

Bad Axe River   14

Ball's Bluff   15

Batoche   15

Baton Rouge   16

Bear Paw Mountains   17

Bear River   17

Beaufort (Port Royal Island)   18

Beaver Dams   18

Beecher's Island   19

Belmont   19

Bennington   20

Bentonville   21

Big Bethel   22

Big Black River	22	Camden	42
Big Hole Basin	23	Camerone	45
Big Meadows	24	Camp Texas (Fort Texas)	46
Billingsport	24	Cedar Creek	46
Black Mingo Creek	24	Cedar Mountain	47
Blackstocks	25	Cedars	48
Bladensburg	25	Celaya	48
Bloody Brook (Pocumtuck, Deerfield)	26	Cempoallan	49
Bloody Swamp (Bloody Marsh, St. Simon's Island)	27	Cerro Gordo	50
Blue Licks	28	Chambly	52
Blue Savannah	28	Champion's Hill	52
Bound Brook	28	Champoton	53
Brandy Station (Fleetwood Hill, Beverley's Ford)	29	Chancellorsville	54
Brandywine	30	Chantilly (Ox Hill)	55
Briar Creek	31	Chapultepec	56
Brice's Cross Roads (Brice's Creek Roads, Guntown, Tishomingo Creek)	32	Charleston (Sullivan's Island)	57
Bristoe Station	32	Charleston	59
Buena Vista	33	Charlotte	60
Bull Run, First (Manassas)	35	Chateaugay (Châteauguay River)	60
Bull Run, Second (Manassas)	37	Chattanooga (Lookout Mountain, Missionary Ridge)	61
Bull's Ferry	39	Cheat Mountain (Elkwater)	63
Bunker Hill (Breed's Hill)	39	Cherry Valley	63
Bushy Run (Edge Hill)	41	U.S.S. *Chesapeake* v. H.M.S. *Shannon*	64
Calderón Bridge (Puente de Calderón)	42	Chesapeake Bay	64
		Chesapeake Capes	65

Chickamauga	66	Fair Oaks (Seven Pines)	88
Chickasaw Bluffs (Chickasaw Bayou)	67	Fallen Timbers	89
Chippewa	67	Falling Waters	90
Chrysler's Farm	69	Farmville and Highbridge	90
Churubusco	70	Fetterman Fight	91
Cloyd's Mountain	71	Fishdam Ford	91
Cold Harbor	71	Fisher's Hill	92
Columbus	72	Fishing Creek (Catawba Ford)	92
Combahee Ferry	73	Five Forks	93
U.S.S. *Congress* v. H.M.S. *Savage*	73	Fort Anne	94
U.S.S. *Constitution* v. H.M.S. *Guerrière*	74	Fort Beauséjour	94
Contreras (Padieras)	74	Fort Caroline	95
Cooch's Bridge (Iron Hill)	75	Fort Clinton and Fort Montgomery	95
Corinth	76	Fort Cumberland	96
Cowan's Ford	76	Fort Donelson	97
Cowpens	77	Fort Erie, First	98
Crampton's Gap	79	Fort Erie, Second	99
The Crater (Petersburg Mine Assault)	79	Fort Fisher (Terry's Expedition)	99
Cross Keys (Union Church)	80	Fort Frontenac	100
Dade's Battle	82	Fort George	101
Danbury Raid	82	Fort Henry	101
Drewry's Bluff	83	Fort Keyser	102
Emuckfau Creek	85	Fort Lee (Fort Constitution)	102
Enitachopco Creek	86	Fort McHenry	102
Eutaw Springs	86	Fort Mercer (Red Bank)	103

Fort Mifflin	104	Gaines's Mill	124
Fort Mims	105	Galveston	125
Fort Motte	105	Garnett's and Golding's Farm	125
Fort Necessity (Great Meadows)	106	Germantown	126
Fort Niagara	106	Gettysburg	128
Fort Pillow	107	Globe Tavern (Weldon Railroad, Six Mile House)	131
Fort Pulaski	108	Glorieta Pass	131
Fort Ridgely	109	Gloucester	132
Fort Stanwix	109	Goliad	133
Fort Stedman	110	Great Bridge	133
Fort Stephenson	111	Great Savannah	134
Fort Sumter	111	Great Swamp	134
Fort Ticonderoga (Fort Carillon)	112	Green Spring	135
Fort Ticonderoga (1775)	113	Guilford Courthouse	136
Fort Ticonderoga (July 1777)	113	Gwynn Island	137
Fort Ticonderoga (September 1777)	115	Hanging Rock	139
Fort Wagner (Battery Wagner)	115	Hanover Courthouse	140
Fort Washington	116	Harlem Heights	140
Fort Watson	117	Harmar's Defeat	141
Fort William Henry	117	Harpers Ferry	142
Franklin	118	Haw River (Pyle's Defeat)	143
Franklin's Crossing (Deep Run)	119	Helena	144
Fredericksburg	119	Hillsborough Raid	144
Frenchtown (River Raisin)	121	Hobkirk's Hill	145
Front Royal	122	Holly Springs	145

Horseshoe Bend	146	Lochry's Defeat	167
Hubbardton	147	Long Island	168
Irish Bend (Bayou Teche)	148	Long Sault	169
Island Number 10	149	Louisbourg (1745)	169
Iuka	149	Louisbourg (1758)	170
Jamestown (1622)	150	Lundy's Lane	171
Jamestown (1676)	151	Lynchburg	172
Johnstown	152	Mackinac Island (Fort Michilimackinac)	173
Julesburg	152	Malvern Hill	174
Kernstown, First	153	McDowell	174
Kernstown, Second	154	Mechanicsville (Ellison's Mill)	175
Kettle Creek	154	Memphis	176
Killdeer Mountain	155	Mesa (La Mesa)	176
King's Mountain	155	Milk Creek	176
Kip's Bay	157	Mill Springs (Logan Cross Road)	177
Klock's Field	157	Minisink	178
Knoxville (Fort Sanders)	157	Mobile Bay	178
Lake Erie (Put-in-Bay)	159	Molino del Rey	179
Lake George (Bloody Pond)	160	Monck's Corner	180
Lake Okeechobee	161	U.S.S. *Monitor* v. C.S.S. *Virginia* (*Monitor* v. *Merrimack*)	180
Lázaro	162	Monmouth	181
Lenud's Ferry	162	Monocacy	183
Lexington and Concord	163	Monongahela (Braddock's Defeat)	184
Lexington	164	Monterrey	185
Little Bighorn (Custer's Last Stand, Greasy Grass)	165	Montreal	186

Moore's Creek Bridge	187	Pea Ridge (Elkhorn Tavern)	209
Munfordville	187	U.S.S. *Peacock* v. H.M.S. *Epervier*	210
Mystic River	188	Pell's Point	210
Nashville	190	Pensacola	211
New London Raid	191	Perryville	211
New Market	191	Petersburg (1781)	212
New Orleans (1815)	192	Petersburg (1864–1865)	213
New Orleans (1862)	194	Philippi	213
New Ulm	195	Pilot Knob (Fort Davidson)	214
Newport	195	Plattsburg Bay (Lake Champlain, Plattsburg)	214
Newtown	196	Pleasant Hill Landing (Blair's Landing)	216
Ninety Six	197	Point Pleasant	217
La Noche Triste (Tenochtitlán)	198	Port Gibson	217
North Anna River (Hanover Junction, Jericho Mills, Taylor's Bridge)	199	Port Hudson	218
Oak Grove (King's Schoolhouse)	201	Port Republic	219
Ocean Pond (Olustee)	202	Port Royal (Annapolis Royal)	220
Okolona	202	Port Royal Sound (Forts Beauregard and Walker)	220
Oriskany	203	Potonchan	221
Otumba	203	Prairie Grove	221
Palo Alto	205	Princeton	222
Paoli	207	Puebla	223
Parker's Cross Roads	207	Puebla (Cinco de Mayo)	224
Parker's Ferry	207	Quebec (Plains of Abraham)	226
Parral	208	Quebec	227
Paulus Hook	208	Queenston	228

Quinby Bridge	230	San Gabriel	245
Quintan's Bridge	230	San Jacinto	246
Ramseur's Mill	231	San Pascual	247
Raymond	232	Sand Creek	248
Resaca de la Palma (Resaca de Guerrero)	232	Sandusky (Crawford's Defeat)	248
Rich Mountain	233	Santa Fe	249
Richmond	233	Saratoga, First (Freeman's Farm)	249
Ridgeway	234	Saratoga, Second (Bemis Heights)	251
Roanoke Island	234	Savage's Station (Allen's Farm, Peach Orchard)	253
Rocky Mount	235	Savannah (1778)	254
Rosebud Creek	235	Savannah (1779)	254
Rush Springs (Rush Creek)	236	Sayler's Creek	256
Sabine Crossroads (Mansfield)	237	Shiloh (Pittsburgh Landing)	257
Sabine Pass (Fort Griffin)	238	Sitka	259
Sackets Harbor	238	Slim Buttes	260
Sacramento River	239	South Mountain	260
St. Augustine (1702)	240	Spencer's Tavern	261
St. Augustine (1740)	241	Spotsylvania	261
St. Charles	242	Springfield	262
St. Clair's Defeat	242	Springfield Arsenal	263
St. Denis	243	Stones River (Murfreesboro)	264
St. Eustache	244	Stono Ferry	266
St. John's (St. Jean's) (May 17, 1775)	244	Stony Creek (Stoney Creek)	266
St. John's (St. Jean's) (September 5–November 2, 1775)	245	Stony Point	267
		Stronghold	267

Summit Springs   268   White Plains   292

Talladega   269   Whitemarsh   293

Tallasahatchee   270   The Wilderness   293

Tarrant's Tavern   270   Williamsburg   294

Tenochtitlán   270   Williamson's Plantation   295

Thames (Moraviantown)   273   Wilson's Creek (Oak Hill)   295

Three Rivers (Trois Rivières)   274   Winchester, First   296

Throg's Neck (Throg's Point)   274   Winchester, Second   296

Tippecanoe   275   Winchester, Third (Opequon Creek)   297

Tlaxcala   276   Wolf Mountain   298

Trenton   277   Wood Lake (Lone Tree Lake)   298

Trevilian Station   278   Wounded Knee   299

U.S.S. *Trumbull* v. *Watt*   279   Wyoming Valley   299

U.S.S. *Trumbull* v. H.M.S. *Iris*   279   Yellow Tavern   301

Tupelo (Harrisburg)   279   Yorktown   302

Valcour Island   282

Veracruz   283   **Glossary**   305

Vicksburg   285   **Appendix 1:** Alphabetical List of Battles   313

Vincennes   287   **Appendix 2:** Chronological List of Battles   321

Wahab's Plantation   289   **Appendix 3:** List of Battles by War   329

Washita   289   **Appendix 4:** Battlefield Sites in
                                                 Alphabetical Order   335
Waxhaws   290

Waynesboro   291   **Appendix 5:** Battlefield Sites Listed by Region   337

Wetzell's Ford   291   **Bibliography**   345

White Oak Swamp (Glendale)   292   **Index**   363

PREFACE

The first obligation is to make clear our definition of battle.

A battle, insofar as this book is concerned, was an armed, violent conflict between two opposing forces of appreciable size, the outcome of which was seen at the time, or has been by historians since, to be significant.

Usually, at least one of the opposing forces, although it need not have been a formal army unit, represented or was sanctioned by a government. Also, in almost all cases an important political, economic, or social issue was affected by the outcome of the battle. In some of the battles we have chosen for this volume, one of these key defining elements may be weak, but on the whole we have clung steadily to these standards.

We believe that we have been comprehensive in our selection of battles but realize that, for practical reasons, our list is not complete—which is to say we have covered almost all kinds of conflicts in time and place in North America, beginning with the first battle between Spaniards and Maya in 1517 (Champoton) and running down to a small but politically significant fight between members of the U.S. Army and a group of Mexican civilians and soldiers almost exactly four hundred years later (Parral), but we have not described every single instance of combat in between.

For example, there have been thousands of battles between Indian groups since prehistoric times in North America, but we can discover little about most of them. We do not diminish the importance of these battles; we simply acknowledge that describing them is beyond our powers. We may know that such a battle took place, but details are so lacking in the public record as to make a description impossible. In addition, we have exercised our own judgment in eliminating a few small engagements that took place between rival Mexican political forces, as well as a few small battles in the western theater late in the American Civil War.

This leaves a large canvas with interested and varied battles, ranging from contests waged with obsidian-bladed swords to battles employing machine guns and barbed wire. It includes battles that are described by such terms as ambush, siege, campaign, skirmish, open field engagement, amphibious landing, and other similar names. We have included battles involving only a few hundred fighters and those involving more than a hundred thousand. We have restricted naval battles to those fought on lakes and rivers or within roughly 250 miles of the coast (the latter standard, adopted for practical reasons, eliminated World War II battles on Pacific islands, including the Aleutians).

For the most part, our entries describe individual battles or closely related battles that may have taken place within the context of a large war or campaign. Therefore, we have tried to make clear the context of each entry and its short-term consequences, but except for a few special cases (Atlanta, for example) we do not have covering entries for overall campaigns and wars. We do supply hundreds of cross-references (designated by small capital letters), which will lead readers to related battle entries.

We acknowledge that most of our descriptions have been specifically designed for a wide-ranging reference book and employ what we judged to be an appropriate level of detail. Generals and commanding officers are identified and given roles in battle that in many cases overestimate their importance; by the same criterion, the average soldier, who did most of the fighting and dying, has been underemphasized. This is an unfortunate but inevitable result of the reference-book approach. (We must also note parenthetically that the battles we describe are almost entirely male activities, and few women participants can be identified, although there may have been women warriors in combat on occasion.)

Readers may find out more about a specific battle and the people involved by consulting the "Further Reading" citations we provide for each entry. We have chosen these references with an eye to accessibility and availability, listing no esoteric sources or sources hard to find for readers in touch with an interlibrary loan program.

We have striven to keep the descriptions relatively free of military jargon and technical words, but a few specialized terms are inevitable and necessary in describing warfare. We have also tried to describe the movements and topography of specific battles as simply and clearly as possible. The detail that we could devote to any one battle entry usually was a function of the size and complexity of the engagement. For example, most of the battles of the American Revolution were on a relatively small scale and took place in restricted space over a short period of time. Moreover, they were usually well described in contemporary official and unofficial sources and have been much studied since. All of these circumstances allowed us to write concise but reasonably detailed entries for that conflict, quite often discussing unit movements and specific field encounters. On the other hand, most of the significant battles of the American Civil War were on such a scale as to make brief description in any detail impossible, and for that war we give in many cases only the gross outlines of maneuver and counter maneuver, and we report on only the largest causes and effects. Descriptions for other wars and circumstances generally lie somewhere between.

While hoping not to offend by verbal sins of commission or omission, we have been forced to make choices as to how to describe groups of people. We used our judgment to select Indian rather than Native American, black rather than African American, Federal or Union rather than Yankee, and Confederate rather than Rebel. Likewise, and meaning no disrespect, we have employed the commonly used term American to refer to the United States, knowing full well that Canadians and Mexicans occupy the American continent as well. Also, we have used the loaded term massacre sparingly.

As a general rule we have used for American Indian leaders proper names that were in common use by whites and historians, supplying whenever possible a version of the name in the person's native language. We acknowledge the shortcomings of this choice—it allows one's enemies the power to name—but the strict use of Native names would be immensely confusing to a large number of readers. Some might recognize Metacomet as King Philip, but we suspect few would know Moketanato as Black Kettle. For clarity and consistency, therefore, we use common anglicized names for individuals, but we have striven mightily to supply the proper name for specific tribes. Likewise, we have struggled to avoid the often derogatory names common to many histories, although we have cited them in passing (for example, using Mexica but explaining that Aztec is the common later name for the same people).

As to place-names and locations, we have chosen to give a modern-day designation whenever possible for clarity's sake, although this inevitably produces historical anachronisms and in some cases conflates geopolitical history; however, it does make it much easier to give consistently locations that a wide range of readers can understand.

The ranks of officers are listed as of the time of the battle, insofar as we could determine. We have generally disregarded the issue of regular rank versus brevet rank or volunteer commission—a briar patch in relation to Union army ranks during the Civil War.

We have supplied casualty figures for almost all entries; however, in many cases the references and sources disagree about the numbers. We have chosen those figures that seem to us to be most plausible and reliable.

In all these matters we have exercised our own judgment.

We very gratefully acknowledge the work of all the writers and historians who have collected and recorded the basic information about all the battles we describe, and we especially acknowledge the work of the librarians who have preserved and made available these resources.

For Mary F. Purcell, wife and mother to the authors, we are grateful.

A to Z Entries

⬷ Adobe Walls

Texas (June 27, 1874) *Buffalo War*

The Comanche of the southern plains included many outstanding war leaders, among them Quanah (Kwanah), the eldest son of a Nocona band leader and Cynthia Ann Parker, a white woman who had been captured as a girl. As a young man, Quanah Parker (as he came to be known) was one of the outstanding warriors of the Kwahadie band of Comanche, a group that strenuously resisted giving up their traditional life of hunting and raiding and that particularly resented the intrusion of white buffalo hunters into the Panhandle region of Texas, which had been reserved for the Comanche by treaty.

In 1874, the Kwahadie's growing anger at the hunters was stirred by the prophecies of a spiritual leader known as Isatai, who introduced the vision-producing sun dance ceremony to the Comanche (prior to this, the ritual had been practiced mostly by tribes on the northern plains). Led by Quanah, a war party numbering as many as seven hundred attacked a group of twenty-eight white buffalo hunters on June 27 at the site of an abandoned trading post known as Adobe Walls.

The Comanche were surprised to discover that the buffalo hunters were able to kill at extreme long range with their highly accurate and powerful .50-caliber Sharps rifles. Even though hugely outnumbered, the white hunters' sharpshooting skills—they were, after all, among the best marksmen in the world—allowed them to hold off their attackers. Some Comanche were killed at distances of more than one thousand yards, which spread discouragement and dissuaded them from an all-out assault that would probably have overrun the hunters. After counting fifteen dead and many more wounded, Quanah and the Kwahadie broke off the fight.

Further Reading

T. Lindsey Baker and Billy R. Harrison. *Adobe Walls: The History and Archaeology of the 1874 Trading Post* (College Station: Texas A & M Press, 1986).

✍ Agua Prieta

Mexico-Arizona border (November 1, 1915)
Mexican Revolution

The U.S. government recognized Venustiano Carranza, the main political and revolutionary rival of Gen. Francisco "Pancho" Villa, as the legitimate ruler of Mexico in October 1915. Villa, who had received American support in the past, was unhappy about the recognition, but his immediate attention was occupied with rebuilding his force after a disastrous defeat at the hands of the Carranzistas at CELAYA in April.

American minister George Carothers suspected that Villa might attack the Mexican village of Agua Prieta on the U.S. border directly across from Douglas, Arizona. Pres. Woodrow Wilson consented to send military supplies to Carranzista general Plutarco Calles to fortify the Mexican town. Both Agua Prieta and Douglas were heavily reinforced with barbed-wire fences, machine-gun, and artillery when Villa's forces attacked in the predawn hours of November 1.

Commanders on both sides of the border had a clear view from the sidelines as Villa's cavalry advanced across an open plain toward Agua Prieta. Just as at Celaya the previous spring, superior technology gave the Carranzista forces a great advantage. Villa had pursued highly effective nighttime attacks in the past, but on this occasion American searchlights (which the Villistas later claimed were operated by American citizens) lit up his approach and blinded the cavalry.

The two sides exchanged heavy fire until the evening, when Villa ordered a charge. His men were caught up in the barbed-wire fortifications and made easy targets for machine-gun crossfire. Villa withdrew to reconsider his position. After meeting with American major general Frederick Funston on the border a few days later, Villa decided not to renew the attack.

Exact casualties totals for the action are unknown, though U.S. observers reported a heavy toll among the Villistas. Many shots strayed across the border, and several U.S. soldiers manning a series of trenches outside Douglas were killed. The defeat at Agua Prieta helped to increase Pancho Villa's resentment against the United States, a resentment he continued to act upon in border raids in 1916 (*See also* COLUMBUS).

Further Reading

Clarence C. Clendenen. *The United States and Pancho Villa: A Study in Unconventional Diplomacy* (Ithaca, N.Y.: Cornell University Press for the American Historical Association, 1961).

✍ Alamance

North Carolina (May 16, 1771)
Regulator Uprising

Throughout the late 1760s and early 1770s, groups of protesters calling themselves "Regulators" agitated against the royal government of North Carolina. The Regulators, who were mostly residents of the western region of the colony, blamed royal governor William Tryon for their lack of representation in the colonial assembly and for the corruption of royal officials. They also protested various imperial measures, such as the Stamp Act and the Townshend Acts. In response to a series of Regulator riots at Hillsborough in September 1770, the North Carolina Assembly passed the "Bloody Act," declaring rioting to be treasonous. When fresh protests erupted in the spring of 1771, governor Tryon led North Carolina militia forces to put down the Regulators.

Tryon's fourteen hundred militia men met the force of twenty-five hundred Regulators, which had gathered at Alamance Creek, on May 16. Before attacking, Tryon paused half a mile from the Regulators' camp and demanded that they surrender up their "outlawed ringleaders." When no answer came, the two forces formed into lines only about three hundred yards apart. Though outnumbered, Tryon's force was armed with artillery, and sometime after 10 A.M. Tryon opened fire on the makeshift Regulator army. After firing grapeshot at the Regulators, many of whom did not even have weapons, Tryon ordered his men to push forward. In less than two hours, the militia force drove the Regulators from the field.

Tryon lost ten men killed and sixty wounded. The Regulators saw nine of their own killed, many more wounded, and twenty or thirty taken prisoner. James Few, one of the Regulators' leaders, was executed for treason on the battlefield on May 17. Twelve others who had taken part in the Regulator uprising were convicted of treason, and six were hanged in June.

William Tryon left almost immediately after the battle to take up his new post as governor of New York, where he was liked much better. More than six thousand western North Carolinians were forced to swear an oath of allegiance to the crown, which many of them would forsake a few short years later when the American Revolution commenced.

Further Reading

William E. Fitch. *The Battle of Alamance* (Burlington, N.C.: Alamance Battle Ground Commission, 1939); Paul D. Nelson. *William Tyron and the Course of Empire: A Life in British Imperial Service* (Chapel Hill: University of North Carolina Press, 1990); and William S. Powell, James Huhta, and Thomas J. Farnham, eds. *The Regulators in North Carolina: A Documentary History, 1759–1776* (Raleigh: North Carolina Department of Archives and History, 1971).

Alamo

San Antonio, Texas (February 23–March 6, 1836)
Texas War of Independence

When Gen. Antonio López de Santa Anna became ruler of Mexico in 1835, he decided to curtail American settlement in the Mexican province of Texas, dissolve its elected legislature, and enforce the Mexican prohibition on slavery in the province. The community of thirty thousand American immigrants in Texas, along with their Tejano allies (Texans of Mexican ancestry), declared their independence and prepared to defend themselves.

The Texans ousted Santa Anna's cousin, Gen. Martin Perfecto de Cós, from San Antonio late in 1835 and established a fortified Franciscan mission, the Alamo, as their base of resistance to the Mexican government. Santa Anna refused to accept his cousin's defeat or the notion of Texas independence. He and an army of five thousand troops marched from south of the Rio Grande into Texas to retake the Alamo.

General Sam Houston, overall commander of the Texas forces, had ordered the Alamo to be destroyed and abandoned. But James Bowie, commander of Texas volunteers in San Antonio (but best known for his namesake knife), decided to hold his ground. He gathered a small force of Texans in the Alamo, including Col. William B. Travis, the famous Tennessee frontiersman Davy Crockett, and Juan Nepomuceno Seguín, who had recruited a volunteer company of Tejanos.

Santa Anna's force arrived in San Antonio on February 23 and announced—with a red flag atop one of the city's churches—that no quarter would be granted to resisters inside the Alamo. The Mexicans then laid siege against the Texans.

On February 24, Colonel Travis, in command while Bowie was in bed with a fever, sent Seguín's men to bring reinforcements. The Tejanos escaped from the Alamo by pretending to be Mexican soldiers, taking with them what became a famous appeal for help from Travis and a ringing proclamation that he sought either "victory or death." Only thirty-two men managed to slip through the siege lines to reinforce the defenders, who now numbered about 185.

Following a preliminary bombardment on March 4, Santa Anna launched an all-out attack against the Alamo on March 6. The Texans fought off two assaults against the north wall of the fort, but a third attack proved to be too much. Mexican soldiers got over the walls, and close combat raged for over an hour inside the compound. With an overwhelming manpower advantage, the Mexicans hunted down and eventually killed all the Texas fighting men trapped within the fort, sparing only women, children, one black slave, and a man named José María Guerrero, who claimed he had been forced to fight.

Even though the Alamo represented total defeat for the Texans, their fewer than two hundred casualties were weighed against a much larger toll among the Mexicans, estimated by some accounts to include more than one thousand dead. It was later rumored, but never proven, that after the battle Santa Anna executed the few men taken alive. It is certain that he had all the bodies of the Texans gathered into three funeral pyres and burned.

While the decision of Bowie and Travis to defend the Alamo to the last man may have been foolish, the defeat gave Texans a rallying point for their revolution: cries of "Remember the Alamo!" spurred Texans to victory six weeks later at SAN JACINTO.

Further Reading

William C. Davis. *Three Roads to the Alamo: The Lives and Fortunes of David Crockett, James Bowie, and William Barret Travis* (New York: HarperCollins, 1998); Stephen L. Hardin. *Texian Iliad: A Military History of the Texas Revolution, 1835–1836* (Austin: University of Texas Press, 1997); C. D. Honeycutt. *The Alamo: An In-Depth Study of the Battle (New London, N.C.: Gold Star Press, 1986); Alan C. Huffines. *The Alamo: An Illustrated Micro History of the Siege and Battle as Told by the Participants and Eye-Witnesses. . . .* (Austin, Tex.: Eakin Press, 1997).

⤜ U.S.S. *Alfred* v. H.M.S. *Glasgow*

Off Block Island, Rhode Island (April 6, 1776)
American Revolution

A tiny American squadron had sailed out of Delaware Bay in early 1776 under Commodore Esek Hopkins and successfully raided the British post at Nassau in the Bahamas. The ships were returning to the eastern seaboard on the night of April 6 when they encountered the twenty-gun British frigate *Glasgow*, commanded by Capt. Trylingham Howe.

The strongest American ship, the *Alfred*, a merchantman converted to a twenty-four-gun frigate and commanded by Hopkins, bore the brunt of the night fight with the British ship.

As was usual in face-to-face sea battles with the highly esteemed Royal Navy—which was the largest and considered to be the finest in the world—the Americans came out second best. During a three-hour battle, the *Glasgow* knocked out the *Alfred*'s steering and raked the American ship from stem to stern several times, inflicting heavy damage and twenty-four casualties.

Having fought his way through five American warships in the dark, Captain Howe escaped with only light casualties and damage to his ship. The American squadron limped into port at Providence, Rhode Island. Hopkins was eventually replaced and censured as a result of the encounter.

Further Reading

John J. McCusker. *Alfred: The First Continental Flagship, 1775–1778* (Washington, D.C.: Smithsonian Studies in History and Technology, no. 20, 1973).

⤜ Allatoona Pass

Georgia (October 5, 1864) *American Civil War*

After he had withdrawn from Atlanta, giving up the city to the Federals, Confederate Lt. Gen. John Bell Hood launched an offensive toward the major Union posts in Tennessee. His first target was the supply depot and rail line at Allatoona Pass. Hood sent Maj. Gen. Samuel G. French with a division of troops, numbering around two thousand men, to seize supplies and tear up the railroad.

Allatoona Pass was defended by a garrison of less than a thousand men under Lt. Col. John F. Tourtelotte, and French expected to overwhelm the Union forces easily.

Unbeknownst to the Confederate commander, however, Maj. Gen. William T. Sherman had ordered the post reinforced by Brig. Gen. John M. Corse, who arrived with an additional thousand men in the early morning hours of October 5. The Union defenses were concentrated at three fortified positions.

When his demand for surrender was rebuffed, French launched an assault at mid-morning that drove the Union defenders out of two of the fortified positions after heavy hand-to-hand fighting. The remaining Federal troops concentrated at the single remaining redoubt. They repulsed three assaults by the Confederates, inflicting heavy casualties. By early afternoon, French abandoned his attacks and began a withdrawal.

The battle claimed a very heavy rate of killed and wounded: French lost about 800 men and Corse lost slightly more than 700.

Further Reading

William R. Scaife. *Allatoona Pass: A Needless Effusion of Blood* (Atlanta: Etowah Valley Historical Society, 1995).

⤜ Allen's Farm

See SAVAGE'S STATION

⤜ Annapolis Royal

(Port Royal)

Canada (September 8–October 6, 1744)
King George's War

Annapolis Royal was the name the British gave PORT ROYAL in Acadia, a region encompassing modern-day Nova Scotia as well as other parts of Canada and the state of Maine, when they captured it in 1710. With the outbreak of King George's War thirty-five years later, the French authorities at Louisbourg tried to retake the lost possession.

Annapolis Royal was commanded by British lieutenant governor Paul Mascarene, whose authority in theory extended to all of modern-day Nova Scotia. In fact, very few British colonists lived in Acadia, which was populated by an independent group of the descendants of French settlers and Micmac and Malecite Indians. (The French Acadians would be forcibly removed to Louisiana in 1755, there to be known as "Cajuns.") Because Mascarene had only one hundred, ill-disciplined British soldiers under arms, he had to treat the Acadians with kid gloves.

Moreover, Annapolis Royal's fortifications had fallen into disrepair. Mascarene, however, was determined to keep the majority of the Acadian population neutral and hold out until reinforcements could arrive from the American colonies, to the south.

The French commandant at Louisbourg, Jean-Baptiste-Louis Duquesnel, had himself few military resources in the way of men and equipment, but he was eager to strike a blow against the British and was under pressure from François Du Pont Duvivier, a rich and politically well-connected merchant and soldier, to organize an expedition against Annapolis Royal. In June, following a successful raid on a British fishing station at Canso, Duquesnel appointed Duvivier to lead the attempt to retake Annapolis Royal and to drive the British entirely from Acadia. The plan was for Duvivier to march with a small detachment of soldiers, recruiting along the way more men among what the French assumed would be sympathetic Acadians and Indians, and two small warships were to join Duvivier at Annapolis Royal. The French soldiers, the Indians, and the ships were all to arrive simultaneously and cow the British into surrender.

As was usual with complex military plans drawn up by inexperienced commanders, the scheme misfired almost from the beginning. The French missionaries among the Micmac in Nova Scotia jumped the gun, setting the Indian forces in motion too soon. Three hundred Micmac, led by Fr. Jean-Louis Le Loutre, descended on Annapolis Royal on July 12, but Duvivier and the warships were nowhere to be seen. Without artillery or disciplined siege tactics, the Micmac had almost no effect on the fortifications, and when seventy British reinforcements from Boston arrived, the Indians departed.

Duvivier did not leave Louisbourg until July 29 (after the Micmac had gone home), and he marched very slowly through Acadia. To his disappointment, the Acadians reacted with almost complete indifference to his call to arms. They were happy to sell him supplies but wanted no part of fighting the British. Only a handful volunteered.

Finally, on September 8, Duvivier arrived at the gates of Annapolis Royal with 280 men, only fifty-six of whom were regulars. He also had the services of about a hundred Micmac and Malecite. The ships failed to appear, and because they carried the only artillery, Duvivier had almost no way to lay an effective siege until they arrived. The British commander, Mascarene, faced dissent among his small force of defenders, but he refused to surrender to Duvivier, since the only thing the French could manage was ineffective musket fire against the fortifications.

The stalemate came to an end on September 26, when three ships appeared carrying fifty Rangers under the command of Capt. John Gorham to reinforce the British garrison. Duviver continued to surround the walls of the town for another two weeks, but there was no longer any question of a serious assault. He returned to Louisbourg to discover that the naval part of the expedition had sailed only after he had withdrawn from Annapolis Royal.

There were few casualties on either side of the fiasco.

Further Reading

Bernard Pothier. "The Siege of Annapolis Royal, 1744." *Nova Scotia Historical Review* 5, no. 1 (1985): 59–71.

Antietam

(Sharpsburg)
Maryland (September 17, 1862)
American Civil War

The engagement between Gen. Robert E. Lee's Army of Northern Virginia and Maj. Gen. George B. McClellan's Army of the Potomac near a small town in Maryland was one of the two or three most important battles fought on the North American continent. It also was the single most costly day in all of American military history.

Lee had brought his redoubtable soldiers north out of Virginia to invade Maryland, where he hoped to defeat the Federals yet again and to rally support among the large proslavery faction in the state. Moreover, a successful thrust northward might convince both northern voters and foreign supporters that the South could win the war. If Lee could inflict a crushing blow on McClellan, the Confederacy might triumph.

Lee had about forty thousand men available, but part of his invasion strategy had been to divide his command. Part had gone with his best commander, Maj. Gen. Thomas J. "Stonewall" Jackson, to HARPERS FERRY. And part, under Maj. Gen. James Longstreet, had marched toward Hagerstown, Maryland. Thus, the Confederate army was vulnerable when a Union soldier found a copy of Lee's special orders and passed it on to the Federal high command. McClellan, the timid commander of the huge Army of the Potomac, was presented with a golden opportunity, but he moved slowly, and Lee managed to find a

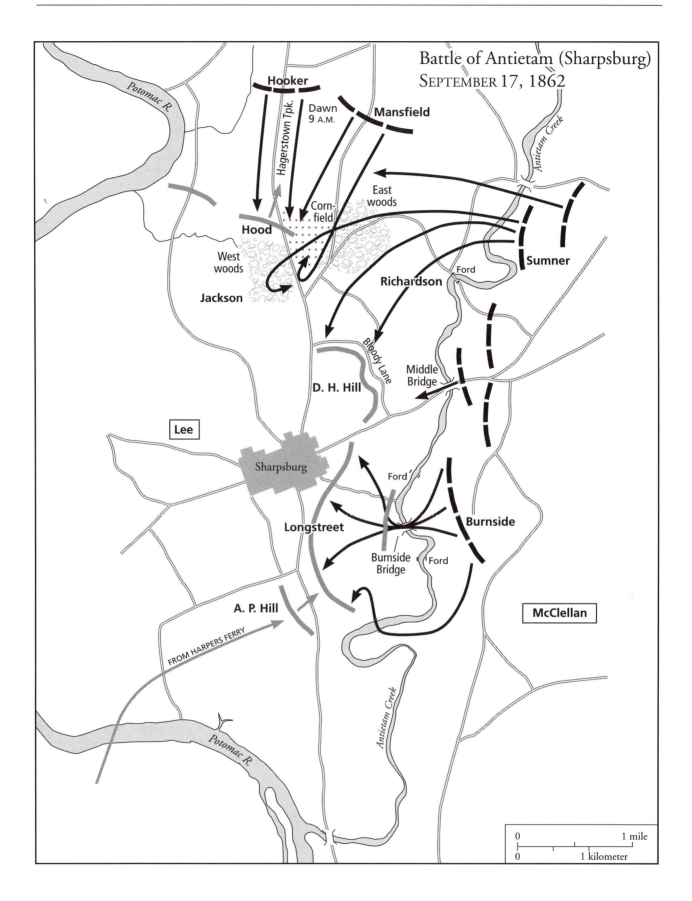

Battle of Antietam (Sharpsburg)
SEPTEMBER 17, 1862

strong defensive position for half of his army near the village of Sharpsburg. There he waited for McClellan to attack and hoped the rest of his troops would arrive in time to fight. Even though they moved fast to consolidate, on the day of battle the Confederates were still badly outnumbered, something on the order of thirty-eight thousand to seventy-five thousand men.

Lee had positioned his army behind Antietam Creek, with Longstreet's corps on the right, Maj. Gen. D. H. Hill's division in the center, and Jackson's men, who had hastened from Harpers Ferry, on the left. All had good places from which to fight a defensive battle, something at which the Army of Northern Virginia was expert. McClellan, with his huge advantage in manpower, apparently had little in the way of a coherent battle plan, other than to attack simultaneously against both wings of the Confederate army. He moved into position cautiously, allowing almost all of Lee's detached troops to join before the main attack came on the morning of September 17.

The first encounter was on the Confederate left, near a small Dunker church and a farmer's cornfield. Union major general Joseph Hooker's corps tried to dislodge Jackson's men, finally sweeping the cornfield nearly clean of enemy soldiers with a withering barrage of artillery fire. As his men appeared close to victory, Hooker was wounded, and at almost the same time, his corps was hit with a vicious counterattack from the West Woods under Brig. Gen. John Bell Hood, who reclaimed the cornfield for the Confederates. Almost immediately, however, Union troops under Maj. Gen. Joseph Mansfield attacked from the nearby East Woods, and the cornfield changed hands again—even as Mansfield took a mortal wound during the assault. Another Federal division, commanded by Maj. Gen. Edwin Sumner, tried to dislodge the Confederates from the West Woods and suffered horrendous losses.

At the center of the battlefield, D. H. Hill's division occupied a farm road that had been worn below the level of the surrounding fields and now served as a well-protected natural rifle trench. When two Union divisions attacked head-on, the Confederates destroyed the advancing bluecoats with musket fire. The carnage was so great that the place was subsequently labeled "Bloody Lane." The first Federal division was broken by the Southerners' firepower, but when one of the Confederate units mistook an order and withdrew from the line, the second Union division, under Maj. Gen. Israel B. "Fighting Dick"

Richardson, dislodged Hill's men and took the position. Had McClellan chosen to follow up this advantage by committing his massive reserve forces (which never saw combat during the entire battle), he might well have swept the Confederates from the field, but with his usual lack of aggressiveness, he held back. His men maintained their hold on Bloody Lane, despite subsequent Confederate counterattacks, but they gained no further advantage.

Another battlefield drama had been enacted on the Confederate right, where a Union corps under Maj. Gen. Ambrose Burnside had been assigned the task of crossing Antietam Creek and attacking the Confederate positions. Instead of finding a ford and wading across the relatively small creek, Burnside's men tried time after time to cross a stone bridge, only to be turned back by fire from Confederates manning entrenchments on a bluff overlooking the site. The Federals finally made it across the bridge, after suffering great losses. They paused to regroup and then began to assault the right wing of the Confederate position. Lee had nearly stripped his right wing of troops earlier in the day to shore up his line, and it appeared that Burnside's men could easily crush the thin ranks in front of them and then roll up the entire Confederate army. At the last minute, however, a Confederate division under Maj. Gen. A. P. Hill arrived, having marched all the way from Harpers Ferry. Despite their fatigue, Hill's men fell on Burnside's flank and drove off the Union attackers. With this engagement, the battle came to an end.

The toll of the battle was horrifying: more than 22,000 men were counted as killed, wounded, or missing after the day's fighting. This made the Battle of Antietam the worst day in the history of American warfare, unsurpassed for single-day casualties even during World War II. (Antietam claimed nearly five times the casualties of D-Day, for example). The numbers of casualties were about equal for each side, with a total of more than 4,800 killed in combat.

On the day following the battle, Lee ordered his army to retreat into Virginia, his hope of an invasion of the North at an end. McClellan was quick to claim victory, but he had allowed Lee to escape destruction, and the Union commander was far too slow in organizing a pursuit of the Army of Northern Virginia. Perhaps the most important consequence of the battle came when Pres. Abraham Lincoln decided that the near victory was enough to allow him to issue the Emancipation Proclamation, thereby putting the war on an entirely new footing, emphasizing the ending of slavery.

Further Reading

Robert I. Cottom, Jr., and Mary Ellen Hayward. *Maryland in the Civil War: A House Divided* (Baltimore: Johns Hopkins University Press, 1994); William A. Fassanito. *Antietam: The Photographic Legacy of America's Bloodiest Day* (New York: Scribner's, 1978); James V. Murfin. *The Gleam of Bayonets: The Battle of Antietam and Robert E. Lee's Maryland Campaign, September 1862* (Baton Rouge: Louisiana State University Press, 1965); and Stephen Sears. *Landscape Turned Red: The Battle of Antietam* (New Haven, Conn.: Ticknor & Fields, 1983).

❧ Ash Hollow

(Blue Lake)

Nebraska (September 3, 1855) *Sioux Wars*

The attack by U.S. troops on a village of the Brulé band of the Teton Lakota (historically—along with the Dakota and Nakota—known as "Sioux") was one of the early encounters in what developed into more than twenty years of hostilities, which became known as the Sioux Wars.

The attack was set off by a previous incident on the North Platte River in modern-day Wyoming when U.S. Army lieutenant John L. Grattan, an inexperienced young officer, attacked a village of the Brulé Lakota in a misunderstanding over a cow stolen from a western immigrant train by a visiting Miniconjou Lakota. The soldiers killed Conquering Bear (Mahtoiowa), who had served as chief spokesman for the Teton Lakota. Grattan and all his men were subsequently killed in a melee. Even though the killings were almost entirely the result of Grattan's poor judgment, the federal government was bent on revenge against the Teton Lakota.

General William S. Harney, a veteran of the Black Hawk War, the Second Seminole War, and the Mexican-American War, was recalled from travels abroad and given command of twelve hundred troops, including dragoons and artillery. His orders were to punish the Lakota and stop their raids on western immigrant wagon trains. Harney was a hard-nosed soldier who advocated no quarter for the Indians, and he set out to find someone to attack.

On September 3, 1855, Harney and his column discovered a village of about two hundred Brulé Lakota at Ash Hollow, on the Blue Water Creek in Nebraska. The Indians attempted to surrender when they saw they were surrounded and heavily outnumbered, but Harney ordered an attack by two columns of his soldiers. The fleeing Brulé warriors were caught between the columns and

almost wiped out. The soldiers then overran the village, killing women and children. Harney's men estimated they killed eighty Indians, with no losses of their own.

Further Reading

Eli R. Paul, ed., "Battle of Ash Hollow: The 1909–1910 Recollections of General N. A. M. Dudley." *Nebraska History* 63, no. 3 (1981): 373–99; and Robert M. Utley and Wilcomb E. Washburn. *The American Heritage History of the Indian Wars* (New York: American Heritage, 1977).

❧ Atlanta

Georgia (May 14–September 2, 1864)
American Civil War

The series of battles fought between Union and Confederate forces over possession of Atlanta, Georgia, in the summer of 1864 were pivotal in the course of the American Civil War. When the Union ultimately prevailed, taking possession of the city in early September, the days of the Confederacy were numbered.

In March 1864, after directing the Federal victory at CHATTANOOGA, Lt. Gen. Ulysses S. Grant was given supreme command of all Union forces. Since he planned personally to direct the campaign in Virginia against Gen. Robert E. Lee, Grant appointed Maj. Gen. William T. Sherman as commander of the western theater, responsible to find and destroy the large Confederate army under Gen. Joseph E. Johnston and to capture the crucial industrial city of Atlanta.

Sherman had at his disposal a huge force, comprising three distinct armies: the sixty-thousand-man Army of the Cumberland under Maj. Gen. George H. Thomas; the Army of the Tennessee, with nearly twenty-five thousand men, commanded by Maj. Gen. James B. McPherson; and the Army of the Ohio, with over thirteen thousand men, under Maj. Gen. John M. Schofield. Starting from northern Georgia, Sherman proposed a three-pronged advance toward Atlanta, across extremely rugged terrain that had been extensively fortified by the Confederates. He hoped to outmaneuver Johnston and destroy the Southern army.

Johnston had two army corps of about forty thousand total under Lt. Gen. William Hardee and Lt. Gen. John Bell Hood, and he was joined by Lt. Gen. Leonidas Polk's corps-strength Army of Mississippi with an additional twenty-five thousand troops. Although heavily outnumbered, Johnston had the great advantage of defending a series of prepared positions, and he was an unusually skillful defensive general. He hoped to make the campaign so costly that Sherman would have to break off before reaching Atlanta.

The first clash came on May 7, 1864, as the Union armies approached Johnston's winter headquarters at Dalton, Georgia, a heavily fortified bastion. Sherman decided on a feint against the Confederate defenses at Dalton, while McPherson and his army swung around to take the town of Resaca, to the south, blocking Johnston's line of retreat. McPherson failed in his task, however, not pushing strongly enough in the face of spirited Southern resistance. Johnston was able to abandon Dalton and withdraw safely to Resaca, setting the pattern for nearly the entire Atlanta campaign: Sherman would try to outflank and cut off Johnston, and Johnston would slip the trap and fall back to yet another strongly fortified position. The Confederate army fell back to Cassville and then to Allatoona Pass, with engagements occurring almost every day.

In late May, Johnston began to move from Allatoona toward Dallas, less than thirty miles from Atlanta. Most of the Union army was trying to maneuver around him there, but Johnston managed to occupy positions around New Hope Church before Sherman could get there. As the two forces closed on each other, both stopped and built breastworks from which they could fight in relative safety. This tendency to build makeshift field fortifications in the presence of the enemy was a unique feature of the Atlanta campaign, and at New Hope Church it led to five days of fighting while Sherman probed for the Southern flank. On May 27, Sherman sent two divisions through heavily wooded ravines to attack Johnston's rear near Pickett's Mill, only to have them run into troops under Maj. Gen. Patrick Cleburne, one of Johnston's best officers. Cleburne stopped the Federals cold and inflicted heavy casualties.

Next, Sherman's cavalry took possession of Allatoona Pass, which forced Johnston to withdraw yet again, this time to a strong line of defenses anchored by several mountains. By late June, Johnston held a fifty-mile-long string of fortifications, with the key point at Kennesaw Mountain. Sherman decided to try a direct attack, in hopes of severely damaging or destroying the Confederate army, but assaults by densely packed Federal formations on the Confederate defensive lines at Kennesaw Mountain produced three thousand Union

casualties in a matter of hours, and Sherman had to call off the attack. Five days later, on July 2, part of the Union force once again slid around Johnston's flank, so the Confederate general was forced to retreat from Kennesaw Mountain to new positions near Smyra. There he could protect the rail lines leading to Atlanta.

In mid-July, there were major changes. Although a great field commander, Johnston was a prickly personality and a poor politician, who disdained explaining himself to the Confederate government in Richmond. By July the Confederate government had grown tired of Johnston, and Pres. Jefferson Davis relieved him of command, replacing him with Lt. Gen. John Bell Hood, a brave but impetuous officer who had lost both an arm and a leg in battle. (Davis might well have chosen his good friend Leonidas Polk, but the general had been killed in fighting in June.) Hood had none of Johnston's skills, and his Union counterparts were encouraged to learn that he was now in charge. Moreover, Grant altered Sherman's objective and ordered him to proceed to take Atlanta without necessarily defeating the Confederate army. As expected, Hood went on the offensive, attacking the Union troops at Peachtree Creek on July 20, but he was repulsed and forced to retreat to trenches just outside the city of Atlanta itself. On July 22, Hood tried again with what was planned as a simultaneous flank and frontal attack, but the timing was off, and the overall assault failed, although Union general McPherson was killed during the fighting.

After another sharp clash near Ezra Church, the Union forces settled into positions facing the Atlanta fortifications and began a constant artillery bombardment of the city. Weeks went by, and Sherman continued to lengthen his lines and pound away with more and more cannon fire. By late August, Sherman's lines encompassed almost the entire western half of Atlanta. Hood tried one last attack, at Jonesboro, but when it failed, he was forced—finally—to withdraw from Atlanta and leave it to the mercies of Sherman and the Union army, which took possession on September 2.

The overall toll of casualties from the long series of battles from May to September was gigantic, probably close to twenty thousand for each side.

With the fall of Atlanta, the Confederacy lost one of its most important manufacturing centers, which in November served as the jumping-off point for Sherman's famous march across Georgia to the sea.

Further Reading

Ronald H. Bailey. *Battles for Atlanta: Sherman Moves East* (Alexandria, Va.: Time-Life Books, 1985); John Cannon. *The Atlanta Campaign: May–November 1864* (Conshohocken, Pa.: Combined Books, 1991); Samuel Carter. *The Siege of Atlanta, 1864* (New York: St. Martin's Press, 1973); Albert Castel. *Decision in the West: The Atlanta Campaign of 1864* (Lawrence: University Press of Kansas, 1992); David Evans. *Sherman's Horsemen: Union Cavalry Operations in the Atlanta Campaign* (Bloomington: Indiana University Press, 1996); Webb B. Garrison. *Atlanta and the War* (Nashville, Tenn.: Rutledge Hill Press, 1995); William Key. *The Battle of Atlanta and the Georgia Campaign* (New York: Twayne, 1958); and Jim Miles. *Fields of Glory: A History and Tour Guide of the Atlanta Campaign* (Nashville, Tenn.: Rutledge Hill Press, 1989).

⚮ Augusta

Georgia (September 14–18, 1780)
American Revolution

Part of the British southern strategy in the second half of 1780 was to secure the Georgia and Carolina backcountry by garrisoning a series of outposts. Augusta was a stronghold of Loyalists and their Creek Indian allies, commanded by Col. Thomas Browne, leader of the King's Rangers and a figure much feared and reviled by the local patriots. Browne had several fortified positions in and around Augusta, including a strong building known as the White House.

Patriot militia under Col. Elijah Clark and Lt. Col. James McCall, numbering a little more than one hundred, assembled northwest of Augusta in mid-September and advanced on the Loyalist base in three columns. They easily beat back the Creek pickets and, after taking two other fortified buildings, laid siege to the White House, where Browne and most of his men had gathered.

The patriots cut off the building's water supply, kept up a peppering of musket fire, and beat off Creek reinforcements, but they had no heavy guns, and their only competent artillerist had been killed early in the engagement. Browne and his men were in an uncomfortable position—Browne himself was wounded—but they refused to surrender.

After two days, a British relief force approached, and the patriots abandoned the siege and dispersed.

There is no record of Loyalist casualties, but about sixty patriots were killed or wounded during the episode.

Afterward, Colonel Browne viciously executed twenty-nine of the patriot wounded by hanging them from the staircase in the White House.

Further Reading

Ronald G. Killion and Charles T. Waller. *Georgia and the Revolution* (Atlanta, Ga.: Cherokee, 1975).

⚮ Augusta

Georgia (May 22–June 5, 1781)
American Revolution

In the spring of 1781, the American commander in the South, Maj. Gen. Nathanael Greene, began a campaign to eliminate the final remaining outposts the British had set up to control South Carolina and Georgia. Greene ordered Lt. Col. Henry "Light-Horse Harry" Lee to seize the Loyalist-garrisoned stronghold at Augusta, which had withstood a patriot assault during the previous September (*see* AUGUSTA).

Lee commanded his own legion, a mixed force of dragoons and infantry, plus several units of militia: South Carolinians under Brig. Gen. Andrew Pickens, North Carolinians under Maj. Pinketham Eaton, and Georgians under Col. Elijah Clarke who had led the unsuccessful attack in 1780. Altogether, Lee's forces may have numbered close to fifteen hundred.

The opposing garrison comprised 330 Loyalists and 300 Creeks under the command of Col. Thomas Browne, a very tough, if vicious, partisan soldier. Browne's defenses were divided between his main position of Fort Cornwallis and a smaller stockade, called Fort Grierson, located a half mile away and commanded by its namesake, a notorious local Loyalist Col. Grierson.

Lee attacked Grierson first and easily took the stockade when its defenders tried, unsuccessfully, to retreat to the safety of Cornwallis. Major Eaton, the North Carolina militia commander, was killed during the fighting at Fort Grierson, as were thirty Loyalists. The rest, including Grierson, were captured. Almost immediately, however, a Georgia militia officer murdered Grierson in retribution for his previous brutalities against patriots.

Lee then turned to taking Fort Cornwallis and defeating Browne, who had proven the previous year that he would neither give up easily nor give any quarter to his opponents. (He had hanged twenty-nine prisoners after the first Battle of Augusta in September 1780.) As usual in such situations in the southern theater, the patriot artillery was too weak to batter the stockaded fort into submission, so Lee had his men begin to dig angled siege trenches that would eventually lead up to the walls. He also ordered construction of a Maham Tower, a tall, hewn-log structure that would give marksmen a sheltered perch from which to fire down on the fort's defenders.

Browne tried to lure Lee's men into a nearby frame house, which he had mined, but Lee refused to be baited, and the house blew up prematurely. One week into the siege, Lee mounted a captured cannon on top of the Maham Tower, and his men poured a hot fire from the gun and their muskets into the fort. Browne's men were driven away from their own gun positions and could put up only an increasingly feeble resistance.

On June 5, Browne surrendered and was taken prisoner along with all his remaining men. He was placed under heavy guard for his own protection and taken to Savannah for parole.

The Loyalists lost fifty-two killed and wounded during the siege, the patriots about forty.

Further Reading

Ronald G. Killion and Charles T. Waller. *Georgia and the Revolution* (Atlanta, Ga.: Cherokee 1975).

Bad Axe River

Wisconsin (August 2, 1832) *Black Hawk War*

The confrontation on the Bad Axe River in 1832 pitted some thirteen hundred militia and regular army soldiers against about four hundred Sac (Sauk) Indian men, women, and children. It was another episode in the continuing saga of Indian resistance to white American expansion into what had been Native-controlled lands.

The main Sac village—the village of Saukenuk—at the confluence of the Rock and Mississippi Rivers, near modern-day Rock Island, Illinois, lay near good bottom farmland and by the late 1820s and early 1830s, white settlers were encroaching on the site, especially during the winter months, when almost the entire Sac tribe scattered in small family hunting groups. Black Hawk (Ma-ka-ta-i-me-she-kia-kiak), a leader of one faction of the Sac, had long opposed American expansion. He had listened to the inspiring words of the Shawnee leader Tecumseh twenty years earlier and had forged close ties to the British. He particularly resented the American tactic of getting chiefs with only small followings to sign land-transfer treaties—the Sac and an allied tribe, the Mesquakie (Fox) Tribes had lost all their land east of the Mississippi in such a treaty in 1804.

In the spring of 1832, Black Hawk moved his followers (most of the tribe remained neutral in the conflict) to the eastern bank of the Mississippi, where they were confronted by a motley force of Illinois militia, commanded by Brig. Gen. Henry Atkinson. The militia had almost no training and few military skills. It was most notable for including among its numbers two future U.S. presidents—Zachary Taylor and Abraham Lincoln—and the future president of the Confederacy, Jefferson Davis. When Black Hawk and his band moved north, the militia followed cautiously, fighting a discreditable skirmish with some of the Sac on May 14. In June, Gen. Winfield Scott took command of the American forces, and Col. Henry Dodge of Wisconsin raised and led a detachment of Wisconsin militia.

Black Hawk realized the futility of fighting such large numbers, and his goal became to escape northward to British territory. But his band, which included about 150 warriors and several hundred women and children, moved slowly as it tried to evade the Americans.

On August 1, Black Hawk's band reached the confluence of the Bad Axe and Mississippi Rivers and paused for the night to build rafts. They hoped to cross the river the next day and escape northward. Instead, they were greeted the next morning by the appearance of the gunboat *Warrior* with a contingent of troops. The *Warrior* opened fire with its small gun, and the soldiers on board fired at the Sac on the riverbank, heedless that the Indians were trying to surrender in the face of the gunboat's superior firepower. As the *Warrior* withdrew upriver to take on fuel, the survivors of the attack began to cross the river. Just then, more troops attacked. The Sac were also fired on by Lakota from the far side of the river.

When the gunfire ended, about 150 Sac had been killed and almost all the rest captured. Only a handful escaped, including Black Hawk, who later turned himself in and was forced to cede even more lands after a period of imprisonment.

Further Reading

Cecil Eby. *"That Disgraceful Affair," The Black Hawk War* (New York: W. W. Norton, 1973); and Donald Jackson, ed. *Black Hawk: An Autobiography* (Urbana: University of Illinois Press, 1964).

⚓ Ball's Bluff

Virginia (October 21, 1861) *American Civil War*

During the fall of 1861, as Pres. Abraham Lincoln was clamoring for military action, Maj. Gen. George B. McClellan was busy training the Army of the Potomac and staging military reviews in Washington. In October, at McClellan's behest, Brig. Gen. Charles P. Stone sent Col. Edward Baker, a former U.S. senator and a close friend of Lincoln's, to make "a slight demonstration" against the Confederates across the Potomac River from the city.

Unfortunately, Baker acted foolishly. Instead of ordering "a slight demonstration," Baker had his men cross the Potomac on October 21 at Ball's Bluff, near Leesburg. There they scaled the sixty-foot cliffs before

Baker could ferry his entire command staff across the river. The Federal troops were surprised in a field just beyond the cliff tops by Col. Nathan G. "Shanks" Evans and his men, who utterly routed them. (Evans was promoted to brigadier general for the action.)

Among those killed as the Federal troops tried to flee back across the river was Baker himself. Forty-eight other Northerners were killed, 158 wounded, and 714 taken prisoner. Confederate casualties totaled 33 killed, 115 wounded, and 1 missing.

In Congress, the newly formed Joint Committee on the Conduct of the War blamed Stone for the defeat, ending his career. He was held in prison, without charges, for six months. McClellan escaped any sanction and continued his temporizing.

Further Reading

Byron Farwell. *Ball's Bluff: A Small Battle and Its Long Shadow* (McLean, Va.: EPM Publications, 1990); and Joseph D. Patch. *The Battle of Ball's Bluff* (Leesburg, Va.: Potomac Press, 1958).

⚓ Batoche

Canada (May 9–12, 1885) *Second Riel Rebellion*

In 1884, Métis (Canadian people of mixed Indian-French heritage, usually Cree or Chippewa [Ojibway]) of the Saskatchewan valley in western Canada asked Louis Riel for help in their struggle against encroachments on their land and to win civil rights. Riel, a Métis politician who had long agitated for Indian and mixed-race rights, had been at the head of a small armed demonstration of Métis in 1869–1870. He then helped to negotiate Manitoba's inclusion in the Canadian confederacy. Riel subsequently suffered a nervous breakdown, then went to work as a schoolteacher for several years in the United States. When the Métis called upon him again in 1884, he returned to Canada and recruited Cree Indian bands under Poundmaker and Big Bear to join the rights movement.

Though Riel championed peaceful resistance, the rebellion turned violent when the Canadian government sent eight thousand troops west on the new transcontinental railroad in order to crush Métis resistance. On March 19, 1885, Riel declared a provisional government in the town of Batoche. This touched off two months of fighting with the North-West Field Force, comprised of army troops and Canadian Mounties led by Maj. Gen. Frederick Middleton. After a series of skirmishes, the main battle between Riel's Métis and Indian forces and Middleton's soldiers took place in Batoche between May 9 and 12.

The final battle was set up when Métis forces wrecked the Canadian supply boat *Northcote* by stretching a line across the Saskatchewan River. On May 9, Middleton marched his men toward Batoche, intent on capturing Riel and putting down the rebellion. Riel's men had constructed an ingenious series of rifle pits outside the town along the river, which allowed them to train concentrated and effective fire on Middleton's force as it arrived.

Middleton's men took cover in an improvised stockade a mile from the line of rifle pits and waited for reinforcements. For three days, Middleton tried the same approach to Batoche, only to be driven back to the stockade. His force had grown to almost nine hundred men—more than four times the number of rebels—but still the defenders held.

The Canadian forces grew impatient to deliver a bayonet charge to clear the rebels away, especially since Riel's men seemed to be running out of ammunition and were firing nails, stones, and slugs from their smooth-bore shotguns. Middleton remained cautious, but on May 12, Col. A. T. H. Williams, who commanded the Midland Battalion, took matters into his own hands and ordered his men to charge. Middleton tried to recall the attack, but when Williams's men pushed forward, Middleton was forced to commit reinforcements. The Métis forces retreated from trench to trench but had to surrender before nightfall.

The Canadian military forces suffered eight killed and forty-six wounded at Batoche, while the Métis lost only sixteen dead and thirty wounded. Gabriel Dumont, one of the chief rebel agitators who had recruited Riel to the Métis cause, escaped to the United States. Riel himself hid in the woods for three days before surrendering.

In July, Riel was tried for treason in Regina and found guilty on counts that stretched all the way back to his first rebellion in 1869. Riel refused an offer of clemency based on insanity and was executed in November. After his death, Métis resistance in western Canada was effectively quashed, though he became a martyr to the causes of Native and mixed-race peoples and of French-speaking Canadians.

Further Reading

Stanley George. *The Birth of Western Canada: A History of the Riel Rebellion* (London: Longmans Green, 1936); Arnold Haultain. *A History of Riel's Second Rebellion and How It Was Quelled* (Toronto: Grip, 1885); and Walter Hildebrandt. *The Battle of Batoche: British Small Warfare . . .* Rev. ed. (Ottawa: National Historical Parks and Sites, 1986).

Baton Rouge

Louisiana (August 5, 1862) *American Civil War*

When the Union fleet steamed up the Mississippi River after taking NEW ORLEANS in April 1862, the Federals took control of Baton Rouge as they passed by, but when they dropped back downriver after VICKSBURG, Confederate irregulars took possession of again. The Federals reoccupied the city in July. The following month, the Confederates attacked in strength.

Union brigadier general Thomas Williams commanded a brigade of twenty-five hundred men who defended Baton Rouge from an attack commanded by Confederate major general John C. Breckinridge, a former vice president of the United States. Breckinridge had six thousand men and three artillery batteries, and the Confederate ironclad ram *Arkansas* was to provide naval support.

On August 5, in the midst of a heavy fog, Breckinridge attacked the city from the east. The initial assault went well for the Confederates, and they pushed back the Union defensive lines and captured the Yankee camps before coming under fire from Union gunboats on the river. When the *Arkansas* attempted to join the battle, her engines failed and she ran aground. She was burned and abandoned by her crew the next day.

Without support from the river, Breckinridge could not sustain his position and was forced to withdraw.

The Union lost 383 casualties, including General Williams, who was killed in the fighting. The Confederates lost 453.

Further Reading

Edward Cunningham. *The Battle of Baton Rouge, 1862* (Baton Rouge, La.: Committee for the Preservation of the Port Hudson Battlefield, 1962); and William A. Spedale. *The Battle of Baton Rouge, 1862* (Baton Rouge, La.: Land and Land, 1985).

Battery Wagner

See FORT WAGNER

Bayou Teche

See IRISH BEND

Bear Paw Mountains

Montana (September 30–October 5, 1877)
Nez Perce War

In 1877, members of the Nez Perce tribe who had resisted treaty conditions for many years were declared outlaw by the federal government, which wanted to take away all but a tiny fragment of the tribe's remaining homeland and turn it over to white settlers and miners. Several bands, led by Chief Joseph (Heinmot Tooyalaket or In-mut-too-yah-lat-lat), his brother Ollikut, Looking Glass (Allalimya Takanin), Toohoolhoolzote, and Poker Joe (Wahwookya Wasaaw) and advised by spiritual leader White Bird (Penpenhihi), made a valiant but doomed dash for freedom, seeking refuge among the Crow of Montana or with Sitting Bull (Tatanka Yotanka or Tatanka Iyotake) in Canada. Five hundred women and children and about 150 warriors traveled seventeen hundred miles during the summer, harassed most of the time by the pursuing U.S. Army. After repulsing army attacks several times (*see* BIG HOLE BASIN), the much reduced group reached a point in Montana within thirty miles of the Canadian border. Believing they had outrun their pursuers, they set up camp to rest.

The army, however, had used the telegraph to set in motion a column of six hundred troops from Fort Keogh under the command of Col. Nelson A. Miles. On the last day of September, Miles's detachment found the Nez Perce camp and launched an attack, supported by Gatling guns and field artillery. Horsemen of the Seventh and Second Country Regiments charged the tipis and captured the Indians' pony herd, but the Nez Perce who survived the initial assault dug into strong defensive positions, and once again staved off defeat. The accurate Nez Perce rifle fire persuaded Miles to forgo more direct assaults and instead to surround the Indians and starve them out.

His tactics quickly worked on the exhausted Indians. Joseph and White Bird were the only remaining leaders—all the others had been killed—and the early freezing weather was killing the children, so on October 5 the Nez Perce surrendered. Joseph, having already fixed his place in history by his brilliant organized retreat, did so still further with an eloquent turn of phrase: "From where the sun now stands, I will fight no more forever," and the moving words that followed.

Although a few escaped to Canada, most of the remaining fugitive Nez Perce were transported to Kansas and then Oklahoma (Indian Territory), where disease killed a large number. Eventually, small remnants of the original bands were settled in Washington State.

Further Reading

Merril D. Beal. *"I Will Fight No More Forever": Chief Joseph and the Nez Perce War* (Seattle: University of Washington Press, 1963); Mark H. Brown. *The Flight of the Nez Perce: A History of the Nez Perce War* (Lincoln: University of Nebraska Press, 1982. Originally, New York: G. P. Putnam's Sons, 1967); Bruce Hampton. *Children of Grace: The Nez Perce War of 1877* (New York: Henry Holt, 1994); and Robert A. Scott. *Chief Joseph and the Nez Percés* (New York: Facts On File, 1993).

Bear River

Idaho (January 27, 1863) *Shoshone War*

One of the largest and bloodiest pitched battles of the western Indian wars was fought in early 1863 between a band of Shoshone and a force of California volunteers serving on federal duty.

During the American Civil War, the frontier region was virtually stripped of troops, and in several places—including the Great Basin region of present-day Utah and Idaho—Indians who opposed white settlement had almost a free hand to raid miners, settlers, and travelers. Led by Bear Hunter (Wirasuap), Shoshone who lived at the edge of the Great Salt Lake in Utah, had indulged in several such violent episodes during 1861 and 1862.

In order to protect whites in the area, the federal government recruited volunteers and swore them into federal service under appointed officers. One such group was the First California Cavalry, recruited in California by Col. Patrick E. Connor, a veteran of the Mexican-American War. Connor led three hundred men across the mountains to Utah, setting up a base at Fort Douglas. In January 1863, despite bitter cold and storms, he set out to attack Bear Hunter's band, which was encamped near the Bear River, north of Salt Lake City.

The Shoshone village, situated on the side of a deep ravine, was exceedingly difficult to approach and the band had built rock and earthwork walls to further improve the natural defenses. There were about three hundred warriors plus their families in the village when the Shoshone detected Connor's approach. Bear Hunter resolved to fight from the fortified position and waited for the Californians to attack.

Connor obliged him with a two-pronged assault, aimed at flanking the Indians' position. The Shoshone defense was stout, but the Californians were better armed and had the advantage of shooting downward from the height of the ravine. Eventually, the battle turned to a hand-to-hand contest that raged for several hours. Bear Hunter was killed, and the rest of the warriors finally gave up and tried to flee.

The casualty toll was high: the Shoshone lost 224 dead and 164 women and children taken prisoner. Connor's command lost 21 dead and 46 wounded. (The Shoshone losses were so steep that the battle has often been referred to as the "Bear River Massacre.")

Afterward, the Shoshone were forced to sign a treaty by which they gave up almost all of their Great Basin lands. Connor was promoted to brigadier general.

Further Reading

Newell Hart. *The Bear River Massacre . . .* (Preston, Idaho: Cache Valley Newsletter, 1982); and Brigham D. Madsen. *The Shoshoni Frontier and the Bear River Massacre* (Salt Lake City: University of Utah Press, 1985).

Beaufort

(Port Royal Island)

South Carolina (February 3, 1779)
American Revolution

During the early stages of the British campaign in the south, British major general Augustine Prevost maneuvered into position across the Savannah River from the American army under Maj. Gen. Benjamin Lincoln. Attacking across the river would have been difficult, so Prevost, one of the ablest British officers in America, sent Maj. William Gardiner with a detachment of two hundred men by ship to take Beaufort, which lay between Lincoln's army and Charleston.

Lincoln, however, learned of the British attempt to establish a position to his rear, and he ordered Brig. Gen. William Moultrie, the hero of the defense of CHARLESTON, to thwart the movement with three hundred North Carolina militia and a handful of Continentals. Moultrie reached Beaufort before the British, occupied the town, and established a position blocking the road down which Gardiner would march.

When the British column arrived, a brief but hot battle followed. Gardiner seems to have had the advantage of cover in adjoining woods for his men, but his only fieldpiece was knocked out of action early on,

which allowed Moultrie to use his own guns to good effect. The Americans began to run out of ammunition after about forty-five minutes, however, and Moultrie ordered a retreat. By then Major Gardiner had had enough, and he also ordered a withdrawal. The battle was a stalemate, but the retreating British left the Americans in control of Beaufort.

American losses were put at eight killed and twenty-two wounded. No figures were reported for the British.

Further Reading

Christopher L. Ward. *The War of the Revolution.* Vol. 2 (New York: Macmillan, 1952).

Beaver Dams

Canada (June 24, 1813) *War of 1812*

Seeking to extend American gains after the capture of FORT GEORGE, Brig. Gen. John Boyd sent a small force against Beaver Dams in June 1813, but his plans ended in utter failure when his men were betrayed by a civilian spy.

Lt. Col. Charles G. Boerstler commanded the American column which hoped to dislodge the British from a position at Beaver Dams, north of Queenston. There, Lt. James Fitzgibbon's small group of British regulars was supplemented by 450 Mohawk and Caughnawaga Indian troops, led by Capt. Dominique Ducharme.

Boerstler kept his attack plan a secret until he arrived in Queenston on the evening of June 23. In Queenston, however, Laura Secord, the wife of a local Canadian militia man, learned of the Americans' route and slipped out to warn Fitzgibbon of the impending attack.

When Boerstler's men marched out of Queenston the next morning, in a loose and unprotected formation, Indians attacked them in the woods outside Beaver Dams. Boerstler himself was wounded early in the skirmish, but the Americans fought off the attack, and Boerstler prepared for an orderly retreat.

Before they could withdraw, however, Fitzgibbon appeared with a flag of truce and demanded their surrender. He played to American fears and prejudices by exaggerating the size of the force of Indians and British regulars who were waiting to attack and assuring Boerstler that the Indians could not be restrained from wanton massacre. Boerstler asked for protection from the Indians and surrendered his 484 men. After Boerstler's men had surrendered their weapons, they realized their superior numbers, but they were unable to regain the advantage.

The Americans suffered fifty-six killed and fifty-six wounded, while the British and Indians counted fifteen killed and twenty-five wounded.

The defeat at Beaver Dams strengthened the British position along the Niagara frontier and hastened the removal of the American theater commander, Maj. Gen. Henry Dearborn, from office. Laura Secord, who betrayed the Americans, was enshrined as a Canadian national heroine.

Further Reading

Ernest A. Cruikshank. *The Battle of Fort George* (Niagara Falls, Ont.: Niagara Historical Society, 1904); Frank H. Keefer. *Beaver Dams* (Thorold, Ont.: Thorold Post Printers, 1914).

Beecher's Island

Colorado (September 17–25, 1868)
Sheridan's Campaign

In a search for tactics to combat the raids of the Great Plains tribes against white settlers after the Civil War, Maj. Gen. Philip Sheridan, who commanded the army in the West, set up a special unit of civilian scouts, led by Maj. George A. Forsyth, which fought a long, drawn-out battle with Cheyenne and Lakota (often known with the Nakota and Dakota as Sioux) in September 1868.

Forsyth recruited fifty men as members of a special strike force and equipped them with the finest arms—Spencer repeating rifles and Colt revolvers—hoping that a mobile detachment of mostly experienced Indian fighters could neutralize bands of raiding Indians. Lt. Frederick H. Beecher was second in command.

In early September, Forsyth's company set out along the Republican River to follow the trail of an Indian war party. On September 17, they were attacked at dawn by a large force of Cheyenne Dog Soldiers (an independent, militant warrior society) led by Tall Bull (Hotoakhihoosis), White Horse, and Bull Bear, and of Oglala Lakota led by Pawnee Killer. The famous Cheyenne warrior Roman Nose (Woquini) was also among the attackers who pinned the U.S. forces down on a long, narrow spit of land in the middle of a dry creek bed. In the first hours of the battle Forsyth's men took heavy casualties, including Beecher, who was killed, but the massed firepower of their repeating Spencers time and again repulsed Indian assaults. They

were, however, immobilized, with almost no food or water, and the Cheyenne and Lakota kept the pressure on.

Forsyth sent out several volunteer messengers to try to get through to help. The siege dragged on, however, for nine days, during which time the scouts were reduced to eating their dead horses. Finally a relief column of Buffalo Soldiers of the Tenth Cavalry (a black unit) under Capt. Louis Carpenter arrived on September 25.

Five of Forsyth's men had been killed and eighteen wounded. The unknown number of Indian casualties included Roman Nose, who died of a gunshot wound.

The concept of an elite force, while attractive in theory, had proven to be less than effective. Forsyth, however, received the brevet rank of brigadier general.

Further Reading

George B. Grinnell. *The Fighting Cheyennes* (Norman: University of Oklahoma Press, 1956); and John H. Monnett. *The Battle of Beecher Island and the Indian War of 1867–1869* (Boulder: University of Colorado Press, 1992).

Belmont

Missouri (November 7, 1861) *American Civil War*

As part of a complex set of movements by Union and Confederate forces along the Mississippi River—both sides hoped to gain strategic control of the West—Brig. Gen. Ulysses S. Grant, a graduate of West Point and a veteran of the prewar regular army, led an attack on the post at Belmont, Missouri, opposite the Confederate stronghold at Columbus, Kentucky. It was Grant's first major battle command of the war.

He left his base at Cairo, Illinois, with three thousand troops and two timberclad gunboats and advanced on the Columbus-Belmont area. Hoping to create a diversion that would draw Confederate forces away from central Missouri, Grant decided to attack the camp at Belmont, which was held by twenty-five hundred Confederate troops under Brig. Gen. Gideon Pillow.

Grant landed his men above Belmont and advanced through a heavily wooded area. The initial attack scattered the Confederates, but Grant's troops, barely trained soldiers only a few months or weeks removed from civilian life, dissolved into a mob of looters and began to ravage the stores left behind in the Confederate camp.

When Maj. Gen. Leonidas Polk crossed from Kentucky with a large number of Confederates in an attempt to cut off the Union force, Grant hastily gathered his men, restored order, and retreated under cover of his gunboats.

Further Reading

Nathaniel C. Hughes, Jr. *The Battle of Belmont: Grant Strikes South* (Chapel Hill: University of North Carolina Press, 1991); and John Seaton. *The Battle of Belmont, November 7, 1861* (Leavenworth, Kans.: Military Order of the Loyal Legion of the United States, 1902).

Bemis Heights

See SARATOGA, SECOND

Bennington

Vermont (August 16, 1777) *American Revolution*

British general John Burgoyne's grand invasion from Canada in 1777 encountered serious problems as his troops marched farther and farther from their base of supply. He had been advised that horses for his German dragoons, food for his men, and the support of Loyalist allies could all be found in the direction of the Hampshire Grants settlements (modern-day Vermont), but a contingent of Burgoyne's German mercenaries met disaster at the

hands of New England militiamen at Bennington, Vermont, while searching for badly needed supplies.

At the end of the first week of August, Burgoyne selected Lt. Col. Friedrich Baum, commander of the Brunswick dragoons, to head a raiding expedition into the countryside. Baum, who spoke no English, was to seek out food, horses, and Loyalist recruits. He had about 375 German mercenaries—including his own dragoons—300 Loyalists, Canadians, and Indians, and another 50 or so British regulars. Burgoyne instructed Baum to be bold but to take no unwarranted chances. He thought there could be little organized opposition to the expedition.

Burgoyne's intelligence reports were completely wrong. The Vermonters had persuaded veteran commander John Stark to take the field. Early on, Stark had been one of the Revolution's best officers, but he was extremely cantankerous and prickly. Passed over for promotion by Congress, he had withdrawn from active duty. The Vermont legislature's appeal, however, broke down his resolve, and he accepted a state commission as brigadier general, on the condition he would not take orders from Congress or Continental army officers. Stark's reputation was such that his call for militia was answered within a week by almost fifteen hundred men. Stark's brigade, innocent of uniforms, discipline, or drill, set out to meet

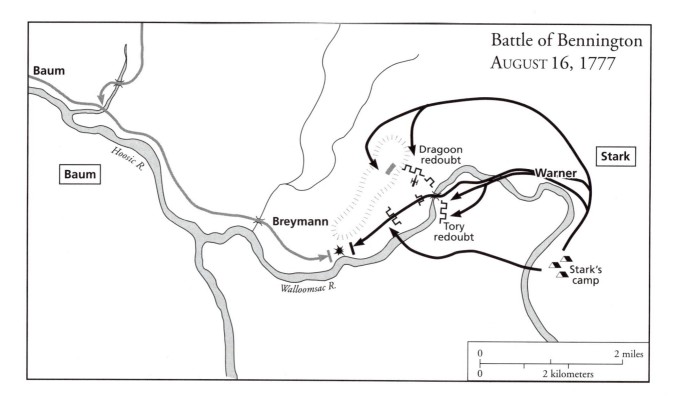

Baum, even though the American command wanted Stark to join the main army on the Hudson. Stark ordered Col. Seth Warner to gather his men (scattered after HUBBARD-TON) and join him near Bennington.

As Baum moved slowly toward Bennington, he received reports of a supply depot there, defended by only a few hundred militia. In fact, by the time Baum's advance troops made first contact at Van Shaick's Mill on August 14, Stark had close to two thousand men to defend Bennington. Though ill equipped, the militiamen were tough fighters.

Baum sent a request back to Burgoyne for reinforcements and then moved forward to positions near the Walloomsac River. He foolishly dispersed his main forces between several locations, which would allow the American militia to attack each in detail. The main position was on a hill that became known as the Dragoon Redoubt, where Baum himself commanded in the midst of his Brunswickers. He sent about 150 Loyalists across the river, where they built a breastwork later called the Tory Redoubt. The rest of the force was scattered piecemeal. Slow-moving reinforcements, in the form of six hundred German grenadiers under Lt. Col. Heinrich Breymann, were on the road to his aid.

In the afternoon of August 16, Stark and his men launched a complicated attack, designed to envelop and surround the Germans. This sort of complex battlefield maneuver almost never succeeded, especially with militia, but in this case it worked perfectly. New Hampshire troops circled to the right and hit the Dragoon Redoubt at about 3:00 P.M. At the same time, three hundred Vermonters looped around the left and came up against Baum's rear guard. The main American assault, with Stark at its head, hit the Dragoon Redoubt itself, lapping around the base of the hill and enveloping the Germans. The Loyalists, Indians, and Canadians holding their scattered positions fought only briefly after the attack began. They soon fled, leaving the field far behind.

Baum's dragoons, however, were professional fighters, and they held their position on the hill for several hours. But their ammunition finally ran out (their reserve wagon exploded), and they were trapped. Baum ordered them to draw their heavy cavalry sabers and cut their way out, but when he was dropped by a musket ball, the Germans surrendered.

Soon thereafter, the grenadiers under Breymann marched into view and prepared to attack Stark's men, who—in the fashion of militia—had lost interest in the battle and were plundering the Germans' equipment and property. Luckily for the Americans, Seth Warner and his troops arrived on the scene at almost the same time. The two new contingents squared off in facing lines and fought a hot battle until the sun began to set. The Germans tried to parley, but the untrained Americans did not recognize the drum call and continued to fire. Breymann ordered a retreat, which turned into a rout, and the American militia ended the day in full triumph—one of the few such militia victories in the whole of the American Revolution.

The Germans lost more than two hundred dead and around seven hundred taken prisoner. Lt. Col. Baum died on the field of his wounds. The Americans had only around forty killed or wounded, and they captured a great trove of weapons.

Further Reading

Frank W. Coburn. *The Centennial History of the Battle of Bennington* (Boston: G. E. Littlefield, 1877); and John Spargo. *The Bennington Battle Monument: Its Story and Its Meaning* (Rutland, Vt.: Tuttle, 1925).

Bentonville

North Carolina (March 19, 1865)
American Civil War

The final significant engagement of the American Civil War occurred near Bentonville, North Carolina, when the sixty thousand troops under Maj. Gen. William T. Sherman met a hastily pulled together Confederate army of less than half that size, commanded by Gen. Joseph E. Johnston. The Confederates had no real chance to do more than bloody the noses of the Federals.

Sherman had marched destructively across the heart of the Confederacy since leaving ATLANTA (where he had faced Johnston during the previous spring and summer), first crossing Georgia to the sea, then marching north through South Carolina. By March, in what everyone understood to be the final days of the war, he commanded two large columns, which moved into North Carolina on more or less parallel courses: the Army of Georgia, commanded by Maj. Gen. Henry Slocum, on the left hand, and the Army of the Tennessee, under Maj. Gen. Oliver O. Howard, on the right.

Johnston, who had been called back to service by Gen. Robert E. Lee, assembled as many men as he could from scattered bits and pieces in the region. Most of the individual units were understrength and top-heavy with officers—Johnston had another full general, Braxton Bragg, and three lieutenant generals, William J. Hardee, Wade Hampton, and A. P. Stewart, as part of his command—but most were veterans, and they represented a tough fighting force.

The Union commander learned that Johnston had been given the Confederate army, but Sherman did not suspect that Johnston intended to go on the offensive.

Johnston saw an opportunity when his cavalry scouts informed him that Slocum's column was strung out and no longer in close contact with the second Union column. Johnston ordered his troops into positions just south of Bentonville and waited for Slocum to march into a trap.

On March 19, Slocum's advance troops encountered Confederate cavalry, but Slocum thought it was only token resistance and signaled to Sherman, who was riding with Howard's column, that he needed no help. However, when Slocum sent ahead two divisions from the Fourteenth Corps, they were hit hard by fire from the entrenched Confederate line. Slocum fed more and more men into the fighting, but eventually he realized he faced a significant battle and called on Sherman for reinforcements. The Federals dug in on the spot, and at 3:00 P.M. their left flank was hit and nearly enveloped by a Confederate assault. Had General Bragg been brisker in committing a division under Maj. Gen. Robert F. Hoke, he might have turned the Federal line completely, but he was slow, and the Federals held on to their log barricades as the charge of the thin Confederate ranks played itself out.

Johnston was forced to pull back and reform his lines as fresh Union troops from Howard's column began to arrive on the scene. After more skirmishing, Johnston understood he could achieve nothing further and withdrew on March 21, aware that he would be unable to offer battle again.

Confederate losses were a little over twenty-six hundred casualties, and the Federals lost about fifteen hundred.

Johnston surrendered his army on April 26.

Further Reading

Mark L. Bradley. *Last Stand in the Carolinas: The Battle of Bentonville* (Campbell, Calif.: Savas Woodbury, 1995); and Nathaniel C. Hughes. *Bentonville: The Final Battle of Sherman and Johnston* (Chapel Hill: University of North Carolina Press, 1996).

Beverly's Ford

See BRANDY STATION

Big Bethel

Virginia (June 10, 1861) *American Civil War*

The skirmish at Big Bethel Church on the Virginia peninsula vies with the Battle of PHILIPPI for the title of "first land battle" of the Civil War—both battles occurred in the months after the bombardment of FORT SUMTER, as the Union and Confederacy were mobilizing for all-out war.

In late May 1861, Maj. Gen. Benjamin F. Butler ordered a Union attack on the Confederate outpost at Big Bethel Church on the Back Creek, eight miles north of Hampton, Virginia, near Fort Monroe. In the early hours of June 10, the first Federal unit, Duryée's Zouaves from New York, marched out to occupy New Market Bridge, between Hampton and Big Bethel. When six other regiments followed them an hour later and moved toward Big Bethel from the direction of Yorktown, they erroneously fired on the New Yorkers, who were dressed in gray uniforms. Two men were killed and twenty-one wounded by the friendly fire.

As the Union commanders tried to restore order, Col. John B. Magruder marched his fourteen hundred Confederates forward to meet the forty-five hundred Federals as they advanced. The Confederates pushed back the Federal attack and forced them to retreat in considerable disarray. Col. D. H. Hill's First North Carolina performed particularly admirably in the short fight.

Union forces suffered eighteen killed in the battle, including the author Maj. Theodore Winthrop, who was a member of Butler's staff. The Confederates lost only one man.

Further Reading

Benjamin R. Huske. "More Terrible than Victory." *Civil War Times Illustrated* 20, no. 6 (1981): 28–31.

Big Black River

Mississippi (May 17, 1863) *American Civil War*

After a long and circuitous march and fighting battles at PORT GIBSON, RAYMOND, and CHAMPION'S HILL, Union major general Ulysses S. Grant advanced from the east toward the Mississippi River stronghold at VICKSBURG. The Confederate commander, Lt. Gen. John Pemberton, could do little to stop the Union juggernaut, which consisted of three full army corps, but a short fight at Big Black River bought a few hours for the Confederate army to retreat behind its fortifications around Vicksburg.

Pemberton thought he might be able to stop, or at least stall, Grant's advance by holding the river crossings. He placed Brig. Gen. John S. Bowen with four thousand men to defend a mile-long trench. It was no contest, however, as Grant threw in ten thousand Federals and brushed Bowen aside in a brief fight.

The Union soldiers captured more than seventeen hundred Confederate prisoners and several field pieces. By the next morning the first Federal units were across the river and advancing on Vicksburg.

Further Reading

Editors of *Civil War Times Illustrated. Struggle for Vicksburg: The Battles That Decided the Civil War* (Harrisburg, Pa.: Stackpole Books, 1967); and Phillip T. Tucker, "Disaster at Big Black River." *Journal of America's Military Past* 19, no. 21 (1992): 85–95.

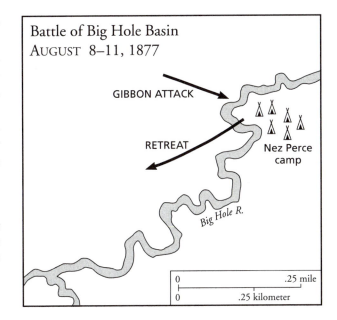

Battle of Big Hole Basin
AUGUST 8–11, 1877

GIBBON ATTACK

RETREAT

Nez Perce camp

Big Hole R.

0 .25 mile
0 .25 kilometer

Big Hole Basin

Montana (August 8–11, 1877) *Nez Perce War*

In the 1870s part of the Nez Perce tribe, living in the region where the present-day states of Oregon, Idaho, and Washington join came into conflict with the federal government over relentless reductions in their recognized homeland. (As usual, this was the result of pressure from whites to allow settlement and mining.) In 1877, bands led by Chief Joseph (Heinmot Tooyalaket or In-mut-too-yah-lat-lat), his brother Ollikut, Looking Glass (Allalimya Takanin), Toohoolhoolzote, and Poker Joe (Wahwookya Wasaaw) eluded or defeated several army columns over the course of a seventeen-hundred-mile flight toward Canada. The most significant of the armed confrontations was a pitched battle at Big Hole in Montana.

The Nez Perce had begun their flight months before, after twice defeating army detachments sent out to subdue them. By the end of the first week of August, even though their numbers included 500 women and children and only about 150 warriors, they had left the original pursuers far behind and had stopped to rest at the head of the Big Hole River. Unfortunately for the Indians, Looking Glass was incautious and failed to post scouts. Col. John Gibbon, who had commanded one of the three columns that had tried to track down Sitting Bull (Tatanka Yotanka or Tatanka Iyotake) in the Black Hills War the year before (*see* LITTLE BIGHORN), approached the Nez Perce camp undetected with a field howitzer, 150 soldiers from his Seventh Infantry, and about 40 civilian volunteers. The soldiers

formed a line of attack before dawn, and when the camp was alerted by an early riser who rode straight into the waiting whites, the soldiers fired a volley and charged the tipis.

The surprise attack created chaos for a while among the Nez Perce, who took heavy casualties during the first moments of the battle, however, Looking Glass and others rallied the well-armed warriors, who set up defensive positions and soon began to pick off the exposed soldiers. A counterattack by the Nez Perce captured Gibbon's field gun and a large store of ammunition, and by late afternoon the soldiers were completely pinned down in hastily dug trenches. During the night, the Nez Perce stole away and resumed their journey, which ended almost a month later at BEAR PAW MOUNTAINS.

The Nez Perce lost about ninety killed and Gibbon's command had thirty-three killed and thirty-eight wounded.

Further Reading

Merril D. Beal. "*I Will Fight No More Forever": Chief Joseph and the Nez Perce War* (Seattle: University of Washington Press, 1963); Mark H. Brown. *The Flight of the Nez Perce: A History of the Nez Perce War* (Lincoln: University of Nebraska Press, 1982. Originally, New York: G. P. Putnam's Sons, 1967); Aubrey L. Haines. *An Elusive Victory: The Battle of Big Hole* (West Glacier, Mont.: n.p., 1991); and Bruce Hampton. *Children of Grace: The Nez Perce War of 1877* (New York: Henry Holt, 1994).

Big Meadows

Oregon (May 27, 1856) *Rogue River War*

The discovery of gold in the Rogue River region of what is now southwest Oregon brought an influx of white miners and settlers into conflict with the Takelma and Tututni Indians who lived there. After considerable tension and a few incidents, a war broke out in 1856.

The region was under the military command of Brig. Gen. John E. Wool, an unusually enlightened officer who worked to keep whites and Indians separated and tried to assure fair treatment for all, but his resources were limited, and the whites coming into the region were bent on running the Indians out or exterminating them. When a simultaneous conflict with the Yakama Indians broke out, Wool diverted most of his troops to deal with them, leaving Capt. Andrew Jackson Smith, a man who shared his views, at Fort Lane to deal with the situation along the Rogue River.

The Takelma and Tututni were represented by leaders known to the whites as Limpy and John (or Old John). Forming a plan to take Smith and his men by surprise, they sent word to Smith that they would come forward to surrender at a place called Big Meadows. The Indians mustered about two hundred warriors, and Smith had only fifty dragoons and thirty infantrymen, whom he positioned atop a hill, along with a small field gun to wait for the Indians to come in to surrender. He was warned by two Indian women of the planned treachery, however, so he and his men were prepared when the attack came on the morning of May 27.

The fight itself unfolded in a way that in retrospect can only be described as enacting one of the mightiest clichés of Indian-white warfare in the nineteenth century. Smith and his men held off their Indian attackers throughout most of the day with the superior firepower of the field gun and a heavy musket fire. The Indians attempted to sneak up the sides of the hill but were unable to come to close range. They were successful, however, in killing or wounding a large number of the soldiers, who were fast running out of ammunition and water.

Just as the Indians were poised for what might have been the final assault, a company of regulars led by Capt. Christopher C. Augur arrived on the scene with a flourish. As Augur attacked the Indians on the hillside, Smith rallied his remaining men and charged down the hill, catching the enemy in a pincer movement. The army had snatched victory from defeat at the last minute, and the

Indians fled the scene. They surrendered shortly thereafter and were removed to a reservation.

Further Reading

Robert M. Utley. *Frontiersmen in Blue: The United States Army and the Indian, 1848–1865* (New York: Macmillan, 1962).

Billingsport

New Jersey (October 2, 1777)
American Revolution

Following a major victory over George Washington at BRANDYWINE, the British wanted to take control of the Delaware River above Philadelphia, but they faced a series of river forts designed to keep their supply fleet from sailing directly to Philadelphia.

The Americans had fortified a point on the river at Billingsport, New Jersey, and had submerged a barrier of timber and spikes between the fort and Billingsport Island. The barrier was formidable, but the fort was thinly defended.

The British commander in chief, Gen. Sir William Howe, sent the Forty-second Regiment (the Royal Highlanders) under Col. Thomas Sterling to clear out the Americans and the obstruction. On October 2, Sterling landed his men near the fort and attacked the rear. Almost before the British began an assault, the few Americans set fire to their barracks, spiked their cannon, and beat a hasty retreat.

Further Reading

Leonard Lundin. *Cockpit of the Revolution: The War for Independence in New Jersey* (Princeton, N.J.: Princeton University Press, 1940).

Black Mingo Creek

South Carolina (September 29, 1780)
American Revolution

The small engagement on Black Mingo Creek near Shepherd's Ferry, South Carolina, was one of several fought between Loyalists and the tiny but active patriot force commanded by militia brigadier general Francis Marion, "the Swamp Fox." The main British forces were operating to the north, and there were almost no organized patriot American fighters in South Carolina after the defeats at CHARLESTON and CAMDEN earlier in the year. Marion was almost alone as the flag-bearer of the Revolution.

Riding with fifty or so men, Marion discovered a camp of about the same number of Loyalists, commanded by Col. John Ball, and attempted to take it unawares, but Loyalist sentries heard Marion's men crossing the creek in the dark and the force went on the alert. Ball deployed his men in a field near the creek and waited for Marion to attack.

The patriots, surprised to find the enemy in the open, tried a frontal assault, which the Loyalists repulsed. Some of Marion's men then flanked Ball's line and drove the Loyalists from the field, bringing the fight to an end after only fifteen minutes.

The patriots lost two killed and eight wounded; the Loyalists had three dead and thirteen wounded.

Further Reading

John S. Pancake. *This Destructive War: The British Campaign in the Carolinas, 1780–1782* (University, Ala.: University of Alabama Press, 1985); and Hugh F. Rankin. *Francis Marion: The Swamp Fox* (New York: Thomas Crowell, 1973).

Blackstocks

South Carolina (November 20, 1780)
American Revolution

Following the defeat at KING'S MOUNTAIN, the British southern commander, Lt. Gen. Lord Cornwallis abandoned his expedition into North Carolina and pulled back into South Carolina, but he continued to be harassed by Brig. Gen. Thomas Sumter and his partisans. Cornwallis ordered Lt. Col. Banastre Tarleton, his most effective officer, to hunt down Sumter with Tarleton's British Legion and portions of the Sixty-third Regiment, which Sumter had repulsed at FISHDAM FORD.

Tarleton moved with his usual speed, catching Sumter and a force of about one thousand patriots at Blackstocks Plantation, on the Tyger River. He had pushed hard with his mounted troops, leaving the infantry to come up as soon as they could, so he had only about 270 men and was badly outnumbered when he found Sumter deployed to meet him.

When Sumter realized how thin were Tarleton's ranks, he ordered Col. Elijah Clarke on a flanking maneuver to cut off the British infantry before it could come onto the field. Sumter himself led a charge on Tarleton's center. The British fought off the assault and counterattacked, driving the patriots back in a remarkable performance against greatly superior numbers.

A secondary flank attack on the legion cavalry nearly succeeded, but when Sumter was hit by a musket ball and severely wounded, the Americans broke off the action and disengaged, retreating under cover of darkness.

Tarleton lost fifty killed and wounded—a high cost for his small force—and the Americans suffered three dead and five wounded.

Further Reading

John Buchanan. *The Road to Guilford Courthouse: The American Revolution in the Carolinas* (New York: John Wiley & Sons, 1997); and John S. Pancake. *This Destructive War: The British Campaign in the Carolinas, 1780–1782* (University, Ala.: University of Alabama Press, 1985).

Bladensburg

Maryland (August 24, 1814) *War of 1812*

In the late summer of 1814, the British decided to capitalize on their control of the Chesapeake Bay and attack Washington, D.C.

Vice Adm. Alexander Cochrane took command of naval operations in the Chesapeake Bay in August and assembled a strong British force of over four thousand men. It included marines and twenty-five hundred regulars under Maj. Gen. Robert Ross, fresh from service in the Napoleonic Wars. The Americans were not expecting an attack against Washington, and they further delayed their defensive preparations when Cochrane deceived them with a feint toward Baltimore.

The main British force started up the Pawtuxet River on August 19, planning to march north through Maryland to Washington. When American defenses along the Pawtuxet failed to halt the British advance, Sec. of War William Armstrong appointed Brig. Gen. William Winder, a political ally of Pres. James Madison, to command the newly created Tenth Military District and reinforce the capital. Winder's incompetence, the slow response of freshly summoned militia forces, and resistance to the idea that the British would really attack all slowed the construction of defenses.

Finally, as the British reached Bladensburg, about six miles east of Washington, it became abundantly clear that they did mean to enter the capital. The opposing forces met at Bladensburg on August 24, as the Americans desperately tried to protect the still underfortified capital.

The American commanders placed their six thousand troops in defensive positions at Bladensburg, but in the process they revealed their lack of tactical prowess. Militia brigadier general Tobias Stansbury at first deployed troops in three lines facing east toward the Potomac River, but Sec. of State James Monroe, who held no formal military command, rearranged two of the lines. Stansbury wrongly assumed that Brigadier General Winder had ordered the change and left them undisturbed. Because of Monroe's meddling, the three American lines were too far apart to support one another, and when the battle began, no solid position could be maintained.

Just before fighting commenced, President Madison and several cabinet members, who had ridden out to urge on the troops, started to cross the Potomac directly into the advancing British front line. They were warned off by a scout at the last moment, but American troops, who had meant to destroy the bridge the presidential party had been about to use, were now unable to do so, leaving the American position open to British attack.

Around 1:00 P.M., Major General Ross led his troops across the Potomac in the initial British advance and quickly flanked the first American line. As militia troops fled, the first line fell back. Ross's men then charged the second American line, and Brigadier General Winder ordered his men to retreat toward Georgetown, where he hoped they could re-form, but the retreat quickly turned into a chaotic rout that would later be derisively referred to as the "Bladensburg races." Confusion reigned on the battlefield. Many British soldiers fired from covered positions on the exposed American lines. In addition, the British fired Congreve rockets, which flamed over the field in noisy, erratic ricochet patterns, frightening the Americans, most of whom were unused to battle.

Only one section of the American force held. Joshua Barney, a hero of the Revolutionary War, who held no formal rank but commanded an American flotilla on the Pawtuxet as a sailing master commandant, arrived with a force of seamen and marines after the battle had begun and attached it to the third American line. Barney's men held their position and fired on the British with heavy naval guns dragged from their ships, but eventually they ran out of ammunition, and when cover from American militia collapsed, the British got around their flank. Barney was wounded and captured, but most of his force escaped.

The three-hour battle was a crushing defeat for the Americans. The British lost 64 killed and 185 wounded versus American totals of just 26 killed and 51 wounded, but the outcome was far more costly for the Americans in overall political and military terms.

After destroying the American force at Bladensburg, the British moved on to burn Washington, D.C., the following night. The destruction of much of the nation's capital marked a low point for the American cause during the War of 1812.

Further Reading

William M. Marine. *The British Invasion of Maryland, 1812–1815* (Baltimore: Society for the War of 1812 in Maryland, 1913); Charles G. Muller. *The Darkest Day: The Washington-Baltimore Campaign* (Philadelphia: Lippincott, 1963); and Neil H. Swanson. *The Perilous Fight* (New York: Farrar and Rinehart, 1945).

Blair's Landing

See PLEASANT HILL LANDING

Bloody Brook

(Pocumtuck, Deerfield)
Massachusetts (September 18, 1675)
King Philip's War

The ambush and destruction of a colonial Massachusetts column near modern-day Deerfield by a mixed force of New England Indians marked the high point of King Philip's War for the Indians and the greatest defeat for the white colonists.

King Philip's War was the largest and most significant conflict between Native Americans and immigrant settlers in the history of colonial New England. It had come about when the pressures applied to the Indians by the New Englanders' cravings for land, religious proselytism, and economic domination grew intolerable. The Wampanoag sachem Metacomet (called King Philip by the New Englanders) was an able, energetic, and persuasive leader, who finally responded in 1675 to repeated provocations by launching a campaign to push out the unwanted whites. The easiest targets were scattered farming settlements in western Massachusetts along the Connecticut River valley, and Metacomet and his allies—the Nipmuc and Narraganset—hit these hard during the summer of 1675. By fall the settlers were in retreat, but they hoped to save one of the most important settlements, at Pocumtuck (what is today Deerfield, Massachusetts).

Realizing the full force of the threat from the Indian alliance, the Pocumtuck settlers sent their women and children to safety, but about fifty men stayed behind to try to preserve the village and the vital harvest of corn, which was ripening in the fields. Capt. Thomas Lathrop led a small company to reinforce Pocumtuck, bringing the total to around sixty-five armed men. They decided to load the corn onto carts and transport it southward along a narrow trail.

When the column slowed to cross a brook about five miles south of the village, the Indians struck from ambush and, during a short, one-sided clash, killed nearly all the white settlers. A relief column arrived too late to do more than survey the scene of the disaster.

The defeat had considerable emotional and psychological effect on the Puritan New Englanders, who needed little prompting to see the hand of Providence in any event, and it intensified the harshness of the war.

Further Reading

Russell Bourne. *The Red King's Rebellion: Racial Politics in New England, 1675–1678* (New York: Atheaneum, 1990); James D. Drake. *King Philip's War: Civil War in New England, 1675–1676* (Amherst, Mass.: University of Massachusetts Press, 2000); Francis Jennings. *The Invasion of America: Indians, Colonialism, and the Cant of Conquest* (Chapel Hill: University of North Carolina Press, 1975); Douglas E. Leach. *Flintlocks and Tomahawks: New England in King Philip's War* (New York: W. W. Norton, 1953); and Richard I. Melvoin. *New England Outpost: War and Society in Colonial Deerfield* (New York: W. W. Norton, 1989).

❧ Bloody Marsh

See BLOODY SWAMP

❧ Bloody Pond

See LAKE GEORGE

❧ Bloody Swamp

(Bloody Marsh, St. Simon's Island)

Georgia (July 7, 1742) *War of Jenkin's Ear*

The colorfully named colonial War of Jenkin's Ear (so called after a British sea captain who claimed that the Spanish had cut off his ear during a dispute) was a conflict between Great Britain and Spain over commercial rights, particularly in the New World. In North America it was focused on the southeastern coast, where Spain had established a strong base at ST. AUGUSTINE in the late sixteenth century to guard her sealanes. In 1732, Great Britain founded a new colony of Georgia just north of Spanish Florida as a buffer against Spanish power and as a potential base for expansion.

When the War of Jenkin's Ear broke out in 1740, the belligerent Georgia governor, James Oglethorpe, a man who had raised a private regiment and had the full backing of the British government, led an unsuccessful expedition to take St. Augustine. Two years later, the Spanish governor of Florida, Manuel de Montiano, struck back at his British opponents, sailing toward Oglethorpe's base on St. Simon Island, off the coast of Georgia, with a large naval and land force numbering between one and three thousand men. His plan was to wipe Georgia off the map.

Oglethorpe's main position was at Fort Frederica, sited to guard the inland passage and surrounded by swamps and marshes. At the sea end of the island were Fort Delegal and Fort St. Simon, designed to protect against a naval attack. The Georgia governor commanded only about seven or eight hundred men, including his regiment of foot, some civilian volunteers, and a few Creek and Chickasaw allies. As the Spanish approached, Oglethorpe abandoned the twin forts at the end of the island and concentrated his troops at Fort Frederica.

Montiano arrived with his forces reduced by storms that had scattered part of his fleet. (This accounts for the great discrepancy in estimates of troops under his command.) But he still had considerable superiority in numbers when he landed his infantry after running past Fort Delegal and Fort St. Simon on July 5. He occupied St. Simon as his headquarters and planned an overland assault on Fort Frederica. However, a Spanish reconnaissance party was detected and repulsed the next day near the British base, and Oglethorpe decided to preempt his enemies. He set up an ambush in the swamps southeast of Frederica along the trail the main Spanish force was bound to use.

On July 7, Montiano's men marched into the trap and suffered a major defeat at the hands of the British and their Indian allies in an engagement that came to be known as "Bloody Swamp." The setback effectively ended the Spanish attempt to eliminate the British from the Georgia coast, and after more maneuvers and aborted plans, Montiano sailed back to St. Augustine.

Further Reading

Larry E. Ivers. *British Drums on the Southern Frontier: The Military Colonization of Georgia, 1733–1749* (Chapel Hill: University of North Carolina Press, 1974).

☙ Blue Lake

See ASH HOLLOW

☙ Blue Licks

Kentucky (August 19, 1782) *American Revolution*

After raiding into modern-day West Virginia, a group of 240 Loyalists and Indians, led by the notorious Simon Girty, a turncoat American who served the British as a leader of irregulars, moved into the Central Kentucky region, threatened Bryan's Station (just north of Lexington), then turned back.

They were pursued by local militia under Maj. Hugh McGary northward to Blue Licks Springs, on the Licking River. Daniel Boone was with the Kentuckians and advised them to wait for the reinforcements that were on the way, but McGary was impatient and led a disorganized attack across a deep ford into the teeth of superior numbers.

Girty's men had no difficulty in picking off the Kentuckians as they tried to wade the river, killing or wounding seventy and sending the rest into retreat.

Further Reading

Samuel M. Wilson. *The Battle of Blue Licks, August 19, 1782* (Lexington, Ky.: n.p., 1927); Bennett H. Young. *History of the Battle of Blue Licks* (Louisville, Ky.: Morton, 1897).

☙ Blue Savannah

South Carolina (September 4, 1780)
American Revolution

Brig. Gen. Francis Marion, "the Swamp Fox," a South Carolina partisan leader, was one of the few American commanders to operate successfully against the British in the Carolinas immediately after the disaster at CAMDEN. He recaptured American prisoners in a swift attack against a British camp at GREAT SAVANNAH and then fled with only fifty men toward the Pedee River.

Two hundred fifty local Loyalists, emboldened by the British victories at Camden and FISHING CREEK, took the field under Maj. Micajah Ganey and set out to find Marion.

The patriots were outnumbered five to one, but Marion set up an ambush for the Loyalists, after routing their advance guard, and at Blue Savannah sprang the trap with his mounted troops. The Loyalist resisted only

briefly before dissolving into the surrounding swamps and heading for home.

Marion suffered only three wounded in the encounter, which defused the Loyalist threat in the area.

Further Reading

John Buchanan. *The Road to Guilford Courthouse: The American Revolution in the Carolinas* (New York: John Wiley & Sons, 1997).

☙ Bound Brook

New Jersey (April 13, 1777) *American Revolution*

During the winter and early spring of 1777, both the main American and British armies were in winter quarters—the Americans at Morristown, New Jersey, and the British at New York City—but both sides had detached outlying units, which were vulnerable to quick attack.

The five hundred Americans under Maj. Gen. Benjamin Lincoln at Bound Brook, New Jersey, on the Raritan River, were wary of the presence of thousands of German mercenaries only a few miles away at Brunswick, but they paid little attention to other enemy forces until an unsuspected attack came from two thousand British troops under Maj. Gen. Charles, Lord Cornwallis.

Aided perhaps by intelligence from a local farmer, Cornwallis's men crossed the river and attacked the American outpost in a surprise maneuver. The American militia sentries did almost nothing to alert Lincoln or his men to the attack. Nonetheless, Lincoln managed to lead most of his troops to safety, losing only three small field guns.

Cornwallis withdrew before a large American reinforcement under Maj. Gen. Nathanael Greene arrived.

The minor incident motivated the commander in chief, Gen. George Washington, to pull in some of the more vulnerable detachments before the beginning of the spring and summer campaign.

Further Reading

T. E. Davis. *The Battle of Bound Brook*, 1895. Reprint ed. (Bound Brook, N.J.: Washington Camp Ground Association, 1981).

☙ Braddock's Defeat

See MONONGAHELA

Brandy Station

(Fleetwood Hill, Beverly's Ford)

Virginia (June 9, 1863) *American Civil War*

After Union cavalry reconnaissance led to a battle at FRANKLIN'S CROSSING on the Rappahannock River on June 5, Maj. Gen. Joseph Hooker learned that the majority of Confederate general Robert E. Lee's army was in Culpeper County, Virginia. Though Hooker wrongly assumed the bulk of the Confederate force to be in the town of Culpeper, he ordered Brig. Gen. Alfred Pleasonton's cavalry to attack across the river, which led to a daylong pitched battle at and around Brandy Station on June 9. The clash, primarily between Union and Confederate cavalry forces, was to make the reputation of Union horsemen and was the largest mounted battle ever fought in North America.

On the evening of June 8, Robert E. Lee and his commander of cavalry, Maj. Gen. J. E. B. Stuart, witnessed a grand review at the Culpeper Court House of his ten thousand cavalry under Brig. Gen. W. H. Rooney Lee (Robert E. Lee's son), Lt. Gen. Richard Ewell, and Lt. Gen. James Longstreet. None of them realized that Pleasonton was arriving from the east, across the Rappahannock from Brandy Station, with eleven thousand troopers of his own. Overnight, Pleasonton's three divisions, under Brig. Gen. John Buford, Brig. Gen. David M. Gregg, and Col. Alfred Duffié, reached the Rappahannock and prepared to attack Stuart's force.

At daybreak on June 9, Buford's forces splashed across Beverly's Ford and surprised the sleeping Confederates in their camp. The attack took a heavy toll, but the Southerners managed to form a horse-artillery line near St. James Church. Buford's orders commanded him to continue south to Brandy Station to join Gregg, but when one of his most effective officers, Col. Benjamin Grimes Davis, was killed, Buford's charge stalled and men fought hand to hand all over the field.

At 8:00 A.M., the Confederate line stretched a long distance from the river toward a rise at Fleetwood Hill, near Brandy Station when one of the most dramatic Union attacks of the war took place. Union horsemen had been ridiculed throughout the war by Confederates, but the Sixth Pennsylvania Cavalry changed that when it charged out of the woods and headed straight into the Confederate line of cannon. Its saber attack did not break through the Confederate position, but it did inspire a new respect and win the Pennsylvanians a reputation for bravery.

After the Sixth was driven back, Buford attacked young Brigadier General Lee's dismounted cavalry line at a stone wall to the north of a force commanded by Brig. Gen. Wade Hampton. Though Lee's men held off their attackers, by midmorning other developments forced them to begin pulling back. Brigadier General Gregg's twenty-four hundred Federals turned up in Brandy Station, behind Stuart's headquarters on Fleetwood Hill. Stuart quickly recalled Brig. Gen. William E. Jones, Rooney Lee, and Hampton from the St. James Church to protect the higher elevation.

The second phase of the battle took place atop Fleetwood Hill, where the fighting raged to the din of horses' hooves and clashing swords. Buford attacked Rooney Lee on the north face as Gregg battled Jones to the south. A British soldier of fortune serving with the Union, Col. Sir Percy Wyndham, at the head of Maryland, Pennsylvania, and New York men, tried to capture a Confederate cannon on the hill's west side, but he was repelled after a strenuous fight by the Twelfth Virginia. The Southerners managed to defend the hill after hours of bitter conflict, but Stuart was outraged that the Federals still controlled the field below, despite the fact that Duffié had been delayed in a separate action at Stevensburg.

Stuart ordered Rooney Lee to attempt one last push against Buford's force to clear the field. Lee's troops made considerable headway, and though Lee was seriously wounded, at last Buford was ordered to retreat back across Beverly's Ford.

Considering the fact that more than twenty thousand total troops, seventeen thousand of them cavalry, were engaged at Brandy Station, the casualties were relatively light. The Northerners lost 868 and the Southerners 515.

Though Stuart's force came away victorious and in possession of both Fleetwood Hill and the field below, the battle at Brandy Station cannot be considered an unqualified Union loss. Most military historians agree that the conflict "made" the reputation of Northern horsemen, who were less a force to be laughed at and more one to be reckoned with after the memorable conflict at Brandy Station.

Further Reading

Heros von Borcke. *The Great Cavalry Battle of Brandy Station, 9 June 1863* (Winston-Salem, N.C.: Palaemon Press, 1976); and Fairfax D. Downey. *Clash of Cavalry: The Battle of Brandy Station, June 9, 1863* (New York: David McKay, 1959).

Brandywine

Pennsylvania (September 11, 1777)
American Revolution

In the fall of 1777, the American commander in chief, Gen. George Washington, needed desperately to stop the British expedition, led by Gen. Sir William Howe, that was moving to occupy Philadelphia, the seat of the American government. Washington's first attempt to quash the British invasion of Pennsylvania was at Brandywine Creek, between Philadelphia and Howe's landing point at Head of Elk, Maryland. Unfortunately for the American cause, Washington's generalship was not up to the task.

Howe had a huge force, numbering perhaps fifteen thousand men, most of them British regulars or German mercenaries, with all the usual attendant artillery and support. He had sailed from his base at New York in late July, keeping Washington guessing as to his intentions, and he now planned to march deliberately toward Philadelphia. Howe hoped to end the rebellion by taking the city. If he could destroy Washington's army in the process, so much the better.

Washington had about eleven thousand men to oppose the British advance. He had positioned most of his

forces around Chadd's Ford on Brandywine Creek, a relatively small waterway that could be easily crossed at many fords in the area. The largest part of the army was divided into two divisions, one commanded by Maj. Gen. Nathanael Greene, the other by Brig. Gen. Anthony Wayne. Most of these troops were deployed on the east side of the creek, with an advance guard of light infantry under Brig. Gen. William Maxwell on the western bank. To the north were troops under Brig. Gen. John Sullivan, who was given the task of defending the fords. To the south was Brig. Gen. John Armstrong.

Even though he was the stranger, Howe approached the Brandywine with a far better understanding of the local geography than that of Washington. The British commander realized that there were enough fords to the north of Washington's position to allow an easy flanking or enveloping movement, and he detached about seventy-five hundred troops under Maj. Gen. Lord Cornwallis to move out to the British left, cross the creek, and take Washington in the rear. Meanwhile, five thousand troops commanded by a senior German officer, Lt. Gen. Wilhelm, Baron von Knyphausen, were to hold Washington's attention with a demonstration at Chadd's Ford.

Starting at dawn, Knyphausen marched forward, shoved Maxwell's light infantry back over the creek, and took up positions just across the ford from Washington. Cornwallis's movements to the north went smoothly, and by afternoon he was in position to attack Washington's rear. Washington learned of the presence of a large force to his north, but his orders to move troops to oppose the British were confused, and no one in the American command seemed to know where the key fords were or what they were called. The American countermovements went astray, and the troops involved ended up miles from the scene of the ensuing battle.

By about 4:00 P.M., Cornwallis was in place and ordered an attack on Washington's rear. Washington had shifted some troops under Maj. Gen. Lord Stirling and Maj. Gen. Adam Stephen to positions on a plowed hill, and they engaged the British while Washington attempted to bring up Greene's division. Before the American commander could arrive with sufficient troops, the British already had the upper hand and were pressing Sullivan's men closely. Washington's dispositions and the tactical confusion they caused had led to impending doom, but his personal courage was never in doubt. Accompanied by the young French volunteer officer the marquis de Lafayette, Washington rode conspicuously up

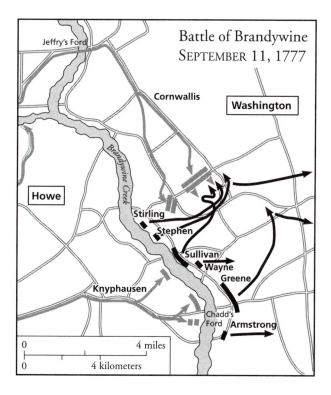

Battle of Brandywine
SEPTEMBER 11, 1777

Jeffry's Ford
Cornwallis
Washington
Brandywine Creek
Howe
Stirling
Stephen
Sullivan
Wayne
Greene
Knyphausen
Chadd's Ford
Armstrong

0   4 miles
0   4 kilometers

and down the American lines, urging his men to greater efforts. The commander was spared, but Lafayette was wounded in the leg.

As the Americans struggled against Cornwallis, Knyphausen finally attacked across the creek at Chadd's Ford and collapsed the remaining American lines. By nightfall both divisions of the British force had made contact, and the American army was in retreat, leaving the road toward Philadelphia open to the British.

The American losses of killed, wounded, and captured were high, perhaps as many as twelve to thirteen hundred altogether. Howe had lost about half that many.

The American army had suffered yet another defeat in a stand-up battle with the British, but once again Howe had been unable to give Washington the death blow. The American army survived, and with it the Revolution.

Further Reading

Henry S. Canby. *The Brandywine.* Reprint ed. (New York: Farrar & Rinehart, 1941); and Samuel S. Smith. *The Battle of Brandywine* (Monmouth Beach, N.J.: Philip Freneau Press, 1976).

Breed's Hill

See BUNKER HILL

Briar Creek

Georgia (March 3, 1779) *American Revolution*

In 1779, the British continued to implement their strategy in the southern states, hoping to win back control of Georgia and the Carolinas and to rally support among southern Loyalists. Major General Augustine Prevost commanded the British armies in Georgia and skillfully directed his field officers to victories over the much less experienced patriots. The British win at Briar Creek was a good example.

The British and the Americans had played cat and mouse across the Georgia countryside during the first two months of the year, with two small American victories but no large engagements. In early March, Brig. Gen. John Ashe was on his way to join the main American army at Purysburg, Georgia, with fifteen hundred militia and about one hundred Continentals, the latter commanded by Lt. Col. Samuel Elbert, when he was surprised en route by a quick-maneuvering British force of about nine hundred.

Ashe had halted his march on the north bank of Briar Creek, a deep waterway surrounded by swampland and crossed by a single bridge. Across the creek, the first battalion of the Seventy-first Highlanders had been stationed as a decoy. The real menace was the heavily reinforced Second Battalion, which Major General Prevost had placed under the command of his younger brother, Lt. Col. Mark Prevost, and sent on a long, quick march across the creek to come up behind Ashe.

Ashe's mounted scouts alerted him that a British force was on the road and approaching but the American militia commander did almost nothing to prepare, even though his back was to a swampy creek and more enemies blocked his retreat on the other side of the waterway.

When Prevost's troops approached the American camp on March 3, Ashe formed his men into two columns, with Lieutenant Colonel Elbert's few loose Continentals to the front. When the enemy came within musket range, Elbert's men began to fire, but with the first shots the entire militia contingent began to collapse. Within minutes, the Continentals found themselves alone on the field—the rest of the Americans were frantically trying to escape across the bridge or through the swamp. Elbert was captured by the advancing British, and dozens of militia were drowned or hunted to death in the swamp.

Altogether the Americans lost between 150 and 200 killed or drowned and 170 captured. The British had only five killed and eleven wounded.

The battle consolidated the British hold on Georgia and sent American fortunes into a spin. General Ashe was convicted by a court-martial of failing to prepare adequately.

Further Reading

David S. Heidler. "The American Defeat at Briar Creek." *Georgia Historical Quarterly* 66, no. 3 (1983): 317–33.

Brice's Cross Roads

(Brice's Creek Roads, Guntown, Tishomingo Creek)

Mississippi (June 10, 1864) *American Civil War*

Brice's Cross Roads was the greatest victory of Confederate major general Nathan Bedford Forrest, the brilliant cavalry leader and tactician, who played havoc with Federal forces in the Mississippi-Tennessee theater during 1864.

The Federal high command wanted to launch a major campaign from Tennessee into Georgia, but the theater

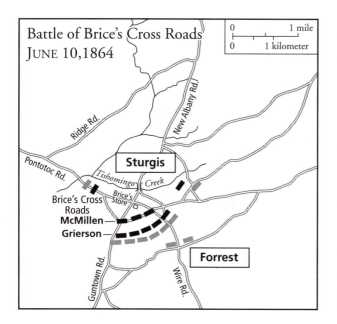

Battle of Brice's Cross Roads
JUNE 10, 1864

commander, Maj. Gen. William T. Sherman, rightly feared that Forrest, with thirty-five hundred fast-moving cavalry troopers, would be able to threaten the Union line of supply. Sherman ordered Brig. Gen. Samuel Sturgis to march with eighty-one hundred men (both infantry and cavalry), twenty-two artillery pieces, and a large train of supply wagons against Forrest's headquarters at Tupelo, Mississippi.

At the same time, Forrest had moved into Alabama, headed toward the Union supply line in Tennessee, just as Sherman had feared. When Forrest learned of Sturgis's movements, he turned his column around and raced back. North of Tupelo, at a swampy, wooded spot called Brice's Cross Roads, Forrest found a position he thought he could use to his advantage against the larger force of Federals. He intended to attack and defeat the Union cavalry before Sturgis could bring up his superior weight of infantry and artillery. The Confederates would then have a tactical advantage over the tired Federals.

The plan worked perfectly. On the morning of June 10, the advance units of Sturgis's cavalry under Brig. Gen. Benjamin Grierson reached the crossroads, where Forrest launched a close-range attack by his own riders. As if following a script, Sturgis called up his infantry, commanded by Col. William L. McMillen, but the foot soldiers had a difficult time covering the muddy, swampy ground in the intense Mississippi heat. By the time they reached the battleground, they were exhausted. Forrest's troopers turned on the Federal infantry and by late afternoon had disrupted the

Union line and turned Sturgis's flank. The Federal troops began to flee toward the rear, and soon the retreat turned into a rout. Many Union soldiers blundered into Tishomingo Creek while trying to escape and drowned.

Sturgis's command completely disintegrated under the Confederate pursuit, losing all its artillery and more than two hundred supply wagons. The Federal units could not be reassembled until they had all reach Memphis, their starting point.

Sturgis lost 223 killed, 394 wounded, and 1,623 captured or missing. Forrest lost only 96 killed and 396 wounded.

Forrest's complete triumph was a morale-builder for the flagging Confederate cause and did much to inflate his reputation as a general; however, Sherman moved on Georgia despite Smith's defeat, and the supply line stayed open.

Further Reading

Edwin C. Bearss. *Protecting Sherman's Lifeline: The Battles of Brice's Creek and Tupelo, 1864* (Washington, D.C.: National Park Service, 1972).

≈ Bristoe Station

Virginia (October 14, 1863) *American Civil War*

In the fall of 1863, Confederate and Union forces were maneuvering back and forth between the Rapidan River and Washington, D.C., in a bid to establish supremacy in the wake of the costly battle at GETTYSBURG. During October, Confederate general Robert E. Lee pushed Union major general George Gordon Meade toward Manassas, seeking to re-create his successful tactic of Second BULL RUN. On October 14, Lt. Gen. A. P. Hill sought to cut off the Federal Third Corps at Bristoe Station, Virginia, to aid Lee's campaign.

When Hill threw his infantry against the Union Third Corps at Broad Run, near Bristoe Station, on October 14, he was unaware that Brig. Gen. John Caldwell had positioned the Federal Second Corps behind a railroad embankment nearby. When Hill's men attacked the strong center of the Third Corps, they were caught in an unexpected cross fire. Brig. Gen. John Rogers Cooke and Brig. Gen. William W. Kirkland, who led the Confederate attacks against Broad Run, were both seriously wounded, and Hill had to order a withdrawal across the Rappahannock River.

Confederate casualties totaled approximately 1,900, while Union forces lost only 548 men.

Hill's disastrous attack allowed Meade time to establish a defensive position near Manassas and thereby contributed to the failure of Lee's strategy.

Further Reading

William D. Henderson. *The Road to Bristoe Station: Campaigning with Lee and Meade, August 1–October 20, 1863* (Lynchburg, Va.: H. E. Howard, 1987).

Buena Vista

Mexico (February 22–23, 1847)
Mexican-American War

At the Battle of Buena Vista, Gen. Antonio López de Santa Anna sought to repair his reputation by besting an army of invading Americans, against whom he bore a grudge for his defeat by an army of Texans at SAN JACINTO eleven years earlier. After returning from exile in Cuba, Santa Anna had taken control of the Mexican army and set out to attack American brigadier general Zachary Taylor, who had encamped at Agua Nueva. Taylor quickly retreated to a more advantageous position at Buena Vista to await the approach of the vastly larger Mexican force.

The hacienda at Buena Vista offered excellent protection from attack, because the main approach, down a narrow road, could be easily covered by artillery. Santa Anna believed that an attack from the foothills to the east of the estate might be effective. Brig. Gen. John E. Wool had proposed the narrows, known as La Angostura, as the best site to make a stand, and he set about constructing a parapet and other fortifications there.

On the morning of February 22, Santa Anna sent a deputation under a white flag to meet Taylor on neutral ground at Saltillo to offer terms if Taylor would surrender. Taylor declined, and he and Wool readied their 4,759 men, only 700 of whom had ever experienced battle, to meet Santa Anna's approximately 16,000 troops.

During the morning, the Mexican army, in full finery and displaying colorful banners, spread out in a long line across the valley before Buena Vista. The Americans did not have enough troops to form a solid opposing line. In addition to the artillery and three regiments stationed at La Angostura, Taylor positioned brigades of infantry and dragoons, along a line leading to foothills in the east, where—on the American left—Col. Archibald Yell's

Arkansas regiment and Col. Humphrey Marshall's Kentucky regiment were stationed.

Around 3:00 P.M., the Mexican artillery opened fire. Maj. Gen. Pedro Ampudia, in command of the Mexican right, took his troops up into the mountains above the Kentuckians' position and began to advance. Marshall's and Ampudia's troops skirmished in the mountains for the rest of the day, but there was no decisive result by the time Taylor recalled the Kentuckians into the valley after dark.

Taylor's men spent the cold night in the field, on the lookout for attack and unable to light fires to warm themselves. Most of Santa Anna's troops were comfortable in their camp. Nonetheless, the Mexican general was facing rising disaffection among his men, many of whom had been forcibly pressed into service and had been underfed for more than a month. Daybreak revealed that the Mexicans had established an artillery battery atop the highest mountain to the east of the American position and had sent a detachment around the Americans' left flank to a position behind the American line. Brigadier General Wool reinforced the left side, where he now expected the main Mexican attack.

Maj. Gen. Francisco Pacheco and Maj. Gen. Manuel María Lombardini pushed their cavalry and infantry against the American left center. Lt. John Paul Jones O'Brien rushed forward with three artillery pieces and held off the Mexicans with only his own small company of cannoneers after the Second Indiana infantry failed to back him up as planned. Vastly outnumbered, O'Brien eventually had to withdraw, leaving one gun behind on the field. On the extreme left, the Kentuckians and Arkansans were also being pushed back, and it looked as if the American left side would give way altogether.

Around 9:00 A.M., Brigadier General Taylor returned from a side trip to Saltillo and rode onto the center of the field. He sat on his horse, "Old Whitey," in full view of all the American troops and, while a company of Mississippi riflemen under Col. Jefferson Davis temporarily held off the Mexican advance, Taylor calmly set in motion his plan to restore order. He sent a mixed group of artillery, riflemen, and infantry east to the rear of town, where they countered a Mexican cavalry charge. The first real American success in the battle came when this group split and drove off the band of Mexican riders.

A large number of Mexican lancers then advanced from the foothills, but their charge was slowed by heavy fire from Capt. Braxton Bragg's artillery. Mississippi and Indiana infantry formed an open V formation, and as the lancers advanced, they were caught in deadly American cross fire. The Mexicans were now being pushed back all across the eastern foothills.

After a short pause in the fighting occasioned by the appearance of a flag of truce, for which no party would take responsibility, the Mexicans formed for one final attack. Brig. Gen. Francisco Pérez led cavalry and infantry in a charge against the new American center (toward the left side). Various batteries of American artillery, first under Lieutenant O'Brien and Lt. George H. Thomas and later under Captain Bragg and Capt. Thomas W. Sherman, held off the charge as American infantry rushed in from other parts of the field. Capt. John M. Washington's heavy guns also fought off an advance of Mexican lancers. The Mexican

attacks could make little headway, and by dusk the fighting had died down.

The American troops again slept in place on the night of February 23, because Taylor expected a renewed Mexican attack the next morning. Instead, after holding a council of war and reviewing his exhausted and hungry troops, Santa Anna decided to withdraw. The Mexican force retreated quietly back to Agua Nueva. Taylor's force awoke on February 24 to find the battle over.

In absolute terms, neither side had won a true victory, but Taylor had held his ground. Both sides suffered heavy casualties. American casualties were 268 killed, 456 wounded, and 23 missing. Mexican losses were estimated at more than two thousand killed and wounded, plus an unknown number of deserters.

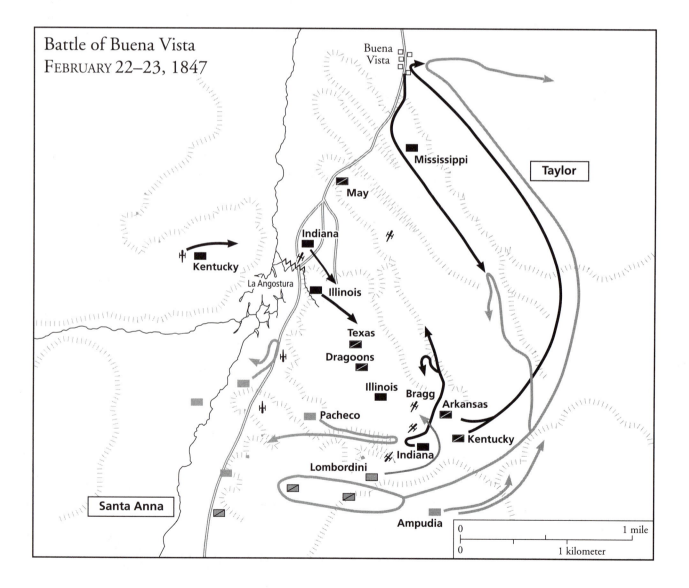

The Battle of Buena Vista effectively ended the war in northern Mexico, where the Americans had won every battle. Though Santa Anna had failed in his only major offensive of the war, he managed to alarm the American public for several weeks after what he falsely claimed had been a victory at Buena Vista. As Pres. James K. Polk prepared to send American reinforcements, Santa Anna returned to Mexico City, where he put down a revolt and was declared president of Mexico.

Further Reading

Henry W. Benham. *Recollections of Mexico and the Battle of Buena Vista* (Boston: n.p., 1871); James H. Carleton. *The Battle of Buena Vista . . .* (New York: Harper and Sons, 1848); and David Lavender. *Climax at Buena Vista: The American Campaign in Northeastern Mexico, 1846–47* (Philadelphia: Lippincott, 1966).

Bull Run, First

(First Manassas)
Virginia (July 21, 1861) *American Civil War*

In July 1861, both North and South were mobilizing for what they expected to be a short war. Federal troops, many of them signed up only for temporary enlistments, gathered in Washington, D.C., under the direction of Gen. Winfield Scott, the commander in chief. Southerners, meanwhile, prepared to defend the Confederate capital at Richmond, Virginia, just one hundred miles to the south. Under constant political pressure to attack and achieve a fast victory, an ailing Scott handed the task of pushing southward to Brig. Gen. Irvin P. McDowell, who gathered an army of thirty-five thousand men and prepared to march. Confederate brigadier general P. G. T. Beauregard and Brig. Gen. Joseph E. Johnston had in mind a vigorous defense of Richmond and contrived to stop the Federal offensive. By the time that the first major battle of the war was over on July 21 between Federal and Confederate troops at Bull Run, Virginia, near the Manassas Railroad junction, it was clear that the conflict would be neither as short nor as clean as either side had imagined.

By mid-July, Beauregard believed that McDowell's offensive was close at hand, so he posted his twenty-two thousand troops along a six-mile defensive line near Bull Run Creek and hoped that Johnston, who had removed to the lower Shenandoah River valley, would be able to reinforce him. McDowell's strategy relied on the advantage of numbers and assumed that Federal major general Robert Patterson, who had taken Harpers Ferry earlier that month, would be able to detain Johnston's men. Patterson's failure to do so played a major role in the battle at Bull Run.

McDowell's force, which had been set up in five divisions, set out from Washington on July 16, but after two days, having only reached Centreville, McDowell decided to pause in order to organize his force further. On July 18, he sent Brig. Gen. Daniel Tyler to reconnoiter Confederate troops commanded by Brig. Gen. Milledge Bonham and Brig. Gen. James Longstreet. Tyler was repulsed in light skirmishing at Blackburn's Ford and Mitchell's Ford.

Tyler's initial defeat confirmed McDowell's decision to delay and gave time for Confederate leaders to order Johnston's force to the scene. For the first time in a North America war, railroads were used to strategic advantage: Johnston slipped away from Patterson in the valley, loaded his men on trains of the Manassas Gap line, and rushed to reinforce Beauregard. Almost ten thousand such reinforcements arrived by July 21, and Johnston assumed command of the Confederate operations.

Early on that same day, McDowell finally decided to push forward with an attack against Stone Bridge, which carried the Warrenton Turnpike over Bull Run Creek. He also sent Col. David Hunter and Col. Samuel Heintzelman to flank the Confederate troops to the north at Sudley Springs, but Daniel Tyler's advance toward the bridge blocked their path for a time. Tyler's men, including several artillery batteries, made such slow progress that Confederate colonel Nathan G. "Shanks" Evans realized their action was a feint.

Evans rushed his one thousand men north toward Sudley Springs, and they arrived at Matthews Hill in time to meet Colonel Hunter's six thousand advancing troops. Though Evans's men and reinforcements from Brig. Gen. Bernard Bee's and Col. Francis Bartow's brigades initially held off Hunter, McDowell pushed so many fresh troops against them that they eventually had to retreat south.

As the Confederates ran south toward the Henry House Hill (which a sickly widow named Judith Henry had refused to vacate during the battle), their situation seemed bleak. But atop the hill they found Brig. Gen. Thomas J. Jackson's brigade calmly formed into a defensive line. Bee exclaimed his famous line, "There is Jackson, standing like a stone wall," and the Confederate troops rallied around Jackson's men.

By early afternoon, Beauregard and Johnston had established a strong line of seven thousand men across the Henry House Hill. The battle began to turn when a Confederate counterattack knocked out two batteries of artillery that McDowell had rushed into action. Johnston effectively brought reinforcements into play on the Confederate left, and about 4 P.M. the Federal right began to fall apart. Beauregard ordered a frontal advance, and the Confederate line swept the field. Federal soldiers were frightened by the ominous "Rebel yell," which they heard for the first time during the assault.

The Federal line broke, and the Confederate push turned the retreat into a rout as Northern soldiers fled in great confusion from Henry House Hill back across Bull Run Creek and on past Centreville. Politicians and other civilians who had ridden out in carriages from Washington to observe what

First Battle of Bull Run (Manassas)
JULY 21, 1861

they assumed would be a picturesque battle scene were caught in the chaos as wave after wave of Federal troops rushed away from the action (or "skedaddled," as the press dubbed their retreat). Though several Confederate units wanted to pursue the fleeing Northerners, Beauregard and Johnston recalled their tired and battered troops and broke off the attack.

Though casualty figures for the First Battle of Bull Run were modest compared to many later in the war, they were much higher than the Northern or Southern public had expected. The Union casualties totaled 2,896, and the Confederate 1,982.

McDowell faced public scorn after the Union defeat at Bull Run, while Beauregard's reputation improved, despite the fact that Johnston had actually performed better on the field. While Northern confidence was damaged by the loss and Southern pride inflated, both sides realized that the war would take far more time, energy, and blood than they had previously assumed.

Further Reading

William C. Davis. *Battle at Bull Run: A History of the First Major Campaign of the Civil War* (Garden City, N.J.: Doubleday, 1977); Alan Hankinson. *First Bull Run, 1861: The South's First Victory* (London: Osprey, 1991); John Hennessy. *The First Battle of Manassas: An End to Innocence, July 18–21, 1861* (Lynchburg, Va.: H. E. Howard, 1989); and R. M. Johnston. *Bull Run: Its Strategy and Tactics* (Boston: Houghton Mifflin, 1913).

⤜ Bull Run, Second

(Second Manassas)

Virginia (August 29–30, 1862) *American Civil War*

After Maj. Gen. John Pope's Federal army was defeated at CEDAR MOUNTAIN in Culpeper County, Virginia, on August 9, 1862, Confederate and Federal forces entered a period of strategic maneuvering between the Potomac, Rappahannock, and Rapidan Rivers that resulted in a climactic battle around Bull Run Creek, where the first large-scale battle of the war had taken place just thirteen months before (*see* FIRST BULL RUN). Confederate general Robert E. Lee sent Maj. Gen. Thomas J. "Stonewall" Jackson to attack Pope's 63,000 men before Maj. Gen. George B. McClellan's 120,000-man Army of the Potomac, which had been recalled from the Virginia Peninsula, could provide reinforcements. Pope, in turn, hoped to engage Jackson's twenty-four thousand troops before Lee could arrive with Maj. Gen. James Longstreet's thirty-one thousand additional men. On August 25 and 26, Jackson's men marched over fifty miles and laid waste to the

Federal supply depot at Manassas before retiring to woods near the previous Bull Run battlefield. Pope struggled to locate the Confederate troops and to begin an all-out fight.

In the early evening of August 28, one of Pope's columns (later known as the Iron Brigade) happened upon Jackson's center near the Warrenton Turnpike, and Jackson ordered an artillery attack against it. Brig. Gen. John Gibbon formed his Wisconsin and Indiana troops into lines of battle and pressed forward. Confederate and Federal infantry met near the Brawner House in two hours of fierce fighting at extremely close range that brought 33 percent casualties. Though both sides broke off as darkness fell, the engagement served notice to both Pope and Jackson that the main battle would begin the next day.

Pope opened the fight on August 29 with artillery shelling as Jackson formed his men into a long line in the railroad cut along Bull Run, stretching from Sudley Springs to the Brawner Farm. Pope went on the offensive, but his attacks were not well coordinated. He sent first two regiments against Jackson's center and then an additional five to attack the Confederate left side. Pope ordered Maj. Gen. Fitz-John Porter to attack the Confederate right, but Porter delayed until afternoon, by which time, unknown to Pope, Longstreet's reinforcements had arrived. Porter refused to move, an action for which he was later cashiered from the service. Around 4:00 P.M., Pope threw three more regiments against Jackson's center. One hour later, Maj. Gen. Philip Kearny, the flamboyant, one-armed Mexican-American War hero, pushed Maj. Gen. A. P. Hill's Confederates up the hill at Stony Ridge, where they made a stand. All the Federal attacks on August 29 made headway, but Pope's failure in every case to send in timely reinforcements meant that Jackson's line was never broken.

Overnight, the Confederate line withdrew a bit in preparation for a flanking maneuver around the Union left, and Pope, still unaware of Longstreet's presence, mistook their actions for a prelude to retreat. In the late morning and early afternoon of August 30, Pope sent ten thousand men to cut off the supposed retreat at Deep Cut. The Confederates, well protected by the rail line and artillery on the left, rebuffed this attack in thirty minutes of carnage.

Lee now sensed an opportunity and ordered Longstreet forward with his entire corps of thirty thousand to strike at the exposed Union left. Longstreet pushed the battered and surprised Federal troops all the way back to Chinn Ridge, where in an hour-long fight Pope scrambled to save his army. By nightfall, the fighting had shifted almost a mile back to Henry House Hill, the site of the

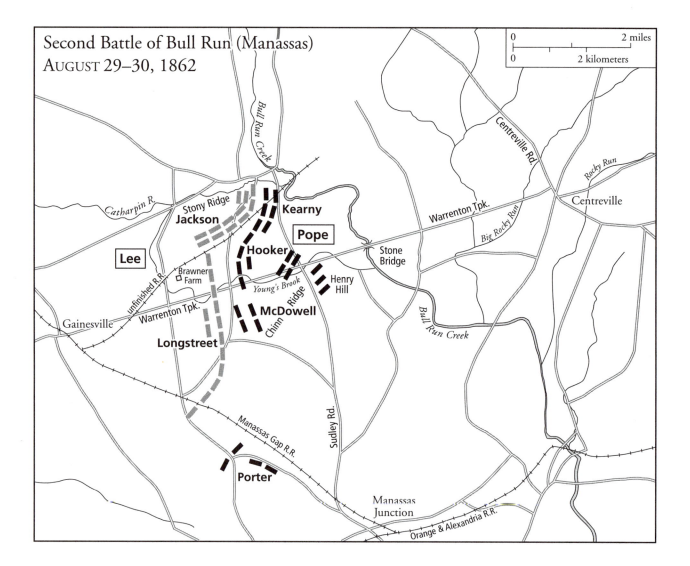

Second Battle of Bull Run (Manassas)
AUGUST 29–30, 1862

most severe phase of the First Battle of Bull Run. There the Federals made a last stand as Longstreet continued to throw his men against the Federal line until darkness ended the fight.

Casualties were heavy. The Union reported 9,931 wounded or dead and another 3,895 missing. Confederate casualties totaled 8,353.

Pope's men retreated toward Washington, D.C., under cover of darkness (finally meeting some of McClellan's reinforcements on the way). Pope and Lee met again two days later at CHANTILLY, where Pope bought his army enough time to escape back to the capital, but the defeat at Bull Run confirmed Lee's ascendance and helped encourage him to invade Northern territory.

Further Reading

Alan D. Gaff. *Brave Men's Tears: The Iron Brigade at Brawner Farm.* Rev. ed. (Dayton, Ohio: Morningside, 1988); David G. Martin. *The Second Bull Run Campaign, July–August 1862* (Conshohocken, Pa.: Combined Books, 1997); and Joseph Whitehorne. *The Battle of Second Manassas: A Self-Guided Tour* (Washington, D.C.: U.S. Army Center of Military History, 1990).

Bull's Ferry

New Jersey (July 21, 1780) *American Revolution*

Even though the war in general was in a stalemate in the northern theater after 1779, there were still occasional skirmishes and conflicts. One such took place at Bull's

Ferry, New Jersey, at a blockhouse that served as a wood-cutting base for a seventy-man Loyalist unit under Capt. Thomas Ward.

The detachment somehow attracted the attention of the American commander in chief, Gen. George Washington, who ordered Maj. Gen. Anthony Wayne to wipe it out. Wayne marched out with his Pennsylvania brigade and four artillery pieces and approached the blockhouse on the morning of July 21.

Wayne attempted to batter the fortification into submission with his cannon, but an hour's bombardment did little noticeable damage. The Loyalists, in reply, had peppered the Pennsylvanians with musket fire from the safety of the blockhouse, and the Americans apparently reacted hastily. Two regiments rushed the blockhouse, hoping to break in, but the place was secure, and they suffered heavily from the Loyalists' fire at close range. Wayne had no choice but to withdraw, having been defeated by a force a fraction the size of his own. He reported fifteen killed and forty-nine wounded.

Further Reading

Charles H. Winfield. *The Block-House by Bull's Ferry* (New York: A. Abbatt, 1904).

☙ Bunker Hill

(Breed's Hill)

Charlestown, Massachusetts (June 17, 1775)
American Revolution

The fierce battle between British regulars and American militiamen at Breed's Hill, on the Charlestown peninsula across from Boston, was the first great, formal passage of arms of the Revolution and influenced battlefield fighting for years to come.

After the first clashes in April 1775 at LEXINGTON AND CONCORD and along the road to Boston, the British, under their commander in chief, Maj. Gen. Thomas Gage, remained holed up in the city with several regiments of regulars and a number of warships in the harbor and on the Charles River. Gage was joined in May by three other major generals: John Burgoyne, Henry Clinton, and William Howe.

Surrounding the city on the landward side was a remarkable "Boston Army," made up of militiamen from Massachusetts, Rhode Island, Connecticut, and New Hampshire. The first fragments of this force were the

Minutemen who had chased the British back from Concord. Over the subsequent two months, more and more troops had joined them, until the patriots numbered around ten thousand. The American army was only loosely organized, however, with a hodgepodge of officers—some locally elected, some commissioned by the various colonial revolutionary committees, and some appointed by the Second Continental Congress, which nominally accepted the troops as the first units in a Continental army.

In theory, the entire army was commanded by Maj. Gen. Artemus Ward, a Massachusetts veteran of the French and Indian War, but he in fact played only a small role. Much more significant during the battle on the heights overlooking Charlestown were the activities of Israel Putnam, a general of Connecticut troops and a celebrated hero of the French and Indian War, and of Massachusetts colonel William Prescott. Also present was Dr. Joseph Warren, one of the main political leaders of the Revolution in Massachusetts, who had recently been designated a major general but had not yet taken up his commission.

Hearing rumors that Gage was about to march out of Boston, the Americans decided to fortify the hills above Charlestown, from which they could command the city and the harbor—provided they could bring sufficient artillery from FORT TICONDEROGA.

On the night of June 16, a force of around twelve hundred men assembled on the Cambridge common and

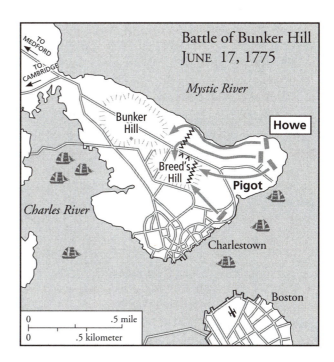

moved out for Bunker Hill, the higher of two commanding hills on the Charlestown peninsula. The chief officers were Putnam, Prescott, Capt. Thomas Knowlton of Connecticut, and Capt. Samuel Gridley of Massachusetts (a skilled military engineer and artilleryman, trained by the British during the French and Indian War). Advancing across a thin neck of land that connected the heights with Cambridge, the force stopped at Bunker Hill. To its left was the Mystic River and to its right was the Charles River. The town itself was at the bottom of the hills, facing the Charles. The American commanders decided to bypass Bunker Hill and instead fortify Breed's Hill, which was closer to the confluence of the rivers, and early in the morning the men began to dig in there, along lines laid out by Gridley. By first light, they had constructed strong earthworks at the top of the hill, with a less stout breastwork and a stone fence trailing down from the heights to the left toward the Mystic River beach.

Ignoring fire from the British ships, the untrained American troops took positions behind the fortifications. Prescott commanded the main fortification, with Knowlton assigned to the breastworks and fence. Ward, the commander in chief, was across the neck of land with several thousand more troops, but he refused to send more than a handful to cross under the fire of the British naval guns to Breed's Hill. Throughout the day no pleas from the forward commanders, principally Putnam, could produce from him more troops or ammunition. In the end, this lack of supply proved crucial. One of the few units to march forward during the day was a group of New Hampshire militia under Col. John Stark, which crossed at a deliberate pace and took up the defense of the American far left near the beach. Dr. Warren asked to serve as a private soldier behind the earthen wall.

When General Gage learned of the activity above Charlestown, he called a council of war, which decided on a frontal assault, despite the apparent strength of the patriot position. The infantry regiments at Gage's disposal were probably among the finest troops in the world—highly trained, well equipped, and superbly led—and they had every confidence that the ragtag militia opposite could not withstand a classic bayonet attack. Howe was assigned to lead the landing and to attack, with Clinton in reserve and Burgoyne in charge of long-range artillery.

At midday, the British landed about twelve hundred troops, resplendent in red coats and full field gear, on the peninsula and moved into position at the foot of the steep Breed's Hill. Howe's plan was to send the Thirty-eighth

and Forty-third Regiments under Brig. Gen. Robert Pigot straight at the main earthworks. On the British right, the grenadier companies of several regiments and batallion companies of the Fifth and Fifty-third aimed for the weak point along the fence near the beach, intending to overrun Stark's New Hampshiremen and then roll up the flank of the American position on top of the hill.

The redcoats marched up to within fifty yards of Stark's position and began to deploy from column to line for a bayonet charge. Stark gave the order to fire at close range, and the British were shattered. Subsequent waves of attackers were likewise blasted by highly accurate American musketry. In a matter of minutes, almost one hundred British soldiers and officers were killed. Nearly the same story was enacted at the center of the American line, where Howe led the attack, and at the summit.

Howe and his men retreated, but within the hour they launched a second frontal attack, the heavily laden British infantrymen struggling up the hill in oppressive afternoon heat and into the face of withering fire. Again they were mowed down as they approached the American positions, with officers accounting for the highest proportion of casualties.

The Americans seemed invincible behind the protection of their earthworks, but they were now almost out of gunpowder and musket balls, and no new supply appeared. General Clinton arrived about this time with four hundred fresh troops, and Howe ordered a third assault.

This time enough British soldiers survived the weakening American fire to reach the embankment and pour over the wall. Their bayonets went to work, and the American resistance crumbled. Under extreme pressure, and with little or no ammunition left, the patriots fled the fortifications, leaving Dr. Warren dead behind the wall.

Total American casualties for the battle were 140 killed and 301 wounded out of around 1,500 actually engaged in the fighting (an equal number of troops stayed to the rear). The British losses were shocking: out of 2,500 in the battle, the British took 1,150 casualties, including 226 killed (19 of them officers) and more than 800 wounded. More than 40 percent of the British troops on the field were killed or wounded in the space of a few hours.

Although they lost the day, the Americans learned that they could go toe to toe with the British army (at least behind secure fortifications). The British command, on the other hand, acquired a caution it never quite shook off for the rest of the war.

Further Reading

John R. Elting. *The Battle of Bunker's Hill* (Monmouth Beach, N.J.: Philip Freneau Press, 1975); Thomas Fleming. *Now We Are Enemies: The Story of Bunker Hill* (New York: St. Martin's Press, 1960); and Richard M. Ketchum. *Decisive Day: The Battle for Bunker Hill* (Garden City, N.Y.: Doubleday, 1974).

❧ Bushy Run

(Edge Hill)

Pennsylvania (August 5–6, 1763) *Pontiac's War*

The expulsion of France from North America at the end of the French and Indian War meant a wrenching realignment for Indian tribes that had long been allied to the French. Faced with the expansion of British power all along the western frontier, many tribes concluded it was better to resist Great Britain than to accede to the new order. Under the military leadership of Pontiac (Ponteach) and the spiritual inspiration of the Delaware Prophet (Neolin), a confederation of Great Lakes and Old Northwest tribes launched a war against British outposts, seizing fort after fort during the spring and summer of 1763. When a mixed force of Delaware (Lenni Lenape), Shawnee, Mingo, and Wyandot laid siege to Fort Pitt (now Pittsburgh), the British North American commander in chief, Jeffrey, Lord Amherst, sent a relief force under a Swiss-born mercenary officer, Col. Henry Bouquet.

Bouquet's force numbered about four hundred regulars from the Forty-second and Seventy-seventh Highlander Regiments and the Royal Americans, plus thirty scouts. The detachment included four hundred packhorses carrying flour and other supplies for the garrison at Fort Pitt. The soldiers were well-trained, well-equipped veterans, although some of the Highlanders suffered from residual malaria picked up at their previous post in the Caribbean.

Waiting for the British in an ambush near Bushy Run creek, about twenty-five miles from Fort Pitt, was a mixed force of Shawnee, Delaware, Mingo, and Wyandot. The Indians sprang the trap on Bouquet's column early in the afternoon of August 5, but they failed to make much impression on the well-disciplined regulars, who formed up and chased off their attackers in a series of charges. Bouquet camped for the night on top of nearby Edge Hill, ordering his men to build a circular barricade out of flour bags around the camp.

As daylight broke the following morning, the Indians attacked again. Bouquet cleverly hid several companies of light infantry and grenadiers on an adjacent spur of the hill and enticed the Indians to attack by feigning retreat. As the Indians pressed forward, the concealed troops emerged and fell on their flank, forcing them into a cross fire. The attack collapsed, and the entire Indian force fled the field.

Bouquet was able to relieve the garrison at Fort Pitt, having recorded one of the few clear-cut victories of British regulars over Indian foes in heavily wooded terrain during the entire colonial era. He reported the loss of fifty killed and sixty wounded. Indian casualties are unknown.

Further Reading

Niles Anderson. *The Battle of Bushy Run* (Harrisburg, Pa.: Pennsylvania Historical and Museum Commission, 1966); and Howard H. Peckham. *Pontiac and the Indian Uprising* (Detroit: Wayne State University Press, 1994).

C

⬚ Calderón Bridge

(Puente de Calderón)
Mexico (January 17, 1811) *Hidalgo Revolt*

Throughout 1810, Don Miguel Hidalgo y Costilla, a priest from the town of Dolores, worked to organize a movement for Mexican social reform and independence from Spain. With the Spanish government distracted by the Napoleonic Wars, in the fall and winter Hidalgo's allies, mainly rural Indians and peasants, captured several cities around Guadalajara and prepared to spread the independence movement. In January 1811, Hidalgo's army of between seventy and eighty thousand rebels gathered outside Guadalajara was defeated at the Calderón River by the much smaller imperial army of Brig. Gen. Félix María Calleja del Rey. Hidalgo's defeat at the Calderón Bridge helped to delay Mexican independence for another eleven years.

Hidalgo had spent December 1810 and the first three weeks of January 1811 gathering troops around Guadalajara with the assistance of Capt. Ignacio de Allende, a rich Creole whose own rebel troops had already been defeated by Calleja in Guanajuato. The new rebel army included cavalry lancers, foot soldiers, archers, and thousands of irregulars. Spies for the Spanish estimated that there were only approximately six hundred firearms among almost eighty thousand men and that most of Hidalgo's fighters were armed with slings, clubs, and Indian-made bows and arrows. Calleja advanced on Guadalajara with only three thousand infantry and three thousand cavalry, but his men were better trained, better disciplined, and better equipped than the rebel force, which vastly outnumbered them. Calleja also had ten of the finest Spanish cannon, which more than matched the greater number of old, clumsy pieces possessed by Hidalgo's force.

When Hidalgo and Allende learned on January 13 that Calleja was marching toward their stronghold, they disagreed about how to array their troops to meet the Spanish imperial onslaught. Hidalgo's plan won out—fortify the hills around the high bridge over the Calderón River outside Guadalajara and engage the entire army in the fight. Calleja's men arrived at the Calderón on January 16, and the two sides faced off in expectation of a pitched battle.

Early on January 17, Calleja began his attack by sending Col. Francisco Flon's division against Hidalgo's right flank. Flon mounted one of the high hills near the bridge and captured a rebel battery even before his own artillery could be dragged up the slope. When his guns arrived, Flon established an effective artillery fire that drove Hidalgo's gunners from the entire right side of the action and sent rebels scurrying to the center for protection.

Calleja, meanwhile, occupied a small hill just to the right of the bridge, a vantage point that allowed him to direct fire at the rebel batteries on the left. He also sent a squadron of the Dragoons of Spain and a cavalry regiment under a Colonel Emparán down the river to attack Hidalgo from behind, and he established a small battery to cover any retreat. As Flon's men pushed against the rebels, they were overwhelmed by Hidalgo's superior numbers, and the rebels also scattered Emparán's cavalry. Only quick action by Calleja in sending reinforcements prevented Emparán's total rout. Superior numbers were foiling military strategy, and although Calleja threw infantry and cavalry charges, as well as concentrated artillery fire, against the rebel center, the line would not give way.

After almost five hours of fighting, a chance shot changed the entire course of the battle. A ball from Calleja's artillery struck a rebel ammunition wagon and caused a huge explosion. The dry grasses in the river valley immediately caught fire, and strong winds blowing toward Hidalgo's forces fanned the flames. The explosion, heat, and smoke were so intense that confusion overtook Hidalgo's troops, and they broke ranks. Rebel troops fled in all directions, and Calleja's regulars, who maintained their battle order, swept the field. It was impossible for Hidalgo and Allende to restore order among eighty thousand men, and Calleja crushed the remaining resistance.

More than twelve hundred of Hidalgo's rebels were killed during the battle, and thousands more surrendered, many of whom were later shot. Calleja lost only around fifty men, including Flon, who was killed near the end of the six-hour conflict. Hidalgo and Allende fled the scene, but they were captured in March and executed at Chihuahua on July 31.

The defeat at the Calderón Bridge ended Hidalgo's hope to take Mexico City and rid his country of imperial Spanish control. Though the rebel cause continued to find support in the countryside among Creoles, Indians, and poor farmers, without Hidalgo the dream of independence was not realized until 1822.

Further Reading

John A. Caruso. *Liberators of Mexico* (Gloucester, Mass.: Peter Smith, 1967); and Hugh M. Hamill, Jr. *The Hidalgo Revolt: Prelude to Mexican Independence* (Gainesville: University of Florida Press, 1966).

Camden

South Carolina (August 16, 1780)
American Revolution

The Battle of Camden, a disaster resulting from a deadly combination of incompetent leadership and cowardice, was one of the worst defeats ever suffered by an American army in the field.

The American commander was Maj. Gen. Horatio Gates, the "hero" of SARATOGA, who had been appointed after the surrender of CHARLESTON in May 1780 to head the Southern Department. Gates assumed command of a force under Bavarian volunteer general Johann de Kalb in North Carolina in late July and ordered a march south toward the British.

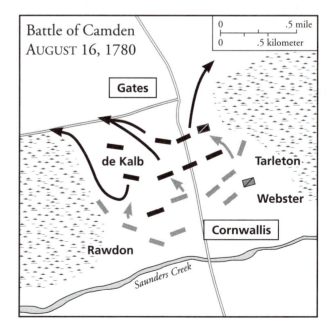

Battle of Camden
AUGUST 16, 1780

The core of Gates's army was formed by de Kalb's twelve hundred or so superb regulars of the Maryland and Delaware Continental regiments. These were among the most experienced and best American soldiers of the war, although fatigued and ill supplied at this juncture. Gates also had a small artillery force, a tiny remnant of the mounted Pulaski Legion, and about two thousand inexperienced militia from North Carolina and Virginia. On the eve of the battle, the American forces may have numbered close to four thousand; however, Gates believed his army totaled at least seven thousand, and he could not be convinced otherwise by his staff. By mid-August the exhausted, sick, and nearly starved Americans were just north of Camden, South Carolina.

The British army they approached was commanded by Lt. Gen. Lord Cornwallis, who had been put in charge of the Carolinas by the commander in chief, Sir Henry Clinton, after the capture of Charleston. Cornwallis believed he was badly outnumbered by the Americans. He had slightly more than two thousand troops, nearly all of them veteran regulars or members of such experienced Loyalist units as Lt. Col. Banastre Tarleton's infamous British Legion. Cornwallis knew that Gates was approaching and had moved north along the road from Camden to meet him.

The first shots were fired about 2:30 A.M. on August 16, when the advance American guard encountered the leading units of the British army at a place where the road opened onto a wide, sandy space broken up by pines and bounded on both sides by swampland. After stumbling into this unplanned contact, both sides ceased firing and waiting for morning.

The commanders' respective dispositions of the opposing forces were among the crucial factors in the battle. On the British right, commanded by Lt. Col. James Webster, Cornwallis placed the Royal Welch Fusiliers, the Volunteers of Ireland (Irish deserters from the American army), and veteran North Carolina Loyalist militia. On the left, Lt. Col. Francis Rawdon-Hastings (known as Lord Rawdon) was in charge of the Seventy-first (Fraser's) Highlanders. Tarleton's mixed force of dragoons and light infantry backed up the Highlanders. On the American side, Gates's fatal decision—one of the few tactical decisions he made all day—was to place the untested Virginia and North Carolina militia on his left, opposite the Royal Welch Fusiliers. Gates put his best troops, the Maryland and Delaware Continentals under Brig. Gen. Mordecai Gist, on the right of the line, with de Kalb in overall charge of the right wing of the army. One Maryland regiment was in reserve.

Gates himself took a position hundreds of yards to the rear, and after giving a few initial orders took no active part in the battle. The actual command fell to his able adjutant, Col. Otho Williams of Maryland, and a few other officers who seized the initiative. The British right wing opened the battle with an advance on the Virginians and North Carolinians. At the first few shots, the American militia opposite the Fusiliers panicked, threw down their muskets before firing a shot, and fled the field as rapidly as they could run. Thus, half of the American line collapsed during the first few minutes of the engagement.

On the British left, however, Lord Rawdon's advance came up against the rock-solid Delawaremen and Marylanders. The American line there held firm at first, despite pressure from the Royal Welch Fusiliers, who had wheeled to their left across the positions vacated by the militia and now took the American regulars on the flank. Otho Williams took command of the Maryland reserve and tried to rally the line, but after two valiant stands he was swept away. For a time de Kalb and the Continentals continued to hold, but they soon came under attack from all sides: British infantry struck the Delaware and Maryland positions from the front and sides, and Tarleton's mounted troops attacked from the rear. De Kalb, at the center of the storm, received multiple musket and saber wounds (he died three days later), and only a few of the Delaware and Maryland regulars escaped the carnage. The surviving Americans disengaged and fled north at top speed with Tarleton's riders in close pursuit.

It was impossible to calculate American losses accurately, but they were severe: only seven hundred of the original four thousand Americans on the field reached the safety of Hillsboro three days later, and it is likely that eight hundred or nine hundred Americans were killed and close to one thousand were taken captive. The British reported only 68 killed and about 350 wounded.

Gates's army—the only significant American force left in the South—had been almost completely destroyed, and General Gates himself was nowhere near the scene. When the American left wing collapsed during the first moments of the battle, the commander turned and ran. As soon as possible, he requisitioned a fast horse and galloped for his life. By nightfall of the same day, Gates was at Charlotte, 60 miles from the battle, and he arrived in Hillsboro (a full 120 miles farther) three days later.

The aftermath of the victory left Cornwallis the complete master of the southern theatre for the time being. Gates was removed from command and replaced by Washington's choice, the redoubtable Nathanael Greene.

Further Reading

Charles B. Flood. *Rise, and Fight Again: Perilous Times along the Road to Independence* (New York: Dodd, Mead, 1976); *U.S. Army War College. The Battle of Camden, South Carolina, August 16, 1780* (Washington, D.C.: U.S. Government Printing Office, 1929).

Camerone

Mexico (April 30, 1863) *Mexican-French War*

When Pres. Benito Juárez declared a moratorium on Mexico's foreign debt payments in 1861, the French emperor, Napoleon III, saw an opportunity to invade and establish French control over Mexico. The French landed in Veracruz in December 1861 (initially supported by British and Spanish troops), but their march on the capital of Mexico City was considerably slowed by the defeat of Gen. Charles Latrille's sixty-five hundred troops at PUEBLA in May. Latrille was recalled to France and replaced as commander of the French expedition by Gen. Elie-Frédéric Forey, who decided early in 1863 that the only way to take Puebla and march on toward Mexico City was to settle in for a long siege. Forey employed two battalions of the French Foreign Legion under Col. Pierre Jeanningros to keep his supply lines open between the siege lines at Puebla and Veracruz. On February 17, 1863, sixty-two of Jeanningros's men fought a large force of the Mexican army at the town of Camerone and suffered defeat in what the Legion has since considered one of its most glorious battles.

Two thousand French Foreign Legionnaires, foreign mercenaries in the employ of the French military, had arrived in Mexico in February to support Forey's troops. In April, Jeanningros's men were assigned to protect a supply convoy that included sixty wagonloads of ammunition and mules carrying three million dollars' worth of gold bullion to pay French troops and France's Mexican allies. The convoy made an appealing target for Col. Francisco de Paula-Milan, a former governor of the state of Veracruz and veteran of the Mexican-American War who commanded a brigade of National Guard troops fiercely loyal to President Juárez. The Third Company of the First Brigade, one of the Foreign Legion's most experienced units, under the command of Capt. Jean Danjou, was assigned to patrol the convoy road between Chiquihuite and Palo Verde and flush out any Mexican ambush parties.

Just after 5:00 A.M. on April 30, Danjou's men advanced on the village of Camerone, thought to be a prime hiding place for Juárista soldiers, but when they found it entirely deserted, they continued on to Palo Verde. Around 7:30 A.M., just as the men were being served their morning ration of coffee from large steel vats, sentinels alerted Danjou that Mexican cavalry, the Cotaxtla Squadron of Capt. Tomas Algonzanas, was approaching quickly along the road from Camerone. When the cavalry unaccountably turned south and avoided contact with the company of legionnaires, Danjou decided to march his men back to Camerone, where they could take cover inside the town's adobe walls and fortify a hacienda called La Trinidad.

As the legionnaires were making their way back to Camerone, Mexican colonel Francisco de Paula-Milan, who was indeed planning an ambush of the supply convoy, decided that he had to wipe them out. Already almost out of water, Danjou's men struggled through the underbrush back to Camerone and quickly searched the village for snipers. Just after 9:30 A.M., as the legionnaires were reconnoitering an Indian village outside Camerone, Algonzanas's Mexican cavalry lancers formed into a long line around the French column on a hill just northwest of the village. When the cavalry hesitated to attack, Danjou formed his men into a defensive hollow square with bayonets fixed and retreated inside Camerone's walls. Algonzanas's cavalry advanced slowly until they were within two hundred feet of the legionnaires, and then they lowered their lances and charged as the defenders opened fire.

Incredibly, the legionnaires' fire knocked out enough lancers to cause the remainder to divert their attack at the last minute, and before they could regroup for a second charge across a cactus-filled ditch, so many Mexicans were shot from their horses that Algonzanas ordered his men to circle the hacienda. Danjou's men had sought refuge in the ditch, from which they emerged and formed another open-square formation in time to catch Algonzanas's men coming around the hacienda. The main section of the Cotaxtla Squadron retreated under heavy fire, but Milan's Mexican reinforcements were arriving by the minute, and the legionnaires had no men to spare.

During a pause in the action, the legionnaires managed to struggle inside La Trinidad, the hacienda where they had determined to defend themselves even though the Mexican forces surrounded them. Several of Algonzanas's men entered the ranch house and fought the legionnaires from room to room. Even under heavy attack, the legionnaires held on, and Danjou made each of his men swear an oath to fight to the death.

At 10:00 A.M., Mexican captain Ramon Laine, son of a French harbormaster, advanced under a white flag and announced that Milan demanded that the French surrender. Danjou refused, and within minutes the fight resumed. Having established protected positions in a stable and on the roof of the hacienda, the Legion held off two thousand Mexican attackers in hand-to-hand fighting for ten more hours. By 6:00 P.M., the last three legionnaires who could still carry on the fight, headed by Cpl. Phillipe Maine, surrendered to Milan's second in command, Maj. Sabastian I. Compos.

Of the sixty-two legionnaires who fought at Camerone, thirty-three were killed (including Danjou), fourteen wounded, and twelve taken prisoner. Mexican forces suffered between three hundred and five hundred casualties.

The sixty-two men of the Third Company of the French Foreign Legion became revered as French military heroes, renowned as having held off an entire Mexican army and dying in supposed glory. The Foreign Legion continued to play a crucial role in the French attempts to besiege Puebla, which finally succeeded on May 17. Napoleon established Maximillian Ferdinand Joseph of Austria in a puppet monarchy over Mexico that lasted until 1867.

Further Reading

James W. Ryan. *Camerone: The French Foreign Legion's Greatest Battle* (Westport, Conn.: Praeger, 1996).

✐ Camp Texas

(Fort Texas)

Texas (May 3–8, 1846) *Mexican-American War*

After a decade of conflict with the United States, brought to a crisis by the American annexation of Texas, and finally sparked by Brig. Gen. Zachary Taylor's encroachment into disputed territory along the Rio Grande, Mexico declared war on April 28, 1846. Following the formal declaration of war, Taylor withdrew his main force from Fort Texas to Point Isabel in anticipation of a Mexican attack on the fort. The first major battle of the Mexican-American War began on the evening of May 3.

Maj. Gen. Ariano Arista, commander of the northern Mexican military forces, had hoped to cut off Taylor's force before it crossed the Rio Grande, but when he realized Taylor was already gone, Arista ordered Maj. Gen. Pedro de Ampudia's brigade to begin a bombardment of Fort Texas instead. The Mexican artillery was too light to do much damage to the fort, and the bombardment was answered by American eighteen- and six-pounders. American firing into the town of Matamoros had little effect, but it held the Mexicans at bay.

On the morning of May 4, Capt. Samuel H. Walker slipped through the Mexican siege line with orders for Maj. Jacob Brown to defend the fort until Taylor could return with reinforcements. That day and the next, Ampudia brought up more guns and 1,230 more troops, but even a steadily increasing bombardment failed to open up the fort to a frontal attack.

Major Brown, however, was mortally wounded (the site is now Brownsville named in his honor), and Capt. Edgar S. Hawkins took command of the American forces inside the fort on the morning of May 6. Ampudia called upon Hawkins to surrender, but he refused. The Mexican siege lasted for two more days, until May 8, when Arista ordered Ampudia's men to join him against Zachary Taylor's troops, who were once more on the march.

During the artillery battle at Fort Texas, two Americans were killed and nine wounded. Mexican casualties are unknown. The successful defense of Fort Texas led directly to the much larger battle at PALO ALTO on May 8.

Further Reading

Charles L. Dufour. *The Mexican War: A Compact History* (New York: Hawthorne Books, 1968); and Robert Selph Henry. *The Story of the Mexican War.* Reprint ed. (New York: Frederick Ungar, 1961).

✐ Catawba Ford

See FISHING CREEK

✐ Cedar Creek

Virginia (October 19, 1864) *American Civil War*

In September and October 1864, Maj. Gen. Philip H. Sheridan's troops subdued the Confederate citizens in the Shenandoah Valley during a campaign of destruction labeled "The Burning." Convinced that the valley had been won, Sheridan left his troops to attend a strategy meeting in Washington, D.C. Confederate lieutenant general Jubal Early, however, was not yet convinced that he was out of the fight, and his force made one last bid at Cedar Creek on October 19, for control of the valley.

Early had rebuilt his force to a strength of twenty-one thousand men with the addition of Maj. Gen. Joseph B. Kershaw's division. In mid-October he took his troops north, recaptured FISHER'S HILL, and approached Sheridan's thirty-two thousand men, who were stretched out along Cedar Creek near the Valley Pike. Sheridan had placed Maj. Gen. Horatio G. Wright in charge when he left for the capital on October 16. He was completely unaware that Confederate major general John B. Gordon and the cartographer Capt. Jedediah Hotchkiss could see his entire line from atop Signal Hill and were busy concocting battle plans for Early.

Gordon proposed to overcome the Union numerical advantage by concentrating on the weak left flank. The plan was almost successful, since Union brigadier general George Crook wrongly convinced Wright that the Confederates had withdrawn. Overnight on October 18, Gordon, Maj. Gen. Stephen Ramseur, and Brig. Gen. John Pegram each led a column of infantry with cavalry support along paths pointed out to them by local residents, converging behind Crook's position early on October 19, ready to attack. Kershaw, whose men marched unseen through the morning fog, opened the fight at 5 A.M., and soon after all three main wings of the Confederate force pushed forward against the Federal line.

Crook was taken by surprise, and the four Federal corps under Wright's command gave way fairly quickly, retreating to form a new line north of Middletown. Only the Second Division of the Sixth Corps, commanded by Brig. Gen. George W. Getty, held its ground, and Early chose to dislodge it rather than pursue the remainder of the Federal forces, as Gordon urged him to do. By around 1 P.M., Getty's holdouts were finally pushed north and there was a break in the action, during which Confederate soldiers looted the Federal camps and took prizes.

Sheridan had returned to Winchester on October 18, and on the morning of the battle, he was riding his horse slowly back to Cedar Creek when he heard gunfire. Becoming concerned as he progressed, he began to encounter stragglers fleeing from the morning's Confederate advance. Sheridan immediately comprehended the danger in letting two of his corps remain beaten, and he galloped ahead, rallying the fleeing men with his enthusiasm as he

went—an event that became immortalized as "Sheridan's Ride." Sheridan and Capt. William McKinley, the future president of the United States, funneled most of the stragglers back to the new Federal position, where Wright was forming a new line.

Sheridan was determined to counterattack while Early's guard was down, and though Gordon urged his commander to send out skirmishing parties to test the new Federal line early in the afternoon, the Confederates were not prepared for the Union thrust when it came. Just before 4:00 P.M. Sheridan's cavalry, led by Brig. Gen. George A. Custer, hit the Confederate left flank hard. Gordon's division was driven back first, and the remainder of Early's force quickly buckled. The Confederates withdrew toward Strasburg, and by dark Sheridan's force had driven them all the way south of Fisher's Hill.

Union casualties were nearly double those suffered by the Confederates. Sheridan lost 5,672 compared to Early's 2,910.

Despite the heavy Federal casualties, Sheridan's force had finally won control of the Shenandoah River valley once and for all.

Further Reading

Thomas Lewis. *The Guns of Cedar Creek* (New York: Harper & Row, 1988); Theodore Mahr. *The Battle of Cedar Creek: Showdown in the Shenandoah, October 1–30, 1864.* 2d ed. (Lynchburg, Va.: H. E. Howard, 1992); and Joseph Whitehorne. *The Battle of Cedar Creek: A Self-Guided Tour* (Washington, D.C.: U.S. Army Center of Military History, 1992).

Cedar Mountain

Virginia (August 9, 1862) *American Civil War*

In August 1862, Pres. Abraham Lincoln and Sec. of War Edwin M. Stanton, backed by Radical Republicans in the U.S. Congress, sent Maj. Gen. John Pope, hero of the battle at ISLAND NUMBER 10 and several other successful western fights, to command a new Army of Virginia and restore order to Union troops commanded by Maj. Gen. John C. Frémont, Maj. Gen. Nathaniel P. Banks, and Maj. Gen. Irvin P. McDowell. Confederate general Robert E. Lee sent Maj. Gen. Thomas J. "Stonewall" Jackson north from Richmond to deal with the growing Union force in Culpeper County after his victory over Maj. Gen. George B. McClellan's Army of the Potomac in the SEVEN DAYS' BATTLES. The subsequent battle at Cedar Mountain, a narrow Confederate victory, would mark Jackson's final independent campaign of the war.

Jackson first attempted to make contact with Pope by pushing his famous "foot cavalrymen" across the Rapidan River on August 8, but bad weather and unclear orders prevented his twenty-two thousand troops from engaging the twelve thousand Union soldiers in Culpeper County.

On August 9, a corps from Pope's army, under the direct command of Major General Banks, arrayed themselves in front of Cedar Mountain, with cavalry covering open farmland at Cedar Run and artillery perched in the hills. Confederate brigadier general Jubal Early, followed by his commander, Jackson, established a counter position, with artillery stationed along the length of the Union line, on a wooded hill called the Cedars, on the opposite side of Cedar Mountain from the Federals, and along the main road leading out of the forest to the Crittenden House. Confederate infantry established a position next to the open farmland at the mountain's foot along the Crittenden Lane.

The battle began with a hot artillery duel before Banks's men had marched on the Confederate positions along the Crittenden Lane. Unaware that they were badly outnumbered, New England and Midwestern volunteers under Brig. Gen. Samuel W. Crawford charged through a wheat field and toward the Confederate line at the edge of the woods, breaking apart the entire Confederate left flank and badly damaging several enemy brigades. The Confederate artillery at the Cedars and Crittenden Road were almost captured by Brig. Gen. Christopher C. Augur's division.

Though Jackson had been concentrating on the artillery duel, he realized that his army was in trouble, and he stormed onto the field carrying both a sword and a Confederate battle flag to rally his troops personally. Spurred on by their commander and encouraged by fresh reinforcements from Maj. Gen. A. P. Hill's brigades, the Confederates turned the tide and chased the Federals from the field as evening came.

Stonewall Jackson nearly tasted unfamiliar defeat at Cedar Mountain, though he later declared the fight "the most successful" of his exploits. The action caused 2,353 Union casualties, compared to a Confederate total of 1,338.

After his narrow victory at Cedar Mountain, Jackson prepared to rendezvous with Lee to march toward the conflict at Second BULL RUN.

Further Reading

Robert K. Krick, *Stonewall Jackson at Cedar Mountain* (Chapel Hill: University of North Carolina Press, 1990); and Edward J. Stackpole. *From Cedar Mountain to Antietam, August–September, 1862* (Harrisburg, Pa.: Stackpole, 1959).

Cedars

Canada (May 16, 1776) *American Revolution*

After the failed attempt to take QUEBEC on New Year's Day 1776, the demoralized American army had lingered in the vicinity for months, hoping for significant reinforcement and some positive change in their situation. The British commander, Gen. Guy Carleton, was happy to stay within the city's walls and wait for Maj. Gen. John Burgoyne, who was on his way from Britain with eight regiments of regulars and two thousand German mercenaries.

By the middle of May, the British began maneuvers to expel the Americans. A force of six hundred marched on the Cedars, a post on the St. Lawrence between Montreal and Quebec. Maj. Isaac Butterfield, the American commander at the Cedars, surrendered without offering any serious resistance. A relief column under Maj. Henry Sherburne was ambushed by a mixed force of British and Indians and also surrendered. A second relief column under Benedict Arnold, who still suffered from a wound sustained while leading one wing of the attack on Quebec, caught up to the British and compelled them to give up the American prisoners but allowed them to return to Quebec unmolested.

The American invasion of Canada had almost completely petered out.

Further Reading

Christopher Ward. *The War of the Revolution.* Vol. 1 (New York: Macmillan, 1952).

Celaya

Mexico (April 8–15, 1915) *Mexican Revolution*

Gen. Francisco "Pancho" Villa joined forces with Emiliano Zapata, Pánfilo Natera, and Venustanio Carranza to oust Victoriano Huerta from power as leader of Mexico in mid-1914. But this alliance of various Constitutionalist military and political forces was soon riven by conflict. Villa and Zapata led the populist wing of the movement, the Conventionists, in the north and south of Mexico, respectively. Throughout 1914 and into 1915, the revolution was plagued by guerrilla fighting on all sides (at an estimated cost of two hundred thousand lives), as Gen. Alvaro Obregón formed a provisional army to support Carranza against Villa and Zapata. The Constitutionalists and Conventionists fought back and forth for control of the capital of Mexico City in 1915 before Obregón finally bested Villa at Celaya and bestowed fairly stable power on Carranza.

At the beginning of 1915, Carranza, Villa, Eulalio Gutiérrez, and Roque González Garza (Zapata's candidate) all claimed to exercise national executive authority, from various regions of the country. At the beginning of April, Villa began a march toward Mexico City from the north, intending to reestablish his control over the capital and to capture essential oil fields at Tampico along the way. Obregón marched north from the capital with the intention of provoking a major battle and wiping out Villa, whom he viewed as Carranza's strongest opposition.

Between April 8 and 15, as the two sides engaged in constant skirmishing, Villa orchestrated two major offensives against Obregón at Celaya, both of which resulted in tactical defeat. Obregón had carefully studied the early progress of World War I in Europe, and when Villa's force of twenty-five thousand men approached his outpost at Celaya, Obregón put the lessons to use. Obregón realized that he could effectively oppose Villa's cavalry by encircling strong defensive positions with barbed wire in the style of the European conflict. Villa was renowned for his military prowess, but he still relied on tried-and-true Mexican cavalry tactics, unaware that technology was about to make them all but obsolete.

During the first attack on Celaya, Villa ordered his cavalry to charge Obregón's position, but artillery and machine guns ripped apart horses and men alike before they could even reach Obregón's front lines. Though Villa had to order a quick retreat, he reported victory to the international press, and newspapers all over the world published word that Villa's force would renew its attack now that it had the city surrounded.

Within days of the first attack, Villa did press forward again, but this time Obregón's barbed-wire fences would utterly stymie his plan. Villa ordered his cavalry all the way to the barbed-wire barrier around Obregón's entrenchments, but the horsemen only became entangled and again made easy targets for machine-gun fire. Villa's force was crushed before it could inflict much damage at all.

Obregón's tactical advantage was amply illustrated by the casualty figures for the week-long battle. Obregón reported 4,000 Villistas killed, 5,000 wounded, and 6,000 taken prisoner, while his force lost only 138 dead and 227 wounded.

While these figures were probably somewhat inflated for the foreign press, their lopsided nature was borne out by the thousands of bodies strewn about the barbed wire.

Villa did not immediately give up after the crushing defeat at Celaya, but his national support was broken. Obregón helped Carranza consolidate power, and in October the United States recognized his government. Villa harbored resentment against the United States that played out several months later when he raided COLUMBUS, New Mexico—drawing the United States even farther into Mexico's military and political predicament.

Further Reading

Charles C. Cumberland. *Mexican Revolution: The Constitutionalist Years* (Austin: University of Texas Press, 1972); and John D. Eisenhower. *Intervention! The United States and the Mexican Revolution, 1913–1917* (New York: W. W. Norton, 1993).

☙ Cempoallan

Mexico (May 28–29, 1520) *Spanish Conquest*

The first pitched battle between Europeans in the New World took place in an Indian town near the east coast of Mexico, and it pitted two competing groups of Spanish conquistadores against each other.

Hernán Cortés had led an expedition of a few hundred well-armed Spaniards from Cuba to the Mexican mainland in 1518. After battling Indians at POTONCHAN and TLAXCALA, he had founded a coastal town, Villa Rica de la Vera Cruz, formed an alliance with several tribes, and crossed the mountains overland to the fabulous capital of the Mexica (called the Aztecs by later writers) at Tenochtitlán where, without fighting, he had virtually taken control of the city by kidnapping the emperor, Montezuma. Although lacking specific authority from the Spanish government to do so, Cortés had captured a huge empire of extraordinary wealth and sophistication.

Meanwhile, however, the governor of Cuba, Diego Velázquez, who had originally commissioned Cortés, became jealous and bitter over the rumored success of the Caudillo, or dictator, as Cortés was known. Velázquez appointed Pánfilo de Narváez to head an expedition that was to sail to Mexico and there find and arrest Cortés. In

March 1520, Narváez left for Mexico with nine hundred men and a complement of artillery and horses. He eventually landed on the coast about forty miles from Villa Rica and founded his own town, near what is today the city of Veracruz. He established relations with the local Indians, most of whom previously had become allies of Cortés, and communicated secretly with members of Cortés's company and even with Montezuma, but Narváez was slow to organize a move over the mountains to Tenochtitlán.

Cortés, however, was quick to react to the news of Narváez's presence on the coast. Although he had relatively few men at his disposal, he designated Pedro de Alvarado as commander in Tenochtitlán—a choice that was to have disastrous consequences (*see also* La NOCHE TRISTE)—and with eighty men and no artillery left immediately to confront Narváez. Along the way, he picked up 260 more men, bringing his total to 350 against Narváez's 900, who by this time had occupied the Indian town of Cempoallan, which Cortés had visited a year earlier. Cortés dispatched messengers to Narváez, hoping to put him off guard, and at the same time offered large bribes—Cortés was flush with confiscated Mexican gold—to key members of Narváez's expedition.

Despite being badly outnumbered, Cortés decided to attack as soon as he was in position. He brought his men to within a few miles of Cempoallan on the night of May 28 and prepared them for the assault by dividing them into companies, each with a specific objective, and declaring that the first to lay hands on Narváez would win a bonus of one thousand *castellanos.*

Narváez had stationed his artillery, horsemen, crossbowmen, and harquebusiers (armed with shoulder-fired guns) outside the town, while he and his staff occupied the top of the ceremonial pyramid at the center of the town. When it began to rain during the evening, the unwary sentries outside the town abandoned their posts for the comfort of dry houses, leaving the horses and artillery unattended.

As Cortés and his men approached Cempoallan in the early morning hours of May 29, they learned from spies that Narváez had isolated himself from most of his army and had only a handful of men with him. Cortés immediately dispatched a group of sixty men under Gonzalo de Sandoval to capture the opposing commander, while Cortés led an assault against Narváez's main body of troops. A frightened sentry alerted Narváez, who was sleeping in a thatched hut at the top of the pyramid, but Cortés's strike force climbed the steps and attacked before

a defense could be organized. During a brief, violent struggle, Narváez's eye was put out by a lance, and most of the thirty or so men with him were killed or wounded. Bleeding profusely, he surrendered to Sandoval. Meanwhile, Cortés had easily defeated the rest of Narváez's men, in part because his prebattle bribes had done their work and there was little determined resistance.

Fifteen of Narváez's force were killed; Cortés lost two.

Cortés soon convinced the defeated Spaniards to join his forces, and he thereby increased his overall army by nearly twofold. Unfortunately, he had little time to savor his victory, since word now reached him of a new crisis in Tenochtitlán.

Further Reading

Salvador de Madariaga. Reprint ed. *Hernán Cortés, Conqueror of Mexico* (Westport, Conn.: Greenwood Press, 1979); William H. Prescott. *History of the Conquest of Mexico . . .* (New York: Modern Library, 1936); and Hugh Thomas. *Conquest: Montezuma, Cortés, and the Fall of Old Mexico* (New York: Simon & Schuster, 1993).

➣ Cerro Gordo

Mexico (April 18, 1847) *Mexican-American War*

Just days after the American capture of the coastal Mexican city of VERACRUZ, Gen. Antonio López de Santa Anna was proclaimed president of Mexico. Determined to thwart Maj. Gen. Winfield Scott's plan to end the Mexican-American War by marching to Mexico City and taking over the Mexican capital, Santa Anna decided to make a stand outside of Jalapa, the capital of the state of Veracruz, at the high pass of Cerro Gordo where he hoped his troops and the oncoming yellow-fever season would stop Scott in his tracks.

Santa Anna's six thousand troops, anchored by the brigades of Brig. Gen. Ciriaco Vásquez and Maj. Gen. Pedro de Ampudia, began fortifying the hills around Cerro Gordo on April 5 as they awaited the American advance from the east.

Winfield Scott dispatched the Second Division under Maj. Levi Twiggs from Veracruz on April 8, but Twiggs's progress along the treacherous national highway to Rio del Plan was slow. Maj. Gen. Robert Patterson set out behind Twiggs with additional men and supplies.

Skirmishing began as the Americans neared Cerro Gordo on April 11 and 12. Several men were wounded, including Lt. Col. Joseph E. Johnston, as he led his men on a reconnaissance in the high hills to the east of the mountain pass. Twiggs wanted to attack the Mexican position at Cerro Gordo on April 13, but Patterson urged caution, and in the evening Twiggs and Patterson received orders to await the arrival of Major General Scott and Brig. Gen. William J. Worth's division. While awaiting Scott's arrival on April 15, Capt. Robert E. Lee reconnoitered the three Mexican batteries in the hills around the peak of Cerro Gordo; he was almost captured but slipped back into camp with full information about the Mexican left flank.

As Scott formed his men into attack position on April 17, he sent Lt. Frank Gardner's infantry to take the hill called Atalaya, and they were so successful at clearing the hill that some troops began to push up the main hill at Cerro Gordo. The remaining American troops were not ready for the assault, however, and the men had to be withdrawn cautiously to Atalaya, covered by fire from Lt. Jesse L. Reno's artillery.

General Santa Anna assumed that this withdrawal signaled a Mexican success, but he was unaware that Scott was actually planning the main attack for the next day, April 18. Scott's plan called for careful coordination of the kind that rarely succeeds flawlessly: Twiggs would push

forward and cut off a Mexican retreat toward Jalapa as Worth brought up his rear, and Maj. Gen. Gideon J. Pillow's brigade would take Twiggs's fire as its sign to break through the Mexican right.

The morning of April 18 began with an artillery duel between Mexican guns atop Cerro Gordo and American guns on Atalaya. Twiggs sent Brig. Gen. Bennett Riley and Brig. Gen. James Shields with Lee beyond Cerro Gordo to attack from behind, but before they were in position, Lt. Col. William S. Harney's men pushed up the front of Cerro Gordo, just as many of them had the day before.

Harney's men quickly mounted the hill, rushed the Mexican breastworks, took the enemy's guns, and ran up an American flag. Brigadier General Vásquez was killed in this furious assault as Riley's men charged up the rear of the hill.

Maj. Gen. Pillow was not yet in position to attack the Mexican right when Twiggs's guns signaled the beginning of the action. His two storming parties nonetheless attacked in an uncoordinated assault toward the right Mexican battery, sustaining heavy losses before Pillow observed Mexican troops waving white flags and halted the action.

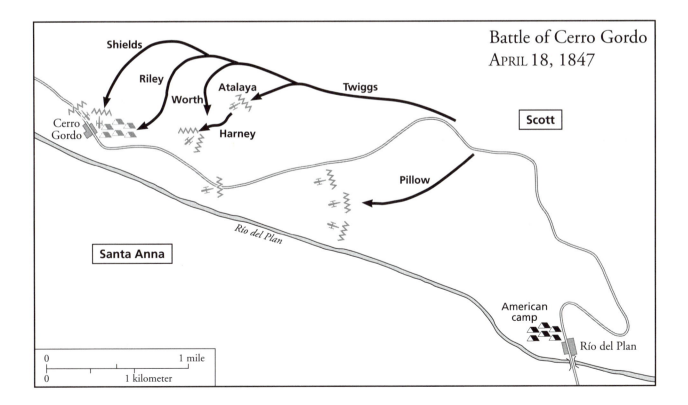

Battle of Cerro Gordo
APRIL 18, 1847

By 11:00 A.M., the American forces had carried the day. Santa Anna had evacuated the field, and most of his troops were either surrendering or fleeing on foot. The Americans pursued them as far as Santa Anna's estate at Encero, but they broke off the chase before reaching Jalapa.

The American forces lost only 337 wounded and 63 killed in the battle. No clear Mexican casualty reports exist, but the Americans claimed to have captured 3,041 Mexicans, including 5 general officers. As many as one thousand other Mexican soldiers escaped as they were going home on parole. One of the most colorful items captured at Cerro Gordo was a wooden leg that the Fourth Illinois claimed belonged to Santa Anna. The leg was displayed for years in the Illinois state capital, and replicas toured several American cities. The American forces took over Jalapa on April 19 and continued their march toward Mexico City.

Further Reading

K. Jack Bauer. *The Mexican War: 1846–1848* (New York: Macmillan, Publishing 1974); John D. Eisenhower. *Agent of Destiny: The Life and Times of General Winfield Scott* (New York: Free Press, 1997); John Edward Weems. *To Conquer a Peace: The War between the United States and Mexico* (Garden City, N.Y.: Doubleday, 1974).

Chambly

Canada (October 18, 1775) *American Revolution*

As it became clear during the summer of 1775 that the armed conflict with Great Britain was likely to continue, the American Continental Congress resolved to send an invasion force to Canada. New Yorker Philip Schuyler, was given command of a New England militia army and moved north toward Montreal and Quebec.

The British had two strong posts on the Richelieu River north of Lake Champlain guarding the approaches to Canada, and Schuyler laid siege to ST. JOHN'S, the most important of the two. St John's had been raided by Benedict Arnold in May, immediately following the fall of FORT TICONDEROGA, but it had since been reinforced by the British. The second British position was at Chambly, where eighty-eight regulars of the Seventh Regiment of Foot were stationed under the command of a Major Stopford, along with nearly one hundred women and children.

In mid-October, the Americans leapfrogged over St. John's and attacked Chambly. Col. Timothy Bedel and

Maj. John Brown, commanding about 625 men and backed by Canadian volunteers, surrounded the post and drove back a British sortie. The Americans then ferried a small field gun around St. John's and began a bombardment of Chambly's walls.

The British surrendered on October 18. The entire garrison became prisoners, and the Americans seized a considerable store of arms and ammunition.

Further Reading

Papers Relating to the Surrender of Fort St. Johns and Fort Chambly (Toronto: Canadiana House, 1971); and Christopher Ward. *The War of the Revolution.* Vol. 1 (New York: Macmillan, 1952).

Champion's Hill

Mississippi (May 16, 1863) *American Civil War*

Federal general Ulysses S. Grant's campaign against Vicksburg, Mississipi, required extremely complex maneuvering because of the nearly impassable terrain surrounding the river city for hundreds of miles on the landward side. In the spring of 1863, after several false starts, Grant crossed his huge army well below the city and began a march north and east, angling away from Vicksburg and around the most difficult swamps and ravines. He defeated Confederate forces at PORT GIBSON and RAYMOND on the way and occupied Jackson, on the Pearl River. He then turned directly west and began to march toward Vicksburg. Confederate lieutenant general John C. Pemberton had come out of Vicksburg with twenty-two thousand men and, after briefly considering an attack on Grant's rear base, turned eastward to face the oncoming Union army at Champion's Hill.

Pemberton had a brigade under Brig. Gen. Stephen D. Lee in possession of Champion's Hill itself, a seventy-five-foot knoll that commanded the surrounding countryside, when the first Union forces came down the road from Jackson. Two of Grant's corps—numbering together more than twenty thousand troops—moved into position to attack. Brig. Gen. Alvin Hovey's corps and Maj. Gen. John A. Logan's corps broke the defenses on Lee's flanks and took possession of the hill, but Maj. Gen. John McClernan was slow to bring up additional units, and the Confederates counterattacked with one of their best brigades, Col. Francis Cockrell's Missourians, and retook the hill.

Cockrell's brigade, along with Brig. Gen. Martin E. Green's men, pushed on and drove the Federal forces back up the road to within several hundred yards of Grant's headquarters. At that point, Union brigadier general Marcellus Crocker sent in two brigades, and Union artillerists got in position to enfilade the Confederate advance. The Southern attack broke up after a desperate fight and retreated, with the Federals once again taking control of the hill.

Pemberton ordered Maj. Gen. William Loring to withdraw from his position and attack the main Federal advance, but Loring refused and did little more than cover the Confederate withdrawal. He and his men were separated from the main force and at the end of the day wandered off to join other Confederate units to the south, rather than retreating with Pemberton back toward Vicksburg.

Grant lost 410 killed, 1,844 wounded, and 187 missing. The Confederates lost 381 killed, 1,800 wounded, and 1,670 missing.

Grant had used only about half of his army to fight the battle, holding William Tecumseh Sherman's troops in reserve all day. With the victory at Champion's Hill, the road to Vicksburg was open.

Further Reading

Editors of *Civil War Times Illustrated. Struggle for Vickburg: The Battles That Decided the Civil War* (Harrisburg, Pa.: Stackpole Books, 1967); H. Grady Howell. *Hill of Death: The Battle of Champion Hill* (Madison, Miss.: Chickasaw Bayou Press, 1993); and Herb Phillips. *Champion Hill!* (Edwards, Miss.: Champion Hill Battlefield Foundation, 1984).

✤ Champoton

Mexico (March 1517) *Spanish Conquest*

The first recorded battle between Indians and Europeans on the North American continent took place on the coast of Yucatán. Unlike in the majority of the battles to follow, the Indians won and put the European to flight.

The Indians were members of one of the fifteen or sixteen tribes of Maya that inhabited most of the Yucatán Peninsula, living in towns and villages at a level considerably below that of the grand era of Maya civilization that had flourished until the thirteenth century but still in the sixteenth possessed of a sophisticated culture. They may have heard of the presence of strange white-skinned, bearded men on the islands to the east, but until 1517 they had seen none close at hand.

The first Europeans to meet the Maya were 110 Spanish conquistadores from Cuba, led by Francisco

Hernández de Córdoba, who had been sent on a mission of exploration by the governor of Cuba. Hernández de Córdoba and his men sailed two *noas* (substantial sailing ships) and a small brigantine from Santiago de Cuba in February 1517. They landed on the Yucatán coast and visited a town they called "El Gran Cairo" because of the Mayan pyramids, the like of which no Spaniard had ever seen in the New World. After a skirmish and threats from the first Maya they met, Hernández de Córdoba and his men moved on along the coast and disembarked near another Maya town, close to the location of the modern-day city of Champoton.

The Spaniards were running short of drinking water and tried to find a water source. This may have been the specific irritant that caused the Maya of the town, led by their chief, Mochcouoh, to turn hostile. Unknown to the Spaniards, drinking water was scarce on the peninsula, and the Maya would have been reluctant to share with these strangers.

After spending an uncomfortable night listening to the drums, flutes, and shouts of the Maya, the Spaniards woke to find themselves surrounded. After a ritual display by the feather-bedecked Mayan leaders, the Indians attacked with stone-throwing slings, bows and arrows, copper-headed axes, and the characteristic obsidian-bladed swords of the region. Even though the Spaniards were armed with superior Toledo-steel swords and had fifteen crossbows and ten harquebuses (a powerful if cumbersome early firearm), they were no match for the Maya. Later conquistadores would be able to defeat vastly greater numbers of Indians by skillful use of weapons and tactics, but Hernández de Córdoba's men apparently were unprepared for the ferocity and organization of the Maya. (They were more accustomed to the less effective Indian warriors of the Caribbean islands.)

Twenty Spaniards were killed and the survivors, most of whom were wounded—Hernández de Córdoba suffered more than thirty wounds—barely managed to reach their boats and withdraw. Two of their number were captured and suffered what the conquistadores came to fear most: they became human sacrifices, in accord with the practice of all the Indian cultures of Mexico. The number of Mayan casualties was unrecorded.

The Spanish ships limped back to Cuba, where Hernández de Córdoba died of his wounds.

Further Reading

Hugh Thomas. *Conquest: Montezuma, Cortés, and the Fall of Old Mexico* (New York: Simon & Schuster, 1993).

Chancellorsville

Virginia (May 1–4, 1863) *American Civil War*

During the fighting at Chancellorsville in early May 1863, Confederate general Robert E. Lee demonstrated unequivocally that he was a military genius. With audacity, intelligence, intuition, and skill he wielded the Army of Northern Virginia, a small but superb fighting force, to defeat utterly a Union army twice its size.

After his victory at FREDERICKSBURG four months earlier, Lee had allowed his army to rest, actually sending a portion of it, under Lt. Gen. James Longstreet, away to find food. He commanded no more than sixty thousand troops by May, most of them still concentrated around the heights above Fredericksburg. Lee's main subordinate on the scene was Lt. Gen. Thomas J. "Stonewall" Jackson, although Lee's army boasted many experienced and talented corps, division, and brigade commanders.

Opposing Lee was Maj. Gen. Joseph Hooker, known as "Fighting Joe," who had taken over the Army of the Potomac from the hapless Ambrose Burnside and had managed to resuscitate the men's spirits and physical condition. Hooker had nearly 130,000 men at his disposal, and he had a sound plan to circle upstream on the Rappahannock and Rapidan Rivers and send a strike force around Lee's left flank. However, Hooker was arrogant and boastful before launching his campaign, and his subsequent behavior mocked his prebattle self-confidence.

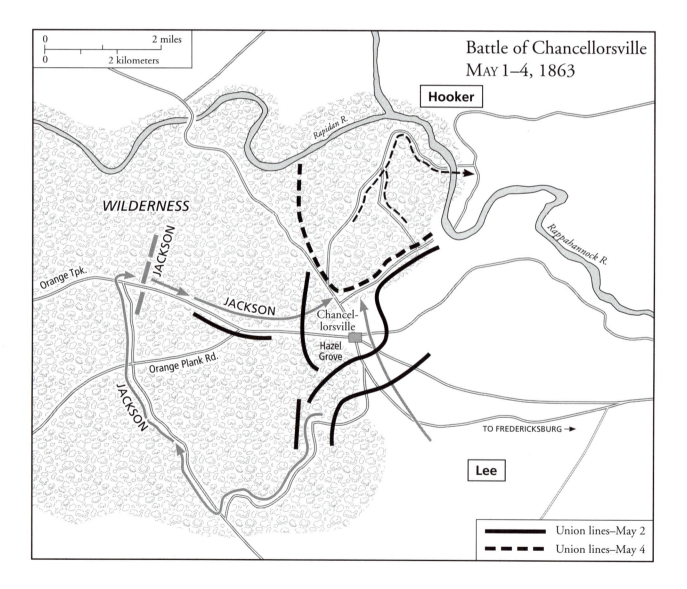

Hooker took three Union corps on a long swing and by April 30 was at the crossroads of Chancellorsville, in a region of heavy, tangled, second-growth forest called the WILDERNESS (site of another battle in 1864). By all the standard rules of warfare, he was in position to deal the Confederates a deathblow, but Lee made his own rules. The Confederate commander, leaving only ten thousand troops under Maj. Gen. Jubal Early to guard the river crossings at Fredericksburg, ordered the bulk of his small army on rapid march north under Jackson to meet Hooker head-on. On the morning of May 1, the two forces clashed near the Chancellorsville crossroads. Despite gaining an early advantage, Hooker timidly declined to press his men forward and ordered a retreat into defenses in the densely wooded Wilderness. Hooker's blustery belligerence had collapsed immediately in the face of Lee's opposition.

Lee then made an extraordinarily daring decision. His cavalry scouts told him that Hooker's right flank was unsupported and vulnerable, so Lee ordered Jackson to take twenty-nine thousand men on a night march around Hooker's right wing, leaving a mere thirteen thousand to face the entire forty- or fifty-thousand-man main Union contingent. If Hooker had understood how Lee had split his forces in the face of overwhelming numbers, he could have swept forward and destroyed Lee's holding force. But Hooker was both cowed and self-deluded. When he received reports that Jackson was on the move, he concluded that the Confederates were retreating.

Late in the afternoon of May 2, Jackson's men emerged from the woods and fell, with crushing effect, on the unsuspecting Union Eleventh Corps, commanded by Maj. Gen. Oliver O. Howard. The Federal troops were snapped up by the veteran Confederates, and only nightfall saved them from complete annihilation.

During the dark evening hours, Jackson and his staff rode forward to reconnoiter. As they rode back toward their lines, troops from North Carolina mistook them for Federals and fired a volley that severely wounded Jackson. (He died eight days later, and Lee lost his best subordinate.)

On May 3 the focus of the fighting shifted back to Fredericksburg, where the Union forces under Maj. Gen. John Sedgwick crossed the river and moved over the heights toward Lee's rear. A Confederate counterattack near Salem Church, however, stopped the Federal advance.

Defying the recommendations of his commanders, Hooker ordered a general withdrawal back across the Rappahannock on May 4, leaving Lee in total control of the battlefield.

Lee lost around 12,800 casualties in the three days of fighting; the Union lost approximately 17,000.

Lee had once again defied the odds and won a great victory in the field. Now he was emboldened to undertake the invasion of the north that ended at GETTYSBURG.

Further Reading

Ernest B. Furguson. *Chancellorsville, 1863: The Souls of the Brave* (New York: Alfred A. Knopf, 1992); Gary W. Gallagher, ed. *Chancellorsville: The Battle and Its Aftermath* (Chapel Hill: University of North Carolina Press, 1996); Augustus C. Hamlin. *The Attack of Stonewall Jackson at Chancellorsville* (Fredericksburg, Va.: Sergeant Kirklands, 1997); Noel G. Harrison. *Chancellorsville Battlefield Sites* (Lynchburg, Va.: H. E. Howard, 1990); Stephen W. Sears. *Chancellorsville* (Boston: Houghton Mifflin, 1996); and Edward J. Stackpole. *Chancellorsville: Lee's Greatest Battle.* 2d ed. (Harrisburg, Pa.: Stackpole Books, 1988).

Chantilly

(Ox Hill)

Virginia (September 1, 1862) *American Civil War*

Two days after Confederate general Robert E. Lee's smashing victory at Second BULL RUN, he sought to follow up with an attack on Maj. Gen. John Pope, who was gathering a force near the town of Chantilly about halfway between Bull Run and the U.S. capital at Washington, D.C. Union forces under the direct command of Maj. Gen. Philip Kearny and Brig. Gen. Isaac Stevens inflicted heavy casualties on the Confederates and allowed Pope's main force to escape safely toward Washington.

The Battle of Chantilly began when Lee ordered a move around the left flank of Union forces stationed at Centreville. This brought his second in command, Maj.

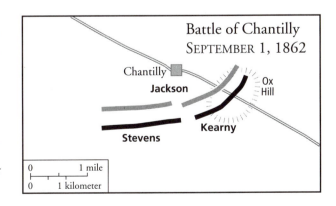

Battle of Chantilly
SEPTEMBER 1, 1862

Gen. Thomas J. "Stonewall" Jackson, into contact with Kearny and Stevens at Ox Hill, near Chantilly, on September 1. The fierce battle lasted all day, even during a severe thunderstorm. Few details of movements during the day are known, but the Federals held their ground until they withdrew at nightfall, sure that Pope was safely within the capital's defenses.

The Confederates reported eight hundred casualties, and the Union thirteen hundred. Both Stevens and Kearny, the brilliant one-armed Mexican-American War veteran, died at Chantilly.

Though Union forces acquitted themselves admirably at Chantilly, the battle ended a campaign around Second Bull Run that had amply demonstrated the superiority of the Confederate command in the eastern theater.

Further Reading

Edward J. Stackpole. *From Cedar Mountain to Antietam, August–September, 1862* (Harrisburg, Pa.: Stackpole, 1959).

⚓ Chapultepec

Mexico (September 13, 1847)
Mexican-American War

After the failure of an armistice and the capture of MOLINO DEL REY on September 8, 1847, in a costly battle that gained little, Maj. Gen. Winfield Scott was left to consider how best to pursue his final attack on Mexico City. Scott hoped to capture the Mexican capital, show his superiority over Gen. Antonio López de Santa Anna once and for all, and win the war outright.

After consulting with his officers, Maj. Gen. Scott decided on September 11 that the American forces would attack the western gates of Mexico City. This meant, however, that they would first have to deal with the fortified castle on the hill at Chapultepec, which lay on the city's western edge. Though the two-hundred-foot-high hill presented a formidable obstacle, its peak was underfortified and was protected by around only nine hundred men, commanded by Maj. Gen. Nicholás Bravo. The south wall was protected by sandbag fortifications, the western slope by a minefield and heavy fortifications. Two batteries covered a ditch behind the castle, and by the northern wall rose a breastwork and a projecting redan.

On September 12, Capt. Benjamin Huger and the American engineers constructed four batteries to bombard Chapultepec from the west, while two thousand of Santa

Anna's men tried to shore up the hill's southern defenses. Maj. Gen. John A. Quitman's division executed a diversionary action near the village of Piedad, effectively distracting attention from Chapultepec. Mexican commanders were further confused by rumors of an attack on Mexico City from the southeast, so when the American batteries opened fire on Chapultepec late in the day, it was too late to rush many reinforcements into place.

By the evening of September 12, American fire had knocked out two of the best Mexican guns, but the Mexicans refused to abandon the hill, even though Santa Anna had rejected Bravo's request for reinforcements. Scott drew up plans for a frontal attack the next morning: Maj. Gen. Gideon J. Pillow's brigade, supported by men led by Capt. Samuel Mackenzie (from among Brig. Gen. William J. Worth's force), would attack from Molino del Rey. Meanwhile, Quitman's men and a storming party under Capt. Silas Casey (from among Brig. Gen. David E. Twiggs's troops) would push up the Tacubaya Road to the castle's southeast.

At dawn on September 13, the attack began, with artillery fire directed first at the castle's fortifications and then at a protected grove of trees farther down the hill. At 8:00 A.M., the infantry push began as Col. William B. Trousdale and Lt. Thomas J. Jackson led infantry and artillery out from Molino del Rey. To the south, Lt. Col. Joseph E. Johnston's four companies broke through the sandbags, poured up the hill, and fired directly on the castle with their muskets. Santa Anna sent the San Blas Battalion to counter Johnston's force, but it was unable to break through to the castle.

As Col. Timothy Patrick Andres led two companies of infantry and Lt. Jesse L. Reno's howitzers toward the grove to the west to meet Johnston's men, he encountered resistance from fifty-one cadets of the Mexican Military College, housed in the castle. Six of the cadets were killed and overnight became martyrs and Mexican patriotic figures, known subsequently as the *Niños Heroicos*.

After Andres cleared the grove, Col. Trueman B. Ransom shouted, "Forward, the Ninth!" but he was immediately shot in the head. His men charged on the fortifications but without scaling ladders, so they took cover and fired at the castle's parapets until they were driven away.

Major General Pillow, who was wounded at the base of the hill, began to panic, and he called in reinforcements. Capt. John G. Reynolds and Maj. Levi Twiggs's companies of marines, accompanied by Capt. Silas Casey's storming party, pushed toward a Mexican battery on the Tacubaya Road, but were repulsed, and both Twiggs and Casey lost their lives. Major General Quitman ordered Brig. Gen. Persifor Smith to try to flank the Mexicans to the right of the road, and he called in fresh troops for the attack up the hill.

These new attackers, parts of Col. Newman Clarke's brigade and some of Brig. Gen. James Shields's men, crossed a minefield with the long-awaited ladders, and the Americans began to scale the castle walls, which were still being defended by Mexican troops. Capt. Moses Barnard planted a flag on the parapet, and hundreds of Americans poured into the castle buildings, trampling on the Mexican wounded. Around 9:30 A.M., Bravo surrendered to Lt. Charles B. Brower of the New York Regiment. The American flag was raised by Lt. George E. Pickett, who had picked it up when Lt. James Longstreet, the previous flag bearer, was wounded. When the castle's guns were silenced, the Mexicans who were contending against Quitman to the east of the hill began to retreat.

Immediately after Chapultepec was captured, the Americans pushed on toward Mexico City. Quitman led almost every man who had swarmed into the castle toward the Belén Garita, which protected two roads on the western edge of the city's gates. There they met 180 infantrymen commanded by Brig. Gen. Andrés Terrés. Terrés's men and additional reinforcements sent by Santa Anna resisted manfully, but the arrival of two American howitzers and Terrés's lack of ammunition caused him to withdraw to the Ciudadela, closer to the city, at around 1:20 P.M. Heavy fire from the Ciudadela stopped Quitman's advance.

Brigadier General Worth led a large force toward the city from the northwest down the San Cosmé Road, but it faced resistance from fifteen hundred cavalry troops led by Brig. Gen. Anastasio Torrejón as well as from fire from the city's rooftops and a hastily constructed redoubt thrown up by Brig. Gen. Matías Peña y Barragán's men.

Finally, Col. John Garland's brigade drew up on the right. Lt. Ulysses S. Grant and Navy Lieutenant Raphael Semmes both had their men drag heavy guns to high points on either side of the road, and the Mexicans began to abandon their positions. Lt. Henry J. Hunt trained an American howitzer on the city from the Belén Garita, and Lt. George H. Terret's marines began to fire on the Mexican position from a three-story house that they had somehow occupied inside the city's walls. The Mexican artillery was knocked out, and by 5:00 P.M. a wounded Brig. Gen. Joaquín Rangel was leading his troops in retreat—taking Santa Anna with them as they swept through the city. Worth's men entered the city by 6:00.

By 1:00 A.M. Santa Anna's men had withdrawn to Guadelupe Hidalgo, and at 4:00 A.M. city officials sent a message of capitulation to Winfield Scott. The American troops made their official entry into the city and flew the American flag over the Mexican capital the next day. Santa Anna's men sniped at the troops until they were finally silenced on September 17.

During the fighting, the Americans lost 130 killed, 703 wounded, and 29 missing. The total of Mexican killed and wounded numbered around 2,000, and another 823 men were taken prisoner.

The American capture of Chapultepec and Mexico City ended Scott's campaign. Once the Mexican siege of PUEBLA was lifted over the next few weeks, the entire war was over. The conflict, begun almost single-handedly by land-hungry Pres. James K. Polk, was a victory for the United States that added vast amounts of territory, including the Southwest and California, to the country.

Further Reading

K. Jack Bauer. *The Mexican War: 1846–1848* (New York: Macmillan, 1974); John D. Eisenhower. *Agent of Destiny: The Life and Times of General Winfield Scott* (New York: Free Press, 1997); J. F. C. Fuller, *Decisive Battles of the U.S.A.* (New York: Beechhurst, 1953); and John Edward Weems. *To Conquer a Peace: The War between the United States and Mexico* (Garden City, N.Y.: Doubleday, 1953).

Charleston

(Sullivan's Island)
South Carolina (June 28, 1776)
American Revolution

An ambitious British expedition to regain the southern colonies in 1776 turned to defeat when South Carolinians repulsed a powerful British fleet at Sullivan's Island in Charleston harbor.

The government in London decided in 1775 to counter the rebellion in the southern colonies, where all the royal governors had been chased from office, by sending an expedition under Lt. Gen. Sir Henry Clinton to land in either Virginia or North Carolina and rally what was thought to be a large number of Loyalists. Clinton was to take charge of an army assembled from Boston and the British Isles, along with a fleet of ten warships. Unfortunately for the British plan, the organization and sailing of the expeditionary force was delayed until after the new year, and long before the naval force arrived on the coast of North America the Loyalist defeat at MOORE'S CREEK BRIDGE had made the plan moot. Nevertheless, Clinton decided to shift his focus to Charleston, South Carolina, which was the principal port of the southern colonies.

When Clinton's army of twenty-five hundred troops arrived off the approaches to Charleston, he discovered not only that the mouth of the harbor (the city itself was several miles away) was a treacherous region of marshes, shoals, and narrow channels but that the Americans had fortified several of the islands guarding the harbor. The principal defense was Fort Sullivan on long, narrow Sullivan's Island, which bent around the northern headland of the harbor and commanded the approach to the city.

The fort was still under construction when the British arrived in May 1776. A parallel, double row of palmetto logs, with sand filling the sixteen-foot gap between, constituted the main work facing the harbor, and a flimsy series of earthworks along the back edge of the island guarded the channel between it and the mainland. There were nearly sixty-five hundred American troops in and around the city, commanded by Continental major general Charles Lee, but the island itself was defended by only about one hundred men of the Second Carolina Regiment under the command of Col. William Moultrie, plus two dozen or so artillerists. The half-finished fort was armed with twenty-five guns, ranging from twenty-four-pounders down to nine-pounders.

Clinton had at his disposal a considerable naval force, commanded by Adm. Sir Peter Parker: *Bristol*, a fifty-gun ship of the line; four twenty-eight-gun frigates, *Active*, *Actaeon*, *Soleby*, and *Syren*; two smaller frigates; a sloop; a schooner; and *Thunderer*, a bomb ketch, designed for long-range bombardment of fortifications. Clinton decided to take Sullivan's Island by first occupying undefended Long Island nearby and then sending troops across the narrow distance between the islands, but to his dismay his men discovered that the gap was a wicked combination of shoals and seven-foot holes. The British troops were stymied. Clinton turned to a naval attack, with an amphibious assault to follow.

Late in the morning of June 28, Parker's squadron sailed toward Sullivan's Island. The bomb ketch anchored a mile and a half away and began to lob ten-inch mortar shells into the fort. The rest of the ships maneuvered to within a few hundred yards and began a terrific bombardment hurling thousands of iron cannonballs at what seemed like the seemingly feeble walls of the fort.

Surprisingly, however, the heavy weight of British cannon fire did little damage. The palmetto logs forming the fort's walls were spongy soft, and the cannonballs simply sank into the wood without splintering or doing serious structural damage. The sand-filled pit between the log walls had the same effect. No matter how fiercely the Royal Navy ships battered at the American position—seven thousand spent cannonballs were gathered at the fort after the battle—they could cause almost no damage to the defenders, who were meanwhile busy firing their own guns with cool effectiveness. The fort was short of powder when the battle began, but Major General Lee managed to get a fresh supply across from the mainland during the day, and the American gunners made good use of the ammunition.

Bristol, with Admiral Parker aboard, was hit hard by fire from the fort. As she drifted out of control, her cable shot away, American shot swept the quarterdeck several times, killing everyone on deck except the admiral himself, who was wounded. The other British ships suffered severely as well, and as the day wore on the casualty lists mounted.

Parker had sent three of his frigates to sail around the island and take the fort in enfilade, but they all three ran aground in the tricky waters. Two of them eventually freed themselves, but the *Actaeon* could not be saved and had to be set afire by her crew and abandoned.

Inside the fort, the American defenders kept up their barrage all day. The only worrisome incident occurred when a British shell hit the fort's flagstaff and dropped the flag outside the walls. Fearing that the British might mistake this for a surrender, Sgt. William Jasper climbed the walls, retrieved the flag, and remounted it for all to see. (His feat made Jasper one of the best-known heroes of the American Revolution in the South; he was killed three years later defending SAVANNAH.)

By late evening the firing finally abated, and twelve hours after they had opened fire, the British ships slipped their cables and left. The attempt to take Charleston had been thwarted at a high cost. The British lost about 225 casualties, including between 40 and 50 killed. The captain of the *Bristol* was dead, and the former British governor of South Carolina, Lord William Campbell, who had served aboard as a volunteer, was severely wounded and later died. The Americans, on the other hand, suffered ten killed and twenty or so wounded.

Charleston and the South were safe from British invasion for another four years.

Further Reading

Jim Stokely. *Fort Moultrie: Constant Defender* (Washington, D.C.: National Park Service, 1985); and Christopher Ward. *The War of the Revolution*. Vol. 1 (New York: Macmillan, 1952).

Charleston

South Carolina (April 1–May 12, 1780)
American Revolution

After a military stalemate had developed in the North following the battle of MONMOUTH in 1778, and after he had consolidated control of Georgia in 1779 with the successful defense of SAVANNAH, the British commander in chief, Lt. Gen. Sir Henry Clinton, began again to think of seizing Charleston, South Carolina, a task at which he had so badly failed in 1776 (*see also* CHARLESTON [SULLIVAN'S ISLAND]). His second expedition was much different, and before the middle of 1780 it resulted in the greatest British victory of the entire war.

Clinton assembled a large invasion force drawn from his main American base in New York City. When he sailed in December 1779—on 90 transports, escorted by 10 warships—he had 8,700 troops and 396 horses in addition to thousands of sailors and marines. The bulk of his army comprised such regular units as the Seventh, Twenty-third, Thirty-third, Sixty-third, and Sixty-fourth Infantry Regiments, plus a corps of light infantry, two British grenadier battalions, four battalions of German mercenaries, and a battalion of New York Loyalist volunteers. Later he was joined by another 1,500 troops, including the dragoons of Lt. Col. Banastre Tarleton's mounted legion. The fleet was commanded by Adm. Marriot Arbuthnot, while Clinton's second in command was Maj. Gen. Lord Cornwallis. The voyage south was extremely difficult, with violent weather causing long delays and a very uncomfortable time for most of the invasion force (all the cavalry horses died at sea, and one ship was swept halfway across the Atlantic). The fleet was forced to put in at Savannah for repairs, but by February 1780 most of the force was ready for the advance on Charleston.

Clinton's plan was to land in force, cut off Charleston (trapping, if possible, the large American army garrisoned there), and take the city by siege. The state of military technology and tactics in the latter part of the eighteenth century was such that a carefully prepared and competently executed siege was nearly certain of success. If no outside relief force arrived and if the besieging army had large enough guns and enough troops to dig trenches, defend the approaches, and make the final assaults, the besieged garrison was doomed.

The defense of Charleston was nominally up to Maj. Gen. Benjamin Lincoln, commander of American forces in the southern theater, but his task was complicated by the interference of civilian authorities. Almost all the organized armed forces of the American cause in the South were gathered inside Charleston: about seven thousand regulars and militia, and a small flotilla of armed ships, most of them purchased from the French, guarded the harbor and river approaches to the city. The defenses of the city were in serious disrepair, having been allowed to deteriorate after the victory over a British fleet four years before. All the important government officials of the state, including Gov. John Rutledge and Lt. Gov. Christopher Gadsden, were present, in addition to a large civilian population.

Charleston was situated on a neck of land bordered by two rivers and guarded by several islands in the harbor, but the harbor forts, including Fort Sullivan (renamed Fort Moultrie), were scarcely in defensible condition. The authorities began to repair the landward defenses as soon as they discerned Clinton's intentions, and by the time the British actually began their siege, the city had a semicircle of strong fortifications from riverbank to riverbank, with a marshy canal and two lines of log-strewn abatis in front.

Clinton moved excruciatingly slowly. He sailed from Savannah to the seaward approaches to Charleston in February and landed his men and most of his supplies on James Island. He then paused for many weeks while more supplies and men arrived and Adm. Arbuthnot got his warships into the harbor and up the Cooper River to cut off the American line of retreat. On March 29, Clinton finally made his move. He had a fleet of flatboats rendezvous with his army on the Ashley River twelve miles upstream of the city. By sending his men onto the neck of the Charleston peninsula, he gained complete control over communication with the city on three sides. Three days later he marched south into positions in front of the city's fortifications, and on April 1 his men began to dig the first of the parallel trenches that would eventually bring the capture of the city.

Meanwhile, more American troops had filtered into Charleston, including the North Carolina and Virginia Continentals who had been fighting with Washington in the north. While General Lincoln and the authorities in

Charleston tried to reach a decision about withdrawal, Tarleton and Maj. Patrick Ferguson seized the initiative and, with victories at MONCK'S CORNER and LENUD'S FERRY, further narrowed the possibility of escape. By late April, the British approach trenches were within a few hundred yards, and Lincoln's ability to save his army was fading rapidly. On April 20, the civilian Governor's Council, led by Lieutenant Governor Gadsden (Governor Rutledge had fled), demanded that Lincoln remain in the city and defend the civilian population, threatening to turn on the soldiers if they refused. Lincoln tried to parley with Clinton on April 21 to ask for a surrender with honors, but Clinton refused. Three days later, a sortie from the city failed to dislodge the siege.

The situation progressed as if by script during the first days of May, with the British lines creeping closer and closer and the Americans becoming more and more desperate. On May 11, the council met again and advised Lincoln to surrender on the best terms he could: Clinton's men were within a few yards of the fortifications and were firing red-hot shot into the city to set houses on fire.

Lincoln surrendered without conditions on May 12. All of the regular American troops in the city became prisoners of war, although the militia were allowed to return to their homes on parole. All of the supplies, arms, and equipment of the Americans were forfeit. The garrison marched out at 11:00 A.M. and stacked their arms.

The surrender of Charleston was a disaster for the American cause, surpassing even the loss of FORT WASHINGTON four years previous. The official British count listed nearly 5,500 prisoners taken and the capture of 33,000 rounds of musket ammunition, 8,400 round shot, and 376 barrels of flour, in addition to food, clothing, and other supplies.

American losses during the siege were put at about 90 killed and 150 wounded. Clinton lost 76 killed and 200 to 300 wounded.

With the fall of Charleston, the major trading seaport in the southern states, and the loss of an entire American army, the cause of the Revolution in the south appeared to be at its lowest ebb.

Further Reading

Franklin B. Hough. *The Siege of Charleston . . .* (Spartansburg, S.C.: Reprint, 1975).

✎ Charlotte

North Carolina (September 26, 1780)
American Revolution

Lt. Gen. Lord Cornwallis was in charge of the British operations in the South following the British seizure of CHARLESTON. In the fall of 1780, he began a slow movement into North Carolina, often encountering American patriot militia.

Cornwallis was moving toward Charlotte with a large force of Loyalists and regulars when he met Col. William Davie's men at a road and stone wall. Although Davie had around one thousand men altogether, only a handful—probably no more than twenty dragoons and seventy infantry—were actually engaged in the fight that followed. Davie had his infantry positioned behind the stone wall, with the dismounted dragoons behind fences along the road.

When the British forces approached, Cornwallis sent Maj. George Hanger, temporarily in command of Lt. Col. Banastre Tarleton's British Legion, forward to clear the road. With little preparation, Hanger charged the fences and was driven back by accurate musket fire. He then attacked the stone wall but was repulsed again, despite the patriots' thin ranks.

Cornwallis himself rode to the front and exhorted his men to better efforts. Finally a larger force of light infantry under Lt. Col. James Webster chased the patriots out of their positions.

The British suffered fifteen killed and wounded; the Americans lost twice that number.

Further Reading

John S. Pancake. *This Destructive War: The British Campaign in the Carolinas, 1780–1782* (University, Ala.: University of Alabama Press, 1985).

✎ Chateaugay

(Châteauguay River)
Canada (October 25–26, 1813) *War of 1812*

The battle of Chateaugay marked a low point in the disastrous American campaign against Montreal in the fall of 1813.

In a bid to cut off British supply outside of Kingston, Sec. of War John Armstrong ordered Maj. Gen. James Wilkinson, one of the most infamous characters in early American history, to march down the St. Lawrence River and rendezvous with Maj. Gen. Wade Hampton, who commanded troops on Lake Champlain. Hampton and Wilkinson had hated one another since the Revolutionary War, but they reluctantly agreed to Armstrong's plan.

Wilkinson was delayed, or hesitated, throughout the first weeks of October, but by October 21 Hampton began to march up the Châteauguay River from his headquarters at Four Corners (now Chateaugay), New York, toward the St. Lawrence. At the Canadian border, Hampton's fourteen hundred New York militia troops refused to leave American soil, so the general continued with four thousand regulars.

On October 25, Hampton was stopped cold by the enemy. A combined force of French-Canadian volunteers, various militia units, and Indians warriors, all under the command of Napoleonic War veteran Lt. Col. Charles de Salaberry, had blocked the road with log abatis and had built fortifications alongside.

Hampton sent Col. Robert Purdy to cross the river and weaken the enemy by an attack from behind, but Purdy's troops got lost in the forest overnight and in the morning faced Canadians on both sides of the river. Purdy skirmished with the Canadians for two days, unable to find Hampton or get a message to him.

Meanwhile, on the night of October 25, Hampton received a letter from Armstrong describing the winter quarters he had ordered constructed back in New York. To Hampton, this signaled only weak support for the attack into Canada. Hampton probably would have withdrawn at once if Purdy's advance had not been in progress.

Around 2:00 P.M. the next day, Hampton decided to attack the enemy position, despite the lack of communication from Purdy. Hampton pursued the attack with something less than full vigor drawing up in formal formation within range of the abatis. The Canadians let out a great yell that, according to Canadian lore, convinced Hampton he faced a much greater force than he did. Over two hours of firing Hampton refused to order a charge on the defensive position, and he eventually retreated. Once Purdy returned, the commanders agreed to withdraw to Four Corners.

The lackluster nature of the battle was reflected in the casualty totals. The Americans lost around fifty men, and the Canadians lost only two killed, thirteen wounded, and three captured.

Hampton's defeat left Wilkinson alone to contend against the British at CHRYSLER'S FARM. The two-pronged campaign against Montreal was never completed, and Hampton's suspiciousness of his superiors led to his resignation in March 1814.

Further Reading

John A. Bilow. *Chateaugay, N.Y. and the War of 1812* (Plattsburgh, N.Y.: Payette & Sims, 1984).

Chattanooga

(Lookout Mountain, Missionary Ridge)

Tennessee (November 23–25, 1863)
American Civil War

After the great Confederate victory at CHICKAMAUGA, the Union's damaged and disorganized Army of the Cumberland, under Maj. Gen. William S. Rosecrans, retreated into the city of Chattanooga. The commander of the Confederate Army of the Tennessee, the unpopular Gen. Braxton Bragg, had declined to pursue the Federals but instead laid siege to the city, occupying the heights of Lookout Mountain and Missionary Ridge, which commanded the Union positions from the south and west, and sending cavalry units to cut off supply lines from the north.

The Federal command underwent a drastic change when Pres. Abraham Lincoln appointed Maj. Gen. Ulysses S. Grant to command of all Union forces in the western theater. Grant relieved Rosecrans, replacing him with Maj. Gen. George H. Thomas, and he ordered a concentration of forces at Chattanooga. Maj. Gen. William T. Sherman arrived from the west with several divisions, and Maj. Gen. Joseph Hooker came from the Virginia front with two corps of the Army of the Potomac. By November, Grant had secured a small but adequate line of supply to his rear and had amassed around seventy thousand troops.

The Confederate command had also been in turmoil, Bragg's subordinates nearly unanimously demanding his removal. Confederate president Jefferson Davis personally visited the army and confirmed Bragg in command for at least one more campaign, but he detached Generals Leonidas Polk, James Longstreet, Nathan Bedford Forrest, and others. Bragg was left with about fifty thousand troops, although he held commanding positions on the high ground.

Grant, determined to break out of Chattanooga, ordered Sherman to cross the Tennessee River and prepare an attack on Missionary Ridge. At the same time, Grant sent Hooker to assault the Confederates at Lookout

Mountain, and Thomas was to make a feint in the center. On November 23, Thomas's men put on a show of drilling in front of a Confederate position at Orchard Knob (a lower promontory in front of the main Confederate positions), but suddenly the drill turned into an attack, and the Federal soldiers ousted the defenders and seized Orchard Knob, which Grant, moving forward, took as his field headquarters.

The next day, Hooker's men attacked up the slopes of Lookout Mountain in an early-morning assault. They dislodged Confederates part way up and continued to the top, where they finished the fighting in thick fog that surrounded

the heights (giving the engagement its nickname, "Battle above the Clouds"). Bragg withdrew his remaining troops, and by nightfall Hooker controlled Lookout Mountain.

Meanwhile, Sherman's men had advanced on Missionary Ridge, but on November 25 Sherman's attacks stalled, and Grant reluctantly called on Thomas to reinforce the Union position by taking rifle pits at the base of the ridge. There followed one of the most extraordinary combat events of the entire Civil War. Thomas's men—who felt strongly the disgrace of their defeat at Chickamauga—overran the rifle pits and, without orders from any officer, continued to charge straight up the steep,

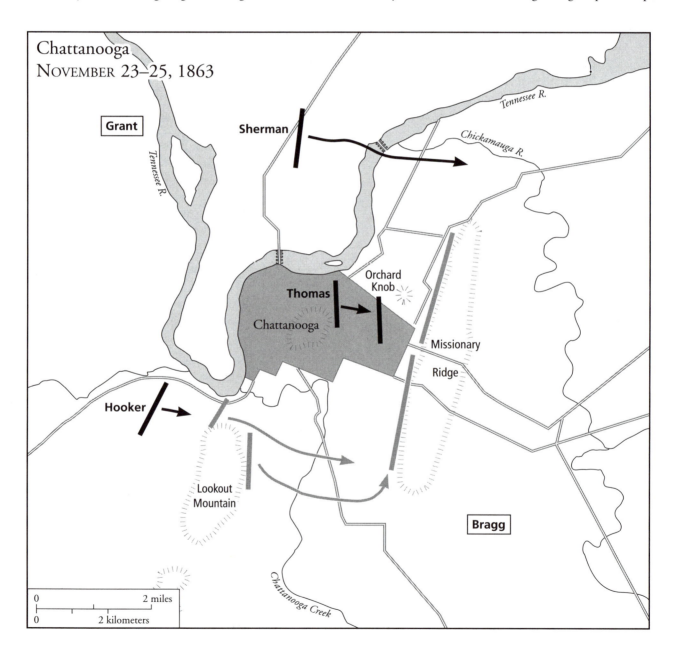

Chattanooga
NOVEMBER 23–25, 1863

Grant

Sherman

Tennessee R.

Chickamauga R.

Orchard Knob

Thomas

Chattanooga

Missionary

Ridge

Hooker

Lookout Mountain

Bragg

Chattanooga Creek

0   2 miles

0   2 kilometers

rugged slope. Against all odds and understanding, they clawed and fought their way to the Confederate defenses at the top of the ridge and not only dislodged the Southerners but sent them fleeing in disarray down the other side. By nightfall, the men of the Army of the Cumberland held the heights of Missionary Ridge and had broken the Confederate hold on Chattanooga.

Overall casualties for the three days of fighting were 5,815 for the Union and 6,667 for the Confederates.

Bragg's defeat finally convinced President Davis to relieve him of command. Conversely, the Union victory confirmed Lincoln's judgment in appointing the controversial Grant (many complained of his excessive drinking) to high command. The way for a Federal invasion of Georgia was now open.

Further Reading

Richard Baumgartner and Larry M. Strayer, eds. *Echoes of Battle: The Struggle for Chattanooga* (Huntington, W. Va.: Blue Acorn Press, 1996); John Hoffman. *The Confederate Collapse at the Battle of Missionary Ridge* . . . (Dayton, Ohio: n.p., 1985); and Charles P. Roland. "Chattanooga," in Francis H. Kennedy, ed. *The Civil War Battlefield Guide* (Boston: Houghton Mifflin, 1990).

⤳ Cheat Mountain

(Elkwater)

West Virginia (September 10–15, 1861)
American Civil War

The clash at Cheat Mountain, West Virginia, in September 1861 marked an inauspicious start for Gen. Robert E. Lee's command of Southern forces in the Civil War, as Lee failed to retake the areas of western Virginia whose capture had catapulted Maj. Gen. George B. McClellan into command of the Federal army a few months earlier.

Lee sought to take two Federal posts, one commanded by Col. Nathan Kimball at the peak of Cheat Mountain and the other by Brig. Gen. Joseph J. Reynolds in the town of Elkwater, positions separated by a seven-mile mountain road. On September 10, Lee's force, which he divided into three parts for the attack, pushed forward. On September 11, Lee's main force met action at Conrad's Mill as Brig. Gen. Samuel R. Anderson's brigade moved against Col. Kimball's right. By the next day, most of the Federal forces had been driven toward Elkwater, but Col. Albert Rust failed to complete a flanking move around Cheat Summit that was to have signaled the beginning of a coordinated Confederate attack, so Lee had to withdraw.

In the early hours of September 13, Reynolds and Kimball reestablished contact. Meanwhile, Lee sent Col. J. A. Washington to reconnoiter an attack position against Elkwater. Washington was fooled into believing that the three hundred Federals on Cheat mountain really numbered four thousand and was killed before he could report any more useful information. Lee decided to abandon his plans and withdrew on September 15.

Lee denied heavy casualties, but Union forces reported taking twenty prisoners and seeing one hundred Confederates killed and wounded. Twenty-one of Reynolds's men were killed or wounded and sixty taken prisoner.

Lee suffered heavy criticism for failing in his first campaign of the war.

Further Reading

Jack Zinn. *Lee's Cheat Mountain Campaign* (Parsons, W.Va.: McClain, 1974).

⤳ Cherry Valley

New York (November 11, 1778)
American Revolution

In 1778, Loyalists and Indian allies of the British conducted a series of raids against western American settlements that had been left relatively undefended due to the demands of the Revolutionary War to the east. One of the most successful expeditions was a raid on the Cherry Valley settlements in New York, which lay close to the Mohawk River valley and formed a strategic salient into the homelands of the Iroquois Confederacy.

The raid was led by Loyalist Walter Butler—son of Maj. John Butler, who was in charge of Loyalist forces at Niagara—and the Mohawk leader Joseph Brant (Thayendanegea). They gathered a force comprised of Butler's Rangers (a Loyalist unit) and several hundred Mohawk and prepared to move on the Cherry Valley settlements.

The American settlements had called on Congress for help in defending themselves, and in July, Col. Ichabod Alden (great-grandson of John Alden of Pilgrim fame) arrived at the head of 250 men of the Seventh Massachusetts regiment. Unfortunately, Alden had no experience in frontier conditions or fighting, and he ignored the sound advice of the locals.

Alden refused to let the settlers and their families into a newly constructed fort, forcing them to stay in their scattered homes despite clear warnings that there was a large force of Loyalists and Mohawk nearby. Moreover, the colonel posted his men and officers in houses outside the stockade, leaving the force unable to concentrate if attacked.

Late on the morning of November 11, Butler and Brant's men stepped out of the woods and began to attack the Americans in their houses. Alden, who had been sleeping in a house four hundred yards from the fort, was killed while trying to reach safety, as were many of his men. The fort itself was too strong for the Loyalists and Mohawk to capture, so they abandoned the attempt by mid-afternoon and turned to capturing and killing settlers and burning their homes. In addition to Alden's men, at least thirty civilians were killed during the day and about seventy women and children captured, although most of them were released the next day before Butler and Brant departed for their base at Niagara.

The raid and the depredations on settlers and their families were characterized by the Americans as a massacre and, along with the attack on the WYOMING VALLEY in Pennsylvania a few months before, served as the motivation for the devastating sweep through Iroquois country by an American army one year later.

Further Reading

William V. Campbell. *Annals of Tyron County, or the Border Warfare of New York, during the Revolution.* 4th ed. (New York: Dodd, Mead, 1924).

✍ U.S.S. *Chesapeake* v. H.M.S. *Shannon*

Off Boston, Massachusetts (June 1, 1813)
War of 1812

The U.S.S. *Chesapeake* became the first U.S. Navy frigate to be captured during the War of 1812 when in June 1813 she was taken by the H.M.S. *Shannon*, under the command of Capt. Philip Broke.

The *Chesapeake*'s fifty guns were a match for the *Shannon*'s fifty-two, but the crews of the two frigates were hardly equal. Capt. James Lawrence had been in command of the *Chesapeake* for less than a month and had been forced to man his ship with fresh recruits, after most of its seasoned crew left with the previous captain. Broke, who had commanded the *Shannon* since 1806, was one of Britain's most capable captains, and his crew was well trained in gunnery techniques, some of which their captain had invented.

On June 1, while the *Shannon* was patrolling the waters just eighteen miles from Boston harbor, Broke sent a letter of challenge to Lawrence, but by the time it arrived the Americans had already sailed, with the intent of finding and fighting the British frigate. The two ships met shortly before 6:00 P.M. and with little ado engaged at close quarters. During the initial exchange of broadsides, the *Chesapeake* inflicted heavy damage on the *Shannon*. Within ten minutes, the two ships maneuvered into parallel courses and began to deliver close range broadsides. When the *Shannon*'s anchor became entangled with the *Chesapeake*, Broke ordered the two ships lashed together as his gunners fired continuously at the American quarterdeck. Under these extreme conditions—the most violent and destructive kind of combat that warships of the period were likely ever to encounter—many of Lawrence's inexperienced crew lost their nerve and abandoned their guns. As the fire from the *Chesapeake* slackened, the veteran British seamen seized cutlasses and pikes and at Broke's command swarmed over the side and onto the American ship. Lawrence was mortally wounded in the melee as the British boarded, and the *Chesapeake* was surrendered less than fifteen minutes after the fight had begun. Lawrence subsequently became famous for uttering the phrase "Don't give up the ship!" as he died.

Sixty Americans were killed and eighty-five wounded. Broke was wounded, along with forty-nine of his countrymen. Thirty-three of his crew were killed.

Though the *Shannon* suffered heavy damage in the battle, the British victory showed the clear advantage of Broke's gunnery techniques and his rigorous training regime. Surviving his wounds, Broke was made a baronet and hailed as a national hero.

Further Reading

Charles Cross. *The Chesapeake: The Biography of a Ship* (Chesapeake, Va.: Norfolk Historical Society, 1968); Peter Padfield. *Broke and the Shannon* (London: Hodder & Stoughton, 1968); and H. F. Pullen. *The Shannon and the Chesapeake* (Toronto: McClelland and Stewart, 1970).

✍ Chesapeake Bay

Off the Maryland Coast (March 16, 1781)
American Revolution

The French navy continued to add to its dismal record during most of the American Revolution with this inconclusive engagement with a British flotilla.

French admiral Chevalier Charles Destouches, who had taken over command of the French squadron in Rhode Island after the death of Admiral Chevalier Charles de Ternay, left Newport on March 8 with eight ships, headed for the Chesapeake Bay. He planned to meet with the marquis de Lafayette, who was leading an American army in Virginia against the raids of turncoat Maj. Gen. Benedict Arnold. As soon as the British learned of Destouches's departure, Adm. Marriot Arbuthnot, usually a slow-moving officer, sailed from New York with eight ships of his own. The British flotilla, despite leaving port a day and a half later, arrived off the capes of the Chesapeake slightly ahead of the French.

The subsequent engagement began with the British holding a slight tactical advantage and having superior firepower, despite the equality in the number of men of war. Arbuthnot, however, scrupulously adhering to the Admiralty's overly rigid fighting instructions, failed to capitalize on his advantages. The hour-long battle ended in a draw, with considerable damage to the ships of both sides.

True to his reputation for timidity, however, Destouches turned away and sailed back to Newport, leaving Lafayette on his own. Arbuthnot, on the other hand, sailed into the bay and eventually made contact with Arnold.

Both admirals were replaced within a few months.

Further Reading

Mark M. Boatner. *Encyclopedia of the American Revolution* (New York: David McKay, 1966).

✒ Chesapeake Capes

Off the Virginia–North Carolina Coast
(September 5, 1781) *American Revolution*

Although the sea battle itself was indecisive, the engagement by the French fleet under Adm. Comte François de Grasse, of a British fleet commanded by Adm. Thomas Graves off the Chesapeake Capes prevented the relief of Lt. Gen. Lord Cornwallis's army at YORKTOWN and was a decisive factor in the ultimate defeat of the British and the triumph of the American Revolution.

The French had been an ally of the Americans since 1778, but little except disappointment had come from the alliance. French naval commanders had uniformly

proven timid, uncooperative, or both, and the hoped-for stifling of British sea power had never materialized. Despite these past disappointments, American commander in chief, Gen. George Washington, had high hopes for Admiral de Grasse, who had arrived in the West Indies with a powerful fleet of twenty-four ships of the line. On August 13, de Grasse left the West Indies for a rendezvous with Washington and Jean de Vimeur, Comte de Rochambeau, in Virginia, carrying three thousand troops to add to the allied investment of Cornwallis. He arrived two weeks later and began to disembark his soldiers on September 2.

British admiral Graves had sailed with a smaller fleet—nineteen ships—from New York hoping to catch de Grasse in open water or to intercept a second French fleet from Newport, but he was too late; de Grasse had already completed delivery of the French soldiers when Graves arrived off Chesapeake Bay on September 5. Surprisingly, de Grasse decided to give battle and immediately ordered his ships out to sea.

The British ships were upwind and could control the beginning of the battle, but Graves handled his fleet poorly. The two battle lines of ships never completely engaged, and only the leading ships from each side exchanged fire. Both sides took considerable punishment, however, during the two-and-one-half-hour battle, which was suspended when darkness came.

For the next two days, the fleets shadowed each other and attempted to maneuver into advantageous positions, but without success. The French finally turned back toward the mouth of Chesapeake Bay so as to maintain their protection of the Franco-American army. Graves loitered for several days off the coast, then set sail for New York on September 14.

The French had 220 seamen killed and wounded and several ships badly damaged. The British lost 90 killed and 246 wounded, and *Terrible*, a 64-gun British ship of the line, had to be destroyed. Two British frigates were so badly damaged that they were captured later. While it did not mark an overwhelming triumph for the French fleet, when the British turned and sailed away, Cornwallis was left to his fate.

Further Reading

Henry Lumpkin. "The Battle off the Capes." *Virginia Cavalcade* 31, no. 2 (1981): 68–77; and Joseph N. Valliant, Jr. *Revolution's Fate Sealed at Sea* (Herndon, Va.: Empire Press, 1995).

Chickamauga

Georgia (September 19–20, 1863)
American Civil War

When VICKSBURG fell to the Union during the summer of 1863, the strength of the Confederacy in the Mississippi River valley was virtually destroyed, but there were still powerful Southern forces in Tennessee and Georgia. The Federal command decided to send Maj. Gen. William S. Rosecrans to take CHATTANOOGA, a crucial rail center whose possession would open the way to ATLANTA.

Rosecrans had a huge force at his disposal, nearly eighty thousand men of the Army of the Cumberland, although nearly twenty thousand were needed to guard his long line of supply and were therefore unavailable for the campaign. Facing him was his old antagonist from the battle of STONE'S RIVER nine months earlier, Confederate general Braxton Bragg, commanding the Army of the Tennessee. Bragg was initially outnumbered by the large Federal force.

Rosecrans marched on Chattanooga, arriving in early September to find that Bragg had withdrawn from the city into the rugged Georgia countryside to the southeast. Rosecrans sent his corps commanders, Maj. Gen. Alexander McCook, Maj. Gen. George H. Thomas, and Maj. Gen. Thomas Crittenden, forging ahead, and for a few days the three parts of the Union army were dangerously separated. This state of affairs was especially hazardous to the Federal position since the Confederate high command had sent Lt. Gen. James Longstreet and fifteen thousand veterans of the Virginia fighting to reinforce Bragg (making a long movement by rail). When Longstreet and other reinforcements arrived, Bragg's forces were a numerical match for the Federals, and Bragg decided to launch an attack across Chickamauga Creek against the Union's left wing, hoping to cut off Rosecrans from Chattanooga.

The chosen battleground was terrible terrain for a fight, a densely overgrown and rugged area that made maneuver almost impossible and left soldiers on both sides fighting at close quarters against enemies who often could not be seen distinctly. Both commanders lost the ability to control their units almost as soon as the battle began, so much of the fighting took place in an isolated, haphazard fashion—success or failure depending on local initiative, courage, and luck rather than overall strategy or tactics. The Confederates pushed forward three major attacks during the day on September 19, successively against the Union left, center, and right. While damaging, none of the three managed to break the Federal defensive line.

On the morning of September 20, Bragg renewed the attacks, and for an hour and a half the Union soldiers held on, bolstered by the strength of fieldworks they had built during the night; however, at 11:00 A.M., Rosecrans made a huge mistake that handed Bragg the victory. Receiving an erroneous report that there was a gap in the Federal line, Rosecrans ordered Brig. Gen. Thomas Woods to move his division to cover the supposed weakness. Just as Woods abandoned his position, Longstreet pushed eight divisions directly at the spot Woods had left open: the Confederates poured through the self-inflicted gap in the Federal defenses, penetrating more than a mile before noon. The entire right wing of the Union army collapsed into a chaotic retreat. Since his headquarters lay squarely in the path of the Confederate advance, Rosecrans himself, along with Crittenden and McCook, was swept off the field and ceased to exercise command.

Maj. Gen. George H. Thomas, a slow-moving but imperturbably courageous fighter, was left in command of what had been the Federal left wing, pressed from front and flank by the surging Confederates. Thomas ordered his troops to fall back to a rise of land called Snodgrass Hill; there they formed a new, hook-shaped defensive position. The full weight of the Confederate force fell on Thomas and his men, but they managed to fight off assault after assault throughout the rest of the day. The Confederates came close to overrunning Thomas's men, but they were unable to collapse the desperate defense even by hand-to-hand assaults late in the afternoon.

As darkness came and the Confederate attacks petered out, Thomas withdrew his men up the road toward Chattanooga to catch up with the shattered, disorganized remains of the Union army. For his work that day, Thomas earned the nickname "Rock of Chickamauga." Bragg, despite the urgings of his subordinate commanders, refused to pursue the Federals and instead allowed them to retreat to the safety of the city.

The Army of the Cumberland lost 16,170 men during the two-day battle and was temporarily destroyed as a cohesive fighting force. Bragg suffered even more casualties—18,454—and was severely shaken by the losses.

The great battlefield victory was more or less frittered away by Bragg's inactivity immediately following the fighting at Chickamauga, and he allowed the Federals to re-form in Chattanooga, which he put under siege over the following weeks.

Further Reading

Richard Baumgartner and Larry M. Strayer, eds. *Echoes of Battle: The Struggle for Chattanooga* (Huntington, W.Va.: Blue Acorn Press, 1996); Glenn Tucker. *The Battle of Chickamauga* (New York: Eastern Acorn Press, 1969).

➢ Chickasaw Bayou

See CHICKASAW BLUFFS

➢ Chickasaw Bluffs

(Chickasaw Bayou)

Mississippi (December 27–29, 1862)
American Civil War

Maj. Gen. Ulysses S. Grant had the devil's own time getting any significant part of his huge army into position to attack the great Confederate stronghold city of VICKSBURG on the Mississippi River. He attempted several approaches by land and water during late 1862, including a massive but unsuccessful assault by Maj. Gen. William Sherman.

Sherman's force, designated a full army corps, numbered around thirty-two thousand, organized into four divisions. He was to attack Vicksburg's defenses on the Yazoo River side while Grant occupied the Confederates with demonstrations on the other side of the city. Sherman moved his men down the Mississippi and into the Yazoo on river transports, and by the day after Christmas he was in position to begin an advance across difficult, swampy terrain.

The rebel defenses were commanded by Maj. Gen. Martin Smith, a West Point–trained engineer who initially had only six thousand men to oppose a Federal force more than five times as large; however, by the time Sherman actually arrived before the Confederate fortifications, six thousand more troops had arrived, and reinforcements continued to trickle in throughout the following days. The Confederate victory at HOLLY SPRINGS had frustrated Grant's advance and freed troops to reinforce Smith, but Sherman was unaware of this development. Smith commanded almost twenty-five thousand well-fortified troops by the day of the battle.

The day after skirmishing on December 27, Sherman sent his assault force in four columns into the swamps. The slow advance came to a halt when the Federal troops ran into a bayou that was within reach of Confederate artillery. The Union field commanders discovered that the only way across the water was by two sand bars, but the Confederates had installed log barriers (abatis) and trained their artillery on the sand bars. On December 29, Sherman ordered an attack. His troops pushed across the sand bars to the bottom of the bluffs, but they could go no farther. Supporting attacks failed to cross the obstacles, and without reinforcements the Federals had to abandon the attempt by midafternoon.

Sherman had lost 208 killed, 1,005 wounded, and 563 missing. The Confederate losses were slight by comparison: 63 dead, 134 wounded, and 10 missing.

When the weather turned bad, Sherman decided to withdraw entirely. It was another six months before a Union army claimed Vicksburg by siege.

Further Reading

James M. McPherson. *Battle Cry of Freedom: The Civil War Era* (New York: Oxford University Press, 1988); and Mark M. Boatner. *The Civil War Dictionary* (New York: David McKay, 1966).

➢ Chippewa

Canada (July 5, 1814) *War of 1812*

Brig. Gen. Jacob Brown invaded Canada on July 3, 1814, in a bid to reestablish American control of the Niagara frontier. On the second day of his forward push, Brown encountered a large army under British major general Phineas Riall at the Chippewa River, and the two sides engaged in one of the most important battles of the entire War of 1812.

Hearing that Brown had taken Fort Erie on July 3, Major General Riall had amassed two thousand troops to defend British positions. Brown's force was pushing steadily northward into Canada, led by an advance party headed by Brig. Gen. Winfield Scott's First Brigade. Riall dispatched Lt. Col. Thomas Pearson to halt Scott's progress and to destroy a major bridge. Scott and Pearson engaged in a series of skirmishes on July 4, but the British were unable to stop the Americans' forward movement (in large part due to Scott's good use of field artillery).

Finally, the Chippewa River stopped the American advance, and Riall fortified its northern bank with regulars, militia forces, and Mohawk Indian allies. Scott encamped one mile to the south at Street's Creek, and Brigadier General Brown decided to send troops to cross the river west of Riall's fortification, where the militia and Indian troops were concentrated.

On the morning of July 5, Brown sent the Third Brigade to attempt the river crossing. The attempt did not last long once the brigade encountered the Indians and militiamen in a patch of forest to the west of their camp. The officer in charge of the advance, Col. Peter B. Porter, who commanded his own group of volunteers and allied Indians from New York and was jealous of the recently promoted Winfield Scott, showed no leadership or military prowess on the field. His men turned and fled back toward the creek.

The attack on the Third Brigade in the forest signaled the beginning of a general British attack across the river. As

British regulars crossed the river with bayonets fixed, Brown urged Scott to re-form his men, who had been preparing for drill after a belated Independence Day celebration.

By the time Scott sent his artillery forward, Riall's troops had advanced into open ground near the American position at the Street's Creek bridge. The two sides traded heavy fire as Riall watched Scott hurry his infantry into order. At first judging the disorganized troops to be militia, in part because they wore gray coats instead of the usual American blue, Riall soon realized the Americans were

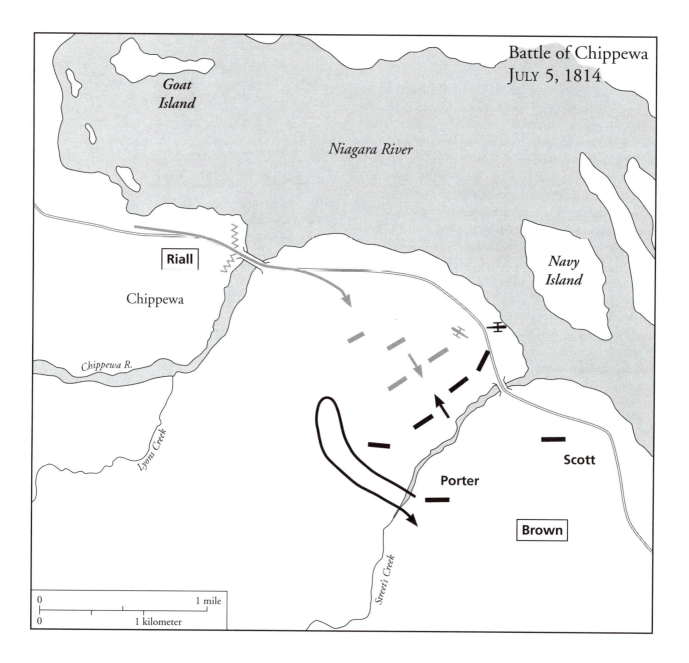

calmly advancing in lines through the artillery fire. He exclaimed, "Those are Regulars, by God!" (a remark that would immortalize him in American military memory).

While the artillery battle raged on, Scott enveloped the British line in a U-shaped formation. The British initially ignored Scott's tactic, but when the two forces came close enough to exchange musketry, the British line was caught in a destructive cross fire.

As the cross fire took its toll, the American artillery regiment exploded a British caisson, in effect ending British ability to return the fire of the American twelve-pounders. Scott ordered an American charge, and, in a reversal of the usual course of events, Riall's British regulars retreated at the sight of advancing American bayonets. Riall surrendered. Scott halted the attack, though some of the Indians allied with the Americans continued across the river to capture prisoners.

The British lost 148 regulars killed, around 100 militia and Indians killed, 221 wounded, and 46 missing or captured. American casualties totaled approximately forty-four killed and another ninety-eight wounded.

The victory for Brown and Scott was significant, because it was the first time during the War of 1812 that a group of American regulars had faced British regulars in open battle and won. For years to come, public praise for the military prowess of the U.S. Army was based on the victory at Chippewa. Unfortunately for Brown, the immediate effect was short-lived. He soon met defeat at the hands of the British at LUNDY'S LANE.

Further Reading

Donald E. Graves. *Red Coats and Grey Jackets: The Battle of Chippewa, 5 July, 1814* (Niagara Falls, N.Y.: Dundurn Press, 1994).

⤜ Chrysler's Farm

Canada (November 11, 1813) *War of 1812*

After Maj. Gen. Wade Hampton's defeat at CHATEAUGAY in late October 1813, Maj. Gen. James Wilkinson was left to carry on by himself the American attack against Montreal ordered by Sec. of War John Armstrong. Wilkinson's march up the St. Lawrence River went badly, and the major general's sickness and incompetence contributed in no small part to his defeat at John Chrysler's farm in November.

Seeking to cut off British supply lines at Kingston in upper Canada, Wilkinson moved up the St. Lawrence

with eight thousand regular soldiers. The journey was difficult, and many men and boats were lost in the broad waters of the river. Wilkinson almost called off the attack, and many sources report that he appeared gradually to lose his mind as his force advanced.

British detachments followed Wilkinson, both behind on the river and alongside on its banks. Lt. Col. Joseph Morrison, commanding the regulars along the north bank, prepared to attack Wilkinson's men as they approached eight miles of rough rapids at Long Sault. Wilkinson sent a party under Brig. Gen. Jacob Brown to clear opposition forces from around the rapids, and it was successful both at keeping the British at bay and at plundering local farms.

By the time Wilkinson encamped at Chrysler's farm on November 11, he was incapacitated, and he placed Brig. Gen. John P. Boyd in command of an operation to defeat Morrison's forces, which continued to harass the Americans. Boyd gathered twenty-five hundred men and approached Lieutenant Colonel Morrison's forces, who had established a defensive line across one end of the farm, with their right flank protected by gunboats on the river. The British line of regulars was further strengthened by detachments of French-Canadian volunteers and Indians, who took positions in front.

Boyd neglected to provide artillery support or to resupply ammunition before he repeatedly ordered his loosely formed men forward. In the confusion, Morrison's troops counterattacked, and only charges against the British right by Wilkinson's adjutant general, Col. John de Barth Walback, prevented Morrison from totally overwhelming the American defenses. Superior British firepower and maneuvering kept the American forces at bay and prevented a mounted charge. Eventually, the Americans fell back across the river, and the battle ended, though no officer would later admit to calling for retreat.

Casualties in the battle were heavy, considering the number of troops engaged. The Americans suffered 102 killed, 237 wounded, and around 100 taken prisoner. The British lost far fewer: 23 killed, 148 wounded, and 9 missing.

Immediately following the battle, Wilkinson received word of the defeat of his hated fellow commander, Wade Hampton, at Chateaugay. He decided to halt the advance toward Montreal and go into winter quarters. Though Wilkinson always blamed Hampton for the failed campaign, he was relieved of command and court-martialed in early 1814. Wilkinson was acquitted, but he added to his reputation for incompetence.

Further Reading

Robert Sellar. *The U.S. Campaign of 1813 to Capture Montreal.* 2d ed. (Huntingdon, Que.: Gleaner Office, 1914); and Morris Zaslow, ed. *The Defended Border: Upper Canada and the War of 1812* (Toronto: Macmillan, 1964).

☙ Churubusco

Mexico (August 20, 1847) *Mexican-American War*

In August 1847, Maj. Gen. Winfield Scott was pursuing Gen. Antonio López de Santa Anna across the valley of Mexico in a bid to capture the capital city and finish the war. To begin their final push, American troops under the direct command of Brig. Gen. Persifor Smith had won a decisive victory in the early hours of August 20 at CONTRERAS. Scott, seeking to capitalize on the victory, directed a bloody attack against Santa Anna's main force at Churubusco later that same day.

After the battle near Contreras, Persifor Smith organized the pursuit of the fleeing remnants of Maj. Gen. Gabriel Valencia's Army of the North. At the village of San Angel, Maj. Gen. Gideon J. Pillow took over command of Smith's force, by then also augmented by Brig. Gen. David E. Twiggs's men, and the combined force pushed on to Coyoacán, where Scott regrouped his army at around 9:00 A.M.

Scott sent Brig. Gen. William J. Worth's men to attack Santa Anna's main headquarters at San Antonio, and he ordered Pillow, now in charge of Brig. Gen. George Cadwalader's brigade, to march around and hit San Antonio from behind. Brigadier General Smith was sent to attack the Franciscan convent church of San Mateo, held by Maj. Gen. Manuel Rincón's fifteen hundred Mexico City National Guard troops, near the fortified bridge over the Churubusco River, while Brig. Gen. Franklin Pierce and Capt. Robert E. Lee would establish a strong position upriver. Meanwhile, Capt. James Mason led Col. N. S. Clarke's brigade in an arc through the eastern edge of a large *pedregal*, or lava field, which had slowed American progress the day before. Col. John Garland's men marched along the road toward San Antonio to cut off any Mexican forces who tried to retreat south from Worth's attack.

To avoid the American attacks, Santa Anna was already leading his main force away from San Antonio and back toward the town of Churubusco, where he hoped to rendezvous with Maj. Gen. Nicolás Bravo, who led another body of troops retreating from San Antonio. American engineers observed the chaotic Mexican movement toward Churubusco from atop a church steeple in Coyoacán, and

Scott signaled Twiggs to take the convent so that further retreat from the San Antonio Road and across the bridgehead at Churubusco could be stopped.

Twiggs's men failed in their first assault, and their second push also failed, when reinforcements got lost in the surrounding cornfields. Inside the convent Rincón's men and the San Patricio Brigade, a unit made up of deserters from the American army and commanded by Lt. Col. Francisco Rosenda Moreno, provided some of the most daring and well-coordinated resistance met by any American troops during the war. They held off the repeated infantry attacks and blasted Taylor's main artillery battery, which had been called up as reinforcement, until it had to be removed.

Pillow and Worth closed in on Mexican troops forming at the bridgehead as Garland and Smith attacked the Mexican left. Meanwhile, Pierce and Lee were engaged in a hot battle at the Portales ranch just north of the bridge, and though Lt. Jesse L. Reno's howitzer fire provided good cover, they were badly outnumbered by the twenty-two hundred highly effective troops Santa Anna sent against them. They barely held on for reinforcements from Scott's main force.

For three hours fighting raged at all three points of attack near Churubusco—the Portales ranch, the convent, and the bridgehead—before the American troops took the upper hand. Brig. Gen. James Shields enveloped the Mexicans at the bridge, as the Fifth Infantry finally charged with bayonets and took the Mexican position after a strenuous hand-to-hand fight.

Once the bridge was taken, Capt. James Duncan aimed toward the convent two guns from the highway and a four-pounder on the bridge. A fifteen-minute exchange with Mexican cannon weakened the convent's outer walls, and the American Third Infantry scaled them. The Mexican troops holed up inside the convent building and refused to raise a white flag. Finally, Capt. James M. Smith of the Third Infantry called a halt to the slaughter inside the convent and gained control of the complex. Over twelve hundred prisoners were taken inside the convent, including Gen. Pedro María Anaya, who had served as interim president of Mexico for several months when Santa Anna was out of favor.

Brigadier General Shields reinforced Pierce's men at the road by the Portales ranch and helped achieve victory there as well. Shields, Worth, Pierce, and Capt. Philip Kearny's dragoons chased the retreating Mexicans along the highway toward San Antonio. Kearny ended the battle with one last push toward a battery at San Antonio Garita, a risky move that cost him an arm.

Overall, the Battle of Churubusco was a disorganized and costly American victory. Out of 8,497 Americans engaged, 133 were killed, 865 were wounded, and 40 went missing. Santa Anna's losses were even heavier. Winfield Scott estimated that over four thousand Mexican troops were killed or wounded.

Immediately following the battle, Santa Anna sent representatives to open truce negotiations with Scott. A military armistice was concluded on August 24, but the war would not end until Scott marched on Mexico City.

Further Reading

Charles L. Dufour. *The Mexican War: A Compact History, 1846–1848* (New York: Hawthorn Books, 1968); John D. Eisenhower. *Agent of Destiny: The Life and Times of General Winfield Scott* (New York: Free Press, 1997); Robert Selph Henry. *The Story of the Mexican War.* Reprint ed. (New York: Frederick Ungar, 1961); and Dennis Wynn. *The San Patricio Soldiers: Mexico's Foreign Legion* (El Paso: Texas Western Press, University of Texas at El Paso, 1984).

➳ Cinco de Mayo

See PUEBLA

➳ Cloyd's Mountain

Virginia (May 9, 1864) *American Civil War*

At the end of April and beginning of May 1864, Lt. Gen. Ulysses S. Grant launched a three-part offensive into Virginia designed to destroy Gen. Robert E. Lee's Confederate Army of Northern Virginia. One part of Grant's plan sent sixty-five hundred troops under Brig. Gen. George R. Crook into the Appalachian Mountains to destroy the Virginia and Tennessee Railroad. On May 9, Crook's three brigades emerged into a clearing after crossing Cloyd's Mountain and ran up against Brig. Gen. Albert G. Jenkins, who had positioned twenty-four hundred Confederate troops and ten heavy guns on the banks of Back Creek. The resulting battle, though it lasted only a short time, saw some of the fiercest hand-to-hand fighting of the entire war.

The morning of May 9 began with an artillery duel. Around noon the Federal West Virginia Brigade assaulted the center of the Confederate line but was only partially successful.

Cook's Ohio division was pinned down on the left, and many men perished when a thick layer of dead leaves caught fire. When Col. Rutherford B. Hayes, who would become one of America's postwar presidents, threw his Ohio brigade against the Confederate right, Jenkins's men fought bitterly hand to hand, though they were vastly outnumbered.

Finally, the Federals' superior numbers won the day, as fresh reinforcements joined the fight, overran the Confederate cannon, and wounded the Confederate commander.

Casualty totals reflect the ferocity of the short battle at Cloyd's Mountain. The Confederates lost 538 men, Federal forces 688. Jenkins was taken prisoner when his arm was shattered near the end of the action. He died from complications after the arm was amputated.

The victorious Union troops marched on to destroy the Virginia and Tennessee Railroad, cutting off one of the Confederacy's last remaining supply lines.

Further Reading

Jay Wertz and Edwin C. Bearss. *Smithsonian's Great Battles and Battlefields of the Civil War* (New York: William Morrow, 1997); and Frances H. Kennedy, ed. *The Civil War Battlefield Guide* (Boston: Houghton Mifflin, 1990).

➳ Cold Harbor

Virginia (June 3, 1864) *American Civil War*

Union commander in chief Ulysses S. Grant's campaign against Confederate general Robert E. Lee in the spring and summer of 1864 was a terrible series of engagements that chewed up men like a meat grinder. The worst single day was June 3, when Grant ordered a frontal assault on Confederate defenses at Cold Harbor. The attackers lost thousands in the space of half an hour.

Grant had tried to corner and destroy Lee's Army of Northern Virginia in battles at the WILDERNESS, SPOTSYLVANIA, and the NORTH ANNA RIVER, after each engagement working his army south toward a position east of Richmond. As the Union Army of the Potomac, commanded by Maj. Gen. George G. Meade but under Grant's direct supervision, moved closer to the Confederate capital, Lee kept maneuvering his forces—only about half the size of Grant's—to protect Richmond's lines of rail and road supply.

During the last days of May, Lee took up strongly fortified positions behind Totopotomy Creek and began to

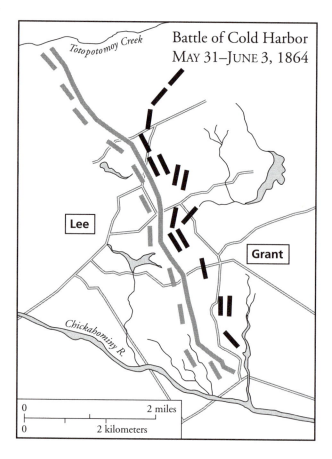

Battle of Cold Harbor
MAY 31–JUNE 3, 1864

Totopotomoy Creek

Lee

Grant

Chickahominy R.

0   2 miles

0   2 kilometers

probe toward a key crossroads at Cold Harbor. Grant, who was getting reinforcements daily, likewise wanted to control Cold Harbor. Grant's new cavalry commander, Maj. Gen. Philip Sheridan, sent in his troopers (many of them armed with new Spencer repeating rifles) and gained hold of the crossroads. In response, Lee shored up his strongly entrenched lines and waited.

On June 3, Grant ordered an all-out attack on the Confederate lines, hoping the weight of his superior numbers could crush the Southern army and bring an end to the conflict. He was hopelessly wrong. More than forty thousand Federal soldiers made the assault, but they were stopped before reaching the Confederate positions. More than seven thousand fell in the space of thirty minutes, about half of them dead. Lee lost only about fifteen hundred men.

The slaughter had been phenomenal, but Grant refused to acknowledge his mistake for several days. Both sides refused a truce to collect the wounded, who were left to die on the battlefield.

Lee had pulled off yet another spectacular victory, but the human mathematics of the campaign were against

him: he had no means to replace the hundreds lost; Grant could call on thousands more from his reserves.

Further Reading

Louis J. Baltz. *The Battle of Cold Harbor, May 27–June 13, 1864* (Lynchburg, Va.: H. E. Howard, 1994); Gregory Jaynes. *The Killing Ground: Wilderness to Cold Harbor* (Alexandria, Va.: Time-Life Books, 1986); R. Wayne Maney. *Marching to Cold Harbor: Victory and Failure, 1864* (Shippensburg, Va.: White Mane, 1995); Noah A. Trudeau. *Bloody Roads South: The Wilderness to Cold Harbor, May–June 1864* (Boston: Little, Brown, 1989).

Columbus

New Mexico (March 9, 1916) *Border Raid*

After Gen. Francisco "Pancho" Villa, leader of northern Mexican revolutionary forces, was defeated by Venustiano Carranza's army under Gen. Alvaro Obregón at CELAYA in April 1915, the U.S. government recognized Carranza as Mexico's legitimate ruler. Villa, who had enjoyed American support in the past, bitterly resented the recognition of his rival, and within a year he began to take revenge on Americans, probably hoping to provoke an all-out war between the two countries. Villa suffered defeat at AGUA PRIETA in November 1915, but after the new year he resumed his anti-American campaign. Fifteen American mining engineers who had been promised Mexican protection were murdered in Santa Isabel, Mexico, by a band of Villistas in January 1916. Villa did not restrict his military action to within Mexico, however. His forces frequently harassed Americans across the border, and in March he raided Columbus, New Mexico, where he encountered the U.S. Thirteenth Cavalry.

Villa's force of 485 men simultaneously attacked the adobe town of Columbus and the nearby cavalry camp in the early hours of March 9, shouting "Viva Villa!" as they rode in. For over an hour, Villa's Mexican troops terrorized, looted, and burned the town. The sleeping American cavalry troopers were slow to respond, and they put up scarcely any resistance during the initial stages of the attack.

Just before daybreak, however, Col. Herbert J. Slocum, the cavalry commander, organized a counterattack and drove the Villistas from the camp and the town. As the Villistas rode south back into Mexico, Maj. Frank Tompkins organized a small detachment to pursue them. At a hill three hundred yards south of the border, Tompkins's thirty-two men attacked a covering detachment of Villistas and captured the summit. Though Tompkins realized he had unwittingly invaded Mexico, Slocum provided reinforcements and encouraged him to continue his pursuit. Over the next three hours, Tompkins engaged the rear guard of the Villistas three times before running out of ammunition and returning to Columbus.

During the raid on Columbus, eighteen Americans were killed and more wounded. Over thirty Villistas died during Tompkins's pursuit.

The Columbus raid immediately raised calls in the United States for an American invasion of Mexico. Pres. Woodrow Wilson commanded Gen. John J. Pershing to march into Mexico, initially with Carranza's approval, to find and bring back Pancho Villa (*see also* PARRAL). Villa's daring raid into the United States made him a national hero to many Mexicans, especially after he continued to elude capture.

Further Reading

William Clark. "The Search for Pancho Villa." *Palacio* 97, no. 3 (1992): 20–23, 47–54; and Craig Smyser. "The Columbus Raid." *Southwest Review* 68, no. 1 (1983): 78–84.

Combahee Ferry

South Carolina (August 27, 1782)
American Revolution

In what was the final engagement of the American Revolution between regular troops, British foragers surprised and defeated a force of American light infantry near Charleston, South Carolina.

Even though the war was essentially over after Lt. Gen. Lord Cornwallis's surrender at YORKTOWN in October 1781, the negotiation of a final treaty and the withdrawal of all British armies took two more years. The British still held New York City in the North and Charleston in the South. Charleston was commanded by Maj. Gen. Alexander Leslie, who had a hard time feeding his troops. He proposed a cessation of hostilities to allow his men to forage, but Maj. Gen. Nathanael Greene refused.

Leslie sent out a foraging party in force—about five hundred regulars and Loyalists—which was opposed by a light brigade under Brig. Gen. Mordecai Gist. Gist tried to block the British movements at Combahee Ferry, and he then ordered Col. John Laurens to march to Cheraw Point with several hundred light infantry to prevent British movement.

The British, however, beat Laurens into position and set up an ambush in tall grass that Laurens and his men walked into. In the subsequent fight, two Americans— Laurens and one other—were killed, and nineteen were wounded.

Gist was unable to dislodge the foragers, who eventually retreated back to Charleston.

Further Reading

Christopher Ward. *The War of the Revolution.* Vol. 2 (New York: Macmillan, 1952).

Concord

See LEXINGTON AND CONCORD

U.S.S. *Congress* v. H.M.S. *Savage*

Off the South Carolina Coast (September 6, 1781)
American Revolution

American privateers (armed private ships sailing under government sanction) were usually too small and weak to engage British men-of-war on the open sea, but the *Congress*, sailing out of Philadelphia under Capt. George Geddes, was well armed, with twenty main-deck twelve-pounders as well as four six-pounders on the upper deck. It also had a contingent of marines commanded by the redoubtable Capt. Allan McLane, who had won fame as a cavalry leader and scout for Gen. George Washington.

Off Charleston, South Carolina, *Congress* encountered H.M.S. *Savage*, a British sloop of only sixteen guns, commanded by Capt. Charles Stirling. Stirling mistook *Congress* for one of her weaker brethren and closed to batter and board her.

The subsequent running battle lasted four hours, and eventually *Congress*'s superior firepower triumphed. She shot away the British ship's mizzenmast, set the ship on fire, and killed or wounded many of her crew. When the Americans began to board *Savage*, Capt. Stirling surrendered.

Further Reading

Mark M. Boatner. *The Encyclopedia of the American Revolution* (New York: David McKay, 1966).

U.S.S. *Constitution* v. H.M.S. *Guerrière*

Off Nova Scotia, Canada (August 19, 1812)
War of 1812

After years of harassment by the French and British navies, the U.S. Navy (despite some resistance from James Madison's administration) was anxious to put to sea once war was declared against Great Britain in June 1812. The first full-scale naval battle of the war occurred 600 miles east of Boston and 250 miles south of Nova Scotia when the U.S.S. *Constitution*, commanded by Capt. Isaac Hull and recently escaped from a British squadron at Annapolis, encountered the H.M.S. *Guerrière*, just returning from a Jamaican raid under the command of Capt. James Dacres.

The *Constitution*, America's most impressive ship, was armed with fifty-four guns and designed expressly to outgun ships like the similarly sized *Guerrière*, which carried forty-nine guns. This superior firepower, and a measure of good luck, helped Captain Hull's ship to win the day.

Captain Dacres opened fire from long range at 4:00 P.M. An hour later, the fight began in earnest as Hull maneuvered to fire his double-shotted guns at close range. The heavy fire destroyed one of *Guerrière*'s masts, causing the ships to collide. Hull extricated the *Constitution*, delivered two broadsides and then raked *Guerrière* with fire. The *Constitution* took fewer hits from the British ship, and after another collision, the *Guerrière* was totally crippled by the loss of two more masts.

Just as Hull was set to resume fire, Dacres surrendered. The battle had lasted less than half an hour, and the Americans had won a surprising victory over the world-dominant British navy. Hull's crew suffered only fourteen casualties, while the British counted seventy-nine officers and sailors dead or wounded. Too badly damaged to make much of a prize, the *Guerrière* was set afire and sunk.

The victory cemented Isaac Hull's reputation as one of America's first naval heroes. The *Constitution*, which gained its nickname "Old Ironsides" by withstanding *Guerrière*'s fire, became an icon of American sea power and continued as one of the mainstays of the navy for the rest of the war and beyond.

Further Reading

Ira N. Hollis. *The Frigate Constitution: The Central Figure of the Navy under Sail* (Boston: Houghton Mifflin, 1931); Thomas P. Horgan. *Old Ironsides: An Illustrated History of the U.S.S. Constitution* (Dublin, N.H.: Yankee Press, 1980); and Tyrone G. Martin, *A Most Fortunate Ship: A Narrative History of Old Ironsides*. Rev. ed. (Annapolis, Md.: Naval Institute Press, 1997).

Contreras

(Padierna)

Mexico (August 19–20, 1847)
Mexican-American War

In August 1847, Gen. Antonio López de Santa Anna, determined to stop Maj. Gen. Winfield Scott from capturing Mexico City, gathered twenty thousand Mexican troops to resist Scott's final push across the valley of Mexico. Establishing his headquarters at CHURUBUSCO, Santa Anna positioned his force across several small valley towns to await Scott's arrival from the west.

Maj. Gen. Gabriel Valencia, a longtime political nemesis of Santa Anna, arrived with his troops from the north in late July, but he expressly disobeyed Santa Anna's orders to hold a position at the town of San Angel. Instead, he advanced on August 17 along the Contreras Road to the village of Padierna to prepare for an American attack.

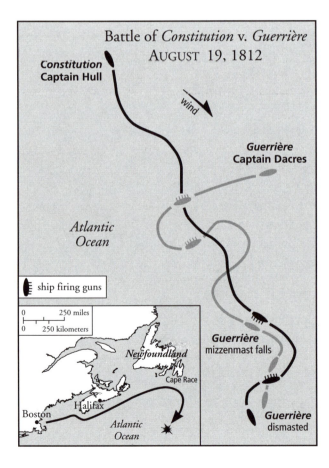

Battle of *Constitution* v. *Guerrière*
AUGUST 19, 1812

Constitution
Captain Hull

wind

Guerrière
Captain Dacres

Atlantic
Ocean

ship firing guns

0   250 miles
0   250 kilometers

Newfoundland

Cape Race

Guerrière
mizzenmast falls

Halifax

Boston

Atlantic
Ocean

Guerrière
dismasted

Not having attacked directly from the south, as Santa Anna had expected, Major General Scott ordered Capt. Robert E. Lee, who had provided essential reconnaissance at CERRO GORDO, to find another approach toward Valencia's position. Lee set out with Lt. P. G. T. Beauregard, elements of the Eleventh Infantry, and two companies of Capt. Philip Kearny's dragoons to explore a large *pedregal*, or lava field, that led east toward the villages of Padierna and Contreras beyond. After a small skirmish with a Mexican advance party, Lee climbed to the top of a tall hill called Zacatepec and located the Mexicans' fortified position on a hill outside Padierna. (Lee wrongly identified the town as Contreras, thereby misnaming the subsequent battle.) With an eye toward eventually reaching more of Santa Anna's men at San Angel, Scott assigned Captain Lee to cut a road through the craggy lava field on August 19.

Between 9:00 A.M. and 1:00 P.M. five hundred troops from Maj. Gen. Gideon J. Pillow's division, under the command of Lee, dug their way almost up to the Mexican fortified position. Since they were protected by more of Pillow's men and by Brig. Gen. David E. Twiggs's division, the diggers made quick progress, even in the face of harassment by Mexican pickets, but when the Mexican batteries opened fire, it became clear Lee would have to withdraw until the gunners could be cleared away. Between 2:00 P.M. and 10:00 P.M., light batteries and rockets, commanded by Capt. John B. Magruder, Lt. Franklin D. Callender, and Lt. Jesse L. Reno, tried to blast away the Mexican resistance, but the Americans were not close enough to their targets to make much progress.

Valencia assumed at this point that he had won the day, but the American forces were actually just regrouping for a predawn attack on August 20. During the fire fight on the nineteenth, Brig. Gen. Persifor Smith had pushed his brigade around the American batteries up to a long ravine near the Mexican position. Col. Bennet Riley had marched around the entire action to the right, across the ravine, and occupied the village of San Gerónimo. Two thousand of Valencia's troops blocked any return for Riley's men, and soon Riley realized he was pinned between Valencia and Santa Anna's main force of five thousand troops, which seemed to be slowly advancing. Captain Lee, who had joined Smith's troops, crossed back to Brigadier General Taylor's camp to report Smith's plan of attack. At 3:00 A.M., Smith and Riley would attack Valencia's troops from behind by marching directly up the ravine, Brig. Gen. Franklin Pierce and Col. Trueman B. Ransom would provide a diversion, and Smith suggested

Scott could charge head-on toward the Mexican position. Smith's plan proved to be brilliant.

Riley led the attack up the ravine to a height above the Mexican position. When the Mexicans began to fire, Riley's men charged down the ravine under cover of fire from an American rifle company. Brig. Gen. George Cadwalader's men followed Riley's attack, while Maj. Justin Dimick's brigade wheeled around to attack Valencia's troops from the left. The three-pronged attack brought the Mexicans under hot fire from Ransom's men across the ravine.

As the artillery fire continued and the Americans charged with bayonets, the Mexican troops began to flee. General Valencia was among the first to abandon the field, which grew chaotic as retreating cavalry rode over Mexican infantrymen. Hundreds of men who tried to escape to San Gerónimo were taken prisoner.

After only seventeen minutes of fighting, and before Winfield Scott even had a chance to attack, the battle ended in a total American victory. Valencia's Army of the North was completely destroyed, with 700 dead and 813 taken prisoner. Twenty-two guns (including two American pieces taken by the Mexicans at BUENA VISTA), and thousands of smaller weapons, as well as ammunition and other supplies, were captured. The Americans lost only sixty men killed or wounded.

The predawn victory at Padierna (still wrongly referred to as Contreras) did not end the fighting on August 20. Before nightfall, the Americans would be almost upon Mexico City, but not before losing many more men at Churubusco.

Further Reading

K. Jack Bauer. *The Mexican War: 1846–1848* (New York: Macmillan, 1974); John D. Eisenhower. *Agent of Destiny: The Life and Times of General Winfield Scott* (New York: Free Press, 1997); and John Edward Weems. *To Conquer a Peace: The War between the United States and Mexico* (Garden City, N.Y.: Doubleday, 1974).

Cooch's Bridge

(Iron Hill)

Delaware (September 3, 1777) *American Revolution*

The British commander in chief, Gen. Sir William Howe, opened his campaign to take Philadelphia, the American seat of government, in 1777 by sailing with a powerful expedition from New York to Head of Elk, Maryland. The American commander in chief, Gen. George Washington, hoped to stall and eventually stop Howe's march toward Philadelphia, beginning this delaying action only a few miles from Howe's landing point.

Washington alerted a newly formed unit of about one thousand light infantry under Brig. Gen. William Maxwell to contest the movement of Howe's army, which was around 15,000 strong. As the advance British units under Maj. Gen. Lord Cornwallis marched forward on the morning of September 3, they encountered Maxwell's men and exchanged fire. Mercenary German troops pushed forward in a bayonet attack and drove Maxwell into retreat.

The Americans fell back to a second delaying position and renewed the fight but only briefly. Once the weight of British and mercenary German numbers were brought to bear, Maxwell had no choice but to withdraw. He eventually left the British advance undisturbed and joined the main American army several miles away.

The action had accomplished little except the deaths of between thirty and forty Americans and thirty or so killed and wounded on the British side.

Further Reading

Edward W. Cooch. *The Battle of Cooch's Bridge, Delaware, September 3, 1777* (Wilmington, Del.: W. N. Cann, 1940).

❧ Corinth

Mississippi (October 3–4, 1862)
American Civil War

Corinth was a crucial rail crossing of lines that could move troops rapidly between theaters in the West. Both sides wanted to control the vital spot, and both made strong efforts to occupy the town. The Confederates had been forced to give it up in May 1862 when threatened by a huge Union army. The occupying Federal forces then strengthened the already formidable defenses of the place, a series of exceptionally strong batteries connected by breastworks and protected by log abatis and successive lines of rifle pits. By October 1862, Maj. Gen. William Rosecrans was in command of twenty-three thousand troops at Corinth.

Confederate major general Earl Van Dorn, who had general orders to support Gen. Braxton Bragg's campaign into Kentucky, had decided to try to take Corinth and had combined his troops with those of Maj. Gen. Sterling Price, whom he outranked. Van Dorn had a total of twenty-two thousand men at his disposal for the assault.

On October 2, Van Dorn's army approached Corinth and took positions around the northwestern side of the defenses. The main field commanders were Price, on the left, and Maj. Gen. Mansfield Lovell, on the right.

Rosecrans planned a series of defensive lines, hoping to fight but ready to fall back strategically if the Confederates attacked the fortifications. Van Dorn followed the script precisely, launching an all-out assault with nearly his entire force on the morning of October 3. Throughout the day, the Confederates pressed the fighting along the defensive perimeter, and the Union troops fought hard and then fell back to ever-tighter positions, finally ending the day in a semicircle around the strongest batteries. The Confederates had been successful, but they had blunted their strength and not achieved a decisive breakthrough.

On the following morning, the Confederates sent a mass attack against Battery Powell and Battery Robinette, the two strongest Union positions. The savage fighting degenerated into a hand-to-hand struggle in front of the batteries, but by noon the Confederates were spent and began to withdraw, eventually leaving the Union in control of the city.

Losses were high from the two-day battle: the attacking Confederates lost 2,470 killed and wounded and had another 1,763 missing. The Federal forces lost 2,520.

Further Reading

Peter Cozzens. *The Darkest Days of the War: The Battles of Iuka and Corinth* (Chapel Hill: University of North Carolina Press, 1997); G. W. Dudley. *The Lost Account of the Battle of Corinth, and Court-Martial of General Van Dorn* (Wilmington, N.C.: Broadfoot, 1991).

❧ Cowan's Ford

North Carolina (February 1, 1787)
American Revolution

Following Daniel Morgan's great victory at the COWPENS, American commander Maj. Gen. Nathanael Greene began a game of pursuit and maneuver with the British commander, Lt. Gen. Lord Cornwallis. The British were trying to catch Greene's army in a vulnerable position and attempted to snap up the American militia rear guard, commanded by Brig. Gen. William Davidson, at Cowan's Ford on the Catawba River.

Cornwallis himself led his troops across the tricky ford, which forked in the middle of the river, with a deep wagon route going one way and a shallower horse ford leading downstream. Second in command on the spot was Brig. Gen. Charles O'Hara, with a contingent of his Coldstream Guards, backed by a German unit, two hundred cavalry, and a detachment of the Royal Welch Fusiliers.

The Guards, led by O'Hara, had waded nearly halfway across the deep river before American sentries spotted them and opened a heavy fire. The Guards struggled on, but they took the wrong fork and encountered deep, rough water in addition to the galling fire of the American militia. O'Hara rallied his men, however, and they finally reached the river bank, even though O'Hara's horse was swept under and Cornwallis's mount was wounded.

Once out of the water, the Guards loaded their muskets, formed up, and advanced against the militia. Davidson was struck down and killed as he tried to rally his men, who thereupon dispersed. The British had gained a river crossing, but the delay caused by the militia allowed the main American force to slip away safely. No casualty figures were reported.

Further Reading

Robert Henry. *Narrative of the Battle of Cowan's Ford, February 1st, 1781* (Greensboro, N.C.: Reece & Elam, 1891).

✎ Cowpens

South Carolina (January 17, 1781)
American Revolution

Daniel Morgan's great victory over Lt. Col. Banastre Tarleton at the Cowpens was—save for YORKTOWN—the high point of American arms during the southern campaigns of the American Revolution. Morgan's brilliant use of militia and his masterful preparation for battle produced one of the few unalloyed victories against the British and allowed Maj. Gen. Nathanael Greene to begin the long series of maneuvers and battles that eventually drove Lt. Gen. Lord Cornwallis north to his fate in Virginia.

Greene had split his small army in two, giving command of the smaller portion to Morgan, who had been called out of a pouting retirement and promoted to brigadier general. Greene's daring plan was to threaten and outmaneuver Cornwallis without falling prey to an attack by the full weight of the British. Morgan's mere presence irritated Cornwallis and made it hard for him to concentrate on Greene. The British commander therefore ordered his most successful subordinate, Lieutenant Colonel

Tarleton, who had administered a string of defeats to the American patriots, to find and defeat Morgan or drive him into Cornwallis's waiting arms.

Morgan ran before Tarleton's pursuit until coming to a place known as the Cowpens, where local farmers herded cows during the winter. It was a large open meadow, with a gradual slope toward two successive high points. There were no natural features on which to anchor his army's flanks, and several of his officers criticized Morgan's choice of battlefields, but he turned out to know what he was about when he ordered a halt on the spot and a restful night of food and sleep by the campfires.

Morgan commanded an unusually high number of veterans: three hundred Maryland and Delaware Continentals (survivors of CAMDEN and the best American troops in the war) under Lt. Col. John Howard; one hundred or so light infantry and dragoons under Lt. Col. William Washington; and two hundred Virginia Continental veterans who had reenlisted as riflemen. Several hundred militia from the Carolinas and Georgia, commanded by Brig. Gen. Andrew Pickens, joined Morgan before the battle, although the exact number is in

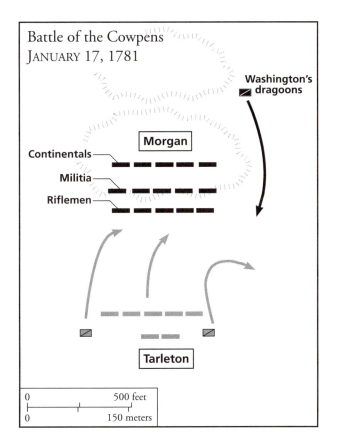

dispute. Depending on who was counting, Morgan had a total force of from eight hundred to eleven hundred.

Morgan carefully planned his deployment and tactics to take advantage of his men's strengths and weaknesses. He knew his militiamen were good shots, but he also knew they would not stand up to the disciplined British in an open field. He also believed that his core of Continental veterans could match anything Tarleton could send forward, if supported properly. Therefore, Morgan arranged his troops in three successive lines. The North Carolina and Georgia militia riflemen were far to the front, in semi-concealed positions. Morgan told them—he limped from campfire to campfire and spoke to nearly all the men personally—that they were to wait until the British were at close range, fire twice, and then they were free to run back to safety behind the rear lines. Pickens commanded a second line of militia (North and South Carolinians), and his orders were similar: fire at close range and then retreat in order behind the third line to reinforce it. In the final line, bayonets fixed, waited John Howard's Continental veterans, with William Washington's cavalry and mounted Georgia infantry in reserve to the rear.

Tarleton had a force of about equal numbers, and most of his men were regulars or veterans: the infantry and cavalry of his own British Legion, the famous Seventy-first Highlanders, recruits of the Seventh Regiment, and a few troopers of the Seventeenth Dragoons. There were almost no local Loyalist militia, save for a few guides and scouts.

When Tarleton learned, on the night of January 16, that Morgan had paused and was within reach, he ordered a quick advance, starting at 3:00 A.M. By early-morning light, Tarleton's men had covered four miles and were ready to deploy and attack.

Tarleton placed his Legion infantry, the Seventh, and three companies of light infantry in his front line, with dragoons on the flanks. The Highlanders and the Legion cavalry were held in reserve. The first contact was between British cavalry and the first line of American militia. The horsemen rode up to the militia, where they were met with a withering fire that turned them back. The first line of Americans then fled as instructed. The British infantry line stepped off to the music of Tarleton's bandsmen and had advanced to within a few yards of the second line of American militia when a blast of musketry hit them hard, causing many casualties, especially among the officers. As planned, the militia then scurried off the field and to the rear. When Tarleton's dragoons tried to pursue the militia, they were effectively counterattacked by

Washington's cavalry; nonetheless, the flight of the American militia caused Tarleton's men to believe they had victory in hand, and they advanced again.

They then came up against the Continental and Virginia veterans, who poured out disciplined volley fire and stunted the British advance. Tarleton ordered the Highlanders into action in an attempt to flank the Americans. Lieutenant Colonel Howard ordered his men to wheel to meet the new threat, but the rest of the American line mistook this for a signal to retreat and began to move, in an orderly way, to the rear. Morgan was irate, but Howard assured him that his men were still under control. At a crucial moment, the Continentals and the Virginians turned about, fired a volley from the hip, and charged with their bayonets. Simultaneously, the American cavalry hit the British flank, and the battle was decided: the British soldiers began to throw down their arms and surrender on the spot.

On the flank, however, the Highlanders of the Seventy-first fought on and refused to surrender until subdued by hand-to-hand fighting from Pickens's militia, who emerged from behind the American lines to maul the Highlanders.

Tarleton himself attempted to rally his Legion cavalry for a final charge, but for once his men failed him and they refused the orders, turned, and fled.

In a final dramatic scene, Tarleton was chased from the field by a small group of horsemen headed by William Washington. The two actually came to close mounted combat, with Washington breaking his saber and Tarleton killing Washington's horse with a pistol, the final shot of the battle. Tarleton managed to disengage and escape.

The British had suffered severe losses: 100 killed, 229 wounded, and 600 captured out of a force of 1,100. The Americans suffered only twelve dead and sixty wounded, and they seized a great store of supplies, tents, and arms from the British supply wagons.

The victory allowed Greene to continue to campaign, set a fire beneath patriot recruiting, and showed that with proper organization, American militia could inflict terrible damage on their opponents.

Further Reading

Burke Davis. *The Cowpens-Guilford Courthouse Campaign* (Philadelphia: Lippincott, 1962); Thomas Fleming. *Cowpens: "Downright Fighting": The Story of the Cowpens* (Washington, D.C.: National Park Service, 1988); and Kenneth Roberts. *The Battle of the Cowpens: The Great Morale Builder* (Garden City, N.Y.: Doubleday, 1958).

Crampton's Gap

Maryland (September 14, 1862)
American Civil War

Although Maj. Gen. George B. McClellan had intercepted Confederate general Robert E. Lee's battle order to split his army into two divisions, McClellan moved slowly to counter Lee's invasion of Union territory in Maryland. As Confederate major general Thomas J. "Stonewall" Jackson closed in on the Federal installation at HARPERS FERRY, the right wing of McClellan's Army of the Potomac engaged Confederate forces at three high passes on SOUTH MOUNTAIN on September 14. The day's fighting began at Turner's Gap and Fox's Gap at the same time as Confederate Maj. Gen. Lafayette McLaws tried to make his way through the nearby Crampton's Gap to attack Harpers Ferry from the north.

At noon, Union major general William B. Franklin was also trying to bring his Sixth Corps through

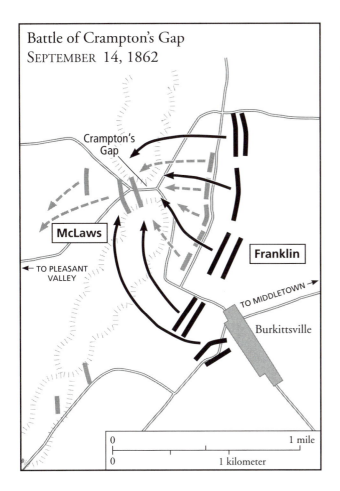

Battle of Crampton's Gap
SEPTEMBER 14, 1862

Crampton's Gap

McLaws

Franklin

← TO PLEASANT VALLEY

TO MIDDLETOWN →

Burkittsville

0   1 mile
0   1 kilometer

Crampton's Gap to relieve Federal forces at Harpers Ferry. Franklin slowed when he realized that McLaws lay ahead, but around 4 P.M. Franklin finally ordered a Union charge, just as the Confederate forces turned to meet him. A fierce fight raged for the rest of the day, as Franklin's men made considerable progress, taking Confederate prisoners, cannon, and battle flags.

By nightfall, the Federal forces had taken Crampton's Gap, and McLaws's men had taken up a new defensive position on the low ground at Pleasant Valley. Though McLaws's position was extremely vulnerable, Franklin halted his advance, probably because he overestimated the Confederate force's strength.

The delay allowed McLaws to regroup and form reinforcements into a stronger line, so that when Franklin did finally try to march on to Harper's Ferry, he found his way completely blocked. Franklin was too late to damage McLaws or keep Stonewall Jackson from defeating the Federal forces at Harpers Ferry.

Casualty estimates for the battle at Crampton's Gap are vague at best. Franklin claimed a total loss of 533 Federal troops, and Confederate losses are unknown.

Franklin's delay at Crampton's Gap, combined with McClellan's general lethargy, contributed to Jackson's victory at Harpers Ferry and helped convince General Lee to concentrate his forces for a bigger attack at Sharpsburg (*see also* ANTIETAM).

Further Reading

Edward J. Stackpole. *From Cedar Mountain to Antietam, August–September, 1862* (Harrisburg, Pa.: Stackpole, 1959).

The Crater

(Petersburg Mine Assault)
Petersburg, Virginia (July 30, 1864)
American Civil War

Starting in June 1863, Lt. Gen. Ulysses S. Grant began a nine-month campaign against the Confederate stronghold of PETERSBURG, Virginia, intending to capture the city and hurry the war to a close. Grant's assaults against the city did not go well, and Confederate general Robert E. Lee turned the fight into a campaign of attrition. One of the most striking actions in the Petersburg campaign, and indeed one of the biggest spectacles of the war, took place on July 30, when Lt. Col. Henry Pleasants's regiment, recruited largely among Pennsylvania coal miners, exploded a massive land mine under Confederate positions in the hope that the resulting breach, shock, and carnage would allow the Federals to break through Confederate lines and enter the city. Though the explosion went as planned, Federal commanders failed to carry out an effective follow-up attack, and the operation turned into a Union bloodbath.

The construction of the mine underneath a Confederate position known as Elliott's Salient was a testimony to Pleasants's engineering genius and his men's construction ingenuity. Though Grant and Maj. Gen. Ambrose Burnside approved the action, they did not provide many supplies or much technical support. Pleasants devised a ventilation system that allowed his men to work safely underground, and between June 25 and July 23 they dug a 511-foot tunnel and deposited 4 tons of black powder in a gallery 20 feet below the Confederate camp.

While the tunnel was being constructed, Burnside instructed Brig. Gen. Edward Ferrero, who commanded a division of African-American soldiers, to train his men for the postexplosion attack. On July 29, Brig. Gen. George G. Meade and Lieutenant General Grant ordered Burnside not to send the African-American division in first, because they feared political criticism if the men were seen to have been used as mere cannon fodder. Burnside made his other division commanders draw straws, and Brig. Gen. James Ledlie wound up with command of the lead Union attack.

In the predawn hours of July 30, the mine was detonated by Lt. Jacob Douty and Sgt. Harry Reese, who crawled into the shaft and lit the fuse by hand. The huge explosion stunned Confederate forces, blowing 300 of them into the air, and blasted a crater 170 feet long, 60 feet wide, and 30 feet deep.

The Union follow-up to the explosion faltered almost immediately. Ledlie languished at the rear, drinking rum in a bombproof shelter, as his division pressed forward. Instead of fanning out around the crater and pushing toward the city walls, however, the Federals (who themselves had been startled by the scale of the blast) poured directly into the huge hole in the ground. Burnside sent in his African-American division, but they too lacked effective command, because Ferrero joined Ledlie at the rear. In fact, they suffered the largest portion of casualties of any Union unit: Southern soldiers targeted them especially because of their skin color. The Confederates recovered from their shock remarkably quickly, and the South

Carolina artillery blasted away at the Federal soldiers in the crater, who were effectively trapped. By 8:30 A.M., the fifteen thousand Union troops in the crater were virtually helpless against Confederate fire, and it took another five hours to bring them out of harm's way.

Union forces lost 3,798 casualties in the debacle, while the Confederates suffered only around 1,500 men killed or wounded.

Ulysses S. Grant called the failed attack "the saddest affair I have witnessed in the war." His troops had been unable to exploit their best chance to clear the Confederates away, and they settled in for another eight months of siege outside Petersburg.

Further Reading

Jeff Kinard. *The Battle of the Crater* (Fort Worth, Tex.: Ryan Place, 1995).

❧ Crawford's Defeat

See SANDUSKY

❧ Cross Keys

(Union Church)

Virginia (June 8–9, 1862) *American Civil War*

After Maj. Gen. Thomas J. "Stonewall" Jackson chased Maj. Gen. Nathaniel Banks's Union army out of the Shenandoah Valley and across the Potomac River at FIRST WINCHESTER on May 25, 1862, Union commanders Maj. Gen. John C. Frémont and Brig. Gen. James Shields pursued Jackson's forces to the town of Strasburg, where they threatened to end his brilliant Shenandoah Valley campaign. Jackson, however, escaped up the Shenandoah Valley, while Frémont and Shields pursued him along parallel courses. Jackson ordered Maj. Gen. Richard S. Ewell to slow Frémont's progress, and Ewell engaged Frémont's men at Cross Keys on June 8.

Ewell positioned his three infantry brigades and four artillery batteries, totaling about five thousand men, in front of a rural tavern at Cross Keys, south of Harrisonburg. He placed artillery in the center and the infantry of Brig. Gen. George H. Steuart and Brig. Gen. Isaac R. Trimble to cover the left and right of his line, respectively. At 9 A.M. on June 8, Frémont marched his 10,500 men up the road from Port Republic.

Encountering Confederate pickets at the Union Church in front of the tavern, he positioned his own ten batteries of artillery on a hill facing Ewell and began an artillery duel.

As the firefight continued, Frémont took the initiative and sent Brig. Gen. Julius Stahel's brigade into the woods on Ewell's right to attack the Confederate line. Unfortunately for Stahel, he was unaware of Trimble's presence in the woods until he had pursued an advance party across a wheat field to within fifty yards of that body of Confederate infantry. Stahel's men were stunned by a surprise volley from Trimble's brigade, and Trimble, with the Fifteenth Alabama Volunteers, pursued them as they retreated. The pursuit along the Keezletown Road continued even as Brig. Gen. Henry Bohlen's brigade arrived, having been sent to reinforce Stahel.

Meanwhile, Brig. Gen. Robert H. Milroy and Brig. Gen. Gustave P. Cluseret held a position near the Confederate center but found their opponents' line too strong to attack. Ewell, worried that Steuart's position on the Confederate left was vulnerable to an advance by Union brigadier general Robert C. Schenck, sent Col. John M. Patton and Brig. Gen. Richard Taylor, whom Jackson had sent to shore up his force, to prevent his line from being turned. Frémont, however, was already so shaken by Stahel's and Bohlen's retreat that he ordered all of the Federal troops to withdraw south along the Keezletown Road. Trimble wanted to attack Frémont's force at their new position, but Ewell broke off the fight, in accordance with instructions from Jackson, who was ready to engage Shields at PORT REPUBLIC.

Casualties in the battle at Cross Keys were relatively light. The Confederates suffered 288 wounded and killed, compared to the Union total of 684.

Though Frémont's men pursued Ewell toward Port Republic the next day, they were unable to cross the South River Bridge, which Ewell had destroyed, and they had to watch as Jackson and Ewell defeated Shields in the final victory of the campaign.

Further Reading

Darrell L. Collins. *The Battles of Cross Keys and Port Republic* (Lynchburg, Va.: H. E. Howard, 1993).

❧ Custer's Last Stand

See LITTLE BIGHORN

Dade's Battle

Florida (December 18, 1835)
Second Seminole War

The resistance of a part of the Seminole of Florida to the federal policy of forced removal of the tribe led to a series of engagements known collectively as the Second Seminole War. The first significant confrontation came in December 1835.

Maj. Francis Dade commanded a force of troops at Fort Brooke at Tampa Bay, and when hostilities appeared to be approaching, he set out to Fort King in north-central Florida with 108 reinforcements for the contingent of troops there, who were commanded by Gen. Duncan Clinch.

On the way, Dade's column was ambushed by a group of around three hundred Seminole warriors under Alligator (Halpatter Tustenuggee), Jumper (Ote Ematha), and Micanopy. The Seminole force included several black men, who were probably former slaves living with the tribe.

The first assault killed around fifty of Dade's men. The balance of the detachment was able to form a defensive formation, but it was badly outnumbered, and all but three men died. The Seminole victory was so complete that Americans afterward usually referred to the battle as "Dade's Massacre." Whatever the title, the conflict set off a long and costly war. (*See also* LAKE OKEECHOBEE.)

Further Reading

Frank Laumer. *Dade's Last Command* (Gainesville: University of Florida Press, 1995); *Massacre!* (Gainesville: University of Florida Press, 1968).

Danbury Raid

Connecticut (April 23–28, 1777)
American Revolution

There were several sharp skirmishes between the British troops raiding into Connecticut in the spring of 1777 and local defenders, with little damage to the British, despite the presence of Benedict Arnold, the Americans' best field general.

William Tryon, former British governor of New York—he had recently been commissioned as a major general—led the British raid with the purpose of destroying a cache of American arms and supplies at Danbury. He landed with around two thousand men at Fairfield, Connecticut, on Long Island Sound, on the night of April 23. The British had collected portions of several regular regiments, including dragoons and artillery, to make up the raiding party.

On April 24, Tryon marched unopposed to Danbury and occupied the town. The 150 American Continentals who had garrisoned Danbury removed some of the stores and fled before the British arrived. The British proceeded over the next two days to destroy the stores that were left and burn a large number of houses and barns.

The American response was weak, since there were few regular troops in the vicinity. Generals David Wooster and Gold Selleck Silliman cobbled together a force of about one hundred Continentals and perhaps five hundred militia and moved into position at Redding, Connecticut, in hopes of harassing the British into withdrawal. They were joined there by Brig. Gen. Benedict Arnold, a hero of the assault on QUEBEC and of the naval battle of VALCOUR ISLAND. Arnold, who had been passed over for promotion, had withdrawn from the war to sulk at his sister's house in New Haven, but news of the British raid sent him flying to join the Americans at Redding.

The British left Danbury on April 27 and headed south. Arnold took the majority of the American forces and set up a blocking position astride the road at Ridgefield. Wooster, with two hundred men, followed the British, hoping to snap at their heels, but after he captured some stragglers the enemy turned on his small force and chased it away, killing Wooster in the process.

Tryon also made short work of Arnold's attempt to block the road. He engaged the Americans head-on and sent detachments around both flanks to take Arnold's men from the rear. The Americans had to beat a quick retreat. Arnold himself had a close call, when his horse was shot and he became tangled in the stirrups (his leg was still weak from a wound he had received at the gates of Quebec). As he struggled on the ground to free himself, a Tory ran up and demanded his surrender. Arnold shot him cold with a pistol and made his escape.

The Americans then set up another blocking position, hoping to stop the British the next day, but Tryon discovered a route around Arnold and set up at Compo Hill, between Arnold and their point of disembarkation. As Arnold prepared to attack, Tryon delivered a preemptive assault under Brig. Gen. William Erskine that completely spoiled Arnold's plan and allowed the British to load their ships and sail away virtually unmolested, having put a satisfying dent in the American supply line.

Further Reading

Robert F. McDevitt. *Connecticut Attacked, A British Viewpoint: Tryon's Raid on Danbury* (Chester, Conn.: Pequot Press, 1974).

Deep Run

See FRANKLIN'S CROSSING

Deerfield

See BLOODY BROOK

Drewry's Bluff

Virginia (May 16, 1864) *American Civil War*

The scheme of the Union commander in chief, Lt. Gen. Ulysses S. Grant, to end the war in 1864 focused primarily on a campaign by the Army of the Potomac against Gen. Robert E. Lee and the Army of Northern Virginia. But Grant also had hopes for a thrust westward toward Richmond from the James River region, by an army under Maj. Gen. Benjamin Butler. The hopes were frustrated when Butler was defeated in mid-May.

Butler was one of the more notorious political generals of the war. Time after time he had demonstrated his incompetence as a general, but his huge political power kept him in command and gave him important assignments. In May 1864, he commanded the thirty-five-thousand-man Army of the James, with the assignment to advance from Bermuda Hundred and assault Richmond while Grant occupied the Army of Northern Virginia, the main Confederate force, to the north. Butler's corps commanders, Major Generals Quincy Adams Gillmore and W. F. "Baldy" Smith, were competent soldiers.

Butler was opposed by the veteran Confederate commander Gen. P. T. G. Beauregard, who had held a variety of important commands during the early days of the war. He had taken over the Richmond defenses in early May and organized a mismatched force of regular units, city troops, and militia that finally numbered more than eighteen thousand.

After several hesitant probes that did little more than destroy railroad tracks, Butler finally moved against the Confederate fortifications at Drewry's Bluff on May 12, driving back Beauregard's outer defenders and taking positions facing the main stronghold, Fort Darling. Despite overall numerical superiority, the Union troops immediately on the field numbered only slightly more than fifteen thousand, so Beauregard was able to outnumber his opponent where it mattered. Gillmore and Smith dug into defensive lines and waited.

Before dawn on May 16, in the midst of a heavy fog, the Confederates came out of their defenses and attacked. The brigade commanded by Maj. Gen. Robert Ransom, Jr., overran the position held by Brig. Gen. Charles A. Heckman, capturing about four hundred prisoners, including the general himself. Other Confederate columns were less successful, and by midmorning the fighting had ground down to a stalemate along a broad front. Beauregard had sent two infantry brigades and his cavalry to flank the Union line, but the sweep failed to come into position for an attack. When a hard rainstorm hit the battlefield, Butler was able to disengage and withdraw his remaining troops back to the safety of Bermuda Hundred.

In the battle at Drewry's Bluff and its preliminaries, the Confederates lost 4,160 casualties, and the Union lost 2,506.

After the battle, Butler settled down behind a fortified line of defense across a narrow neck of land between the Appomatox and James Rivers, effectively removing the Army of the James from the war.

Further Reading

Mark M. Boatner. *The Civil War Dictionary*. Rev. ed. (New York: David McKay, 1988

$\mathcal{E}$

✒ Edge Hill

See BUSHY RUN

✒ Elkhorn Tavern

See PEA RIDGE

✒ Elkwater

See CHEAT MOUNTAIN

✒ Ellison's Mill

See MECHANICSVILLE

✒ Emuckfau Creek

Alabama (January 22, 1814) *Creek War*

The bloody Creek War that followed the annihilation of several hundred white settlers at FORT MIMS by the pro-British Red Stick faction of the Creek Nation (the Red Stick faction supported war; the White Stick faction peace) involved thirty-five hundred Tennessee and one thousand Georgia militia as well as several hundred pro-American Indians, all under the command of Maj. Gen. Andrew Jackson. The Americans won victories at TALLASAHATCHEE and TALLADEGA but suffered during the late fall of 1813 from a severe lack of supplies and dwindling manpower as enlistments expired.

After facing down militiamen who wanted to return home in January 1814, Jackson launched an assault on the Red Stick town at Emuckfau Creek. His force consisted of eight hundred militia, two hundred Indian allies, and one six-pounder cannon. He faced a larger number of Creek, probably as many as nine hundred warriors.

Jackson approached the Red Stick camp during the night of January 21, stopping to reconnoiter before dawn. As Jackson formed up his men in preparation for an attack, the Red Sticks launched a surprise assault from the cover of the heavy undergrowth. The Americans, in a hollow-square formation, held off the first waves. When daylight illuminated the battlefield, Jackson sent Brig. Gen. John Coffee with four hundred men to counterattack.

Coffee's men charged out of the American position and pushed the Red Sticks back toward their village. Coffee had to retreat in his turn, however, when he realized how badly he was outnumbered. Thus heartened, the Creeks again attacked Jackson's main formation and were again driven off by Coffee. At that stage, Jackson disengaged and began a full retreat toward his base at Fort Strother.

The Americans lost twenty killed and seventy-five wounded; the Red Stick casualties are unknown.

Further Reading

Angie Debo. *Road to Disappearance: A History of the Creek Indians* (Norman: University of Oklahoma Press, 1941); David S. and Jeanne T. Heidler. *Old Hickory's War: Andrew Jackson and the Quest for Empire* (Mechanicsburg, Pa.: Stackpole Books, 1996); Joel W. Martin. *Sacred Revolt: The Muskogees' Struggle for a New World* (Boston: Beacon Press, 1991); and Frank L. Owsley, Jr. *Struggle for the Gulf Borderlands* (Gainesville: University Presses of Florida, 1981).

✑ Enitachopco Creek

Alabama (January 24, 1814) *Creek War*

The Creek War, set off in the summer of 1813 by an attack on white settlers at FORT MIMS, was fought between the pro-British Red Stick faction of the Creek Nation and an opposing army of American militiamen and their Indian allies. (The Red Stick faction supported war; the White Stick faction peace.) The Americans, commanded by Maj. Gen. Andrew Jackson, had a very difficult time sustaining themselves over the winter so far away from their base of supply and reinforcement. In addition, Jackson's men were roughly treated by the Red Sticks at the Battle of EMUCKFAU CREEK in late January and at Enitachopco Creek a few days later.

Jackson and his one thousand men were on the move back toward their base at Fort Strother after the nasty fight at Emuckfau when they stumbled upon a major Red Stick concentration near Enitachopco Creek. Jackson crossed the stream with his main force, but the Red Sticks attacked his rear guard before it could ford the creek. Jackson had been alert for just such an attack and had instructed his two columns of troops in that case to turn back and recross the creek both above and below the Indian position, so as to catch the enemy in a pincer movement. Unfortunately for Jackson, his unreliable militia refused to attack, abandoning the field and leaving only a small force to fend off the Red Stick assault. Jackson's army was saved by the timely intervention of his six-

pounder fieldpiece, which broke up the Red Stick attack with grapeshot.

The exact extent of the casualties from the battle was unreported, but the Red Sticks appeared to have suffered significant losses in the final engagement.

Further Reading

Angie Debo. *Road to Disappearance: A History of the Creek Indians* (Norman: University of Oklahoma Press, 1941); David S. and Jeanne T. Heidler. *Old Hickory's War: Andrew Jackson and the Quest for Empire* (Mechanicsburg, Pa.: Stackpole Books, 1996); Joel W. Martin. *Sacred Revolt: The Muskogees' Struggle for a New World* (Boston: Beacon Press, 1991); and Frank T. Owsley, Jr. *Struggle for the Gulf Borderlands* (Gainesville: University Presses of Florida, 1981).

✑ H.M.S. *Epervier*

See U.S.S. PEACOCK

✑ Eutaw Springs

South Carolina (September 8, 1781)
American Revolution

In what was the last major stand-up battle and one of the hardest-fought engagements of the American Revolution, the main southern army, under Maj. Gen. Nathanael Greene, inflicted on the British an unusually high casualty rate, despite losing overall.

The British army that had been commanded by Lord Rawdon at HOBKIRK'S HILL had passed to Lt. Col. Alexander Stewart when Rawdon returned to England. Stewart had about eighteen hundred men, including a so-called "flank battalion" (made up of light infantry and grenadiers from several regiments) under Maj. John Majoribanks as well as the Third, Nineteenth, Thirtieth, Sixty-third, and Sixty-fourth Regiments of regulars and some Loyalist infantry and cavalry, camped on the Santee River.

Greene's army, which comprised about twenty-two hundred in all, included South Carolina and North Carolina militia and partisans, but mostly it was made up of Continentals from North Carolina, Virginia, Maryland, and Delaware. Both Lee's Legion and William Washington's dragoons were with Greene as he approached the British camp, hoping to take Stewart by surprise.

The advance American units encountered British foragers out on an early-morning yam-digging expedition and

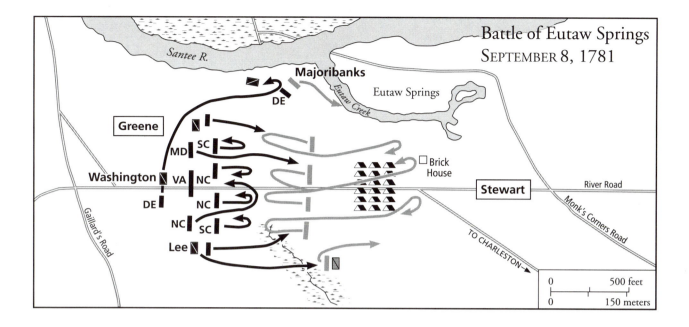

took several captives, but Boston Loyalist cavalry commander Maj. John Coffin escaped and warned Stewart of Greene's presence. Stewart formed a line of battle in front of his camp, with Majoribank's flank battalion anchoring the right wing in an overgrown thicket. The first assault came at 9:00 A.M. from the Carolina militia, who pressed forward, pouring seventeen volleys at the waiting British before a counterattack drove them into retreat. Greene then sent in a newly recruited regiment of North Carolina Continentals, who drove the British back to their original line. He followed with a bayonet charge by the veteran Marylanders and Virginians. The British were sent flying straight through their own camp, and it appeared that Greene had finally won a battle against the British.

At a fatal moment, however, the Americans stopped to plunder the British tents. They quickly lost all cohesion and disintegrated into a mob. At the same time, William Washington attacked Majoribank's strong position with his dragoons. The horsemen could not penetrate the thick growth, and they were cut down—Washington himself was unhorsed, bayoneted, and captured. Majoribanks then led his men in a race for a brick house, beating the Americans by a narrow margin. Once in the building, the British fired muskets and swivel guns on the nearby Americans, who used captured British officers as shields while escaping out of range. Majoribanks then organized a sortie that swept down on the looting Continentals and chased them from the field, snatching a victory for the British at the last moment. Majoribanks was killed in the final attack. Greene, struggling to regain control of his troops, ordered yet another retreat.

The toll of the battle was fierce; the British took the highest proportionate losses of the entire war, losing 693 killed, wounded, or missing out of an initial force of 1,800. The Americans reported losses of five hundred.

Despite his battlefield victory, Stewart realized his army was too depleted to offer much resistance to a renewed offensive by Greene, so he retreated toward Charleston. Within little more than a month, the British cause was lost irretrievably at YORKTOWN.

Further Reading

Christopher Ward. *The War of the Revolution.* Vol. 2 (New York: Macmillan, 1952).

F

Fair Oaks

(Seven Pines)
Virginia (May 31–June 1, 1862)
American Civil War

The campaign of Union major general George B. McClellan in the James River peninsula in the spring of 1862 reached to within a half-dozen miles of the Confederate capital of Richmond before he began to fumble away his advantage with timidity and irresolute decision making, despite a failed Confederate attack at Fair Oaks.

McClellan had positioned his Army of the Potomac on either side of the Chickahominy River, thereby splitting his forces and providing a tempting target for the Confederate commander, Gen. Joseph E. Johnston. The Chickahominy was in spring flood and was a major barrier to troop movements. Johnston planned a complex, three-pronged attack against the Federal troops south of the river, but he was hampered by very poor staff work: orders to his corps and division commanders were received in garbled verbal versions instead of in writing, and much confusion resulted.

Maj. Gen. James Longstreet was supposed to make the main attack on the Union positions, with support from Maj. Gen. Benjamin Huger and a secondary attack by Maj. Gen. D. H. Hill, but Longstreet's men took the wrong road and jammed up the entire Confederate advance. The attack ordered for early morning did not get under way until afternoon, and instead of throwing the entire weight of three divisions against the Federals, the Confederate assaults were made piecemeal.

Moreover, the Union troops, especially the Fourth Corps, commanded by Maj. Gen. Erasmus Keyes, put up a fierce resistance and blunted the Confederate assaults. Because of the delayed and fragmented attack, McClellan was able to reinforce his troops south of the river by sending a division under Maj. Gen. Edwin "Bull" Sumner across the Chickahominy in time to stifle the Confederate advance at the end of the day.

General Johnston was seriously wounded during the latter stages of the battle on May 31, and Maj. Gen. G. W. Smith assumed command, ordering a renewed attack for the next morning. The second day went even worse for the Confederates. The initial attacks were repulsed by the

Federals, and Longstreet failed to respond when ordered to come up with reinforcements. The fighting was eventually broken off at the orders of the new Confederate commander, Gen. Robert E. Lee, who had ridden out from Richmond.

The two sides had been almost evenly matched, with about forty-two thousand men each on the field. The Confederates lost around sixty-one hundred casualties; the Federals lost about five thousand.

The most significant effect of the battle was to reinforce McClellan's natural timidity. He declined to follow up on the Confederate failures, wrongly believing, as always, that he was vastly outnumbered by his opponents, and he allowed the audacious Lee eventually to take control of the situation.

Further Reading

Steven H. Newton. *The Battle of Seven Pines, May 31–June 1, 1862* (Lynchburg, Va.: H. E. Howard, 1993).

Fallen Timbers

Ohio (August 20, 1794) *Little Turtle's War*

After suffering two devastating defeats at the hands of a confederation of Indians of the Old Northwest (*see also* HARMAR'S DEFEAT; ST. CLAIR'S DEFEAT), the fledgling U.S. government finally found a competent general who was capable of organizing and leading a frontier army to victory.

The tremendous shock of losing more than one thousand soldiers and noncombatants under Arthur St. Clair in 1791 had pushed the U.S. Congress, timid and suspicious of the military, to reorganize and expand what had been a minuscule regular army. At the urging of Pres. George Washington, Congress authorized five "legions" of 1,250 men each, with a full complement of trained infantry, artillery, and cavalry. The legions were to be commanded by brigadiers, with a major general in overall command. After due consideration, Washington chose the American Revolution veteran Anthony Wayne (known as "Mad Anthony" for his occasional impetuousness) as the new army commander.

Wayne was an extremely capable general, combining administrative and planning ability with ferocious combat abilities on the battlefield. He set to work to build the Legion of the United States, as the new army was to be known, a difficult task that consumed months. It became clear that Wayne would be unable to take the field before late 1793 and that he would be unable to recruit and train more than three thousand regulars. Nonetheless, Wayne's preparations resulted in an American army vastly more capable than any that had existed since the siege of Yorktown thirteen years before. In December 1793, Wayne marched from Fort Washington (present-day Cincinnati) on the Ohio River up the same path taken by previous American armies to the site of St. Clair's Defeat on the Wabash, not far from the principal Miami village of Kekionga (known as Miami Town to non-Indians). After burying the grisly remains of the previous army, which had lain abandoned for two years, Wayne's men built a strong post, called Fort Recovery, on the spot.

The main campaign against the tribes began the following summer. The great Miami war leader Little Turtle (Michikinikwa), who had destroyed the two previous American armies sent into the region, had withdrawn from leadership and in fact now advocated peace. His place had been taken by Blue Jacket (Weypapiersenwah), a Shawnee of considerable ability but no peer of Little Turtle as a field commander. The British exerted a strong influence among the tribes, having not only held on to their western posts following the Revolution but built a new fort on the Maumee River, as a strong provocation. At one point it appeared likely that Wayne might have to fight his old British foes on the frontier as well as the new ones, but at the last minute Great Britain shied away from direct conflict.

When Wayne's force was finally assembled at Fort Recovery, it included two thousand regulars and sixteen hundred militia, the latter—good, high-quality fighters—commanded by Kentucky brigadier general Charles Scott and comprising most of Wayne's mounted troops. There were also about one hundred Indian scouts, mostly Chickasaw and Choctaw from Tennessee.

Wayne struck for a point midway between the principal concentrations of Indians, leaving fortified bases behind as he marched. He caught up with a large force of warriors from a mixture of tribes, including Shawnee, Miami, Wyandot (Huron), and others, led by Blue Jacket, at a spot near modern-day Toledo, Ohio, called Fallen Timbers. (It had been ravaged by a tornado and was a twisted mass of felled trees.) The one thousand Indians, aided by sixty white Canadian militia dressed in Indian garb, planned an ambush among the natural obstacles, with warriors posted on nearby hills to fire into what Blue Jacket believed would be the confused American column after the trap was sprung.

Anthony Wayne was not a general to be easily taken in by ruses, however. He had formed up his men in a powerful marching formation that allowed them to change from moving to fighting at a moment's notice. He also had warned his officers that he expected an attack at any time. As the army's advance guard, under Maj. William Price, slowly moved into the tangle of trees at Fallen Timbers, some of the Indians who had grown tired of lying in wait for several days fired prematurely on the Americans, driving the skirmishers back to the main column. Wayne immediately ordered his mounted militia to split and ride around the obstacles so as to attack the Indians on the flanks. He wanted to drive a disciplined bayonet attack directly through the tangle while a dragoon detachment penetrated along the river's edge.

The American soldiers executed the attack perfectly. The infantrymen formed up, picked their way through the trees until they could deploy into a line, fired a devastating volley at the Indian positions, and launched a straight-ahead bayonet attack. The warriors broke and ran almost immediately, retreating toward the nearby British fort so rapidly that the mounted Kentucky militia could not catch up. Wayne's dragoons, however, caught many of the fleeing Indians as they crossed the river and killed and wounded many with sabers. The British remained inside their walls and offered no aid to their erstwhile allies.

The battle was a complete triumph for Wayne. He lost only thirty-three men killed and one hundred wounded. The Indian casualties were not accurately counted but amounted to several hundred.

The power of the Miami-Shawnee confederation that Little Turtle had led so well was now broken.

Further Reading

Douglas R. Hurt. *The Ohio Frontier: Crucible of the Old Northwest* (Bloomington: Indiana University Press, 1996); Dave R. Palmer. *1794: America, Its Army, and the Birth of a Nation* (Novato, Calif.: Presidio Press, 1994); and Wiley Sword. *President Washington's Indian War: The Struggle for the Old Northwest, 1790–1795* (Norman: University of Oklahoma Press, 1985).

❧ Falling Waters

West Virginia (July 14, 1863) *American Civil War*

As Confederate general Robert E. Lee retreated south after the pitched battle at GETTYSBURG, Pennsylvania, in July 1863, he divided his army into three parts. The main body

of troops, led by Lee himself, encamped on the eastern bank of the Potomac River at Williamsport, Maryland, on July 6, and began to construct pontoon bridges in order to cross the storm-swollen river. By the evening of July 13 flood waters had receded enough to make the bridges passable, and Lee marched his men back into Confederate territory in Virginia. He left two divisions at Falling Waters under Maj. Gen. Henry Heth to cover the retreat.

When the hot-headed Union brigadier general Judson "Kill Cavalry" Kilpatrick stormed Williamsport on July 14 and found Lee's troops gone, he charged on toward Heth's divisions at Falling Waters. The fight was brief and at close quarters—the southerners knocked many of Kilpatrick's cavalrymen from their horses with fence rails and axes. Heth's men fought off a second cavalry attack that afternoon by Kilpatrick and Brig. Gen. John Buford.

No precise casualty figures exist, but the southerners probably suffered at least five hundred killed, including Brig. Gen. James J. Pettigrew, who had led Heth's men in Pickett's Charge at Gettysburg.

While Heth's divisions did well to hold off their attackers while Lee's troops got safely away, the Northern public, disappointed at the lack of a conclusive victory at Gettysburg, exaggerated the Confederates' marginal victory.

Further Reading

R. T. Coles. *From Huntsville to Appomattox* (Knoxville: University of Tennessee Press, 1996).

❧ Farmville and Highbridge

Virginia (April 6–7, 1865) *American Civil War*

On April 6, 1865, Confederate Gen. James Longstreet retreated toward Farmville, Virginia, while the rest of Gen. Robert E. Lee's army was being pounded at SAYLER'S CREEK. The following day Lee tried to rally his troops around Longstreet's men, but despite Confederate stands at Farmville and Highbridge, Union victories set the stage for Lee's ultimate surrender at Appomattox Courthouse.

On April 6, Maj. Gen. Fitzhugh Lee's cavalry turned on the pursuing Federal column of Maj. Gen. Edward Ord and killed or captured every man. This success allowed the remaining Confederates to escape across the elaborate 126-foot Highbridge (part of the Southside Railroad) early on April 7. But Maj. Gen. William "Little Billy" Mahone, who later became president of the Southside Railroad but who was for now covering Lt. Gen. John B. Gordon's movements, failed to set fire to the entire bridge after the Confederate crossing, and Federal troops commanded by Maj. Gen. Andrew Humphreys frantically beat out the flames and crossed behind the Southerners. Mahone attempted to counterattack, but it was clear that the Federals had established a position from which they could disrupt the Confederate resupply operation at Farmville.

Lee's main Confederate force crossed the Appomattox River, this time thoroughly burning the bridges behind it, and formed a battle line at the Cumberland Church. Mahone finally held Humphreys in check, beating off several waves of Federals through the afternoon. Maj. Gen. George Crook and Col. John I. Gregg's cavalry forded the Appomattox River to attack Lee's force, but they were countered by Fitzhugh Lee's horsemen, and Gregg was captured.

Casualty totals for the skirmishing are uncertain.

Though Lee's army managed to hold off its Union attackers at Highbridge and Farmville, the Confederates were not able to gain possession of the supplies they so badly needed after weeks of fierce fighting and withdrawals. On the evening of April 7, Lt. Gen. Ulysses S. Grant arrived in Farmville with eighty thousand men, and Lee retreated farther toward Appomattox Courthouse. Grant sent his first demand for Lee's surrender from Farmville.

Further Reading

Jay Wertz and Edwin Bearss. *Smithsonian's Great Battles and Battlefields of the Civil War* (New York: William Morrow, 1997).

≈ Fetterman Fight

Wyoming (December 21, 1866)
Bozeman Trail War

Immediately after the Civil War, the U.S. Army in the West turned to a program of subduing the resident Indian tribes and attempting to protect a flood of settlers. As part of this effort, the army set up a series of forts to protect travelers on the Bozeman Trail, but these outposts proved to be provocations to the Indians of the region. Moreover, the army discovered, to its sorrow, that military skills that had prevailed against the Confederacy did not translate immediately to success in the Indian wars, as the fate of Capt. William J. Fetterman demonstrated.

Fetterman, who had established a good record and held brevet rank as a major during the war, was assigned to Fort Phil Kearney in Wyoming under the command of Col. Henry B. Carrington, but he found Carrington's conservative approach to the army's assignment constricting. Fetterman boasted that with eighty men he could ride through the entire Sioux (Dakota, Lakota, Nakota) Nation, which revealed his lack of experience in the sort of warfare that typified confrontations in the West.

When Indians harassed wood-cutting parties from the fort, Fetterman requested permission to punish the offenders. Carrington expressly warned Fetterman to stay in sight of the fort and not to go beyond Lodge Trail Ridge, a hill three miles away. Fetterman picked a mixed force of cavalry and infantry numbering almost exactly eighty men, with Lt. George W. Grummond in charge of the mounted troopers and Capt. Frederick H. Brown and two civilians along as observers, and moved out of the fort.

Fetterman disregarded orders and took his men over the hill and out of sight of the fort, running directly into a classic ambush that had been set by 1,500 Cheyenne and Lakota warriors, led by Oglala-Brulé Lakota Crazy Horse (Ta-sunko-witko or Ta-shunca-Uitco). The soldiers were apparently overwhelmed by superior numbers, with many falling at the first assault. Some evidence at the site suggests that Fetterman and a few others may have made a last stand, but the command was wiped out to the last man, and no one knows for certain how the battle unfolded. A relief column from the fort found only mutilated bodies.

The disaster was the worst defeat of the army at the hands of the western Indians up until that time and was to be surpassed only by the losses at the LITTLE BIGHORN.

Further Reading

Dee A. Brown. *The Fetterman Massacre: An American Saga* (Lincoln: University of Nebraska Press, 1984).

≈ Fishdam Ford

South Carolina (November 9, 1780)
American Revolution

In October 1780, Thomas Sumter was promoted to militia brigadier general and encouraged to continue to harass the British in South Carolina while the American patriots struggled to reorganize their military effort in the South. The British commander, Lt. Gen. Lord Cornwallis, on the other hand, wanted to be rid of Sumter, so he ordered Maj. James Wemyss to march on him with mounted infantry and dragoons from the Sixty-third Regiment and Lt. Col. Banastre Tarleton's British Legion, hoping to take the partisan band of three hundred by surprise. Unfortunately for Wemyss, his men ran into Sumter's pickets in the middle of the night, and the surprise was spoiled. In fact, Wemyss himself was wounded by the exchange of fire. A subsequent mounted charge into Sumter's camp was repulsed, and after some hot fighting, both sides withdrew from the field. Sumter narrowly escaped capture when dragoons found his tent, but he hid during the night along a riverbank.

The next morning, Sumter and his men returned to the camp and claimed the British wounded—including Wemyss—as prisoners. No reliable casualty figures were reported by either side, but American losses must have been light.

Cornwallis's scheme failed badly, in that the minor victory invigorated local patriots to rally to Sumter.

Further Reading

John Buchanan. *The Road to Guilford Courthouse: The American Revolution in the Carolinas* (New York: John Wiley and Sons, 1997); Jerome J. Nadelhaft. *The Disorders of War: The Revolution in South Carolina* (Orono: University of Maine at Orono Press, 1981); and John S. Pancake. *The Destructive War: The British Campaign in the Carolinas, 1780–1782* (Tuscaloosa: University of Alabama Press, 1985).

⮑ Fisher's Hill

Virginia (September 22, 1864) *American Civil War*

At the end of a hard-fought battle for Winchester, Virginia, on September 19, 1864, Confederate lieutenant general Jubal Early's crippled force retreated to a strong position on Fisher's Hill, overlooking the town of Strasburg (*see also* WINCHESTER, THIRD). Federal major general Philip Sheridan, under strict orders to wipe out Early and to secure Union control of the Shenandoah Valley, engaged Early's force at its new position three days later.

Early deployed his twelve-thousand-man force, which had been considerably thinned at Winchester, across a four-mile stretch of rocky hills protected by trenches and a variety of natural impediments. Early ordered Maj. Gen. Lunsford Lomax's cavalry to dismount and fill in gaps along the line of infantry, and he placed his limited artillery where it could protect his weak eastern side. Sheridan arrived with twenty thousand troops and ordered Brig. Gen. George Crook's Eighth Corps to approach the Confederate rear secretly. As the Federal cavalry took up a position along the New Market Road to prepare in case of retreat, Brig. Gen. James Ricketts led the Union Sixth Corps up a ravine called Tumbling Run to within several hundred yards of the Confederate line.

By 4 P.M., Crook had finally completed his flanking move around Early's force, and his men executed a surprise attack. At the same time, the Sixth Corps rushed directly up the hill, as Sheridan and his officers rode the line shouting, "Forward! Forward everything!" Taken by surprise and greatly outnumbered, the Confederates slowly began to turn and run. Early's cavalry held open his corridor of withdrawal, and the Confederate force retreated to Edinburgh.

Federal troops suffered only 528 casualties in their assault, compared to a Confederate total of 1,235. Though Early's force was not quite broken, Sheridan convinced his superiors to call off his pursuit. Instead, Federal forces marched back into the Shenandoah Valley and began a mouth-long scorched-earth campaign referred to by civilians as "the Burning." Federal control of the Shenandoah Valley was finally accomplished not through pitched battles but through wholesale destruction of both military and civilian property—a hint of the strategy that would finally end the war.

Further Reading

Joseph W. A. Whitehorn "Fisher's Hill," in Frances H. Kennedy, ed. *The Civil War Battlefield Guide* (Boston: Houghton Mifflin, 1990).

⮑ Fishing Creek

(Catawba Ford)
North Carolina (August 18, 1780)
American Revolution

Following his demolition of the southern American army at CAMDEN, Lt. Gen. Lord Cornwallis invaded North Carolina hoping to eradicate pockets of patriot resistance by sending Lt. Col. Banastre Tarleton after the struggling Americans.

The chief remaining concentration of Americans was six hundred militia and one hundred Continentals under North Carolina partisan militia Col. Thomas Sumter, who had seized a British wagon train and was moving slowly with his booty along the banks of the Wateree River, well ahead of Cornwallis. He did not reckon, however, with the speed and determination of Tarleton, who was ordered by Cornwallis to catch the Americans.

By pushing his 350 dragoons and infantry at a furious pace, Tarleton came upon Sumter at Fishing Creek on August 18. Many of his men had dropped out in exhaustion, but Tarleton still had about 160 troopers when he discovered Sumter's camp.

The Americans had been careless, and they were in a state of complete relaxation—their arms stacked, cook fires going, and many of them swimming in the river. Tarleton charged immediately and totally routed the patriot camp, sending Sumter riding bareback for his life. Only a few Continentals rallied long enough for a brief resistance.

The Americans lost 150 killed and wounded, with 300 more taken prisoner. Tarleton lost only sixteen killed or wounded. He captured forty-four supply wagons and released one hundred British prisoners.

Further Reading

John Buchanan. *The Road to Guilford Courthouse: The American Revolution in the Carolinas* (New York: John Wiley & Sons, 1997); Jerome J. Nadelhaft. *The Disorders of War: The Revolution in South Carolina* (Orono: University of Maine at Orono Press, 1981); and John S. Pancake. *The Destructive War: The British Campaign in the Carolinas, 1780–1782* (Tuscaloosa: University of Alabama Press, 1985).

❧ Five Forks

Virginia (March 30–April 1, 1865)
American Civil War

In anticipation of Maj. Gen. Philip Sheridan's arrival at Petersburg, Virginia, Gen. Robert E. Lee ordered Maj. Gen. George Pickett and Maj. Gen. Fitzhugh Lee to march on Five Forks (where strategic roads converged) in order to protect the Southside Railroad. This, he hoped, would keep supply lines open and enable Confederate troops to escape and rendezvous with Gen. Joseph E. Johnston's force in North Carolina. After three days of fighting and maneuvering in and around Five Forks, the Confederate forces were utterly defeated at what some historians consider the Confederacy's "Waterloo."

On March 29, Federal major general Gouverneur K. Warren took up an entrenched position at the Boydton Plank Road with twelve thousand infantry troops. The next day Sheridan and Maj. Gen. Wesley Merritt's supporting cavalry struck out from there toward Five Forks. They made only limited progress before Pickett's men hit the Union left flank and pushed the Federal forces back toward Dinwiddie Courthouse. An additional Confederate attack caused Warren to move his men to a new post at the White Oak Road. Sheridan took stock of the enemy and decided that the battle would turn on the ability to defeat Pickett's men.

Much heavier action commenced on March 31. The day began when Confederate major general

Bushrod Johnson pushed Warren's forces all the way back to Gravelly Run. They held there until Sheridan sent reinforcements that helped Warren to smash Johnson back across the White Oak Road, where he was isolated from Pickett's line by a distance of three miles. Pickett struck out from Five Forks across Chamberlain's Bed of Stony Creek and forced Sheridan's men once again back toward Dinwiddie. Warren sent a brigade around behind Pickett toward Five Forks, and then marched his remaining troops overnight to join Sheridan's main force. Sheridan and Warren's combined force of twenty-two thousand men was nearly double the Confederates' strength, so Pickett once more retreated toward the safety of Five Forks, which Lee had directed him to "hold . . . at all hazards."

Under the misimpression that the Union attack would be delayed, Pickett and Fitzhugh Lee attended a fish bake on the afternoon of April 1. At 4:00 P.M., Warren moved his three divisions and many of Sheridan's dismounted cavalry troopers back across the Gravelly Run toward the White Oak Road, but they wheeled around three-quarters of a mile short of Pickett's line, which was farther west, nearer to Five Forks. Before Pickett and Lee returned from their picnic, however, Warren's men made up the gap and attacked the Confederate line from the north while Brig. Gen. George A. Custer's cavalry hit from the south.

Though protected by Col. Willie Pegram's artillery in the center of the line, the Confederates could offer only weak resistance, especially in the absence of their commanders. The Federal force swept across Ford's Road, to the north of Five Forks, and captured over thirty-two hundred prisoners, as Pickett's men fled into the nearby pine forest. Confederate brigadier general Montgomery Corse tried to cover the retreat, but chaos reigned until darkness ended the fight.

Total Federal casualties over the three days of action equaled only about 800, far fewer than the 4,444 Confederates wounded, killed, or captured.

The Confederate defeat at Five Forks, and the capture of the Southside Railroad immediately following on April 2, contributed to the Confederate withdrawal from Petersburg and the surrender of the Confederate capital at Richmond. The southern army could not sustain much more action.

Further Reading

Edwin C. Bearss. *The Battle of Five Forks.* 2d ed. (Lynchburg, Va.: H. E. Howard, 1985).

❧ Fleetwood Hills

See BRANDY STATION

❧ Fort Anne

New York (July 8, 1777) *American Revolution*

When Maj. Gen. John Burgoyne moved toward Albany after taking FORT TICONDEROGA as part of his invasion of the northern rebel states, some of his most advanced detachments were close on the heels of the slowest American units.

On July 7, 1777, Burgoyne sent Lt. Col. John Hill with about 190 men of the Ninth Regiment to chase a 150-man American detachment, under Col. Pierce Long, that had moved ahead of the British down a rugged wilderness road to within a mile of Fort Anne. Long and his men halted for the night and camped at the bottom of a narrow, wooded area between a creek and a steep hill. During the evening, a supposed American deserter came into Hill's camp and reported that there were one thousand Americans with Long. In fact, the "deserter" was a spy, who slipped away and informed Colonel Long of the British weakness.

Long had been reinforced with four hundred New York militia men under Col. Henry van Rensselaer, and, feeling in command of the situation, he ordered an attack for the next morning.

The Americans hit the British hard about 10:30 A.M., but Hill rallied his men to the top of the steep incline and kept up a hot fire for two hours. Just as his ammunition was running low, Hill heard an Indian war whoop in the distance and assumed it meant the imminent arrival of Indian allies. The Americans assumed the same, and they quickly disengaged and fled.

In fact, the war cry was a ruse—only one British officer appeared—but it was enough to chase away the Americans.

No reliable casualty figures were recorded for the brief battle.

Further Reading

Robert B. Roberts. *New York's Forts in the Revolution* (Cranberry, N.J.: Associated University Presses, 1980).

❧ Fort Beauregard

See PORT ROYAL SOUND

❧ Fort Beauséjour

Canada (June 4–17, 1755) *French and Indian War*

The French stronghold of Fort Beauséjour, located on the Missaquash River in Nova Scotia just opposite the British Fort Lawrence, fell easily to a British-American expedition in mid-1755, consolidating the hold of Great Britain on Nova Scotia and providing one of the few bright spots for the British during the early phases of the French and Indian War (known in its later incarnation as the Seven Years War). For many of the French-speaking inhabitants of the region, known as Acadians, the fall of Beauséjour was a disaster: they were expelled by the British and forcibly transported to Louisiana.

After the British took control of Nova Scotia following the end of King George's War, the French decided to build Fort Beauséjour to provide a buffer against renewed conflict. It was a large, impressive-looking structure, built along classic lines as a five-sided palisade, but in fact the buildings were never really finished, and the fortifications were in poor repair. In 1755, there were only sixty-six French regulars and about four hundred Indians manning the fort, under Capt. Louis Du Pont Duchambon de Vergor. The French plan was to recruit Acadians from the surrounding villages in case of a threat.

The British commander at Fort Lawrence, Lt. Col. Robert Monckton, learned of the weakness of the French, and, with the support of Gov. Charles Lawrence of Nova Scotia and Gov. William Shirley of Massachusetts, he set about planning and executing an expedition to take Fort Beauséjour. He was appointed co-commander with John Winslow, whom he met in Boston to organize their forces. They sailed to Halifax in early June and then on to Fort Lawrence with two thousand New England and Nova Scotian militia and 250 British regulars.

On June 4, Monckton crossed the river, brushed aside a small force of Acadians and Indians, and set up a siege around Fort Beauséjour. By mid-June the British siege trenches were close enough to the walls to begin bombardment. The French defenses were weak to begin with, and the Acadians who had come inside the walls were reluctant to fight, making Vergor's position untenable. On June 16, the British demolished one of the fort's casements with a mortar shell, and the demoralized French surrendered the next day.

Monckton took possession of the fort and rebuilt it as an important position that gave Great Britain control of the Chignecto Isthmus, which connect Nova Scotia to the Canadian mainland. The somewhat ambiguous role of the Acadians in the campaign as well as the subsequent refusal of many of them to swear allegiance to the British crown resulted in their forced removal to Louisiana (where their descendants became known as Cajuns). Monckton went on to distinction during the British campaign against QUEBEC in 1759.

Further Reading

Jacau de Friedmont. *The Siege of Beausejour in 1755: A Journal of the Attack on Beausejour* (St. John's, Nfld.: n.p., 1936); Dominick Graham. "The Planning of the Beausejour Operation and the Approaches to War in 1755." *New England Quarterly* 41 (1968): 551–566; and John Clarence Webster. *The Forts of Chignecto: A Study of the Eighteenth Century Conflict between France and Great Britain* (n.p.: author, 1930).

✍ Fort Carillon

See FORT TICONDEROGA (FORT CARILLON)

✍ Fort Caroline

Florida (September 20, 1565)
French-Spanish Colonial Wars

Fort Caroline, located on the south bank of the St. Johns River about ten miles from modern-day Jacksonville, was founded in 1564 by a group of French Huguenots (Protestants) led by René Laudonnière. Part of a larger expedition under the command of Jean Ribault, it became the first French settlement on the southern coast of America. The presence of Frenchmen was a direct and immediate challenge to the power of the Spanish, who until then had total control over the Caribbean and Florida. The fort—oriented to defend against attack from the river—was a strong triangular structure with moats along the sides and a large stone gate. The garrison was relatively small and suffered from a lack of supplies and support.

The Spanish could not tolerate this challenge, especially since Fort Caroline's position threatened the sea lanes used by the Spanish treasure fleets, and an expedition was launched under the command of Pedro Menéndez de Avilés in the fall of 1565 to eradicate the French post. Menéndez de Avilés was a skilled and experienced sailor and commander, who established his base at Saint Augustine, thereby founding a city. Meanwhile, Ribault

had returned from France in late summer, bringing fresh supplies for the garrison at Fort Caroline.

The first French-Spanish encounter was at sea, on September 4 resulting in an inconclusive engagement, from which the French fled back to the safety of their base and Menéndez de Avilés returned to Saint Augustine.

Laudonnière was ill, but the other French officers decided to organize an attack on the Spanish home base, hoping to catch the Spanish while they were unloading their ships. The French left a force of around 175 at Fort Caroline and sailed to the attack. Unfortunately for the French plan, Menéndez de Avilés was on the alert and got his own flagship under way as soon as the French ships appeared off Saint Augustine. When a storm drove the French ships southward down the coast, Menéndez de Avilés realized he had the advantage and led an attack force overland to Fort Caroline, coming up on the lightly defended landward side early in the day on September 20. The French defenders were too few, and they were easily defeated by the Spanish.

The French lost 135 men in the initial fight, and when the rest of the garrison, including Ribault, tried to return, they were captured and executed by the Spanish on the banks of the Matanzas River.

The disaster killed French hopes of establishing bases or settlements at the southern end of the American coast.

Further Reading

Charles E. Bennet. *Laudonnière and Fort Caroline: History and Documents* (Gainesville: University Presses of Florida, 1964); Eugene Lyon. *The Enterprise of Florida: Pedro Menéndez de Avilés and the Spanish Conquest of 1565–1568* (Gainesville: University Presses of Florida, 1976); and ———, ed. *Pedro Menéndez de Avilés* (New York: Garland, 1995).

✍ Fort Clinton and Fort Montgomery

New York (October 6, 1777) *American Revolution*

During the fall of 1777, Lt. Gen. Sir Henry Clinton was in charge of the main British base in New York City, while the commander in chief, Gen. Sir William Howe, campaigned in Pennsylvania. Clinton had ambiguous orders regarding British major general John Burgoyne's expedition from Canada, which was moving down the Hudson River valley. There were vague plans and even vaguer orders for him to support Burgoyne, if needed, by a thrust up the Hudson from New York City, but under what circumstances and in what force were not spelled out. When he learned Burgoyne might be in trouble (in fact, Burgoyne had been stopped in his tracks at First SARATOGA, which Clinton did not know), and since he had just been reinforced with fresh troops from home, Clinton assembled about three thousand men—British regulars, German mercenaries, and Loyalists—and marched north to take Forts Clinton and Montgomery, which guarded the river approaches to the vital Hudson highlands.

The twin forts were situated on the west bank of the Hudson about five miles south of West Point. Both were sturdily fortified on the river side, and Fort Montgomery was the anchor of a series of obstructions strung across the river to bar British warships. Fort Clinton, across a deep gorge from Montgomery, was designed to protect the latter. The topography was so rugged to the west behind the forts that the American defenders thought it unnecessary to secure that side.

The forts were manned by about six hundred New York militia and a sprinkling of regular Continentals. The overall commander—operating from Fort Montgomery—was New York governor George Clinton, who had recently been confirmed by Congress as a brigadier general, although he was innocent of military experience or training. Fort Clinton was commanded by Brig. Gen. James Clinton, the governor's brother and a competent soldier.

However uncertain he was about the overall British objectives, Sir Henry Clinton demonstrated firm professional skills in conducting his operation against the American forts. He sailed up the river and landed his men on the eastern shore at Verplanck's Landing, a tactic that drew troops out of the garrisons. Clinton then transported his men swiftly to the other bank of the river and moved them into position to attack.

He sent a force of around nine hundred regulars and mercenaries to circle through a pass in the rugged terrain and behind Fort Clinton. His other troops marched straight for the forts, brushing aside small American units sent out by Governor Clinton to delay the British approach.

By late in the afternoon of October 6, Sir Henry Clinton's forces were in position, and the double assault began.

Fort Montgomery was attacked by a mixed group of regulars, Germans, and Loyalists, commanded by Lt. Col. John Campbell of the Fifty-second Regiment. It overran the defenses relatively easily, chasing the governor and many of his men out of the fort and across the river. Lieutenant Colonel Campbell was killed in the brief, sharp fighting.

Across the gorge at Fort Clinton, the British and Germans had a more difficult time. The only practical approach was a frontal assault against strong defenses, but the troops attacked with trained skill and tenacity, and they took the fort, inflicting heavy losses on the American defenders. By nightfall, the British were in command of both Fort Clinton and Fort Montgomery.

Losses on both sides were significant: the Americans had 250 casualties, although more than half the defenders escaped; the British and Germans suffered around 300 killed or wounded, mostly during the assault on Fort Clinton.

After taking the forts, the British destroyed the river obstructions and sent a naval detachment to Kingston, New York, which was burned. But Sir Henry Clinton did not push on to link with Burgoyne, and under subsequent orders from Howe, he withdrew from the region and gave up occupation of both forts by the end of the month.

Further Reading

Robert B. Roberts. *New York's Forts in the Revolution* (Cranberry N.J.: Associated University Presses, 1980).

Fort Constitution

See FORT LEE

Fort Cumberland

Canada (November 7–29, 1776)
American Revolution

In a little-noticed campaign in 1776, overshadowed by the clash of armies at New York City, a small force of rebels attempted to capture this British outpost in Acadia, formerly known as FORT BEAUSEJOUR when it was the site of a colonial conflict in 1755.

The American effort was based on the relatively large number of transplanted New Englanders living in Acadia (modern-day Nova Scotia). Jonathan Eddy, formerly of Massachusetts and a veteran of the French and Indian War, along with a recent Scots immigrant named John Allen, led the attempt to take Fort Cumberland. Allen was promised help by the revolutionary government of Massachusetts but could muster fewer than two hundred men to lay siege to the British garrison, which had about an equal number of militia and local residents, under the command of Col. Joseph Goreham.

Eddy and Allen's men captured a sloop anchored nearby on November 7 and began attacking the fort—unsuccessfully—on November 13. A second attack on November 22 also failed, and a relief force from the large

British naval base at Halifax arrived soon after. A determined sortie broke the siege and scattered the American force; however, Goreham offered a pardon, and more than half the rebels returned to the fort and surrendered.

Further Reading

Ernest Clarke. *The Siege of Fort Cumberland, 1776: An Episode in the American Revolution* (Buffalo, N.Y.: McGill-Queen's University Press, 1995).

Fort Donelson

Tennessee (February 13–15, 1862)
American Civil War

Fort Donelson on the Cumberland River at the border of Tennessee and Kentucky was crucial to Confederate control of a wide swath of territory, from the Cumberland Gap to the Mississippi River, and holding it would allow a Confederate campaign into the key border state of Kentucky. In early 1862, the Union launched a drive to challenge Confederate power in the West by sending Brig. Gen. Ulysses S. Grant to take FORT HENRY on the Tennessee River and then move on to Fort Donelson. His victory at Donelson was the most important to date for the Federal cause in western states and propelled Grant to national prominence.

After easily capturing Fort Henry on February 6, Grant moved his fifteen thousand troops down the Tennessee and then back up the Cumberland (the two rivers ran parallel with each other at a distance of about ten miles) to assault Ft. Donelson. His river gunboat fleet, commanded by Flag Officer Andrew Foote, lagged behind when Grant's infantry took positions virtually surrounding Fort Donelson on February 12.

Donelson was a very well designed fort, consisting of a ring of strong earthworks and rifle pits that were positioned to protect two tiers of artillery batteries commanding the river. The fatal weakness, however, was human: the

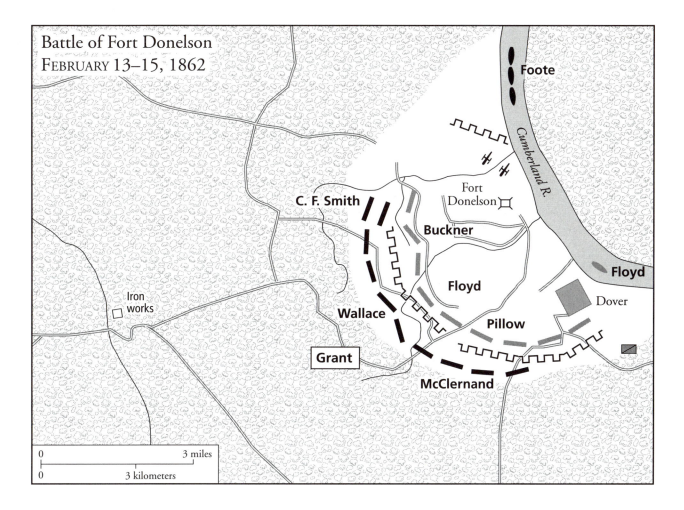

Battle of Fort Donelson
FEBRUARY 13–15, 1862

Confederate department commander, Gen. Albert Sidney Johnston (a man of ability himself), had placed not one but two of the South's worst generals in charge shortly before Grant appeared. The ranking commander was Brig. Gen. John B. Floyd, a dishonest former U.S. secretary of war who had no field experience and who owed his commission to political influence. His immediate subordinate was Brig. Gen. Gideon J. Pillow, an incompetent political appointee who had performed poorly as a general officer during the Mexican-American War. The only worthwhile Confederate general on the scene was Brig. Gen. Simon Bolivar Buckner, a West Pointer (and former classmate of Grant) who, despite a fine record from the Mexican war, was relegated to third in command. There were about twenty-one thousand Confederate troops in the garrison.

After investing the fort, Grant sent in probes under Brig. Gen. Charles F. Smith and Brig. Gen. John A. McClernand, only to discover that the Confederate lines were strong and unlikely to yield to direct assault. During the night, however, Flag Officer Foote arrived with the gunboats, and Brig. Gen. Lew Wallace appeared with twelve thousand Union reinforcements.

Foote tried a naval assault on February 14, sailing his fleet up to the fort's batteries and opening fire. The Confederate guns were too strong and the gunners too accurate, however, and Foote's gunboats had to withdraw. Foote himself was wounded by splinters, one of the gruesome hazards of fighting aboard wooden ships.

The next day, while Grant was consulting with Foote aboard ship, the Confederates launched an attack against the Union right, held by McClernand's men. For a while it appeared that the Confederates would be able to break through the Union lines and roll up part of the Federal army; however, the Confederate attack stalled, and Grant returned to take control of the battle. He ordered a Union counterattack all along the line, and by the end of the day he had restored the original positions.

At that point, the Confederate command disintegrated. General Floyd was afraid that if captured he would be indicted for stealing funds as a U.S. cabinet officer, so he turned command of Fort Donelson over to General Pillow and escaped by ship, with about two thousand Tennessee troops. Pillow had no more courage than Floyd; he relinquished command to Buckner and made his escape as well.

Buckner realized the futility of his position and asked Grant under what terms he would accept surrender. Ulysses S. Grant's reply became a classic: "No terms except an unconditional and immediate surrender." Buckner was stung by the demand, but he had no choice but to comply, surrendering to his friend on February 15.

The Union casualties numbered 2,832 killed or wounded. The Confederates lost about two thousand killed or wounded, but fifteen thousand became Federal prisoners at the surrender, and the South lost a large number of guns and supplies.

News of Grant's victory provided a much-needed boost to the Union cause, which had lost regularly to the Confederates in the East, and his no-nonsense demand for unconditional surrender provoked widespread admiration (he was promoted immediately to major general). He was ordered to pursue the campaign to dislodge the Confederates' hold on Tennessee.

Further Reading

B. Franklin Cooling. *Fort Donelson's Legacy: War and Society in Kentucky and Tennessee, 1862–1863* (Knoxville: University of Tennessee Press, 1977);———. *Forts Henry and Donelson—The Key to the Confederate Heartland* (Knoxville: University of Tennessee Press, 1987); and James J. Hamilton. *The Battle of Fort Donelson* (South Brunswick, N.J.: T. Yoseloff, 1968).

Fort Erie, First

Canada (August 15, 1814) *War of 1812*

After being defeated at LUNDY'S LANE in July 1813, the American army on the Niagara frontier withdrew to Fort Erie, on the eastern end of Lake Erie. Lt. Gen. Gordon Drummond, commander of the British army in Upper Canada, decided to follow and attempt to recapture the strategically important fort.

When Drummond arrived at Fort Erie in early August, he discovered that the Americans had been busy building a long wall, a line of log-strewn abatis, and a stone redoubt to guard their position. Instead of attacking head-on, Drummond brought heavy guns from FORT GEORGE and on August 13 laid siege.

By August 15, it was clear that the British weaponry was not effective against the fortifications, so Drummond ordered a three-column infantry attack on the fort. The attacks of the first two columns, led by Lt. Col. Victor Fisher and Col. Hercules Scott, respectively, failed because the American commander, Brig. Gen. Edmund P. Gaines, was well prepared for the British onslaught and the Americans mowed down the attackers before they could reach the fort.

The third column, commanded by Col. William Drummond, fought its way inside one of the fort's exterior bastions but struggled in vain for several hours to break through the fort's main stone wall. The battle ended when the powder magazine stored in the bastion unexpectedly exploded, instantly killing dozens of British soldiers.

The failed attack on Fort Erie cost the British heavy casualties. Lieutenant General Drummond's force lost 366 men killed and 539 wounded or taken prisoner. Both William Drummond and Hercules Scott were killed. The Americans inside the fort recorded eighty-four total casualties.

Lt. Gen. Gordon Drummond continued his bombardment of Fort Erie until he was attacked by Brig. Gen. Jacob Brown on September 7 (see FORT ERIE, SECOND).

Further Reading

David A. Owen. *Fort Erie: An Historical Guide* (n.p.: Niagara Parks Commission, 1986).

Fort Erie, Second

Canada (September 7, 1814) *War of 1812*

A month after his first assault on Fort Erie was repulsed on August 15, 1814 (see FORT ERIE, FIRST), British lieutenant general Gordon Drummond resumed his artillery bombardment of the American fort. Instead of waiting for reinforcements or another British infantry attack, American brigadier general Jacob Brown, still nursing wounds received at LUNDY'S LANE, ordered a preemptive strike against Drummond's batteries outside the fort.

Brown organized two attack parties, to be led respectively by Brig. Gen. Peter B. Porter and Col. James Miller, and called an extra one thousand militia volunteers to the fort. Drummond remained unaware of the American attack preparations, even as Brown's men cut a new trail through the forest directly toward one of his batteries.

The Americans took advantage of the element of surprise, attacking in a driving rain on the afternoon of September 7. Porter's men quickly captured a battery to the left of Drummond's line, then joined Miller's force to overrun a second battery, spiking the British guns at both. However, after a thirty-minute fight with Drummond's best troops at the remaining battery, Brown was forced to call off the attack.

American casualties totaled more than five hundred, and British totals were greater than six hundred.

Drummond gave up the attempt to capture Fort Erie and withdrew. Less than a month later, American forces destroyed Fort Erie as they retired into New York.

Further Reading

David A. Owen. *Fort Erie: An Historical Guide* (n.p.: Niagara Parks Commission, 1986).

Fort Fisher

(Terry's Expedition)

North Carolina (January 12–15, 1865)
American Civil War

Union major general Benjamin Butler had tried to destroy Fort Fisher, which protected Wilmington, North Carolina, in December 1864, by exploding the U.S.S. *Louisiana* in the harbor and landing troops near the fort, but his plan had been an utter failure. Fort Fisher's seventy-five heavy guns and more than six thousand defenders, commanded by Col. William Lamb, were a stubborn bulwark against Union advances into North Carolina and allowed supplies to continue trickling through the Union naval blockade to the ever-weaker Confederate army. Butler was relieved of duty after the fiasco, but the Union commander in chief, Lt. Gen. Ulysses S. Grant, remained determined to control North Carolina. He authorized Brig. Gen. Alfred H. Terry to lead a fresh attack against Fort Fisher just after the new year. The success of Terry's operation helped to bring about the end of the war.

For his expedition, Terry assembled a provisional corps consisting of the largest fleet of the entire war—58 ships with 627 guns—and 8,000 troops (including 2 African-American brigades). The force arrived at Fort Fisher from Bermuda Landing on January 12 and immediately began to bombard the Confederate earthworks. Rear Adm. David D. Porter, who had assisted Butler in his December effort and now commanded part of Terry's squadron, targeted specific points at the fort and was able to destroy almost all of its heavy guns during the two-and-a-half-day bombardment.

As the fort's defenses were being damaged, Terry gradually put his men ashore. On January 13, infantry dug into two lines opposite Maj. Gen. Robert Hoke's men, whom Gen. Braxton Bragg had sent to reinforce the Confederate force. Union brigadier general Newton Curtis's brigade took up a position to the west of the fort (Curtis's promotion to brigadier general took effect on the day of the assault). Once the mixed force was in place, on January 15, the main attack came. A total of twenty-two hundred sailors and marines (led by Capt. K. R. Breese) splashed ashore to the north of the fort, and though they made little progress in a frontal assault against the fort, they did draw attention away from a simultaneous army attack to the south side.

Bragg never ordered Hoke's Confederate division to attack, and the Union army troops faced no outside resistance as they rushed the fort. Curtis's brigade, covered by a small number of sharpshooters, hacked through the fort's palisades and captured the main parapet, as Col. Galusha Pennypacker's brigade moved out to the right. These and several other army brigades fought hand to hand inside the fort until the final Confederate resistance at Battery Buchanan was crushed around 10 P.M. and the fort was surrendered.

Federal forces took nineteen hundred Confederate prisoners inside the fort, though other Confederate casualty totals are uncertain. Both Colonel Lamb and Maj. Gen. William H. C. Whiting, who commanded Wilmington's overall defense, were wounded in the fight. The Union army reported 955 casualties, and the navy and marines a total of 686. Pennypacker and Curtis both received the Medal of Honor for their actions at Fort Fisher. On January 16, twenty-five more Union troops were killed when two drunken sailors set fire to thirteen thousand pounds of gunpowder inside the fort.

After the surrender of Fort Fisher, Union troops streamed onto Cape Fear, and a whole series of Confederate forts were abandoned. The Confederate vice president, Alexander Stephens, called the action "one of the greatest disasters which had befallen our Cause from the beginning of the war," and those who agreed with him began to press even harder for an end to the war.

Further Reading

Chris E. Fonielle. *The Wilmington Campaign: Last Rays of Departing Hope* (Campbell, Calif.: Savas, 1997); and Rod Gragg. *Confederate Goliath: The Battle of Fort Fisher* (New York: HarperCollins, 1991).

≈ Fort Frontenac

Canada (August 25–27, 1758)
French and Indian War

Situated at the head of the St. Lawrence River, and therefore commanding the head of Lake Ontario, Fort Frontenac was one of several important bases that allowed the French to control traffic and trade on the Great Lakes. When an expedition of British colonial troops seized the fort in mid-1758, it began a reversal of fortunes for the French and the beginning of the British ascendancy in the French and Indian War.

Although its location was crucial, the French had only a small garrison at Frontenac, not more than 110 soldiers, commanded by Pierre Payen de Noyan et de Chavoy. The main defense of the post relied on a flotilla of naval vessels, which turned out to be less than effective at this task. Perhaps the French had become slightly complacent after their great victory over the British at FORT TICONDEROGA in July 1758, for they certainly did not expect an attack in force on Frontenac.

The British expedition was the brainchild of Lt. Col. John Bradstreet, a soldier and entrepreneur of mixed Anglo-Irish and Acadian birth who had proven himself capable in moving men and materiel through the wilderness region of upper New York and the Great Lakes. He was also an adroit politician, managing to stay in favor through several changes of overall command in North America. He convinced Maj. Gen. James Abercromby to allow him to take a small army of colonial troops across Lake Ontario and attack Frontenac. Abercromby, who was responsible for the massive British defeat at Ticonderoga, agreed.

Bradstreet's force left Fort William Henry in mid-July, traveling by water on a fleet of bateaux (shallow-draft boats typical of the lakes region). He had twenty-five hundred colonial troops from New York, New Jersey, Massachusetts, and Rhode Island and only 150 regulars. In addition, Bradstreet's force included three hundred bateau men and forty Indian scouts (probably Mohawk). By August 21, he was at Oswego and ready to launch his attack across the lake.

On August 25, Bradstreet and his men rowed within sight of the fort. Fortunately for them, the French flotilla was completely unprepared: only two small ships were armed, and the majority lacked rigging and were unable to sail. Bradstreet landed his troops and seized an abandoned breastwork only 250 yards from the fort, a perfect place to site the siege guns that his men dragged ashore from the bateaux. His troops also set up another artillery position even closer to the fort and began to bombard the French, whose own guns could make but a feeble reply.

Within two days, the pounding had done its work—one shell set off an explosion in the French powder magazine—and de Noyan surrendered.

Bradstreet's expedition not only removed one of the more strategically important posts from French control but also seized a huge amount of supplies and munitions that were stored at Frontenac. All in all, it was a serious blow to the French, and it began a string of British victories.

Further Reading

William G. Godfrey. *Pursuit of Profit and Preferment in Colonial North America: John Bradstreet's Quest* (Waterloo, Ont.: Wilfrid Laurier University, 1982); Frederick A. Rahmer. *Dash to Frontenac: An Account of Lt. Col. John Bradstreet's Expedition to and Capture of Fort Frontenac* (Rome, N.Y.: n.p., 1973); and R. A. Preston, ed. *Royal Fort Frontenac* (Toronto: Champlain Society, 1958).

⚓ Fort George

Canada (May 27, 1813) *War of 1812*

Fort George, located at the meeting-point of the Niagara River and Lake Ontario, was the strategic key to British positions along the Niagara frontier in early 1813. American general Henry Dearborn and Commodore Isaac Chauncey designed an attack on the fort as part of a campaign against several positions along the Niagara, and the subsequent battle was one of the best-planned American victories of the war.

Fort George was defended by eleven hundred regular soldiers and militia commanded by Gen. John Vincent, who prepared for an attack when American artillery opened fire on the nearby town of Newark on May 24. Col. Winfield Scott, Commodore Oliver Perry, and Commodore Chauncey carefully planned the American approach—warships would bombard the fort from the lake, while Scott led an amphibious river landing behind the fort.

The plan began well with the assault on Fort George on May 27. Perry led the naval attack from the *Hamilton,* which along with four other schooners knocked out the fort's lake-shore defenses. Covered by the fire from the lake, the river landing was successful. The Scots Glengarries, sent by General Vincent to attack the first wave of Americans, were cut to pieces. A British counterattack, aided by militia and a company of African-American pioneers, temporarily pushed Scott's force back toward the beach, but soon the Americans' superior numbers and naval strength convinced Vincent to evacuate the fort.

The British suffered 52 killed, 44 wounded, and 262 captured in the battle, while the Americans lost only 39 killed and 111 wounded.

Scott wanted to follow the British south and attack, but his senior, Gen. Morgan Lewis, ordered him to remain at the fort. The capture of Fort George provided the Americans with a stronghold in the Niagara region and led directly to the Battle of STONY CREEK in early June.

Further Reading

Robert S. Allen. "A History of Fort George, Upper Canada." *Canadian Historical Sites* 2 (1974): 61–93; Margaret Coleman. *The American Capture of Fort George, Ontario* (Ottawa: Department of Northern and Indian Affairs, 1977); and Ernest A. Cruikshank. *The Battle of Fort George* (Niagara Falls, Ont.: Niagara Historical Society, 1904).

⚓ Fort Griffin

See SABINE PASS

⚓ Fort Henry

Tennessee (February 6, 1862) *American Civil War*

In early 1862, the Union launched an offensive in the West calculated to dislodge the Confederates from their strong line of positions across southern Kentucky and northern Tennessee. The first step was a movement against the river Forts Henry and DONELSON, located on the parallel-flowing Tennessee and Cumberland Rivers, respectively.

Fort Henry, separated from Fort Donelson by only about ten miles of intervening land, was an incomplete earthwork, located poorly on low ground and mounting seventeen cannon. The Confederate commander, Brig. Gen. Lloyd Tilghman, had evacuated all of his garrison troops, save for one hundred artillerymen.

The Union campaign against the fort was entrusted to Brig. Gen. Ulysses S. Grant, who had fifteen thousand troops and a force of four ironclad river gunboats and three wooden vessels, commanded by Flag Officer Andrew Foote.

As it turned out, Grant's infantry, slowed by a muddy route, never came into action against Fort Henry. Foote had moved upriver ahead of Grant's line of march, and, on February 6, his gunboats opened fire on the fort. After only two hours, Tilghman surrendered.

The Confederates lost five killed and eleven wounded. Foote's squadron had eleven killed and thirty-one wounded.

With the fall of Fort Henry, Grant had successfully completed the first step in the campaign.

Further Reading

Franklin B. Cooling. *Fort Donelson's Legacy: War and Society in Kentucky and Tennessee, 1862–1863* (Knoxville: University of Tennessee Press, 1997); and ———. *Forts Henry and Donelson: The Key to the Confederate Heartland* (Knoxville: University of Tennessee Press, 1987).

Fort Keyser

New York (October 19, 1780)
American Revolution

Col. Sir John Johnson, organizer and leader of Loyalist and Indian raids along the New York border during the American Revolution, set out from Oswego in September 1780 with a mixed force numbering perhaps fifteen hundred.

He had raided extensively along the Mohawk River valley for a month when New York militia general Robert Van Rensselaer began a pursuit with several hundred men. Van Rensselaer sent orders ahead to Col. John Brown, who commanded a small garrison at Fort Paris, in the village of Stone Arabia, telling Brown to attack Johnson's main column while Van Rensselaer caught up and came to his support.

In a brave but rather foolish move, Brown and his 130 men moved out and assaulted Johnson's column near the ruined Fort Keyser. Brown and forty of his men were killed in a brief battle, and Rensselaer was nowhere in sight.

Johnson was delayed long enough, however, for the New Yorkers to catch up with him later in the day at KLOCK'S FIELD.

Further Reading

Mark M. Boatner. *The Encyclopedia of the American Revolution* (New York: David McKay, 1966).

Fort Lee

(Fort Constitution)

New Jersey (November 20, 1776)
American Revolution

When the British took Fort Lee with scarcely a shot and seized a large store of flour and other goods, it was the final seal on the British campaign in New York in 1776.

The fort (previously known as Fort Constitution) had been established on the opposite side of the Hudson River from FORT WASHINGTON to help secure a line of obstacles that the Americans hoped would prevent the British war fleet from sailing up the river. The hope was futile, however, and British ships moved between the forts and up the waterway with impunity, making Fort Lee strategically worthless.

When British and German mercenary troops under commander in chief Gen. Sir William Howe captured Fort Washington in mid-November, the last bastion of American defense on Manhattan Island was gone. American commander Gen. George Washington had already withdrawn into New Jersey, and only the two-thousand-man garrison at Fort Lee remained in the path of the British. Howe was usually the most deliberate of generals, but he moved quickly to take Fort Lee. On November 20, he sent Maj. Gen. Lord Cornwallis and four thousand men across the Hudson to attack the fort. The Americans, however, under Maj. Gen. Nathanael Greene, learned of the approach of the British and evacuated Fort Lee in great haste, leaving behind tents, blankets, and a large supply of flour and other provisions. Greene personally returned to the fort and pried away several hundred stragglers, who may have been drunk on abandoned liquor. His men skirmished with the advancing British, and several were killed or wounded, but the bulk of the garrison got away to join Washington in the retreat across New Jersey.

Further Reading

Jacob Judd. *Fort Lee on the Palisades: The Battle for the Hudson* (Tarrytown, N.Y.: Sleepy Hollow Restorations, 1963).

Fort McHenry

Baltimore, Maryland (September 12–14, 1814)
War of 1812

After winning a significant victory at the Battle of BLADENSBURG and burning Washington, D.C., the British sought to cap off their Chesapeake campaign by capturing Baltimore, Maryland. Vice Adm. Alexander Cochrane's attack on Fort McHenry proved unsuccessful, however, and the British withdrew from the Chesapeake.

Cochrane, who commanded forty-five ships of various sizes, landed five thousand men and eight cannon at North Shore on September 11 and instructed Maj. Gen. Robert Ross to lead them overland to capture Fort McHenry. The commander of the group of fortifications at Fort McHenry, Maj. Gen. Samuel Smith (who was also at the time a U.S. senator), sent Brig. Gen. John Stricker with thirty-two hundred militia volunteers to stop Ross's advance.

Stricker took up a secure defensive position between North Shore and the fort on the morning of September 12. Meanwhile, Ross's men wasted time plundering local farms. Stricker sent an attack party under Maj. Richard Heath to take Ross by storm, and in the midst of a confused fight through the woods, Ross was killed. Col. Arthur Brooke took command of the British force and counterattacked. When Stricker withdrew a short distance and rallied his men, Brooke called off his men and made camp. In this initial engagement, the British lost 46 killed and 300 wounded, while the Americans suffered 24 killed, 139 wounded, and 50 captured.

On the same day, Vice Admiral Cochrane brought his ships through a difficult, narrow passage and into range of Fort McHenry. Maj. Gen. Samuel Smith had worked for over a year to strengthen the fort, and the time it took Cochrane to come into position was the first hint that his preparations might ultimately thwart British plans.

When Cochrane got sixteen ships within two miles of the fort, he began a long-range bombardment. He planned to wear down the American defenses with heavy fire while keeping a safe distance from the Americans' shorter-range batteries.

Major George Armistead's one thousand troops inside the fort weathered almost twenty-five hours of continuous pounding. During the extended bombardment, the British fired over fifteen hundred rounds of all kinds, including exploding shells and Congreve rockets. More than four hundred rounds hit the fort, but overall damage was light, and only one American gun was temporarily disabled. Five people were killed inside the fort and twenty-four wounded, but the Americans were nowhere near ready to surrender when Cochrane halted his fire, thinking the fort had been terribly damaged. As Cochrane's ships approached the fort, the Americans' heavy guns hit them hard and forced them to withdraw quickly.

By September 14, Col. Brooke's force had finally made its way to the outskirts of the fort and was prepared to attack in concert with an amphibious force that Cochrane promised to land nearby. Capt. Charles Napier sailed the frigate *Euryalus* to land the troops, but he became lost in a heavy fog and was caught by American fire from all sides. When Napier retreated, Brooke decided Cochrane's maneuver had been unsuccessful and withdrew his own men to North Point.

In the early hours of September 15, the British gave up their campaign against Baltimore. The American victory was henceforth celebrated by the poem "Defence of Fort M'Henry," written by Francis Scott Key, an American diplomat who had been detained on board a British ship. The poem was set to music as "The Star-Spangled Banner" and in 1931 became the American national anthem.

The failure of the British to capture Fort McHenry further lifted public morale already raised by the victory at the Battle of PLATTSBURG BAY. American success also stimulated negotiations to end the war.

Further Reading

Walter Lord. *The Dawn's Early Light* (New York: W. W. Norton, 1972).

Fort Mercer

(Red Bank)

New Jersey (October 22–November 21, 1777)
American Revolution

In the early fall of 1777, the British commander in chief Gen. Sir William Howe launched a seaborne expedition from his base at New York City and sailed up the Chesapeake Bay, landing a large army at Head of Elk. He then marched into Pennsylvania, twice defeated the main American army, under Gen. George Washington, and occupied Philadelphia, the rebel capital. However, Howe needed free navigation of the Delaware River in order to supply his army, and the way was barred by river obstacles defended by Fort Mercer at Red Bank, New Jersey, and FORT MIFFLIN, located opposite, on an island in the river.

Fort Mercer was a substantial earthwork fortification with fourteen guns and a garrison of four hundred Continentals from Rhode Island, under the command of Col. Christopher Greene. The landward walls had the additional protection of a ditch and log-strewn abatis. During the course of preparation for defense, the French volunteer officer Thomas Du Plessis consulted with Greene and suggested that the fort was too large to defend with so few soldiers; consequently, Du Plessis supervised the building of a new wall inside the existing north wall of the fort.

Howe believed the fort could be taken from the landward side, and he selected one of his experienced German mercenary officers, Col. Count Carl Emil von Donop, to lead the attack. Von Donop commanded a German jaeger corps of five hundred. To his own unit he added three battalions of grenadiers and a battalion of infantry, making an assault force of around two thousand men, all Germans.

On October 22, the Germans marched up to the fort and demanded its surrender, threatening to give no quarter if the attack proceeded. Greene rejected the demand—one that was particularly insulting since it came from a representative of the hated German mercenaries—and von Donop prepared to assault the fortifications.

The Germans attacked on two sides simultaneously. One column of grenadiers and infantry hit the north side of the fort, and von Donop himself led his jaegers and the rest of the detachment across the abatis and ditch to the base of the wall on the landward side. While all this took place, the defenders held their fire, allowing the Germans to approach. Von Donop's column discovered somewhat belatedly that the wall in front of them was too high to scale without ladders, of which they had none. As the attackers swarmed at the foot of the wall, Colonel Greene gave the order to fire, and his men poured down grapeshot and musketballs on the exposed Germans, breaking their ranks and killing and wounding many, including von Donop, who fell with a mortal wound. A second attack on the south wall met exactly the same fate.

The column attacking the north wall had a similar lack of success. The men stormed over the outer wall unopposed but discovered the second wall, built by Du Plessis, blocking their path. The American defenders caught the Germans in the gap and devastated them with withering fire.

The Germans lost between four hundred and five hundred killed and wounded in the futile attack. At least one hundred were captured after being stranded without cover at the base of the fort's walls. The Americans lost fewer than thirty.

Unfortunately for the Americans, however, Fort Mercer became untenable a month later, when the weaker Fort Mifflin fell to a heavy bombardment, leaving Fort Mercer vulnerable. Greene and his men evacuated the fort during the night of November 21, giving the British a free run up and down the Delaware.

Further Reading

Christopher Ward. *The War of the Revolution.* Vol. 1 (New York: Macmillan, 1952).

Fort Michilimackinac

See MACKINAC ISLAND

Fort Mifflin

Pennsylvania (October 10–November 15, 1777)
American Revolution

Fort Mifflin, along with FORT MERCER, anchored a formidable barrier across the Delaware River, designed to keep the British from sailing unobstructed into Philadelphia after Gen. Sir William Howe's land forces had seized the American capital in September 1777. If the forts could bar the river to traffic, the British would have a difficult time supplying their army.

Mifflin had been built on Port Island, close to the west bank of the river, and it was the smaller and less substantial of the two forts. Between Mifflin and Mercer, located on the New Jersey shore at Red Bank, the Americans had built a triple chain of submerged obstructions that were capable of tearing the bottom out of any British ship attempting to run past. But both forts had to be held securely if the river defenses were to work. Mifflin was not well built to withstand pounding from heavy guns, and its defenders, commanded by Lt. Col. Samuel Smith, numbered only 450.

Since the British had control of the region around the Pennsylvania side of the fort, they were able to place guns on Province Island and begin pounding Fort Mifflin on October 10. Nonetheless, the American defenders dealt the British flotilla a severe blow on October 23, when the *Augusta,* a sixty-four-gun ship of the line, and the sloop *Merlin* attempted to run through the obstructions. The fort's gunners drove both ships onto shoals and destroyed them.

Two and a half weeks later, the British made a more determined attack, increasing the number of guns on Province Island and bringing a heavy gun barge that mounted twenty-four-pounders to within a few dozen yards of the fort. The British bombardment was too much for the feeble fort, and it began to disintegrate under the pounding. Lieutenant Colonel Smith was wounded, and command passed to Maj. Simeon Thayer.

More British ships joined the attack, and on November 15 the surviving members of the American garrison evacuated the fort, fleeing across the river to Fort Mercer. More than two hundred had fallen.

Further Reading

Jeffery W. Dowart. *Fort Mifflin of Philadelphia: An Illustrated History* (Philadelphia: University of Pennsylvania Press, 1998).

Fort Mims

Alabama (August 30, 1813) *Creek War*

An attack by members of an aggressive, pro-British faction of the Creek tribe in Alabama killed several hundred American settlers at Fort Mims during the summer of 1813 and brought a long-brewing conflict to a head resulting in a series of battles known as the Creek War.

The Creek, a large and powerful southern tribe (one of the so-called Five Civilized Tribes), lived in Georgia and Alabama and by the time of the War of 1812 were divided into several factions. The more aggressive Red Sticks were generally pro-British and favored a policy of violence and war. The opposing White Sticks supported peace and leaned toward a pro-American position. The Red Sticks, the traditional warriors, were headed by William Weatherford (known as Lamochatte or Red Eagle), an able leader of mixed Creek and white ancestry. Weatherford and several other Red Sticks had been incited against American domination by a visit from the great Shawnee leader Tecumseh in 1811, and a contingent of Red Sticks had fought with the British at FRENCHTOWN in January 1813.

In August, Weatherford led one thousand Red Stick warriors against five hundred American settlers who had gathered at the weakly stockaded farm of Samuel Mims, at the confluence of the Alabama and Tombigbee Rivers. The Americans were poorly organized and led. The officer in charge, Maj. Daniel Beasley, showed little military skill and even less common sense. Despite warnings from black slaves (who had been outside the fort) that a large force of Creek was nearby, Beasley failed to post sentries and carelessly left the gates of the stockade open.

At midmorning on August 20, the Red Stick warriors emerged from the tall grass surrounding the fort to overrun the first defenders, killing Beasley in the process. Many of the Americans, including large numbers of women and children, managed to reach the farmhouse, but they were eventually driven out by fire arrows and killed on the spot, with only a handful escaping. The Creek spared most of the black slaves, but they were merciless with the white settlers.

Approximately four hundred Americans died at Fort Mims; fewer than thirty-six survived.

The fall of Fort Mims and the heavy death toll produced a demand for revenge and led directly to the government's mobilization of troops and the continued Creek War.

Further Reading

Angie Debo. *Road to Disappearance: A History of the Creek Indians* (Norman: University of Oklahoma Press, 1941); David S. and Jeanne T. Heidler. *Old Hickory's War: Andrew Jackson and the Quest for Empire* (Mechanicsburg, Pa.: Stackpole Books, 1996); and Frank L. Owsley, Jr. *Struggle for the Gulf Borderlands: The Creek War and the Battle of New Orleans* (Gainesville: University Presses of Florida, 1981).

Fort Montgomery

See FORT CLINTON

Fort Motte

South Carolina (May 12, 1781)
American Revolution

Despite losing all his major battles with the British in the South, American commander Nathanael Greene managed to win the campaign by wearing away at British strength and knocking off the small posts the British relied on to protect their lines of communication.

Fort Motte was one such strategic spot—a fortified house at the confluence of the Congaree and Wateree Rivers. The patriot owner, Rebecca Motte, had been ousted by the British, who built a stockade, a ditch, and a log-filled abatis to protect the 150 members of the garrison, commanded by a Lieutenant McPherson.

Lt. Col. Henry "Light-Horse Harry" Lee and Brig. Gen. Francis "Swamp Fox" Marion had combined forces to harass the British, laying siege to Fort Motte early in May. They had no artillery to batter the British to submission, and it appeared likely that Lord Rawdon would sooner or later appear to relieve the garrison, so time was at a premium. They attempted to dig approaching trenches, but that proved too slow.

Finally, when they saw Rawdon's beacon fires, the Americans took direct action. At Lee's instigation (and with Motte's approval), they fired blazing arrows onto the roof of the building while simultaneously launching an assault. The pressure was too much, and Lieutenant McPherson surrendered.

The only casualties were two Americans killed.

Further Reading

Christopher Ward. *The War of the American Revolution.* Vol. 2 (New York: Macmillan, 1952).

≈ Fort Necessity

(Great Meadows)

Pennsylvania (July 3, 1754) *French and Indian War*

The French and Indian War (an opening salvo in the worldwide Seven Years' War), broke out in 1754, when a very young George Washington, a lieutenant colonel of Virginia militia, clashed with French troops and their Indian allies at Great Meadows in what is now Pennsylvania. The question of which European power would control the rich lands and trading opportunities of the Ohio River valley motivated the fighting.

The French had previously expelled a small force of Virginians from a key position at the falls of the Ohio (modern Pittsburgh) and had begun to build a strong point called Fort Duquesne. Washington's orders from Gov. Robert Dinwiddie of Virginia were to take the fort.

The twenty-two-year-old Virginian had been appointed as joint commander of the expedition, which probably numbered around three hundred men, along with the older and more experienced Joshua Fry, but Fry was killed in a riding accident, leaving Washington in sole command.

He reached Grand Meadows in May 1754 and began work on a crude stockade and earthwork fortification, which became known as Fort Necessity. While most of the Virginians worked on the fort, Washington took forty men and carried out a surprise attack on a small party of French, killing most of them, including the commanding officer, Ens. Joseph Coulon de Villiers, sieur de Jumonville, on May 27. By mid-June, Fort Necessity was finished, and Washington began slowly to advance toward Fort Duquesne. But on June 29 scouts informed Washington that a large continent of French and Indian troops was on its way to attack him, led by Capt. Louis Coulon de Villiers, a brother of the officer killed by the Virginians in May. Washington retreated to Fort Necessity and waited for the French to attack.

Washington showed inexperience and lack of sound military understanding in his conduct of the ensuing fight. He arranged his men in a thin line outside the stockade in preparation for an attack across open ground, and when the French arrived just before midday, he allowed them to take sheltered positions unmolested in the ring of trees about sixty yards away. The Virginians were forced to take shelter in shallow trenches, as a dismal rain began. The French were well within range, and throughout the afternoon they kept up a steady musket fire that inflicted heavy casualties among Washington's ill-protected troops.

By evening, the Virginians were tired, hungry, wet to the bone, and discouraged by the continued heavy musketry of the French and Indians. When Coulon de Villiers called for a parley, Washington complied and shortly thereafter surrendered.

French losses were put at three killed and seventeen wounded, and the Virginians' at a combined one hundred.

Washington was forced to accept a humiliating set of terms specifying that the English would stay out of the Ohio River valley for the next eighteen months and remain east of the Alleghenies. He and his men began a miserable trek home after abandoning almost all their supplies and personal effects. The French, who destroyed Fort Necessity, were in control of the forks of the Ohio, and Coulon de Villiers went on to distinguished service during the ensuing war before dying of smallpox in 1757. Washington returned to the region a year later as part of Gen. Edward Braddock's ill-fated expedition (*see also* MONONGAHELA).

Further Reading

Robert C. Alberts. *A Charming Field for an Encounter: The Story of George Washington's Fort Necessity* (Washington, D.C.: National Park Service, 1975); John P. Cowan. "George Washington at Fort Necessity." *Western Pennsylvania Historical Magazine* 37, no. 3 and 4 (1955): 12–14, 92–111; William B. Hindman. *The Great Meadows Campaign and the Climactic Battle of Fort Necessity* (Leesburg, Va.: Potomac Press, 1967); John K. Lacock. *Washington's Military Expedition, 1754* (Farmington, Pa.: Fort Necessity National Battlefield Site, 1940); Henry M. Smith. "Fort Necessity." *Virginia Magazine of History and Biography* 41 (1933): 204–214; and Frederick Tilberg. *Fort Necessity National Battlefield Site* (Washington, D.C.: National Park Service, 1956).

≈ Fort Niagara

New York (July 6–July 25, 1759)
French and Indian War

The fort at the mouth of the Niagara River, which guarded the portage around Niagara Falls, was one of several important posts that had allowed the French to dominate trade and the expansion of settlement in the Great Lakes region. Its loss to the British during the French and Indian War marked another significant loss for French power and pointed toward the eventual hegemony of Great Britain in what had been French-dominated territory.

The fort was in bad repair at the beginning of the war, with the wooden stockade badly deteriorated, but the French rebuilt the fortifications along classic lines, constructing a very strong projecting earthwork section that transformed the place into a formidable base for French and Indian expeditions south into the Ohio River valley and for communications with Louisiana. The fort was defended by a six-hundred-man garrison under the command of Capt. Pierre Pouchot de Maupas.

The British expedition to take the fort was entrusted to Brig. Gen. John Prideaux of the Fifty-fifth Regiment. He was given command of a force of twenty-five hundred regulars and colonial troops, plus a contingent of one thousand Indians (principally Mohawk) under Indian superintendent William Johnson. The British sailed from Oswego and landed near Fort Niagara on July 6. Prideaux was unaware that the French had rebuilt the fort, and he had expected to be able to batter down easily a dilapidated wooden stockade. Instead, he was forced to set up a siege operation with inexperienced engineers and too-small cannon.

The British began to dig their approach trenches on July 10, and within the week they had placed a mortar battery within range and begun to bombard the French garrison. More batteries were added over the next two days, and the siege appeared to be on track. Then Prideaux was killed when he thoughtlessly stepped in front of a mortar as it was fired. A council of war among the remaining British officers elected the command to William Johnson, who held a king's commission in addition to the office of Indian superintendent and who had won the battle of LAKE GEORGE four years previously. The digging continued, and within five more days the British had guns firing on the fort from a distance of only one hundred yards.

When a siege operation had proceeded this far, the only hope was for the arrival of a relief column, but the British detected and routed a French column on the morning of July 24, sealing the fate of the garrison. The following day, Pouchot surrendered.

Fort Niagara was held by the British until well after the American Revolution, and it played a key role in frontier warfare for many decades.

Further Reading

Brian Leigh Dunigan. *Siege—1759: The Campaign against Niagara* (Youngstown, N.Y.: Old Fort Niagara Association, 1960); and ———. "Vauban in the Wilderness: The Siege of Fort Niagara, 1759." *Niagara Frontier* 21 (1974): 37–52.

⇜ Fort Pillow

Tennessee (April 12, 1864) *American Civil War*

Fort Pillow was a Confederate earthwork fortification on the Mississippi River that had been captured by Union forces during their river campaign in 1862. In the spring of 1864, it was the site of what became one of the more controversial engagements of the war. A large force of Confederate cavalry under Maj. Gen. Nathan Bedford Forrest (a former slave trader who, after the war, founded the Ku Klux Klan) overwhelmed a Federal garrison at Fort Pillow comprised in large part of black soldiers, then proceeded to murder both black and white prisoners.

Fort Pillow's original defenses had been modified by the Federals by the construction of an inner bastion, reducing the area a garrison needed to defend, but engineers had introduced a fatal defect: the walls of the inner defenses were extremely thick and lacked a slope on the outer wall, so that defenders could not fire down on attackers without exposing themselves completely. The defective design of the fort offered nearly as much protection to attackers as to defenders.

The fort was garrisoned in 1864 by 262 black soldiers and 295 white, commanded by Maj. Lionel F. Booth. A Union gunboat, the U.S.S. *New Era,* commanded by Capt. James Marshall, was stationed on the river to provide support.

General Forrest decided to attack Fort Pillow as part of his campaign into Tennessee during the spring of 1864, and he sent Brig. Gen. James R. Chalmers with twenty-five hundred troopers to invest the fort. The Confederate cavalrymen easily took the outer works and held commanding positions surrounding the fort when Forrest arrived at midmorning of April 12 to take charge himself. The *New Era* was unable to find a position on the river from which it could support the garrison, and the Union defenders soon discovered the defects of the inner bastion's design. They were at the mercy of Confederate sharpshooters, who kept up a steady fire into the fort, killing Major Booth, among others.

At 3:30 P.M., Forrest sent a demand for unconditional surrender to Booth's replacement, Maj. William F. Bradford. Bradford asked for an hour to consider a surrender, but Forrest allowed only twenty minutes. When Bradford declined, Forrest ordered an all-out assault that relatively easily swept over the walls and into the fort. Many of the defenders were driven to the river's edge, there to be shot or drowned.

Although Northern and Southern accounts disagreed and the facts have long been a matter of fiercely partisan dispute—involving as they do the reputation of Forrest and charges of racist murder—most historians now agree that the Confederates shot most of the black prisoners and Major Bradford after the surrender, in a genuine racial massacre. In total, the Confederates killed 231 Union defenders and wounded 100. Only 58 black soldiers survived as prisoners (in addition to 168 whites). Forrest lost fourteen killed and eighty-six wounded. Since he could not hope to hold the place, and his movements into Tennessee were really in the nature of a raid in force, Forrest withdrew from Fort Pillow on the evening of the same day—his only accomplishment having been to annihilate the garrison.

Immediately, Northerners charged there had been a brutal massacre, including such atrocities as burying prisoners alive and burning the wounded in their tents. A committee of the U.S. Congress investigated the affair, and Pres. Abraham Lincoln pressed for reprisals, but little could be done after the fact. Confederate officials and many Southerners since have claimed that the battle was no more than a one-sided victory, disregarding declarations by Confederate leaders before the attack that they sanctioned execution of free black Union soldiers and their white officers. Black Union troops in later battles raised the cry of "Remember Fort Pillow."

Further Reading

Albert Castel. "The Fort Pillow Massacre: A Fresh Examination of the Evidence." *Civil War History* 4 (1958): 37–50; John Cimprich and Robert C. Mainfort, Jr. "Fort Pillow Revisited: New Evidence about an old Controversy." *Civil War History* 28 (1982): 293–306; and Richard L. Fuchs. *An Unerring Fire: The Massacre at Fort Pillow* (Rutherford, N.J.: Fairleigh Dickinson University Press, 1994).

Fort Pulaski

Georgia (April 10–11, 1862) *American Civil War*

Fort Pulaski, built over a long span between 1829 and 1847 as one of more than twenty similar installations along the East Coast, was situated on Cockspur Island near the mouth of the Savannah River and thought to be impregnable, with seven-and-a-half-foot-thick brick walls and wide moats. Confederate troops from Georgia had seized the fort at the beginning of the Civil War, and nearly all Southern military authorities and commanders agreed that nothing could take the place short of a costly close-range assault. They were wrong.

When Federal forces took command of Tybee Island, one mile away, Fort Pulaski's commander, Col. Charles Olmstead, thought that he and his 384 men had little to fear. Conventional military wisdom held that no artillery, however large in caliber, could do much harm to

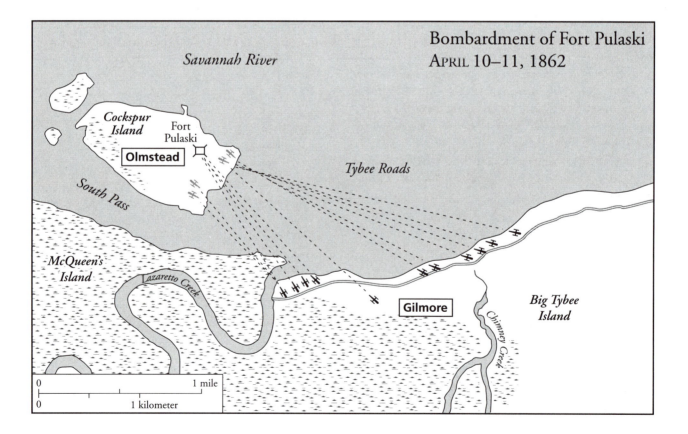

well-constructed masonry walls at that extreme range. Olmstead's own guns seemed more than adequate to counterbalance any possible Union attack.

Federal captain Quincy A. Gillmore, however, hoped to surprise the Confederates by using ten new rifled cannon—guns with machined spiral grooves inside the barrels that fired bulletlike projectiles accurately over a long distance. He supervised the laborious placement of his rifled guns, as well as smooth-bores and mortars, and prepared to batter down Fort Pulaski's walls. On April 10, he opened fire. The burrowing projectiles from the rifled guns had no difficulty reaching the fort, and immediately the thick mortared walls began to crumble under the barrage. The Confederates were astounded to see several breaches open under the impact of the bombardment. Their own guns were knocked out of action before doing any damage to the Union batteries, so the garrison was left helpless as the fort began to crumble. By noon on April 11, the Federal rifled cannon were ranging shots through breached walls onto the roof of the fort's main magazine. Olmstead had no choice but to surrender, which he did at 2:30 P.M.

The assault by the rifled cannon cost only one Confederate life, but in the space of a few hours it demonstrated the effectiveness of a new technology that rendered masonry forts completely useless.

Further Reading

Herbert H. Schiller. *Sumter Is Avenged: The Siege and Reduction of Fort Pulaski* (Shippensburg, Pa.: White Mane, 1995).

❧ Fort Ridgely

Minnesota (August 21–22, 1862) *Santee Uprising*

The Santee (Dakota), or eastern branch of the huge Sioux Nation (as the Dakota, Lakota, and Nakota were collectively known), rose up in a bloody struggle against white settlers and the thin frontier army during the Civil War resulting in a heavy death count from combat and its aftermath.

The Santee had signed a treaty in 1851 giving up their traditional lands and agreeing to move to a region on the Minnesota River, where the government promised to supply them with food through two local Indian agencies. Like almost all agents of the period, however, the men in charge were marked by both corruption and bad judgment. In 1862, while most white men of fighting age were off to the Civil War, the agents, Maj. Thomas J. Galbraith and Andrew J. Myrick, provoked the Santee by refusing to disburse food sup-

plies on schedule and insulting tribal representatives. Tensions escalated, and in August warriors of the Mdewkanton band of the Santee killed a family of settlers and then, led by a reluctant Little Crow (Cetan Wakan Mani), killed Agent Myrick and began a series of attacks on settlers and the meager forces stationed at Fort Ridgely, near the settlement of New Ulm. Capt. John S. Marsh, the commander of the fort, died in an ambush while trying to rescue refugees, leaving a handful of soldiers at the fort, commanded by Lt. Thomas P. Gere.

Gere was reinforced by Major Galbraith's company of volunteers, called the Renville Rangers, but the so-called fort, which lacked a stockade, relied mostly on the firepower of four artillery pieces and the skill of Sgt. John Jones, the only artillerist in the garrison. When Little Crow and a large war party arrived outside the fort on August 19, the defenders probably numbered no more than 180 men.

On August 21, after an attack on nearby NEW ULM, Little Crow attacked Fort Ridgely with four hundred warriors. The defenders held off the attack with grapeshot from their cannon, and a heavy thunderstorm swept in and blunted the Dakota's attack. The first assault petered out without a decisive blow from either side.

On the following day, Little Crow's Mdewkanton were joined by four hundred or so warriors of the Sisseton and Wahpeton bands of Santee, bringing the attacking force up to nearly eight hundred and giving them a better than four-to-one advantage in numbers. They again attacked the fort, trying unsuccessfully to set the buildings alight with fire arrows, but the defenders made good use of their superior firepower, and after a sharp struggle the Dakota broke off the attack and withdrew.

Casualties were not reported accurately for the assaults on Fort Ridgely, but overall deaths from raids and the battle were several hundred on each side. Some estimates claim as many as eight hundred settlers were killed altogether in the uprising.

The Santee were subsequently defeated (*see also* WOOD LAKE) and thirty-eight were hanged in a mass execution.

Further Reading

Kenneth Carley. *The Sioux Uprising of 1862* (St. Paul: Minnesota Historical Society, 1976).

❧ Fort Stanwix

New York (August 3–23, 1777) *American Revolution*

Part of Maj. Gen. John Burgoyne's grand scheme to invade New York and split the American states in 1777 was to send an expedition under Lt. Col. Barry St. Leger to advance through the Mohawk River valley and take the American stronghold at Fort Stanwix as a diversion.

St. Leger, appointed to the temporary rank of brigadier general, had two thousand men in his force, about one thousand of them Indian auxiliaries (mostly Mohawk) and three hundred or so Loyalists. The rest were British regulars and a handful of German mercenaries. The expedition moved much more easily through the wooded and watered region of upstate New York than did Burgoyne's main force, and St. Leger reached Fort Stanwix on August 3, after a relatively quick passage from Montreal.

The fort was held by 550 Continentals of the Third New York Regiment, commanded by Col. Peter Gansevoort and Lt. Col. Marinus Willet, who proved to be tenacious defenders. They had managed to repair the fort's walls and defenses before St. Leger arrived, and they were determined and able to withstand a considerable siege, especially since St. Leger lacked artillery sufficiently powerful to batter them to submission.

St. Leger surrounded the fort and called for surrender, but the Americans refused, especially when they saw the large numbers of Indians in St. Leger's force. They believed that surrender probably meant torture and death. Since he could not attack the walls directly, St. Leger settled in for a siege.

When an American relief force was stopped—mostly by St. Leger's Mohawk auxiliaries—at the battle of ORISKANY on August 6, the British chances should have improved, but a sally by Willet while the Indians were away destroyed the Indians' clothes and supplies. Coupled with the lack of plunder and the tediousness of siege warfare, the loss of their possessions began to sap the Mohawk's interest.

Meanwhile, the redoubtable Maj. Gen. Benedict Arnold had convinced his commanding general, Philip Schuyler, to send a relief force from the main American army camped near Stillwater. The decision was confirmed when Willet, who had sneaked out of the fort and through St. Leger's lines, arrived in Stillwater for a parley. On August 9, Arnold led a force of eight hundred New Yorkers and Massachusetts men on the road toward Fort Stanwix. When he arrived at the gates of the fort, on August 23, he discovered that St. Leger had abandoned the siege and disappeared into the woods, hastened by exaggerated rumors about the strength of Arnold's column.

Further Reading

John A. Scott. *Fort Stanwix (Fort Schuyler) and Oriskany: The Romantic Story of the Repulse of St. Leger's British Invasion of 1777*

. . . (Rome, N.Y.: Rome Sentinel, 1927); and William L. Stone. *The Campaign of Lieut. Gen. John Burgoyne and the Expedition of Lieut. Col. Barry St. Leger* (New York: DaCapo Press, 1970).

✍ Fort Stedman

Virginia (March 25, 1865) *American Civil War*

In March 1865, as Southern military resistance was crumbling, Confederate president Jefferson Davis ordered a last-ditch attack at Petersburg, Virginia, hoping that in the commotion Gen. Robert E. Lee would be able to escape and march to North Carolina to engage Maj. Gen. William T. Sherman. Lt. Gen. A. P. Hill was on sick leave, so Lee ordered Maj. Gen. John B. Gordon to command the assault. Gordon decided to attack Fort Stedman, on the outskirts of town, but despite initial success, his operation turned into a fresh Confederate disaster.

Gordon, a very able commanding officer and tactician, decided that Fort Stedman, which was only about 150 yards from the Confederate line, was a good target for attack, because if in response Lt. Gen. Ulysses S. Grant were to concentrate his forces to cover a nearby military railroad, Lee might be able to dislodge several divisions. At 4 A.M. on March 25, Gordon sent teams of pioneers to hack through the underbrush in front of the fort and clear the way for three companies of volunteers, who posed as deserters, and planned to overwhelm the fort at the last minute. Federal forces inside Fort Stedman were caught asleep; the fort and its batteries quickly fell under Confederate control.

Once additional infantry divisions began to spread out toward the Federal line, however, they faced stronger resistance and failed to reach their objectives. By 7:30 A.M., Confederate forces had been pushed back into the fort by Union troops and artillery fire from Fort Haskell and Batteries Ten and Eleven. Lee ordered Gordon to withdraw, but as his men were preparing to move back, Federal brigadier general John F. Hartranft sent a new division against them. Instead of braving a withering crossfire that cut them off from Confederate lines, almost nineteen hundred Confederates surrendered.

Union casualties totaled 1,044, and Confederate losses (including those surrendered) reached almost 3,500.

After the disaster at Fort Stedman, Lee began to plan for a total evacuation of Petersburg.

Further Reading

William H. Hodgkins. *The Battle of Fort Steadman . . .* (Boston: Author, 1889).

Fort Stephenson

Ohio (August 1–2, 1813) *War of 1812*

After failing to take the American position at Fort Meigs in July 1813, British major general Henry Proctor decided to attack Fort Stephenson, on the Sandusky River. On August 1, Proctor's regulars and his Indian allies, part of Tecumseh's pro-British confederacy, surrounded the fort, which occupied a strategic position below Detroit.

U.S. major general William Henry Harrison wanted to abandon Fort Stephenson and had left it held only by Maj. George Croghan's two companies of artillerymen. Croghan refused to surrender to Proctor and settled in for a fight, despite the fact that his only artillery piece was an eighteenth-century French cannon known as "Old Betsy."

Proctor bombarded the Americans on August 2, but the fort sustained little damage. During the afternoon, Proctor determined to take the fort by storm. Lt. Col. William Short led a frontal attack, but his ill-equipped infantrymen and Indian warriors could neither climb nor cut through the fort's outer walls. The Americans answered their advance with grapeshot from "Old Betsy." After half an hour, the British withdrew, though the Indians wanted to keep fighting.

The British suffered heavy casualties for such a small engagement: twenty-six killed, forty-one wounded, and around thirty taken prisoner. The Americans lost only one killed and seven wounded.

The attack on Fort Stephenson ended the British offensive in the Lake Erie region and increased Indian dissatisfaction with British command. Proctor's military reputation suffered, but Croghan was promoted to brevet lieutenant colonel at the young age of twenty-one.

Further Reading

Bruce Bowlus, "A 'Signal Victory': The Battle for Fort Stephenson, August 1–2, 1813." *Northwest Ohio Quarterly* 63 (1991): 43–57.

Fort Sumter

South Carolina (April 12–14, 1861)
American Civil War

Fort Sumter was the most important Federal military establishment in any of the seven states that had seceded from the Union. Pres. Abraham Lincoln's resolve to resist secession and Federal attempts to resupply Fort Sumter's

defenders led to a conflict, which became the opening battle of the four-and-a-half-year American Civil War.

Fort Sumter, an imposing pentagonal structure with forty-foot-high walls, was built on an artificial island at the mouth of Charleston Bay. It was intended to supplement Fort Moultrie, on Sullivan's Island, which had played an important role in the defense of CHARLESTON in 1776. Construction on the fort began in 1829, but it was still incomplete on December 26, 1860, when Maj. Robert Anderson moved his eighty-four U.S. soldiers there to escape the South Carolina militia, which was threatening to surround Fort Moultrie. Upset over Lincoln's election as president and fearful that the federal government would end slavery, South Carolina had seceded from the union on December 20, leaving Anderson, who was a native Southerner but loyal to the union, effectively in hostile territory.

In January, the state of South Carolina, now a leader of the rapidly forming Confederate States of America, built batteries in Charleston Harbor that targeted Fort Sumter from several surrounding points. Though outgoing U.S. president James Buchanan still sought compromise over secession, he decided to maintain the fort and to reinforce Anderson with two hundred additional soldiers and supplies. A federal supply ship, *Star of the West,* was fired upon and turned away, however, when it attempted to enter the harbor on January 9, 1861. Anderson did not open fire, but the stage was set for future conflict.

When Lincoln was inaugurated president in March, he announced his intention to hold Fort Sumter as a bastion of federal power in the heart of the Confederacy, though Gen. Winfield Scott and many cabinet members argued that the fort was too costly to defend. In the meantime, Major Anderson's men were running critically low on food and supplies. Lincoln sent supply ships and warships to the mouth of Charleston Harbor, and on April 6, 1861, he notified Gov. Francis Pickens that the warships would attack only if the peaceful resupply mission was interfered with.

Brig. Gen. P. G. T. Beauregard, the commander of Confederate forces in Charleston Harbor, notified Anderson on April 10 that he had been ordered to secure evacuation of the fort, or he would have to attack. When Anderson replied that he would evacuate by April 15 unless he was resupplied, Beauregard responded that he would be forced to fire on Fort Sumter on April 12.

The resupply mission was unsuccessful, and Beauregard opened fire on the fort at 4:30 A.M. on April 12. Confederate batteries trained eighteen mortars and thirty heavy guns on the fort, which was underarmed, with only forty-eight guns. Capt. Abner Doubleday ordered the first return shot at around 7:30 A.M., and a thirty-three-hour fire-fight ensued, during which Confederate guns fired four thousand rounds and the fort answered with one thousand more.

By afternoon of the first day of the fight, a lack of ammunition had reduced Fort Sumter's firepower to just six guns, and parts of the fort had been set afire by Confederate hot shot. More hot shot was poured into the fort on April 13, which caused the fires to spread disastrously. At around 1:30, the flagstaff was shot away, and eventually Anderson decided he must surrender.

On April 14, Anderson lowered the Stars and Stripes (from a newly improvised flagstaff) and evacuated his troops. The only federal soldier killed in Fort Sumter, Pvt. Daniel Hough, died when a gun exploded during a one-hundred-gun salute to accompany the surrender.

Total Union casualties totalled eleven men, and only four Confederates were wounded.

Despite these moderate casualty totals, the bombardment of Fort Sumter began the bloodiest war in American history. Northern resistance to secession was galvanized by the loss of Fort Sumter, and both sides mobilized for war. Fort Sumter would not become a federal fort again until April 1865, when Robert Anderson supervised the raising of the original American flag.

Further Reading

Richard N. Current. *Lincoln and the First Shot* (Chicago: Waveland Press, 1990); Webb B. Garrison. *Lincoln's Little War* (Nashville, Tenn.: Rutledge Hill Press, 1997); Robert Hendrickson. *Sumter, The First Day of the War* (Chelsea, Mich.: Scarborough House, 1990); Maury Klein. *Days of Defiance: Sumter, Secession, and the Coming of the Civil War* (New York: Alfred A. Knopf, 1997); Roy Meredith. *Storm over Sumter: The Opening Engagement of the Civil War* (New York: Simon and Schuster, 1957); and W. A. Swanburg. *First Blood: The Story of Fort Sumter* (New York: Charles Scribner's Sons, 1957).

Fort Texas

See CAMP TEXAS

Fort Ticonderoga

(Fort Carillon)

New York (July 8, 1758) *French and Indian War*

As if to complete the frustration of their efforts during the first years of the French and Indian War, the British launched a massive but unsuccessful assault on the French fortress of Carillon (known subsequently as Fort Ticonderoga), located at the key juncture of Lake Champlain and Lake George.

The huge fortress had been built by the French in 1755 and had served as the point of departure for Gen. Louis-Joseph de Montcalm's expedition that destroyed the British post at FORT WILLIAM HENRY in 1757. French control of Ticonderoga was a constant threat to all of upper New York and even the Hudson River valley, so the British government directed the new commander in North America, Maj. Gen. James Abercromby, to organize a campaign to capture the fort.

Abercromby was, unfortunately, a poor commander with few battlefield skills, as events would prove. His second in command, Lord Howe, was an extremely capable man, but he was killed in an ambush before reaching Ticonderoga, leaving Abercromby to face Montcalm. The British commander assembled the largest field force seen in North America prior to the Civil War, and sailed on July 5, 1758, with nearly fifteen thousand men, including a large contingent of British regulars as well as such specialized units as the recently formed Rogers's Rangers and about nine thousand colonial troops.

When they arrived at Ticonderoga, they confronted a fortress with massive walls and well-engineered corner bastions that contained heavy guns. In addition, Montcalm had built a wooden wall and a wide abatis (a ditch strewn with sharpened logs) in advance of the main walls as a further obstacle to attackers. Nonetheless, Abercromby's field artillery was heavy enough to have destroyed the wooden obstacles and made serious inroads against the walls had it been employed in the usual fashion of European siege warfare. For some reason, however, Abercromby left his artillery to the rear and ordered a series of disastrous frontal assaults against the French defenses.

Beginning early in the afternoon, the British sent column after column marching up to the abatis and wooden wall under a withering fire from the muskets of the defenders behind the main wall and the guns of the fort. Despite reckless and resolute courage, the British had no chance, not even the elite regulars of the Black Watch Regiment. When a weak attempt at a flank attack was shattered, the end was in sight for the British, although they continued to attack and a handful of men even got over the main walls before being bayoneted by the French. That evening the British gave up and began a retreat back the way they had come, leaving the field in front of the fortress strewn with bodies. Abercromby's army lost a reported 1,900 casualties during the afternoon, the French only 377.

While they reigned supreme for the moment, losses elsewhere rendered Carillon of little use to the French within a year.

Further Reading

Edward P. Hamilton. *Fort Ticonderoga: Key to a Continent* (Boston: Little, Brown, 1964); and Douglas E. Leach. *Arms for Empire: A Military History of the British Colonies in North America, 1607–1763* (New York: Macmillan, 1973).

≈ Fort Ticonderoga

New York (May 10, 1775) *American Revolution*

Only three weeks after the beginning of armed hostilities at LEXINGTON AND CONCORD, American rebels captured the British fort at Ticonderoga, New York, at the southern narrows of Lake Champlain. The nearly bloodless seizure was important to the overall American cause, since it captured a considerable cache of artillery along with the fort, but the manner and style of the assault on the British stronghold demonstrated the confusion and military amateurism that infected many of the colonists' first efforts at waging war.

Ticonderoga was a classically designed fort, built by the French in 1755 to guard Canada from invasion from the south, but it had been allowed by the British to fall into sad disrepair and was garrisoned by a force of only about forty soldiers and their dependents under the command of Capt. William De la Place.

There was no central direction of American effort in the first weeks after Lexington and Concord, so the planning of an expedition against Ticonderoga was fragmented, the desirability of seizing the fort having occurred to several people at the same time. One project came from the Connecticut Assembly, which set afoot a plan to seize Ticonderoga with a small force built around the so-called Green Mountain Boys, who were a semiorganized local militia from the Hampshire Grants (the eventual state of Vermont) led by Ethan Allen. By May 7, Allen had gathered about two hundred men and was positioned a few miles from Ticonderoga.

While this was going on, the Massachusetts Committee of Safety formed its own plan to attack the fort by giving a colonel's commission to a Connecticut merchant, Benedict Arnold, who had gone to Cambridge from his home in New Haven soon after Lexington and Concord. He was given the charge to recruit a force of volunteers and to take the fort. When Arnold heard of the Connecticut project, he left others to recruit and went alone to meet Allen. Finding Allen's camp on May 9, Arnold demanded to be given command of the expedition. Allen and his men refused, although they allowed Arnold to accompany them on the assault planned for the next day.

The Americans hoped to take the British garrison by surprise. When enough boats for the entire force failed to arrive, Allen and Arnold crammed eighty-three men into two scows before dawn and rowed for the fort. A rainstorm helped cover their movements, and the Americans landed undetected at the foot of the south wall and proceeded to rush into the fort, taking the sleeping garrison completely unprepared: the only shot attempted was a misfire by a British sentry. Allen beat a second sentry on the head with the flat of his sword and demanded to be taken to the officers' quarters.

When Allen and Arnold reached the top of the stairs leading to the barracks, Allen pounded on the door and demanded that the British come out. Lt. Jocelyn Feltham, the sleepy second in command, opened the door only half dressed and asked what was going on. According to an account he wrote much later, Allen maintained he took possession of the fort "in the name of the Great Jehovah and the Continental Congress"—others present at the time failed to mention anything but Allen's crude exclamations. Whatever was said, commander De la Place appeared and agreed to surrender.

Most important was the capture of a train of more than seventy heavy guns, crucial articles of war hitherto missing from the American arsenal. Eventually the guns of Ticonderoga were dragged across country to Boston and used by Gen. George Washington to impel the British to evacuate the city.

Further Reading

Edward P. Hamilton. *Fort Ticonderoga, Key to a Continent* (Boston: Little, Brown, 1964).

≈ Fort Ticonderoga

New York (July 2–5, 1777) *American Revolution*

The old French fort at Ticonderoga became the focus of British and American strategy during the early stages of Maj. Gen. John Burgoyne's 1777 invasion from Canada, with the British taking the key position with a minimum of difficulty.

The Americans had held Ticonderoga since its seizure early in the war by Ethan Allen and Benedict Arnold (*see* FORT TICONDEROGA). Following the defeat of the American army at QUEBEC early in 1776 and the subsequent retreat southward, the fort had become one of the principal American bases, with considerable symbolic importance. It was defended by almost three thousand men, both Continentals and militia, under the command of Maj. Gen. Arthur St. Clair, and some steps had been taken to improve the defenses, which had fallen into almost

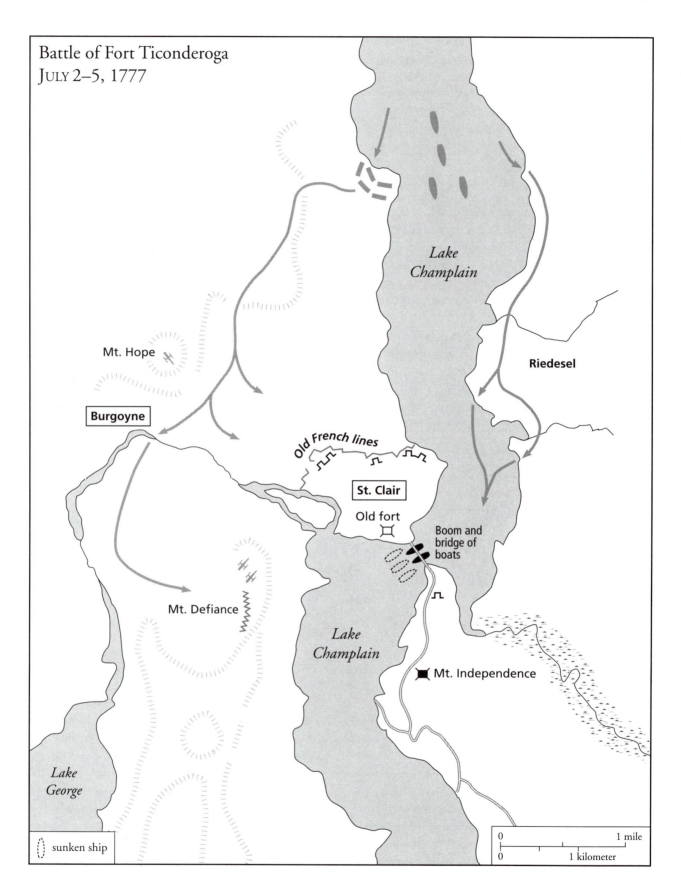

Battle of Fort Ticonderoga
JULY 2–5, 1777

Lake
Champlain

Mt. Hope

Riedesel

Burgoyne

Old French lines

St. Clair

Old fort

Boom and
bridge of
boats

Mt. Defiance

Lake
Champlain

Mt. Independence

Lake
George

sunken ship

0   1 mile

0   1 kilometer

complete disrepair since the French and Indian War. Still, the position was inherently weak unless there were enough troops and artillery to fortify the surrounding high ground. St. Clair had some men on Mount Hope to the northwest of the main fort and at Mount Independence to the southeast, across the lake, but he had no forces to the southwest on Mount Defiance, which loomed close enough to the fort to allow commanding artillery fire if the British could get guns to the summit.

Against the Americans, Burgoyne brought an overwhelming force—close to ten thousand men in all, including large numbers of British Army regulars and well-trained German mercenaries—that was just setting out on a mission to split the rebellion in two. As he approached Ticonderoga, Burgoyne sent Maj. Gen. Baron Riedesel with the German corps across the lake to the eastern shore to threaten Mount Independence. On July 2, the main British force marched up to Mount Hope, which the Americans abandoned with no resistance after burning their works. The British then advanced to within sight of the main fortifications, drawing a great barrage of musket and cannon fire, which had almost no effect. Slowly it dawned on St. Clair that he faced a huge, well-equipped British army. On July 3, the British placed guns on Mount Hope and began to bombard the American positions. The following day, Burgoyne sent engineers to scout Mount Defiance and decided to build a crude road to the top and mount artillery there. By late on July 5, four guns were in place and ready to open fire.

Observing the British preparations on Mount Defiance, St. Clair decided that his position was hopeless, and he ordered a stealthful evacuation across a flimsy bridge to the eastern shore of the lake, hoping to escape Burgoyne. His subordinates proved incompetent, and many of his men drank themselves to incapacity during the evacuation, but the bulk of the American troops got away, with Burgoyne's men in close pursuit.

Further Reading

Edward P. Hamilton. *Fort Ticonderoga, Key to a Continent* (Boston: Little, Brown, 1964).

Fort Ticonderoga

New York (September 18, 1777)
American Revolution

Although he had easily taken Fort Ticonderoga from the Americans in July 1777 (*see* FORT TICONDEROGA, July 2–5, 1777), British general John Burgoyne had perilously

extended his line of supply as he marched down the Hudson River toward his goal of attacking Albany. In September, a fifteen-hundred-man American detachment under Col. John Brown sneaked in behind Burgoyne and raided Ticonderoga.

Brig. Gen. William Powell, in command at Fort Ticonderoga, had about nine hundred men, but he had grown careless, assuming the war had moved far away, and he failed to post adequate outlying guards. The American attack force was able to reach Ticonderoga and reconnoiter undetected for two days.

At dawn on September 18, the Americans attacked, easily seizing all the posts surrounding the fort itself on the western side of Lake Champlain. Powell was secure inside the walls of the old fort, however, since Brown's artillery was too weak to batter a way in. After four days of firing his small field pieces, Brown withdrew.

While the material gain from the raid was slight, the bold move gave a boost to the troops of the main American army lying in wait for Burgoyne at SARATOGA.

Further Reading

Edward P. Hamilton. *Fort Ticonderoga, Key to a Continent* (Boston: Little, Brown, 1964); Richard P. Northey, "The Letters of Colonel Samuel Johnson of Andover Relating to an Expedition in September 1777 to Recapture Fort Ticonderoga." *Essex Institute Historical Collections* 123, no. 3 (1987): 287–95.

Fort Wagner

(Battery Wagner)

South Carolina (July 10–11 and 18, 1863)
American Civil War

In a bid to gain access to Charleston, South Carolina, in July 1863, Union forces attacked Fort Wagner, a sand and palmetto-log fortification on Morris Island, less than two miles from FORT SUMTER. The second of two bloody attacks became renowned as the first engagement of the Massachusetts Fifty-fourth, a regiment comprised of African-American soldiers, who took the opportunity at Fort Wagner to prove their battle-worthiness to skeptical Union commanders. The battle achieved little in military terms, but symbolically it has remained vastly important.

The first Union assault against Fort Wagner came on July 10, when Brig. Gen. George C. Strong's brigade established a position on the southern part of Morris Island. Confederate brigadier general William Taliaferro, in command of the fort, prepared to resist any Federal attack. On July 11, Strong pushed his men across the wetlands and beach in a frontal assault against the fort, but the attack was easily repulsed.

Federal artillery pounded the fort in preparation for the second attack on July 18. Col. Robert Gould Shaw, the son of prominent white Boston abolitionist parents, led the Massachusetts Fifty-fourth in the dawn attack. Although raked by heavy musket and rifle fire, the men of the Fifty-fourth charged onto the parapet, followed by wave after wave of Federal reinforcements from Strong's brigade. Though several Federals did break into the fort, they were eventually repulsed.

The Union forces who had charged the strong Confederate position suffered extremely heavy casualties. The Fifty-fourth lost fully one-quarter of its men, and only one regimental commander from Strong's brigade escaped unscathed. Both Strong and Shaw were killed. Altogether Union casualties totaled 1,515, while the Confederates lost only 174 men.

The assaults on Fort Wagner accomplished very little (the Confederate forces abandoned the position in September). The Massachusetts Fifty-fourth went on to prove its bravery on still other battlefields, and Sgt. William H. Carney, the regiment's color-bearer, became the first African American to receive the Medal of Honor, bestowed for his actions at Fort Wagner.

Further Reading

Peter Burchard. *"We'll Stand by the Union": Robert Gould Shaw and the Massachusetts Regiment* (New York: Facts On File, 1993); Luis F. Emilio. *A Brave Black Regiment: History of the Fifty-fourth Regiment of Massachusetts Volunteer Infantry, 1863–1865.* 3d ed. (Salem, N.H.: Ayer, 1990); and Stephen R. Wise. *Gate of Hell: Campaign for Charleston Harbor, 1863* (Columbia: University of South Carolina Press, 1994).

❧ Fort Walker

See PORT ROYAL SOUND

❧ Fort Washington

New York (November 16, 1776)
American Revolution

Gen. Sir William Howe's 1776 campaign to take New York as his main base of operations against the American rebels culminated in the capture of Fort Washington. His victory was a nearly crushing blow to the Americans because of his large haul of prisoners and war matériel.

After scoring a victory on LONG ISLAND and hurting the Americans badly at HARLEM HEIGHTS and WHITE PLAINS, Howe had chased Gen. George Washington and the main American army to the north end of Manhattan Island. He had bypassed the American stronghold at Fort Washington, but by mid-November, with Washington apparently in retreat into New Jersey, Howe was ready to turn his attention back to the fort.

Fort Washington was built on the eastern bank of the Hudson River, across from corresponding FORT LEE, on the New Jersey side, and was intended to be the anchor for an impassable obstruction to British navigation up the river, but the British warships had no trouble from the beginning of the campaign in running past the obstacles and the forts. Thus, Fort Washington had almost no military purpose throughout the New York campaign, but the American high command failed to understand this point and regarded the fort as a major asset to be defended to the last.

The fort seemed, on cursory examination, to be formidable: it was sited atop a high cliff over the river and surrounded by what appeared to be defensible outposts. The fort itself, however, was not much more than an impressively high five-sided earthwork, with few of the classic design elements or permanent fortifications that might have allowed the defenders to withstand a siege. There were no buildings, for example, inside the fort—no stores or barracks—and no source of drinking water closer than the river itself.

Col. Robert McGaw, one of the builders of the fort, was in command of the garrison, which comprised around twelve hundred men, mostly regulars from several state Continental regiments. Before the British assault, he received about seventeen hundred reinforcements. McGaw decided to disperse his defenses to nearby outposts: he positioned Maryland and Virginia riflemen under Col. Moses Rawlings on Cox Hill, to the north; Pennsylvania militia under a Col. Baxter at Laurel Hill, to the east; and a large contingent under Lt. Col. Lambert Cadwalader in the old fortifications at Harlem Heights, to the south.

Against these defenders, General Howe brought nearly three times the number of men. He devised a complex, three-prong scheme of attack. He moved his army by barge on the Hudson and Harlem Rivers, and by November 15, he was in position. The traditional call for surrender was made, and McGaw declined. The next morning, Howe ordered three thousand of his German mercenaries under the command of Lt.

Gen. Baron Wilhelm von Knyphausen to begin the main assault from the north of the fort. From the south, Gen. Lord Percy led a force of two thousand mixed British and German regiments against the positions held by Cadwalader. A smaller force, under the general command of Maj. Gen. Lord Cornwallis, crossed the Harlem and prepared to attack from the base of Laurel Hill. Part of Cornwallis's detachment was the Forty-second Highlanders (the Black Watch), under Lt. Col. Thomas Sterling, who were to make a feint toward the south.

As was usual with three-pronged attacks in difficult terrain, there were delays and miscues in moving all the parts of the British assault force into place, and the American defenders aggressively contested the movements. Lord Percy attacked Cadwalader, while Colonel Sterling's diversion turned into a hot fight with Baxter's Pennsylvanians. Cornwallis wisely seized the initiative and reinforced the Forty-second until this latter fight became one of the focal points of the battle. Sterling's unit took severe casualties but finally pushed Baxter out of his defensive position and back toward the fort, opening Cadwalader's flank to attack. To the north, Knyphausen's Germans had a very difficult time advancing in rough, wooded terrain against effective American artillery fire, but the regiment of Col. Jacob Rall finally scattered the defenders, who withdrew inside the walls of the fort. By early afternoon, the American plan had collapsed and all the troops were crowded into the fort, with no food, water, or shelter. Colonel McGaw surrendered at 3:00 P.M., and his men marched out as prisoners of war.

The overall American loss was immense. Washington (who had rowed across the Hudson to the fort during the battle but could do nothing and returned unscathed) lost his last foothold on the New York island; worse was the loss of nearly three thousand troops who had been captured—most faced a horrible fate aboard prison hulks in New York harbor—and much of the American supply of guns, ammunition, and equipment. American casualties were never accurately reported, but there were probably around fifty killed and two hundred wounded. The British paid for their victory with 458 killed and wounded, about three-fourths of these among the Germans.

Further Reading

Charles B. Flood. *Rise, and Fight Again: Perilous Times along the Road to Independence* (New York: Dodd, Mead, 1976).

Fort Watson

South Carolina (April 15–23, 1781)
American Revolution

As he maneuvered against the main British army of Lt. Gen. Lord Cornwallis, American commander Maj. Gen. Nathanael Greene dispatched one of his best subordinates, Lt. Col. Henry "Light-Horse Harry" Lee with his legion of mixed mounted troops and light infantry, along with a company of Maryland Continentals and one artillery piece, to join forces with Brig. Gen. Francis Marion and attack the Loyalist stronghold at Fort Watson—a move that would threaten Cornwallis's lines of communication.

Fort Watson was a strongly stockaded post, sited on a hill with three log-filled abatis and garrisoned by Loyalists under a Lieutenant McKay. The defenders had dug a well and so had a good supply of water, and the fort appeared to be difficult to take for the patriots, especially since they had no true siege guns.

One of Lee's officers, Col. Hezekiah Maham, came up with an ingenious solution: he constructed a tall tower out of stout, notched logs with a protected rifle platform on the top. The "Maham Tower" was put up at night, close enough to the fort to allow patriot marksmen to pour plunging fire on the garrison. Combined with a concerted ground assault, the pressure proved too much for the Loyalists, and they surrendered.

The patriots suffered two dead and six wounded; the Loyalist casualties were not recorded.

Further Reading

John S. Pancake. *This Destructive War: The British Campaign in the Carolinas, 1780–1782* (Tuscaloosa: University of Alabama Press, 1985).

Fort William Henry

New York (August 3–9, 1757)
French and Indian War

The fall of Fort William Henry and what was thought at the time to have been a large-scale massacre by the Indian allies of the French were severe blows to the British strategic position in North America, as well as to British and colonial morale.

The fort had been built by the British at the lower end of LAKE GEORGE to consolidate their control of the lower lakes region after their victory over the French in 1755. It was a well-built, heavily constructed earthwork fort with well-designed corner bastions and artillery positions. It was small, however, accommodating only five hundred men. Still, the fort had demonstrated its strength in March 1757 when an assault by a mixed French and Indian force of fifteen hundred had been easily fought off.

Matters were different a few months later, when Fort William Henry became the focus of a large-scale campaign by Gen. Louis-Joseph de Montcalm, the commander of French forces in North America. Montcalm was determined to take the fort, and he assembled an army of eight thousand men—sixty-two hundred French and Canadians and eighteen hundred Indian allies drawn from more than thirty tribes as far away as the Mississippi River valley—backed by siege artillery and a fleet of bateaux and canoes. He advanced on the fort in late July, arriving on August 3 to begin siege operations.

The fort was under the command of Lt. Col. George Monro, a regular officer of the Thirty-fifth Regiment, who had slightly more than twenty-three hundred troops. Since the fort could hold only a fraction of that number, most of the troops were outside the fort in an entrenched camp, where they were almost immediately cut off and surrounded by Montcalm's superior numbers.

The French had invented siege warfare and were masters of its tactics, even in the wilderness of North America. Within a few days they had dug trenches that allowed their siege cannon to be sited to great advantage, and their gunners proceeded to knock out many of the fort's heavy guns. By August 7, the French were pounding the fort almost at will, with the British response growing weaker and weaker. A British sortie was unsuccessful, and on August 9 Monro concluded that his only course was to surrender.

The situation then became extremely difficult. Montcalm's Indian allies had grown increasingly unhappy during the siege—as was almost always the case when they accompanied European armies—and they were eager to collect on promises of plunder, scalps, and prisoners. Montcalm, however, extended extremely lenient terms to Monro: most of the garrison were to be allowed to leave unmolested with arms and possessions intact, under a parole to not fight the French for the next eighteen months.

The Indians took matters into their own hands as soon as they gained access to the fort, killing several British wounded and seizing loose plunder. The French tried to protect their prisoners and spirit them away during the night, but the Indians killed more wounded and captive Indians and black soldiers who had served with the British. They then attacked the column of retreating British, killing some, taking most of the prisoners' private possessions, and seizing more prisoners before making a general exodus from the scene. Most of the British then dispersed and made for the safety of Fort Edward on their own.

The first reports failed to account for the fates of almost five hundred British or colonial soldiers, an omission that, added to accurate reports of the killing of the wounded by the Indians, led to a widespread story of a massacre after the battle. In fact, most of the supposedly killed five hundred made their way back to British posts, and the French made a serious effort to reclaim many more from the hands of their allies. About seventy British or colonial prisoners were actually known to have been killed, and about another hundred were never accounted for. The stories of hundreds massacred continued to spread, however, long after the fact.

The capture of Fort William Henry, the high point of the French military effort during the French and Indian War, gave them temporary control of almost the entire lakes region.

Further Reading

Ian K. Steele. *Betrayal: Fort William Henry and the "Massacre"* (New York: Oxford University Press, 1990).

Franklin

....

Tennessee (November 30, 1864)
American Civil War

Confederate lieutenant general John Bell Hood invaded Tennessee from the south after abandoning Atlanta to Maj. Gen. William T. Sherman in October 1864. The Confederate offensive was an attempt to divert Sherman from a campaign to the southeast, but the Union's western commander was not to be deflected from his purpose of marching toward the sea. Instead, Hood found himself facing another Union army as he approached the Federal stronghold at Nashville. Hood tried to trap a part of the Union force, commanded by Maj. Gen. John M. Schofield at Franklin, Tennessee.

Hood with about 38,000 men had been chasing Schofield and 32,000 Federal troops for several days. Schofield reached Franklin but had trouble crossing his forces to the other side of the Harpeth River, allowing

Hood to catch up. Schofield had no choice but to put his men into defensive positions and await Hood's attack. Luckily for the Union general, he was able to take advantage of strong fortifications that had been built during the previous year.

At 4:00 P.M., Hood ordered a frontal assault on the Union fortifications by 23,000 men. The first attack swept a forward Federal unit back up the approaching road and into the works, but when the Confederates got close to the fortifications, the Union defenders unleashed massed musketry and grapeshot. The Confederates were slaughtered as they tried to press home the attack. A few breached the Union lines but were pushed back by a counter attack led by Col. Emerson Opdyke. The fighting continued until after nightfall with no clear conclusion.

Schofield withdrew across the river on the following day.

The Federals reported 2,300 casualties, and the Confederates counted more than 6,200, including five generals killed.

Further Reading

Winston Groom. *Shrouds of Glory: From Atlanta to Nashville: The Last Great Campaign of the Civil War* (New York: Atlantic Monthly, 1995); James L. McDonough and Thomas C. Connelly. *Five Tragic Hours: The Battle of Franklin* (Knoxville: University of Tennessee); and Wiley Sword. *Embrace an Angry Wind: The Confederacy's Last Hurrah* (New York: HarperCollins, 1991).

Franklin's Crossing

(Deep Run)

Virginia (June 5, 1863) *American Civil War*

After the Union defeat at CHANCELLORSVILLE in May 1863, Union forces had withdrawn north of the Rappahannock River, where Maj. Gen. Joseph Hooker tried to reorganize his army of seventy-five thousand men. On June 5, believing that the Confederates were retreating from the town of Fredericksburg on the south side of the river, Hooker assigned Maj. Gen. John Sedgwick to cross the river at Franklin's Crossing and gather reconnaissance on Confederate movements.

Sedgwick, whose attack at Chancellorsville had been pushed back across the Rappahannock, led parts of his Sixth Corps across the river but met with resistance from Confederates stationed in rifle pits at Deep Run, on the Maryland side. When artillery and small arms proved unable to clear the Confederates away, Sedgwick ordered infantry to cross the river on pontoon boats. The Union force gained the opposite bank, took thirty-five prisoners, and drove off the remaining Confederates.

In addition to the thirty-five Confederate riflemen taken prisoner at Deep Run, six Union infantrymen were killed and thirty-five wounded.

After the skirmish at Franklin's Crossing and Deep Run, Sedgwick told Hooker he believed that Gen. Robert E. Lee's Confederate army was still strongly positioned in Maryland. Hooker ordered further reconnaissance, which led directly to the battle at BRANDY STATION.

Further Reading

Mark M. Boatner. *The Civil War Dictionary* (New York: David McKay, 1988).

Fredericksburg

Virginia (December 13, 1862) *American Civil War*

With Maj. Gen. George B. McClellan's failure to pursue Lee's army following the battle of ANTIETAM, Abraham Lincoln's patience finally ran out, and the president relieved McClellan of command of the Army of the Potomac and gave it to Maj. Gen. Ambrose Burnside, one of the army's corps commanders. Burnside's only full-scale battle as army commander, fought at Fredericksburg, Virginia, resulted in one of the worst Union defeats of the war and one of Lee's easiest and most complete victories.

Burnside began well. He decided to avoid the usual routes toward Richmond along the rail lines, instead shifting the Army of the Potomac to Fredericksburg, where his 120,000 men could cross the Rappahannock River on pontoon bridges and get in behind Gen. Robert E. Lee's main force. Lee was caught off guard by Burnside's maneuver to the Fredericksburg area, but Burnside's logistical support failed miserably, and the promised pontoons did not show up for nearly three weeks—giving Lee ample time to concentrate his army on the other side of the river and to dig extremely strong defensive positions. He placed a corps under Lt. Gen. James Longstreet to occupy the heights above the city, with Lt. Gen. Thomas J. "Stonewall" Jackson's corps downstream on the Confederate right. Altogether, Lee commanded about seventy-eight thousand men.

Burnside organized the Union army into three "grand divisions": the right wing, under Maj. Gen. Edwin "Bull" Sumner; the center, under Maj. Gen. Joseph

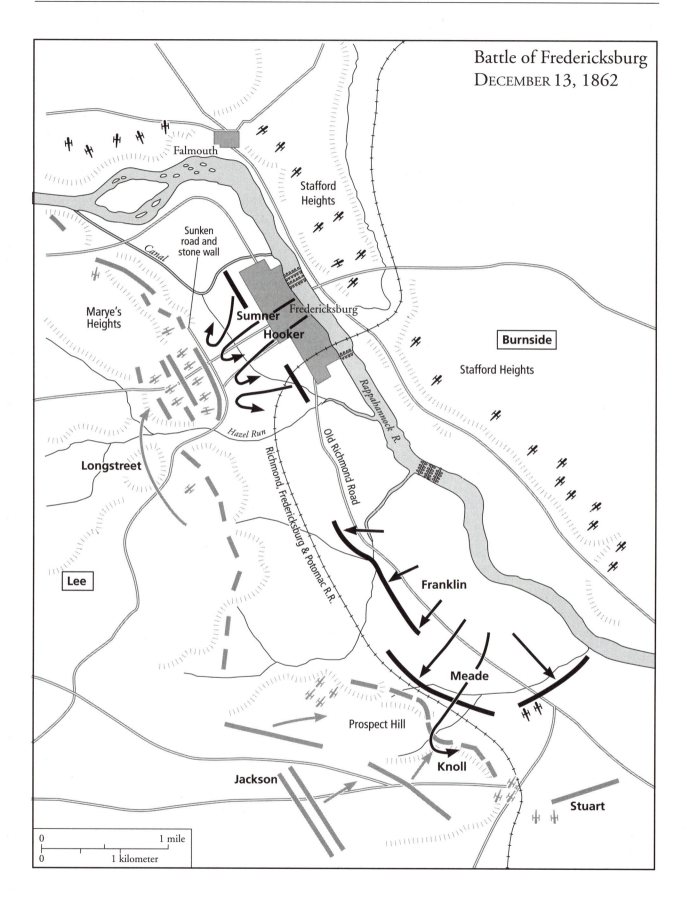

Battle of Fredericksburg
DECEMBER 13, 1862

Falmouth

Stafford
Heights

Canal

Sunken
road and
stone wall

Sumner   Fredericksburg

Marye's
Heights   **Hooker**

Burnside

Stafford Heights

Longstreet

Hazel Run

Rappahannock R.

Old Richmond Road

Richmond, Fredericksburg & Potomac R.R.

Franklin

Lee

Meade

Prospect Hill

Knoll

Jackson

Stuart

0   1 mile
0   1 kilometer

Hooker; and the left wing, under Maj. Gen. William B. Franklin. Franklin and Hooker had disputed Burnside's appointment; as it turned out, their reluctance to take orders from him played a major role in the Union defeat. Before dawn on December 11, Union engineers began to assemble the pontoon bridges across the river opposite the town, but as soon as there was light, Confederate sharpshooters picked them off and drove them to cover. The Federals unleashed a massive artillery bombardment that did nothing to dislodge the Confederates, who were finally chased away by Union infantry crossing on boats. These Federal advance forces then proceeded to loot and burn the abandoned town. The bulk of the Union army finally crossed the river on December 12 and prepared to attack all along the Confederate front.

On the Confederate right, Jackson had his brigades deployed to meet Franklin's grand division. As the Union soldiers began to advance across open ground, Maj. John B. Pelham unlimbered two guns of the Confederate horse artillery to meet them and did serious damage to the Federal formations. Soon thereafter, Jackson's main batteries opened up, and the casualties began to mount rapidly. Nonetheless, Pennsylvanians under Brig. Gen. George Meade fought through the artillery barrage and breached the Confederate defensive line. General Franklin, however, petulantly refused to follow Burnside's slightly ambiguous order to follow up Meade's breakthrough, and the opportunity evaporated; Jackson's troops counterattacked and drove back the entire Union assault.

Meanwhile, on the Confederate left, Longstreet's men had dug into positions on Marye's Heights, behind a sunken road and stone wall. With supreme but utterly futile courage, the Union regiments of Sumner's command formed up and made charge after charge across open fields against the massed Confederate musket fire. The entire area in front of the Confederate defensive became a killing field through which none could advance. Despite wave after wave of attackers, not a single Union soldier reached the sunken road and stone wall alive. The Union dead accumulated in piles at the foot of Marye's Heights before the assaults were finally called off.

The Union losses were extreme: more than twelve thousand total casualties, at least seven thousand of them at Marye's Heights. Lee lost less than half as many, about fifty-three hundred casualties.

The Army of the Potomac withdrew across the Rappahannock, and after a botched attempt to flank Lee with a march over roads made impassable by winter rains, Burnside was relieved of command.

Further Reading

Bradley Finfrock. *Across the Rappahannock: From Fredericksburg to the Mud March* (Bowie, Md.: Heritage Books, 1994); Frank A. O'Reilly. *"Stonewall" Jackson at Fredericksburg.* 2d ed. (Lynchburg, Va.: H. E. Howard, 1993); Edward J. Stackpole. *Drama on the Rappahannock: The Fredericksburg Campaign.* 2d ed. (Harrisburg, Pa.: Stackpole Books, 1962); and Vorin E. Whan. *Fiasco at Fredericksburg* (University Park: Pennsylvania State University Press, 1961).

✒ Freeman's Farm

See SARATOGA, FIRST

✒ Frenchtown

(The River Raisin)
Ohio (present-day Michigan)
(January 18 and 22, 1813) *War of 1812*

Militia major general William Henry Harrison, the newly appointed American commander of the northeastern theater, wanted to clear upper Ohio and lower Michigan of the Indian allies of the British in preparing to retake Detroit, which had been surrendered to the British in an American disaster during the summer of 1812. He dispatched U.S. Army brigadier general James Winchester to fortify the Maumee River (at present-day Perrysburg, Ohio). However, Winchester was asked for protection by the citizens of Frenchtown (present-day Monroe, Michigan), and he decided to attack the British and Indians in the local area.

On January 18, Col. William Lewis and Col. John Allen led 560 men, mostly Kentucky volunteers, along the frozen River Raisin to surprise the 250 Canadian militia and Indians that British commander Col. Henry Proctor had stationed in Frenchtown. Helped by the element of surprise, the Americans easily expelled the Canadians and Indians from the town, but they later lost twelve killed and fifty-five wounded in a hand-to-hand fight in the forest (the number of Canadian and Indian casualties is unknown.)

Winchester did a poor job of fortifying Frenchtown against further attack, establishing himself in a grand house on the edge of town and dispersing his 934 troops throughout the town, which was guarded only by a weak palisade. Colonel Proctor, now aware of the potential American threat to Detroit, transported a mixed force of British regulars from the Forty-first Regiment, Canadian militia, and Indians led by Wyandot (Huron) chief Roundhead across icy Lake Erie and prepared for a new fight five miles north of Frenchtown.

Though Proctor paused first to form his troops into lines, his attack surprised the Americans in Frenchtown when the new battle began on January 22. An Indian attack across the River Raisin broke the American right and threw Winchester's troops into chaos. Winchester was captured by Roundhead, stripped of his clothing, and delivered to Proctor. He then surrendered his troops, despite the fact that a Kentucky rifle regiment in town on his left wing was still acquitting itself well.

Proctor's forces marched their American prisoners to Brownstown (modern Trenton, Michigan), but the Indians left behind killed between thirty and sixty wounded Americans who had been too weak to march out of Frenchtown. This incident, described as a post-surrender massacre by survivors and the American press, caused "Remember the River Raisin!" to become a rallying cry against the British, and particularly Indian, troops throughout the remainder of the War of 1812.

All told, the British took five hundred prisoners and killed four hundred. British losses are unknown but are estimated at approximately one-third of their total force. Proctor was promoted to brigadier general; Harrison retreated south, his plans to take Detroit in complete disarray.

Further Reading

Dennis Carter-Edwards, "The War of 1812 along the Detroit Frontier: A Canadian Perspective." *Michigan Historical Review* 13 (1987): 21–34; and Robert S. Quimby. *The U.S. Army in the War of 1812: An Operational and Command Study* (East Lansing: Michigan State University Press, 1997).

Front Royal

Virginia (May 23 and 30, 1862)
American Civil War

The two battles at Front Royal, Virginia, in late May 1862 marked the midpoint of Maj. Gen. Thomas J. "Stonewall" Jackson's Shenandoah Valley campaign, a campaign that

sealed his reputation as a great Confederate military leader. After defeating Union troops at MCDOWELL (in an action that caused heavy Confederate casualties), Jackson continued to pursue the forces commanded by Maj. Gen. Nathaniel Banks, in an attempt to push Federal troops out of Virginia.

After the victory at McDowell, Jackson marched his troops south toward Strasburg, where Banks's main force of seven thousand soldiers was stationed. Instead of attacking straightaway, Jackson left his cavalry commander, Col. Turner Ashby, to cover the western valley while he crossed the Massanutten Mountains at New Market to march north and take Banks by surprise. On May 21, Jackson joined Maj. Gen. Richard S. Ewell, whose division brought the Confederate force to a total strength of seventeen thousand.

The combined Confederate force quick-marched to the town of Front Royal, site of a Federal outpost, commanded by Col. J. R. Kenly, that Banks little suspected would come under attack. On May 23 at Front Royal, Belle Boyd, the daughter of a local hotel owner and head of one of the most famous Confederate spy operations of the war, provided detailed information about the Federal outpost to the commander of the Confederate advance party, Brig. Gen. Richard Taylor, son of former U.S. president Zachary Taylor and brother-in-law of Confederate president Jefferson Davis. Taylor ordered an immediate attack and was joined by Jackson at 2:00 P.M. for an all-out assault on the Federal camp.

The Federal troops were taken totally by surprise, and the fight did not last long. By 5:00 P.M., Kenly was trying to make a last stand north of town when his men were swarmed by Col. Thomas Flournoy's Virginia Cavalry and the majority (including Kenly himself) taken prisoner. The Confederates suffered fewer than 50 casualties in the battle, while 904 out of 1,063 Federals were captured, wounded, or killed. Jackson's men also captured a cache of supplies worth an estimated three hundred thousand dollars.

Immediately following the action on May 23, Jackson continued north toward WINCHESTER, hoping to engage Banks's main force, but he left Col. Zephaniah Turner with the Twelfth Georgia to guard the captured men and matériel. On May 30, when Col. Nathan Kimball (in peacetime an Indiana doctor) led a Union division to near Front Royal, Turner panicked and immediately decamped to find Jackson at Winchester, leaving his force without a commander. His men set their captured supplies afire and retreated under the direction of Capt. William F. Brown.

The Federals retook Front Royal, recaptured twenty-four of the prisoners taken on May 23, and arrested Belle Boyd, who had been betrayed as a spy, apparently by her lover. The First Rhode Island Cavalry rode after Brown's retreating men and managed to take 156 Confederate prisoners. Fourteen Union soldiers were killed in the process.

When Jackson learned of Turner's precipitous departure from Front Royal, he placed the colonel under arrest. The recapture of Front Royal was only a temporary setback for Jackson's Confederate forces, who went on to brilliant victories at CROSS KEYS and PORT REPUBLIC.

Further Reading

Mark M. Boatner. *The Dictionary of the Civil War* (New York: David McKay, 1988).

G

Gaines's Mill

Virginia (June 27, 1862) *American Civil War*

The battle at Gaines's Mill was one of the largest of the series of engagements, known since as the Seven Days Battles, that took place along the Chickahominy River near Richmond between Maj. Gen. George B. McClellan's Federal Army of the Potomac and the Army of Northern Virginia, newly commanded by Gen. Robert E. Lee. McClellan's campaign to take the Confederate capital by advancing from the James River continued to come unraveled, despite poor tactics by Lee and his lieutenants.

Thirty thousand men of the Union Fifth Corps (out of McClellan's total force of more than a hundred thousand men) were positioned north of the Chickahominy under the command of Maj. Gen. Fitz John Porter. They had fought off two major assaults by the Confederates, including a sharp encounter on June 26 near the village of MECHANICSVILLE, and Porter now had them in very strong defensive positions on a raised plateau behind a swampy stream called Boatswain's Creek. Porter had a strong reserve behind his main lines to guard the bridges crossing the Chickahominy, which were his corps's means of escape.

Lee had massed around fifty-six thousand soldiers north of the river in an attempt to smash Porter and severely wound McClellan's army. His plan was to attack from woods across open ground facing Porter's position. He gave the orders to Maj. Gen. A. P. Hill, who sent the first of his men out of the woods at about 2:30 P.M. As soon as they emerged into the open, the Confederates came under heavy fire from the well-placed Federal artillery. Despite the pounding, however, the Confederate attackers—members of Brig. Gen. Maxcy Gregg's South Carolina brigade—managed to advance close to the center of the Federal line, whereupon they were hit by a flank attack from Col. Gouverneur K. Warren's Fifth New York Brigade, including a regiment of fancy-dress Zouaves. A fierce, hand-to-hand melee developed in front of the Union positions, with the South Carolinians gradually forced back. Throughout the afternoon, similar encounters took place along other parts of the Union lines, with the Confederates advancing against artillery fire, only to be thrown back by spirited infantry counterattacks.

The Confederate assault suffered overall from a lack of coordination—Lee's staff work was still poor a month after he had taken command—and the usually reliable Maj. Gen. Thomas J. "Stonewall" Jackson failed (as he had during the two previous battles) to bring his troops into the fray as expected. Jackson had wandered around behind the battlefield for several hours, and it was not until late in the day that Lee had all of his forces on hand.

At 7:00 P.M., Lee ordered a general attack all along the front, hoping to finally break the Union lines. The greatest force, brigades under Brig. Gen. John Bell Hood, was sent again against the Union center, where Hill had failed earlier. Hood's men swept across the open field, now littered with the dead and wounded of the previous assaults, and rushed the Union line, despite devastating cannon and musket fire. In the face of the ferocious Confederate attack, Porter's men finally buckled and began to retreat, moving toward the river crossings as the day's light faded and the battle came to a close. A final, futile charge by the Union's Fifth and Second Cavalry failed to stop the Confederates but nearly annihilated the Federal horsemen.

The Union lost 893 killed, 3,107 wounded, and 2,836 missing. The Confederates suffered 8,750 killed and wounded.

Lee's hard-won victory finally pushed Porter over the river and hastened McClellan's retreat from Richmond.

Further Reading

Clifford Dowdey. *The Seven Days: The Emergence of Lee*. Reprint ed. (Lincoln: University of Nebraska Press, 1993); James M. McPherson. *Battle Cry of Freedom: The Civil War Era* (New York: Oxford University Press, 1988); and Time-Life Staff. *Lee Takes Command: From Seven Days to Second Bull Run* (Alexandria, Va.: Time-Life Books, 1984).

Galveston

Texas (January 1, 1863) *American Civil War*

During the final months of 1862, both sides took a renewed interest in the Texas theater, appointing new commanders and planning campaigns along the coast.

The Union navy had taken control of the port of Galveston in October. In December, the new Federal commander for the Gulf Department, Maj. Gen. Nathaniel Banks, a former Massachusetts politician and—as it turned out—a poor field commander, sent a force of about 250 men under Col. I. S. Burrell to fortify the wharf area of the city, as well as five gunboats under commodore W. B. Renshaw to defend the harbor.

On January 1, 1863, the new Confederate commander in the region, Maj. Gen. John B. Magruder, a veteran of battles in Virginia, challenged the Federal hold on the city with an early-morning attack over land that failed to carry the Union defenses. He then ordered his river fleet—two "cottonclads" (river steamers protected by deck barricades of projectile-absorbing cotton bales)—to attack the Union gunboats.

The first Confederate ship sank, but the second came alongside one of the Federal boats and boarded and captured her. The other Federal gunboats tried to escape, but one ran aground and was burned by her crew to avoid capture. Commander Renshaw was killed when his ship blew up while attempting to flee.

Without support from its river fleet, the Union garrison was in a hopeless situation, and Burrell surrendered.

The Federal forces lost three hundred men as casualties or prisoners as well as two riverboats. The Confederates reported 27 killed and 180 wounded.

The Confederates kept control of Galveston until after the surrender at Appomattox.

Further Reading

Robert M. Franklin. *The Battle of Galveston, January 1, 1863* (Galveston, Tex.: San Luis Press, 1975); and Donald S. Frazier. *Cottonclads! The Battle of Galveston and the Defense of the Texas Coast* (Abilene, Tex.: McWhiney Foundation Press, McMurray University, 1998).

Garnett's and Golding's Farm

Virginia (June 27–28, 1862)
American Civil War

Federal commander Maj. Gen. George B. McClellan's plan to capture Richmond by a thrust from the James River peninsula in 1862 brought his one-hundred-thousand-man Army of the Potomac to within a few miles of the Confederate capital, but when Gen. Robert E. Lee took command of the Southern army, McClellan lost his nerve and began a retreat, despite several Northern victories or stalemates in what became known as the Seven Days Battles.

On the same day as a large battle took place at GAINES'S MILLS north of the Chickahominy River, the relatively small

Confederate holding force south of the river, facing the main Federal army, probed the Union dispositions. Col. George T. Anderson's brigade attacked the Federal right wing but was easily repulsed. The Confederate assault was followed up by Brig. Gen. Robert Toombs (a former secretary of state of the Confederacy), whose brigade attacked during the evening and then again at first light the next day.

The fighting was inconclusive, although the Confederates lost 461 casualties and the Union 368.

Further Reading

Clifford Dowdey. *The Seven Days: The Emergence of Lee.* Reprint ed. (Lincoln: University of Nebraska Press, 1993); James M. McPherson. *The Battle Cry of Freedom: The Civil War Era* (New York: Oxford University Press, 1988); and Time-Life Staff. *Lee Takes Command: From Seven Days to Second Bull Run* (Alexandria, Va.: Time-Life Books, 1984).

～ Germantown

Pennsylvania (October 4, 1777)
American Revolution

Following his victory over the Americans at BRANDYWINE on September 11 and his subsequent occupation of the American capital of Philadelphia on September 26, the British commander in chief, Gen. Sir William Howe, seemed to be in control—indeed, to have won—his 1777 campaign into Pennsylvania. His main forces, numbering around nine thousand, went into camp at Germantown, with three thousand more in Philadelphia under Maj. Gen. Lord Cornwallis, and other troops had been detached to aid in bringing up supplies from the Chesapeake.

The defeated American army under Gen. George Washington was camped at some distance, and surprisingly, it had gained in strength after the loss at Brandywine through the addition of considerable numbers of Maryland and New Jersey militia. By the first days of October, Washington had around eleven thousand men in camp, and he began to entertain ideas of an aggressive attack on Howe's base at Germantown.

Washington and his staff devised an elaborate plan, the sort of tactical scheme the amateur American generals loved—but were seldom able to execute successfully with the ill-trained "regulars" of the Continental regiments and the raw militia that made up Washington's army.

The American plan was to divide the army into four divisions and attack the British camp at Germantown with a double envelopment. The strongest division, with nearly two-thirds of the army, under Maj. Gen. Nathanael Greene, was to hit the British right wing. To Greene's right, a division under Maj. Gen. John Sullivan would attack what was thought to be the weaker British left wing. Two more, smaller, divisions, comprised entirely of militia, were to move in wide flanking movements around each side of the British lines and close the double pincers around Germantown. All of these units were to march over rough terrain at night, and Washington expected them all to reach the jumping-off points simultaneously at 2:00 A.M.—even though they had no means of coordination or communication—wait there for two hours, and attack at 4:00 A.M.

From the American perspective, things began to go wrong from the beginning, and the battle developed on its own terms, with the elaborate tactical plan collapsing almost immediately. The British were caught by surprise, but individual leaders responded rapidly and vigorously and turned a possible defeat into yet another British victory.

To begin with, General Sullivan's division was late getting into place, and when it was ready to step off to the attack around dawn, it was hampered by an early morning fog that developed into a thick blanket, preventing soldiers and officers from seeing what was going on (the proverbial "fog of war" was real during much of the battle of Germantown). One of Sullivan's units, under Brig. Gen. Thomas Conway, surprised the British pickets and thereby alerted the main British force to the attack. The British Fortieth Regiment was formed up by its commander, Lt. Col. Thomas Musgrave, and attacked Conway and subsequently the entire front of Sullivan's column, by itself stopping the American advance in its tracks. Eventually, Sullivan brought his numbers to bear—sending Brig. Gen. Anthony Wayne's men forward—and Musgrave's men had to retreat, but Musgrave occupied a solidly built stone house, owned by a Loyalist, Judge Benjamin Chew, with several companies. They barred the windows and doors and began to fire from the second story on Americans passing by on their way to attack the main British camp.

Washington was persuaded by his staff to stop and eliminate this strong point, which would be to his rear, but Musgrave's position proved to be impossible to take. American field artillery was too puny to damage the stone walls of the house, and British musket fire was too hot to allow the building to be taken by storm. Courageous attempts to set the house afire failed. The

American advance was stalled by the futile attempt to take the Chew House.

Meanwhile, the division of Nathanael Greene seemed to be having more success. Greene's units vigorously met the British who came out of camp to meet his advance. Virginia Continentals under Brig. Gen. John Peter Muhlenberg drove through the enemy line with a spirited bayonet charge and advanced all the way to the British rear, where they came upon the British tents. Penetrating the farthest were the men of the Ninth Virginia, commanded by Col. George Matthews, who had taken one hundred prisoners and were far in front of Greene's main attack.

However, one of Greene's commanders, the incompetent Brig. Gen. Adam Stephen pulled out of the attack without orders and swung over to attack behind Sullivan's column. The result was total confusion. Stephen's men met those of Anthony Wayne coming from the other direction, mistook them for the enemy, and opened fire. Wayne's men fired back. Both columns dissolved into chaos and fled into an unorganized retreat.

Sullivan's advance units came under attack from British units organized by Maj. Gen. Charles Grey at about the same time as Stephen blundered down the road to the rear. Sullivan's men had fought hard, but they were almost out of ammunition, and the new blows were too much for them, especially with the British stronghold of Chew House at their rear. They began to disengage and retreat. Reverses struck Muhlenberg and Greene's column as well. Matthews's men had driven too far, and a brisk British counterattack cut them off and captured almost the entire regiment. The rest of the Americans

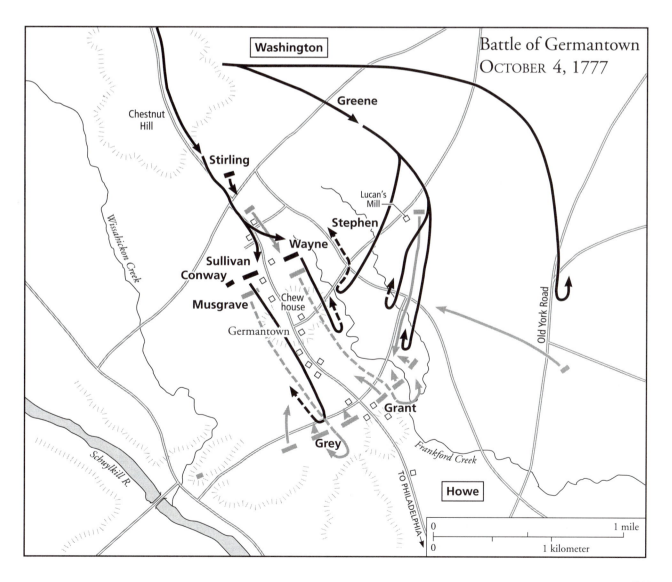

Battle of Germantown
OCTOBER 4, 1777

began to falter, and they too turned and began to go back the way they had come.

By the time Cornwallis arrived on the scene with fresh troops from Philadelphia, the battle was over. All of the Americans were in full retreat, and nothing could stop them, not even Washington's vigorous exhortations. By nightfall the American army was more than twenty miles from the battlefield.

The Americans had lost 152 killed, 521 wounded, and more than 400 captured (most of the prisoners were Matthew's Virginians). The British lost 70 killed and 450 wounded.

Howe's possession of Philadelphia was now secure, and Washington had no recourse but to withdraw and go eventually into winter quarters at Valley Forge.

Further Reading

John W. Jackson. *With the British Army in Philadelphia, 1777–1778* (San Rafael, Calif.: Presidio Press, 1979); Thomas J. McGuire. *The Surprise of Germantown . . .* (Gettysburg, Pa.: Thomas, 1994); and Ray Thompson. *Washington at Germantown* (Fort Washington, Pa.: Bicentennial Press, 1971).

✍ Gettysburg

Pennsylvania (July 1–3, 1863) *American Civil War*

The titanic, three-day struggle near a small town in southern Pennsylvania was probably the most significant battle of the American Civil War. The victory by the Union, although not followed up to a satisfactory conclusion, nonetheless meant that Confederate general Robert E. Lee's second attempted invasion of the North was a failure and that, in the long run, the Confederacy was unlikely to win the war.

Encouraged by his great offensive victory at CHAN-CELLORSVILLE and supremely confident in his Army of Northern Virginia, Lee convinced the Confederate government in May 1863 that he should march into Pennsylvania, shifting the war away from battered Virginia and creating a military and political crisis for the Federal government. He began to move his seventy-five thousand troops northward in June, dispatching Maj. Gen. J. E. B. Stuart and his cavalry division to scout. (Stuart, however, went off on a long ride around the Union army and failed to supply Lee with information or support until the middle of the subsequent battle at Gettysburg.)

The Federal Army of the Potomac, physically and psychologically battered by defeats at FREDERICKSBURG and Chancellorsville, was still a formidable fighting force, as usual outnumbering the Confederates and able to fight well if led competently. In late June, the command of the Union army passed from the ineffective Maj. Gen. Joseph Hooker to Maj. Gen. George G. Meade, a corps commander, and the fortunes of the hitherto nearly hapless Army of the Potomac took a step forward. Meade was not Lee's equal—scarcely any general in American history was—but he was competent, resolute, and had the respect of his subordinate commanders. He began to maneuver his eighty thousand or so men against Lee's line of march.

Advance elements of the two armies met by accident on July 1 at the outskirts of Gettysburg, a small town but the site of crucial road junctions. A Union cavalry brigade under Brig. Gen. John Buford moved out of Gettysburg and encountered two Confederate divisions under Lt. Gen. A. P. Hill. The engagement grew hotter with the appearance of Union reinforcements under Maj. Gen. John F. Reynolds, who was shot down and killed at long range while directing placement of his troops. Almost reluctantly, both sides poured more and more men into the fight, and the commanders began to concentrate their manpower north of the town, wrapping around the high ground to the west and south. The first day's fighting came to an end after vicious back-and-forth attacks, with the Union securing its strongest defenses at a point called Cemetery Hill.

Lee was faced with an unusual situation. He did not command the kind of defensive positions that had allowed him to defeat so often Union opponents, and he had only Lt. Gen. James Longstreet left as principal subordinate, after Maj. Gen. Thomas J. "Stonewall" Jackson's death from friendly fire at Chancellorsville. Nonetheless, Lee determined to go on the offensive the following day, despite the Union army's strong positions. Meade, meanwhile, had rapidly brought up the bulk of his forces and had them arranged in a long defensive line hooking around from Culp's Hill and Cemetery Hill on the north, along Cemetery Ridge, and then south toward two small hills called Little Round Top and Big Round Top. The Federal units were thin on Meade's left flank near Little Round Top, but they were dug in securely behind strong natural barriers, which the soldiers improved with improvised breastworks.

Lee wanted to attack the Union positions at Culp's Hill at the extreme right-hand end of the Federal defenses, but Lt. Gen. Richard S. Ewell, the corps commander, convinced him that his troops could not take that strong point. Lee then shifted his attention toward the middle of the long north-south Union line, along Cemetery Ridge, ordering Longstreet to attack. The Federal deployment

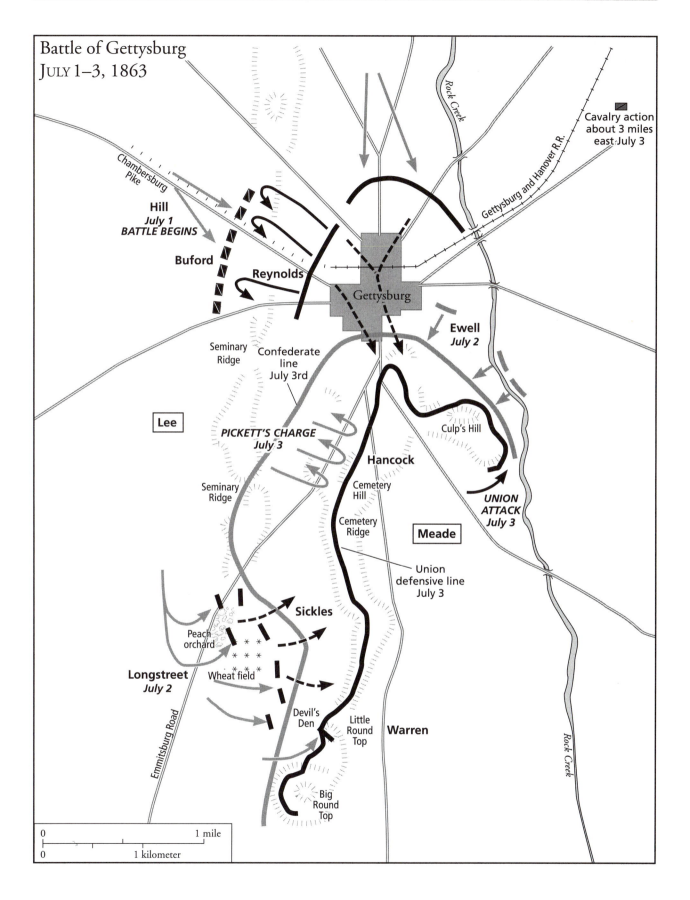

Battle of Gettysburg
JULY 1–3, 1863

Cavalry action
about 3 miles
east July 3

Rock Creek

Gettysburg and Hanover R.R.

Chambersburg Pike

Hill
July 1
BATTLE BEGINS

Buford

Reynolds

Gettysburg

Ewell
July 2

Seminary
Ridge

Confederate
line
July 3rd

Lee

PICKETT'S CHARGE
July 3

Culp's Hill

Seminary
Ridge

Hancock

Cemetery
Hill

*UNION
ATTACK
July 3*

Cemetery
Ridge

Meade

Union
defensive line
July 3

Peach
orchard

Sickles

Longstreet
July 2

Wheat field

Devil's
Den

Little
Round
Top

Warren

Emmitsburg Road

Big
Round
Top

Rock Creek

0			1 mile

0		1 kilometer	

was disarranged when Maj. Gen. Daniel Sickles advanced his corps to form a dangerous salient in the Union lines near a peach orchard and a wheat field, with his left flank in a tangled, boulder-strewn ground known as the Devil's Den, leaving Little Round Top and the entire left flank of the Federal line in jeopardy.

The Confederate attack was led by the troops under Maj. Gen. John Bell Hood, who was soon severely wounded, but the Southerners pressed on, taking the heights at Big Round Top and moving to the north to try to occupy Little Round Top. At the last moment, they were met by Federal troops hastily gathered by Brig. Gen. Gouverneur K. Warren, a topographical engineer and not a combat officer, who had been scouting the location. In desperate fighting, the Union soldiers defending Little Round Top, the extreme left flank of their army, held against the Confederate attacks. Col. Joshua Chamberlain, a professor of modern languages in civilian life, was conspicuous in leading his Twentieth Maine in a countercharge that drove off Alabamans who threatened to take the hill.

At the center of the Union line, where Sickles had positioned his men, the battle was the most intense. Longstreet's troops attacked the peach orchard, wheat field, and Devil's Den time after time, and possession of the disputed ground changed hands repeatedly throughout the afternoon. Meade fed in reinforcements, however, and as the fighting ended for the day, the Union continued to hold Cemetery Ridge as well as Cemetery Hill and Culp's Hill to the north.

Taking counsel during the night, Lee then made what military historians since have considered one of his few major mistakes of judgment. Overruling Longstreet's objections, Lee decided that his men could take the Union strongpoints at the center of the line. He ordered a massive artillery barrage, to be followed by a massed attack of infantry across open ground. The infantry divisions of Maj. Gen. George E. Pickett, Brig. Gen. Johnston Pettigrew, and Maj. Gen. Isaac Trimble, representing units from Virginia, North Carolina, Alabama, Tennessee, Mississippi, and Florida, assembled in open formation in front of Cemetery Ridge. At 3:00 P.M. they launched an assault, led personally by Brig. Gen. Lewis Armistead, who waved his black slouch hat on the point of his saber as he started the advance across nearly a mile of gently rolling ground.

The romantic bravery of what came to be called "Pickett's Charge" was magnificent, but it was doomed.

Federal gunners knocked apart the charging Confederate formations while still in open ground, and massed musket fire from the dug-in defenders finished the job. Armistead and a few others reached the stone wall and the batteries that marked the leading edge of the Union positions, but they were destroyed— Armistead was mortally wounded just over the Union side of the wall—and of the twelve thousand men who stepped off from the Confederate lines, only about seven thousand stumbled back alive. Lee's grand assault had failed, and with it his chance of defeating the Union army at Gettysburg.

The Confederates suffered more than twenty-eight thousand casualties during the three-day battle. The Union lost twenty-three thousand.

Lee was devastated by the huge losses, but he organized an orderly retreat back toward Virginia, and since Meade refused to pursue the Confederates, the Army of Northern Virginia escaped. The victory allowed the Federal government to continue the war effort and to pin Lee in Virginia, but the failure to destroy the Confederate army meant the war would continue for nearly another twenty months, with tens of thousands more deaths.

Further Reading

Bruce Catton. *Gettysburg: The Final Fury* (Garden City, N.Y.: Doubleday Books, 1974); Gary W. Gallagher, ed. *The First Day at Gettysburg: Essays on Confederate and Union Leadership* (Kent, Ohio: Kent State University Press, 1992); ———, ed. *The Second Day at Gettysburg* (Kent, Ohio: Kent State University Press, 1993); ———, ed. *The Third Day at Gettysburg and Beyond* (Chapel Hill: University of North Carolina Press, 1994); ———, ed. *Three Days at Gettysburg* (Kent, Ohio: Kent State University Press, 1999); JoAnna M. McDonald. *The World Will Long Remember: A Guide to the Battle of Gettysburg* (Shippensburg, Pa.: White Mane, 1996); Gerald A. Patterson. *Debris of Battle: The Wounded of Gettysburg* (Mechanicsburg, Pa.: Stackpole Books, 1997); Harry W. Pfanz. *Gettysburg: The Second Day* (Chapel Hill: University of North Carolina Press, 1987); ———. *Gettysburg: Culp's Hill and Cemetery Hill* (Chapel Hill: University of North Carolina Press, 1993); Carol Reardon. *Pickett's Charge in History and Memory* (Chapel Hill: University of North Carolina Press, 1997); Edward J. Stackpole and Wilber Nye. *The Battle of Gettysburg: A Guided Tour.* Rev. ed. (Harrisburg, Pa.: Stackpole Books, 1988); and Peter G. Tsouras. *Gettysburg: An Alternate History* (Mechanicsburg, Pa.: Stackpole Books, 1997).

✎ H.M.S. *Glasgow*

See U.S.S. *ALFRED*

✎ Glendale

See WHITE OAK SWAMP

✎ Globe Tavern

(Weldon Railroad; Six Mile House)

Virginia (August 18–21, 1864) *American Civil War*

During August 1864, Gen. Robert E. Lee had succeeded in turning Lt. Gen. Ulysses S. Grant's assault on the Confederate stronghold of PETERSBURG, Virginia, into a virtual campaign of attrition. After an attempt to blast through Confederate lines and gain access to the city failed at the end of July (*see also* THE CRATER), Grant ordered Maj. Gen. Gouverneur K. Warren to march against the Weldon Railroad in a bid to extend his siege to the west of Petersburg. The Union forces started dismantling the railroad line near the Globe Tavern to cut off communications to Petersburg, and the Confederates rushed to counterattack on August 18.

Union brigadier generals Romeyn Beck Ayers and Charles Griffin were leading a largely unopposed attack on the rail line on the afternoon of August 18 when they were surprised by Maj. Gen. Henry Heth's Confederate division. Ayers had to withdraw his left flank toward the tavern, though he held off Heth with a late-afternoon counterattack. Overnight, both sides sent for reinforcements and prepared for a larger engagement.

On August 19, Confederate lieutenant general A. P. Hill led five infantry brigades and one cavalry brigade directly against Ayers and against Brig. Gen. Samuel W. Crawford's division of Warren's force. Hill executed a double envelopment of the Union troops and almost destroyed Crawford's flank. Warren delivered a counterattack, however, and managed to regain most of the lost ground.

On August 20, both sides gained further reinforcements, and the Federals established a defensive line stretching in front of the tavern and east to the Jerusalem Plank Road.

The next day Hill tried another attack against this new Union position, but he could find no weak point and was unable to pierce the defensive line. General Lee brought in fresh troops that afternoon, but he called off

the attack when he realized that his intended target, the Union flank, had been shored up with men from the Ninth Corps. Casualties were fairly heavy for what started out as a small action against a railroad: the Northerners counted 1,303 killed and wounded and 3,152 missing, compared to the Southerners' 1,200 killed and wounded and 419 missing.

The Union victory at the Globe Tavern meant that Grant's siege lines at Petersburg had been effectively extended to the west. The severing of the rail line meant that Confederate supplies and information from Wilmington, North Carolina, could not get through to Petersburg.

Further Reading

John Horn. *The Destruction of the Weldon Railroad, Deep Bottom, Globe Tavern, and Ream's Station . . .* (Lynchburg, Va.: H. E. Howard, 1991).

✎ Glorieta Pass

New Mexico (March 26 and 28, 1862)
American Civil War

The two battles fought in 1862 at Glorieta Pass in New Mexico Territory were inconclusive by military standards, but they stopped dead the Confederate attempt to take control of the far West.

The Confederate army in New Mexico was comprised mostly of twelve hundred Texans commanded by an army veteran, Brig. Gen. Henry Sibley, who had sided with the South. With the support of the Confederate high command in Richmond, Sibley set out to seize the considerable amount of supplies and materiel left in New Mexico by U.S. Army troops when the war began. Starting in the southern part of the territory, he had marched along the line of prewar forts, occupying Albuquerque and Santa Fe. His goals were a large Union supply depot at Fort Union and, eventually, Denver. Sibley himself was in Albuquerque when his subordinates fought at Glorieta Pass.

The Union force was made up of miners and frontiersmen from Colorado, commanded by Col. John P. Slough, along with a few regular infantry and cavalrymen. Slough had 1,340 men altogether. He set up a blocking position on the Santa Fe Trail near Glorieta Pass and waited for the Confederates.

On March 26, an advance party of Confederates under the command of Maj. Charles Pyron of the Second Texas Mounted Rifles encountered the First Colorado

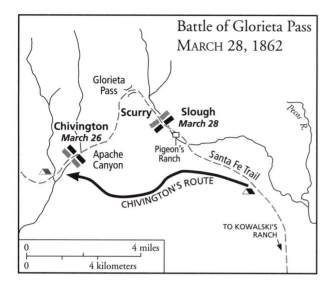

Battle of Glorieta Pass
MARCH 28, 1862

Glorieta
Pass

Scurry   **Slough**
                March 28

Chivington
March 26

Apache   Pigeon's
Canyon   Ranch

Pecos R.

Santa Fe Trail

CHIVINGTON'S ROUTE

TO KOWALSKI'S
RANCH

0		4 miles

0		4 kilometers

Volunteers, commanded by Maj. John Chivington, and a hot fight developed, without the involvement of the main bodies. Chivington outflanked his opponents several times and drove them back down the trail to Apache Canyon, where a vigorous charge pushed the Confederates back into camp and won the day for the Coloradans. Chivington withdrew to Koslowski's Ranch, a way station twelve miles distant. Four Texans were killed and twenty wounded; Chivington had five killed and fourteen wounded.

After a day-long pause in the action, the main Confederate force under Lt. Col. William Scurry advanced on the Union camp, catching the troops filling canteens at Pigeon's Ranch, just east of Glorieta Pass. The Union forces were not at full strength, since Chivington had taken about five hundred men on a long cross-country movement to attack the Confederate camp.

Scurry had the advantage of better artillery during the main battle at Pigeon's Ranch, and he eventually forced Slough and the Colorado troops to withdraw several times, following up his cannon barrages with flanking movements. Although they clearly held the upper hand, the Confederates could not administer a decisive blow, and the battle petered out as the day ended. The Confederates had forty-eight killed and sixty wounded, and the Union forces had similar losses.

Meanwhile, Chivington had descended on the Confederate camp to the rear and played havoc. Finding the supplies virtually unguarded, he destroyed almost everything the Confederates had left behind that morning: eighty wagons were burned, along with all the clothes, food,

forage, medicine, and ammunition. Chivington then rejoined Slough at the Union position at Koslowski's Ranch.

Although they were not defeated in the major engagement at Glorieta Pass, the Confederates had to give up their campaign after losing all their supplies, and the attempt to take over New Mexico and Colorado failed.

Further Reading

Don E. Alberts. *The Battle of Glorieta: Union Victory in the West* (College Station: Texas A&M Press, 1998); Thomas S. Edrington. *The Battle of Glorieta Pass: A Gettysburg in the West, March 26–28, 1862* (Albuquerque: University of New Mexico Press, 1997); Robert Scott. *Glory, Glory, Gloryieta: The Gettysburg of the West* (Boulder, Colo.: Johnson Books, 1992).

Gloucester

Virginia (October 3, 1781) *American Revolution*

Gloucester, located on a point of land directly across the York River, was vital to the support of the British position in YORKTOWN, Virginia, to which commander Lt. Gen. Lord Cornwallis had retreated in the fall of 1781. Control of Gloucester would allow British ships—should they appear as Cornwallis hoped—to enter the river and rescue the stranded British army from Yorktown. If that plan failed, Cornwallis would need possession of Gloucester as a possible overland escape route.

The British commander had posted a strong garrison at Gloucester under Lt. Col. Thomas Dundas, and on October 2, Lt. Col. Banastre Tarleton crossed the river with the dragoons and light infantry of his famous Legion to reinforce the town. Opposing him were fifteen hundred experienced Virginia militia under Gen. George Weedon, and the Duc de Lauzun, who had arrived with six hundred men of his mounted legion in late September. Lauzun was a veteran officer, commander of the French cavalry wing during the last years of the American Revolution, who had been sent to Gloucester by Washington and Rochambeau to forestall a possible British breakout. On October 1, the Marquis de Choisy took command of the Allied forces.

On October 3, Dundas and his men were on a foraging expedition when they encountered Lauzun's dragoons, who were the vanguard of an allied advance toward the town. Tarleton's riders were covering the withdrawal of the British infantry when they clashed on the road with the French troopers. Lauzun's men charged into Tarleton's formation three times, and the British line finally broke, with Tarleton and Lauzun nearly coming to arms face to face.

Tarleton retreated behind a company of Royal Welch Fusiliers (Twenty-third Regiment), who proceeded to drive off the French dragoons. However, a battalion of Virginia militia under Lt. Col. John Mercer appeared on the scene and stopped the British infantry cold. Tarleton and the fusiliers retreated into the town, where they remained neutralized during the siege at Yorktown.

The French had three men killed and sixteen wounded. Reports of other losses are sketchy, but Tarleton is said to have lost twelve men.

Further Reading

Christopher Ward. *The War of the Revolution.* Vol. 2 (New York: Macmillan, 1952).

Golding's Farm

See GARNETT'S AND GOLDING'S FARM

Goliad

Texas (March 18–19, 1836)
Texas War of Independence

Several weeks after Gen. Antonio López de Santa Anna's Mexican army defeated Texas forces at the ALAMO, it overwhelmed a second makeshift Texan defense at Goliad. Santa Anna's execution of prisoners after the surrender of Goliad added further fuel to the vengeful fire that eventually inspired the Texans to victory at SAN JACINTO.

Gen. José Urrea led a division of Mexican soldiers against the Texans' fortification in the town of Goliad, where he encountered James Walker Fannin's company of four hundred Texas volunteers. Fannin had been ordered by Gen. Sam Houston to abandon Goliad, but he decided instead to fight the Mexicans when they captured several of his scouts.

Fannin formed his volunteers and artillery into a square in an open field outside the town, while the Mexican forces took advantage of natural cover nearby. Capt. Albert C. Horton's horsemen, patrolling in front of Fannin's line, warned of the vulnerability of the Texans' position, but Fannin held his ground and ordered his men to fire their weapons only at point-blank range. Fannin's riflemen held off repeated Mexican advances, and the two sides traded artillery fire throughout a hot day of fighting. Urrea ordered Fannin's oxen killed, immobilizing his force, and repeated Mexican cavalry and infantry attacks depleted the ranks of the Texans, who now had no way to escape.

At dusk, the Texans improvised a breastwork and spent the night trying to regroup. By morning, however, it was clear that Urrea's reinforcements far outnumbered the Texans. Fannin decided to surrender, and Urrea granted him general terms.

During the battle, the Texans suffered 9 killed and 51 wounded; the Mexicans lost 50 killed and 140 wounded.

Three hundred sixty-five Texas prisoners were taken to the town of Victoria to await parole, but on March 27 General Santa Anna declared them to be pirates and ordered their immediate execution. All 365 were killed, in violation of the terms of surrender that Urrea had originally granted.

The memory of those slain at the Alamo, now augmented by the 365 executed after Goliad, left Gen. Sam Houston's loosely organized Texas military force hungry for revenge. The Texans also harbored a personal hatred for General Santa Anna, which they would unleash at the Battle of San Jacinto.

Further Reading

Stephen L. Hardin. *Texian Iliad: A Military History of the Texas Revolution* (Austin: University of Texas Press, 1997); Jakie L. Pruett. *Goliad Massacre: A Tragedy of the Texas Revolution* (Austin, Tex.: Eakin Press, 1985); and Craig H. Roell. *Remember Goliad! A History of La Bahia* (Austin: Texas State Historical Association, 1994).

Greasy Grass

See LITTLE BIGHORN

Great Bridge

Virginia (December 9, 1775)
American Revolution

John Murray, the earl of Dunmore and royal governor of Virginia, strove mightily but unsuccessfully during 1775 to keep the colony in the British fold. Lord Dunmore was a pugnacious official, opposed by equally determined and aggressive Virginia patriots who chased him from his capital in June. Dunmore responded by threatening to free the black slaves and white indentured servants in the colony, and he set about organizing a military force of a few British regulars, Loyalist militia, backwoodsmen, Indians, and black slaves—the latter known as Dunmore's Ethiopians. By late in the year, Dunmore had assembled his main force in the coastal town of Norfolk.

The opposing patriots had organized two regular Virginia regiments as part of the fledgling Continental army and had much support from militia and irregulars.

In early December, American colonel William Woodford led one of the Virginia regiments, reinforced by several companies of riflemen, toward Norfolk. Dunmore took the bait and sent about twelve hundred men out to meet the Americans at Great Bridge, a crossing of the Elizabeth River south of Norfolk. The British built a hasty fortification on the eastern end of the bridge, and Woodford constructed a breastwork on the western end. The patriot commander left a relatively small detachment of less than one hundred men under a Lieutenant Travis at the bridge and encamped his main force at a nearby church.

On December 9, Dunmore ordered a force of six hundred, including many of the black slaves and two hundred regulars, to attack the Americans across the long bridge. A Captain Fordyce marched out at the head of a column of regulars and got within fifty yards or so of the patriot breastworks when the Americans opened fire and shattered the British. Fordyce rallied his men and tried a second attack, but the relatively few Americans again blasted the British at close range, killing Fordyce and wrecking the assaulting force.

Colonel Woodford now appeared with the main body of American troops, crossed the bridge, and surrounded the British defenders behind their own fortifications. During the night, the British evacuated all their troops back along the road to Norfolk. Woodford chased them out of the city and took possession a few days later.

The British counted twelve dead and seventeen wounded. As usual in the early engagements of the Revolution, when the British relied on frontal assaults against strong patriot field positions, the royal officers suffered disproportionately: three lieutenants and Captain Fordyce died at the point of attack. The Americans had only one man slightly injured.

Dunmore's hopes of holding Virginia for the crown were crushed by the defeat at Great Bridge.

Further Reading

Elizabeth B. Wingo. *The Battle of Great Bridge* (Chesapeake, Va.: Norfolk County Historical Society, 1964).

Great Meadows

See FORT NECESSITY

Great Savannah

South Carolina (August 20, 1780)
American Revolution

In the chaos that enveloped the American cause after Horatio Gates's defeat at CAMDEN, one of the few bright spots was the activity of a South Carolina partisan leader, Brig. Gen. Francis Marion (known as the "Swamp Fox"). He made a splash by a small but morale-boosting action at Great Savannah a few days after Gates had lost his entire army and Col. Thomas Sumter had been routed at FISHING CREEK.

Marion had a small force of dragoons and infantry, most of whom he had organized on his own. When he learned that a British detachment was camped on the Santee River with American prisoners from the battle at Camden, Marion swiftly moved in on it.

Capt. Hugh Horry was sent with sixteen men to block the main escape road, and Marion led most of his men in a direct surprise attack. The British regulars from the Sixty-third Regiment and the Prince of Wales Regiment scarcely put up a fight, and with the loss of only one killed, Marion liberated 150 American prisoners and killed or captured 24 British.

Further Reading

Mark M. Boatner. *The Encyclopedia of the American Revolution* (New York: David McKay, 1966).

Great Swamp

Rhode Island (December 19, 1675)
King Philip's War

The climactic battle of King Philip's War took place in a frozen swamp near modern-day West Kingston, Rhode Island, when a combined force of New Englanders wiped out the main village of the Narragansett.

The war had began earlier in 1675, when the pressures of a growing and expanding white presence in New England finally proved too much for several of the local tribes. Led by their chief sachem, Metacomet (called King Philip by the white New Englanders), the Wampanoag formed a loose alliance with the Nipmuc and gained cooperation from the more numerous Narragansett. Throughout the summer and fall of the year, Indian warriors attacked outlying white settlements, primarily in the Connecticut River valley, with considerable success. They destroyed an entire column of white settlers at BLOODY BROOK in September and threatened to push back the farming frontier to the coastline.

The governments of Massachusetts Bay, Plymouth, and Connecticut joined to form a combined military force (with the passive cooperation of Rhode Island, which did not contribute troops) and set out to defeat Metacomet's alliance. Their major goal was to prevent the Narragansett from joining Metacomet, so the New Englanders marched in December against the main fortified Narragansett village, which was in the middle of a large swamp in southwestern Rhode Island. The colonial army of one thousand men, most of them assembled from local militias and including 150 Mohegan Indian allies, was commanded by Plymouth governor Josiah Winslow. The Narragansett, led by Canonchet, may have numbered as many as four thousand, with between one thousand and two thousand warriors.

The weather was bitter cold and the swamp frozen solid when the New England army approached the Narragansett village on the afternoon of December 19. The village's fortifications were incomplete, and the New Englanders spotted a breach in the outer wall, which they made the focus of a frontal assault. The fighting was fierce, with heavy casualties on both sides, but the Narragansett could not withstand the superior firepower of the New Englanders. As soon as the white troops got the upper hand, they set the stockade and houses afire, killing many women and children who had taken shelter from the fighting.

The New England army lost twenty killed during the battle and had about two hundred wounded, many of whom subsequently died from the severe cold and exposure. The Narragansett losses are impossible to calculate accurately, but it is likely that at least one thousand perished in the battle or along the trail while trying to escape. Some estimate that one-third of the entire tribe died as the result of the battle.

The victory for the New Englanders was the turning point of the war, and Metacomet was unable thereafter to muster much resistance. He was hunted down and killed in August of the following year. He was treated in typical fashion by the New Englanders: his corpse was beheaded and quartered; his head was displayed at Plymouth and his body parts hung in trees; and his wife and children were sold as slaves to the West Indies. With his defeat, the power of the local tribes of New England was crushed forever.

Further Reading

Russell Bourne. *The Red King's Rebellion: Racial Politics in New England, 1675–1678* (New York: Atheneum, 1990); James D. Drake. *King Philip's War: Civil War in New England, 1675–1676* (Amherst, Mass.: University of Massachusetts Press, 2000); Francis Jennings. *The Invasion of America: Indians, Colonialism, and the Cant of Conquest* (Chapel Hill: University of North Carolina Press, 1975); Douglas E. Leach. *Flintlocks and Tomahawks: New England in King Philip's War* (New York: W. W. Norton, 1953); and Stephen S. Webb. *1676, The End of American Independence* (New York: Alfred A. Knopf, 1984).

Green Spring

Virginia (July 6, 1781) *American Revolution*

Throughout the spring and summer of 1781, the Marquis de Lafayette, a major general in the American army, played a game of maneuver in Virginia with Lt. Gen. Lord Cornwallis. The British commander hoped to trap "the boy," as he called his young opponent, and destroy the American army, which he greatly outnumbered. Lafayette, who had been reinforced by the arrival of Maj. Gen. Anthony Wayne in June, knew his force was too weak to fight a full-scale battle with the British, but he hoped to deplete and divert Cornwallis. When Cornwallis appeared to be taking his army across the James River, Lafayette ventured dangerously close and brought on a near disaster at Green Spring.

Cornwallis cleverly duped the Americans by giving indications he was crossing the river with his entire force of nearly seven thousand, but in fact, he sent only a small detachment and hid the bulk of his forces in woods. He then sent members of Lt. Col. Banastre Tarleton's British Legion down a road to impersonate a rear guard and to entice the Americans to march into a vulnerable position.

General Wayne was in command of about nine hundred Continentals—mostly his Pennsylvanians and some troops from Connecticut—and he pushed forward after Tarleton's men, across a marsh, and right up to the edge of the woods where Cornwallis waited. The British commander hoped to lure Lafayette forward with the rest of the American army, but when Wayne made contact, Cornwallis was forced to attack.

Wayne had deployed his troops and was preparing to attack what he still thought was merely a rear guard when the entire British army emerged from the woods, formed a long line, and struck, seeming about to overwhelm the Americans with sheer weight of numbers.

Although stunned to find himself facing Cornwallis's full force, Wayne was quick to recover. In an act of supreme courage and spirit, he ordered his men to fix bayonets and charge forward directly at the British army. The maneuver was so startling and the Americans' attack so spirited that the British were momentarily stopped in their tracks. After a hot exchange of musketry at close range, Wayne's men were able to retreat in good order and avoid annihilation.

Lafayette, who had meanwhile discovered the truth of Cornwallis's strength, covered Wayne's withdrawal and then managed to disengage entirely and remove his army from harm's way.

The Americans lost twenty-eight killed and ninety-nine wounded in the uneven fight. The British suffered seventy-five killed and wounded.

Cornwallis failed to follow up on the battle, allowing Lafayette to extricate himself.

Further Reading

Page Smith. *A New Age Now Begins: A People's History of the American Revolution.* Vol. 2 (New York: McGraw-Hill, 1976).

H.M.S. *Guerrière*

See U.S.S. CONSTITUTION

Guilford Courthouse

North Carolina (March 15, 1781)
American Revolution

Although he proved in the end to be the strategic master of his British foe, the American southern commander, Maj. Gen. Nathanael Greene, never defeated Lt. Gen. Lord Cornwallis on a battlefield. The engagement at Guilford Courthouse was typical: Cornwallis sent Greene into flight, but the triumph was costly to the British in the long run.

After the American victory at the COWPENS in January 1781 and Greene's successful withdrawal across the Dan River, Cornwallis was stymied in his campaign to destroy Greene's army and invade Virginia from the south. Moreover, his army had shrunk in size, and he probably commanded no more than nineteen hundred or so men, although they were nearly all veteran professionals. He was a long way from his base of supply and perhaps frustrated by Greene's harassing tactics.

Greene, on the other hand, had gained strength from an influx of militia and recrossed into North Carolina. By mid-March, he had more than four thousand troops, though a large percentage were raw and inexperienced. Confident that he could use his numbers to good advantage, Greene marched his army to Guilford Courthouse and waited for Cornwallis, who was twelve miles away, to give battle.

Since Greene had large numbers of militia and only a small core of seasoned Continentals, he followed the example set at the Cowpens by Daniel Morgan and arranged his troops in depth, hoping to use the militia to best advantage before relying on his veterans for a decisive blow. He chose a position across one of the main roads in the region, with heavy woods on each flank and to the rear, as well as a long, open field that the British would have to cross before attacking. Greene deployed his untested North Carolina militia, about one thousand strong and commanded by Brig. Gen. John Butler and Brig. Gen. Pinketham Eaton, in a line closest to the British avenue of approach. He instructed them to fire twice and then retreat, knowing full well that they would never stand up to a disciplined British bayonet charge. Greene positioned the Virginia rifle brigades of Gens. Edward Stevens and Robert Lawson three hundred yards farther to the rear, just inside the edge of the woods. Even farther back, in an open area near the courthouse, Greene stationed his elite troops, the Maryland Continentals, under Col. Otho Williams, and the Virginia Continentals, under Brig. Gen. Isaac Huger. Guarding the wooded flanks were the mounted troopers of William Washington and Henry Lee.

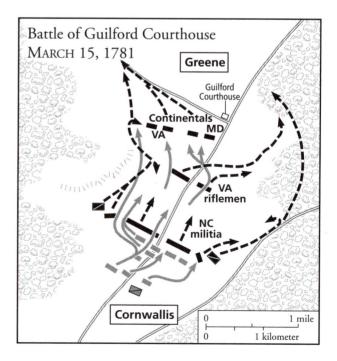

Battle of Guilford Courthouse
MARCH 15, 1781

Greene

Guilford Courthouse

Continentals
MD
VA

VA riflemen

NC militia

Cornwallis

0   1 mile
0   1 kilometer

Cornwallis got his men on the road at dawn for the long march to meet the Americans. Lt. Col. Banastre Tarleton's cavalry skirmished briefly with American riders before the main British force came up to the battleground, and by about noon the first redcoats had come into view and were under fire from two six-pounders that constituted the only American battery on the field. While the British gunners exchanged harmless shots with the Americans, Cornwallis formed up his troops into a main line of attack, with the Thirty-third and Twenty-third Regiments of Foot, under Lt. Col. James Webster, on the left, and the Seventy-first and the German Bose Regiments, commanded by Maj. Gen. Alexander Leslie, on the right. Two brigades of Guards were to the rear in reserve, along with Tarleton's riders.

The battle opened when the British line stepped off toward the first line of North Carolina militiamen, who opened fire at long range. The British continued to within one hundred yards, paused to fire a volley, and launched a bayonet charge. As if on cue, the North Carolinians broke and ran for the rear. The British formed up again and moved toward the second American line, the Virginia riflemen. Firing from the cover of the trees, the sharpshooting Americans did great damage to the British formations, but the British veterans showed—as they did throughout the battle—their extreme discipline and courage, pressing home an attack that forced the Virginians to abandon their positions and flee to the rear.

The British stepped out into the open ground and dressed their formations yet again for a bayonet attack against the third American line. When the redcoats came to within one hundred yards, however, a disciplined volley revealed the presence of the Continental veterans, who followed up with a bayonet countercharge that took the British line head-on. From the flanking woods, Col. William Washington's cavalry charged into the mass of British soldiers, and the fighting turned into a confused, hand-to-hand melee, with neither side willing or able to disengage. At this point in the battle, Cornwallis demonstrated his professionalism with a decision from which most amateur generals would have shrunk: over the objections of his subordinates, he ordered his artillery to fire devastating grapeshot into the mass of fighting infantry. Although there were British casualties from the friendly fire, the artillery attack ended any chance that the Americans would overwhelm the redcoat infantry. At the same time, Cornwallis ordered his reserve Guard brigades into the battle and directed Tarleton to charge into the melee. The weight of the British reserve was too much even for the hardy Continentals, and they began to waver and break.

When Greene realized what was happening, he ordered a general retreat, fearing the destruction of his army if he continued to press the issue. The Americans managed to disengage and withdraw in relatively good order, leaving the victorious Britons in command of the contested ground.

The British losses were severe. They counted 532 casualties, with 93 killed during the battle and 50 more dying of wounds soon after. The Guards were particularly hard hit, losing eleven of nineteen officers and close to 50 percent of the enlisted ranks. The American losses were proportionately lighter, with 78 killed and 183 wounded.

Greene led his army to the safety of camp a night's march away, where he once again regrouped. Cornwallis, although the victor, saw that his small army was severely depleted and his chances of pursuing the Americans were nil. After resting on the battlefield for three days, he began the trek toward his base in Wilmington.

Further Reading

Thomas E. Baker. *Another Such Victory: The Story of the American Defeat at Guilford Courthouse* (New York: Eastern Acorn Press, 1981); Burke Davis. *The Cowpens-Guilford Courthouse Campaign* (Philadelphia: Lippincott, 1962); and Hugh F. Rankin. *Greene and Cornwallis: The Campaign in the Carolinas* (Raleigh, N.C.: Department of Cultural Resources, Division of Archives and History, 1976).

≈ Guntown

See BRICE'S CREEK ROADS

≈ Gwynn Island

Virginia (July 8–10, 1776)
American Revolution

John Murray, the earl of Dunmore, the royal governor of Virginia, fought an aggressive but doomed campaign during 1775 and 1776 to keep his colony within British control. He commanded a few hundred regulars and recruited hundreds of black slaves (known as Dunmore's Ethiopians), white indentured servants, and backwoodsmen. By mid-1776, the Virginia patriots had beaten and harassed Dunmore nearly out of the colony. His last stronghold was on Gwynn Island at the mouth of the

Rappahannock River, where he had a small squadron of ships and his remaining troops.

Virginia brigadier general Andrew Lewis brought a column of troops and artillery to assault the island on July 8. A barrage from the Americans guns damaged the British ship *Dunmore* and wounded the governor himself. The other ships offered no resistance and attempted to escape, although several ran aground. The Virginians then turned their artillery on the island and bombarded it, with no reply, for several hours. An American landing force the next morning discovered that nearly all the defenders of the island had been stricken with smallpox, and only the sick and the dead remained.

Dunmore had been routed again, at the cost of only one American casualty—an officer killed in the explosion of a defective mortar.

Further Reading

Peter J. Wrike. *The Governor's Island: Gwynn's Island, Virginia, during the Revolution* (Gwynn, Va.: Gwynn's Island Museum, 1993).

⚒ Hanging Rock

South Carolina (August 6, 1780)
American Revolution

There were several engagements in South Carolina during the summer of 1780 between American patriot militia and British-sponsored units of Loyalists. The success of the patriots at Hanging Rock, though lessened by their lack of discipline, was important to the ebbing cause of the Revolution in the South.

The British had set up a series of outlying posts to help protect their base at CAMDEN, garrisoning most of them with Loyalist units from the North (who had come to the Carolinas as part of Lt. Gen. Sir Henry Clinton's expedition against CHARLESTON) and with South Carolina Loyalists who had organized after the British success. The South Carolina patriots, however, had some success in attacking the isolated posts, and the ranks of the militia had grown significantly under Col. Thomas Sumter. In early August, Sumter decided to attack ROCKY MOUNT,

meanwhile sending a column under Maj. William Davie toward Hanging Rock, twelve miles away.

The British post at Hanging Rock was defended by five hundred men—Loyalist members of the Prince of Wales Loyal American Volunteers, a few of Lt. Col. Banastre Tarleton's British Legion, North Carolina Loyalist militia, and Col. Thomas Brown's South Carolina Rangers. Maj. John Carden, commander of the Prince of Wales Volunteers (a unit of Connecticut Loyalists), was in charge of the defense.

As he approached the main Loyalist camp, Davie encountered and defeated a small unit of Loyalists at an outlying farm, and by August 5 he had brought his men into position. He was joined during the night by Sumter and his men, mostly mounted infantry, who had been frustrated at Rocky Mount. By morning on August 6, Sumter was ready to attack, planning a three-part assault all along the Loyalists' defensive front.

The patriot plan went awry almost at once, when guides misdirected Sumter's troops and almost all his force ended up facing North Carolinians, under Col. Morgan Bryan, who were stationed slightly apart on the left wing. Sumter's heavy attack collapsed Bryan's position, and the Loyalists pulled back toward their own center.

As Sumter's men pressed their attack, Major Carden made a daring movement with his Prince of Wales Volunteers. He left his position, circled the field, and assaulted Sumter from the flank just as the patriots were about to defeat the bulk of the Loyalist center. Despite the surprise, Sumter's men turned, fought off Carden, and took possession of the Loyalist camp.

Thereupon occurred the kind of episode so common in militia battles during the American Revolution: discipline broke down, and what had been a reasonably efficient fighting force became a mob of looters. Sumter's force lost all coherence, and the men began to plunder the Loyalists' possessions and supplies as fast as they could, many of them drinking themselves into a state of defenselessness.

Meanwhile, Carden regrouped his regiment of Connecticut Loyalists, formed a hollow square, and began to fire on the disorganized patriots. At about the same time, a troop of the British Legion showed up and added its weight to the British resurgence. Sumter could rally only a small number of his men—most of them were too drunk or preoccupied with looting to pay attention—but he managed to get them on the road and out of the way of further harm.

The patriots lost 12 killed and 41 wounded; the Loyalists recorded total casualties of 192.

Further Reading

John S. Pancake. *This Destructive War: The British Campaign in the Carolinas, 1780–1782* (University, Ala.: University of Alabama Press, 1985).

❧ Hanover Courthouse

Virginia (May 27, 1862) *American Civil War*

Federal major general George B. McClellan brought a huge army into eastern Virginia in the spring of 1861 in an attempt to capture the Confederate capital at Richmond. He was exceedingly timid and slow in his advance, however, and was eventually repulsed by a much smaller Confederate force.

One of the first engagements in this peninsular campaign came near Hanover Courthouse, toward which units of the Union Fifth Corps under Brig. General Fitz-John Porter had moved during the early morning hours of May 27, hoping to find and drive off Confederate troops that might constitute a threat to McClellan's flank. Porter's men ran into North Carolinians, commanded by Brig. Gen. Lawrence O. Branch.

After a brief but intense fight, the Confederates withdrew, leaving more than two hundred casualties and losing more than seven hundred prisoners. The Union lost 355.

Further Reading

Mark M. Boatner. *The Civil War Dictionary.* Rev. ed. (New York: David McKay, 1988).

❧ Hanover Junction

See NORTH ANNA RIVER

❧ Harlem Heights

New York (September 16, 1776)
American Revolution

The relatively small battle at Harlem Heights provided one of the few bright spots in the American attempt to stave off British seizure of Manhattan in 1776, but in the end it had little effect.

After evacuating his defeated army from LONG ISLAND to Manhattan, the American commander in chief, Gen. George Washington, set up his new defenses at Harlem Heights, an easily fortified high and narrow place between the Hudson River on the west and the Harlem River on the east. Washington had three divisions: Maj. Gen. Nathanael Greene's thirty-three hundred, at the southern limits of the American position, closest to the line of British advance; Maj. Gen. Israel Putnam, half a mile farther back with twenty-five hundred troops; and forty-two hundred men, under Maj. Gen. Joseph Spencer, behind the first of three defensive lines along the top of the heights. The rest of the American army was to the north, inside FORT WASHINGTON and at King's Bridge.

After landing at KIP'S BAY, the British commander, Gen. Sir William Howe, brought his main force of regulars and German mercenaries up from the southern part of the island to face the American positions at Harlem Heights, a distance of about two miles. With two regiments held in reserve to the rear, he had a large advantage in numbers as well as in commanding a much better trained and more experienced body of soldiers than did Washington.

By a quirk of topography, the Americans holding the most advanced position on the right could not see the British opposite them, hidden in a wooded area on the other side of a depression known as the Hollow Way. On the morning of September 16, General Washington ordered Lt. Col. Thomas Knowlton, one of the heroes of Bunker Hill, forward with about 150 Connecticut rangers to discover and report on the British dispositions. Knowlton's men crossed into the woods and found three regiments of British regulars, including the Forty-second Highlanders (known as the Black Watch). After a brisk exchange of fire, the American rangers retreated toward their own lines.

When Washington observed the skirmish and when he heard derisive fox-hunting bugle calls from the British lines, he ordered a feint toward the British and directed a second American force to steal around to the right and make a surprise flank attack. A mixed force from both New England and the southern colonies advanced on the British and boldly stood up to the regulars in the open field. Unfortunately for Washington's plan, the encircling American detachment discharged their muskets too soon and alerted the British, who withdrew toward the woods.

The major engagement of the day then developed in and around a field of buckwheat, and it continued as the afternoon wore on. Both sides poured more and more troops into the fight. The Americans, who had seen some of their militia compatriots abandon Kip's Bay the day before without a shot, were now emboldened by their success in driving the British redcoats back, and they pressed the attack. The British commander on the left, Brig. Gen. Alexander Leslie, called forward the reserves, including two regiments of Germans, to stiffen the British lines.

At this stage, Washington decided that a full-scale battle was to be avoided, and he ordered a retreat to the fortified lines on the heights. The American troops withdrew in good order, leaving the British in their positions.

Overall, the Americans were more successful in this battle than in any other during the New York campaign, and to some degree they repaired their sagging morale. Altogether, they lost about 30 killed (Knowlton among them) and 100 wounded. The British and Germans suffered 14 killed and 154 wounded. In overall strategic terms, not much was done to prevent the British moving onward toward capture of all of Manhattan.

Further Reading

Henry P. Johnston. *The Battle of Harlem Heights, September 16, 1776* (New York: Columbia University Press, 1897); William R. Shepherd. *The Battle of Harlem Heights* (New York: G. P. Putnam, 1898).

Harmar's Defeat

Indiana (October 19 and 22, 1790)
Little Turtle's War

Part of the Old Northwest (principally modern-day Ohio and Indiana) became the focus of intense conflict between the United States and several Indian tribes during the 1790s. The Miami, Shawnee, Delaware (Lenni Lenape), Wyandot (Huron), and other tribes resisted the encroachment of Americans and inflicted severe military defeats on the frontier armies of the United States. The first such blow came in 1790, when the Miami, under Little Turtle (Michikinikwa), destroyed an American expeditionary force.

For reasons both of cost and widespread political fear of a large standing army, the United States under its new constitution had only a token force of regulars: a few hundred men in one infantry regiment stationed on the Ohio frontier, commanded by Lt. Col. Commandant Josiah Harmar, a Revolutionary War veteran. When conflict escalated with the Indian tribes of the region (who often raided into Kentucky and refused to hand over land coveted by speculators), the nation had to rely on militia called up by the states. In 1790, Pres. George Washington and Sec. of War Henry Knox directed Harmar, who had been breveted as a brigadier general, to campaign against the tribes, ordering Kentucky and Pennsylvania militia to join the regulars at Fort Washington, near present-day Cincinnati.

Harmar was a reasonably competent officer, but he was completely inexperienced in frontier warfare, and like most of his American military colleagues, he greatly underestimated the caliber of his Indian foes. Moreover, when the militia arrived—about eleven hundred of them—they proved to be low-quality hired substitutes rather than reliable and experienced fighting men. The Kentucky troops were led by Lt. Col. James Trotter, and the Pennsylvanians by Lt. Col. Christopher Truby. Col. John Hardin was in overall command of the militia, which, together with 320 of Harmar's regulars, formed the American army.

Harmar planned a march against the large Miami village of Kekionga (known as Miami Town to non-Indians), situated at the head of the Maumee River in modern-day Indiana. Kekionga was surrounded by smaller villages and served as a central trading post for Indian commerce with the British. Harmar and his column set out for Kekionga in late September, and although his main body took a circuitous route, the object of his march was soon discerned by the Indians, who prepared a trap.

The chief war leader facing Harmar was Little Turtle, an extraordinary combat leader of mixed Miami and Mohican parentage. In addition to warriors from his own Miami tribe, there were also fighters from the Shawnee, Delaware, Wyandot, and others, forming an army of fluid size that at any one time may have numbered nine hundred warriors available to fight. Little Turtle's prime tactic was the ambush, the traditional and typical Indian battlefield maneuver, and he used it masterfully.

On October 13, Harmar learned from scouts that Kekionga was nearly deserted and that most of the inhabitants had fled. He sent Colonel Hardin ahead with a detachment of mounted Kentucky militia and followed with the main force, reaching Kekionga on October 17. Hoping to catch lingering Indians in the area, Harmar ordered Hardin to reconnoiter with 180 militia and 30 regulars, the latter commanded by Capt. John Armstrong. On October 19, Hardin and his men marched out of camp and down a well-traveled trail. When the advance patrol spotted a few fleeing Indians, Hardin allowed an ill-organized pursuit that broke up his formation. The militia ran directly into Little Turtle's main camp and found fresh campfires and abandoned equipment. As they stumbled around the camp clearing in a fit of looting, Little Turtle sprang his ambush.

From a position hidden in trees at the edge of the village clearing, the Indians poured musket fire on the disorganized militia. When the Americans turned to fire back, they were hit by another volley from the rear. Overcome by confusion and fear, the militia broke and ran for their lives, many falling to Indian fire and tomahawks. Captain Armstrong held his handful of regulars in place, but they were soon overrun by Little Turtle's warriors. Armstrong and a few others escaped into a nearby swamp and hid, surviving only because the Indians were preoccupied with killing the wounded and prisoners. At least 120 Americans were killed in the ambush or its aftermath.

Harmar saw little choice but to retreat, so he ordered his remaining men to destroy a few smaller Indian villages and prepare to march back to Fort Washington. On October 22, however, he received a report that a few Indians had returned to Kekionga, and hoping to recoup

something from his failed expedition, Harmar ordered a regular officer, Maj. John Wyllys, to take a detachment of sixty regulars, forty mounted militia, and four hundred picked militia infantry back to the site of the ambush, where they were to attack the Indians as they drifted back to their village.

Wyllys split his force and planned a double envelopment of the village, with his mounted troops to attack up the middle. Little Turtle, however, was once again ahead of his opponents. Even though many of his warriors had left the area, he still had a force sufficient to set another trap. As Wyllys and his mounted men crossed the Maumee near Kekionga, they were attacked. When the Americans fought back, the Indians appeared to flee, and Wyllys set out in rapid pursuit. When the Americans reached a burned-over cornfield, Little Turtle unleashed his full strength, overwhelming the whites with sheer numbers and killing most of them at close range. Wyllys and all but ten of his regulars died on the spot, and the militia support arrived too late to engage the Indians, who had slipped away. The surviving militia abandoned the dead and wounded and fled back to Harmar's main column.

The American losses overall for the two engagements were around two hundred; there are no figures for the Indians' casualties, but one soldier reported seeing forty bodies left at the ambush site on October 22.

The defeat of an American army by western Indians was devastating to the new nation. Harmar was disgraced, and the national administration immediately began to look for a replacement to revenge the losses (*see also* ST. CLAIR'S DEFEAT).

Further Reading

Harvey Carter. *The Life and Times of Little Turtle: First Sagamore of the Wabash Indians* (Urbana: University of Illinois Press, 1987); Douglas R. Hurt. *The Ohio Frontier: Crucible of the Old Northwest* (Bloomington: Indiana University Press, 1996); John A. Murphy. *Harmar's Defeat: Letters, Journals, and Narratives* (Pataskala, Ohio: Brockston, 1990); Dave R. Palmer. *1794: America, Its Army, and the Birth of a Nation* (Novato, Calif.: Presidio Press, 1994); and Wiley Sword. *President Washington's Indian War: The Struggle for the Old Northwest, 1790–1795* (Norman: University of Oklahoma Press, 1985).

❧ Harpers Ferry

Virginia (West Virginia) (September 12–15, 1862)
American Civil War

The town of Harpers Ferry, at the confluence of the Potomac and Shenandoah Rivers (in what become West

Virginia in 1863), was one of the Union's most strategically important points: it housed the large Federal arsenal that John Brown had attacked in 1859 and was home to both the Baltimore & Ohio Railroad and the Chesapeake & Ohio Canal. When Confederate general Robert E. Lee invaded northern territory in the fall of 1862, he split his army and dispatched Maj. Gen. Thomas J. "Stonewall" Jackson to capture Harpers Ferry, assuming that the thirteen thousand Union troops stationed there would withdraw. Instead, Federal colonel Dixon S. Miles was ordered "to hold Harper's Ferry to the last extremity," but daring Confederate moves and the delay of Union reinforcements due to engagements at SOUTH MOUNTAIN and CRAMPTON'S GAP enabled Jackson to capture the Union stronghold.

On September 10, 1862, three separate columns of Confederates began to close in on Harpers Ferry, where Colonel Miles tried to prepare his vastly less experienced men by dividing them between the Maryland and Bolivar Heights. Though Confederate major general Lafayette McLaws's approach from the Maryland Heights was to be slowed by his engagement at Crampton's Gap, Maj. Gen. John G. Walker's division of two thousand men and Major General Jackson's three divisions of fourteen thousand battle-tested soldiers made rapid progress toward the Loudon Heights (southeast of town) and the Bolivar Heights (west of town), respectively.

Fighting near Harpers Ferry broke out on September 13, when Walker's men easily seized the Loudon Heights from the green Federals assigned to protect them. McLaws initially seized the Maryland Heights but had to pause on September 14 to fight with Union major general William B. Franklin. Jackson's three divisions also pushed toward the Bolivar Heights and took the School House Ridge on the evening of September 13.

Capturing these hill positions allowed Confederate artillery to target the city directly, and at 2 P.M. on September 14 it began a heavy bombardment that lasted until nightfall. The inexperienced Federal troops barely held on to the Bolivar Heights and, despite the heavy fire, continued to hold the town as well.

Late on September 14, Stonewall Jackson received news that the other wing of General Lee's army was in trouble: Brig. Gen. D. H. Hill's division had been forced to abandon South Mountain, and Maj. Gen. George B. McClellan (who had captured General Lee's orders for the action) was bearing down on Lee himself. If Harpers Ferry could not be taken on September 15, the entire northern invasion would have to be canceled.

Overnight on September 14–15, Jackson sent Maj. Gen. A. P. Hill's three thousand men around the Union left flank on Bolivar Heights, just as Col. Benjamin F. "Grimes" Davis's thirteen hundred Federal cavalrymen escaped from town. Hill's move was effective, and he was able to establish an additional line of infantry and artillery at the Chambers farm beyond the Union left.

At dawn on September 15, the Confederates resumed their bombardment, now made all the more effective by Hill's new position. Miles was mortally wounded and finally ordered white flags to be raised around 8 A.M. The formal surrender, delivered to Lee atop School House Ridge, meant that the Confederates had captured more than twelve thousand Federal soldiers, the largest single-day surrender of U.S. troops up to that time. (It would not be surpassed until 1942, at Bataan.) Jackson also captured a number of artillery pieces, small arms, and supply wagons.

The lopsided casualty totals at Harpers Ferry reflect the severity of the Union surrender. The Confederates lost only 286, while Federal losses totaled 12,719 (including those captured).

Jackson's success at Harpers Ferry prompted Lee to fall back to Sharpsburg, Maryland, where he decided to engage McClellan's army. The subsequent battle of ANTIETAM was to be the bloodiest single day in American military history.

Further Reading

Edward J. Stackpole. *From Cedar Mountain to Antietam, August–September, 1862* (Harrisburg, Pa.: Stockpole, 1959).

Harrisburg

See TUPELO

Haw River

(Pyle's Defeat)
North Carolina (February 25, 1781)
American Revolution

After successfully eluding Lt. Gen. Lord Cornwallis, and crossing the Dan River into Virginia, the American southern commander, Maj. Gen. Nathanael Greene, sent a strong mobile detachment comprised of Lt. Col. Henry "Light-Horse Harry" Lee's legion and two companies of

Maryland regulars under Brig. Gen. Andrew Pickens back into South Carolina to harass Cornwallis and discourage Loyalist organization. A ruse by Lee resulted in a sharp victory at Haw River.

Lee's men wore short green dragoon jackets that were very similar in appearance to the uniforms of Lt. Col. Banastre Tarleton's famed British Legion. Lee decided to impersonate Tarleton and infiltrate a group of four hundred mounted Loyalist militia commanded by Capt. John Pyle. Pickens led the Maryland infantry into nearby woods, while Lee and his troopers, with sabers drawn, rode directly up the road to Pyle's men, asking that they move aside to allow "Tarleton" to pass.

Pyle obligingly pulled his men to the edge of the road and permitted Lee's men to ride alongside in a column. Lee was about to disabuse Pyle of his identity when a Loyalist spotted the Maryland infantry and gave the alarm. Lee's troopers wheeled and attacked with blade and pistol, taking the Loyalists completely by surprise, killing ninety of them on the spot and wounding many more. None of Lee's men were injured, and the will of the local Loyalists to aid the British was further weakened.

Further Reading

John S. Pancake. *This Destructive War: The British Campaign in the Carolinas, 1780–1782* (Tuscaloosa: University of Alabama Press, 1985).

➷ Helena

Arkansas (July 4, 1863) *American Civil War*

At the same time that the battles at GETTYSBURG and VICKSBURG reached their climaxes, Confederate forces attempted unsuccessfully to retake the Mississippi River port of Helena, Arkansas, which the Union had captured a year earlier.

The city was stoutly fortified against a land attack, with strong earthworks dominated by four batteries placed in protruding, enclosed redoubts. The garrison had been reduced to around four thousand when all spare troops were ordered away for the siege of Vicksburg, but the remaining numbers were enough to man the defenses, which were commanded by Maj. Gen. Benjamin Prentiss, a veteran of SHILOH. Prentiss anticipated the arrival of a fleet of river gunboats to assist him, but only a single wooden ship, the U.S.S. *Tyler*, showed up in time for the battle.

The Confederate assault was under the overall command of Lt. Gen. Theophilius H. Holmes, but the direct commander in the field was Maj. Gen. Sterling Price, who had around sixty-five hundred men in his force, which struck at the Union defenses in the early morning.

The initial assault against Battery C was successful, and the Confederates drove the Union defenders out of the fortifications, which they left after spiking the guns. There were too few Confederates, however, both to hold the captured redoubt and concentrate strength at other points. When the *Tyler* began a bombardment from the river, the Confederates were unable to continue the attack and began to withdraw by mid-morning.

The Confederates lost four hundred killed and twelve hundred captured. The Federals lost 239.

The fall of Vicksburg made the attack on Helena moot, even had the Confederates won.

Further Reading

Jay Wertz and Edwin C. Bearss. *Smithsonian's Great Battles and Battlefields of the Civil War* (New York: William Morrow, 1997).

➷ Hillsborough Raid

North Carolina (September 12, 1781)
American Revolution

Col. David Fanning, a backcountry North Carolina Loyalist, was a thorn in the side of the patriots throughout the war in the South, but his greatest exploit came after it was too late to affect the course of the war: he captured the entire patriot government of North Carolina and carried it off to captivity. Unfortunately for Fanning, Gen. George Washington was about to close in on Lt. Gen. Lord Cornwallis to the north on the YORKTOWN peninsula, so Fanning's accomplishment had small practical impact.

Fanning operated off and on during the war from a base near Cox's Mill, his activity increasing with the rise in British fortunes in the region during late 1780 and early 1781.

In September 1781, Fanning gathered a Loyalist militia force of 950 and marched in a surprise attack on Hillsborough, where the patriot government had its headquarters. He brushed aside the weak patriot defense, capturing Gov. Thomas Burke, the state council, several legislators, and more than seventy Continentals. By noon, he was on the road with his prisoners, but he was attacked at Lindley's Mill by four hundred Continentals under Brig. Gen. John Butler. The battle stretched throughout the afternoon, and Fanning finally won, although he and several other Loyalists were badly wounded, and the prisoners were delivered to Wilmington. Fanning lost a total of 115 casualties; the patriots about the same number.

Further Reading

Mark M. Boatner. *The Encyclopedia of the American Revolution* (New York: David McKay, 1966).

➷ Hobkirk's Hill

South Carolina (April 25, 1781)
American Revolution

Following the Battle of GUILFORD COURTHOUSE, American commander Nathanael Greene turned toward South Carolina to confront the British army, commanded by Brig. Gen. Francis Rawdon-Hastings (known during this period of his life as Lord Rawdon), that had been left there by Lt. Gen. Lord Cornwallis to guard British posts. The two forces fought a sharp battle at Hobkirk's Hill, near the old battle site of CAMDEN.

Marching with about fifteen hundred men, including Continentals and militia, Greene hoped to surprise Rawdon and attack the British before the young commander could gather his forces, but Rawdon had good intelligence information and was ready when the Americans arrived in the vicinity of Camden. Greene was forced to halt about a mile and a half away from Rawdon's position, setting up camp at Hobkirk's Hill. He deployed the Virginia Continentals under Isaac Huger to the right, facing the British camp, and the Marylanders under Otho Williams to the left, astride the main road leading to Camden. A company of Delaware Continentals camped in front of the main deployment, and William Washington's dragoons and some North Carolina militia were to the rear. The Americans relaxed, not anticipating a fight.

Rawdon had other ideas. He had about eight hundred men, the majority of them in experienced Loyalist units, and he was expecting the arrival of five hundred more troops who had been on detached duty, but he decided not to wait for the reinforcements. On the morning of April 25, he marched out of his camp in Camden and deployed his troops into attack formation as they neared Hobkirk's Hill. Greene's scouts alerted the Americans, who were cooking their breakfasts, and they hastily prepared to meet Rawdon's men.

When Greene looked down the hill, he saw that Rawdon's front line comprised only three units—the King's Americans, the New York Volunteers, and the Sixty-third Regiment—and that the rest of Rawdon's under-strength force was to the rear. Greene decided to use his superior numbers and outflank Rawdon's relatively narrow front, so he ordered his front line to attack the British line in a double envelopment, and he told Washington to sweep around and attack Rawdon from the rear.

Greene's tactic failed when Rawdon, after a brief check, brought up his reserve units on the flanks of his front line, so that he overlapped the American flanks instead of vice versa, as Green had envisioned. Even more disastrously for the Americans, the usually rock-solid First Maryland Continentals of Col. John Gunby for once failed in the clutch. They began to waver, and their formation turned ragged. Gunby ordered a halt, which soon turned into a retreat that was rapidly joined by the other frontline Continental units until the entire American battle line disintegrated into flight. Greene himself had to help rescue his army's field artillery. Washington's dragoons had to abandon two hundred noncombatant prisoners they had taken at the rear of the British lines and race to catch up to the retreating American army.

By midafternoon, Greene and his men were three miles from the battlefield; Rawdon, after surveying his sharp little victory, marched back to Camden. The Americans lost 18 killed and 248 wounded. Rawdon reported 38 killed and 220 wounded.

Further Reading

Christopher Ward. *The War of the Revolution*. Vol. 2 (New York: Macmillan, 1952).

➷ Holly Springs

Mississippi (December 20, 1862)
American Civil War

Confederate major general Earl Van Dorn dealt a serious blow to Union major general Ulysses S. Grant's first attempt to attack VICKSBURG when he raided the major Federal supply depot at Holly Springs with thirty-five hundred cavalrymen.

Van Dorn achieved an easy and complete victory over a small Union garrison commanded by Wisconsin colonel Robert Murphy, even though Murphy had advance word of the attack. Van Dorn took fifteen hundred prisoners and destroyed mounds of supplies and several buildings, thereby wrecking the logistical support of Grant's army.

Following the raid, Van Dorn returned to his base, raiding other small Union posts on the way. Murphy was dismissed from the Federal service the following month.

Further Reading

Jay Wertz and Edwin C. Bearss. *Smithsonian's Great Battles and Battlefields of the Civil War* (New York: William Morrow, 1997).

Horseshoe Bend

Alabama (March 27, 1814) *Creek War*

The Creek War was fought between the Red Stick faction of the Creek Nation and an army of American militia, which was supplemented by many pro-American Indian allies. Events came to a head in the spring of 1814 after seven months of fighting deep in Alabama Territory. (The Red Stick faction supported war; the White Stick faction peace.)

The Red Sticks were led by William Weatherford (Lamochattee or Red Eagle), a warrior of mixed Scottish and Creek ancestry, and even though they had suffered heavy losses at TALLASACHATCHEE and TALLADEGA, they were still a powerful force. They had prepared a strong fortified village called Tohopeka with an angled log stockade that stretched across a horseshoe bend in the Tallapoosa

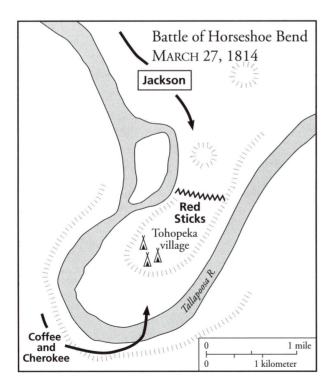

Battle of Horseshoe Bend
MARCH 27, 1814

Jackson

Red Sticks

Tohopeka village

Tallapoosa R.

Coffee and Cherokee

0   1 mile

0   1 kilometer

River and presented a formidable defense against an attack from the landward side. The village sheltered nearly fifteen hundred warriors and their families and black slaves. The Indians had assembled a fleet of canoes on the river side of the fortress, ready for escape, if need be.

Opposing the Red Sticks was a mostly volunteer army made up of Tennesseans and Georgians and commanded by Maj. Gen. Andrew Jackson. Jackson had barely been able to keep a viable force in the field during the winter, when poor supply and lapsing enlistments had at times reduced his army to a few hundred. By spring, however, his ranks had swollen with new militia and the six hundred regular troops of the Thirty-ninth Infantry Regiment. Jackson probably commanded forty-five hundred men on the eve of the battle.

When he learned of the strength of the Red Stick fort from the reports of his Indian scouts, Jackson ordered Brig. Gen. John Coffee across the river to provide a diversionary threat to the rear of the Creek position. After Coffee got into position, a group of daring Cherokee allies swam across and stole all of the Red Stick canoes, stranding the Creek warriors with their families.

Jackson began his assault with a cannonade by his light fieldpieces, but the six-pounders made little impression on the heavy log construction of the stockade. Meanwhile, Coffee's men set many of the Red Stick houses ablaze with fire arrows. After these preliminaries, Jackson ordered a frontal assault with the bayonet by the regulars of the Thirty-ninth. Their discipline and training proved decisive, and their attack drove the majority of the Red Stick defenders away from the fortified wall. The battle was essentially over at that stage, but the Americans continued to hunt down and kill Creek for several hours. Many drowned in the swift-flowing river.

By Jackson's tally, 917 Red Stick warriors were killed, and 300 women and children were taken captive. The American troops lost 47 killed and 159 wounded, and the Americans' Indian allies lost 23 killed and 47 wounded.

The defeat ended the war and broke the power of the Creek Nation, which had been a dominant force in the South since before the American Revolution. Jackson subsequently forced a confiscatory treaty on all the Creek, hostile and allies alike, and parlayed his victories into a national military and political reputation. William Weatherford, who had been absent during the Battle of Horseshoe Bend, surrendered and was pardoned.

Further Reading

Angie Debo. *Road to Disappearance: A History of the Creek Indians Tribe* (Norman: University of Oklahoma Press, 1941); David S. and Jeanne T. Heidler. *Old Hickory's War: Andrew Jackson and the Quest for Empire* (Mechanicsburg, Pa.: Stackpole Books, 1996); Joel W. Martin. *Sacred Revolt: The Muskogee's Struggle for a New World* (Boston: Beacon Press, 1991); and Frank L. Owsley, Jr. *Struggle for the Gulf Borderlands* (Gainesville: University Presses of Florida, 1981).

Hubbardton

Vermont (July 7, 1777) *American Revolution*

When the American army under Maj. Gen. Arthur St. Clair abandoned FORT TICONDEROGA in the face of British general John Burgoyne's invasion force, it fled rapidly toward Vermont, but the rear guard was caught and surprised at Hubbardton.

Most of St. Clair's 2,500 troops cleared Hubbardton on July 6, but he ordered Vermont's Col. Seth Warner to hold the town with 150 men until the army's rear guard caught up. By nightfall, Warner's men were joined by the rear guard, the Eleventh Massachusetts, under Col. Turbott Francis, and the Second New Hampshire, commanded by Col. Nathan Hale (not the famous school teacher and spy). The one thousand or so men settled in for the night in Hubbardton, despite St. Clair's orders to keep moving. Moreover, Warner and his fellow commanders were careless and set out too few guards.

The British pursuit, led by Brig. Gen. Simon Fraser, was close on the Americans' heels. Fraser had about 750 light infantry and a few Indian scouts, plus Brunswick grenadiers and jaegers (riflemen) under Maj. Gen. Baron Friedrich von Riedesel. Pausing to rest his men after he discovered the American detachment in Hubbardton, Fraser prepared an early morning attack.

Shortly before 5:00 A.M., the British light infantry assaulted Hale's camp, achieving complete surprise. The New Hampshiremen fled the scene and played almost no role in the rest of the battle.

Fraser then turned on Warner and Francis, but the remaining Americans had had time to rally and form a long line of battle, anchored on the extreme left by Zion Hill, steep, wooded, and 1,200 feet high. As the British moved forward, the Americans delivered several effective volleys, stalled the attack, and killed several officers. Fraser then decided to try to flank the American line by sending troops up Zion Hill, hoping they could fire down on the enemy or reach the Americans' rear. The going was difficult, however, and the British could barely climb the rugged hillside. The Americans shifted their front to face the new attack, and the flanking movement failed.

Worse for Fraser, he had taken troops from his left to make the attack on his right, and now the Americans pushed forward, threatening to collapse the weakened British line and sweep it off the field. At the crucial moment, Riedesel arrived with his jaegers (and a regimental band playing as it marched) and drove straight into the Americans who threatened Fraser's flank. The blow struck the Massachusetts men hard. Colonel Francis fell, and the rest of the regiment melted away.

When he realized his Vermonters were the only Americans left on the field, Warner ordered a piecemeal retreat with the command "Scatter and meet me in Manchester."

For the numbers involved, the sharp encounter produced heavy casualties. The Americans had 40 or so killed and more than 300 captured, including Colonel Hale and many of his men who had tried to flee. The British and Germans lost 35 killed and 145 wounded.

Further Reading

Ebenezer Fletcher. *The Narrative of Ebenezer Fletcher, a Soldier of the Revolution, Written by Himself.* 4th ed. (Freeport, N.Y.: Books for Libraries Press, 1970); and John A. Williams, *The Battle for Hubbardton: The American Rebels Stem the Tide* (Montpelier: Vermont Division for Historic Preservation, 1988).

I

⚓ H.M.S. *Iris*

See U.S.S. *TRUMBULL*

⚓ Irish Bend

(Bayou Teche)

Louisiana (April 12–14, 1863) *American Civil War*

One of Union general Nathaniel Banks's campaigns in the West was against Port Hudson, a Confederate stronghold on the Mississippi River. As part of his plan, Banks tried to take control of the west bank of the river by occupying Irish Bend. He was opposed by Confederate lieutenant general Richard Taylor, brother-in-law of Pres. Jefferson Davis and a skillful field general.

Banks had around fifteen thousand men and therefore vastly outnumbered the Confederates, who could muster only about four thousand, but the Union forces were never concentrated and found it difficult to move in the swampy region.

Banks, believing he had Taylor trapped, sent various parts of his army to flank or take the Confederates in the rear; however, the Union detachments failed to get into position. One, attempting to move around a nearby lake, was stymied when an escorting gunboat ran aground. A second detachment managed to cross the bayou and attack Taylor's main body on April 13, with some success, but Taylor was able to disengage and withdraw during the night.

On the following day, Taylor turned the tables and attacked one of the larger Union detachments, commanded by Brig. Gen. Cuvier Grover, bringing the Federal movements to a halt again. Taylor then retreated out of harm's way.

The engagements around Irish Bend cost the Union 350 casualties.

Further Reading

Mark M. Boatner. *The Civil War Dictionary.* Rev. ed. (New York: David McKay, 1988).

148

Iron Hill

See COOCH'S BRIDGE

Island Number 10

Tennessee (April 7, 1862) *American Civil War*

At the same time Ulysses S. Grant was staving off defeat at SHILOH, Tennessee, another Union force took the important Mississippi River fort at Island Number 10.

The Confederate position in the West had suffered grievously with the loss of both FORT HENRY and FORT DONELSON, but the South still controlled all of the lower Mississippi. Island Number 10 (named for its position as tenth island downriver from the confluence of the Ohio and Mississippi Rivers) was at the head of a contorted double bend in the river, a spot that formed a natural strong point. Maj. Gen. John McCown, in command of the island's defenses, had pulled his seven thousand troops out of New Madrid, Missouri. The island was susceptible to a land assault if an army could run past the fifty guns and deploy troops below the post, but this was a difficult task.

The Union forces were commanded by Brig. Gen. John Pope, a career officer whose campaign was supported by a powerful fleet of ironclad gunboats and mortar boats under Flag Officer Andrew Foote. Foote opened a heavy bombardment of the island, but no amount of pounding seemed to do much damage; Foote feared a disaster, however, if his gunboats attempted to run past the Confederate batteries. Meanwhile, army units cut a canal through a swamp to allow shallow-draft Union transports to deposit Pope's infantry downriver from the island.

Finally, on the night of April 4, Cmdr. Henry Walke ran his gunboat *Carondelet* past the island fort and he was followed two nights later by the *Pittsburg*. The two boats were sufficient to guard the river crossing, and the next day Pope's men were behind Island Number 10 and had cut off the Confederate line of escape. The Confederates surrendered, giving up 7,000 prisoners and 158 pieces of artillery. The Union land forces suffered no casualties, although the navy reported seventeen killed and thirty-four wounded.

Further Reading

Larry J. Daniel. *Island No. 10: Struggle for the Mississippi Valley* (Tuscaloosa: University of Alabama Press, 1996).

Iuka

Mississippi (September 19, 1862)
American Civil War

Iuka was important because of its proximity to CORINTH, a key rail junction that in mid-1862 both the Confederacy and the Union wanted to control. Confederate major general Sterling Price had occupied Iuka on September 13, and Union major general Ulysses S. Grant sent two columns—one under Maj. Gen. Edward Ord and the other commanded by Maj. Gen. William Rosecrans—to take it back.

The Federal plan was for Rosecrans to take up a blocking position, but as his leading brigade passed within two miles of the town during the late afternoon, the Confederates, now under the command of Brig. Gen. Lewis Henry Little, attacked in strength. Heavy fighting developed between two full brigades of Confederates and the three brigades under Rosecrans, with the Southerners pushing back the Union line until about sunset, when Rosecrans's men stabilized their positions.

Ord had been waiting for the sound of battle before he attacked, but a freak of topography and wind, called an acoustic shadow, prevented him from hearing anything of the clash that was only a few miles away, and he remained in place throughout the entire afternoon and evening.

The Confederates withdrew the following day in the face of superior numbers. They had lost 263 killed, 692 wounded, and 561 missing. General Little died on the battlefield. The Union reported 144 killed, 598 wounded, and 40 missing.

Further Reading

Peter Cozzens. *The Darkest Days of the War: The Battles of Iuka and Corinth* (Chapel Hill: University of North Carolina Press, 1997); and Ben Earl Kitchens. *Rosecrans Meets Price: The Battle of Iuka, Mississippi* (Florence, Ala.: Thornwood Books, 1987).

J

Jamestown

Virginia (March 22, 1622) *Virginia-Indian Wars*

The violent attack on English settlements around Jamestown, Virginia, on the morning of March 22, 1622, was probably the most notable event in a long series of conflicts between the Powhatan Indians and the settlers of the area, and it touched off an intermittent warfare that lasted for twenty years.

The first English had sailed into the mouth of the James River in 1607 and founded a small settlement that barely survived its first years. The region was under the sway of Powhatan (Wahunsonacock), a strong leader who had consolidated an alliance founded by his father into a confederacy of around thirty-two Algonquian-speaking bands in the James, York, and Rappahannock River drainages shortly before the English arrived. (The bands are usually termed "Powhatan" collectively and are often called the Powhatan Confederacy, although more accurately they were allies who all acknowledged Powhatan as

their principal chief.) Powhatan's policy was to tolerate the Europeans, even after the colonists began to expand their settlements around 1610, following their discovery that tobacco was a profitable cash crop. By the time of Powhatan's death in 1618, there were more than one thousand English colonists in the area, and their tobacco farms were beginning to spread for miles along the banks of the James, displacing Indian cornfields.

Powhatan's position was assumed by his second brother, Openchancanough, who had never been as tolerant of the European invasion. As conflict with the settlers increased, fueled by more arrivals, more tobacco farms, and annoying attempts to convert the Indians to Christianity, Openchancanough planned a reversal of Powhatan's policies and an attempt to rid his land of the English. When settlers murdered Nemattanew, a famous Powhatan warrior, Openchancanough had his excuse.

The actual violence, scarcely a battle, may be one of the few incidents between Europeans and Indians that actually deserves the term massacre. Openchancanough's warriors struck the outlying farmsteads suddenly on the morning of Good Friday, meeting little resistance. They killed all the whites they could find, a total of 347, including men, women, and children. The people of Jamestown proper were spared because they retreated to their strong triangular stockade in the middle of the town. The Powhatan probably suffered few casualties, if any.

The result of the 1622 attack was a long period of military conflict. The English organized raids into Powhatan territory to destroy the corn crops, and the Indians retaliated with raids on farmsteads and settlements. The struggle lasted, off and on, until 1644, when Openchancanough—by then a very old man—was finally captured and killed.

Further Reading

Francis Jennings. *The Founders of America* (New York: W. W. Norton, 1993); William S. Powell, "The Aftermath of the Massacre." *Virginia Magazine of History and Biography* 66 (1958): 44–75; Helen Rountree. *The Powhatan Indians of Virginia* (Norman: University of Oklahoma Press, 1989); and Ian K. Steele. *Warpaths: Invasions of North America* (New York: Oxford University Press, 1994).

✎ Jamestown

Virginia (September 16, 1676) *Bacon's Rebellion*

In 1676, Nathaniel Bacon, a wealthy tobacco farmer and member of the provincial council of the colony of Virginia, led a makeshift army against Susquehannok, Ocaneechi, and Pamunkey Indians, some of whom had attacked settlers on the outskirts of colonial settlements, though some of whom were perfectly friendly. Bacon galvanized the support of Virginians, many of whom feared Indian incursions and blamed the royal governor Sir William Berkeley for adopting too conciliatory an attitude toward them. By September 1676, Bacon had turned against Berkeley, who objected to his leading military expeditions without proper crown authority, and Bacon's rebels laid siege to the capital of Jamestown to drive Berkeley from office.

Berkeley took up a position across the Chesapeake from Jamestown on Virginia's Eastern Shore, where he gathered more than 500 soldiers and militiamen and prepared to send ships against Bacon's camp (of only 136 rebels) outside of Jamestown. Bacon's men built fortifications on Block House Hill, from which they repulsed Berkeley's main naval attack on September 14. Though Berkeley's cannon caused some damage to Bacon's newly constructed palisades, the governor's men were unable to overwhelm the rebel position, and Berkeley realized that only an all-out assault would dislodge the rebel force. Though Berkeley's military force outnumbered Bacon's, the rebels' cause enjoyed support among Virginia's colonial settlers, so Bacon was confident he could find reinforcements.

The main attack came on September 16, when Berkeley tried to coordinate naval action with a sortie of loyalists from Jamestown itself. Berkeley positioned servants and conscripts in the front line of attack, followed by militia officers and prominent men of the colony. When they approached Bacon's fortifications, the front ranks collapsed quickly, and those in the rear panicked and fled. Bacon had made it even more difficult for Berkeley to rally by deploying a line of female prisoners, including the wives of several provincial Council members, in the front of his fortification. Berkeley's men would have had to fire on their own wives in order to reach Bacon's rebels.

Twelve of Berkeley's men were killed in the assault on Bacon's camp.

Bacon's rebels continued to take and display prisoners throughout September. They even bombarded Jamestown. Berkeley returned to the Eastern Shore, from where he watched as Bacon ordered Jamestown burned to the ground on October 18. Bacon hoped to govern the colony, but his hold began to slip when he caused fear and suspicion among his more elite supporters by recruiting indentured servants and even slaves to his cause. Bacon died of dysentery on October 26, and Berkeley quickly regained control of Virginia.

Further Reading

Robert Middlekauf, ed. *Bacon's Rebellion* (Chicago: Rand MacNally, 1964); Stephen S. Webb. *The End of American Independence*. Reprint ed. (Syracuse, N.Y.: Syracuse University Press, 1995); and Thomas J. Wertenbaker. *Torchbearer of the Revolution: The Story of Bacon's Rebellion and Its Leader* (Princeton, N.J.: Princeton University Press, 1940).

✎ Jamestown Ford

See GREEN SPRING

✎ Jericho Mills

See NORTH ANNA RIVER

Johnstown

New York (October 25, 1781) *American Revolution*

The last in a long series of raids and battles in upper New York State pitting patriots against British-sponsored Loyalists and Indians, the battle at Johnstown was itself inconclusive, with the American patriots allowing a large raiding party to slip away.

Col. Marinus Willet, one of the heroes of FORT STANWIX, had been placed in charge of guarding the New York frontier against Loyalist and Indian raids in the summer of 1781, but he had a force of only about four hundred men, scattered across a wide area, with which to defend the farmers and settlers of the region.

In the fall, British major John Ross assembled a large force of Loyalists, probably around 550, and about 150 Indian allies at the post at Oswego and headed toward the Mohawk River valley to raid, coming within a few miles of Schenectady before starting back toward his home base.

Colonel Willet gathered all his troops and set out in pursuit, catching Ross on October 25. The men on both sides were exhausted from moving in the deep mud caused by heavy rains, and Ross's men were short of food and supplies.

Willet attacked Ross, who had taken position in a wooded area with his main force, and sent a smaller body under Col. Aaron Rowley to flank the Loyalists. Ross's men temporarily captured Willet's only fieldpiece, which caused Willet's left to waver. By the time he had corrected this problem, Willet's militia on his right began to collapse. Darkness called a halt to the fighting before either side could claim a clear victory. Ross was able to disengage and slip away, and Willet could not give chase until three days later. Save for a brief firefight while crossing a river at Jerseyfield, Ross managed to escape with little further harm. Willet reported seven dead Loyalists and three dead among the patriots.

Further Reading

James F. Morrison. *The Battle of Johnstown, October 25th, 1781* (n.p.: Third Battalion of Tryon County, 1991).

Julesburg

Colorado (January 7 and February 2, 1865)
Colorado War

After the massacre of two hundred peaceful Indians at SAND CREEK by Colorado volunteers, a general Indian-white war broke out in Colorado. A blow in retribution for the massacre was struck at the small town of Julesburg, a stagecoach stop guarded by a small detachment of troops at Fort Rankin.

On January 7, 1865, one thousand Cheyenne and Sioux (Dakota, Lakota, Nakota) warriors surrounded the town and tried to bait the garrison into an ambush by sending forward a small advance party, which turned and ran when troopers—members of the 7th Iowa Cavalry, commanded by Capt. Nicolas J. O'Brien—emerged from the fort to give chase. The ambush was sprung prematurely, however, and the troopers were able to retreat behind the fort's walls, along with the town's civilian population and passengers from a newly arrived stagecoach. The Indians could do little more than destroy the town, after carrying off as much loot as they could.

After leading a column of soldiers on a fruitless chase for several weeks, the Indians returned on February 2 to Julesburg, where they razed and burned the few remaining buildings.

The garrison and townspeople suffered sixteen dead during the attacks.

Further Reading

Robert M. Utley. *Frontiersmen in Blue: The United States Army and the Indian, 1848–1865* (New York: Macmillan, 1962); and Eugene F. Ware. *The Indian War of 1864* (Lincoln: University of Nebraska Press, 1994).

Kernstown, First

Virginia (March 23, 1862) *American Civil War*

In March 1862, the preparations for Maj. Gen. George B. McClellan's campaign against the Confederacy on the Virginia Peninsula received a blow from Maj. Gen. Thomas J. "Stonewall" Jackson. Jackson's attack against Federal troops in Kernstown failed but nonetheless signaled the vulnerability of the capital city of Washington, D.C.

Union major general Nathaniel Banks had occupied the city of Winchester in the lower Shenandoah Valley on March 12 with thirty thousand troops, but less than ten days later two of his divisions were called to Manassas to join McClellan on the Peninsula. Major General Jackson, who had received orders to prevent the reinforcements from leaving, force-marched his men to the scene and decided to attack.

On March 22, Col. Turner Ashby, Jackson's cavalry commander, began the attack, but he vastly underestimated the strength of Banks's remaining division, under the command of Brig. Gen. James Shields. Ashby told Jackson that Shields had only four infantry regiments, but in reality Shields had a full nine-thousand-man division in Winchester.

When Jackson arrived and began his attack on March 23 at Kernstown, just south of Winchester, he relied on Ashby's underestimation of Shields's troop strength and assumed that he would quickly and easily defeat the Federals. Jackson sent two brigades against the Union right, while Ashby's cavalry blocked avenues of retreat. Jackson's initial attack did push back the Federal line, but when Col. Nathan Kimball's brigade moved forward with reinforcements, Jackson realized his forty-two hundred troops were outnumbered.

Maj. Richard Garnett, one of Jackson's officers, ordered his "Stonewall" Brigade to retreat when it ran low on ammunition. Jackson relieved him of command. But lack of ammunition plagued the Southerners generally, and they were entirely defeated. Jackson withdrew south to Newton, leaving Ashby to stop Federal pursuit of his force a mile and a half south of Kernstown.

Casualties totaled 590 Northerners and 700 Southerners.

Though the battle at Kernstown was an unqualified Union victory, strategically the South benefited. Since Jackson's attack suggested he had reinforcements,

Washington, D.C., was now looked upon in the North as a viable Confederate target. All of Banks's troops were recalled to the lower Shenandoah Valley, Maj. Gen. Irvin McDowell's thirty-five thousand men were stationed outside the capital city, and McClellan was left to pursue his Peninsula campaign without them.

Further Reading

Gary L. Ecelbarger. *We Are In for It! The First Battle of Kernstown, March 23, 1862* (Shippensburg, Pa.: White Mane, 1997).

Kernstown, Second

Virginia (July 23–24, 1864) *American Civil War*

After his victory at MONOCACY on July 9, 1864, Confederate lieutenant general Jubal Early unsuccessfully attacked Washington, D.C., and was forced to retreat across the Potomac River into the Shenandoah Valley. Maj. Gen. Horatio Wright and Maj. Gen. David Hunter—the latter having been defeated by Early at LYNCHBURG in June—pursued Early. After some skirmishes near Winchester they left Brig. Gen. George Crook's ninety-five hundred men to cover what they assumed would be Early's continued withdrawal. Instead, Early turned and fought Crook's force at Kernstown, where Maj. Gen. Thomas J. "Stonewall" Jackson had dealt an effective blow to Federal forces two years before (*see also* KERNSTOWN, FIRST).

Crook established his position at Kernstown on July 23, when Col. Rutherford B. Hayes, a future president of the United States, led his brigade against the Confederate force stationed there. In the midst of hot cavalry skirmishing on July 23, Early learned that Wright and Hunter had pulled back, and so he rushed Maj. Gen. John C. Breckinridge, Maj. Gen. John B. Gordon, and Brig. Gen. Gabriel C. Wharton to Kernstown in hopes that their superior combined force of fourteen thousand men would crush Crook's smaller one.

Early's main attack began before noon on July 24, as Gordon's infantry pushed against the Federal center. Fearful that the center would give way and that Confederate cavalry on either side would deliver a death-blow to the Union line, Colonel Hayes and the Irish-American brigadier general James A. Mulligan rushed their forces into position behind a series of stone walls around the Opequon Presbyterian Church. The Confederate soldiers, many of whom had fought near the same church two years earlier, cleared the Federals from behind the walls fairly quickly. A Confederate sweep through the right side of the Union line, to the west, opened the Union left flank, under Hayes, to withering fire from Brig. Gen. Gabriel C. Wharton's infantry. Gordon's men simultaneously charged the Union center a second time, and Crook had to withdraw. Colonel Hayes's brigade managed to cover a retreat by Capt. Henry A. du Pont's artillery, and the Union withdrawal proceeded in a generally orderly manner all the way back to Bunker Hill.

Confederate casualty totals are unknown, but Union forces lost 1,185 men, including Brigadier General Mulligan, who was mortally wounded while trying to rally his troops one last time. That figure includes 479 Federal soldiers who were taken prisoner.

The Confederate victory at Kernstown gave Early new energy, and he penetrated again into Union territory and burned Chambersburg, Pennsylvania, several days later. Union lieutenant general Ulysses S. Grant was prompted to reorganize the Federal command structure and to send Maj. Gen. Philip H. Sheridan to reestablish control in the Shenandoah Valley.

Further Reading

Jeffrey Wert, "The Old Killing Ground: The Second Battle of Kernstown, 1984." *Civil War Times Illustrated* 23, no. 6 (1984): 40–47.

Kettle Creek

Georgia (February 14, 1779) *American Revolution*

The seizure of the initiative by the British in Georgia in late 1778 and early 1779 emboldened many Georgia and Carolina Loyalists to declare themselves and organize into military units. Seven hundred such Loyalists rallied under the command of a Colonel Boyd in Anson County, North Carolina, and marched to join the gathering of Loyalists under Lt. Col. John Hamilton in Georgia. Along the way, they disrupted life for patriots by an aggressive campaign of depredation.

A patriot militia force of about 350, under Col. Andrew Pickens, trailed Boyd's line of march and planned an attack when Boyd went into camp at Kettle Creek, Georgia, near the confluence of the Savannah and Broad Rivers. Boyd's men suspected nothing and set an inadequate guard on their camp while they occupied themselves by slaughtering a herd of cattle.

Pickens formed a line of battle and advanced on the Loyalists, hoping to sweep them up in a double envelopment, but Boyd rallied his men into a defensive formation. Sharp fighting lasted for an hour, but Boyd was fatally wounded, and his men were finally subdued.

The Loyalists lost forty killed and seventy captured; the patriots lost only nine killed and twenty-three wounded.

The seventy captives were later tried for treason, all were convicted. Five were hanged by the patriots, the rest pardoned.

Further Reading

Robert S. Davis. *Georgians in the Revolution: At Kettle Creek . . .* (Easley, S.C.: Southern Historical Press, 1986); Robert S. Davis and Kenneth H. Thomas. *Kettle Creek: The Battle of the Cane Brakes* (Atlanta: Georgia Department of Natural Resources, 1975); and Janet H. Standard. *The Battle of Kettle Creek: A Turning Point of the American Revolution in the South* (Washington, Ga.: Wilkes, 1973).

Killdeer Mountain

North Dakota (July 28, 1864) *Sioux Wars*

The battle at Killdeer Mountain in what is modern-day North Dakota was an extension of the Santee Uprising, which had taken place in Minnesota two years before (*see also* FORT RIDGELY, NEW ULM, and WOOD LAKE). Members of the Santee (Dakota) or eastern division of the Sioux Nation (collectively the Dakota, Lakota, and Nakota) had fled west and north after their defeat, taking refuge with their kin the Teton Lakota. During the summer of 1863, Brig. Gen. Alfred Sully led a large expedition to find and punish hostile Sioux in the western region.

Sully was supposed to coordinate his campaign with a column commanded by Col. Henry H. Sibley, the victor at the battle of Wood Lake, but Sibley remained in Minnesota while Sully led about three thousand troops (with a large number of immigrants and prospects in tow) into Teton Lakota territory. After a sharp encounter resulting from a search for the infamous Inkpaduta, a warrior responsible for killing white settlers in Iowa in 1856, Sully's column approached the Killdeer Mountain region, site of several large Lakota camps. Sully claimed the villages held as many as six thousand warriors, but the Lakota themselves later put the figure at far fewer, perhaps no more than fifteen hundred.

Sully employed an unusual tactic, dismounting his men and forming them into a traditional hollow square and advancing on the Lakota camp in that ponderous formation—a configuration that limited mobility but gave

great protection. He used his field artillery to support the movements of the square. At one stage, Maj. Alfred E. Brackett attempted a cavalry charge, but the ground was too rugged, and it had little effect. Sully concentrated on his slow advance. After unsuccessfully attacking the American formation, the Lakota gave up and withdrew, leaving behind a large store of food and supplies.

Sully lost five killed and ten wounded, and by his estimate the Lakota suffered 150 dead.

The campaign and victory at Killdeer Mountain cleared the way for more white intrusion into Sioux lands.

Further Reading

Louis Pfaler, "The Sully Expedition of 1864." *North Dakota History* 31 (1964): 1–54.

King's Mountain

South Carolina (October 7, 1780)
American Revolution

The victory of backcountry patriot militia over an army of British-backed Loyalists at King's Mountain was one of the signal American triumphs in the South and one of the best military performances by untrained troops during the entire American Revolution.

The only regular soldier, and only non-American, at the battle was Maj. Patrick Ferguson, the Loyalist commander. He was an experienced and talented British officer—he had invented a practical and ingenious breech-loading rifle and was reputed to be the best shot in the British army—who had been deputized by Maj. Gen. Lord Cornwallis to rally Loyalist support and find and defeat patriots wherever he could, while Cornwallis led the main British army into North Carolina. The nucleus of Ferguson's force was his King's American Rangers rifle corps, which he had brought south from New York and New Jersey. To these were added about one thousand Carolina Loyalists, giving Ferguson a total force of around twelve hundred, about two hundred or so of whom were detached and missed the battle.

Ranged against Ferguson and his Loyalists were fourteen hundred patriots, led by a remarkable collection of good commanders. The most glamorous contingent were "over mountain men" from the settlements along the Watauga River over the Appalachians in what is now Tennessee. Led principally by Col. Isaac Shelby and Col.

John Sevier, the frontier riflemen had responded to the threat from Ferguson by organizing and marching on a pre-emptive mission to stop the Loyalists before they could invade the Watauga region. These frontiersmen were joined by hundreds of patriot militia from North Carolina, South Carolina, and Virginia. The outstanding leaders were Col. Arthur Campbell and his brother-in-law William Campbell, both from Virginia, and Col. Benjamin Cleveland, Col. Charles McDowell, and his brother Maj. Joseph McDowell, all from North Carolina. After a series of rendezvous—they were joined on the march by Maj. Joseph Winston and Col. James Williams—the patriots set out to find and destroy Ferguson's forces.

After several days of maneuver, Ferguson brought his troops to King's Mountain, a 60-foot-high, flat-topped ridge, with a summit about 500 yards long, 70 yards wide at one end but broadening to 120 yards at the other. The slopes were steep and heavily wooded. Ferguson believed he could defend the position with his better-trained and -equipped troops, and he settled in to await the patriots.

They arrived on October 7, surrounded the mountain, and prepared to make a simultaneous assault up the slopes. A majority of the patriots were riflemen and accustomed to frontier-style combat, where formations counted for little and cover for a great deal. As it turned out, Ferguson had baited them into a situation perfectly suited to their skills and experience. Perhaps most surprising was the ability of so many different commanders and units to deliver what turned out to be a well-coordinated attack.

The patriots launched themselves up the slopes on all sides of Ferguson's position, aiming to infiltrate, surround, and envelope the Loyalists. Many of them were well up the slopes before the Loyalists went on the alert and began to open fire. Ferguson sent a bayonet charge down the hill against Shelby and his men, stopping their ascent. Shelby's men, however, simply took to the trees and began to pour a deadly rifle fire at the Loyalists. On the other side of the mountain, William Campbell's Virginians charged up the slope with screams and aimed fire. Ferguson's bayonet counterattacks failed to stop the patriots, who melted away in front of the massed Loyalists and picked them off, one by one. When Shelby's men made it over the top, the end was inevitable.

Ferguson, conspicuous in a black-and-white-checked rifleman's shirt, raced back and forth trying to rally his men, but he was singled out and cut down by the patriot sharpshooters. He died on the spot.

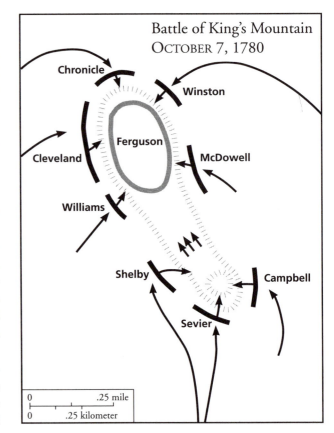

Battle of King's Mountain
OCTOBER 7, 1780

Chronicle
Winston
Ferguson
Cleveland
McDowell
Williams
Shelby
Campbell
Sevier

0   .25 mile
0   .25 kilometer

The battle soon turned into a rout, with most of the Loyalists huddling in a disorganized mass, surrounded by roused patriots, who fired for some time into the circle of unresisting men, refusing to accept surrender and meeting the Loyalists white flags with shouts of "Buford, Buford," a reference to Lt. Col. Banastre Tarleton's actions at WAX-HAWS. Eventually, their officers gained control and the slaughter stopped.

The victory was one of the most complete recorded during the war of the Revolution: the Loyalists lost 157 killed, 163 badly wounded, and 698 taken prisoner. Virtually the entire Loyalist force was killed, wounded, or captured. The patriots lost only twenty-eight killed and sixty-four wounded.

The Loyalist prisoners were marched off to Gilbert Town, where thirty were convicted in a rump trial and nine were hanged. The rest of the prisoners were eventually taken to Hillsboro, from which most of them escaped over the following months.

The defeat ended Cornwallis's attempts to rally significant Loyalist support, and he withdrew from his expedition into North Carolina.

Further Reading

Lyman C. Draper. *King's Mountain and Its Heroes: History of the Battle of King's Mountain, October 7th, 1780 . . .* Reprint ed. (Spartansburg, S.C.: Reprint, 1967); Hank Messick. *King's Mountain: The Epic of the Blue Ridge "Mountain Men" in the American Revolution* (Boston: Little, Brown, 1976); and Katherine K. White. *The King's Mountain Men: The Story of the Battle . . .* (Baltimore: Genealogical, 1966).

King's Schoolhouse

See OAK GROVE

Kip's Bay

New York (September 15, 1776)
American Revolution

Following a crushing defeat on LONG ISLAND at the hands of Gen. Sir William Howe, the American commander in chief, Gen. George Washington, managed a brilliant withdrawal of his army across the East River to Manhattan, but his troop dispositions and the large concentration of men and matériel at FORT WASHINGTON left the Americans vulnerable.

The British controlled the waters surrounding Manhattan. Then were skilled at amphibious operations and had their choice of several promising points along the eastern shoreline at which to land an army. Howe selected Kip's Bay, and on September 14, less than three weeks after his victory on Long Island, he positioned five of his warships offshore. The relatively few American defenders were members of Connecticut militia regiments under William Douglas and James Wadsworth, supplemented to the south by units under Samuel Parsons.

About 10:00 A.M. the next morning, four thousand British and German troops embarked on barges. An hour later, the British warships unleashed a massive bombardment on the feeble American defenses. When the troops landed from their transports, they discovered that virtually all the American militiamen had turned and run. The British took the landing beach unopposed.

To the rear, General Washington was irate at the behavior of his militia troops, but no amount of ranting and remonstration could rally them to their positions on the shore.

Further Reading

Robert B. Roberts. *New York's Forts in the Revolution* (Cranbury, N.J.: Associated University Presses, 1980).

Klock's Field

New York (October 19, 1780)
American Revolution

During the fall of 1780, Sir John Johnson led a mixed force of around fifteen hundred Loyalists and Indians on an extended raid into the Mohawk River valley. They were so successful that they attracted the attention of New York State authorities, and a force of 850 militia under Gen. Robert Van Rensselaer set out after them.

Johnson's march was slowed on the morning of October 19, when he was attacked by militia at FORT KEYSER, and by afternoon, Van Rensselaer had caught up. When the New Yorkers crossed the Mohawk River and formed up for an attack, Johnson turned his column around and took up defensive positions behind an improvised breastwork. He had only one company of regulars, but they were backed by experienced Loyalist units and three small field guns. On his left flank, Johnson placed his Indian auxiliaries and a company of riflemen.

The patriot attack was led by Col. Morgan Lewis, with Capt. Robert McKean heading a picked unit of volunteers on the right wing. Late in the day the battle finally began, and McKean's men overran Johnson's right flank and turned to attack his center from the rear. After strong resistance, Johnson gave up the fight and ordered a retreat.

The timid Van Rensselaer refused to allow a pursuit until the next day. Casualties were not reported by either side.

Further Reading

Lou D. MacWethy. *The Battle of Klock's Field. . . .* (St. Johnsville, N.Y.: Enterprise and News, 1930).

Knoxville

(Fort Sanders)

Tennessee (November 29, 1863)
American Civil War

Following the Confederate victory at CHICKAMAUGA, Maj. Gen. James Longstreet was detached from the command of Gen. Braxton Bragg at Chattanooga and sent with ten thousand infantry and five thousand cavalry to retake the city of Knoxville, which had been occupied virtually unopposed in early September by the Federal Army of the Ohio, commanded by Maj. Gen. Ambrose Burnside. The subsequent siege and assault on the city once again pitted two opposing generals who had faced each other on several battlefields in the East, including at ANTIETAM and FRED-ERICKSBURG (where Burnside had engineered a disaster as the commander of the Army of the Potomac).

After a skirmish with Union cavalry at Campbell's Station on November 13, Longstreet's army moved close to Knoxville and began a siege operation. The city was strongly fortified with earth works (one side was protected by the Tennessee River), and the defenders were well supplied with food and ammunition. Burnside may have been a disaster as an overall army commander, but he was more than competent to plan a sound defense, and he was eager to burnish a reputation that had been so tarnished in the East. This time it was Burnside who controlled a strong defensive position and Longstreet who was forced to make a difficult assault.

Longstreet aimed his main attack at a redoubt known as Fort Sanders. On the morning of November 29, pressured by the defeat of Bragg at CHATTANOOGA, Longstreet launched his men from a dry riverbed about one hundred yards away from the walls of the redoubt. It was a bitterly cold day, with snow cover on the ground that made footing treacherous; moreover, as they charged full speed across the open ground in front of Fort Sanders, the Confederates discovered that the Federals had strung trip-wires from tree stumps. To make matters worse, once they crossed the field, Longstreet's men were forced to plunge across a deep, ice-filled moat and then climb a slippery wall without scaling ladders.

The waiting Union defenders blasted the attackers at close range as they floundered at the foot of the fortifications. Within a few moments it became obvious that the assault could not succeed. In less than half an hour, Longstreet called his men back and gave up the idea of taking Fort Sanders.

Longstreet lost a total of 813 men, while Burnside's command suffered the loss of only 100 casualties.

Ten days after the attack on Fort Sanders, upon hearing of the approach of a Federal relief column, Longstreet ended the siege and withdrew.

Further Reading

Robert Armour. *The Attack upon and Defense of Fort Sanders, Knoxville, Tennessee, November 29, 1863: An Eyewitness Account.* . . . (Knoxville, Tenn.: Fine Arts Press, 1991).

Lake Erie

(Put-in-Bay)

Ohio (September 10, 1813) *War of 1812*

After months of posturing on Lake Erie by both the British and American navies, twenty-seven-year-old American commodore Oliver Hazard Perry directed an attack against Capt. Robert H. Barclay's fleet in September 1813 and handed the British one of their most significant defeats during the War of 1812.

After Commodore Isaac Chauncey put Commodore Perry in charge on Lake Erie in 1813, Perry assembled a fleet of nine ships to challenge British dominance of the lake. Despite difficulties, by early August Perry's fleet, manned by seamen, Kentucky sharpshooters, and army regulars, was anchored at Put-in-Bay and awaiting an opportunity to attack.

Captain Barclay, who had lost an arm serving under Lord Nelson at Trafalgar, commanded just six ships and faced a shortage of men and supplies due to frequent American blockades and the large number of Indian warriors at Amherstburg whose families the British had to feed. Barclay installed guns from Fort Malden on several ships, and when only one day's rations remained in British storehouses, he decided to engage Perry and attempt to reopen his supply lines.

The two fleets came in sight of one another on the morning of September 10. Perry commanded the American squadron from the twenty-gun brig Lawrence, flying a banner reading "Don't Give Up the Ship" in memory of Capt. James Lawrence, who had been killed in June (*see also* U.S.S. *CHESAPEAKE* v. H.M.S. *SHANNON*). Barclay's flagship was the Detroit, a captured American twenty-one-gun corvette.

Barclay planned to fight the battle from a distance, using his superior long-range gunnery, but the wind soon shifted to the Americans' backs, which gave them control of the prebattle maneuvering. Perry preferred a close-range engagement, and by 11:45 A.M. the American fleet was in position to come to grips with the enemy. When Barclay

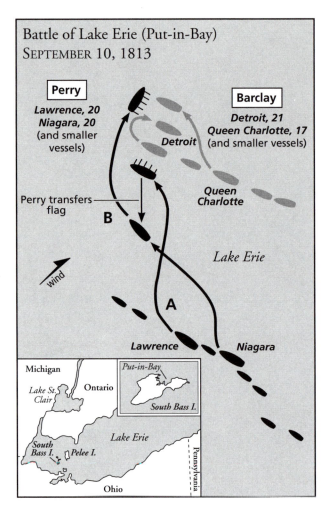

Battle of Lake Erie (Put-in-Bay)
SEPTEMBER 10, 1813

Perry
Lawrence, 20
Niagara, 20
(and smaller vessels)

Barclay
Detroit, 21
Queen Charlotte, 17
(and smaller vessels)

Detroit

Perry transfers flag

B

Queen Charlotte

Lake Erie

wind

A

Lawrence   *Niagara*

Michigan
Lake St. Clair   Ontario

Put-in-Bay

South Bass I.

Lake Erie

South Bass I.   *Pelee I.*

Pennsylvania

Ohio

British faced a command crisis at this point, because so many officers had been wounded. Junior officers commanded five of the six ships in the fleet.

As Perry maneuvered around the crippled *Lawrence*, the *Queen Charlotte* and the *Detroit* became entangled. Perry was able to rake *Detroit* with close-range fire and break the British line. Within half an hour, the *Detroit* and *Queen Charlotte*, along with two other British ships, surrendered. The last two British ships were captured while trying to flee at the end of the action.

British casualties in the Battle of Lake Erie totaled forty-one killed and ninety-four wounded. On the American side only twenty-seven were killed and ninety-six wounded.

As a result of the action, Commodore Perry became a hero, and he and several other officers received large bounties from Congress. Perry's assessment of the battle in a letter to Maj. Gen. William Henry Harrison—"We have met the enemy and they are ours"—immortalized him in national memory.

Perry's victory, undoubtedly the most important action ever fought on the Great Lakes, ensured American control of Lake Erie for the remainder of the War of 1812 and opened the way for William Henry Harrison's successful invasion of Canada in October.

Further Reading

Richard Dillon. *We Have Met the Enemy: Oliver Hazard Perry, Wilderness Commodore* (New York: McGraw-Hill, 1978); Robert and Thomas Malcomson. *HMS Detroit: The Battle for Lake Erie* (Annapolis, Md.: Naval Institute Press, 1990); David C. Skaggs and Gerald T. Altoff. *A Signal Victory: The Lake Erie Campaign, 1812–1813* (Annapolis, Md.: Naval Institute Press, 1997); William J. Welsh and David C. Skaggs, eds. *War on the Great Lakes: Essays Commemorating the 175th Anniversary of the Battle of Lake Erie* (Kent, Ohio: Kent State University Press, 1991); and Joseph Whitehorne. *While Washington Burned: The Battle for Lake Erie* (Baltimore: Nautical and Aviation, 1992).

opened fire at two thousand yards, Perry formed his ships into a line and closed in.

Lawrence made for *Detroit* but came under heavy fire from the H.M.S. *Queen Charlotte*, which was not being effectively challenged by Perry's second ship, *Niagara*. L. Jesse Duncan Elliot, in command of the *Niagara*, stayed at long range during the first hour of fighting, as the Lawrence exchanged broadsides with both the *Detroit* and *Queen Charlotte*. All three ships suffered heavy damage.

By the early afternoon, Perry had lost most of his crew and was unable to keep up a steady fire. Instead of surrendering, he pulled off a daring individual feat, leaving the *Lawrence* in a small boat and rowing half a mile under heavy fire to take personal command of the *Niagara* for the rest of the battle.

Leaving Elliot in command of the gunships, Perry sailed back to reengage the main British fleet. Captain Barclay had been wounded and carried below, and Lt. George Inglis became de facto British commander. The

⌁ Lake George

(Bloody Pond)
New York (September 8, 1755)
French and Indian War

Part of the overall British strategy against the French in North America in 1755 was to seize Fort Frédéric (Crown Point) at the lower end of Lake Champlain, but the British expedition ran head-on into a French column moving south to take British positions on Lake George. In the end, the hard-fought, two-stage wilderness battle gave the British the upper hand.

The British commander appointed to march against the French at Fort Frédéric was the redoubtable Col. William Johnson, a transplanted Irishman who had established himself as the most influential Indian trader and local landowner in the Mohawk River valley of upper New York. He not only had great political power with the British and colonial governments, but his influence among tribes of the Iroquois Confederacy, particularly the Mohawk, was unparalleled. The home government appointed him superintendent of Indian affairs at the same time that he was named to command the Fort Frédéric expedition. He assembled an army of around three thousand colonial militia and three hundred or so Mohawk, the latter led by his father-in-law, Tiyanoga (Chief Hendrick), and set out for Lake George, reaching the head of the lake in late summer.

Opposing Johnson was a formidable army under the command of Maj. Gen. Jean-Armand de Dieskau, a veteran French regular-army officer who had been sent from France to command an invasion of the British colonies. At his disposal was a large force, from which he drew a smaller assault column of slightly more than 200 regulars, 684 Canadian militia, and about 600 Indian allies, mostly Onondaga and Seneca, with a few from other tribes. Dieskau was well aware of Johnson's intentions, since a copy of the British strategic plan had been captured by the French from the British when they defeated Maj. Gen. James Braddock at MONONGAHELA. Dieskau had been misled, however, by a prisoner who had understated the strength of the British force. He moved south in early September, hoping to intercept Johnson.

On the morning of September 8, as the two armies drew close to each other, Johnson detached one thousand colonials under Col. Ephraim Williams and two hundred Mohawk under Tiyanoga and sent them northward to probe for the French. Dieskau was alerted to their approach and set an ambush, hoping to annihilate the British force. The British allies spotted the trap before it could be sprung most effectively, yet Williams's force was caught in a tough spot as the French allied Indians and the Canadian militia attacked, with the French regulars following up. Williams and Tiyanoga were killed, but the bulk of their force managed to reorganize and withdraw toward the main British position, doing considerable damage to the French in a fierce rear-guard action.

Alerted by the sound of the ambush, Johnson had

time to throw up a barricade of trees and overturned wagons and to site three cannon to repel the French if they tried a frontal assault. In fact, Dieskau foolishly did just that: his regulars marched out of the woods and directly at the British barricade, while the militia and the Indians flung themselves at the flanks. The British cannon tore into the French infantry, and a counterattack over the barricades by Johnson's men nearly destroyed the entire force. Dieskau, who was severely wounded, surrendered as the cohesion of his army collapsed and his men fled the field. Exact casualties were not reported.

With Johnson's victory, one of the few by British arms in the early years of the French and Indian War, the British took control of the lower lakes region.

Further Reading

Douglas E. Leach. *Arms for Empire: A Military History of the British Colonies in North America, 1607–1763* (New York: Macmillan, 1973); and W. Max Reid. *Lake George and Lake Champlain: The War Trail of the Mohawk and the Battle-Ground of France and England . . .* (New York: G. P. Putnam's Sons, 1910).

Lake Okeechobee

Florida (December 25, 1837)
Second Seminole War

During the late 1830s, a long, drawn-out conflict arose between the U.S. government and a portion of the Seminole tribe of Florida over the removal of the tribe to Indian Territory. The dispute soon became violent (*see also* DADE'S BATTLE) and continued at a low level of fighting for several years. One of the few large-scale battles took place at Lake Okeechobee in 1837.

Maj. Gen. Thomas S. Jesup was in overall command of American forces, but a procession of field commanders had failed to make much headway against the Seminole, who were skillful fighters and operated in terrain that was almost impossible for regular troops. Jesup tried subterfuge to capture or subdue the Seminole, but for the most part these efforts served only to antagonize further the Indians, who were supported by significant numbers of black freed or runaway former slaves. After Jesup captured Osceola, one of the principal Seminole leaders, by treachery and the warrior died in captivity, the American commander launched an offensive.

Overall, the U.S. forces numbered nearly nine thousand troops, under the command of Col. Zachary Taylor, a seasoned veteran who would become a hero of the Mexican-American War and eventually president of the United States. Taylor took the field in late 1837 with one thousand men and finally brought the Seminole to battle near Lake Okeechobee. The Seminole and their black allies were led principally by Wild Cat (Coachoochee), Alligator (Halpatter Tustenuggee), and Arpeika.

Although the actual fighting was inconclusive and ended with a retreat by the Seminole, the Indians inflicted nearly 150 casualties on Taylor's force while taking only about twenty-four casualties themselves.

The Second Seminole War continued until 1842, but there were few large-scale confrontations. The Third Seminole War was fought from 1855 to 1858. Although some tribe members agreed to move to Indian territory, many did not.

Further Reading

John K. Mahon. *History of the Second Seminole War* (Gainesville: University of Florida Press, 1967); and Willard Steele. *The Battle of Lake Okeechobee* (Miami, Fla.: Archaeological and Historical Conservancy, 1987).

◈ Lázaro

Mexico (May 27, 1518) *Spanish Conquest*

Dissatisfied with the failure of an expedition by Francisco Hernández de Córdoba the previous year (*see also* CHAMPOTON), Diego Velázquez, the governor of Spanish Cuba, commissioned his nephew, Juan de Grijalva, to go on a second mission to Yucatán to search for gold and a possible place of settlement.

Grijalva sailed from Cuban waters in April with two hundred men, including twenty harquebusiers armed with primitive firearms. The expedition also boasted two pieces of artillery, called culverins, and a few of the vicious dogs that became part of the typical Spanish combat force in the New World. The conquistadors were clad in steel armor and carried steel-bladed swords, weapons vastly superior to any used by the Indians of the mainland.

After exploring the island of Cozumel, Grijalva's expedition landed on May 26 on the Yucatán Peninsula at Lázaro, a town named by Hernández de Córdoba, near Champoton. Speaking through an interpreter captured by the previous year's expedition, Grijalva demanded gold and fresh water from the Maya living in Lázaro. Since there was no gold to be found in Yucatán, the Maya had little to offer, and they strongly resented the Spanish request for water, which was in short supply in the region.

The next morning the Spaniards woke to find themselves surrounded by what they estimated to be three thousand painted Maya, who appeared to be ready for battle. The Maya told the Spaniards to go immediately or die. The Spaniards refused, and the Maya attacked with their slings, bows, and arrows, war axes, and obsidian-bladed swords. As in most combat by the Indians of Mexico and Yucatán, the tactics were designed to capture prisoners for ritual human sacrifice, which played a central role in their public and religious life. Consequently, the Spaniards usually were able to defeat large numbers of opponents.

The conquistadores fired their cannon, the sound of which alone had a devastating effect on the Mayan warriors, and killed several at long distance with crossbow darts. When the Maya closed for hand-to-hand fighting, they were at a disadvantage, in attempting to capture rather than kill. They inflicted wounds on forty of the Spanish but killed only one.

The Maya broke off the contest, and Grijalva sailed away the following night.

Further Reading

Hugh Thomas. *Conquest: Montezuma, Cortés, and the Fall of Old Mexico* (New York: Simon and Schuster, 1993).

◈ Lenud's Ferry

South Carolina (May 6, 1780)
American Revolution

With Charleston and almost all the American armed forces in the southern theater on the verge of surrender to the British, the few American units still on the loose managed only weak resistance to the lightning attacks of Lt. Col. Banastre Tarleton, whom British commander Sir Henry Clinton sent to hunt down the remaining rebels. Having routed a contingent of Americans at MONCK'S CORNER and taken their horses, Tarleton struck again at Lenud's Ferry on the Santee River, where the fleeing rebels had taken refuge with about 350 Continentals under Col. Abraham Buford and Col. William Washington.

Buford had been on his way to reinforce Maj. Gen. Benjamin Lincoln's garrison at Charleston, but paused at Lenud's Ferry when he learned of the imminent surrender of the city. On the afternoon of May 6, Buford was joined by a troop commanded by Col. Anthony White, who had captured one of Tarleton's officers who had been on a foraging mission.

Just as the two rebel groups greeted each other, Tarleton and 150 of his men sprang a surprise attack that swept everything before them. The Americans barely put up a resistance, and many—including Washington and White—escaped only by swimming the river. Buford also escaped, but he lost about forty men, killed or wounded. Tarleton lost not a man.

Further Reading

John Buchanan. *The Road to Guilford Courthouse: The American Revolution in the Carolinas* (New York: John Wiley and Sons, 1997).

Lexington and Concord

Massachusetts (April 19, 1775)
American Revolution

The shots fired on the village green at Lexington, Massachusetts, during the early morning hours of April 19, 1775, and the subsequent events of the day at Concord and on the road back to Boston changed the long-simmering political conflict between the British government and the people of the thirteen American colonies into a violent military confrontation.

The British commander in Boston, Maj. Gen. Thomas Gage (who also served as royal governor of Massachusetts), commanded a garrison of around four thousand professional troops, most of whom had been sent to Boston to enforce punitive British imperial policies following the infamous Boston Tea Party. Opposing Gage

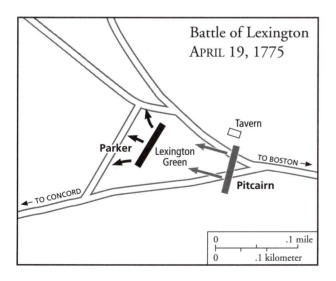

Battle of Lexington
APRIL 19, 1775

Tavern

Parker

Lexington
Green

TO BOSTON

TO CONCORD

Pitcairn

0   .1 mile

0   .1 kilometer

was an extralegal Massachusetts Provincial Congress, directed by a handful of American patriot leaders, which had called on the armed militia companies of the small towns near Boston to prepare for military resistance if the British attempted to occupy the countryside.

Gage, under heavy pressure from his superiors in Britain to suppress the potential rebels, decided to send an expedition from Boston to Concord with orders to arrest patriot leaders and to find and seize any caches of military supplies and equipment. He gave command of a force of seven hundred light infantry and grenadiers to a veteran officer, Lt. Col. Francis Smith, with Maj. John Pitcairn as second in command, and directed them to march to Concord. The redcoats formed up on the Boston Common during the night of April 18 and prepared to march out of the city. Patriot dispatch riders Paul Revere and William Dawes got on the road ahead of the British troops and warned militiamen in villages along the route to Concord.

Capt. John Parker and about 130 Minutemen—civilians pledged to respond instantly to a military summons—assembled on the green at Lexington during the early morning hours of April 19, but when no threat appeared, many drifted away. The remainder warmed themselves in a tavern next to the green. At 4:40 A.M., Dawes warned Parker that a British column was only a half-hour's march down the road and would pass the green on its way toward Concord. Parker assembled his remaining seventy militiamen and formed them into two lines facing the approaching British.

As daylight broke, Major Pitcairn came into view at the head of the British advance guard. Parker told his men to stand their ground but gave no order to resist the overwhelming numbers of redcoats, who appeared to be headed around the green and down the Concord road. Pitcairn rode forward and ordered the Americans to disperse, and most of them began to comply, although they refused to lay down their muskets.

At that stage, someone fired a shot—it has never been learned exactly who—and a junior British officer shouted a command to open fire. Despite Pitcairn's orders to desist, the troopers fired two volleys and charged the patriots with their bayonets. By the time Pitcairn regained control of his men, eight Americans were dead on the green and ten more had been wounded. The Revolution had begun with this small, one-sided engagement.

Soon afterward, the balance of the British force under Lieutenant Colonel Smith arrived, joined the advance guard, and turned down the road toward Concord.

Meanwhile, word began to spread, and militiamen from all over the region began to stream toward the area. A messenger reached Concord well ahead of the British column, and the patriots there, commanded by Col. James Barrett, had time to hide or remove their stores of arms and supplies and form up into their militia companies to await the British. When Smith's column arrived, however, the Americans retreated to a ridge outside of town near the Old North Bridge and waited while reinforcements poured in from the countryside. The British stationed a guard under Capt. Walter Laurie near the bridge and proceeded with a leisurely search of the town for arms.

When the patriots saw smoke from British-set fires at the courthouse and a blacksmith's shop, several of the militia officers, principally Maj. John Buttrick, urged an attack to prevent the ruin of the town and moved to the west end of the Old North Bridge, facing Captain Laurie's British troopers, who had assembled at the east end. The British opened fire, wounding three patriots and killing two. The militiamen fired back, killing three British soldiers and wounding several others. The British retreated, but the Americans lacked leadership and failed to follow up on the first moments of success, allowing Lieutenant Colonel Smith to regroup his command and begin a retreat down the road toward Boston at about noon.

The withdrawal soon turned into a nightmare for the British. Hundreds of American militiamen had arrived to reinforce the companies from Concord, and they spread out along the British route, crouching behind walls and trees. When the British fired on a house about a mile out of Concord, the hidden Americans opened fire, killing and wounding more of Smith's men. Over a sixteen-mile length of road, the patriots raced ahead of the redcoats and raked the British soldiers with musket fire from the safety of concealed positions. Smith himself was wounded, and Major Pitcairn unhorsed, before the straggling British reached the temporary safety of Lexington. There they were met by a relief column under Brig. Gen. Lord Percy and began a further retreat toward Boston.

Despite the British reinforcements, which tripled the number of redcoats, the Americans continued to harass and snipe at the column. The British responded by attacking houses along the road, killing any males they could find, and burning and looting buildings. After a torturous march, they finally reached the Charlestown Peninsula, across from Boston proper, and the protection of the guns of British warships at anchor in the Charles River.

Despite the terror of the retreat down the Boston road, the British had only 273 casualties, 72 of them killed. Had the American militiamen been more organized and better trained as marksmen, the redcoats would have suffered far worse. As for the Americans, their dead numbered forty-nine, with forty-six more wounded.

The strung-out battle began what would be a bloody, eight-year war. The immediate result was the gathering of a New England militia army to bottle up Gage's troops in Boston.

Further Reading

David Hackett Fisher. *Paul Revere's Ride* (New York: Oxford University Press, 1994); Thomas Fleming. *The First Stroke: Lexington, Concord, and the Beginning of the American Revolution* (Washington, D.C.: National Parks Press, 1978); John R. Galvin. *The Minute Men: The First Fight* (Washington, D.C.: Pergaman-Brassey's International Defense, 1989); and Arthur B. Tourtellot. *William Diamond's Drum: The Beginning of the War of the American Revolution* (Garden City, N.Y.: Doubleday, 1959).

➤ Lexington

Missouri (September 18–20, 1861)
American Civil War

Following his victory at WILSON'S CREEK, Confederate major general Sterling Price hoped to consolidate his advantage by marching into the northern part of Missouri. His army of several thousand men was made up mostly of untrained recruits and newly enlisted soldiers, and he lacked equipment and arms. Nonetheless, he set out on an aggressive campaign.

In September, Price approached the Union-held town of Lexington, not far from Kansas City on the Missouri River, where Col. James A. Mulligan, a former Irish-American politician from Chicago, commanded a garrison of about thirty-five hundred troops. The town's defenses seemed strong, with stout earthworks and artillery, and Price hesitated to attack, choosing instead to surround and lay siege to the town.

After five days of waiting and hoping for a resupply of ammunition, Price decided to take the initiative. On September 18, his men moved to cut off Mulligan's water supply and began to bombard the defenses with artillery. Mulligan pulled back into a tighter perimeter but could do little over the following two days to resist Price's greater numbers. Finally, on September 20, the Confederates opened fire at point-blank range, and Mulligan surrendered the garrison. Few casualties were reported on either side.

Price's second victory in two month's time brought him little in the long run: a greatly superior Union army moved into the state, and he was forced to retreat southward.

Further Reading

Jay Wertz and Edwin C. Bearss. *Smithsonian's Great Battles & Battlefields of the Civil War* (New York: William Morrow, 1997).

✒ Little Bighorn

(Custer's Last Stand, Greasy Grass)
Montana (June 25, 1876) *Black Hills War*

In one of the most famous battles fought in the United States, and perhaps the most controversial, several thousand Teton Lakota and Cheyenne warriors overwhelmed and wiped out 215 men of the Seventh Cavalry, including their flamboyant commander, Lt. Col. George Armstrong Custer.

The bands of the Lakota Nation were, collectively with the Dakota and Nakota, the largest and most powerful tribe of the northern plains, and they—along with the Cheyenne to the south—long resisted the attempts of the U.S. government to move them into a static life on reservations. Although some Lakota agreed to change to the sedentary ways urged by the U.S. government, the majority continued to roam during the early 1870s across the modern-day states of North and South Dakota, Montana, and Wyoming. Their fate was more or less sealed, however, when an army expedition commanded by Custer discovered gold deposits in the Black Hills, the center of the Lakota's most sacred and important territory. The pressure to allow in white miners and settlers was irresistible, and a new war broke out when the federal officials ordered all Lakota onto reservations. The resistance was led by Sitting Bull (Tatanka Yotanka) of the Hunkpapa band of the Teton Lakota. One of the great leaders in all of American Indian history, Sitting Bull combined intelligence with great spiritual authority. The Lakota also had highly talented combat leaders, such as Crazy Horse (Ta-sunko-witko or Tashunka Witco), a Brulé Oglala Teton, and Gall (Pizi) of the Hunkpapa, and had perfected tactics that almost always gave them victory when the U.S. Army allowed the Lakota to fight on their own terms.

The army's plan was to squeeze the Lakota in Montana along the Yellowstone or Bighorn River valleys between the pincers of a three-pronged campaign. Brig. Gen. George A. Crook marched from Fort Fetterman, to the south; Col. John Gibbon advanced from Fort Ellis, in the west; and Brig. Gen. Alfred H. Terry set out from Fort Abraham Lincoln, to the east. Terry's command included the Seventh Cavalry, under Custer, a colorful hero of the Civil War (he had risen to brevet major general by age twenty-three) whose subsequent career as a western Indian fighter had been disappointing. Despite his bluster and extravagant buckskin costumes, Custer had little to show for ten years on the frontier other than a disputed "victory" over a nearly defenseless Indian village at WASHITA and a court-martial conviction for desertion of his post and cruelty to his men.

The army's grand scheme came unraveled on June 17, when Crook's camp on the ROSEBUD CREEK was attacked by a large Lakota force led by Crazy Horse. Crook retreated, leaving Gibbon and Terry to face what they mistakenly thought were no more than seven or eight hundred Lakota. Terry ordered the Seventh to pursue and seek the Lakota, and Custer moved out up the Rosebud to the Little Bighorn, where he intended to attack and pin down the Lakota.

Unbeknownst to any of the army commanders, however, nearly all the free-roaming Lakota, plus hundreds of Cheyenne, had made a large summer encampment on the Little Bighorn River, in a place they called Greasy Grass. There were probably between six thousand and eight thousand Indians in camps strung along the river valley, and several thousand of these were skilled and experienced warriors, many of them equipped with the best repeating rifles of the day. On June 25, Custer's Crow and Arikara scouts told him there was a large number of Indians camped ahead, but he apparently disregarded their estimates of numbers and decided to push on hard, lest the enemy escape. Of course, no one knows what was in Custer's mind or his precise tactical plans, since neither he nor any of his immediate confidants survived the day, and reconstructing his intentions and movements has become a matter of considerable controversy. It does seem clear, however, that he intended to proceed with an attack without waiting on Terry and Gibbon to come up in support.

Leaving his pack train behind, Custer detached Capt. Frederick W. Benteen with 125 men as a blocking force to the south. He also ordered Maj. Marcus A. Reno to take 140 others and cross to the other side of the Little Bighorn and attack the first village they came to. Reno and his men pushed to within sight of a Lakota camp (most of the Indian tepees were out of view farther up the valley) and were surprised to see hundreds of warriors swarming toward them. Reno's men formed a defensive formation,

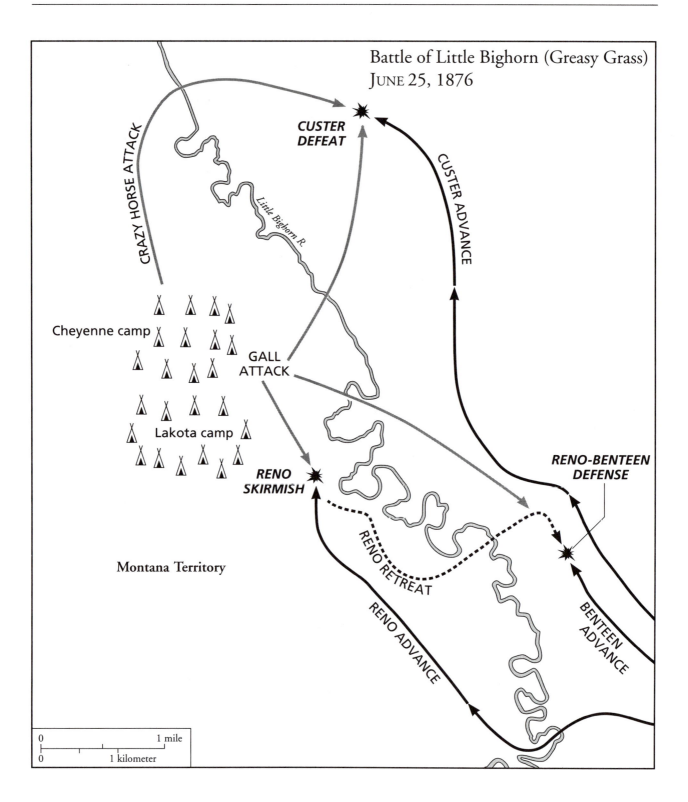

Battle of Little Bighorn (Greasy Grass)
JUNE 25, 1876

CRAZY HORSE ATTACK

CUSTER
DEFEAT

CUSTER ADVANCE

Little Bighorn R.

Cheyenne camp

GALL
ATTACK

Lakota camp

RENO-BENTEEN
DEFENSE

RENO
SKIRMISH

Montana Territory

RENO RETREAT

RENO ADVANCE

BENTEEN
ADVANCE

0   1 mile
0   1 kilometer

but this was soon broken up, and Reno ordered the survivors to mount and flee across the river. Many were caught and killed, or shot down as they tried to get back across the river. The remnant of Reno's command finally rallied on a hilltop when their pursuers broke off contact. Reno and the others could hear the sounds of a battle to the north, although they could see nothing.

The gunfire was the sound of Custer and the remaining five companies of troopers, 215 men altogether, putting up a futile struggle. Custer had demonstrated over and over again during his career that his preferred tactic was to find an enemy and charge hell for leather into their midst, and he apparently had indulged this habit for the last time. According to Indian eyewitnesses, when Custer and his men appeared on the bluffs above the Lakota camps, thousands of warriors quickly grabbed their weapons and streamed out to surround and overwhelm the horse soldiers. There is no grand description of the battle, since the Indian accounts are limited to individual viewpoints, but eyewitness stories combined with archaeological evidence from a survey conducted in the 1980s suggest that most of the men of the Seventh were simply cut off in small groups and killed. By some Indian accounts, many committed suicide rather than face capture. Custer and a few others apparently made a last stand on the north end of the ridge behind a barricade they formed by shooting their horses. Late in the afternoon, after an hour or so of fighting, the gunfire began to abate. Every man of the five companies under Custer's immediate command had been killed, and most of their bodies had been mutilated.

Benteen and Reno joined forces and managed to fight off several more attacks, which stretched into the next day, but by the following afternoon, all the Lakota and Cheyenne had quietly packed up and dispersed under the cover of a grass fire.

Although there had been other Indian victories over white armies nearly as complete (*see also* HARMAR'S DEFEAT, DADE'S BATTLE, ST. CLAIR'S DEFEAT, and FETTERMAN FIGHT), none had the immense public and historical impact of Custer's defeat. He was a famous national character—he had testified to the U.S. Congress at the impeachment trial of Sec. of War W. W. Belknap shortly before joining his command at Fort Abraham Lincoln, for example—and a great deal of attention was focused on the struggle for the gold-filled Black Hills. To this day, a vocal faction of whites refuses to accept the simple explanation of the defeat of the Seventh, and on the other side, Indian adherents have struggled to have the events on the Little Bighorn commemorated from the Lakota point of view.

Army commanders in the West seemed immobilized in the months immediately following Custer's demise, but eventually they responded to an aroused public opinion and increased the pressure on the Lakota. Within a year, Crazy Horse had been defeated (*see also* WOLF MOUNTAIN), Sitting Bull had fled to Canada, and the majority of the Lakota had surrendered.

Further Reading

Richard Allan Fox, Jr. *Archaeology, History, and Custer's Last Battle* (Norman: University of Oklahoma Press, 1993); John S. Gray. *Centennial Campaign: The Sioux War of 1876* (Fort Collins, Colo.: Old Army Press, 1976);————.*Custer's Last Campaign: Mitch Boyer and the Little Big Horn Reconstructed* (Lincoln: University of Nebraska Press, 1991); Richard G. Hardoff. *Cheyenne Memories of the Custer Fight: A Source Book* (Spokane, Wash.: Arthur H. Clark, 1995); Orin G. Libby. *The Arikara Narrative of the Campaign against the Hostile Dakotas, June 1876* (Glorieta, N.Mex.: Rio Grande Press, 1976); Mari Sandoz. *The Battle of the Little Bighorn* (Philadelphia: Lippincott, 1966); Robert M. Utley. *Custer and the Great Controversy: The Origin and Development of a Legend* (Lincoln: University of Nebraska Press, 1998); and James Welch and Paul Strekler. *Killing Custer: The Little Big Horn and the Fate of the Native Americans* (New York: W. W. Norton, 1995).

❧ Lochry's Defeat

Ohio (August 24 or 25, 1781) *American Revolution*

Col. Archibald Lochry, a Pennsylvania militia officer, set out with a force of about one hundred men to journey down the Ohio River and join George Rogers Clark in Indiana on one of Clark's planned raids. Unfortunately for the Pennsylvanians, the eight-man advance party was captured by the famous Mohawk leader Joseph Brant (Thayendaga), and a letter in their possession revealed Lochry's plan and route.

Brant set an ambush that caught Lochry's main body when the men landed near the confluence of the Ohio and Big Miami Rivers. The battle was swift and one-sided. The Americans lost five officers and thirty-six men killed outright. Several of the sixty prisoners taken, including Lochry, were killed by Brant's warriors later in the day. About thirty members of the expedition eventually escaped and returned to Pennsylvania.

Further Reading

Mark M. Boatner. *The Encyclopedia of the American Revolution* (New York: David McKay, 1966).

∾ Lone Tree Lake

See WOOD LAKE

∾ Long Island

New York (August 27, 1776) *American Revolution*

The British began their conquest of New York with a victory over the bumbling American army on Long Island, pushing aside the inexperienced rebels with a show of European military professionalism.

After evacuating his original headquarters at Boston, the British commander in chief, Gen. Sir William Howe, wisely decided to seize New York as a base from which to fight the rebels. He amassed a huge force of British army regulars, augmented by mercenaries from several German states (known collectively to the Americans as Hessians) and backed by a powerful fleet of Royal Navy warships. Howe's ground troops may have numbered as many as thirty-two thousand, almost all of them highly trained, disciplined, professional fighting men, led by experienced officers. The fleet of ten ships of the line and numerous frigates and smaller vessels promised to give Howe complete control of the waters surrounding Long Island and Manhattan.

Opposing the British was a smaller American army under the command of Gen. George Washington. The Americans probably numbered no more than nineteen thousand troops, almost all of them untried, untrained, poorly equipped, and lightly disciplined. Worse still, the corps of American officers, including the commander in chief himself, were rank amateurs at the business of warfare, and although both men and officers lacked little in courage, they often flunked the most basic tests of military knowledge and skill.

On August 22, Howe transported fifteen thousand troops from the tip of Staten Island to Long Island and prepared to advance against the Americans, who had built defenses along the commanding Brooklyn Heights, a natural line of defense that stood between the British landing point and the American base at Brooklyn. The high ridge was a formidable obstacle, but it was pierced at four points by passes and roads. Maj. Gen. Nathanael Greene, the most knowledgeable American on the scene, fell ill before the British began to move, and local command fell to Israel Putnam and John Sullivan, neither of whom knew the topography of Long Island. Four days later, Washington himself arrived and directed reinforcements to Brooklyn Heights—the total number of Americans in the lines was probably about nine thousand men. Unfortunately, no one thought to cover adequately the northeasternmost gap, at Jamaica Pass, and only a handful of men and one officer were sent to guard a road that led completely around the American left.

Howe devised a clever plan: demonstrations in front of the main American forces were to be carried out by British and German troops, while Lt. Gen. Sir Henry Clinton, followed by Earl Percy and the main British force, was to march silently around the Americans on the heights and seize the Jamaica Pass. Clinton and his men executed the plan brilliantly, and by morning on August 27 held Jamaica Pass and the road. The main British column poured through and turned to attack the American flank and rear. The American commander Sullivan was captured when he foolishly led a small contingent forward to reconnoiter.

Meanwhile, Gen. Leopold von Heister, commander of the German mercenaries, attacked the main American defenses on the heights, which were by then commanded by Brig. Gen. William Alexander (who insisted on being called Lord Stirling by his American compatriots). Stirling's men put up a spirited resistance and several times drove the Germans back, but they did not realize that Clinton and the bulk of the British army were behind them. When Clinton attacked, the American defenses collapsed, most of the men turning and running for safety. Stirling and several hundred of his men stood and fought fiercely but were finally forced to surrender (both Stirling and Sullivan were later exchanged).

The British victory—due in part to good planning and execution and in part to American carelessness—was nearly complete. Howe lost around 400 casualties, with about 65 men and officers killed. The Americans, however, suffered nearly one thousand casualties and lost more than one thousand more as prisoners.

Despite the one-sided result of the battle, Howe was slow to follow up, and he allowed Washington to fall back and regroup the American defenses. The British and Germans, however, were cheered by their easy victory in the first open battle with the Americans since BUNKER HILL.

Further Reading

Eric I. Manders. *The Battle of Long Island* (Monmouth Beach, N.J.: Philip Freneau Press, 1978).

Long Sault

Canada (April 1659) *Indian Wars*

Although the French in North America generally strove for good relations with Indian tribes, especially those such as the Huron (Wyandot) who could provide furs, there was a long tradition of hostility between the French and members of the Iroquois Confederacy. In 1659, following several Iroquois attacks on French missionaries, a small band of Frenchmen engaged a much larger Iroquois army in one of the more memorable battles between the French and the Indians.

Adam Dollard, sieur des Ormeaux, a young man "of good family" who had recently arrived in Montreal, decided on a plan to provoke and engage Iroquois Confederacy hunting parties. He convinced sixteen other Frenchmen to join him in the exploit and won the reluctant permission of the French commander, Simon de Maisonneuve, to undertake the mission. The small band left Montreal in late April, hoping to find Iroquois in small enough numbers to attack. The Frenchmen were not experienced woodsmen, however, and after a brief skirmish with a band of Indians near Île Saint-Paul, the adventurers had a difficult time canoeing the rivers of the area, which were high with spring flood waters.

Dollard and his band finally reached an abandoned stockade on the Ottawa River, called Long Sault. Within a few days, the Frenchmen were joined by a party of forty-four Huron and Algonkin, led by Anahotaha and Mitiwemeg. Almost immediately, the Huron discovered evidence of a large party of Iroquois nearby, and Dollard and his men decided to strengthen the neglected fortifications at Long Sault. Just as they began to cut trees and repair the existing log stockade, however, a party of two hundred Iroquois appeared on the river and drove the French and their Indian allies behind the walls of the fort.

After an unsuccessful attempt to parley, the Iroquois attacked the stockade but were driven off with great loss by the gunfire of the French. Dollard showed the usual bloody-minded brutality of white-Indian warfare by cutting off the head of one of the fallen Iroquois and mounting it atop the stockade walls. Infuriated by their losses and Dollard's provocations, the Iroquois settled in for a siege, knowing there would be no reinforcement or relief for the cornered Frenchmen. For seven days the Iroquois sniped at the stockade and feinted attacks, only once actually making an assault, which was turned back by French firepower.

The situation came to a head with the arrival of five hundred new Iroquois warriors. Most of the Huron inside the fort defected to the Iroquois, and the Frenchmen and their few remaining Indian allies prepared for the end, which came in a massive frontal assault by the attackers. The Frenchmen managed to withstand the first wave, but when they attempted to throw a lighted keg of gunpowder over the swall, the improvised bomb hit a tree branch and rebounded back into the stockade, where it exploded in the midst of the defenders. The Iroquois then breached the wall and made short work of the remaining French and Huron inside. Four Frenchmen were captured and led away to villages for ritual torture and execution. None of Dollard's party survived the siege and battle.

The defeat was a severe blow to the French in Canada and greatly depleted the manpower of the settlement at Montreal.

Further Reading

T. W. Paterson, "Siege at the Long Sault." *Canada West* 6, no. 3 (1990): 114–118.

Louisbourg

Canada (May 11–June 17, 1745) *King George's War*

The French stronghold of Louisbourg, a fortress at the tip of Cape Breton Island in what became Nova Scotia, fell to an army of amateur militia soldiers from New England during the colonial phase of King George's War (called the War of the Austrian Succession in Europe).

The conflict started in Europe primarily over the question of which major powers would dominate Belgium (then the Austrian Netherlands), and it involved a grueling land campaign between Great Britain and France as well as large-scale naval battles. In North America, the struggle was fought almost entirely by colonial forces and centered on commercial rivalries between French Canada and British New England. Most politicians and business leaders in New England saw the declaration of war against France as an opportunity to quash a rival for the great cod fishing grounds off the Maine and Nova Scotia coast and to extend New England's economic influence northward. Louisbourg, founded in 1713 and constructed along the lines of a traditional European fortress, was the main object of their aggression.

The chief instigator of the war in New England was Gov. William Shirley of Massachusetts, who represented powerful trading interests. Shirley took the lead in organizing a coalition of militia forces from the New England colonies. When the French attacked the British base at ANNAPOLIS ROYAL, Shirley was able to convince the Massachusetts assembly to fund a military expedition. By April he had assembled an army of around forty-three hundred militiamen from Massachusetts, New Hampshire, Rhode Island, Connecticut, New York, New Jersey, and Pennsylvania, and he embarked his force on a fleet of ninety transports, escorted by armed privateers. The New Englanders were joined on the way by a squadron of British warships under the command of Adm. William Pepperill, Jr., and arrived off Louisbourg (which was unprotected from naval attack) to begin a siege on May 11.

The French commander, Louis Dupont, sieur Duchambon, was in a weak position. While the massive walls of the fortress looked impressive, in fact they were vulnerable to bombardment and likely to crumble under a determined assault. The fort had been designed to withstand only a few weeks' siege, and there was no hope of relief from anywhere in French Canada. Moreover, Dupont had too few cannon to cover his walls and only about six hundred regular troops as a garrison, although he had assembled around twelve hundred more colonial militia inside the fort.

Dupont's tactics were less than forceful. He failed to oppose the landing of the New England troops, and after taking a pounding for several weeks from the New Englanders' siege guns (including thirty extra-heavy cannons captured by the New Englanders when the French panicked and abandoned an outlying battery), Dupont surrendered on June 17.

Unfortunately from the point of view of the New England colonists, the treaty ending the war in 1748 returned Louisbourg to the French.

Further Reading

Raymond F. Baker. *A Campaign of Amateurs: The Siege of Louisbourg, 1745* (Ottawa: Parks Canada, 1995); John S. McLennan. *Louisbourg from Its Foundation to Its Fall, 1713–1748.* 4th ed. (Halifax, N.S.: Book Room, 1979).

✎ Louisbourg

Canada (May 30–July 27, 1758)
French and Indian War

The strategic fortified town and harbor of Louisbourg, at the tip of Cape Breton Island, gave the French control of the Gulf of St. Lawrence and provided a convenient base for a French fleet and a home port for French-Canadian privateers who preyed on New England merchantmen. A colonial army of new Englanders had seized the fortress in 1745 during King George's War (*see also* LOUISBOURG, 1745), but the treaty at that war's end had returned it to the French. In 1758, during the subsequent French and Indian War (part of a conflict known as the Seven Years' War in Europe), the British government made the capture of Louisbourg one of its major goals. The campaign against Louisbourg involved the sort of large-scale amphibious assault and combined land-sea operation seldom seen before the twentieth century.

Against this array, the British commander, Brig. Gen. Jeffrey Amherst, a favorite of the British high command, brought more than thirteen thousand troops plus a significant fleet, commanded by Adm. Edward Boscawen. Amherst was fortunate in his lieutenants, who included Brig. Gens. James Wolfe and Edward Whitmore and Gov. Charles Lawrence of Nova Scotia. The British fleet and troop transports arrived off Louisbourg on May 30, but bad weather kept them from moving closer for a few days.

Amherst divided his command into three brigades and planned a three-pronged amphibious assault on the beaches of the harbor, to be carried out by small boats after the warships had pounded the shore defenses with their big guns. Once ashore, the three brigades were to combine and push inland. The British went into action on June 8, beginning with the predawn bombardment of the defenses. Brigadier General Wolfe, commanding the main assault force, judged it impossible to land at his assigned spot, so he directed his boats to a nearby undefended stretch of beach and landed his men. He then proceeded to attack the French defenses on the flank, which caught them completely by surprise and drove them away from the other beaches, where the remaining British columns landed with little difficulty. The British lost only 108 casualties during the landings and managed to drive the French entirely off the beaches and back behind the walls of the fort.

As soon as weather permitted, Amherst landed his heavy guns and on June 19 began a siege bombardment from relatively close range. Within a week, the French were driven from their island battery. A sortie from the fortress killed some of the attackers but did not seriously impede the British. The most serious obstacles were the two remaining French warships, both ships of the line, which kept Boscawen's ships from controlling the harbor. During the night of July 25, a force of British seamen performed a classic cutting-out operation, a surprise assault from small boats, and captured the French ships.

De Drucour realized he was defeated and asked for surrender terms, which were agreed to on July 27.

Amherst's victory at Louisbourg eliminated a strong French base and to some degree compensated for the defeat of Abercromby at FORT TICONDEROGA on July 8, 1758.

Further Reading

J. Mackay Hitsman and C. C. J. Bond, "The Assault Landing at Louisbourg, 1758." *Canadian Historical Review* 35 (December 1954): 314–330; Douglas E. Leach. *Arms for Empire: A Military History of the British Colonies in North America, 1607–1763* (New York: Macmillan, 1973); John S. McLennan. *Louisbourg from Its Foundation to Its Fall, 1713–1758.* 4th ed. (Halifax, N.S.: Book Room, 1979); and George A. Rawlyk. *Yankees at Louisbourg* (Orono: University of Maine Press, 1967).

Lundy's Lane

Canada (July 25, 1814) *War of 1812*

After defeating the British at the battle of CHIPPEWA on July 5, Brig. Gen. Jacob Brown prepared to renew his invasion of the Canadian Niagara territory. British major general Phineas Riall was waiting to fight again at Lundy's Lane, in what developed into the war's bloodiest conflict.

For two weeks General Brown planned his new attack and waited for supplies and reinforcements from Commodore Isaac Chauncy, but Chauncy declined to subordinate his fleet to army needs, and he never appeared. Finally, Brown sent Brig. Gen. Winfield Scott, who had performed brilliantly at the Battle of Chippewa, to push north toward Niagara Falls in preparation for a larger offensive.

Lt. Gen. Gordon Drummond, commander of the British army in Upper Canada, was determined to resist the American invasion. He sent Major General Riall to fortify a hill at Lundy's Lane, just west of Niagara Falls, as he gathered a large force to oppose Brown's main army.

When he arrived at Lundy's Lane, Winfield Scott spied Riall's forces forming up on the hill and he sent several skirmishing parties ahead to take measure of the enemy forces. Scott also immediately sent for Brown, who arrived to strengthen the American force to a total of twenty-one hundred men. Perhaps hoping to avoid a replay of his defeat at the Chippewa River, Riall ordered a retreat.

As Riall was organizing his withdrawal, he was brought up short by the arrival of Drummond, with fresh

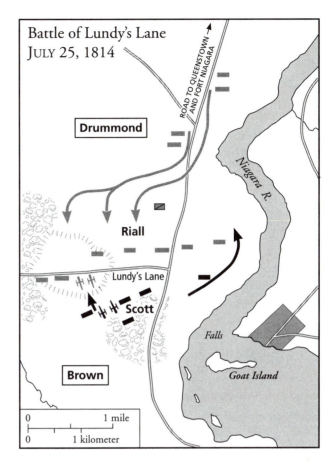

Battle of Lundy's Lane
JULY 25, 1814

ROAD TO QUEENSTOWN
AND FORT NIAGARA

Drummond

Niagara R.

Riall

Lundy's Lane

Scott

Falls

Brown

Goat Island

0   1 mile
0   1 kilometer

troops and artillery. Drummond ordered Riall to hold the hill with a total British force of around three thousand men, including militia and Indian allies.

By the evening of July 25, two large armies faced one another across Lundy's Lane. Since occupying the hill offered the British obvious tactical advantages, Brown first considered alternatives to a frontal attack. He ordered Maj. Thomas S. Jesup and several companies of militia and regulars around his opponent's left flank. They were too weak to destroy the British from behind, but they did capture General Riall, who had been wounded.

As night fell, the last of Brown's reinforcements arrived, and he determined to take the hill in order to halt the heavy cannon fire that the British were raining down on the Americans. Brig. Gen. Winfield Scott and Col. James Miller led two attack waves up the hill. The Americans engaged British infantry troops at close range in a chaotic and bloody firefight. Confusion was so great that at one point two British units apparently attacked each another.

Colonel Miller's regiment eventually gained the crest of the hill and fired directly on the British artillerymen. Several gunners were bayoneted standing at their weapons. The attack broke Drummond's line, and as fresh waves of American reinforcements stormed the hill, the British retired.

As the Americans gained control of the hill at around 9:00 P.M., Lt. Col. Hercules Scott arrived with British reinforcements. Although confusion reigned, the Americans took the arrival of new troops to mean that another attack would follow shortly. At midnight, Drummond tried three times to push the Americans off the hill. Both Winfield Scott and Jacob Brown were seriously wounded during the struggle to repel these attacks.

With nearly all the American officers wounded and ammunition and water growing short, Brown decided to withdraw his dwindling force from the hill. The Americans, now totalling only around seven hundred men, retreated south toward Fort Erie, and Drummond did not follow. The next day, in a weak effort to retake the hill, Brown sent Maj. Gen. Eleazar Ripley, whose men had performed exceptionally well in the confusion of battle, back to Lundy's Lane, but by then Drummond had reinforced the position, and the effort came to naught.

Casualties at the Battle of Lundy's Lane were the heaviest of the War of 1812. The British lost 81 killed and 562 wounded, and the Americans suffered 171 killed and 573 wounded. So many British and American corpses littered the hill that many were gathered and burned on the field. Veterans of the European wars who were present maintained that the fight was every bit as fierce.

Though nominally a defeat, the Battle of Lundy's Lane once again proved that American regulars could acquit themselves well against British troops, albeit at a grim price. The American attack into Upper Canada was halted, and Winfield Scott, whose command had been key to American successes on the Niagara frontier, had to retire from the war because of the severity of his wounds.

Further Reading

Donald E. Graves. *The Battle of Lundy's Lane: On the Niagara in 1814* (Baltimore: Nautical and Aviation, 1993).

Lynchburg

Virginia (June 17–18, 1864) *American Civil War*

In June 1864, Union major general David Hunter advanced through the Shenandoah Valley, intent on attacking the Confederate railroad and supply depot at Lynchburg, Virginia. Although Hunter was informed that Maj. Gen. Philip H. Sheridan's cavalry had been defeated at TREVILIAN STATION and so would be unable to join the action, Hunter proceeded toward Lynchburg on his own. On the evening of June 17 and morning of June 18, Hunter engaged Lt. Gen. Jubal Early's Second Corps at Lynchburg. Though he possessed superior numbers, Hunter was driven back into West Virginia.

Gen. Robert E. Lee sent Early to Lynchburg by train on June 12, as soon as he learned of Hunter's impending attack. By the time Early arrived with the first part of his corps on the evening of June 17, Hunter was already in position. The Federals attacked Lynchburg from the southwest and pushed back the cavalry protecting the Confederate supply depot. Hunter did not finish off his opponents on June 17, however, and by the next morning more of Early's men had arrived by train.

Hunter launched a second series of attacks, but he was pushed back by Early's troops and two brigades under the command of former U.S. vice president John C. Breckinridge. Hunter assumed that more Confederate reinforcements were on the way, and he called off the attack.

No reliable casualty figures exist for the engagement at Lynchburg.

Hunter retreated out of Virginia entirely, and Early was so encouraged by his successful defense of Lynchburg that he began his own offensive through the Shenandoah Valley and on toward Washington, D.C.

Further Reading

Charles M. Blackford. *The Campaign and Battle of Lynchburg, Virginia* (Lynchburg, Va.: Warwick House, 1994); Henry DuPont. *The Campaign of 1864 in the Valley of the Virginia and the Expedition to Lynchburg* (New York: National Americana Society, 1925); and George S. Morris. *Lynchburg in the Civil War.* . . . 2d ed. (Lynchburg, Va.: H. E. Howard, 1984).

Mackinac Island

(Fort Michilimackinac)

Canada (Michigan) (August 4, 1814) *War of 1812*

The British captured Fort Michilimackinac on Mackinac Island (in modern-day Michigan) in July 1812. Two years later, in August 1814, American forces tried to retake the fort, which protected vital fur-trading routes to the north and seemed practically unassailable.

Capt. Arthur Sinclair, American naval commander of Lake Erie, transported seven hundred of Lt. Col. George Croghan's troops to the island. Croghan, the young hero of the Battle of FORT STEPHENSON, planned a direct attack despite the extreme natural protection that geography provided the two British fortifications on the island.

British lieutenant colonel Robert McDouall commanded the British defenses, and he readied his 140 regular troops and 400 Indian and militia allies for the fight.

On August 4, Sinclair's ships *Lawrence* and *Niagara* bombarded the British fortifications but did little damage, because their thirty-two-pound guns could not be aimed at a high enough elevation to reach the fort. Croghan landed on the north side of the island, but his force was unable to break through a strong British artillery position there. Croghan then tried to flank McDouall's troops, but he and his men became lost in woods, where they were attacked by the British Indian allies. After about two hours both sides withdrew, and the Americans gave up trying to capture the island.

The Americans lost twelve killed, fifty-nine wounded, and two missing. British casualties are unknown.

The British maintained control of the fort on Mackinac Island until after the War of 1812 was concluded.

Further Reading

Ernest A. Cruikshank, "The Defense of Mackinac." *Canadian History Readings* 1 (1900): 195–201; and Walter Havinghurst. *Three Flags at the Straits: The Forts of Mackinac* (Englewood Cliffs, N.J.: Prentice-Hall, 1966).

Malvern Hill

Virginia (July 1, 1862) *American Civil War*

In the last of the series of engagements that became known as the Seven Days Battles, the Union Army of the Potomac, commanded by Maj. Gen. George B. McClellan, and the Army of Northern Virginia, under its new commander, Gen. Robert E. Lee, met at Malvern Hill. The costly battle resulted in McClellan's abandoning his campaign to capture Richmond, despite his army's apparent victory.

The Union army, after retreating from within a few miles of the outskirts of Richmond—a retreat due more to the commander's timidity than to battlefield failure—held a superb defensive position at Malvern Hill, a long, high elevation whose flanks were protected by rugged creeks. In total, there were three full corps of about eighty thousand Union soldiers entrenched at Malvern Hill, supported by 250 cannon. Generals Fitz-John Porter, Edwin Sumner, and Samuel Heintzelman commanded the troops.

A nearly equal number of Confederates assembled near the base of the hill, with two artillery positions to the rear. General Lee's plan was to have the artillery, part of the commands of Maj. Gens. James Longstreet and Thomas J. "Stonewall" Jackson, bombard the Federal positions and then to launch a massed infantry attack under Maj. Gens. John B. Magruder and D. H. Hill. With the best of execution, it would have been a desperate enterprise; as it transpired, the plan was a near disaster.

Longstreet discovered that his guns could not be sited properly to hit the Union lines, and only a handful were able to fire as planned, and those were soon knocked out by Union counterbattery fire. Without the hoped-for artillery barrage, the Confederate infantry was terribly exposed, and worse, was fed into the battle in a piecemeal, uncoordinated fashion when Lee lost control of his divisions and the field commanders failed to communicate with each other.

Troops under Brig. Gen. Lewis Armistead on the far right of the Confederate line launched an unsupported attack against the Union fortifications late in the afternoon, but they were hit hard by the Federal artillery and pinned down on the field. Major General Magruder, hearing Armistead's engagement, mistook the noise for a signal for a general attack. Shortly before 5:00 P.M., Magruder ordered Maj. Gen. Benjamin Huger to send his men forward. On the left wing of the Confederate line, Maj. Gen. D. H. Hill committed his troops to an assault an hour later. Magruder's own command eventually followed, later still.

None of the Confederate infantry were able to reach or break the Union defensive lines, although at several points they came within a few yards. All along the line the Confederates were pinned down by massive Federal artillery and musket fire that turned the approaches into a killing field. Grapeshot was especially effective in stopping the Confederate foot soldiers.

The end of daylight signaled the end of the battle. The following day, despite the terrible damage his army had inflicted on the Confederates, McClellan continued his withdrawal and abandoned his campaign.

The Confederates suffered 5,355 casualties in the fighting; the Union reported 3,000.

Further Reading

Clifford Dowdey. *The Seven Days: The Emergence of Lee.* Reprint ed. (Lincoln: University of Nebraska Press, 1993); James M. McPherson. *Battle Cry of Freedom: The Civil War Era* (New York: Oxford University Press, 1988); and Time-Life Staff. *Lee Takes Command: From Seven Days to Second Bull Run* (Alexandria, Va.: Time-Life Books, 1984).

Manassas, First

See BULL RUN, FIRST

Manassas, Second

See BULL RUN, SECOND

Mansfield

See SABINE CROSSROADS

McDowell

Virginia (May 8, 1862) *American Civil War*

During May 1862, the actions of Maj. Gen. Thomas J. "Stonewall" Jackson in Virginia were among the few bright spots in the Confederate military situation. Southern forces had suffered a major defeat at SHILOH, and Union forces were preparing to march on the Confederate capital at Richmond, but despite his own defeat at KERNSTOWN in March, Jackson continued to pursue his campaign in the Shenandoah Valley. One of Jackson's first successes in the campaign came at McDowell on May 8.

Union major general John C. Frémont, the former western explorer and Republican presidential candidate, wished to push his small army west from Virginia into Tennessee, but he decided first to put pressure on Jackson in the valley. In early May, Frémont detached Brig. Gen. Robert H. Milroy with thirty-five hundred men, who were soon joined by Brig. Gen. Robert C. Schenck's twenty-five-hundred-man brigade, to approach Jackson's position from the Allegheny Mountains. When the Federal soldiers paused near the town of McDowell, Jackson moved out to meet them.

Jackson's force of nine thousand, which included twenty-eight hundred men under Brig. Gen. Edward "Allegheny Ed" Johnson, marched ninety-two miles and rode trains for twenty-five miles more in four days to reach the Federal position and engage in battle. The Union soldiers were encamped by the Bull Pasture River when Jackson's troops arrived, establishing a position across the river on Sitlington's Hill. Despite being outnumbered, Milroy and Schenck decided to go on the offensive, and Col. Nathaniel McLean's Ohio regiments led an afternoon attack against the Confederate position.

The progress of the fight was influenced by the topography of the densely wooded Sitlington's Hill, which provided ample cover for the advancing Union soldiers and allowed them to take clear shots at the Confederates in the open field atop the hill. Confederate casualties were very heavy, particularly among the Twelfth Georgia, whose men held the center of the line and refused to retreat even when their commander directed them to run for cover. General Jackson, riding his lines during the battle, ordered Brig. Gen. William B. Taliaferro to march his men down the hill to the right and halt the stinging Union advance.

Though heavy fighting continued until nightfall, the Union forces were unable to make significant progress or to mount the top of the hill. After dark, the Federals withdrew and evacuated McDowell altogether.

Despite the Union loss, Milroy's force suffered only 256 casualties compared to Jackson's 500. Brigadier General Johnson was among those severely wounded.

On May 9 and 10, Jackson continued his pursuit of Milroy toward Monterey, finally feeling he had gained the upper hand. He sent the Confederate government in Richmond a heartening one-line report of the action: "God blessed our arms with victory at McDowell yesterday."

Further Reading

Richard L. Armstrong. *Jackson's Valley Campaign: The Battle of McDowell, March 11–May 18, 1862* (Lynchburg, Va.: H. E. Howard, 1990).

Mechanicsville

(Ellison's Mill)
Virginia (June 26, 1862) *American Civil War*

The day after a battle at OAK GROVE, Confederate commander Robert E. Lee took the initiative away from Federal major general George B. McClellan with the second of what have since been called the Seven Days' Battles. Even though poor logistics resulted in a defeat for Lee, he pushed the Union's huge Army of the Potomac away from Richmond.

Knowing that his ninety-thousand-man Army of Northern Virginia was outnumbered by McClellan's force of one hundred thousand, Lee had nonetheless split his own forces, leaving only twenty-five thousand men to face sixty thousand Union soldiers south of the Chickahominy River, in order to bring to bear superior numbers against the thirty thousand men of Maj. Gen. Fitz John Porter's Fifth Corps, who had been left isolated on the other side of the river by McClellan's dispositions. Lee hoped to concentrate his troops and gain the upper hand, especially if Maj. Gen. Thomas J. "Stonewall" Jackson's division arrived from the Shenandoah Valley in time to add its weight to the attack.

For once, however, Jackson failed. Not only was he slow to reach the area, but on the day of the fighting at Mechanicsville he and his men moved so sluggishly and indifferently that they never got into the battle. Jackson's orders were to descend on Porter's unsecured right flank in an early-morning attack coordinated with the divisions of Maj. Gens. A. P. Hill and James Longstreet. The men of Porter's corps were well dug in and secure behind Beaver Dam Creek and in the town of Mechanicsville, waiting for the Confederate attacks. Hill and Longstreet waited as well, as hour after hour went by with no sign of Jackson.

Finally, at the middle of the afternoon, Hill decided to cross the river at the Meadow Bridge and assault the Union positions. His men made earnest efforts but little headway against the well-situated Federal defenders. As usual during the Civil War, the defensive had the advantage, and the Confederate attacks petered out by late afternoon. Meanwhile, Jackson's division finally reached its assigned point, but since neither Hill nor Longstreet were in sight, Jackson was undecided and instead of pressing on to an attack, he allowed his men to camp. Hill sent in two final attacks to dislodge the Federals just as the day ended, but they were stopped with a high rate of loss.

When the firing ceased at 10 P.M., the Confederate losses totaled between fourteen and fifteen hundred. The Union had suffered only 49 killed, 207 wounded, and 105 missing.

Despite the clear-cut victory, McClellan ordered Porter to withdraw during the night to a new position five miles to the rear, near GAINES'S MILL.

Further Reading

Clifford Dowdey. *The Seven Days: The Emergence of Lee.* Reprint ed. (Lincoln: University of Nebraska Press, 1993); James M. McPherson. *Battle Cry of Freedom: The Civil War Era* (New York: Oxford University Press, 1988); Time-Life Staff. *Lee Takes Command: From Seven Days to Second Bull Run* (Alexandria, Va.: Time-Life Books, 1984).

∽ Memphis

Tennessee (June 6, 1862) *American Civil War*

This river battle fought on the Mississippi at Memphis, Tennessee, pitted ironclad against ironclad, but also featured uniquely designed Union ram ships, which brought the Federals victory and handed them an important base for operations in the western theater.

The Union squadron of five ironclads—*Benton, Louisville, Carondelet, Cairo,* and *St. Louis*—was commanded by Capt. Charles H. Davis. Voluntarily attached to his command were unarmed rams built and commanded by Col. Charles Ellet, an engineer who had devised a way to strengthen the structures of ordinary river steamers, turning them into deadly rams even without guns. Ellet himself commanded the ram *Queen of the West.* The Union plan was to attack the Confederate squadron of ironclads based at Memphis and open the city to capture.

Before dawn on the morning of June 6, the Union ironclads steamed into range of the Confederate ships and began the battle. Davis feinted a retreat upriver, and when the Confederate ships came in pursuit, Ellet's rams swept out, moved rapidly between the Union ironclads, and attacked the Confederates. The rams proved effective, sinking several of the Confederate ships, although at the cost of Ellet's life, and after a brief fight, the remaining Confederates steamed away downriver.

The garrison of the city withdrew during the afternoon, and Federal troops marched in.

Further Reading

Jay Wertz and Edwin C. Bearss. *Smithsonian's Great Battles & Battlefields of the Civil War* (New York: William Morrow, 1997).

∽ *Merrimack*

See U.S.S. *MONITOR*

∽ Mesa

(La Mesa)

California (January 9, 1847)
Mexican-American War

The day after their victory at SAN GABRIEL, American troops led by Commodore Robert F. Stockton, part of a small force sent to wrest California away from Mexico, were scouting for hostile California troops around the Los Angeles River when they met and engaged three hundred of Capt. José María Flores's men in a clearing at La Mesa.

Flores had deployed his troops in a long line in front of a ravine, with artillery on the left, ready to challenge the advancing Americans. Stockton quickly arranged his men in a square and advanced toward the Californians' left. Flores's ineffective artillery was no match for the Americans' heavy fieldpieces, and after a fifteen-minute firefight the Californians were pushed back.

Flores attacked again, sending mounted lancers against the American left, but they were driven back almost immediately by heavy fire. Unable to make any progress, the Californians withdrew.

Only one man was killed on each side, and five Americans and an unknown number of Californians were wounded.

The small battle at La Mesa was the last gasp of Californian resistance to the American capture of Los Angeles, which proceeded the next day. Pres. James K. Polk's plan to conquer California in the course of the larger war with Mexico was one large step closer to success.

Further Reading

La Battalla de la Mesa: The Battle of the Mesa (Los Angeles: East Side, 1926).

∽ Milk Creek

Colorado (September 29–October 5, 1879)
Ute War

The Ute, who inhabited the mountain regions of western Colorado and northern Utah, came under the pressure to change their way of life and become sedentary farmers, as did nearly all tribes of the Great Plains, and like other tribes, they resisted. In 1879, the callous and arrogant agent at the White River Agency in Colorado, Nathan Meeker, provoked the tribe to violence when he called for troops to back up his demands that the Ute plow up their grazing lands.

When Maj. Thomas Thornburg arrived on the scene with 150 men, the Ute perceived a threat and prepared for conflict—which was set off, probably unintentionally, on September 29, when Thornburg's column crossed Milk Creek and rode up to the agency. A band of Ute warriors attacked the soldiers, killing Thornburg with the first shots and sending his men into hastily devised defensive positions. The Ute had command of the surrounding high ground and completely pinned down the column. Agent Meeker and several others at the agency were killed, and his wife and daughter were captured.

Capt. J. Scott Payne took over command of the stranded army detachment and sent out pleas for help. A relief column of Buffalo Soldiers', an all-back regiment, under Capt. Francis Dodge approached the scene on October 2, but the Ute killed all of their horses before the troopers could get close enough to help. Finally, on October 5, Col. Wesley Merritt arrived with a larger detachment, and the Ute faded away in the face of superior numbers.

Diplomacy during the aftermath of the battle prevented further armed confrontations, and the Ute were eventually exonerated, but they were forced to relocate to a reservation.

Further Reading

Marshall Sprague. *Massacre: The Tragedy at White River* (Boston: Little, Brown, 1957).

❧ Mill Springs

(Logan Cross Road)

Kentucky (January 19, 1862) *American Civil War*

The Union triumph at Mill Spring was one of the first decisive victories of the war in the West for the Federal cause, and it pushed the Confederates out of Kentucky and back into Tennessee.

The Confederates had taken control of the Cumberland Gap in late 1861 and decided to protect this position by moving forward into eastern Kentucky. Brig. Gen. Felix Zollicoffer, an inexperienced political appointee, was given command of two thousand troops and told to camp on the south side of the Cumberland River at Mill Spring. Zollicoffer, however, unwisely chose to cross the unpredictable waterway and establish his base with the river at his rear. He was reinforced by another several thousand troops and joined by Maj. Gen. George Crittenden, a Mexican-American War veteran and West Pointer who had just taken over command of the District of East Tennessee. Crittenden decided to make the best of the situation and ordered Zollicoffer to make a surprise attack on the Union forces of Brig. Gen. George H. Thomas, who had been advancing slowly along muddy roads with eight thousand Union troops and was now stopped near Logan Cross Road to wait out the rains.

Zollicoffer marched out during the morning hours of January 19, but Thomas detected his approach and was prepared, having been reinforced by a brigade under Brig. Gen. Albin Schoepf.

The battle began in the midst of an early morning rainstorm with a vigorous attack by Zollicoffer on the Tenth Indiana. A Unionist Kentucky unit commanded by Col. Speed Fry came to the support of the Indianans (as often was the case, there were Kentucky units on both sides of the battle) and checked the Confederate advance.

Two incidents illustrated the inexperience of many of the key officers involved in the first battles of the war. Discovering that Confederate troops were using a convenient ravine to mask their movements into the line, Fry climbed atop a fence and loudly denounced their unsporting tactics. Less comically, Fry was approached during a lull in the fighting by an officer on horseback wearing a long, white raincoat. The mystery officer told Fry to order his troops to cease fire, and Fry was on the verge of doing so when he became suspicious. Fry and several other Union officers drew their weapons and shot the man dead. The mystery officer turned out to have been General Zollicoffer himself, who had apparently become disoriented during the battle and mistaken Fry for a Confederate.

Some of the zeal went out of the Confederates when they learned of the loss of the popular Zollicoffer. Renewed assaults were blunted, and the Union forces eventually pushed back the Confederate lines, despite the arrival of Crittenden, who made efforts to rally the troops. A bayonet attack by the Tenth Ohio finally drove the Confederates into full retreat.

The Union forces reported a loss of 55 killed and 191 wounded, while the Confederates lost 150 killed and 383 wounded.

Crittenden managed to get his men across the Cumberland and to safety, but he lost most of his stores, arms, guns, horses, and mules to Thomas, who overran the Confederate camp. Thomas was prevented from a vigorous pursuit, however, by continued rain.

Further Reading

Mark M. Boatner. *The Civil War Dictionary.* Rev. ed. (New York: David McKay, 1988); Raymond E. Meyers. *The Zollie Tree* (Louisville, Ky.: Filson Club, 1964).

Minisink

New York (July 22, 1779) *American Revolution*

In the summer of 1779, Joseph Brant (Thayendanegea) led a group of about sixty Indians (probably most of them Mohawk) and a few Loyalists on a raid into Tryon County, New York, where they met and defeated a force of American militia.

Brant and his men descended the Delaware River to the town of Minisink, New York, and during the night of July 19–20 they burned the village and scattered the inhabitants, withdrawing afterward with a load of captured goods and a herd of cattle.

The next day, militia under Lt. Col. Benjamin Tusten assembled at Minisink, and after considerable debate—they knew their foe was Brant, and many were properly cautious, in view of his reputation—they decided to pursue the Mohawk and Loyalists. On the morning of July 22, the original militia force was joined by a few more men, led by Col. John Hathorn, a New Jersey militia officer. Hathorn claimed command by virtue of his superior rank and directed the pursuit to continue.

Within a few miles, the Americans came on the remains of Brant's camp. Hathorn and Tusten now decided to give up the chase, since it appeared they were outnumbered (Brant had left a deceptively large number of fires smoldering at his campsite). Others in the party, however, were eager to fight, and they pushed on, initially under the leadership of Capt. Bezaleel Tyler, until he was killed by a hidden sharpshooter soon after.

Topping a rise, the Americans sighted Brant's force at a ford on the Delaware, and they decided to quick-march and catch the enemy before he could cross. Unfortunately for the militiamen, Brant saw them as well and easily outmaneuvered them. As soon as the Americans dropped out of sight, Brant and his men circled away from the ford and took positions astride the Americans' probable line of withdrawal. When they reached the ford, no one was there, and the Americans turned for home, only to walk straight into Brant's ambush.

At the beginning of the fight, Brant cut off a significant part of the American force and tried to persuade the rest to surrender, but they refused and formed a defensive square on top of a hill. For several hours the Americans held their ground, but late in the afternoon Brant spotted a weakness in the defenses and led his men through. A slaughter ensued. Tusten was killed, along with seventeen men who had been wounded earlier; many others drowned in the river trying to escape. Altogether, the Americans lost forty-five killed.

Further Reading

Vernon E. Leslie. *The Battle of Minisink: A Revolutionary War Engagement in the Upper Delaware Valley.* 2d ed. (Middletown, N.Y.: T. E. Henderson, 1976).

Mobile Bay

Alabama (August 5, 1864) *American Civil War*

Mobile, Alabama, was the only remaining major Confederate port on the Gulf of Mexico after the fall of NEW ORLEANS, and it did not succumb to Union naval forces until mid-1864, when a brief but large battle delivered its approaches into Federal hands.

Mobile Bay was protected by strong island forts on either side of the mouth. The Confederates, commanded by Adm. Franklin Buchanan, had strengthened their defenses by laying more than two hundred underwater mines, called "torpedoes," along the main channel. Buchanan's squadron was small, however, comprising his flagship, the *Tennessee,* and three other ironclads, the *Selma, Morgan,* and *Gaines.*

The Union fleet was commanded by Rear Adm. David G. Farragut, who had a variety of powerful ships: his flagship, the *Hartford;* five ironclad monitors, the *Manhattan,* the *Chickasaw, Winnebago, Metacomet,* and *Tecumseh;* the iron-prowed *Monongahela* and *Lackawanna;* plus a number of gunboats and wooden, oceangoing warships.

Farragut aligned his ships in two columns, ironclads in one and gunboats and wooden-hulled ships together in the other, and sailed into the main channel early on the morning of August 5, immediately meeting fire from one of the Confederate forts. The ironclads forged ahead, and as Capt. Tunis A. M. Craven maneuvered the *Tecumseh* toward the *Tennessee*, the Union monitor hit a torpedo, blew up, and sank with almost all hands in a matter of minutes. The Union line of ships came to a halt and jammed up behind the minefield, at which point Farragut, who had climbed into the *Hartford*'s rigging to get a better view of the battle, ordered his ships to press on. He was later alleged to have exclaimed, "Damn the torpedoes! Full speed ahead!" which, accurate or not, became one of the most famous phrases of American naval warfare.

In fact, most of the torpedoes were duds, and the Federal ships began to close on the Confederate squadron. The *Gaines,* hammered out of action, was burned by her own crew; the *Selma* surrendered to the *Metacomet;* and the *Morgan* sought refuge under the protection of one of the forts. Admiral Buchanan continued to fight on with only the powerful *Tennessee,* which eluded major damage, but he too was forced to withdraw temporarily in the face of superior numbers.

After a brief pause, however, Buchanan rejoined the battle, attacking Farragut's flagship, the *Hartford,* avoiding the Federal ram ships. Finally, the Union monitor *Chickasaw* maneuvered into position and blasted away the Confederate ship's smokestack and steering mechanism. Buchanan, who was wounded, was forced to surrender.

Despite losing the battle, the Confederates suffered only 12 dead and 20 wounded, although 243 sailors were captured with their ships. The Union fleet lost 92 when the *Tecumseh* went down, in addition to another 250 killed or wounded.

The result of the naval battle and a subsequent land assault against the forts was to turnover control of the approaches to Mobile Bay to the Union navy, but the city itself resisted capture until the final days of the war in April 1865.

Further Reading

W. Norman Fitzgerald, Jr. *President Lincoln's Blockade and the Defense of Mobile* (Madison: Lincoln Fellowship of Wisconsin, 1954); and Chester G. Hearn. *Mobile Bay and the Mobile Campaign: The Last Great Battles of the Civil War* (Jefferson, N.C.: McFarland, 1993).

≋ Molino del Rey

Mexico (September 8, 1847)
Mexican-American War

On August 24, 1847, a military armistice between the United States and Mexico went into effect, barring Maj. Gen. Winfield Scott from entering Mexico City and

ending the war, which he had sought to do since landing at VERACRUZ in March. Gen. Antonio López de Santa Anna had lost the confidence of most citizens within the capital city, but Scott was afraid an immediate attack on the city would leave Santa Anna at large to gather additional reinforcements in the countryside and that he would prevent negotiations with the Mexican government. Peace negotiations failed on September 6, and Scott notified Santa Anna that the armistice would end the next day if his frequent violations of its terms did not cease.

Reports circulated that Santa Anna had built up his military force to eighteen thousand (twice the number of American troops present) and that he was having church bells cast into cannon at a foundry in Molino del Rey, one mile from the American position at Tacubaya and one thousand yards west of the fortified castle of CHAPULTE-PEC. Santa Anna responded to the challenge from Scott with the declaration that he was willing to do anything to save "the first city of the American continent."

Scott decided the truce was over and sent Brig. Gen. William J. Worth, who commanded his own division, Brig. Gen. George Cadwalader's brigade, Capt. Simon H. Drum's battery of three six-pounders. Capt. Benjamin Huger's two twenty-four-pounders, and three hundred dragoons under Maj. Edwin V. Sumner—a total force of thirty-one hundred—to attack Molino del Rey. Worth wanted to delay the raid until a plan to take Chapultepec as well could be formed, but Scott quashed the idea, ordering Worth forward at 3:00 A.M. on September 8.

Molino del Rey presented a formidable objective, situated up a gentle slope from Tacubaya. Santa Anna had stationed Maj. Gen. Juan Álvarez's four thousand cavalry at the foundry in Molino del Rey, where the main series of low buildings was defended by the Oaxaco Brigade, commanded by Brig. Gen. Antonio León, and additional troops under Brig. Gen. Joaquín Rangel. Fifteen hundred regulars under Brig. Gen. Francisco Pérez protected earthworks around a massive stone building called the Casa Mata, and Brig. Gen. Simeon Ramírez's brigade manned seven guns behind a cactus hedge overlooking a drainage ditch.

Worth ordered a three-column assault at 5:45 A.M. after only a weak preliminary bombardment (his reconnaissance having wrongly reported that the Mexicans had abandoned the foundry). As the Americans approached the complex of buildings, they were driven back by heavy Mexican fire. Lt. Col. Miguel María Echeagaray simultaneously attacked Worth's force from Chapultepec, his men, the Americans later claimed, slitting the throats of everyone they encountered. To the left, Col. James S. McIntosh made better headway under cover from Col. James Duncan's battery, but when McIntosh's men accidentally masked Duncan's guns, they too were turned back by fire from Casa Mata and a Mexican counterattack. Both McIntosh and his second in command were killed.

The American troops began to flee, unmasking Duncan's guns, which now directed heavy, effective fire on Casa Mata. Pérez then withdrew from the stone building as Alvarez's cavalry prepared to strike McIntosh's flank. Before the cavalry could attack, Col. T. P. Andrews led his Voltigeur Regiment to the ravine as Sumner's dragoons rode across toward Molino del Rey.

The battle was finally decided in a series of back-and-forth pushes on the right. American troops broke through two gates at the southern and northwestern corners of the city and began an arduous hand-to-hand fight from building to building. The Eleventh Infantry prevented the Mexicans from retaking the guns at Casa Mata, and the Ninth Infantry helped Garland's men repel Brig. Gen. Matías Peña y Barragán's Mexican troops, who were moving down from Chapultepec to counterattack. With great effort, the Americans finally held the compound.

The American forces lost 116 men killed, 665 wounded, and 18 missing in the confused assault. Mexican losses were estimated at 2,000 killed or wounded and 685 taken prisoner. Later in the morning, the Casa Mata, which had been set afire, exploded, killing several more Americans.

The Battle of Molino del Rey marked an inglorious start for Winfield Scott's final assault on Mexico City. American troops found only a few gun molds and no completed pieces within the complex, and holding the town did nothing to make the assault on Mexico City easier to plan or more successful.

Further Reading

K. Jack Bauer. *The Mexican War: 1846–1848* (New York: Macmillan, 1974); John D. Eisenhower. *Agent of Destiny: The Life and Times of Winfield Scott* (New York: Free Press, 1997); and John Edward Weems. *To Conquer a Peace: The War between the United States and Mexico* (Garden City, N.Y.: Doubleday, 1974).

Monck's Corner

South Carolina (April 14, 1780)
American Revolution

While his main army invested Charleston, South Carolina, the British commander in chief, Lt. Gen. Sir Henry Clinton, sent a strong force up the Cooper River to close off the last American line of retreat out of the doomed city and to seize, if possible, a rebel supply depot at Monck's Corner.

Brig. Gen. Isaac Huger held the position with several hundred Continental cavalry and militia, but he had been careless in his dispositions and failed either to protect adequately the key crossing at a bridge or send out patrols.

Bearing down on Huger and his men was a British officer who now came to notice for the first time but who would become the bane of the Americans in the southern theater: Lt. Col. Banastre Tarleton. The vigorous Tarleton had organized a so-called legion of mixed mounted infantry and cavalry, most of them Loyalists, and it was to be one of the most effective and fastest-moving units in all of the war of the Revolution. On this occasion, Tarleton was paired with Maj. Patrick Ferguson, another brilliant but unorthodox British officer.

Tarleton and Ferguson caught Huger and his patriots unawares between midnight and dawn on April 14 and routed them completely. Lt. Col. James Webster arrived during the day with two regiments to hold the captured stores. Perhaps of greatest value to the British was the capture of several hundred cavalry horses, which allowed him to outfit his legion, its own mounts having died at sea the previous winter.

The Americans had 25 killed and about three times that number captured. The British suffered only three wounded.

Further Reading

John Buchanan. *The Road to Guilford Courthouse: The American Revolution in the Carolinas* (New York: John Wiley & Sons, 1997).

U.S.S. *Monitor* v. C.S.S. *Virginia*

(*Monitor* v. *Merrimack*)

Hampton Roads, Virginia (March 9, 1862)
American Civil War

During the first year of the Civil War, the Union navy enjoyed generally uninterrupted success in capturing Confederate outposts and enforcing a blockade against the South. The Confederates pinned hopes for improving their fortunes in 1862 on converting the hulk of the raised Union ship *Merrimack* (which had been scuttled the previous year) into an ironclad attack vessel. At the end of 1861, however, the Union navy built its own ironclad gunboat, the radically designed *Monitor,* which was ready to sail by February 1862. In March, the U.S.S. *Monitor* met the C.S.S. *Virginia* (as the *Merrimack* was rechristened) in the first-ever battle between two ironclad ships.

The *Virginia's* hull had been cut down to the waterline and covered with crossed wrought-iron bars. Consequently, the ship rode low in the water with an awkward-looking armored superstructure perched above the decks. Though armed with six nine-inch smoothbore and two rifled guns, her main weapon was a cast-iron prow intended to be used as a battering ram. However, the ship was ungainly, and her two engines could move her at a maximum speed of only four knots. Cmdr. Franklin Buchanan commanded *Virginia* and her crew of 350 when she arrived off the coast of Virginia on March 8, 1862.

The *Monitor* was a much different vessel, conceived from the beginning as an unusual departure in naval design by the innovative engineer John Ericsson. Constructed in just over one hundred days, the *Monitor* had a flat deck, above which rose a nine-foot-high revolving turret reinforced with eight inches of iron plates. The turret, which housed two eleven-inch smoothbore guns, and a small pilot house were the only prominent features when *Monitor* was afloat, causing her to be dubbed a "Yankee cheesebox on a raft" or a "tin can on a shingle." Lt. John Lorimer Worden supervised an inexperienced crew of only fifty-eight.

On the afternoon of March 8, the *Virginia* and her two supporting gunboats, the *Beaufort* and the *Raleigh,* steamed into the midst of a Union squadron anchored at Hampton Roads and attacked two frigates, the *Cumberland* and the *Congress.* The *Cumberland* sank within an hour and a half, taking *Virginia's* ram with it, and after constant shelling the *Congress* surrendered at 4:30 P.M. Lt. Catesby ap Roger Jones, who took over command of the *Virginia* when Buchanan was severely wounded, tried to attack a third Union ship, the *Minnesota,* which had run aground, but he was unable to get into position before the *Monitor* arrived on the scene at 10 P.M.

The next morning, the fight between the two ironclads began. The Virginia opened the action with two shots, one of which struck the Monitor broadside but glanced off. The battle continued for several hours at close range. While the Virginia possessed superior firepower, Monitor had greater agility, and her heavy armor prevented even direct blows from inflicting much damage. Jones spent a full hour maneuvering his ship into position to ram the Monitor, but the Union ship merely moved away undamaged, continuing its fire at *Virginia's* stern.

The Southerners finally gained a slight advantage at noon, when a shot exploded at the eye-slit of *Monitor's* pilothouse, permanently blinding Worden in one eye, and putting the ship briefly out of command. Gunnery officer Lt. S. Dana Greene took over and tried to continue the fight, but *Monitor* had drifted into shallow water, taking her away from the *Virginia.* Jones assumed the Union ship was breaking off, and after one last run at the *Minnesota* he steamed away toward the Elizabeth River. The four hours of continuous battle finally came to a close.

In tactical terms, the battle was a draw, and neither ship suffered much damage, proving how admirably ironclads could perform. Casualty totals are unknown.

The *Virginia* was scuttled two months later when the Federals captured the Norfolk Navy Yard, and the *Monitor* was lost in a storm off North Carolina in December. Since the *Monitor* had successfully defended the *Minnesota,* and the *Virginia* had performed equally well, both sides immediately ordered more ironclad construction. The Union navy ultimately achieved the greater benefit, building fifty-eight ships patterned after the *Monitor.*

Further Reading

Robert W. Daly. *How the Merrimack Won: The Strategic Story of the C.S.S. Virginia* (New York: Crowell, 1957); James T. deKay. *Monitor: The Story of the Legendary Civil War Ironclad . . .* (New York: Walter, 1997); Galland E. Hopkins. *The First Battle of Modern Naval History* (Richmond, Va.: House of Dietz, 1943); Arthur Mokin. *Ironclad: The Monitor and the Merrimac* (Novato, Calif.: Presidio, 1991); Gene A. Smith. *Iron and Heavy Guns: Duel between the Monitor and the Merrimac* (Fort Worth, Tex.: Ryan Place, 1996); and William C. White. *Tin Can on a Shingle* (New York: E. P. Dutton, 1957).

Monmouth

New Jersey (June 28, 1778) *American Revolution*

Commander in chief George Washington's near victory in what turned out to be the last large-scale battle in the northern theater during the American Revolution demonstrated the progress his army had made toward becoming a professional force, but confusion at the command level allowed a large British army to escape destruction.

The British had taken Philadelphia, the American capital, in the fall of 1777, but with the defeat of Maj. Gen. John Burgoyne at SARATOGA, and Washington's demonstrated ability to keep his army intact despite defeats at BRANDYWINE and GERMANTOWN, it became increasingly apparent that holding Philadelphia afforded little advantage. Soon after Lt. Gen. Sir Henry Clinton took over as commander in chief from Sir William Howe in May 1778, he decided to abandon Philadelphia and return to the main British base at New York City.

The movement would be dangerous and difficult, however, since the British lacked sufficient shipping to make the evacuation entirely by water. Clinton sent some of his equipment and about three thousand Philadelphia Loyalists (who feared to remain behind) to New York by way of the Delaware River, but the bulk of his army—about ten thousand troops and all their baggage—set out on June 17 to march across New Jersey. The column stretched out along the hot, dusty roads, with a strong contingent under German general Baron Wilhelm von Knyphausen leading the way, a twelve-mile baggage train in the middle, and Clinton and Maj. Gen. Lord Cornwallis with several thousand of the best British troops at the rear. The weather was ghastly hot, with temperatures hovering for days at nearly one hundred degrees.

Washington and his army were still in quarters at Valley Forge, where they had suffered horribly over the winter from cold, exposure, and lack of food and clothing.

However, the army's fighting abilities had been significantly improved through the efforts of Friedrich von Steuben, a former Prussian officer whom Washington had appointed as inspector general of the Continental army. In an amazing effort, von Steuben had taught the Americans the discipline and drill needed to meet the British and German professionals on even terms. Washington now had the finest instrument he had ever had at his command, but the question was how to use it.

Washington set his men in motion, dogging Clinton's route and guessing at which of several options the British would take to reach the Jersey shore. Washington's commanders were divided as to the proper course. Most—including Nathanael Greene and the marquis de Lafayette—wanted to fall on the vulnerable British column full force, but the senior major general, Charles Lee, a former British officer and the best-trained and most experienced member of the American officer corps, thought it would be folly to offer battle. Washington could not quite make up his mind and rather stumbled into the subsequent battle without a coherent plan. After considerable confusion, Washington appointed a reluctant Lee to command a four-thousand-troop

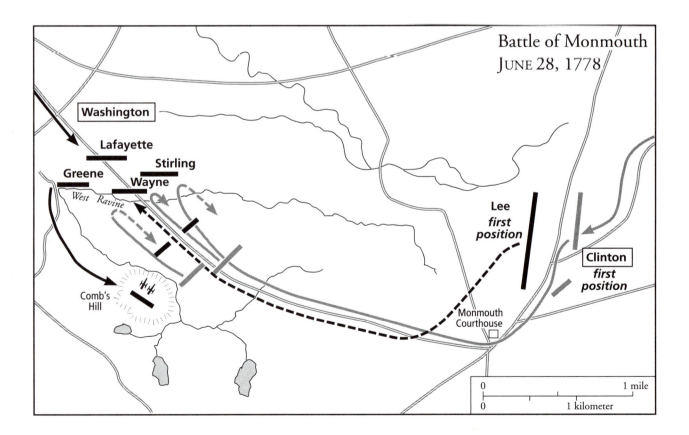

Battle of Monmouth
JUNE 28, 1778

Washington

Lafayette

Stirling

Greene

Wayne

West Ravine

Comb's Hill

Lee
first position

Clinton
first position

Monmouth Courthouse

0   1 mile
0   1 kilometer

force in an attack on the British, who had settled into a defensive position at Monmouth. Washington himself would hold the main American concentration a short distance away, ready to move up.

Lee began to move toward the British camp early on June 28. Clinton had ordered Knyphausen to resume the march, and so a significant portion of the British army was on the road and played no role in the subsequent fighting. Clinton retained some of his best troops as a rear guard, and they became the object of Lee's advance. Unfortunately, Lee's performance on the battlefield was one of the worst by any American commander during the war. Either from lack of conviction about the attack or simple confusion, he botched what should have been a relatively simple assault on an inferior force. His contradictory orders (the record of exactly what happened is muddied and no two firsthand accounts agree in detail) resulted in a full-scale retreat from the British.

As the American troops streamed back from the engagement, they met Washington, who could scarcely credit what he saw. When Lee himself arrived, Washington confronted him with bitter recriminations—some accounts have Washington swearing vehemently at his second in command. Washington and his other senior officers managed to staunch the retreat and organize a new line of defense behind a swampy declivity known as the West Ravine, a strong position with good artillery support. By the time Clinton decided to move forward and counterattack with his elite light infantry and grenadier units, the Americans presented an organized front with regiments under Anthony Wayne at an advanced center position, Lord Stirling in command of the left wing, and Nathanael Greene on the right.

During the ensuing fight the Americans demonstrated fully that they were no longer the amateur rabble that the British had so easily defeated in open-field combat during the first two years of the war. Urged on by Washington and Steuben, who ranged back and forth on the field, the Continentals met the best Clinton had to offer and turned them back time after time with disciplined maneuver and firepower. The British light infantry and grenadiers made several assaults on Wayne's exposed position, but the Americans held firm, devastating the tight British formations with well-timed musket volleys. During one exchange, Lt. Col. Henry Monckton of the Forty-fifth Regiment of Foot led his grenadiers to within yards of Wayne's front line, but he was shot down and his body and the British colors were hauled in by the Americans.

By late afternoon, the American lines had contracted to a degree—Wayne had withdrawn from his salient—but the troops were ready to receive more assaults. The previous days' long marches, the vicious heat, and the effectiveness of the American resistance now convinced Clinton that his men could not renew the battle. As darkness fell, the troops of both sides more or less collapsed where they stood, as Washington busily brought up reserves and made plans for a morning attack.

When the sun came up, however, the British side of the field was empty. Clinton and his army had slipped away during the night and were now on the road toward the coast to meet the ferries and ships that would carry them back to the safety of New York City.

The total casualties from the day-long battle were surprisingly light. The Americans reported 72 killed, 161 wounded, and 132 missing. Thirty-five or forty Americans may have died from sunstroke. The British losses were not accurately reported, but the estimate was around 350 total casualties, with a high percentage killed in action or dead from heat exhaustion. One authority put total losses much higher. Around six hundred, the majority Germans, deserted during or immediately after the battle.

The accounting of the battle gave Washington a slight edge at the end of the day, and the American commander must have known how close he had finally been to a complete victory, had only General Lee performed better. Clinton, on the other hand, was lucky to have escaped with most of his army intact.

Further Reading

Samuel S. Smith. *The Battle of Monmouth* (Trenton: New Jersey Historical Commission, 1975); and Theodore Thayer. *The Making of a Scapegoat: Washington and Lee at Monmouth* (Port Washington, N.Y.: Kennikat Press, 1976).

✎ Monocacy

Maryland (July 9, 1864) *American Civil War*

After defeating Union major general David Hunter at LYNCHBURG in June, Lt. Gen. Jubal Early reinforced his Second Corps, forming the fourteen-thousand-man Army of the Valley, and went on the offensive toward Washington, D.C. Union major general Lew Wallace commanded fifty-eight hundred troops in Maryland, with which he hoped to slow Early down, observe the Confederate's strength, and provide time for reinforcements to reach the capital. Wallace fortified two positions where the Baltimore and Ohio Railroad, the Georgetown Road, and the National Road crossed the Monocacy River south of Frederick and there waited to engage Early, whose force arrived on the morning of July 9.

The first skirmishes broke out around 6:30 A.M. at the Georgetown Road, when Confederate major general Stephen Ramseur's division pushed back Union pickets and established a position at the Best Farm. Ramseur hesitated to cross the Monocacy by a covered bridge in the midst of an artillery duel, and while he waited to consult with Early, Maj. Gen. Robert E. Rodes's Confederate division hit Brig. Gen. Erastus B. Tyler's brigade near the National Road. As the fight continued into the afternoon, Brig. Gen. John McCausland's Confederate cavalry troopers were twice pushed back by fire from Brig. Gen. James B. Ricketts's veteran infantrymen to the south of the railroad at the Worthington-McKinney Ford.

Federal troops burned the covered bridge, after which a late-afternoon Confederate attack focused on the Union left side, as McCausland regrouped his troops. A bitter fight broke out in the wheat fields at the Thomas Farm, east of the river. Confederate artillery continued to blast away, and the Confederates' superior numbers began to make themselves felt. By 4:30 P.M., Wallace realized that his force might be wiped out, as were his men in the wheat field, and he withdrew along the National Road. Ramseur and Rodes gave chase, but Early called them off, and Wallace got away.

The lopsided casualty totals reflect the scale of the Confederate victory. The southerners lost between 700 and 900 men, while the northerners counted 1,968 casualties.

Though Early achieved a victory at Monocacy, Wallace had gained an accurate impression of his strength and intentions in time to provide the information for the defense of Washington, D.C. Wallace lost the battle but helped save the capital.

Further Reading

B. Franklin Colling. *Monocacy: The Battle That Saved Washington* (Shippensburg, Pa.: White Mane, 1997); and Glenn H. Worthington. *Fighting for Time: The Battle That Saved Washington.* Rev. ed. (Shippensburg, Pa.: White Mane, 1988).

Monongahela

(Braddock's Defeat)

Pennsylvania (July 9, 1755) *French and Indian War*

In a battle that was the high point of the first years of the French and Indian War, a large British expedition was destroyed as it approached the French post at Fort Duquesne, handing the French an advantage in the North American war that belied their slim resources.

The French had first established a base at Fort Duquesne, at the confluence of rivers forming the Ohio River, in 1754 and had successfully defended it against an inept Virginia militia expedition led by twenty-two-year-old Lt. Col. George Washington (*see also* FORT NECESSITY). The post was a key factor in controlling all of the Ohio Valley, and as long as the French commanded the river, they could enforce their will as to trade and settlement on the western frontier of the British colonies. The French were chronically short of men, especially trained soldiers; however, they had superb relationships with a host of Indian tribes and recruited heavily among these allies in order to flesh out their North American armed forces. At Fort Duquesne, for example, the French in the summer of 1755 had only 108 regulars and 146 Canadian militia, under the command of Capt. Daniel Hyacinthe-Marie Liénard de Beaujeu, but they also had 637 Indian allies from a mixture of several tribes from the Great Lakes region.

The British home government appointed Maj. Gen. Edward Braddock as commander in chief in North America in 1754 and ordered him to execute a large-scale plan to defeat the French, the key point of which was to take Fort Duquesne. He sailed to Virginia with two undersized and poorly manned regiments, hoping to fill out his expedition with colonial recruits. Although a long-serving officer from a military family, Braddock was an administrator, with virtually no combat or campaign experience. He apparently hoped to rely on superiority of numbers to intimidate the French. He received only grudging support from the colonial governors and was thwarted in attempts to recruit Indian scouts (the governor of South Carolina apparently discouraged Cherokee and Catawba from joining), and his force might have starved in camp had not Benjamin Franklin arrived with a wagon train of supplies at a key juncture.

Braddock set out overland for Duquesne in June with a total of slightly more than two thousand men and virtually no Indian scouts. George Washington, who had resigned his Virginia militia commission in a dispute over rank, marched as Braddock's aide de camp. The expedition moved slowly—as British columns always did when confronted with American forests—but steadily toward its goal. Partway there, at Little Meadows, Braddock detached about six hundred men and left them there, under the command of Col. Thomas Dunbar, with most of the army's baggage.

Tiring from the hard going, and running out of food and water, the British stopped ten miles short of Fort Duquesne on July 8 and set up camp. The French commander, de Beaujeau, learned of Braddock's presence from his Indian scouts and prepared a sortie to cut off the British.

On the morning of July 9, Braddock and his men crossed the Monongahela, circled back around a difficult bit of terrain, recrossed the river, and prepared to make their approach on the French post. To the complete surprise of the British, who still operated without scouts, the much smaller French force, comprised largely of Indians, fell on Braddock's vanguard and rapidly sent it reeling back on the main column, where it collided with a detachment Braddock had sent forward in response to the sound of firing. The confusion among the British was complete, and while they stumbled about in panic, mixing up units and losing discipline and cohesion, the French and Indians poured on a vicious fire from atop a commanding hill and from hidden flank positions among the surrounding trees. Many British troops were hit in the confusion by fire from their own side.

After three hours of merciless French and Indian attack, the British turned and ran, most of them not stopping until they reached Dunbar's base camp, fifty miles away. Washington organized Virginian militia to cover the retreat, which just missed being a complete and headlong rout. Braddock was carried from the battlefield with a severe wound, and overall the British suffered 977 casualties. Captain de Beaujeau was killed in the first moments of battle, but otherwise the French casualties were light.

After pausing to burn most of their supplies and ammunition, the British began a retreat back to Virginia on July 13. Braddock died before the withdrawal began and was buried in a disguised grave. With his defeat on the Monongahela the British strategy in the Ohio Valley collapsed.

Further Reading

Paul Kopperman. *Braddock at the Monongahela* (Pittsburgh, Pa.: University of Pittsburgh Press, 1977); and Ronald D. Martin, "Confrontation at the Monongahela: Climax of the French Drive into the Upper Ohio Region." *Pennsylvania History* 37 (1948): 133–150.

⤳ Monterrey

Mexico (September 20–24, 1846)
Mexican-American War

For four months after the first major battle of the Mexican-American War, at RESACA DE LA PALMA, Brig. Gen. Zachary Taylor gathered American volunteers, planning to march cross-country to attack the Mexican city of Monterrey, the capital of the state of Nuevo León. The main northern force of the Mexican army, commanded by Maj. Gen. Pedro Ampudia, and a large garrison of men headed by Brig. Gen. Francisco Mejía built up the city's fortifications and waited for the Americans. The attack finally came in September 1846.

Even after months of preparation, Taylor's advance from the city of Camargo to Monterrey proceeded slowly. On September 19, the American forces arrived at the outer walls of Monterrey and discovered the city to be extremely well fortified, with forts blocking attack from the east and north. The next day, Taylor devised a complicated plan and began his attack.

Taylor sent Brig. Gen. William J. Worth with two thousand soldiers and five hundred mounted rangers around the city to the northwest to approach a weakly fortified hill at Independence Heights. Taylor planned to attack with the rest of his seven thousand troops from the east. After drawing the fire of a Mexican nine-pounder atop a western hill, Taylor's men encamped for the night at Walnut Springs.

On the morning of September 21, the two sides exchanged artillery fire as Worth began his attack and Taylor sent two divisions in a diversionary move to the northeastern side of the city. One part of the diversionary attack, under Lt. Col. John Garland, came under heavy fire from three separate Mexican fortifications and broke apart, leaving only Capt. Braxton Bragg's artillerymen to work their way into the city. Eventually, all the Americans had to withdraw under heavy Mexican fire.

Capt. Electus Backus's infantrymen managed to seize briefly a fortified tannery on the eastern edge of town, but Mejía retook the guns there in time to ward off another attack by a mixed force of regulars and Ohio volunteers led by Col. Alexander M. Mitchell and Brig. General John A. Quitman. The Americans finally took the tannery in the afternoon, after taking heavy casualties, and Capt. Randolph Ridgeley established an American artillery position there.

After securing the tannery, Col. Mitchell's Ohioans pushed unsuccessfully against the town, having to fight off two Mexican cavalry regiments commanded by Brig. Gen. José María García Conde. John Garland's troops had reorganized for another attack by early afternoon, but they too were pushed back. The Americans, however, succeeded in driving the Mexican cavalry within the city walls just before darkness halted the fight for a few hours.

Around 3:00 A.M., Brigadier General Worth sent his men up Independence Hill in a surprise attack. They charged Fort Libertad at its peak and took over the Mexican position there, although Lt. Col. Francisco de Berra still held the Obispado, an abandoned bishop's palace, halfway down the slope. Throughout the day on September 22, the Americans fired a twelve-pound howitzer at the Obispado to cover repeated infantry attacks. De Berra's men left the palace to try and retake the heights, but they were chased off the hill altogether. With the capture of the Obispado, the Americans had secured the western edge of the city, and around midnight Ampudia ordered his men on the outer fortifications to the east and north to abandon their positions.

On the morning of September 23, Taylor moved to occupy the empty fortifications, and by 11 A.M. Quitman had secured the entire eastern end of town. Worth, still occupying Independence Hill, assumed that the gunfire from the east meant a general attack had begun and ordered his men into the town. Throughout the day on September 23, the Americans fought from house to house, trying to reach the central plaza, where the Mexican general command was located. At dusk Taylor ordered a tactical retreat, though his forces were close to taking the plaza with the aid of artillery fire directed into the center of town.

Before dawn on September 24, Gov. Francisco Morales and Brig. Gen. Ampudia began negotiations with Taylor to surrender the city. The Mexicans resisted American demands that they surrender their munitions, the town, and all public property. Finally, a commission of officers from both sides, including Col. Jefferson Davis and Maj. Gen. José María Ortega, decided that the city would be evacuated but that Mexican forces could retain their side arms and one battery of artillery. Taylor agreed to an eight-week armistice, as long as the Mexican army withdrew beyond the Rinconada pass. On September 25, the U.S. flag was raised over the city of Monterrey.

During the five days of fighting at Monterrey, the American forces lost 120 killed, 368 wounded, and 43 missing; the Mexicans lost 367 killed or wounded.

Ampudia's withdrawal after his defeat at Monterrey opened the way for Zachary Taylor to push deeper into

Mexican territory when the two governments invalidated the eight-week armistice.

Further Reading

Jack K. Bauer. *The Mexican War, 1846–1848* (New York: Macmillan, 1974); and John Edward Weems. *To Conquer a Peace: The War between the United States and Mexico* (Garden City, N.Y.: Doubleday, 1974).

Montreal

Canada (September 25, 1775)
American Revolution

During the late summer of 1775, the American Continental Congress commissioned an invasion of Canada and sent an army under New York general Philip Schuyler north along Lake Champlain. Vermonter Ethan Allen, who had seized FORT TICONDEROGA the previous May, had been ousted from command by his Green Mountain Boys, and attached himself to Schuyler's force.

Allen grew impatient when Schuyler laid siege to ST. JOHN'S, deciding he could push ahead and take the British post at Montreal on his own. He recruited a group of about one hundred Canadians and joined forces with American major John Brown, who had another one hundred Canadian volunteers under his command. They planned to cross the St. Lawrence River and attack Montreal from two sides simultaneously.

Gen. Guy Carleton, the British commander in chief in Canada, held the city with a handful of regulars and about two hundred volunteers. Carleton, as events later in the winter would prove, was a soldier skilled in both tactics and strategy, and he was much more than a match for the amateurish Americans. Allen had only a few canoes for his men, and it took three trips to ferry them across the river during the night. Brown and his men failed to cross at all. When Allen discovered he was unsupported, he ordered a withdrawal, but the lack of transport marooned him. He and his men were at the mercy of a sortie by Carleton. Allen's volunteers melted into the countryside, and Allen himself was captured.

Further Reading

Harrison Bird. *Attack on Quebec: The American Invasion of Canada, 1775* (New York: Oxford University Press, 1968); Hal T. Shelton. *General Richard Montgomery and the American Revolution: From Redcoat to Rebel* (New York: New York University Press, 1994); and George Stanley. *Canada Invaded, 1775–1776* (Toronto: Hakkert, 1973).

Moore's Creek Bridge

North Carolina (February 27, 1776)
American Revolution

The defeat of a colorful army of Scots Loyalists at Moore's Creek Bridge in North Carolina temporarily quashed British hopes of using loyal Americans to help regain control of the state.

The British believed during most of the Revolution that in the southern states were thousands of Loyalists who could be recruited to fight for the crown. In 1776, North Carolina's royal governor, Josiah Martin, encouraged a group of transplanted Scots highlanders to rally to the king and support Gen. Sir Henry Clinton's expedition to take CHARLESTON. Many of the backwoods highlander leaders were aged veterans of the Battle of Culloden and the uprising in Scotland inspired by "Bonny Prince Charlie." Nonetheless, they preferred the cause of the Hanoverian king to American independence. By mid-February, almost one thousand men had gathered in the Cross Creek region under the leadership of Donald McDonald, Donald McLeod, and Allan McDonald, intending to march to Cape Fear and join Clinton.

A patriot force marched out from Wilmington to stop the Scots Loyalists. The core of the American army was the First North Carolina Regiment of Continentals, under Col. James Moore. He was joined by smaller groups of militia and volunteers, notably a unit commanded by Col. John Lillington. Their plan was to cut off the highlanders' march and prevent them from reaching the coast. Hearing that reinforcements under Col. Richard Caswell were on their way to stiffen his forces, Moore decided to stop the Loyalists at a bridge over Moore's Creek, about eight miles from Wilmington.

Building and then abandoning breastworks on the west end of the bridge, the Americans withdrew to the east end. They cleverly removed the planking from the bridge and may have greased the log stringers, to make it difficult for the Loyalists to cross. Lillington and Caswell were in charge of the American position, with Moore some distance away.

During the night of February 27, the highlanders arrived at the bridge and prepared to attack. Donald McDonald was ill, so Donald McLeod took command. The highlanders' plan was simple, based on generations of warfare in their native land: to the sound of the pipes they would send forward an advance assault force armed with traditional two-handed broadswords, called claymores, and defeat the Americans by sheer valor and the terror of medieval weaponry. The main body would mop up with muskets and rifles.

In what must have been a magnificent spectacle, McLeod and Capt. John Campbell led the attack, shouting "King George and the broadswords!" When the Scots got to within thirty yards, the Americans cut loose a hail of musket balls and shot from two artillery pieces. The highlanders were destroyed. McLeod and Campbell were killed, along with most of the attack force, and many of those who were not gunned down slipped off the bridge and drowned in the creek. The battle was over in a matter of minutes.

The Americans promptly replaced the bridge planks and crossed the creek to capture 850 Loyalists with all their equipment and supplies. The defeat ended the threat of a Loyalist uprising in North Carolina for several years.

Further Reading

Hugh F. Rankin. *The Moore's Creek Bridge Campaign, 1776.* Reprint ed. (Conshocken, Pa.: Eastern National Parks and Monuments Association, 1993).

Moraviantown

See THAMES

Munfordville

Kentucky (September 14–17, 1862)
American Civil War

Gen. Braxton Bragg led a force of thirty thousand Confederates north from Tennessee into Kentucky in 1862 as part of the South's campaign in the West. His advance hit a bump at Munfordville, but he gained the surrender of his opponents in one of the most unusual incidents of the entire Civil War.

Bragg was marching toward central Kentucky when an advance force under Brig. Gen. James R. Chalmers attacked a fortified Union position guarding a railroad bridge over the Green River near Munfordville. The fortifications were defended by a relatively small force commanded by an amateur, Col. John T. Wilder, who rebuffed Chalmers's assault on March 14. Overnight, the Union post was reinforced to more than four thousand men.

The next day, however, Bragg brought up his entire army to surround Wilder and his men. Wilder—who had been a businessman before the war and had no experience to help him—decided on a direct if unconventional plan when the Confederates called on him to surrender. Wilder crossed the lines to parley with Confederate major general Simon Bolivar Buckner, a native of the region, and asked Buckner's advice, as a gentleman, as to what to do. Buckner showed Wilder the artillery batteries now ready to bombard the Union position, and Wilder decided on the spot to surrender. Surprisingly, his action at Munfordville did not squash his military career, and he later became famous as a leader of cavalry.

The Union lost 15 killed and 57 wounded during the fighting, and the Confederates lost 35 killed and 253 wounded.

Further Reading

Hal Engerud. *The Battle of Munfordville, September 14–17, 1862* (Munfordville, Ky.: Hart County Historical Society, 1984).

≈ Murfreesboro

See STONES RIVER

≈ Mystic River

Connecticut (May 26, 1637) *Pequot War*

The first large-scale conflict between the Indians of New England and the early English immigrant settlers came seventeen years after the Europeans first arrived at Plymouth, and it resulted in the virtual annihilation of a powerful local tribe, the Pequot.

Less numerous than the neighboring Narragansett and the Wampanoag tribes, the Pequot nevertheless controlled much of the Connecticut River valley, the region into which the English settlers wished to expand. Pressed politically and economically by both their Indian rivals and the New Englanders, the Pequot adopted an energetic defensive stance; also, they opened trade with the Dutch in the Hudson River valley, which further alienated the English settlers. A full-scale war broke out in 1636 following the killing of an English trader off Block Island and subsequent indiscriminate English attacks on Pequot villages (attacks that also mistakenly killed Narragansett).

Led by their sachem, Sassacus, the Pequot launched a long-term campaign to rid Connecticut of non-Indian settlers. Unable to negotiate a treaty with the Narragansett, the Pequot were still powerful enough to strike at settlements at Fort Saybrook and Wethersfield, sending out expeditions from their two villages.

By April 1637, the Pequot War had cost the New Englanders about thirty deaths, and the Connecticut General Court voted to raise an army and exterminate the tribe. Capt. John Mason was given command of between eighty and one hundred men and ordered to attack the main Pequot settlement. This force was joined by an unknown number of Mohegan, a dissident group of Pequot, led by Sassacus's son-in-law, Uncas, which had split from the Pequot several years earlier, and about twenty more Connecticut volunteers from Fort Saybrook, under Capt. John Underhill. The combined force moved by boat along the coast, adding more allies from the Narragansett and Niantic, but Mason decided to ignore the larger Pequot village, on the Thames River, and instead attack the secondary village near the mouth of the Mystic River.

On the morning of May 26, the combined English and Indian attack force surrounded the circular palisade of the Pequot village in lines two deep, the English in front and the Indians behind them. The English charged simultaneously into the two opposite openings in the village stockade, but the aroused Pequot repulsed the attacks and drove the attackers back outside the palisade. The English then changed tactics and set fire to the houses of the village. As the Pequot fled the flames, the New Englanders and their allies cut them down, killing almost everyone they could catch. Within an hour, as many as seven hundred Pequot men, women, and children died either in the fire or at the hands of the attackers. No more than eighteen Pequot were taken prisoner, and fewer than ten managed to escape the ring surrounding the burning village. Two New Englanders were killed and twenty-five wounded, while their Indian allies suffered the loss of forty. The attacking force withdrew after skirmishing with Pequot warriors from Sassacus's village on the Thames.

The attack on the Mystic River village effectively destroyed the Pequot. Sassacus was unsuccessful in finding new allies; when he approached the Mohawk about an alliance, they killed him. In July the remaining several hundred Pequot surrendered to a force of New

Englanders after a confrontation in a swamp near modern-day Hartford. Under the subsequent treaty, the Pequot tribe was completely disbanded, and the remaining members were distributed among the Mohegan, Narragansett, and Niantic or sold into slavery in the West Indies. The tribe was not reconstituted until the late twentieth century.

Further Reading

Laurence M. Hauptman and James D. Wherry. *The Pequots in Southern New England: The Rise and Fall of an American Indian Nation* (Norman: University of Oklahoma Press, 1990); Francis Jennings. *The Invasion of America: Indians, Colonialism, and the Cant of Conquest* (Chapel Hill: University of North Carolina Press, 1975); and Ian Steele. *Warpaths: Invasions of North America* (New York: Oxford University Press, 1994).

N

⋙ Nashville

Tennessee (December 15–16, 1864)
American Civil War

Having been forced to abandon Atlanta in October 1864, Confederate lieutenant general John B. Hood attempted to take the offensive by moving his Army of Tennessee toward the strongly held Union base at Nashville. After fighting battles at ALLATOONA PASS and FRANKLIN, Hood reached the vicinity of Nashville in the first days of December.

The city was one of the strongest Union posts in the entire western theater and its defenses had been built up and improved over a long period. The fortifications were manned by nearly 50,000 men, commanded by Maj. Gen. George H. Thomas, one of the North's best officers.

Hood, on the other hand, had only 23,000 men remaining after his extensive battle losses at Franklin, but he nonetheless took up an aggressive stance in positions south of the city, building four detached redoubts to anchor his left.

On the foggy morning of December 15, Thomas sent a diversionary attack by black troops under Maj. Gen. James B. Steedman against Hood's right, but the main Union attack was on the Confederate left by Maj. Gen. A. J. Smith's corps and the corps of Brig. Gen. Thomas J. Wood. Early in the afternoon, the Federals overran the Confederate redoubts on the left, and by nightfall the Southern lines had collapsed.

Hood, however, did not withdraw during the night but rather established a new, tighter line about a mile and a half south of his previous position.

On the morning of December 16, Thomas again sent black troops in a feint against the Confederate right but ordered the brunt of the Federal attack against the weaker Confederate left. The issue was settled in the late afternoon when troops commanded by Brig. Gen. John McArthur captured a knob that had anchored Hood's left. Thomas saw his chance and threw in all of his available forces in a powerful follow-up attack. Hood's army disintegrated. More than four thousand Confederates surrendered or were captured, and the bulk of the Army of Tennessee turned and fled in disorder. Thomas's victory eliminated the last serious threat to Union control of the western theater.

Thomas reported 387 killed (a surprisingly small number), 2,562 wounded, and 112 missing. Hood's losses were never officially tallied, but a later estimate placed total casualties at around 1,500.

Further Reading

Winston Groom. *Shrouds of Glory: From Atlanta to Nashville: The Last Great Campaign of the Civil War* (New York: Atlantic Monthly, 1995); Stanley F. Horn. *The Decisive Battle of Nashville* (Baton Rouge: Louisiana State University, 1956); Paul L. Stockdale. *The Death of an Army: The Battle of Nashville and Hood's Retreat* (Murfreesboro, Tenn.: Southern Heritage, 1992); and Wiley Sword. *Embrace an Angry Wind: The Confederacy's Last Hurrah* (New York: HarperCollins, 1991).

New London Raid

Connecticut (September 6, 1781)
American Revolution

The fighting connected with a vicious British raid on New London, Connecticut, was the final engagement of the war in the North.

The British were led by turncoat Brig. Gen. Benedict Arnold, a native of the New London area. He had proposed the raid to his British superiors in New York City as a way to divert American attention from Lt. Gen. Charles, Lord Cornwallis and YORKTOWN (Arnold himself had raided in Virginia during the previous summer), and he hoped to seize or destroy American supplies stored at New London.

New London, at the mouth of the Thames River, was guarded by two small forts, Trumbull and Griswold. Fort Trumbull, on the west bank, had only twenty-four defenders and no fortifications at all on the landward side. Fort Griswold, on the east bank, was larger, had much better fortifications, and was garrisoned by 150 militia under Lt. Col. William Ledyard.

Arnold divided his forces—seventeen hundred men from two regular British regiments, two Loyalist units, a detachment of German jaegers (riflemen), and artillery—and landed one group under his command on the west bank; the other group under Lt. Col. Edmund Eyre landed on the opposite bank. A smaller detachment marched on Fort Trumbull, whose defenders fired one volley and then escaped across the river to Fort Griswold.

The defenders of Fort Griswold put up a hot struggle, surprising the British with their effective resistance. Lt. Col. Eyre was killed during the assault, which may have explained his troops' subsequent actions. When the fort finally surrendered, after a forty-minute fight, there was a massacre of the defenders. Colonel Ledyard surrendered his sword to Lt. Col. Abraham Van Buskirk, a commander of a New Jersey Loyalist battalion, and Van Buskirk promptly stabbed Ledyard with his own weapon. Ledyard was then bayoneted to death, and the Loyalists and Germans turned on the remaining garrison shooting and bayoneting many of them.

Meanwhile, Arnold marched into the town, sweeping aside a few residents who fired on his column, and proceeded to burn 143 houses and 12 ships in New London and nearby Groton. He and his men then reboarded their ships and sailed back to New York City.

Eighty-five American militia had been killed at Fort Griswold, all but six of them after the surrender, and sixty more wounded. The British forces lost 48 killed and 145 wounded in assaulting the fort.

The raid accomplished little except wanton destruction and killing, and it blackened Arnold's reputation among his former countrymen even more.

Further Reading

Jonathan Rathbun. *The Narrative of Jonathan Rathbun, of the Capture of Fort Griswold, the Massacre That Followed, and the Burning of New London . . .* Reprint ed. (New York: W. Abbatt, 1911).

New Market

Virginia (May 15, 1864) *American Civil War*

In May 1864, as Federal troops were making progress in the Appalachians at CLOYD'S MOUNTAIN, Maj. Gen. Franz Sigel pushed into the Shenandoah Valley with nine thousand men, hoping to tighten the Union stranglehold on Virginia. Instead, Sigel, the highest-ranking German-born officer in the war, was defeated at New Market by Brig. Gen. John C. Breckinridge, former vice president of the United States and unsuccessful prewar presidential candidate.

As Sigel's men advanced through the Shenandoah Valley, their progress was slowed by constant harassment from Brig. Gen. John D. Imboden's cavalry. The delay allowed Breckinridge time to gather at New Market a force that included 264 cadets from the Virginia Military Institute (VMI), whom Gen. Robert E. Lee had recently certified eligible to go into battle.

Early on May 15, Breckinridge established a line south of town, where he waited as Sigel arrived and gathered his forces into an opposing line at the farm of the Jacob Bushong family. Both sides held steady until Breckinridge finally decided to attack. Fighting continued throughout the afternoon, but the Union line held, despite being pushed back about eight hundred yards. When a gap appeared in the Confederate line, Breckinridge sent in the VMI cadets, whose appearance rallied the other Confederate troops to drive against the eastern and western flanks of the Federal position at the Bushong farm.

By 4 P.M., facing a renewed Confederate attack and in a heavy downpour of rain, Sigel ordered a general retreat. As the Federal troops fell back toward Strasburg, a total rout was prevented by Capt. Henry du Pont, who placed artillery posts along the retreat route on the Valley Turnpike.

Casualties in the battle included 831 Federal troops and 577 Confederate troops. Ten of the VMI cadets were killed, including Thomas Garland Jefferson, a descendant of Pres. Thomas Jefferson.

The Union defeat at New Market seriously hampered Lt. Gen. Ulysses S. Grant's plans to crush quickly Confederate resistance in the Shenandoah Valley. Sigel was removed from command on May 19.

Further Reading

William C. Davis. *The Battle of New Market*. 2d ed. (Harrisburg, Pa.: Stackpole Books, 1993); James Grindlesperger. *Seed Corn of the Confederacy: The Story of the Cadets of the Virginia Military Institute at the Battle of New Market* (Shippensburg, Pa.: Burd Street Press, 1997); and Joseph A. Whitehorne. *The Battle of New Market: Self-Guided Tour* (Washington, D.C.: Center of Military History, U.S. Army, 1988).

≫ New Orleans

Louisiana (January 8, 1815) *War of 1812*

The largest and most decisive battle of the War of 1812 was fought after the treaty ending the war had been signed in Europe. News of the Treaty of Ghent concluded on December 24, 1814, had not yet crossed the Atlantic when Gen. Andrew Jackson's mixed force of militia and American regulars defended New Orleans, Louisiana, against a larger British army commanded by Lt. Gen.

Edward Pakenham. Jackson won such a stunning victory at New Orleans that the United States was able to claim overall victory in what had been for the Americans an ignominious war, and General Jackson cemented a reputation for military heroism that would help catapult him into the presidency thirteen years later.

When Gen. Andrew Jackson arrived in New Orleans on December 1, 1814, he found that Col. Arthur P. Hayne, whom he had sent ahead while he swept Mobile and Pensacola, had done little to prepare the city against an expected British attack. British Admiral Alexander Cochrane had been building up forces in Jamaica as he awaited Pakenham's arrival from Europe with reinforcements, and it seemed likely that the Crescent City would be their initial target, since its capture would open access to the whole southern United States. Jackson immediately set about preparing for an onslaught: he raised Creole militia from the city, appealed to free African Americans to enlist with his regulars, welcomed a force of Tennessee riflemen, and secured the cooperation of Jean Laffite's infamous Baratarian pirates (a group of raiders whose allegiances had been unclear, at best, up to that time). The Baratarians contributed vital supplies as well as artillery skills, and Laffite became Jackson's virtual right-hand man.

New Orleans, situated near the Gulf of Mexico on the Mississippi River and surrounded by smaller rivers, lakes, and bayous, was vulnerable to attack from at least seven different directions, and over the month of December skirmishes broke out at several of the most important positions. Cochrane's fleet arrived from Jamaica on December 13. The admiral decided to attack across Lake Borgne while he waited for the remainder of the British army. On December 14, Cochrane sent Capt. Nicholas Lockyer's forty-five boats to attack American lieutenant Thomas ap Catesby Jones, who occupied the lake with only five gunboats. All of Jones's 185 men were killed, wounded, or captured, and the British took over the lake and established a post on Pea Island. The British then slowly pushed across the lake and through several bayous to a point on the Mississippi just eight miles south of the city, where on December 23 they captured the Jacques Villeré plantation and established a headquarters.

Deciding to test British strength before Pakenham could arrive, Jackson ordered an attack on the Villeré plantation that same night. Two American ships, the fourteen-gun *Caroline* and the twenty-two-gun *Louisiana,* bombarded the British position, and in the early hours of December 24 Jackson's eighteen hundred men attacked.

British major general John Keane's soldiers were taken by surprise, and a confusing hand-to-hand fight ensued. Neither side established clear lines or made much progress. The Americans suffered 215 casualties in the action, the British 275. While Jackson lost men and did not succeed in pushing the British out of the plantation, he did gain valuable time to continue reinforcing New Orleans, as well as valuable information about British strength.

Pakenham finally arrived on December 25, along with troops that brought the total British strength to four thousand men. Jackson used his time well, and the two American ships continued to bombard the British camp until heavy gunboats challenged them on December 27 (only the *Louisiana* escaped). The Americans entrenched behind the Rodriguez Canal two miles away, set up four batteries of heavy artillery, and employed Tennessee and Choctaw sharpshooters to harass further the British.

On December 28, Pakenham tried to rid himself of these annoyances by attacking the American position,

firmly nestled between the Mississippi and an impenetrable cypress swamp, while Cochrane to drive across Lake Pontchartrain. Neither push made much progress, under heavy fire from the Americans and a hail of shot from the *Louisiana,* so after taking fifty-five casualties Pakenham again withdrew (the Americans lost only about thirty-five in the action). Jackson again took the opportunity to reinforce his defensive position; he ordered the construction of four more artillery batteries, extended his main line into the swamps, established two fall-back entrenchments closer to the city, and organized another defensive position to the west of the Mississippi. Additional Tennessee and Kentucky militia reinforcements arrived, while at the same time Pakenham's reinforcements were having trouble getting through.

The immediate prelude to the "main" battle began on January 1, when British artillery began to bombard the American lines. Not only did the British guns overshoot their targets, but most were quickly knocked out

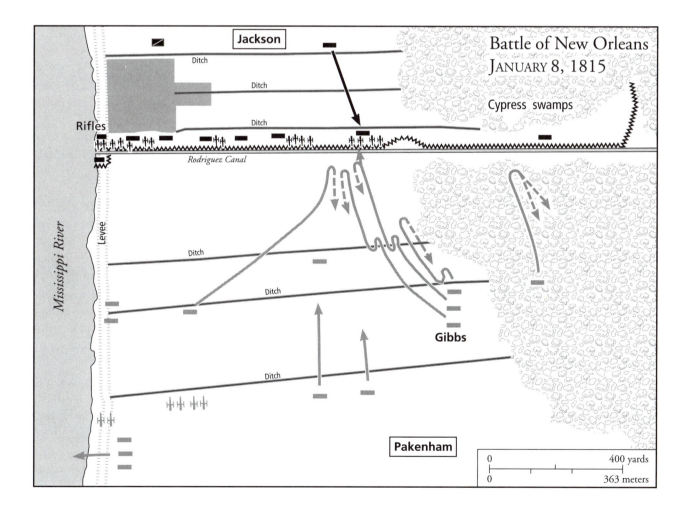

when American artillery answered their fire. In just over two hours, Pakenham's artillery expended much of its ammunition, suffering far greater damage than it inflicted. It took another week for the British to prepare for their final attack.

Though Pakenham had almost six thousand highly trained regulars, as against Jackson's motley force of fifty-three hundred, British plans for the major assault went awry. Col. William Thornton was supposed to attack with six hundred men across the Mississippi, to divert attention away from Pakenham's main attack to the east. Thornton's attack was to take place during the night on January 7, but his men did not get across the river (to take over guns protected by Gen. David Morgan's Louisiana and Kentucky militia) until early on January 8.

Meanwhile, the main British attack, on the American line by the canal, was a complete disaster. Maj. Gen. Samuel Gibbs pushed against the American left, which Pakenham believed to be weak—it was actually Jackson's strongest point and the British made no dent in the American line before they were destroyed by heavy artillery fire. Pakenham had hoped that a heavy fog would mask his advance against the eastern bank, but as his men marched toward the American line, the fog suddenly lifted, exposing them directly to a deadly hail of American fire. Wave after wave of steady British advance was cut down by steady cannon, rifle, and musket fire. The American fire was so accurate that British troops barely made it within one hundred yards of their opponents' line, and bodies quickly piled up before the American defenses. Pakenham himself was killed, and the assault was such a shambles that Maj. Gen. John Lambert, who assumed overall command, halted the entire action, calling off Thornton's men before they could capitalize on their limited victory.

The casualty totals on January 8 are some of the most lopsided in North American history, and they testify to the effectiveness of Jackson's defensive positions and the accuracy of American shooting. Three hundred British were killed, 1,262 wounded, and 484 taken prisoner. The Americans counted only seventy casualties, including only six killed and seven wounded in Jackson's line, which had faced Pakenham's main assault. During the entire month of action before New Orleans, the British suffered 2,450 casualties, compared to an American total of only 350.

News of the peace treaty soon arrived in North America, and the War of 1812 was over. The American victory at New Orleans allowed Americans to snatch victory from the jaws of stalemate and, despite their many losses during the war—including the embarrassing British capture of Washington, D.C., and the burning of the White House—to claim that they had stood up to a superior British military force. Many men, including Jackson, the Tennessee and Kentucky riflemen, and the free African-American soldiers of New Orleans, found that the glorious victory boosted their reputations for years to come.

Further Reading

Harry Albright. *New Orleans: Battle of the Bayous* (New York: Hippocrene Books, 1990); Samuel Carter. *Blaze of Glory: The Fight for New Orleans, 1814–1815* (New York: St. Martin's Press, 1971); Donald Barr Chidsey. *The Battle of New Orleans* (New York: Crown, 1961); Jack C. Ramsay. *Jean Lafitte: Prince of Pirates* (Austin, Tex.: Eakin Press, 1996); and Robin Reilly. *The British at the Gates: The New Orleans Campaign* (New York: G. P. Putnam's Sons, 1974); and Robert V. Rimini. *The Battle of New Orleans* (New York: Viking, 1999).

ᘰ New Orleans

Louisiana (April 18–24, 1862) *American Civil War*

When the Union seized the great port of New Orleans, near the mouth of the Mississippi River, with very little trouble, it gained a big advantage in the West. The Union now controlled both ends of the great waterway. Even though troops under Maj. Gen. Benjamin Butler were at hand, the U.S. Navy won and occupied the city, all on its own.

New Orleans lay seventy miles upstream from the two principal forts, Jackson and St. Philip, that guarded the city at the actual mouth of the river. Both were strongly built masonry forts—St. Philip dated back to the War of 1812—mounting heavy guns that commanded the river passage. Confederate major general Mansfield Lovell was in command of the forts and of the defense of the city of New Orleans itself, although he had few troops and had to rely on the cooperation of the Confederate navy, which had two ironclads and about eight other ships on the river.

The Union water assault was entrusted to Capt. David Farragut, an undistinguished, sixty-one-year-old navy veteran (he began his career as a midshipman during the War of 1812). The plan was to reduce the forts by a massive bombardment, run past them to New Orleans, and there meet Butler's troops, who were to have marched overland from Lake Pontchartrain.

The Union naval force consisted of twenty-four heavily armed wooden ships and nineteen specially equipped schooners mounting thirteen-inch mortars. On April 18, the mortar ships, commanded by Commodore David D. Porter, began a long-range bombardment of forts Jackson and St. Philip, firing almost three thousand shells in one day. The firing continued until April 20, when Farragut reached the conclusion that the massive artillery assault was having almost no effect on the Confederate forts. During the night, Union volunteers aboard two gunboats steamed up to the forts, where they managed to ram and break a huge chain the Confederates had strung across the river to bar Union ships.

In the early morning hours of April 23, Farragut sent his fleet, less the mortar ships, past the forts, steaming in a single column and firing as they passed. Upriver from the forts, they were attacked by the Confederate fleet. A fire raft damaged one of the Union ships, and a Confederate ship rammed another, but no really significant damage was done to Farragut's force. Once past the forts, the way to New Orleans was clear.

The next day, Farragut steamed into the port of New Orleans and claimed it for the Union. Soon after, the isolated Confederate garrisons at Jackson and St. Philip mutinied and surrendered. A week later, General Butler arrived to take over the occupation of the city.

Despite the tremendous expenditure of ordinance, the Confederates lost only nine killed and thirty-three wounded in the Union passage of the river. The Union lost 37 killed and 146 wounded.

Further Reading

Charles L. Dufour. *The Night the War Was Lost* (Garden City, N.Y.: Doubleday, 1960); and Chester G. Hearn. *The Capture of New Orleans, 1862* (Baton Rouge: Louisiana State University Press, 1995).

✍ New Ulm

Minnesota (August 23, 1862) *Santee Uprising*

The Santee (Dakota), the eastern branch of the Sioux Nation—as the large tribe composed of the Dakota, Lakota, and Nakota are often referred to—staged a bloody war with frontier settlers and the army in Minnesota in 1862. The settlement of New Ulm was the focus of an attack in August.

The Santee had been driven to violence by the venality and arrogance of their government Indian agents, who had refused to release food to the starving Indians. After a small group of young warriors killed a family of white settlers, the Mdewkanton band of the Santee, led by Little Crow (Cetan Wakan Mani), launched a series of raids and attacks on the scattered white farms and on the concentration of whites at FORT RIDGELY and nearby New Ulm.

Temporarily bypassing Fort Ridgely on August 20, a force of about one hundred Santee made a halfhearted attack on New Ulm, but a handful of armed settlers and militia chased it off after a fierce thunderstorm dampened the attackers.

Three days later, Little Crow himself led four hundred Santee warriors in a concerted attack on New Ulm. Settlers from the countryside had gathered to reinforce the defenders of the community, but they were essentially untrained volunteers (most of the better equipped and trained fighters were at the fort), commanded by Judge Charles Flandrau. The first assaults were nearly successful, but the judge managed to organize a defense and to hold the Indian warriors at bay. After a stiff struggle throughout the day, the Santee withdrew, leaving most of the town afire or in ruins.

The white defenders suffered thirty-six dead and twenty-three wounded. Santee casualties are unknown.

Although they had beaten off the attack, the two thousand or so remaining inhabitants evacuated to the safety of Mankato. Later in the fall, the Santee were defeated at WOOD LAKE by the U.S. Army and forced to surrender. Thirty-eight Santee were subsequently hanged for taking part in the uprising. Little Crow escaped but was killed by settlers the following year.

Further Reading

Kenneth Carley. *The Sioux Uprising of 1862* (St. Paul: Minnesota Historical Society, 1976).

✍ Newport

Rhode Island (July 29–August 31, 1778) *American Revolution*

For the United States, the first fruit of the new alliance with France was the appearance off the eastern coast, in 1778, of a fleet of sixteen ships and four thousand soldiers commanded by Adm. Comte Charles d'Estaing. When the French found they could not attack the British fleet at New York because of shallow water, Washington persuaded d'Estaing to undertake a joint land-sea operation to recapture Newport, Rhode Island, which the British had held for almost two years. It seemed like a prospect of certain victory, one that would cement the alliance, but the venture in fact was a complete disaster.

Newport is at the southern end of a large island at the mouth of Narragansett Bay. The passage between island and mainland is narrow at the northeast, opposite Tiverton across the Sakonnet River, and it provided easy access for an invading force.

The Americans had a thousand men stationed in Providence under the command of Maj. Gen. John Sullivan, who issued a call for militia that produced several thousand volunteers within weeks. The American commander in chief, Gen. George Washington, appointed Sullivan to command the American part of the project and sent Maj. Gen. Nathanael Greene and the Marquis de Lafayette to join him, along with John Glover's and William Varnum's brigades, two of the best veteran Continental units. By late July, Sullivan had close to ten thousand men at his disposal.

Defending Newport was British major general Sir Robert Pigot, one of the heroes of BUNKER HILL, with only about three thousand troops. The British fleet at Newport consisted of two thirty-two gun frigates and several smaller ships. Pigot appealed to his commander in chief, Sir Henry Clinton, and to Adm. Lord Howe for help, but any help seemed likely to arrive too late to keep the British in possession of Newport.

Sullivan and d'Estaing agreed on a plan of attack—the French ships were to sail up the Sakonnet, and Sullivan was to cross with his army at Tiverton—but there was much friction between the two commanders: the plebeian Sullivan seems to have resented the aristocratic d'Estaing's attitude, and d'Estaing showed contempt for his American allies, referring to Varnum's and Glover's elite troops as mere militia, for example, and complaining bitterly about supplies and arrangements. Difficulties notwithstanding, d'Estaing started the operation, sending Adm. Pierre de Suffren into the Sakonnet River with two frigates. The British panicked and ran their own warships deliberately aground and burned them. Meanwhile, Sullivan was poised at the embarkation point, and when he discovered the British had abandoned the northern end of the island, he crossed over with his entire force, neglecting to coordinate with d'Estaing ahead of time.

For reasons that seem hard to understand, d'Estaing was outraged that Sullivan had moved without consultation,

but he was faced with worse difficulties, since Admiral Howe's reinforced fleet had appeared off the mouth of the river, in Long Island Sound. D'Estaing reboarded his troops and set sail for Howe's fleet, holding the all-important position upwind of his enemy. Howe turned and ran before the French, hoping for an advantageous change in the wind, but before any general action could take place, a storm dispersed both fleets.

While this was going on at sea, Sullivan marched his troops to within cannon shot of Newport and built entrenchments. By August 20, the French fleet had reassembled, and Sullivan requested that d'Estaing land his infantry to support an assault on Newport. To Sullivan's dismay, d'Estaing refused and abruptly sailed away to the safety of Boston, leaving Sullivan and his men alone on the island with a British relief force on its way from New York. When word of the French withdrawal spread, Sullivan's militia began to desert and his army shrank to five thousand, meaning that Pigot now outnumbered him.

Sullivan had no choice but to retreat, with Pigot in close pursuit. On August 29, as the Americans reached the northern end of the island and prepared to recross to the mainland, Pigot attacked. Despite vigorous flanking movements by the British, the American lines held during a daylong battle, which finally ended when Maj. Gen. Nathanael Greene led a counterattack that scattered Pigot's men. The next day, Sullivan had his men ferried across to Bristol, Rhode Island, and then marched back to Providence, just ahead of the British relieving force, commanded by Maj. Gen. Sir Henry Clinton himself.

American losses were 30 killed, and 181 wounded or missing. The British lost 38 killed and 222 wounded or missing.

The dismal failure was a disappointing beginning for the Franco-American alliance.

Further Reading

Harford Powel. *Account of the Battle of Rhode Island and the Defenses of Newport* (Newport, R.I.: Newport Historical Society, 1923); and Page Smith. *A New Age Now Begins: A People's History of the American Revolution.* Vol. 2 (New York: McGraw-Hill, 1976).

❧ Newtown

New York (August 29, 1779) *American Revolution*

In the summer of 1779, the American commander in chief, George Washington, ordered a large expedition to proceed against the Iroquois confederation tribes that had allied themselves with the British and had been raiding with Loyalists into New York and Pennsylvania, causing much damage at WYOMING VALLEY and CHERRY VALLEY. The Americans wanted to destroy the Indian strongholds and take hostages against further border raids.

The huge American force was three pronged, with Maj. Gen. John Sullivan, in overall command, leading a column from the Wyoming Valley in Pennsylvania northward into Iroquois country. Sullivan was extremely slow in organizing his expedition and then spent weeks moving only short distances. It took him from May until August to reach his objective. He had at his command about twenty-five hundred men, including many veteran regular units from New England, New Jersey, and Pennsylvania, plus a company of Col. Daniel Morgan's riflemen and artillery. It was a cumbersome army, but its fighting capacities were far above those usually exhibited by the American militia in the region.

As the American force moved up the Chemung River, it came up against a smaller force of Loyalists and Indians at Newtown and fought the only open battle of the expedition.

Maj. John Butler, leader of the Loyalist forces, along with his son Walter and the Mohawk leader Joseph Brant (Thayendanegea), had about 250 Loyalists rangers, a handful of British regulars, and 800 Indians. Deciding to lay an ambush for the American column at Newtown, New York, they had constructed a log breastwork parallel to the river, hiding it from view with undergrowth. The plan was to let the American column come abreast of the Loyalists and Indians hidden behind the secure defensive position, and then blast it.

However, when the Americans approached, on the morning of August 29, the Virginia riflemen easily detected the ambush well ahead of time. Sullivan deployed his Continentals to attack the hidden breastwork and sent his artillery to a nearby hill to set up an enfilading fire. Brig. Gen. Enoch Poor, a veteran of both SARATOGA and MONMOUTH, led his New Hampshiremen against the Indians in a bayonet charge just as the artillery opened fire.

Brant and his men put up a fierce resistance, however, and managed to prevent being overrun. In fact, they threatened to successfully counterattack against the Second New Hampshire until the First New Hampshire turned and added its weight to disperse the Indian attack. When even more Americans appeared on his other flank, Brant signaled a retreat, and his men escaped.

The Americans lost only three killed and thirty-three wounded. The losses to Brant's force are hard to calculate, but one report says eleven dead were left on the field.

While this relatively easy victory should have invigorated Sullivan's venture, in fact he failed to follow up, and it meant little in the long run.

Further Reading

Albert H. Wright. *The Sullivan Campaign of 1779* (Ithaca, N.Y.: A. H. Wright, 1943).

Ninety Six

South Carolina (May 22–June 19, 1781)
American Revolution

The fortified post at Ninety Six was one of the strongest in a series established in 1780 by the British to protect their control of South Carolina and one of the last to withstand the American southern counteroffensive in 1781. American commander, Maj. Gen. Nathanael Greene, wanted to take the post and eliminate the final backcountry British establishment, and British Carolina commander, Brig. Gen. Lord Rawdon, would have been happy to evacuate the position, but his message to do so was intercepted, and the defenders refused to give in to Greene.

Ninety Six was held by 350 veteran Loyalists troops from New York and New Jersey, along with 200 South Carolina Loyalist militia, all under the command of Col. John Cruger. They garrisoned a strongly fortified stockade that had a star-shaped redoubt with a ditch and log-filled abatis commanding one side, and a weaker outpost, called Fort Holmes, on the other, guarding the water supply. Cruger had only a few small cannon, but they were well served, and he had adequate food and supplies to withstand a siege.

When Greene arrived at Ninety Six, he had only about a thousand troops, having detached Lt. Col. Henry Lee's Legion and Francis Marion's partisans to other tasks. Greene's main tactical advice on how to proceed came from Col. Tadeusz Kosciuszko, a Polish volunteer officer trained in military engineering. The American commander decided to attack the fort's strongest point, the star redoubt, but he made a considerable tactical error by starting to dig the first approach trench at a distance of only seventy yards from the walls. His men had scarcely begun when artillery fire and a sally from the fort overran their position. Greene then drew back and began classic angled approaches, at a distance of 400 yards.

After several days' digging, the trenches had zigzagged their way to within a few dozen yards of the wall, despite several sorties by the garrison. Greene's men then built a Maham Tower (a tall, shielded, log platform from which riflemen could fire into the stockade) and tried to set the buildings alight with fire arrows. Cruger had sandbags piled on top of the walls to protect his men from marksmen on the tower, and he pulled off the roofs of his buildings to frustrate the incendiaries. He also attempted—unsuccessfully, due to an inadequate furnace—to set the tower ablaze with hot shot.

On June 8, Lt. Col. Henry Lee arrived with his legion to reinforce Greene, but the next night Cruger sent out a strong raid from the fort, seizing a patriot gun battery and wounding and capturing several of the attackers. Two days later, Lee sent ten of his men under cover of a thunderstorm to set the stockade on fire, but they were discovered and half of them were killed, and the others were driven off. A subsequent attempt to cut off the fort's water supply likewise failed. It was apparent that the Loyalists would fight to the last and that half measures would not win for the patriots—and there was news of a British relief column on its way.

Greene decided under the circumstance to launch an all-out assault on June 18. He gave orders for coordinated attacks on Fort Holmes and the star redoubt: Lee was to command the assault on Fort Holmes, and Col. Richard Campbell of Virginia was in charge of the effort at the star redoubt. Lee's attack succeeded with relative ease, since Cruger had elected to shift forces from Fort Holmes to defend the redoubt.

The patriots sent against the redoubt a "forlorn hope" (a suicide squad) with axes to cut through the log abatis, bundles of brush to fill in the defensive ditch, and long poles with hooks to pull down the sandbags on top of the wall. A large force waited to follow up the forlorn hope and breach the redoubt. At first the attack went well for the patriots. The advance party got through the abatis, over the ditch, and began to pull down the sandbags, but at that point the Loyalists sent out a sortie from the rear of the redoubt. The force divided in two and circled to attack the patriots from two sides. They drove Campbell's men back from the wall, and one of their three-pounders broke up the patriot formation. The attack had to be called off.

Greene was stymied, and with the British relief force coming closer and closer (and rumored to outnumber the Americans heavily), he decided to abandon the siege. On June 19, Greene and his army began a retreat. Lord Rawdon's relief column arrived two days later to the rejoicing of the Loyalist defenders. The post, however, could not be defended in the long run, and Rawdon ordered its evacuation.

The Loyalists lost 27 killed and 58 wounded during the siege, and the patriots lost 185 killed and wounded.

Further Reading

Page Smith. *A New Age Now Begins: A People's History of the American Revolution.* Vol. 2 (New York: McGraw-Hill, 1976).

La Noche Triste

(Tenochtitlán)
Mexico (July 1, 1520) *Spanish Conquest*

Hernán Cortés, who had controlled the Mexican capital of Tenochtitlán virtually without violence for the previous eight months, was forced into a disastrous retreat from the city on the night of July 1, 1520, a date the Spanish later remembered as *la noche triste*, "the night of sorrow."

Cortés had landed on the Mexican mainland with slightly more than five hundred well-armed conquistadores in 1518. This expedition was equipped with steel swords, armor, crossbows, harquebuses (primitive shoulder-fired guns), artillery, war dogs, and horses, and the Spaniards soon discovered, in battles at POTONCHAN and TLAXCALA, that their superior military technology, added to the ineffective tactics of their opponents, made it possible for a small number of conquistadores to defeat huge Indian armies with small loss. Not only did the horses, artillery, and steel swords give the Spanish an advantage, but the Indian armies of Old Mexico focused on capturing enemies for later human sacrifice rather than killing them on the battlefield, which made them easier prey for the ferocious Spanish swordsmen.

Cortés and his men crossed the mountains from the coastal region and in November 1519 entered the magnificent city of Tenochtitlán. The huge city was built in the middle of a lake, connected to the shore by a series of causeways, and was the capital of the empire of the Mexica people (called the Aztec by later writers), which encompassed most of modern-day central Mexico. Through intimidation and trickery, Cortés managed to kidnap Montezuma, the Aztec emperor, and assume control of the city with almost no violence. In May 1520, Cortés was forced to return to the coast to deal with a rival Spanish expedition (*see also* CEMPOALLAN), leaving his second in command, Pedro de Alvarado, in charge of Montezuma and Tenochtitlán. When Cortés returned to the city, with several hundred new recruits, he discovered chaos. Alvarado had treacherously trapped and murdered hundreds of Aztec political and religious leaders as they danced at a religious festival. The result was a full-scale uprising by the several hundred thousand people of Tenochtitlán and the surrounding lakefront cities. The Spaniards, increasingly isolated, were unable to do more than maintain a foothold in the immediate vicinity of their headquarters, losing many troops and horses in street fighting that was directed by the surviving Aztec leaders. When Cortés exhibited Montezuma on a rooftop in an attempt to quell the attacks, the Aztec emperor was fatally wounded by stones hurled by his own disillusioned subjects. Short of food and water and running out of gunpowder, the Spaniards had to try to escape.

Cortés organized conquistadores into companies and planned to leave at midnight, since the Aztec disliked fighting in the dark. He chose one of the few causeways still in relatively good condition (the Aztec had broken most of them in order to trap the Spaniards), and he ordered portable wooden bridges built to span the gaps. An immense amount of gold and jewels confiscated and stolen from the Aztec was secreted on the bodies of the men, and the "Royal Fifth" reserved for the king of Spain was loaded onto a single mare, which disappeared during the night and was lost forever.

The Spaniards moved quietly through the city and reached the causeway proper before they were discovered and the alarm was raised. Responding to the sound of a war drum atop the huge central pyramid, thousands of Aztec swarmed into canoes and attacked the Spanish column from the lake, firing a storm of arrows, hurling spears, and leaping onto the causeway to fight at close quarters. A frenzy of pent-up Aztec hatred and aggression swept away all but the most determined resistance by individual conquistadores. The horses that usually gave such an advantage to the Europeans were useless on the broken causeway, and groups of Spaniards were surrounded and overwhelmed. The Aztec ignored their usual practice of seeking to capture and instead killed Spaniards whenever possible. Spanish discipline and organization collapsed, and the conquistadores escaped as best they could, especially after the rear guard disintegrated. Several Spaniards had to turn back to the city, where they were eventually hunted down, captured, and sacrificed in the great temple square.

The Aztec declined to pursue immediately the surviving Spaniards who reached the safety of the lakeshore, and Cortés and the remnant of his expedition managed to

get away. While no accurate figures are possible, it is believed that around six hundred Spaniards were killed or captured during the night.

Despite the massive blow to his plans to take permanent control of Tenochtitlán and the Aztec Empire, Cortés managed to escape and begin to regroup and rebuild his small army. The Aztec celebrated their victory and tried to reorganize their leadership, which had been almost completely destroyed by Alvarado's massacre.

Further Reading

Serge Gruzinski. *The Aztecs: Rise and Fall of an Empire* (New York: Harry N. Abrams, 1992); Salvador de Madariaga. *Hernán Cortés, Conqueror of Mexico.* Reprint ed. (Westport, Conn.: Greenwood Press, 1979); William H. Prescott. *History of the Conquest of Mexico.* . . . (New York: Modern Library, 1936); and Hugh Thomas. *Conquest: Montezuma, Cortés, and the Fall of Old Mexico* (New York: Simon & Schuster, 1993).

North Anna River

(Hanover Junction, Jericho Mills, Taylor's Bridge)
Virginia (May 23–27, 1864) *American Civil War*

After the heavy fighting at the WILDERNESS and SPOTSYLVANIA in early May 1864, Confederate general Robert E. Lee hoped that Federal troops would pause to rest and resupply, as Union armies had always done earlier in the war, but Lt. Gen. Ulysses S. Grant defied Lee's expectations and pushed on toward the Confederate capital at Richmond, where he hoped to rendezvous with Maj. Gen. George Meade. Lee established a defensive line north of Richmond at the North Anna River, where Grant's quick advance on May 23 caught his men by surprise. Lee recovered quickly, however, and brilliant tactical maneuvering over the next few days beat off the superior Northern force and allowed him to continue defending Richmond.

On May 21 and 22, Lieutenant General Grant tested Lee's troop strength by sending a corps near his position at Milford Station, and when the Confederates declined to attack, Grant took it as a sign of vulnerability. The following day, Grant marched his army south along Telegraph Road to the North Anna River to take on Lee. Maj. Gen. Winfield S. Hancock's Second Corps approached the Telegraph Road bridge as Maj. Gen. Governeur K. Warren's Fifth Corps forded the river to its north, at Jericho Mill, and constructed a pontoon bridge. Lee, anticipating only a minor skirmish, committed only one brigade (of Lt. Gen. A. P. Hill's troops) to a line of defense north of the river. In the early evening, two waves of Federal attacks beat back the small Confederate force, despite additional opposition from Southern artillery, and Grant's infantry captured Telegraph Bridge.

Having crossed the river at both points, the Union troops relaxed for the evening, expecting to pursue their main assault the next day, but when Hill learned of their advance he ordered an immediate counteroffensive at the Jericho Mill. Hill's attackers were eventually beaten back by three artillery batteries and Union infantry reinforcements, but the engagement convinced Lee that more serious fighting than he had expected was at hand.

Grant had captured control of the river line, and Lee was wary of being pushed too far back toward Richmond without a backup position, so he concocted an ingenious scheme to keep Grant at bay. Lee formed his army into an inverted V that stretched out from his still-solid position along the river at Ox Ford, with Hill's troops on the left and Maj. Gen. Richard H. Anderson's and Lt. Gen. Richard S. Ewell's men on the right. Lee reasoned that he could split Grant's line as it crossed the V and then concentrate his strength on one part at a time.

With no Confederates in sight at either of the Union-controlled bridges, Grant assumed that Lee's force had retreated, and so he pushed forward, right into the V,

on May 24. Grant's force was effectively splintered, and Maj. Gen. Ambrose Burnside's Ninth Corps was torn apart in the V's center at Ox Hill. One of Hancock's divisions on the left also faced destruction on that evening, because the Confederate formation cut it off from reinforcements. Late in the evening, Grant realized that Lee's formation had stymied his plans, and he ordered his men to dig in and build earthworks.

Skirmishing on May 25 and 26 failed to gain an advantage for either side, and Lee was too ill to lead personally the decisive attack, as he wished. Grant decided to cut his losses and seek another approach to Richmond.

Out of 53,000 Confederates and 68,000 Federals engaged in the battle, the Southerners suffered 2,517 casualties and the Northerners 2,623.

While Lee had managed to hold off Grant's larger army with quick thinking and an inventive formation, he was extremely dismayed that he had not delivered a death blow to Grant's force. Lee was right to worry, for Grant's forces continued their advance on Richmond.

Further Reading

J. Michael Miller. *The North Anna Campaign: "Even to Hell Itself," May 21–26, 1864.* 2d ed. (Lynchburg, Va.: H. E. Howard, 1989); ———, "North Anna River," in Frances H. Kennedy, ed. *The Civil War Battlefield Guide* (Boston: Houghton Mifflin, 1990).

O

Oak Grove

(King's Schoolhouse)

Virginia (June 25, 1862) *American Civil War*

The first of what came to be known collectively as the Seven Days' Battles was a relatively small encounter between part of Maj. Gen. George B. McClellan's huge Army of the Potomac, which was only a few miles from the outskirts of the Confederate capital at Richmond, and the Army of Northern Virginia, which had just been named by its new commander, Gen. Robert E. Lee. Uncharacteristically, McClellan initiated the fighting, even though—as usual—he erroneously imagined himself to be outnumbered.

McClellan had about a hundred thousand troops, but he had stationed the majority of them south of the Chickahominy River after the battle of FAIR OAKS. Only the thirty thousand men of the Fifth Corps, command-ed by Maj. Gen. Fitz-John Porter, remained north of the river. Before Lee could bring his smaller forces into play to attack the isolated Federal corps, McClellan ordered a limited advance, more or less a reconnaissance in force, against Oak Grove. He hoped to establish new positions close enough to reach Richmond with his big siege artillery.

Federal major general Joseph Hooker's division moved down the road toward the Confederates early on the morning of June 25, but it soon ran into heavy fight-ing and stopped. McClellan himself appeared on the field and ordered a renewed attack early in the afternoon, which pushed the Confederate defenders out of their positions by nightfall, when the fighting ceased.

McClellan lost 626 casualties, and the Confederates lost 441.

Further Reading

Clifford Dowdey. *The Seven Days: The Emergence of Lee.* Reprint ed. (Lincoln: University of Nebraska Press, 1993); and Edward G. Longacre, "The First of Seven: A Battle at Oak Grove." *Civil War Times Illustrated* 25, no. 9 (1987): 10–19.

Ocean Pond

(Olustee)

Florida (February 20, 1864) *American Civil War*

In early 1864, the Federals landed an expedition under Maj. Gen. Quincy A. Gillmore at Jacksonville, Florida, with the intent of securing a base for later operations and disrupting the Confederacy's transportation net from the south. A part of the Federal force, commanded by Brig. Gen. Truman Seymour and numbering around five thousand men, including two black regiments, marched inland along the line of the Atlantic & Gulf Central Railroad, where it met a defending force of Confederates under Brig. Gen. Joseph Finegan.

Seymour had mistaken intelligence that Finegan had only a small militia force at Ocean Pond, so he pushed hard on February 20, hoping to catch the Confederates unprepared. Seymour's troops were fresh and well equipped—two of his New England regiments had repeating rifles—and he was confident he could brush aside the opposition. The Confederate commander, however, had almost the same number of troops as did his Federal opponent, including a brigade of Georgia veterans under Brig. Gen. Alfred Colquitt, and they were well entrenched with their flanks protected by Ocean Pond on one side and a swamp on the other.

Union cavalry ran into the outlying Confederate positions in midafternoon, and the battle was on. Finegan sent Colquitt's Georgians out of their trenches to attack the Union infantry as it formed up, and the successful Confederate attack broke Seymour's regiments and sent them into retreat. A second line of Union troops held longer but eventually also broke under the Confederates' assault. As a last measure, Seymour threw in the black Fifty-fourth Massachusetts and Eighth U.S. Colored Regiment, but despite hard fighting they could not contain the Confederates. As the sun went down, the entire Federal army began a retreat to Jacksonville.

The Confederates lost 946 killed and wounded, while the Federals lost 203 killed, 1,152 wounded, and 506 missing.

Further Reading

William H. Nulty. *Confederate Florida: The Road to Olustee* (Tuscaloosa: University of Alabama Press, 1990).

Okolona

Mississippi (February 22, 1864) *American Civil War*

The Union seemed to take overall control of the war in the West after the surrender of VICKSBURG, but remaining Confederate armies and skillful generals, such as Maj. Gen. Nathan Bedford Forrest, made life very difficult for the Federal commanders in Tennessee and Mississippi.

In February 1864, Union brigadier general William "Sooey" Smith led a column of around seven thousand cavalrymen south from Memphis toward a rendezvous with Maj. Gen. William Tecumseh Sherman, who had set his sights on a campaign into Georgia. Unfortunately for Smith, he met one of the South's best fighters when he encountered Forrest, with twenty-five hundred hastily trained Confederate recruits, near West Point, Mississippi, on February 20. The hard-hitting, quick-moving, highly aggressive Forrest (an uneducated but extremely wealthy slave trader, who had enlisted in 1861 as a private) presented a sharp contrast to Smith, who at his best moved with methodical slowness and behaved with a lack of imagination.

Smith, alarmed by the minor attacks near West Point, turned his large column—swollen with hundreds of ex-slaves—around and headed back toward Memphis. Near Okolona, Forrest attacked Smith's rear guard before dawn on February 22, beginning a daylong running fight. By late afternoon the Federals had retreated nine miles, and Forrest was prevented from overrunning Smith's entire force only by a desperate charge by the Union Fourth Missouri Cavalry.

Smith lost 319 men; Forrest had only a handful of casualties.

Smith continued his disorganized retreat all the way to Memphis, forcing Sherman to cancel his movements for the time being.

Further Reading

Mark M. Boatner. *The Civil War Dictionary.* Rev. ed. (New York: David McKay, 1988); and Jay Wertz and Edwin C. Bearss. *Smithsonian's Great Battles & Battlefields* (New York: William Morrow, 1997).

Olustee

See OCEAN POND

Opequon Creek

See WINCHESTER, THIRD

Oriskany

New York (August 6, 1777) *American Revolution*

A one-thousand-man British expedition, comprising mostly Indians and Loyalists, commanded by Lt. Col. Barry St. Leger, had been sent up the Mohawk Valley by Maj. Gen. John Burgoyne in 1777 as part of his grand invasion scheme. St. Leger arrived at American-held FORT STANWIX in early April and laid siege.

The patriot militia of Tryon County, New York, was headed by Brig. Gen. Nicholas Herkimer, who sent out a call for a muster at Fort Dayton. Eight hundred men responded, and Herkimer marched out on August 4 to relieve Stanwix.

St. Leger learned of the departure of the relief column and planned a cunning ambush at Oriskany, four miles below Stanwix on the Mohawk River. The only road was at the bottom of an extremely steep gorge, surrounded by heavily wooded hillsides. St. Leger arranged his Indians, mostly Mohawk led by the able Joseph Brant (Thayendanegea), and Loyalist troops so as to cut off and surround the American column as it passed through the narrowest part of the gorge.

Even though Herkimer had sixty Oneida scouts with his party, no one detected the several hundred enemy laying in ambush—Herkimer probably failed to send out any advance scouts—and he marched his men straight into the trap.

The only flaw in the British attack was that the trap was sprung slightly too early, allowing Herkimer's rear guard to escape; otherwise, all the Americans were encircled and apparently at the mercy of their enemies. Herkimer himself was shot from his horse early in the fight. He had himself hauled up with his back to a tree, where he directed the battle while nursing a serious leg wound.

The Americans were unable to form any sort of coherent line of battle, since firing came from all sides. They finally arranged themselves in a loose circle, which allowed them to cover their neighbors' backs. The ground was thick with cover, however, and many Americans fell to tomahawk and knife attacks as Indians crept unseen to close quarters.

In the middle of the fight, a torrential rainstorm fell, stopping the hostilities completely. When the rains stopped, the Americans regrouped in a tighter formation and fought two by two, one man firing and the other reloading and watching for Indian infiltration. Loyalist reinforcements arrived at one stage but were driven off by hand-to-hand fighting.

Finally, the Indians had had enough and withdrew, leaving the Loyalists and the British officers no choice but to disengage. They had failed to destroy the American column completely, but they had stopped the relief of Ft. Stanwix.

Casualties from the battle were severe, proportionately among the worst in the entire American Revolution. The figures are disputed, but as many as 160 Americans may have died at Oriskany, with another 40 or 50 wounded or captured—a loss of two-thirds of the original force. Gen. Herkimer died several days later, bleeding to death after a botched amputation. The British Indian forces probably lost seventy to one hundred killed.

Further Reading

John A. Scott. *Fort Stanwix (Fort Schuyler) and Oriskany: The Romantic Story of the Repulse of St. Leger's British Invasion of 1777* . . . (Rome, N.Y.: Rome Sentinal, 1927); William L. Stone. *The Campaign of Lieut. Gen. John Burgoyne, and the Expedition of Lieut. Col. Barry St. Leger* (New York: Da Capo, 1970).

Otumba

Mexico (July 7, 1520) *Spanish Conquest*

Hernán Cortés and the survivors of a disastrous escape from the Mexican capital of Tenochtitlán (*see also* La NOCHE TRISTE) fought off a huge pursuing army near the town of Otumba in the greatest Spanish feat of arms during the conquest of Mexico.

The Spaniards were in bad condition after fleeing Tenochtitlán in the middle of the night on July 1, 1520. Around six hundred conquistadores had been killed or captured (those taken prisoner became human sacrifices), and most of their horses, artillery, gunpowder, and looted treasure had been lost when almost the entire population of the city attacked them on the causeway leading to the shore of the lake on which Tenochtitlán was situated. Cortés had only 340 Spanish fighting men left, all but a handful wounded, and 27 horses, in addition to an unknown number of Tlaxcalan Indian allies. For the immediate future, the conquistadores would have to rely on cold steel and their skill as swordsmen.

As the slow-moving column approached Otumba, it was overtaken by an army of warriors, tens of thousands strong, which had been dispatched by the new emperor, Cuitláhuac, to destroy the invaders. The army was commanded by an official known as the *cihuacoatl,* and the Mexica (known to later writers as the Aztec) were arrayed in full ceremonial military regalia of extraordinarily elaborate feather costumes and armed with their typical weapons: bows and arrows, spears, slings, and obsidian-bladed wooden swords. They were highly organized and experienced in warfare, but they were hampered against the Spanish by ingrained tactics designed not to kill but to wound the enemy. Generations of Mexica had fought to secure prisoners for sacrifice as the highest goal of combat, and they could not easily change their ways even when confronted by vigorous Spanish swordsmanship that cut down the Mexica in large numbers, usually with little loss to the Europeans.

At Otumba, however, the Spaniards were weary and wounded, and the onslaught of such numbers began to wear them down after several hours of exhausting hand-to-hand combat, even though their fatalities were few. Despite the advantage of weapons and tactics, it appeared likely the Mexica would eventually wipe out the Spaniards.

At this crucial point in the battle, Cortés himself took the initiative and changed the balance with a bold and desperate move. Mounting a cart horse, he rallied five other horsemen, and armed with lances they rode through the entire Indian army toward the conspicuously dressed Mexican commanders. Cortés knocked the *cihuacoatl* to the ground, and a second conquistador killed him with a lance thrust, capturing the leader's feather standard. Almost at once the Mexican warriors were thrown into confusion by the loss of leadership—the standard was used to direct battlefield movements, and there was little aptitude among the Mexica for improvisation. They broke off the fighting and withdrew, leaving the Spaniards free to continue their retreat toward friendly territory.

The casualties of the battle are not known, but Cortés reported losing two fingers from his left hand during the fighting.

Further Reading

Salvador de Madariaga. *Hernán Cortés, Conqueror of Mexico.* Reprint ed. (Westport, Conn.: Greenwood Press, 1979); and Hugh Thomas. *Conquest: Montezuma, Cortés, and the Fall of Old Mexico* (New York: Simon & Schuster, 1993).

❧ Ox Hill

See CHANTILLY

☙ Padierna

See CONTRERAS

☙ Palo Alto

Texas (May 8, 1846) *Mexican-American War*

On May 6, 1846, shortly after Mexico declared war on the United States, Brig. Gen. Zachary Taylor set out with twenty-two hundred American troops and two hundred supply wagons from his fort at Point Isabel, Texas, to the aid of American forces under attack at CAMP TEXAS, near the town of Matamoros. Before Taylor reached Camp Texas, however, he met and engaged Maj. Gen. Ariano Arista's Mexican army in battle.

Arista had prepared for Taylor's approach by calling off Maj. Gen. Pedro Ampudia's attack on Camp Texas on the morning of May 8. The addition of Ampudia's men brought Arista's total force to a strength of four thousand men. The Mexicans took up a well-covered position in woods known as "Tall Timber," which surrounded an open plain just outside Palo Alto. During the afternoon, Taylor's men advanced slowly toward the Mexican force across the open ground. When the two armies were within eight hundred yards of one another, the Mexican artillery opened fire.

Taylor halted his advance and swung forward his own artillery. Maj. Samuel Ringgold and Capt. James Duncan commanded two flying batteries of highly mobile, horse-drawn light artillery, which now pounded the Mexican front line, and two American eighteen-pounders brought from Point Isabel tore apart Mexican cavalry on the left.

Arista sent Gen. Anastasio Torrejón's cavalry and lancers around the American right, but Col. James McIntosh's infantry formed a square and stopped the mounted attack with one volley. A second attack by Torrejón against Taylor's wagon train was beaten back by heavy fire from American infantry.

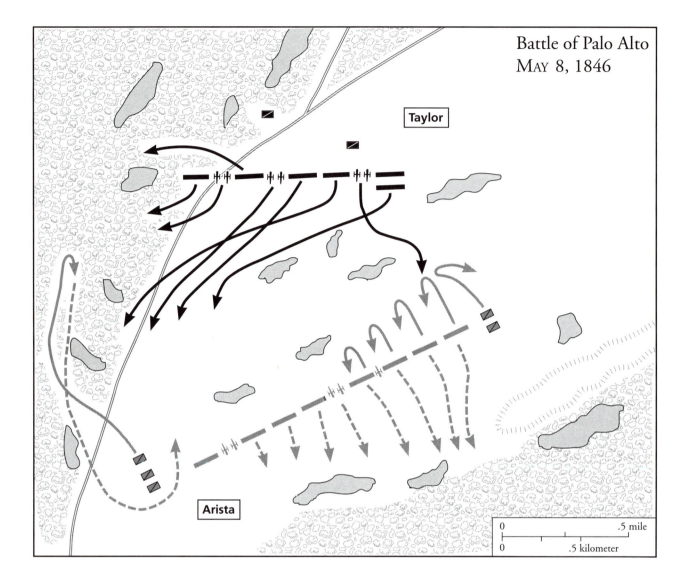

Battle of Palo Alto
MAY 8, 1846

Taylor

Arista

0   .5 mile

0   .5 kilometer

During the first hour of battle, the tall prairie grass on the Palo Alto plain was set afire by artillery, and soon the smoke grew so thick that fighting was all but suspended for a full hour. During the lull, both Taylor and Arista adjusted their lines and shifted men to their respective right wings.

When fighting resumed, Captain Duncan moved his guns to the American left and enfiladed the Mexican line. Taylor sent Capt. Charles May to attack the Mexican left also, but this time Torrejón's cavalry held off the American infantry. Repeated Mexican efforts to capture Duncan's guns and end the enfilade failed, and the Mexican formations progressively weakened. At nightfall Arista was forced to fall back in considerable confusion. Arista encamped his men a few miles from the field, and Taylor declined to follow until the next day.

In the battle of Palo Alto the Mexicans lost between 252 and 400 killed, while the Americans had only 25 killed and 33 wounded.

Though Maj. Samuel Ringgold was killed in the battle, the flying batteries of mobile artillery, which he had devised, proved to be one of the winning elements in the American attack. Calm did not last long after the battle at Palo Alto, one of the first to be reported by telegraph: Taylor and Arista's forces met again the next day at RESACA DE LA PALMA.

Further Reading

Charles M. Haecker. *On the Prairie of Palo Alto: Historical Archaeology of the U.S.-Mexican War* (College Station: Texas A&M Press, 1997). Peter F. Stevens, "The Proving Ground." *American History Illustrated* 23, no.3 (1988): 38–44.

Paoli

Pennsylvania (September 21, 1777)
American Revolution

After the defeat at BRANDYWINE on September 11, the American commander in chief, Gen. George Washington, was forced to retreat from the army of British commander Gen. Sir William Howe, clearing a path for Howe's troops to march on to Philadelphia, the object of the British expedition. However, Washington detached about 1,500 men under Brig. Gen. Anthony Wayne and sent them quietly into camp at Paoli, hoping that Wayne would go unnoticed and be able to attack the British rear guard or baggage train once the main army had passed. Unfortunately for Wayne and his men, Howe learned of their presence and sprang his own nasty surprise.

On the night of September 20, British major general Charles Grey led three regiments of British regulars on a night march. Two more regiments followed, under the command of Col. Thomas Musgrave. Grey's object was to take Wayne by surprise, and the British general ordered men to unload their weapons or remove the flints from the firing mechanisms. The night attack was to be by bayonet alone, cutting down the chances of confusion in the dark, since anyone discharging a firearm would, perforce, be an American. (This stratagem earned Grey the nickname "No Flint.")

The British approach to Wayne's camp was silent, and shortly after 12:00 A.M., Grey gave the order to attack. His men achieved complete surprise, and Wayne's troops were at their mercy. The carnage was considerable: at least 150 Americans were killed or wounded, while the British reported only 6 killed and 22 wounded. Wayne himself escaped and managed to rally the survivors the next morning, but the British had triumphed yet again.

Further Reading

J. Smith Futhey. *The Massacre of Paoli* Reprint ed. (Philadelphia: J. Carbutt, 1990; and Donald G. Brownlow. *A Documentary History of the Paoli "Massacre."* 2d ed. (West Chester, Pa.: Horace F. Temple, 1977).

Parker's Cross Roads

Tennessee (December 31, 1862)
American Civil War

Coming at the end of what came to be known as his "Christmas Raid," this defeat of Confederate brigadier general Nathan Bedford Forrest was one of the rare setbacks suffered by the canny cavalry leader.

Forrest had begun his raid with twenty-one hundred men in mid-December, aiming to disrupt Federal major general U.S. Grant's slow advance on Vicksburg. Most of the raid had gone Forrest's way, and by the last day of the year he and his men were headed back toward their base in middle Tennessee, content with having destroyed railroad tracks that Grant needed to move his huge army. The Confederates had encountered few Federals and had had little trouble shooing away those they did.

Northeast of Jackson, Tennessee, however, Forrest met and engaged a brigade of Federal infantry under Col. Cyrus Dunham. Forrest had a good position near some woods, and his artillery got the early advantage in the battle, driving the Federals back from their first positions. Although he established a new defensive line, Dunham found Forrest's men attacking both of his flanks and his rear. The situation seemed hopeless, although Dunham refused Forrest's demand for surrender.

At a crucial moment, as Forrest was preparing for a final, crushing attack, a second Federal division, under Col. John W. Fuller, arrived on the scene undetected by Forrest's scouts and immediately attacked the Confederate rear in a devastating surprise attack. Forrest ordered simultaneous counterattacks in both directions, but he could do no better than force a slight gap in Fuller's line, allowing his men to flee the field.

Forrest lost about three hundred prisoners and had to leave behind much of the booty from his raid.

Further Reading

Dan Kennerly. *Forrest at Parker's Crossroads.* 6th ed. (Houston, Tex.: D. Kennerly, 1993).

Parker's Ferry

South Carolina (August 13, 1781)
American Revolution

In one of the quick-moving strokes for which he was justly famous, Brig. Gen. Francis "Swamp Fox" Marion helped local patriot militia defeat a force of Loyalists while the main American army in South Carolina, under Maj. Gen. Nathanael Greene, rested in the Santee Hills.

Marion's two hundred men made a forced march of a hundred miles to join Col. William Hardin and his local militia at Parker's Ferry, about thirty miles from

Charleston. Harden was facing Loyalist major Thomas Fraser, who had around four hundred men in his command. Marion had traveled at night, and the Loyalists had no notion that he had arrived to reinforce the local patriots.

Marion set up an ambush, hiding his infantry along a causeway and then enticing Fraser to charge between the hidden troops. The first discharge caught the Loyalists unawares, but they rallied and charged twice more in the face of overwhelming fire. They were nearly destroyed by the encounter, losing around one hundred dead or wounded, while Marion and the patriots had not a single casualty.

Marion and his force immediately left the area and returned to Greene's army.

Further Reading

Mark M. Boatner. *The Encyclopedia of the American Revolution* (New York: David McKay, 1966).

✒ Parral

Mexico (April 12, 1916) *Border Raids*

Gen. Francisco "Pancho" Villa, upset at U.S. recognition of his revolutionary political rival Venustiano Carranza as ruler of Mexico, raided COLUMBUS, New Mexico, in March 1916. When Maj. Frank Tompkins of the Thirteenth Cavalry had to break off his pursuit of Villa following the raid, Pres. Woodrow Wilson authorized Gen. John J. Pershing to command an expedition to hunt down Villa inside Mexico. Though the Carranza government initially supported Pershing's mission, the Mexican populace was none too pleased to see American troops marching ever southward through the countryside. Hostility toward the Americans broke into open battle at the town of Parral in April.

Maj. Frank Tompkins, who was now leading part of the Thirteenth Cavalry as an element of Pershing's expeditionary force, later claimed that he had been invited into Parral by a Carranzista officer, but when his troops arrived on April 12 they met only a hostile crowd. A large mass of people shouting "Viva Villa!" harassed the Americans to the edge of town, and Tompkins subsequently claimed it was joined by several Carranzista soldiers and at least one man who appeared to be German. Eventually, even as the American cavalrymen withdrew, shots rang out. Tompkins's men exchanged fire with the crowd as they quickly left the town. Two Americans were killed in the melee, and

Tompkins, among several others, was wounded. Several Mexicans were also shot down.

The small battle at Parral got the American force no farther toward capturing Pancho Villa and served only to help turn the Carranza government against Pershing's mission. Though facing increasing hostility, the American force was not recalled until January 1917. Pancho Villa was never captured, a fact that helped elevate his status as a Mexican revolutionary folk hero.

Further Reading

John D. Eisenhower. *Intervention! The United States and the Mexican Revolution, 1913–1917* (New York: W. W. Norton, 1993).

✒ Paulus Hook

New Jersey (August 19, 1779) *American Revolution*

This daring raid against a strong British position on the New Jersey side of the Hudson River, opposite New York City, showed considerable courage and dash but accomplished almost nothing to change the military stalemate that had developed in the North after the battle of MONMOUTH.

Paulus Hook occupied a sandy salient of land sticking out into the river, nearly cut off from the New Jersey mainland by an artificial ditch and swampy salt march. The main fortifications were blockhouses and breastworks, protected on the landward side by an abatis (a cut timber obstacle). At high tide, the ditch and marsh could not be crossed.

The British garrison, commanded by Maj. William Sutherland, consisted of about two hundred men drawn from the Sixty-fourth Regiment and a few light infantry and German mercenaries. There were also several women and children, families of the soldiers. An additional 150 Loyalists under Col. Abram Van Buskirk were usually stationed at Paulus Hook, but they were away on a foraging mission.

The American attack was led by twenty-three-year-old Maj. Henry "Light-Horse Harry" Lee, Jr., who had convinced the commander in chief, Gen. George Washington, that the escapade would be worth trying. Lee had as his assault force about two hundred Virginia troops (half of them commanded by Maj. Jonathan Clark), two companies of Marylanders, and a troop of dismounted dragoons from Allan McLane's unit.

Lee's plan was much like the one used at STONY POINT: the attackers were to approach the objective in silence at night; then suicide squads, called "forlorn hopes" in the military jargon of the day, would rush forward, hack a way through the abatis, and open the fort to the following main body. Muskets were to be unprimed, and the men were instructed to use only their bayonets in the attack. The original plan was for three columns to hit the defenses simultaneously.

The most logistically difficult part of the operation was getting to the jump-off point on time. The Americans had to march sixteen miles in darkness, cross the marsh and ditch before high tide made them impassable, and arrive ready to go into action just as dawn broke—all without alerting the British. The approach march went badly for Lee. About half of his Virginians either deserted or got lost on the way, and he was led off the main road by his local guide, who may have done so deliberately. Despite these difficulties, Lee and his remaining men were in position by 4:00 A.M. and ready to attack, although the loss of part of his command meant he had to revise his plan and send in only two columns.

At his signal, the forlorn hope rushed forward and scrambled through the obstacles despite belated musket fire from the British garrison. Lt. Archibald McAllister of the Marylanders, the first over the parapet, captured and struck the British colors. Few of the garrison were able to offer much resistance, and most of those who did were bayoneted by the onrushing Americans, who, firing not a shot, forced the surrender of the British defenders. Only a small group of Germans under Major Sutherland put up a determined resistance, taking refuge in a blockhouse and refusing to give up. Since the Americans' powder was wet from slogging the marshes, there was little they could do.

Indeed, their victory was very short-lived. Alarm guns were heard from New York City across the river, and it was possible that Van Buskirk might return at any moment. Lee decided on a quick withdrawal without further fighting. His men herded together their prisoners and left the fort without even spiking the guns or burning the buildings.

The weary Americans, who had marched a long way, waded a marsh, and rushed a British fort since supper the evening before, reached a planned rendezvous with boats on the Hackensack River, but they discovered that the officer responsible for their transport had given up and rowed away. They had no choice but to march on, hoping to find a relief column commanded by Maj. Gen. Lord Stirling. Along the way, Lee found part of his missing Virginians and posted them as a rear guard, which was a wise precaution—Loyalist colonel Van Buskirk caught up with the retreating Americans and attacked, but he was beaten off and by afternoon Lee and his men had reached safety.

The affair cost the Americans only two dead and three wounded, and the British lost about fifty dead or wounded, all from the bayonet attack. Lee captured 158 of the defenders and hauled them back with him.

Other than securing the prisoners, the attack achieved nothing, even though it was a demonstration of daring. Lee was forced into a court martial by jealous fellow officers, who claimed he had exceeded his authority, but he was acquitted.

Further Reading

William H. Richardson. *Washington and "The Enterprise against Powles Hook"*. . . (Jersey City: New Jersey Title Guarantee and Trust, 1929).

Pea Ridge

(Elkhorn Tavern)

Arkansas (March 7–8, 1862) *American Civil War*

After their victory at WILSON'S CREEK in the summer of 1861, the Confederates in western Missouri under Maj. Gen. Sterling Price, a prewar Missouri politician and Mexican War veteran, enjoyed considerable success, but eventually they had to retreat southward in the face of advancing Union forces under Brig. Gen. Samuel Curtis, a West Pointer and Mexican-American War officer who had served in the U.S. Congress. A reinforced Confederate army met Curtis at Pea Ridge in extreme northwestern Arkansas. The Confederate forces had been taken over by Maj. Gen. Earl Van Dorn, a veteran of both the Mexican-American War and western Indian fighting, who combined Price's army with troops under Brig. Gen. Benjamin McCulloch. Altogether, Van Dorn had 16,500 men, including a contingent of 800 Cherokees commanded by Brig. Gen. Albert Pike and Col. Stand Watie (Degataga). His intent was to bowl over Curtis and retake Missouri for the Confederate cause.

Curtis was badly outnumbered, with no more than 10,250 troops, but he had established a good defensive position on a creek near Pea Ridge and Elkhorn Tavern. He had divided his command, sending two of his divisions with Brig. Gen. Franz Sigel, but learning the Confederates were approaching, he ordered Sigel to rejoin the main army. The Union troops had fortified their positions facing south along the creek, with the heights of Pea Ridge behind them to the north.

Van Dorn decided on a tricky double-envelopment maneuver, using a detour to swing part of his army left to the rear of the Union lines and sending other troops to flank the Union positions on the right, in the direction of Elkhorn Tavern. The actual movements became confused during the day of March 7, but in general Van Dorn succeeded in getting a large part of his forces in position to the north of Curtis's lines.

However, Curtis managed to reorient completely his position from south to north, a difficult maneuver. By the time the Confederates were ready to attack, the Union troops were once again facing them from strong positions. Curtis beat Van Dorn to the punch and launched attacks first, despite his deficiency in numbers. Fierce fighting developed during the day at two points on the front, one on the Union left near Leetown and the other on the right at Elkhorn Tavern. The Federals fought with great tenacity and skill, and the Confederates, though they had the advantage of numbers, could not dislodge them.

General McCullough was leading the fight for the Confederates at Leetown when he was killed by a musket volley. His second in command, Brig. Gen. James McIntosh, took over, but he too was killed. The third in command, Col. Louis Hébert, assumed command, but he was soon captured, leaving the inexperienced Brigadier General Pike in charge, and the Confederate attack slowed and then ceased altogether. With nightfall, the two armies tried to regroup, the Confederates concentrating all their remaining men near Elkhorn Tavern.

On the morning of March 8 the battle was resumed. The Confederates placed artillery on Pea Ridge, hoping to sweep the entrenched Union troops from the field, but Curtis was a stubborn fighter. He ordered Sigel's guns to counter the Southern batteries, which they did effectively. The Union commander then ordered an advance that pushed back the Confederates, who were suffering from a shortage of ammunition, and eventually chased them from the field.

The Union lost 1,384 killed and wounded during the two-day battle; the Confederates suffered about 1,500 losses.

Curtis had achieved a remarkable victory and destroyed entirely the Confederate campaign to invade Missouri.

Further Reading

Hugh Park, ed. *Pea Ridge: The Place Where the South Lost the Civil War* (Van Buren, Ark.: Press-Argus, 1961); William L. Shea. *Pea Ridge: Civil War Campaign in the West* (Chapel Hill: University of North Carolina Press, 1992); and ————. *War in the West: Pea Ridge and Prairie Grove* (Worth, Tex.: Ryan Place, 1996).

Peach Orchard

See SAVAGE'S STATION

U.S.S. *Peacock* v. H.M.S. *Epervier*

Off the Florida Coast (April 29, 1814) *War of 1812*

Master Commandant Lewis Warrington's eighteen-gun sloop, the U.S.S. *Peacock,* was sailing through the Bahamas in the spring of 1814 on a secret supply mission when he encountered the British brig *Epervier*. The battle that followed was the first in *Peacock*'s career as a noted American prize taker.

Capt. Richard H. Wales, commanding officer of the eighteen-gun *Epervier*, cruising to protect merchant shipping, was less prepared for combat than Warrington, who had slipped through the British blockade of the American seaboard at New York and had his ship in a state of alert.

The battle between the *Peacock* and the *Epervier* lasted less than an hour, but both ships were damaged by broadsides. The *Epervier* suffered the greater harm, however, and was eventually crippled by a heavy shot to the hull. The American crew outpaced the British, who refused to board the *Peacock* at an advantageous moment and whose gunnery was inadequate. Wales eventually realized the disadvantage and surrendered.

The British suffered eight killed and fifteen wounded, while the Americans counted only two wounded.

Warrington took the *Epervier* as a prize into Savannah, once again breaking the British blockade, and headed out again to take fourteen more prizes before October 1814.

Further Reading

Donald Shomette. *Flotilla Battle for the Patuxent* (Solomons, Md.: Calvert Marine Museum, 1981).

Pell's Point

New York (October 18, 1776) *American Revolution*

In the fall of 1776, the British commander, Gen. Sir William Howe, had Gen. George Washington and the

American army outnumbered and pinned in a poor position at HARLEM HEIGHTS on Manhattan Island. Having been mildly repulsed in a frontal attack on the heights, Howe decided to leapfrog around Long Island Sound and get to Washington's rear. His first attempt at a landing, at THROG'S NECK, failed due to a bad choice of a landing point and a spirited, if sparse, resistance. After resting for several weeks, Howe tried again three miles farther up the shore, at Pell's Point.

The landing was opposed by four small Massachusetts regiments, numbering about 750 men altogether, under the command of Col. John Glover, leader of the famed Marblehead Mariners. The British put ashore four thousand men and seven guns on the morning of October 18. Glover sent forward a small delaying force and arranged the bulk of his troops to block the road leading from the beach.

The British brushed aside the small American advance force, but when the redcoats marched up to a stone wall, one of the defending American regiments rose up and delivered several volleys at close range. The British were thrown back, while the Americans made an orderly retreat. Eventually the British brought up their guns and bombarded the new American positions. Glover abandoned them during the night, leaving the road open, although the British had paid a price of three killed and twenty wounded. The Americans lost twenty-one casualties.

Further Reading

William Abbatt. *The Battle of Pell's Point (or Pelham) October 18, 1776 . . .* (New York: W. Abbatt, 1901).

❧ Pensacola

Florida (March–May 9, 1781) *American Revolution*

The role of Spain in the American Revolution was equivocal and confined to the margins of the conflict, but the Spanish seizure of the British post at Pensacola in West Florida had important consequences for postwar diplomacy.

Spain wanted to gain from the war in America but did not want to seem to endorse the American Revolution, which the Spanish quite correctly judged to be an ideological menace to their own New World empire. Consequently, when Spain declared war on Great Britain in 1779, she did so out of alliance with France (the kings of the two countries were uncle and nephew) and refused to sign a treaty with the United States.

For the most part Spain's military activities against the British were at sea, but the young governor of Louisiana, Bernardo de Gálvez, was an experienced and energetic soldier. He decided to seize Pensacola, a fortified city held by Brig. Gen. John Campbell with a motley garrison of nine hundred worn-out veterans, Irish deserters from the American army, ill-equipped German mercenaries, and untrained Loyalist troops.

Gálvez landed an army of between eight and ten thousand troops in March and laid siege to Pensacola. Campbell was able to put up a more spirited defense than might have been anticipated, given the nature of his men, and the Spaniards made little headway until, on May 8, a lucky shot dropped a shell into the British magazine. It exploded, killing or wounding about one hundred defenders and completely destroying the main redoubt. Gálvez immediately attacked and placed infantry in the ruins of the outer fortifications, from where they could pour musket fire on the British. Campbell was compelled to surrender the following day.

The capture of the city later provided Spain a pretext for claiming all of East and West Florida in the treaty that officially ended the war.

Further Reading

Eric Beerman, ed. and trans. *Yo Solo: The Battle Journal of Bernardo de Gálvez during the American Revolution* (New Orleans: Polyandros, 1978); Nixon O. Rush. *The Battle of Pensacola, March 7 to March 8, 1781: Spain's Final Triumph over Great Britain in the Gulf of Mexico* (Tallahassee: Florida State University Press, 1966); and James A. Servies, ed. *The Log of H.M.S. Mentor, 1780–1781: A New Account of the British Navy at Pensacola* (Pensacola: University Presses of Florida, 1982).

❧ Perryville

Kentucky (October 8, 1862) *American Civil War*

For several weeks following his victory at RICHMOND in August 1862, Confederate general Braxton Bragg had virtual control of the key border state of Kentucky, ranging north almost to Cincinnati and installing a pro-Confederate state government, but a major battle at Perryville destroyed his grip on the commonwealth.

Bragg's forces in Kentucky consisted of his own Army of Mississippi and an army commanded by Maj. Gen. Kirby Smith. Misjudging the movements of his Union opponents in the days before the engagement at Perryville, Bragg had much of his troop strength in the wrong place, and he commanded no more than sixteen thousand men at the crucial stage. The Confederate corps commanders on hand were Maj. Gen. William Hardee and Maj. Gen. Leonidas Polk. Smith's men were miles away during the battle.

Bragg's opposite number at Perryville was Maj. Gen. Don Carlos Buell, still commander of the Army of the Ohio, despite having received orders a few days before to relinquish his post to Maj. Gen. George Thomas (Thomas had declined, on the grounds that the eve of battle was no time to change commanders). Buell heavily outnumbered Bragg, and he managed to have most of his men—almost thirty-seven thousand—on the scene. His corps commanders were Maj. Gens. Alexander McCook, Charles Gilbert, and Thomas L. Crittenden.

Neither army commander planned the time and place of the battle. It began when both sides sent out patrols to find water in the small creeks and streams around Perryville, a drought-plagued area. Skirmishers fired on each other during the afternoon and evening of October 7 in efforts to take control of the few pools of water available, and before first light the following morning Maj. Gen. Gilbert ordered Brig. Gen. Phil Sheridan to send his division forward to secure the water supply. Sheridan's troops pushed back the forward-most Confederates and took their immediate objective.

During the morning and throughout most of the day, Union commander Buell was ignorant that a battle was going on. His headquarters house was in a so-called acoustic shadow, a quirk of topography and wind, and neither he nor his staff could hear the sounds of the nearby combat. Not until late in the afternoon, when one of his field commanders sent a message to his headquarters, did Buell realize almost his entire army had been committed.

Two hours before, Bragg had ordered a Confederate division under Maj. Gen. Benjamin Cheatam to attack the Union center, under General McCook, which had become slightly separated from its supporting wings, and Cheatam's men had driven their opponents back. Sheridan had a chance to take some of the Confederates in the flank, but he hesitated, and the moment was lost. The fighting was extremely heavy—two Union brigadiers were killed on the field—but McCook's forces resisted complete collapse, and by late afternoon they had established new defensive lines.

Shortly after McCook's men stopped the Confederate advance, other Confederates, under Col. Samuel Powell,

attacked Sheridan's position, which he had held quietly since early in the day. Sheridan's men repulsed the assault and, with the help of reinforcements, drove the Confederates back through the streets of the village of Perryville, ending the battle. Buell expected the Confederate commander to renew the fighting on the next day, but Bragg decided he was too badly outnumbered and during the night he began a withdrawal toward Tennessee that eventually led to the complete abandonment of Kentucky. Buell—a notoriously slow general—failed to follow up his advantage; he was finally relieved of his command later in the month.

The Confederates lost 3,145 casualties, and the Union forces lost 3,696.

Further Reading

Kenneth A. Hafendorfer. *Perryville: Battle for Kentucky* (Louisville, Ky.: KH Press, 1991); Hamilton Tapp. *The Confederate Invasion of Kentucky, 1862, and the Battle of Perryville, October 8, 1862* (Lexington, Ky.: n.p., 1962); and JoAnn B. Wilkerson. *400 Days to Perryville* (Perryville, Ky.: Perryville Battlefield Development Association, 1970).

Petersburg

Virginia (April 25, 1781) *American Revolution*

Turncoat Benedict Arnold, commissioned as a major general by the British after his defection, led a punitive expedition to Virginia in late 1780, and in the spring of the following year he was joined by Maj. Gen. William Phillips, with reinforcements. In April, they raided Petersburg, a central storehouse of tobacco and military supplies for the American army.

Petersburg's defense was in the hands of Brig. Gen. John Peter Muhlenberg, at the head of one thousand militia. Muhlenberg realized he was badly outnumbered by the British—Phillips was in command of the raid—but he wanted to exact a price. He took a position at a village just outside Petersburg and invited a frontal assault by Phillips's twenty-five hundred troops.

Phillips sent his light infantry, a few mercenary German jaegers (riflemen), and the Loyalist New York Rangers of Lt. Col. John Simcoe on flanking movements, while Lt. Col. Robert Abercromby led an attack on Muhlenberg's main position. After a hot fight, the British managed to place artillery where it brought the Americans under heavy fire. Muhlenberg withdrew across the Appomattox River, leaving Petersburg to be ransacked.

The Americans lost approximately sixty or seventy total casualties; the British losses were not recorded.

Further Reading

Christopher Ward. *The War of the Revolution.* Vol. 2 (New York: Macmillan, 1952).

Petersburg

Virginia (June 1864–April 1865)
American Civil War

Union commander in chief Ulysses S. Grant's plan to destroy Gen. Robert E. Lee's outnumbered Army of Northern Virginia and take the Confederate capital at Richmond, Virginia, failed when the battle of COLD HARBOR showed the futility of attacking Lee directly when he had had time to prepare defenses. Grant switched strategies and made an end run against Petersburg, Virginia, the main transportation center south of Richmond. Union troops failed to seize Petersburg, however, and the confrontation developed into a ten-month siege.

Grant understood that Petersburg was a key position, because it was a hub for the rail lines and roads that Lee needed to supply Richmond and his army. After Cold Harbor, Grant ordered troops of Maj. Gen. William F. "Baldy" Smith's Eighteenth Corps to move rapidly to capture the Petersburg defenses facing east. Although they took some of the lightly held Confederate defenses—commanded by general P. G. T. Beauregard, who had just repulsed another Federal army at DREWRY'S BLUFF—Smith's brigades did not push forward and overrun the Confederates immediately. By the time Grant and the balance of the Union army arrived, it was too late; Lee had marched into the entrenched Petersburg defenses and effected a stalemate.

Over the following weeks and months, both sides dug and constructed more and more elaborate defenses, extending them to the south and west until eventually the lines stretched more than thirty miles in length and closely resembled the static, wasteland battlefields that later became so familiar on the western front in World War I. The Confederate defenses were far too strong to be taken by frontal assaults, and even the most determined artillery bombardments had little real effect.

Both sides tried stratagems and maneuvers to break the stalemate, resulting, for example, in the battles of the CRATER in July and GLOBE TAVERN in August, but by fall it was apparent that Grant was stymied and that Lee was pinned down. Throughout the winter months Grant extended his lines even more, but he gained no significant advantage. However, Lee's supply lines were fragile and thin, and by the coming of spring it was obvious that he had either to break out or give up. Lee launched an attack in late March against FORT STEDMAN, but it ultimately failed. When Maj. Gen. Philip H. Sheridan's cavalrymen seized the last remaining rail line after a victory at FIVE FORKS on April 1, Lee saw that the fate of his army was sealed.

The next day, Lee evacuated his army and set it on a march that ended a few days later with his surrender to Grant at Appomattox Court House.

Overall, the battles and siege warfare cost around seventy thousand casualties on both sides.

Further Reading

John Horn. *The Petersburg Campaign: June 1864–April 1865* (Conshohocken, Pa.: Combined Books, 1993); Richard W. Lykes. *Campaign for Petersburg* (Washington, D.C.: United States Park Service, 1970); Richard J. Sommers. *Richmond Redeemed: The Siege at Petersburg* (Garden City, N.Y.: Doubleday Books, 1981); and Noah A. Trudeau. *The Last Citadel: Petersburg, Virginia, June 1864–April 1865* (Boston: Little, Brown, 1991).

Petersburg Mine Disaster

See THE CRATER

Philippi

West Virginia (June 3, 1861) *American Civil War*

After the April 1861 attack on FORT SUMTER in South Carolina, both Union and Confederate forces mobilized for all-out civil war. One of the first areas to see fighting was the western part of Virginia, a fiercely loyal Unionist area that would separate from secessionist Virginia in 1863. In June 1861, Union and Confederate forces came to blows over control of the Baltimore & Ohio Railroad in the first land battle of the war, at Philippi. It was a small fight that predicted nothing of the carnage to come.

At the end of May, Brig. Gen. Robert Garnett sent Col. George Alexander Porterfield and his fifteen hundred men from his Confederate headquarters at Beverly, Virginia, to raid the B&O at Philippi, west of Harpers Ferry. Determined to secure Union access to the strategic railroad, Maj. Gen. George B. McClellan, commander of army operations in Ohio and western Virginia, marched out to attack the Confederates in early June.

McClellan's forces first captured the railroad town of Grafton before making a night raid on the Confederate post at Philippi on June 3. The attack took the Confederates completely by surprise, routed them, and established firm Union control of the railroad system.

Only two of McClellan's men were wounded in the action, and the Confederates suffered a mere fifteen casualties.

The Union victory at Philippi helped Confederate commanders decide to evacuate Harpers Ferry, and it set in motion events that would lead to battles at CHEAT MOUNTAIN and CARRICK'S FORD later in June.

Further Reading

Boyd B. Stutler, "The Civil War in West Virginia." *West Virginia History* 47, no. 1 (1988): 29–38; and Barbara J. Howe, "The Civil War at Bulltown." *West Virginia History* 44, no. 1 (1982): 1–40.

Pilot Knob

(Fort Davidson)

Missouri (September 27, 1864) *American Civil War*

Confederate major general Sterling Price, a prewar Missouri politician, led a raid in force from Arkansas into his former state in the fall of 1864, with the hope of capturing supplies and diverting Federal strength from the more important campaigns east of the Mississippi River. Price, who had defeated a Union army at WILSON'S CREEK early in the war, commanded more than twelve thousand men, although many were untrained and ill-equipped recruits.

The Federals moved a large number of troops into St. Louis in response when Price crossed the border and started north, diverting them from a journey to Georgia as reinforcements for Sherman. Price's first goal was achieved, even though St. Louis was now too strong for him to attack. However, eighty miles to the south, at Fort Davidson, near the town of Pilot Knob, Federal brigadier general Thomas Ewing commanded a force of no more than eleven hundred men. Ewing's men, although in thin numbers, were well entrenched and ready for an attack by Price, who surrounded the fort on September 26.

Price attacked the following day, but despite fierce fighting, the Federals withstood the assault for six hours, when it petered out, with heavy casualties on the Confederate side. Price assumed he could carry the fort

with a new attack the next day, but during the night Ewing and his men quietly slipped out of the fortification and escaped through a gap in the Confederate lines.

Price had lost fifteen hundred casualties, compared to the loss of two hundred by the Union defenders.

Price achieved little from the costly battle: the Federals spiked their guns and blew up their powder supply as they departed, leaving nothing for the Confederates to appropriate.

Further Reading

Cyrus A. Peterson and Joseph M. Hanson. *Pilot Knob: The Thermopylae of the West.* Reprint ed. (Cape Girardeau, Mo.: Ramfire Press, 1964).

Pittsburgh Landing

See SHILOH

Plains of Abraham

See QUEBEC (1759)

Plattsburg Bay

(Lake Champlain, Plattsburg)

New York (September 11, 1814) *War of 1812*

Maj. Gen. Sir George Prevost planned a major British invasion into the United States at the confluence of the Richelieu River and Lake Champlain in the fall of 1814 to coincide with the British attack on the Chesapeake, but his force was turned back by the Americans at Plattsburg, New York.

Just as Prevost, the governor-general of Canada, entered the United States with almost seventeen thousand well-trained soldiers on the last day of August, the American Secretary of War, John Armstrong, decided that no northern invasion would occur. Armstrong ordered Maj. Gen. George Izard, commander of American forces at Plattsburg, to leave the well-constructed defense he had erected between the Saranac River and Lake Champlain, and to remove to Sackett's Harbor.

Brig. Gen. Alexander Macomb, who was left in charge of the defenses at Plattsburg, commanded just thirty-five hundred men, but when he heard of the British advance Macomb quickly pressed thirty-three hundred Vermont and New York volunteers into service. As Prevost

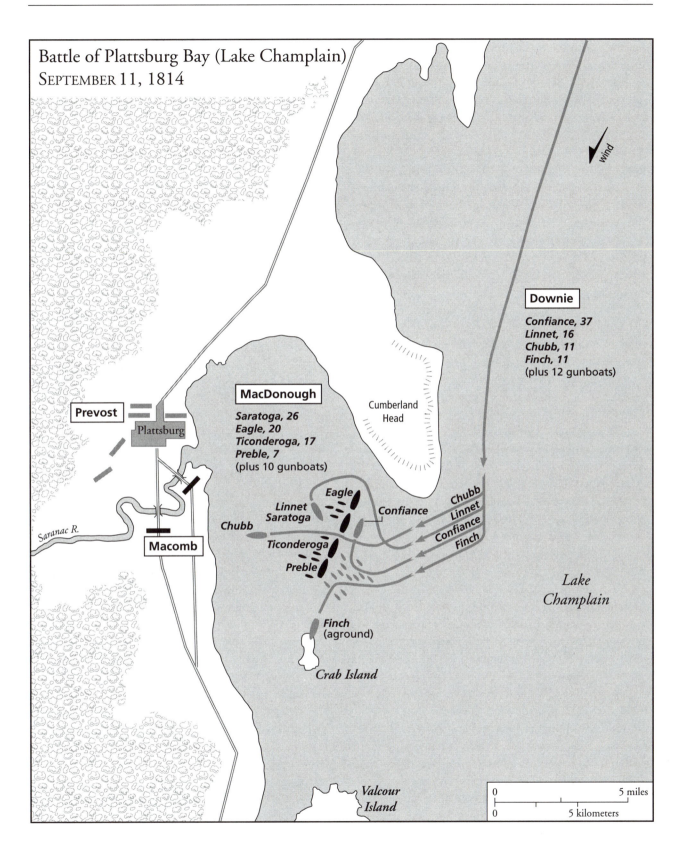

Battle of Plattsburg Bay (Lake Champlain)
September 11, 1814

Prevost

Plattsburg

Saranac R.

Macomb

MacDonough

Saratoga, 26
Eagle, 20
Ticonderoga, 17
Preble, 7
(plus 10 gunboats)

Cumberland
Head

Downie

Confiance, 37
Linnet, 16
Chubb, 11
Finch, 11
(plus 12 gunboats)

wind

Eagle

Linnet
Saratoga

Chubb

Confiance

Ticonderoga

Preble

Chubb
Linnet
Confiance
Finch

Finch
(aground)

Crab Island

Lake
Champlain

Valcour
Island

0		5 miles
0		5 kilometers

marched south, Macomb tried to stop the advance of his solid column with frequent raiding parties, but he succeeded only in slightly slowing British progress toward Plattsburg. Macomb also strengthened the American defenses and destroyed all bridges leading to Plattsburg.

Unable to find a ford across the Saranac River, Prevost decided to pause on September 6 and wait for naval support. Three days later, Capt. George Downie arrived with a considerable fleet that included *Confiance, Linnet, Chub, Finch,* and twelve gunboats. While the new thirty-seven-gun *Confiance* was superior to any American ship, her construction was incomplete, and she was not quite ready for battle. On the American side, Lt. Thomas Macdonough commanded *Saratoga, Eagle, Ticonderoga, Preble,* and ten gunboats.

Vastly outranged by the British cannon, Macdonough prepared for battle by anchoring his ships to draw the British in, so as to take advantage of superior American short-range firepower.

When the battle commenced on the morning of September 11, the American ships at first took heavy blows from long range, as expected. H.M.S. *Confiance* hit the U.S.S. *Saratoga* with broadsides but was unable to come to close quarters, and when the *Saratoga* struck back, captain Downie was killed. The U.S.S. *Preble* fought off an attack against the U.S.S. *Ticonderoga* by H.M.S. *Finch.* The *Preble* was disabled by the British gunboats but not before sending the *Finch* reeling onto the shoals of Crab Island, where she was pounded apart.

At the front of the line, the Americans seemed beaten when the U.S.S. *Eagle* was knocked out of action by H.M.S. *Confiance* and H.M.S. *Linnet* raked the U.S.S. *Saratoga.* The *Saratoga's* starboard guns were unable to fire, but Macdonough dropped anchor and maneuvered his ship to fire on the *Confiance* with his portside weapons. Lt. James Robertson, now in command of *Confiance,* tried a counter-maneuver but failed. *Saratoga's* fire was so heavy that the crew of the *Confiance* began to waver, and at 10:30 A.M., the British ship surrendered.

Major General Prevost had ordered a land attack simultaneous with the naval engagement. Maj. Gen. Frederick Robinson pushed his forces across the river and fought off the front lines of American militia. As Robinson paused for reinforcements, Prevost learned of the naval defeat and ordered Robinson to retreat, fearing that even if the land invasion was successful, his supply lines would be completely cut off without control of the lake.

Casualties were fairly light, considering the severity of the engagements. The British reported 92 killed, 119 wounded, and over 300 captured or deserted. American casualties included 89 killed and 120 wounded.

The defeat was an unmitigated disaster for the British, who lost the chance to control Lake Champlain. American morale, suffering after the defeat at BLADENSBURG and the destruction of Washington, D.C., received a boost—as did the American position at the peace negotiations in Ghent.

Further Reading

Virgina M. Burdick. *Captain Thomas Mcdonough: Delaware Born Hero of the Battle of Lake Champlain* (Wilmington: Delaware Heritage Press, 1991); Allen S. Everest. *The War of 1812 in the Champlain Valley* (Syracuse, N.Y.: Syracuse Univ. Press, 1981); Dennis M. Lewis. *British Naval Activity on Lake Champlain during the War of 1812* (Plattsburg and Elizabethtown, N.Y.: Clinton County Historical Association and Essex County Historical Association, 1994); and Charles G. Muller. *The Proudest Day: Macdonough on Lake Champlain* (New York: Curtis Books, 1960).

～ Pleasant Hill Landing
(Blair's Landing)
Louisiana (April 9, 1864) *American Civil War*

The Federal high command launched an ill-conceived campaign into northern Louisiana in the spring of 1864, aiming to move an army along the Red River and capture the Confederate theater headquarters at Shreveport. The real impetus for the campaign was not the military objective, since the real issues of the war were being fought out in Virginia and Georgia, but the prospect of capturing a large store of cotton in order to invigorate the Northern economy. The government in Washington also wanted to demonstrate its power in the region to the French regime that had seized Mexico.

Maj. Gen. Nathaniel Banks, who had already demonstrated his military incompetence but had been an important prewar politician, was given command of a large army, supported by a squadron of Federal gunboats. He proceeded to blunder into a severe defeat at SABINE CROSSROADS at the hands of Confederate major general Richard Taylor, a veteran of the battles in Virginia and son of former president Zachary Taylor. Banks had not been on the field on April 8, when the Confederates had mauled his advance units, but he ordered a retreat to the nearby town of Pleasant Hill Landing to await developments.

Taylor was reinforced overnight and had about twelve thousand men ready to advance by the morning of April 9. He planned an elaborate flanking attack, whereby Brig. Gen. Thomas J. Churchill would lead his brigade on a fast march around Banks's left flank. When alerted by the sounds of battle, the rest of the Confederate force, under brigadiers Jean Jacques Mouton and John G. Walker, would assault the Union positions straight on. Unfortunately for Taylor, the plan misfired. Churchill's men, who had marched hard the day before to reach the battlefield, were slow to move into position, and in any case, Churchill misjudged his location and turned short, toward the Union positions, without enveloping their flank. When they finally launched their attack late in the afternoon, Churchill's men found heavy resistance, and they were eventually thrown back from the edge of the town. With the flank attack mistimed and misdirected, Taylor's other attacks failed to dislodge the Federals from their defensive positions.

Taylor lost 1,200 killed and wounded and 426 captured; Banks had 150 killed, 844 wounded, and 375 missing.

Despite the inconclusive battle at Pleasant Hill Landing, Banks's expedition was on the skids. He began a long and painful withdrawal from a campaign that had become a fiasco.

Further Reading

Ludwell H. Johnson. *The Red River Campaign: Politics and Cotton in the Civil War* (Kent, Ohio: Kent State Univ. Press, 1993).

Pocumtuck

See BLOODY BROOK

Point Pleasant

West Virginia (October 10, 1774)
Lord Dunmore's War

The background to the Battle of Point Pleasant illustrated the mischievous currents and undercurrents of Indian-white relations on the expanding western frontier. Although white settlement was prohibited by the Treaty of Fort Stanwix, both Virginians and Pennsylvanians were eager to expand westward across the Ohio River and the governments of both colonies asserted conflicting claims

in the region. When Virginia's royal governor, John Murray, the earl of Dunmore, supported provocations against the Indians in the area—including the massacre of the family of Mingo John Logan (Tah-gah-jute) and the killing of the brother of Shawnee leader Cornstalk (Wynepuechsika) while on a peace mission—he set off a short-lived "war" bearing his name. The real purpose of the conflict was to push back the Shawnee and other tribes from a region coveted by British-American farmers, speculators, and traders.

Lord Dunmore organized a two-pronged force of militia. He took personal command of about fifteen hundred men and set out from Fort Pitt for a rendezvous with Col. Andrew Lewis and his fifteen hundred militiamen at the confluence of the Ohio and Kanawha Rivers (in modern-day West Virginia). Along the way, Dunmore decided to divert his force and march overland toward the main Shawnee villages in central Ohio, but Lewis and his men continued to the meeting point, where they were surprised on October 10 by a force of around a thousand warriors, mostly Shawnee, supported by a few Delaware (Lenni Lenape), Wyandot (Huron), and Ottawa, led by Cornstalk.

The fight lasted all day and resulted in relatively heavy casualties. The Virginians had fifty dead and nearly one hundred wounded. The number of Indian casualties is not known exactly but was probably higher. At the end of the day, the Indians withdrew and left the area. Cornstalk was persuaded by the battle of the futility of resisting the white influx across the Ohio, and he signed a treaty on Dunmore's terms. Dunmore himself was to be preoccupied within the year by the outbreak of the American Revolution.

Further Reading

Gregory E. Dowd. *A Spirited Resistance: The North American Indian Struggle for Unity, 1745–1815* (Baltimore: Johns Hopkins University Press, 1992); R. Douglas Hurt. *The Ohio Frontier: Crucible of the Old Northwest, 1720–1830* (Bloomington: Indiana University Press, 1996); and Virgil A. Lewis. *History of the Battle of Point Pleasant . . .* (Charleston, W. Va.: Tribune, 1909).

Port Gibson

Mississippi (May 1, 1863) *American Civil War*

The Union commander, Maj. Gen. Ulysses S. Grant had tried unsuccessfully since the fall of 1862 to get his forces into position to attack VICKSBURG, the great Confederate stronghold on the Mississippi River, but he had been stymied by the extremes of topography in the region, which made maneuvering large armies almost impossible, and the Confederates' efforts to short-circuit the Union plans. Grant launched what turned out to be a successful effort by crossing the river below Vicksburg with most of his army on April 30. The Union victory at Port Gibson the next day was the first in a series of hard-fought battles that led eventually to the surrender of Vicksburg.

Grant brought forward about twenty-four thousand troops at Port Gibson, commanded in two divisions by Maj. Gens. John A. McClernand and James B. McPherson. Their objective was to push the Confederates, commanded by Brig. Gen. John S. Bowen, out of the town and thereby both secure the river landings to Grant's rear and allow the movement toward Vicksburg to begin. The Federal troops greatly outnumbered the Confederates, but the deeply cut terrain made movement difficult and simplified the task of defense.

General Bowen, a skillful soldier, had about eight thousand men, organized in two brigades. One, commanded by Brig. Gen. Edward D. Tracy, he placed on the Bruinsburg Road, which ran atop a high, rugged ridge, flanked by impassable ravines. The second Confederate brigade, under Brig. Gen. Martin E. Green, defended the Rodney Road, which ran parallel about two miles away, separated by hollows and canebrakes.

The Confederates set up blocking positions on the roads, hoping to delay the Union advance until reinforcements could arrive. The fighting began on Green's front and spread as Grant fed more troops into the developing battle. The Union men on the Rodney Road dislodged Green by midmorning, and after falling back to a new position, Green was sent across to the other road, leaving Bowen to defend the Rodney route. On the Bruinsburg Road fighting had been fierce—General Tracy was killed during a fight with Brig. Gen. Peter Osterhaus's brigade—and the weight of Union numbers began to tell as the day wore on, despite a desperate defense by the Confederates.

Meanwhile, Bowen launched a counteroffensive along the Rodney Road, hoping to pin down and then outflank the Union advance, which had been slowed by the difficult terrain. The crack Missourians of Col. Francis M. Cockrell smashed into the Union brigade of Col. James R. Slack and seemed on the point of winning when fresh Federal troops attacked in turn and pushed Cockrell off the field. Bowen had no choice but to begin a retreat, leaving Port Gibson to Grant.

The Confederates reported 60 dead, 340 wounded, and 387 missing. The Union losses were 131 dead, 719 wounded, and 25 missing.

Further Reading

Edwin C. Bearss, "Port Gibson," in Frances H. Kennedy, ed. *The Civil War Battlefield Guide* (Boston: Houghton Mifflin, 1990).

Port Hudson

Louisiana (May 22–July 9, 1863)
American Civil War

Port Hudson had been built by the Confederates as a fortified strong point on the Mississippi River to complement VICKSBURG to the north and control a vital segment of the river. It was an exceedingly well built and defended base that defeated Union attempts at assault and siege.

After two futile attempts by the Union navy to cut off Port Hudson from the river side, Federal major general Nathaniel P. Banks, a former Speaker of the House of Representatives, moved on the bastion from the landward side. He had nearly thirty thousand troops and thought he could overpower the seventy-five hundred Confederate defenders, who were commanded by Maj. Gen. Franklin Gardner, a former classmate of Ulysses S. Grant.

Although smaller, in many ways the setting of Port Hudson resembled that of Vicksburg. It was situated on a sharp bend in the river, which allowed its guns to hammer attacking Union gunboats, and much of the landward side was cut with deep, impassable ravines. Banks discovered that it was physically difficult to bring his manpower advantage into play. He began a siege of Port Hudson on May 22 by positioning troops opposite the Confederate fortifications, and he planned an assault against strong points named Commisary Hill, Fort Desperate, Slaughter's Field, and the Priest Cap.

On May 27, Banks launched his attack, but his men immediately ran into difficulty trying to cross the rugged landscape in order to approach the fortifications. The Confederate defenders easily repulsed the first assaults at Commisary Hill and Fort Desperate, on the northern end of the defensive line, before the rest of Banks's units moved forward, so they were free to shift manpower as needed during the day. When the Federals attacked at Slaughter's Field and the Priest Cap, the defenders were ready and drove them off. Only a fragment of the Union force was engaged at any one time, and the terrain made the attack so difficult and the determined Confederate musketry made it so deadly that the Federals had almost no chance. The casualty figures for the day tell the story: the Union lost two thousand men, the Confederates only five hundred.

A notable feature of the Union assault on May 27 was the presence of two units of African-American troops fighting for the Federal side. The First Louisiana Native Guards had been a prewar New Orleans militia company, comprised of socially and educationally elite free blacks, which had switched to the Union cause when rejected for service in the Confederate army. During the siege of Port Gibson, the unit was known as the First Corps d'Afrique (many of its Creole members spoke French). A second unit, the Third Louisiana Native Guard, was made up of former slaves commanded by white officers and had been organized by the Federal government during the war. Both African-American units fought extremely well in some of the hottest parts of the Union assault.

Despite the heavy cost and lack of result, Banks still thought he could take the Confederate bastion. On June 13, the Federal artillery conducted a heavy one-hour bombardment, which Banks followed up with a demand for surrender. General Gardner declined. Early the next morning, Banks ordered another frontal assault on the Priest Cap by the division commanded by Brig. Gen. Halbert E. Paine, an attack that cost another eighteen hundred casualties but made little impression on the defenders.

Banks turned finally to siege warfare, cutting off all supplies to the Confederates and having his engineers dig the usual trenches and approaches. They were still at it when the Confederates learned that Vicksburg had surrendered. Since Port Hudson was now irrelevant, General Gardner surrendered on July 9. The Confederates had lost around a thousand killed, wounded, or dead from disease, but the Union had suffered a loss ten times that size.

With the surrender, the Union took command of the entire length of the Mississippi River.

Further Reading

Lawrence Le Hewitt, "Port Hudson," in Frances H. Kennedy, ed. *The Civil War Battlefield Guide* (Boston: Houghton Mifflin, 1990); and Howard C. Wright. *Port Hudson: Its History. . .* Reprint ed. (Baton Rouge, La.: Eagle Press, 1978).

⤞ Port Republic

Virginia (June 9, 1862) *American Civil War*

The battle at Port Republic, Virginia, on June 9, 1862, marked the conclusion of Maj. Gen. Thomas J.

"Stonewall" Jackson's brilliant Shenandoah Valley campaign, during which his Confederate army of around seventeen thousand men defeated parts of four separate Federal armies of more than sixty thousand men. After the battle at First WINCHESTER on May 25, Federal commanders Maj. Gen. John C. Frémont and Brig. Gen. James Shields pursued Jackson's forces along parallel routes up each side of the Shenandoah Valley. Jackson planned to defeat Shields first and then to turn on Frémont. Maj. Gen. Richard S. Ewell engaged Frémont's army, to delay his progress, at CROSS KEYS on June 8, while Jackson prepared his position at Port Republic, across the Shenandoah River, to meet Shields's advancing force.

The battle at Port Republic got off to a chaotic start. Jackson narrowly avoided being captured by a party of Union cavalry from Brig. Gen. Erastus B. Tyler's regiment that stormed into Port Republic on June 8. The Federals unlimbered a gun in town as Jackson fled to his camp on a hill above the North River, and the two sides began shelling one another. Col. Samuel Fulkerson's Virginia regiment chased the Federals from town, and Jackson prepared to attack Tyler and Shields the next day.

Tyler, a former fur trapper and merchant from Ohio, stationed his three thousand infantry soldiers in a half-mile line across the south fork of the Shenandoah River, with his left flank protected by seven guns posted at a charcoal plant on a high hill. When Jackson sent Brig. Gen. Charles Winder's Brigade to attack Tyler, Winder's men were stopped cold on a wide-open plain by Tyler's combined infantry and artillery fire. It took quite a while for Brig. Gen. Richard Taylor to bring his Louisiana men across the river to Winder's aid and attack the guns at the charcoal plant.

Though still outnumbered, Winder pushed his men forward under cover of Confederate artillery fire until they reached a position two hundred yards from Tyler's line. After holding that position for a solid hour, they ran out of ammunition and charged blindly at Tyler's men. At that moment, Ewell's reinforcements arrived and attacked the Union left head-on.

Just as Ewell arrived, Richard Taylor, the brother-in-law of Confederate President Jefferson Davis and son of former U.S. President Zachary Taylor, captured the Union guns at the coal facility, after pushing his men through three attacks and a bloody hand-to-hand fight. At the Federal center, Tyler turned his attention from Winder and Ewell and sent his men up the hill at Taylor's force, now in control of the guns. Before the Federals could overwhelm Taylor, however, Jackson brought up reinforcements and rallied Winder's forces to renew their attack. John C. Frémont, whose Federal troops had recovered from their defeat at Cross Keys the day before, arrived to help but was unable to cross the South River—Ewell had destroyed the bridge—and his men watched as Ewell, Winder, and Jackson overwhelmed Shields's entire force at Port Republic. The Federal line broke, and Confederates pursued the fleeing blueclad soldiers for five miles.

The battle at Port Republic exacted eight hundred Confederate casualties, but Jackson's men captured more than five hundred Federal soldiers and killed or wounded another five hundred.

Jackson withdrew his men to Brown's Gap, where he decided, when it was clear that Shields and Frémont would not renew their attacks, that he had concluded his campaign. The Union commander, Maj. Gen. George B. McClellan, realized that his plan to bottle up Confederate forces and contrive a completely decisive battle at Richmond had been thwarted. Jackson's victories in the Shenandoah Valley held out hope that the Confederacy, struggling in many other areas, might yet survive the war.

Further Reading

Darrell L. Collins. *The Battles of Cross Keys and Port Republic* (Lynchburg, Va.: H. E. Howard, 1993).

Port Royal (Canada)

See also ANNAPOLIS ROYAL (1744)

Port Royal

Annapolis Royal

Canada (September 24–October 1, 1710)
Queen Anne's War

When war broke out in 1702 in Europe over whether a member of the Bourbon family could take the vacant throne of Spain, which would have tied that country closely to France, the conflict spread to the New World, where it was known as Queen Anne's War. The British colonists along the Atlantic seaboard launched several attacks against French and Spanish colonies, and following a futile expedition in 1707, a colonial force from New England took Port Royal, on the Bay of Fundy, in 1710.

The town, the chief port of the region, called Acadia, had been founded by the French in 1605 and had functioned as a base for French privateers, who preyed on British shipping with the cooperation of the French governor, Daniel d'Auger de Subercase. People in Massachusetts and the other New England colonies were eager to rid themselves of this menace, and they gave general support to the British home government's plan to capture the port, pledging troops for a united colonial army.

The British sent a thirty-six-ship fleet, including four men-of-war, under Capt. George Martin, and assigned Col. Francis Nicholson to command the regiment of Royal Marines and thirty-five hundred colonial militia. The expedition sailed from Boston on September 18 and began a siege of Port Royal six days later.

Within a week, Gov. Subercase gave up and surrendered to Nicholson. The British took possession of the town and renamed it Annapolis Royal. They held the port until the French and Indian War, despite a French assault in 1744 (*see also* ANNAPOLIS ROYAL).

Further Reading

John B. Brebner. *New England's Outpost: Acadia before the Conquest of Canada* (New York: B. Franklin, 1973).

Port Royal Island (South Carolina)

See BEAUFORT

Port Royal Sound

(Forts Beauregard and Walker)

South Carolina (November 7, 1861)
American Civil War

After disastrous defeats at First BULL RUN and BALL'S BLUFF, Union commanders looked to the U.S. Navy for a much-needed victory in November 1861.

Capt. Samuel Francis Du Pont commanded a squadron of U.S. Navy warships, carrying 148 guns and 13,000 of Brig. Gen. Thomas W. Sherman's soldiers, that sailed from New York in October to attack what was considered the South's best port, at Port Royal Sound, South Carolina. After Du Pont's fleet arrived at Port Royal Sound on November 4, his gunboats spent several days shaking off resistance from Confederate captain Josiah Tattnall and reconnoitering Fort Walker on Hilton Head Island and Fort Beauregard on Phillips Island, which between them provided the sound with most of its protection.

Du Pont moved into the Port Royal channel and began his attack at 9 A.M. on November 7. He ordered his ships to steam in an oval formation to maximize firepower as they bombarded Fort Walker at an estimated rate of one round per second. Fort Walker lacked heavy guns, ammunition, and experienced defenders, and so it was taken by 2 P.M. The guns at Fort Beauregard were even less effective, since they were out of range of the Union gunboats, and Fort Beauregard's green defenders abandoned their posts when they heard Federals cheering their success at Fort Walker. By nightfall, the Union forces controlled all of Port Royal Sound.

Thirty-one Union casualties and sixty-eight Confederate casualties were reported after the battle.

Following the Union's capture of Port Royal Sound, Gen. Robert E. Lee ordered Confederate forces to evacuate all the sea and barrier islands between Charleston and Fernandina, Florida, leaving only Fort Pulaski in Southern control. Hilton Head Island became a major supply and staging area for Union operations in the South, and the barrier islands became the first testing ground for the Union project to build a better life for freed slaves.

Further Reading

Jay Wertz and Edwin C. Bearss. *Smithsonian's Great Battles & Battlefields of the Civil War* (New York: William Morrow, 1997).

Potonchan

Mexico (March 25, 1519) *Spanish Conquest*

The first New World battle commanded by Hernán Cortés, destined to become the conqueror of all of Old Mexico, came on the Yucatán Peninsula, against Mayan warriors of the town of Potonchan.

Cortés had been a moderately successful Spanish conquistador when named in the fall of 1518 by Diego Velázquez, the governor of Cuba, to lead an expedition to explore Yucatán (two previous Spanish expeditions had visited Yucatán, in 1517 and 1518). He immediately showed his great energy and drive by assembling an eleven-ship fleet and recruiting 530 Spaniards within a few weeks, sailing in mid-February. Cortés's force included thirty crossbowmen and ten harquebusiers (armed with primitive firearms), as well as fourteen pieces of artillery, sixteen horses (previously unknown in North America), and several vicious war dogs.

After stopping first on the island of Cozumel, the Spaniards arrived at Potonchan on March 22, near a river

visited in 1518 by Juan de Grijalva (*see also* LÁZARO). The local Maya were descendants of the great Mayan civilization and still possessed a sophisticated culture. They had experience with the previous Spanish expeditions and were eager to see the invaders leave as soon as possible. The Maya gave Cortés and his men a minimum of food and water and a few gold objects, but they insisted that the Spaniards not visit the Mayan town and that they depart as soon as possible. After two days, the Spaniards' demands became more insistent, and both sides prepared for armed conflict. On March 25, soon after Cortés had a notary read a proclamation of the supremacy of the king of Spain, the Maya, probably about five hundred strong, attacked.

As was usual among the Indians of the region, they were armed with bows and arrows, slings for throwing stones, spears flung from atlatls (a throwing device that added leverage and power), and the characteristic obsidian-bladed sword. Mayan tactics were designed to wound and capture the enemy rather than kill them on the battlefield. (All the Indians of Mexico aimed at taking prisoners for the ritual human sacrifice that was the center of their public life.)

The Spaniards replied to the attack with artillery fire, which had a stunning effect on the Maya, and then came to close combat with their superior steel swords, dealing death and inflicting terrible wounds. Twenty conquistadores were wounded in the fighting, but none were killed. A flank attack by a contingent of Spaniards routed the Maya.

After the battle, Cortés occupied the town and remained for three more weeks, skirmishing several times with Maya from the surrounding area, before reembarking for a voyage farther north along the coast (*see also* TLAXCALA).

Further Reading

William H. Prescott. *History of the Conquest of Mexico* . . (New York: Modern Library, 1936); and Hugh Thomas. *Conquest: Montezuma, Cortés, and the Fall of Old Mexico* (New York: Simon & Schuster, 1993).

Prairie Grove

Arkansas (December 7, 1862) *American Civil War*

After the Confederate defeat at PEA RIDGE in March, Arkansas was a quiet theater of the war, but in the fall of 1862 a local general, Thomas Hindman, raised an army and tried to expel all the Union troops from his native state. In December, forestalling an order to send his men to fight at VICKSBURG, Hindman marched against Brig. Gen. James G. Blunt's division, the only Federal force that had not withdrawn to Missouri.

Hindman had about eleven thousand men, Blunt only seven thousand. When he learned of the Confederate movements, Blunt sent north for reinforcements. Two divisions under Brig. Gen. Francis Herron immediately started toward Blunt from their camp 125 miles away, near WILSON'S CREEK. Blunt was near Cane Hill, where his cavalry had clashed with Confederate horsemen the week before, and Herron's divisions, having made a remarkable forced march, neared his camp on December 6.

Hindman, learning of Herron's approach, had decided to ignore Blunt and to try for a devastating blow upon Herron, after which he could dispose of the outnumbered Blunt. Hindman took up a line on a ridge overlooking the village of Prairie Grove and waited for Herron. At a little after midnight of the 7th, the two armies engaged and began a long battle that lasted until nightfall of the following day.

Herron attacked Hindman's positions several times during the day but could not gain the upper hand, despite poor performance by some of the recently recruited Arkansas infantry (one entire regiment deserted during the battle, and other elements refused to fight). At 11:00 A.M. Blunt brought his troops into the fray in a flank attack on Hindman, but he was repulsed by the steady Confederate cavalry. The fighting finally petered out as darkness came. By the next morning the Confederates had retreated, leaving the Union in command of the battlefield. Blunt and Herron failed to pursue Hindman's troops, but they had stopped his projected invasion of Missouri.

The Union casualties were numbered at 1,271 and the Confederates reported 1,317 losses.

Further Reading

William L. Shea. *War in the West: Pea Ridge and Prairie Grove* (Fort Worth, Tex.: Ryan Place, 1996).

Princeton

New Jersey (January 3, 1777) *American Revolution*

Following his great victory at TRENTON on the day after Christmas in 1776, the American commander in chief, Gen. George Washington, consolidated his forces—

persuading several thousand men whose enlistments were up to stay on—and recrossed the Delaware River to positions north of Trenton. He had about five thousand infantrymen in addition to artillery, and he hoped to engage the British forces at an advantage.

Washington's opponent, Maj. Gen. Lord Cornwallis had been stung by the loss of the German brigade at Trenton. Calling scattered units out of winter quarters and concentrating a force of 8,000, Cornwallis left a garrison of about 1,200 at Princeton and marched toward Washington's position, arriving within sight of the American lines on January 2 and halting for the night.

After taking counsel with his commanders, Washington ordered four hundred men to stay in the lines during the night and tend the campfires while the main body of the American army slipped silently around Cornwallis's troops toward Princeton. At 1:00 A.M., the Americans quietly took to roads, which had, luckily, frozen. Washington detached a small force of 350 under Brig. Gen. Hugh Mercer at a stone bridge east of Trenton at Stony Brook to delay any pursuit by Cornwallis.

As most of the Americans marched toward Princeton, British lieutenant colonel Charles Mawhood left the town with troops to reinforce Cornwallis. Near the bridge at Stony Brook, Mawhood's and Mercer's men spotted each other and maneuvered for position, both of them making for a nearby orchard. The Americans reached the cover of the trees first and opened fire. Mawhood ordered a bayonet attack—a tactic usually successful against the inexperienced Americans—and the subsequent charge drove the Americans into retreat. General Mercer was fatally injured by multiple bayonet wounds. Just as the British sensed victory, more American troops, under militia brigadier general John Cadwalader, arrived and renewed the battle.

Washington had heard the firing and, with only his staff, galloped toward the fighting. Finding the troops wavering he rode to the front, waving his hat to rally them against Mawhood's force. He was within about thirty yards of the British when they loosed a volley of musket fire at him. Washington somehow escaped injury and continued to exhort his men, who then re-formed and charged the British positions, firing at point-blank range.

Mawhood and most of his men broke free and began a rapid retreat toward the safety of the British lines at Trenton, with Washington and a troop of Philadelphia dragoons in close pursuit. The remaining British broke and ran, leaving weapons and equipment behind.

Most of the British troops who had been left to hold Princeton either fled or surrendered as the main body of the American force entered the town, but a few took shelter in one of the college buildings and attempted to resist. They were persuaded to give up by a round from an American artillery battery commanded by Alexander Hamilton.

Although it was a relatively small engagement, the battle near Princeton was one of the few in which the Americans could claim victory. The Americans recorded forty killed (General Mercer and the able Maryland commander Col. John Haslet among them) and one hundred wounded. The British took more than 250 casualties and had been chased from both the field and the town.

Washington was not deceived as to his position, however, and he knew his men were exhausted and that Cornwallis would soon be on the road from Trenton with overwhelming force. The American commander ordered a withdrawal toward Morristown, New Jersey, where the army could go into winter quarters. Cornwallis's men were delayed in their pursuit by having to ford Stony Brook on foot (the Americans had destroyed the bridge), reaching Princeton only to see the last of Washington's men disappear up the road.

The chance nature and small scale of the victory did not diminish the importance of another American success, to go along with Trenton, after a long series of defeats at the hands of the British during the preceding months. As the new year began, the American cause was still alive.

Further Reading

Alfred Hoyt Bill. *The Campaign of Princeton, 1776–1777.* (Princeton, N.J.: Princeton University Press, 1948); William H. Dwyer. *The Day Is Ours!! November 1776–January 1777: An Inside View of the Battles of Trenton and Princeton* (New York: Viking Press, 1983); Samuel S. Smith. *The Battle of Princeton* (Monmouth Beach, N.J.: Philip Freneau Press, 1967); Ray Thompson. *Washington along the Delaware: The Battles of Trenton and Princeton . . .* (Fort Washington, Pa.: Bicentennial Press, 1970); and Kemble Widmer. *The Christmas Campaign: The Ten Days of Trenton and Princeton* (Trenton: New Jersey Historical Commission, 1975).

✒ Puebla

Mexico (September 14–October 12, 1847)
Mexican-American War

The Mexican-American War largely concluded with Maj. Gen. Winfield Scott's troops capture of the fortified castle at CHAPULTEPEC and entry into the capital of Mexico City on September 13, 1847. However, peace negotiations stretched into the next year, and some Mexican troops never fully gave up until the Treaty of Guadalupe Hidalgo was concluded. Immediately after the takeover of Mexico City, Brig. Gen. Joaquín Rea laid siege to the American-held city of Puebla and attempted to rally the Mexican cause.

Rea's four thousand troops and guerrilla fighters captured most of the American garrison's food supply when they pushed into Puebla on September 14. Brevet Col. Thomas Childs, who commanded three American posts inside the city—at Fort Loretto, the citadel of San José, and a convent—had already survived harassment by several skirmishing parties in the month of August, and his men were determined, despite the lack of supplies, to wait out their Mexican attackers.

Rea's siege of the town lasted twenty-eight days, during which he made frequent attacks on the American positions. He called for Childs's surrender on September 16, and when Childs refused, Rea sent Mexican horsemen against San José to no effect. A second attack on September 18 was similarly rebuffed by American artillery fire.

Gen. Antonio López de Santa Anna, who had split his army after Chapultepec in a bid to hold on to his military power, arrived to take control of the siege on September 22. On September 23, five hundred Mexican troops stormed the convent unsuccessfully, but Santa Anna demanded Childs's surrender once again. Childs refused, and Santa Anna renewed the siege until the early hours of October 1.

On that day, Brig. Gen. Joseph Lane approached with American reinforcements and supplies. Santa Anna marched out to meet him, leaving Rea to continue the siege. After Santa Anna's and Lane's forces fought to a standstill between the towns of Huamantla and Querétaro, Lane allowed his men to plunder Huamantla, not reaching Puebla until October 12. Heavy rains prevented additional troops and supplies from leaving Mexico City in the meantime. Col. Lewis D. Wilson set out from Veracruz to aid his countrymen, but he died from fever just before his force was turned aside by fifteen hundred guerrillas led by Padre Calendonio Domeco Jaruta and Juan Aburto, two of Mexico's most famous partisan fighters, at the Paso de Ovejas.

American sorties against the Mexican positions in Puebla had reduced the strength of Rea's force, and on October 2 Capt. William F. Small marched out of the citadel at San José and blew up a Mexican shelter, killing seventeen of Rea's men. Capt. John Herron's company of Pennsylvanians cleared the Mexican forces from another building in front of San José on the fifth. Rea pushed forward again three days later, but both sides agreed to a temporary truce after the death of the archbishop of Puebla.

When Lane's men finally reached Puebla on October 12, still suffering the ill effects of their drunken raid on Huamantla, they fought Rea's remaining force through the streets of town and finally liberated Childs's men from their long siege. There are no accurate estimates of casualties from the siege.

Apart from several forays against guerrillas in the late fall, the action at Puebla was the last of the war in central Mexico. Santa Anna renounced the presidency of Mexico after his failed raid on Puebla and was left to rally the pitiful remains of his dispirited army.

Further Reading

K. Jack Bauer. *The Mexican War: 1846–1848* (New York: Macmillan, 1974); Robert Selph Henry. *The Story of the Mexican War.* Reprint ed. (New York: Frederick Ungar, 1961).

Puebla

(Cinco de Mayo)

Mexico (May 5, 1862) *Mexican French War*

After the civil conflict known as the War of Reform (1857–1861) had died down in Mexico, Pres. Benito Juárez declared a two-year moratorium on payment of Mexican foreign debt in an effort to restore the domestic economy. In response, between December 1861 and January 1862, six thousand Spanish troops, seven hundred British marines, and two hundred French soldiers invaded Veracruz, a city on Mexico's Gulf coast with relatively easy access to the capital, Mexico City (*see also* VERACRUZ for a description of the U.S. landing there in 1847). The British and Spanish withdrew their troops after negotiations with the Mexican government, but Napoleon III, the emperor of France, had the larger conquest of Mexico in mind. Within a month, French general Charles Latrille, comte de Lorencez, led sixty-five hundred French troops toward Mexico City, expecting to establish a new French empire. The defeat he met at the city of Puebla in May came as a shock, though he eventually did drive Juárez from office and install Maximilian Ferdinand Joseph of Austria as head of a French puppet monarchy in 1863.

Latrille, who expected to be greeted happily by Mexican citizens, as the French minister in Mexico City, and as exiles from the Mexican civil wars had assured him they would, was thoroughly surprised by the resistance he met at Puebla, known to be a conservative enclave. President Juárez had instructed Gen. Ignacio Zaragoza, who had fled his home in Texas during that republic's war of independence in 1836 and had risen through the ranks of the Mexican military, to defend the city. Zaragoza, who had seen great success as military leader of liberal troops during the War of Reform, commanded only five thousand militia and regular soldiers, but nonetheless, he decided to engage the French in a pitched battle.

The Mexican troops made a stand when Latrille's French troops, many of them seasoned veterans of the Crimean War, attacked the city on May 5. Latrille underestimated the tactical strength of the Mexican position. Zaragoza had not only planned for defensive and offensive infantry actions but had installed troops in the eastern hills around Puebla and covered Latrille's approach with artillery and a cavalry patrol.

Latrille began his attack on Puebla at 5 A.M. He immediately had trouble establishing his own artillery position. Latrille's men finally reached the outskirts of town by 11 A.M., but Zaragoza's quick tactical thinking countered their every move, and three French advances were pushed back. Latrille threw his troops against the walls that surrounded the city, but none of his men, many of them weakened by sickness, was ever able to scale them. Instead, huge numbers of dead and wounded French soldiers piled up in the deep ditch outside the city's fortifications. After two hours of fighting, Latrille had used over half his ammunition and had made no progress.

Zaragoza took the upper hand in the afternoon, when Latrille sent another attack against his right side. Zaragoza ordered Brig. Gen. Porfirio Díaz, who was later Mexico's president for thirty years, to counterattack with his Second Brigade, and the French were repelled. Latrille retreated to the town of Orizaba to plan another route to Mexico City, a route that the French did not pursue until a year later, after Latrille had been replaced by Gen. Elie Frédéric Forey.

The French suffered 482 casualties in their attack on Puebla, almost twice the Mexican total of 250.

The French established control over Mexico in 1863. When Mexico regained its independence, in 1867, the anniversary of the battle at Puebla, May 5 (Cinco de Mayo), became a national holiday as a celebration of victory over the Europeans. Though the holiday is now of minor importance in Mexico, it remains an extremely important celebration for Mexicans and Mexican-Americans living in the United States.

Further Reading

Roberto Cabello-Argandoña. *Cinco de Mayo: A Symbol of Mexican National Resistance* (Encino, Calif.: Floricanto Press, 1997); Maria Cruz Viramontes de Marin. *Cinco de Mayo: A Review of the Battle of Puebla* (San Diego, Calif.: Marin Publications, 1994).

Puente de Calderón

See CALDERÓN BRIDGE

Put-in-Bay

See LAKE ERIE

Pyle's Defeat

See HAW RIVER

Q

Quebec

(Plains of Abraham)
Canada (September 13, 1759)
French and Indian War

The British and the French fought the first European-style, stand-up, open-field battle in North America on a broad plain outside the French capital of Quebec. The death of both army commanders and the dramatic array of forces later obscured the fact that the British failed to follow up their victory on the field.

The British were commanded by Maj. Gen. James Wolfe, a young but experienced officer who had been given the assignment to take Quebec as part of Prime Minister William Pitt's overall strategy to divest France of its North American possessions. Wolfe sailed up the St. Lawrence River with 8,500 regulars and several companies of colonial rangers aboard a British fleet of 49 men-of-war and 119 transports and supply ships. He faced a formidable task, since the walled defenses of Quebec, perched on a rocky promontory that jutted into

the confluent channels of the St. Lawrence and St. Charles Rivers, were intimidating, and the French defenders were able.

The French military commander was Lt. Gen. Louis-Joseph, marquis de Montcalm-Gozon de Saint-Véran, a long-serving veteran of the Continental wars who had successfully directed the French war effort in North America since 1756. He had several thousand troops, but the majority of them, twenty-five hundred Canadian militia, were untrained. His regulars numbered around two thousand. Nonetheless, Montcalm was confident that the British navy would be able neither to navigate the treacherous river approaches to Quebec nor to sustain a siege into the fall months, with the threat of early formation of ice.

The British ships, commanded by Vice Adm. Sir Charles Saunders, made much better progress than the French anticipated, however, they took control of the water approaches to the city and landed troops and heavy guns on the opposite shore. The British guns pounded the city for weeks during the summer, and Wolfe's rangers raided into the countryside, but overall, there was little

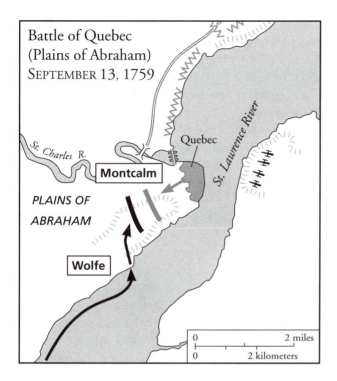

Battle of Quebec
(Plains of Abraham)
SEPTEMBER 13, 1759

St. Charles R.

Quebec

Montcalm

St. Lawrence River

PLAINS OF
ABRAHAM

Wolfe

| 0 | 2 miles |
| 0 | 2 kilometers |

British guns on the field added to the carnage, and ultimately Wolfe—although seriously wounded—led his grenadiers in a charge that smashed the French formation and sent it reeling back toward the city walls.

At the climactic moment, however, Wolfe was hit full in the chest by a musket ball and died on the spot. His subordinates became confused and failed to block the French retreat or to pursue vigorously. Montcalm himself was also mortally wounded, but the surviving members of his army reached safety in a fortified area guarding the northern flank of the city, and many of them eventually escaped the area altogether. The absence of pursuit allowed the French to maintain their force and dissipated for the British the full fruits of the victory.

The French had suffered high losses on the Plains of Abraham, around two hundred dead and twelve hundred wounded. The British losses were put at fewer than one hundred dead.

Five days later, the remaining French garrison surrendered the city, but the question of final victory had not yet been answered. The final expulsion of the French from Canada did not come until 1763.

Further Reading

Gordon Donaldson. *Battle for a Continent: Quebec, 1759* (Garden City, N.Y.: Doubleday, 1973); W. J. Eccles, "The Battle of Quebec: A Reappraisal." *French Colonial Historical Society Proceedings* 3, no. 1 (1978): 70–81; Duncan W. Grinnell-Milne. *Mad Is He? The Character and Achievement of James Wolfe* (London: Bodley Head, 1963); Christopher Lloyd. *The Capture of Quebec* (London: Batsford, 1959); and Francis Parkman. *Montcalm and Wolfe.* Reprint ed. (New York: F. Ugar, 1965).

Wolfe could do to defeat the garrison unless he could force or entice Montcalm from behind the walls.

Wolfe decided on an aggressive approach. Ordering nearly four thousand troops aboard barges and slipping past the city, he unloaded his men on the northern shore of the river west of the citadel itself. His leading troops found a route from the river's edge up to the Plains of Abraham, a broad, flat area facing the city's western walls. Montcalm at first thought the movement upriver was a feint, and he failed to respond until the British appeared in battle formation on the plain. At that stage, the French commander decided that his relatively thin ranks and weak western walls could not stand an assault, so he ordered his regulars and militia to deploy on a ridge just outside the city, facing the British lines at a distance of only a few hundred yards.

The French opened fire with their six cannon, doing considerable damage to the British formations with grapeshot, and after the initial softening-up, Montcalm ordered an assault across the battlefield. He had intermixed the untrained Canadian militia with his regular troops, and as the French began to move forward, the plan fell apart when the militia became disoriented and began to hinder the movements of the trained infantrymen. At forty yards' distance, Wolfe gave the order for the British to open fire, and the volleys from the steady regulars devastated the already faltering French advance. The two

Quebec

Canada (December 31, 1775–January 1, 1776)
American Revolution

An attempt to capture Quebec by Brig. Gen. Richard Montgomery and Col. Benedict Arnold unsuccessfully concluded the American invasion of Canada in 1775.

Montgomery, a longtime veteran of the British army and a recent immigrant to the colonies turned patriot, had marched north up Lake Champlain from FORT TICONDEROGA with an American army, as second in command to Maj. Gen. Philip Schuyler. When Schuyler took ill, the well-liked Montgomery took over the army and advanced toward Quebec, seeking to fulfill the goal of seizing Canada that had been approved by members of the Continental Congress in June.

Arnold, on the other hand, had reached Quebec by an extraordinary journey through the wilderness forests of Maine and New York. He was a former Connecticut merchant and bookseller who had volunteered his services to the Massachusetts Committee of Safety in April and had helped take Fort Ticonderoga in May. In September, he had set forth from Massachusetts at the direct order of the Continental commander in chief, Gen. George Washington, with an army of about eleven hundred men. They crossed the wilderness in a horrific march that saw many turn back and many others die from exposure, disease, and exhaustion. Arnold arrived at the St. Lawrence across from Quebec on November 9 with fewer than seven hundred starving soldiers. Montgomery and Arnold soon joined forces and began to plan an assault on the great fortified city.

Quebec was a fortress of immense strength, situated on a point jutting out into the confluence of the St. Lawrence and St. Charles Rivers. The upper town, with its central citadel, was protected by massive walls and a system of well-planned battlements and stood high above the river and the Plains of Abraham, where James Wolfe had won his great battle against the French in 1759. The lower town was less well fortified but featured a labyrinth-like system of crooked streets and passageways, which could be easily defended.

The British commander, Gen. Guy Carleton, was a talented officer with long years of experience—he had been wounded at Quebec as an officer in Wolfe's army—and he had very steady nerves. He did not have many proven soldiers, however. He had lost most of the men of his only two regiments of regulars, the Seventh and the Twenty-sixth, defending the outlying posts at ST. JOHN'S and CHAMBLY. He was left with a motley crew of a few regulars, a small number of Scots emigrant veterans, sailors from the river fleet, and unreliable French-Canadian militia. Even with the deficiencies of his garrison, however, Carleton knew he outnumbered his American attackers, and he knew how to defend his city.

Montgomery and Arnold decided on a two-pronged attack on the lower town: Arnold would assault from the north and Montgomery from the south, while a few other Americans created a diversion. The commanders were keenly aware that the enlistments of many of their troops would run out at the end of the year, but they resolved to wait for a storm to cover their movements.

Finally, on New Year's Eve 1775, a howling blizzard set the stage, and at 4:00 A.M. a rocket signaled the beginning of the assault.

Montgomery led his three hundred men on foot along miles of an icy and drift-choked path to Point Diamond, where they encountered a series of barricaded and defended streets. They sawed through one of the barricades and moved boldly forward. Montgomery himself was at the head of a small group that approached a fortified house. The British defenders let the Americans come within a few feet and then blasted them with muskets and three-pounder field guns. The withering fire killed Montgomery instantly, along with at least a dozen others; only a few men of the advance party escaped death. The body of the brave Montgomery—fated to become one of the first and most beloved martyrs of the Revolution—was retrieved, but the assault was over, and his troops retreated to the safety of the countryside.

Meanwhile, Arnold's column had entered the lower town by the palace gate and attacked a series of street barricades. Arnold himself was wounded in the leg during the early moments and had to withdraw. Virginia rifleman Dan Morgan took command and led the men against the British barricades—he was blown off his feet at one stage but miraculously was not seriously wounded. All the bravery in the world was futile, however, and the Americans were trapped and surrounded in the narrow streets. When his position became clear, Morgan surrendered.

At the end of the day, Carleton surveyed a nearly complete triumph. The Americans had lost 60 men and officers to death or wounds, and 426 more had been captured. The British lost only five killed and thirteen wounded. Arnold gathered the remnants of the American invasion force and began a long retreat.

Further Reading

John Bayley. *In Another Country.* Reprint ed. (New York: Oxford University Press, 1986); Harrison Bird. *Attack on Quebec: The American Invasion of Canada, 1775* (New York: Oxford University Press, 1968); Charles B. Flood. *Rise, and Fight Again: Perilous Times along the Road to Independence* (New York: Dodd, Mead, 1976); Robert McConnell Hatch. *Thrust for Canada: The American Attempt on Quebec in 1775–1776* (Boston: Houghton Mifflin, 1979); Hal T. Shelton. *General Richard Montgomery and the American Revolution: From Redcoat to Rebel* (New York: New York University Press, 1994); and George Stanley. *Canada Invaded, 1775–1776* (Toronto: Hakkert, 1973).

Queenston

Canada (October 13, 1812) *War of 1812*

In the wake of the disastrous American surrender of Detroit to the British in August 1812, New York militia major general Stephen Van Rensselaer sought to take the heights of Queenston, Canada, in order to advance the campaign on the Niagara frontier, which he commanded. Van Rensselaer's mixed force of American militia and regular soldiers advanced against British regulars, black pioneers, Canadian militia, and British-allied Iroquois Confederacy warriors, all under the command of Gen. Isaac Brock.

An American regular army officer, Brig. Gen. Alexander Smith, was to have helped with the attack, but he refused to submit to Van Rensselaer's command. Van Rensselaer's commissioning of his nephew, militia colonel Solomon Van Rensselaer, to lead the initial attack on Queenston caused further resentment among regular officers under his command, including Lt. Cols. Winfield Scott, John R. Fenwick, and John Chrystie, who were to play decisive roles in the battle.

The campaign got off to a rocky start on October 10, when American forces were unable to cross the Niagara River after the disappearance of a boat carrying all the company's oars. Colonel Van Rensselaer finally set out across the river two days later, with three hundred militia volunteers from New York and three hundred members of the Sixth and Thirteenth Infantry Regiments, under Lieutenant Colonel Chrystie. Other forces were left in the rear to provide reinforcements when ordered.

General Brock had reinforced Queenston and the heights outside of town overlooking the river with almost two thousand men, many of them highly trained and experienced soldiers, including the grenadier and light infantry companies of the Forty-ninth Regiment. The British had also positioned at least four cannon in the area.

Almost as soon as the first Americans crossed the river, Capt. James Dennis's grenadiers opened fire from the heights. Van Rensselaer was severely wounded, and Chrystie's boat was carried downstream from the main action, so it was left to Capt. John Wool of the Thirteenth Infantry to lead the American forces to a protected position at the base of the hill.

The wounded Van Rensselaer ordered Wool to attack the heights, and when a volunteer remembered a little-used fishing path up the side of the hill, Wool led the bulk of the troops up secretly and established a position above the British troops on the heights and in the town of Queenston.

General Brock, who had arrived earlier with reinforcements from Fort George, personally led two British charges up the hill. Brock was mortally wounded, and his aide-de-camp, Lt. Col. John MacDonell, was killed leading a third push.

Though battered, the Americans survived the British attacks, and by daybreak they had established a position on the upper edge of Queenston. There Winfield Scott assumed command from the wounded Captain Wool, and with the help of Capt. Joseph G. Totten of the engineers he established a solid defensive position between Dennis's entrenchment and the redcoat reinforcements who were surely coming, from the north. Major General Van Rensselaer ordered the wounded to be sent back across the river, from where the boats could transport American militia reinforcements to support Scott.

During the afternoon, however, British reinforcements under Maj. Gen. Roger H. Sheaffe, along with several hundred Mohawk led by the famous war leader Joseph Brant, surrounded and attacked the American position on the heights. When Van Rensselaer's inexperienced militia forces across the river saw the boats filled with wounded and heard that the much-feared Mohawk Indians were on the hill, they refused to leave American soil and join the fight. Despite Van Rensselaer's entreaties, most of the militia ran away, and Van Rensselaer had to report to Scott that no further American reinforcements could be expected up the hill.

The Indians led the British attack on the American position, while Sheaffe pushed from the rear. Scott and Brig. Gen. William Wadsworth of the New York militia quickly agreed that the best hope for their outnumbered troops was an immediate withdrawal. The retreat quickly degenerated into panicked chaos, however, some men even jumping from the heights into the river below, and Scott was forced to surrender his entire force.

The British took 958 prisoners, including stragglers and deserters, who had not fought much. The American forces lost 90 men killed and 150 wounded. Among the British regulars and Canadian militia there were fourteen killed and seventy-seven wounded, and the Indians reported five killed and nine wounded.

The defeat marked one in a series of disasters for the Americans along the Canadian border. Three days after the battle, Major General Van Rensselaer resigned. While the British victory protected Queenston and nearby Fort George, the loss of Isaac Brock would be keenly felt.

Further Reading

Smith C. Compton. *The Battle of Queenston Heights, Upper Canada* (Toronto: McGraw-Hill, 1968); Carol Whitfield, "The Battle of Queenston Heights." *Canadian Historical Sites* 11 (1974): 9–59.

✑ Quinby Bridge

South Carolina (July 17, 1781)
American Revolution

During the summer of 1781, the patriot Americans in South Carolina fought a series of engagements with British and Loyalists who had occupied parts of the backcountry for the previous year. Much of the fighting was by small units of partisans, such as those under Brig. Gen. Thomas Sumter and Brig. Gen. Francis ("Swamp Fox") Marion. As the summer wore on, Sumter became less and less cooperative with other commanders, and his behavior at Quinby Bridge solidified their disaffection from him.

Sumter had extracted from southern commander Maj. Gen. Nathanael Greene permission to use Marion's troops as well as the legion of Lt. Col. Henry Lee to track down a detachment of British regulars from the Nineteenth Regiment, commanded by Lt. Col. John Coates. After several preliminary skirmishes, Coates was brought to bay at Quinby Bridge on the Cooper River. His main force had crossed the bridge, and he was waiting for his rear guard and baggage train when Lee's cavalry charged over the river and dispersed most of the British infantry. Coates rallied his men, however, and forced the cavalry back across the bridge.

Lee and Marion—two of the best American officers in the war—realized that Coates's position was too strong to attack, but when Sumter arrived on the scene he ordered an assault over their objections. Setting Marion's and Lee's troops on the flank, Sumter placed a regiment of militia under Col. Thomas Taylor in the center and ordered it forward. Taylor's men charged across open ground and were driven back. Sumter's other men, who were supposed to provide support, declined to leave the safety of cover, and Sumter refused to bring up his artillery to counter a gun that Coates used effectively against Taylor's assault.

Outraged at the foolish orders and lack of support, Taylor resigned from Sumter's command, and both Marion and Lee withdrew as well. There was no reliable report of casualties.

Further Reading

John Buchanan. *The Road to Guilford Courthouse: The American Revolution in the Carolinas* (New York: John Wiley & Sons, 1997).

✑ Quintan's Bridge

New Jersey (March 18, 1778) *American Revolution*

This small but sharp engagement, resulting in a victory by the British, came about as a consequence of the foraging of both armies as they lay in winter quarters. The British under Gen. Sir William Howe occupied Philadelphia, with several strong units stationed in the countryside. Gen. George Washington's army was enduring its terrible winter at Valley Forge.

British colonel Charles Mawhood was foraging on the countryside with a detachment of regulars from the Seventeenth Regiment and Maj. John Simcoe's Loyalist rangers when he learned that around three hundred American militia under Col. Asher Holmes were also foraging nearby. Holmes had established a base at Quintan's Bridge on Alloway Creek, and Mawhood saw an opportunity to deceive and ambush the Americans.

Mawhood moved his men quietly into the area across the bridge opposite Holmes's camp, occupying a brick tavern and hiding in nearby woods. Mawhood had a few of the troops of the Seventeenth stage a conspicuous withdrawal, while the majority of his soldiers remained hidden.

The American militiamen took the bait, and two hundred crossed the bridge in pursuit of what they assumed was a smaller number of British troops. When the Americans passed the tavern, the British emerged at their rear, cut them off from retreat, and attacked.

The Americans lost thirty to forty men in the brief battle, several of whom apparently drowned in the creek trying to escape. The British reported only one casualty.

Further Reading

George B. Macaltioner. *150th Anniversary of the Skirmish at Quinton's Bridge* . . . (Salem, N.J.: Sunbeam, 1928).

⚬ Raisin River

See FRENCHTOWN

⚬ Ramseur's Mill

North Carolina (June 20, 1780)
American Revolution

Having secured control of South Carolina and captured or destroyed all organized American armed forces in the southern theater during the first half of 1780, the British wanted to expand the war into North Carolina, by rousing Loyalists. The patriots of North Carolina struck this scheme a blow with a victory in a partisan battle at Ramseur's Mill.

Loyalist colonel John Moore assembled thirteen hundred untrained and ill-equipped men at Ramseur's Mill in mid-June, anticipating a move into North Carolina later in the year by regulars under Lt. Gen. Lord Cornwallis.

Meanwhile, patriot militia responded to a call from Brig. Gen. Griffith Rutherford, and twelve hundred assembled under the command of Col. Francis Locke at a point not far from the Loyalist camp. Neither the patriots nor the Loyalists presented much in the way of military formation or appearance—they were closer to armed mobs than armies—but such was often the case in the bitter partisan warfare of the backwoods in the South during 1780 and 1781. The conflicts could be described as much as civil war as rebellion.

On June 20, the patriots under Locke marched on Moore's camp and attacked the disorganized Loyalists, who took up defensive positions on a nearby hill, although a goodly number who had been without arms fled the scene. The patriots advanced in a ragged line, and the battle seesawed for a while, degenerating into hand-to-hand fighting with clubbed muskets. Finally, the Loyalists were overwhelmed, and they began to flee.

Only a fraction of the patriots had actually entered the fight, perhaps as few as 400, and they had about 150 killed or wounded. The Loyalists lost about the same number.

Although a small engagement, the victory offered the patriots of North Carolina a breathing space.

Further Reading

John Buchanan. *The Road to Guilford Courthouse: The American Revolution in the Carolinas* (New York: John Wiley & Sons, 1997); and John S. Pancake. *This Destructive War: The British Campaign in the Carolinas* (University, Ala.: University of Alabama Press, 1985).

⚓ Raymond

Mississippi (May 12, 1863) *American Civil War*

Following his victory at PORT GIBSON, Maj. Gen. Ulysses S. Grant continued to move on VICKSBURG, his ultimate goal, although he was uncertain of the exact strength and composition of his opposition. The battle at Raymond helped clarify the situation.

From his headquarters in Vicksburg, the Confederate commander, Lt. Gen. John C. Pemberton, ordered Brig. Gen. John Gregg to march from Jackson to Raymond with his four thousand men and contest the movements of the Union army. Gregg arrived on May 11 and set up roadblocks on the road to Utica, the route the Federals would have to take to Raymond, and positioned troops for attacks on both flanks.

The next morning, two divisions of Union troops, totaling twelve thousand, under Maj. Gen. James B. McPherson, came down the road, the vanguard stepping into the Confederates' view as it topped a rise three miles from the town. Brig. Gen. Elias Dennis's and Brig. Gen. John E. Smith's brigades formed into line and marched toward the waiting Confederates. The ensuing fight lasted until late in the afternoon. The Union had an overwhelming advantage of numbers—twelve thousand to four thousand—but McPherson was an inexperienced general, and he failed throughout most of the day to concentrate his assaults, allowing the Confederates to fight off them piecemeal. During the afternoon, the movements of many Union units were uncoordinated and confused by the smoke, terrain, and lack of clear orders.

Finally, however, the sheer weight of numbers prevailed, and Gregg was compelled to break off the fight and retreat toward Jackson. McPherson's men took possession of Raymond.

Gregg lost 72 men killed, 252 wounded, and 190 missing. McPherson reported 66 killed, 339 wounded, and 37 missing.

Grant inferred from the stiffness of the Confederate resistance at Raymond that larger forces were nearby, and he altered his scheme of advance on Vicksburg.

Further Reading

Jay Wertz and Edwin C. Bearss. *Smithsonian's Great Battles & Battlefields of the Civil War* (New York: William Morrow, 1997).

⚓ Red Bank

See FORT MERCER

⚓ Resaca de Guerrero

See RESACA DE LA PALMA

⚓ Resaca de la Palma

(Resaca de Guerrero)

Texas (May 9, 1846) *Mexican-American War*

The day after fighting Brig. Gen. Zachary Taylor's American army at PALO ALTO, Texas, in one of the first battles of the Mexican-American War, Maj. Gen. Ariano Arista retreated with his four thousand troops to a position about seven miles from the Rio Grande at Resaca de Guerrero. Taylor followed and again attacked the Mexicans.

The *resaca*, the remains of an alluvial river bed, was covered by thick chapparal, which provided Major General Arista's troops an excellent defensive position. On the morning of May 9, Arista posted infantry and cavalry under Gen. Anastasio Torrejón to guard the road from Palo Alto, where Taylor's troops remained. Taylor had his men spend the morning building earthworks to defend his two hundred supply wagons before he decided to pursue Arista.

Taylor sent Capt. George A. McCall and Capt. Charles F. Smith ahead from the Resaca de la Palma to take stock of the Mexican position. When they reported that the thicket of chaparral protected almost the entire Mexican line. Taylor decided to focus his attack on a small clearing along the road to Matamoros.

Capt. Randolph Ridgeley, now commanding the "flying" battery of highly mobile horse-drawn artillery devised by Maj. Samuel Ringgold, who had been killed the day before, pushed his guns forward despite an attack by Torrejón's lancers to open the battle. Ridgeley's guns cleared away the front line of Mexican artillery and prepared the way for an American infantry advance.

When the American infantry charged into the thick growth of brush, it engaged the Mexican troops in hand-to-hand combat. The Mexicans, tired, hungry, and lacking a commander in the field—Arista stayed in camp, occupied with paperwork—eventually fell back.

While the fight progressed, Taylor ordered an attack on the Mexican artillery on the far right side of the *resaca*. Ridgeley's guns began a duel against the Mexican gunners and initially drove them off, but before Capt. Charles May's dragoons could reach the abandoned cannon the gunners resumed their posts and repulsed May's attack. Eventually, two companies of American infantry overran and captured the Mexican guns.

Arista roused himself from his tent and ordered one last charge up the road, but the attack was driven back. Exhausted and with the bulk of their artillery captured, the Mexicans fled across the Rio Grande.

Arista's losses totaled 160 killed, 228 wounded, and 159 missing, while Taylor lost only 33 killed and 89 wounded.

Taylor decided not to cross the Rio Grande to pursue Arista and crush his army, since the Americans recognized the river as their southern border. On the same evening back in Washington, D.C., Pres. James K. Polk was composing his war message to the U.S. Congress, and the fighting would soon shift into Mexican territory.

Further Reading

Peter F. Stevens, "The Proving Ground." *American History Illustrated* 23, No. 3 (1988): 38–44.

➤ Rich Mountain

West Virginia (July 11, 1861)
American Civil War

Both sides in mid-1861 wanted to take control of the key region of western Virginia (most of modern-day West Virginia), but the Union was able to assemble more troops than the Confederacy and thereby gain the upper hand.

Maj. Gen. George B. McClellan, an Ohio militia commander, crossed the Ohio River into western Virginia with about twenty thousand men in May and June 1861. His goal was to find and defeat a smaller Confederate force commanded by Brig. Gen. Robert S. Garnett, which had been sent to defend the transportation routes that led to the Shenandoah Valley. Garnett held defensive positions in two mountain passes south of PHILIPPI, where he had been bested by McClellan in

the first battle of the war. McClellan, made bold by his initial success and supported by good subordinates, hoped to sweep Garnett aside and take command of the road system.

On July 11, McClellan sent a column under Brig. Gen. William S. Rosecrans to attack the Confederates' rear at Rich Mountain, while a smaller Union force attacked head-on and another feinted at the Confederates holding the pass at Laurel Mountain. Outnumbering his opponents by about two to one, Rosecrans attacked as planned, destroyed the Confederate defenses, and drove Garnett's men into retreat toward the town of Beverly, trapping many of them before they could get clear. The next day, Garnett withdrew toward the Cheat River, where his rear guard was caught by Union troops on July 13, and he and several of his men were killed near Carrick's Ford. Garnett was the first general on either side to die in combat.

Overall Federal losses were light, reported as fewer than a hundred, and the Confederates lost fifty or sixty killed or wounded and nearly seven hundred captured.

Further Reading

James M. McPherson. *Ordeal by Fire: The Civil War and Reconstruction.* 2d ed. (New York: McGraw-Hill, 1992).

➤ Richmond

Kentucky (August 29–30, 1862)
American Civil War

In mid-1862 the Confederacy launched a new offensive into Kentucky. Maj. Gen. Edmund Kirby Smith, with about nine thousand troops, moved from Cumberland Gap toward the central bluegrass region with the objective of menacing Cincinnati. Smith met and defeated a smaller Union force near Richmond, Kentucky.

Maj. Gen. William Nelson, the Union commander in Kentucky, sent two brigades of newly raised and little-trained troops to hold Richmond under brigadier generals Charles Cruft and Mahlon Manson, while Nelson himself gathered reinforcements at Lexington. There were about sixty-five hundred Union troops in the area, all told.

Confederate cavalry began skirmishing south of Richmond on August 29, and soon infantry under Brig. Gen. Patrick Cleburne advanced to within a few miles of the town, where it encountered Manson's brigade. The fighting died down at the end of the day, with Manson occupying a defensive position in the village of Rogersville.

The next day the Confederates, led by Cleburne, delivered a series of attacks that pushed Manson and then the combined forces of Cruft and Manson back through a succession of defensive lines. The raw Union recruits were no match for the Confederate veterans, and they were badly outnumbered. Nelson tried to rally the Federals with fresh support from Lexington, but by the end of the battle General Manson had been captured, Nelson was wounded, and the Federals were in full flight toward Louisville. The way was open for Kirby Smith's army to advance all the way to the Ohio River.

The Federals lost 206 killed and 844 wounded, with 4,303 missing. The Confederates lost 78 killed and 372 wounded.

Further Reading

D. Warren Lambert. *When the Ripe Pears Fell: The Battle of Richmond, Kentucky* (Richmond, Ky.: Madison County Historical Society, 1997).

≈ Ridgeway

Canada (June 2, 1866) *Fenian Raid*

In 1866, William Roberts organized a group of Irish-American Fenians, including thousands of American Civil War veterans, to invade Canada in order to weaken British rule in North America and thereby bolster the campaign for Irish independence. Lt. Col. John O'Neill led eight hundred Fenians into Canada from Buffalo, New York, on May 31 and established a camp at Fort Erie. When O'Neill learned that the American gunboat U.S.S. *Michigan* had cut off his access to reinforcements by Lake Erie, he marched south and attacked an approaching column of Canadian militia at Ridgeway.

Canadian militia colonel Alfred Booker arrived in Ridgeway with his column of nine hundred men by train on the evening of June 1, expecting to join Lt. Col. George Peacocke's detachment from Hamilton, Ontario, before marching north to meet the Fenians. Booker was unaware that Peacocke had not yet arrived and that O'Neill's men had taken up a fortified position at Limestone Ridge, just north of the train station, waiting to attack.

A confused battle ensued on the morning of June 2, in which the militia drove Fenian advance parties back toward their camp. After about an hour the Fenians ran low on ammunition, and O'Neill contemplated retreat. At this point, the Canadian militia troops mistook mounted Fenian scouts for cavalry and convinced their commander that a mounted attack was about to begin. As Booker tried to form his men into an open-square formation to counter it, confusion reigned, and the militia made easy targets for the Fenian's superior-quality repeating rifles—many Canadians simply fled. The remainder of the Canadian militia troops were driven from the field by a Fenian bayonet charge.

Booker's Canadians lost ten killed and thirty-eight wounded at Ridgeway. The Fenians probably lost somewhat fewer, though no certain figures exist. Most of O'Neill's men escaped back into the United States, but they were apprehended by American forces led by Gen. Ulysses S. Grant and Maj. Gen. George G. Meade, who had been sent to keep peace on the Canadian border.

Sporadic Fenian raids continued throughout 1866, though hopes for American support of the movement were quashed when Pres. Andrew Johnson issued an official denouncement. When a large uprising in Ireland failed in 1867, the American Fenian movement fractured.

Further Reading

George T. Denison. *History of the Fenian Raid on Fort Erie; with an Account of the Battle of Ridgeway* (Toronto: Rollo & Adam, 1866).

≈ River Raisin

See FRENCHTOWN

≈ Roanoke Island

North Carolina (February 8, 1862)
American Civil War

In January 1862, Brig. Gen. Ambrose Burnside began a Union expedition against North Carolina. The capture of Roanoke Island would allow him access to his main target, the railroad junction at Goldsboro.

Roanoke Island, off the coast of North Carolina between Pimlico and Albemarle Sounds, provided well-fortified coastal defense, but the sand forts and batteries on its north end were severely undermanned. Former Virginia governor Brig. Gen. Henry Wise was ill and bedridden, and his command over the Confederate troops on the island proved ineffective.

Burnside arrived with fifteen thousand soldiers and landed on the south end of Roanoke Island on February 7, protected by the heavy guns of Capt. Louis M. Goldsborough's naval squadron, which more than outmatched the small Confederate "mosquito fleet" of gunboats that harassed it. On February 8, Brig. Gens. Jesse Reno, John G. Foster, and John G. Parke led Burnside's three brigades, respectively, toward the Confederate line of defense on the island's north side.

Wise wrongly assumed that his line was protected by the wetlands on either side. In fact, Reno's forces plunged through the wetlands to flank his position, while Foster's soldiers pounded the center of the Confederate line. The Confederates were unable to hold for long, and they retreated to a narrow strip of land at the far north of Roanoke Island.

Wise had to concede defeat, and Burnside's force took twenty-five hundred Confederate prisoners.

The capture of Roanoke Island left the North Carolina coastline open to Federal attack and proved a good beginning to Burnside's expedition against the rebel state.

Further Reading

John Davis, "Up the Beach and into Battle." *Civil War Times Illustrated* 25, no. 6 (1986): 32–34, 43; and Ivan Musicant, "Hot Pursuit Up the Sound." *Proceedings* 122, no. 19 (1996): 68–72.

Rocky Mount

South Carolina (August 1, 1780)
American Revolution

American patriots and Loyalists fought a series of battles in South Carolina in the weeks between the British capture of CHARLESTON and the Battle of CAMDEN. In most cases, few if any British troops or officers were involved, and the clashes usually had something in the nature of civil war about them. The battle at Rocky Mount, in which the patriots under Col. Thomas Sumter tried to seize a Loyalist strong point, was one such engagement.

The British had set up a string of outposts to protect the approaches to Camden, including Rocky Mount, which comprised three fortified log cabins, protected by a ditch and a log-filled abatis. The post was garrisoned by Lt. Col. George Turnbull with a 150 New York Loyalists and a few South Carolina Loyalist volunteers.

Sumter, deciding the post was vulnerable, led an attack by about six hundred of his South Carolina patriot militia, sending at the same time another unit to attack HANGING ROCK. Unfortunately for Sumter, he had no artillery and no feasible means of broaching the Loyalists defenses, other than a headlong assault. Sumter sent a suicide squad (called a "forlorn hope") led by Lt. Col. Thomas Neal across the ditch and abatis, but it was cut down. Sumter then attempted to set the log cabin afire by rolling a fire wagon against the walls, but this failed also when a sudden rainstorm quenched the flames.

Frustrated, Sumter had no choice but to withdraw and leave the Loyalists in peace. Each side may have lost twelve or so casualties, but the reports are sketchy.

Further Reading

John Buchanan. *The Road to Guilford Courthouse: The American Revolution in the Carolinas* (New York: John Wiley & Sons, 1997); and John S. Pancake. *This Destructive War: The British Campaign in the Carolinas* (University, Ala.: University of Alabama Press, 1985).

Rosebud Creek

Wyoming (June 17, 1876) *Black Hills War*

After gold was discovered in the Black Hills of South Dakota, the federal government became more anxious than ever to drive the Dakota, Lakota, and Nakota (often collectively referred to as the Sioux) out of the heart of their tribal homeland in order to allow white settlers and miners in. The Sioux—especially the western division, called Teton or Lakota—were the largest and most powerful tribe on the northern plains, and significant numbers had resisted white attempts to subdue their nomadic life. In the summer of 1876, the U.S. Army launched a major offensive against the Teton Lakota, only to meet disappointment and defeat at the hands of the great Lakota war leader Crazy Horse (Tahunka Witco).

In May, Brig. Gen. George Crook led one wing of a three-part campaign to catch the Lakota in a pincer movement. He had thirteen hundred men, including cavalry and infantry, plus several hundred Crow and Shoshone allies (traditional enemies of the Lakota). His column moved slowly along the Bozeman Trail, hoping to flush out a concentration of Indians.

On July 17, Crook's encampment on the Rosebud Creek was taken by surprise by a large force of Lakota led by Crazy Horse of the Brulé and Oglala bands of Teton Lakota and Gall (Pizi), a war leader of the Hunkpapa band of Teton Lakota. The Lakota made a highly organized and disciplined attack on the army camp and managed to break up Crook's defense into several small sections, but the firepower of the soldiers was too great to allow the Lakota to overrun any significant defensive position. The Lakota withdrew after several hours of combat.

Crook lost about ten killed and twenty-three wounded in the battle, and he retreated to his base camp, effectively withdrawing his forces from the campaign. Crazy Horse and the majority of the Lakota moved on to join Sitting Bull on the LITTLE BIGHORN, where they were soon attacked by Lt. Col. George A. Custer and the Seventh Cavalry.

Further Reading

John Finerty. *War-Path and Bivouac or the Conquest of the Sioux* (Norman: University of Oklahoma Press, 1961); and Neil C. Mangum. *The Battle of the Rosebud: Prelude to the Little Bighorn* (El Segundo, Calif.: Upton and Sons, 1987).

❧ Rush Springs

(Rush Creek)

Oklahoma (October 1, 1858) *Indian Wars*

Hoping to strike a blow against the decades-long problem of raids by Comanche bands in the Texas region, U.S. Army major Earl Van Dorn, a veteran of the Mexican-American War, took command of a force of 350 dragoons and about 135 Indian allies and set out on what was called the "Wichita" expedition, crossing the Red River from Texas into what is now Oklahoma in the fall of 1858.

On October 1, Van Dorn launched a dawn attack on the village of Buffalo Hump (Pochanaw-quoip), a Comanche leader of long standing who had a record of raids and depredations. The mounted dragoons charged the village at first light and caught the Comanche by surprise. The fighting was vicious and hand to hand, the warriors grabbing whatever weapons came to hand and attempting to defend their women and children. The melee lasted an hour and a half before the Comanche broke and scattered, leaving fifty-six dead warriors behind. Van Dorn had several men killed or wounded, and he himself suffered two severe arrow wounds.

Further Reading

Robert M. Utley and Wilcomb E. Washburn. *The American Heritage History of the Indian Wars* (New York: Barnes & Noble, 1977).

$\mathcal{S}$

≈ Sabine Crossroads

(Mansfield)

Louisiana (April 8, 1864) *American Civil War*

In the spring of 1864, as the war was approaching its climactic phases in Georgia and Tennessee, the Union launched an ill-considered and ill-fated campaign to capture the headquarters of the Confederate Trans-Mississippi Department, in Shreveport, Louisiana. The major objects of the campaign were to seize the valuable hoard of baled cotton that the Confederacy had stored in Louisiana and to intimidate the French, who had invaded Mexico and captured Mexico City.

Maj. Gen. Nathaniel P. Banks, an incompetent politician turned officer, was given command of nearly thirty thousand men, supported by a squadron of river gunboats under Rear Adm. David D. Porter. After taking Alexandria, Louisiana, Banks continued with twenty thousand of his troops along the Red River toward Shreveport.

In the vicinity of Sabine Crossroads he was brought up short by Confederate major general Richard Taylor (son of former U.S. president Zachary Taylor) and a badly outnumbered Confederate army.

Taylor had no more than eighty-eight hundred troops under his command in his defensive position at the crossroads, but fortunately for the Confederates, the Federals were unable to bring more than a small fraction of their numbers into the fighting. At best, only between five and six thousand Union troops were engaged. Brig. Gen. Jean Jacques Mouton commanded the infantry on the Confederate left, Brig. Gen. John G. Walker the right. Brig. Gen. Thomas Green was in charge of the Southern cavalry.

The first Union soldiers appeared at about noon on April 8. Misreading the strength of the Confederate lines, they pushed to within close range, whereupon the Confederates withered the Union advance with musketry, forcing the Federals to retreat to a line of defense. Local command—Banks and the other high-ranking officers were far to the rear—fell first to cavalryman Brig. Gen. Albert L. Lee and then to Brig. Gen. Thomas E. G. Ransom, who positioned his infantry and cavalry to receive the expected Confederate attack.

At 4:00 P.M., Mouton's Confederates charged across the open fields toward the Federal lines, taking heavy casualties, but they pushed the Union defenders out of their line and into retreat. Federal brigadier general Robert A. Cameron rallied about thirteen hundred men to form a new defensive line, but a renewed Confederate attack swept it away after about an hour of fighting. Brig. Gen. William H. Emory then formed a third Federal line, which the Confederates attacked late in the day but could not dislodge before nightfall.

The Union losses were 113 killed, 581 wounded, and 1,541 missing, in addition to the loss of twenty cannon and the entire cavalry-supply wagon train. The Confederates lost about one thousand killed and wounded.

During the night, the Union troops withdrew from the field to new positions at nearby PLEASANT HILL.

Further Reading

Ludwell H. Johnson. *The Red River Campaign: Politics and Cotton in the Civil War* (Kent, Ohio: Kent State University Press, 1993); and Alonzo H. Plummer. *Confederate Victory at Mansfield. . .* (Mansfield, La.: United Daughters of the Confederacy, 1969).

✐ Sabine Pass

(Fort Griffin)

Texas (September 8, 1863) *American Civil War*

The important pass at the mouth of the Sabine River had been a point of contention in September 1862, when Union forces landing from gunboats briefly captured Sabine City, but the major battle—a heroic exploit by a handful of Confederate defenders—took place at Fort Griffin a year later.

The Federals, deciding to retake the pass, assembled a formidable expedition of five thousand infantry under Maj. Gen. William B. Franklin, twenty transport ships, and four gunboats under the command of Lt. Frederick Crocker. The Federal boats entered the pass and moved upriver toward Fort Griffin on the morning of September 8.

The Confederate command in the region considered the fort indefensible and had ordered it to be abandoned. However, Lt. Richard Dowling stayed behind with forty-six civilian Irish dockworkers. Dowling refused to give up

the fort to the Federals and organized the dockworkers into a defense force. After waiting out a barrage by the Union gunboats, Dowling bombarded the Federal flotilla as soon as it came in range of the fort's powerful guns. He crippled two of the Federal gunboats, including Crocker's ship, and when a Confederate ship appeared, the damaged Union vessels surrendered to Dowling. General Franklin, intimidated by the loss of half of his naval escort, ordered the transports to turn back, leaving Dowling and his dockworkers to celebrate: they had not had a man killed or wounded but had inflicted a hundred casualties on the enemy and captured 350 more.

The victory was cause for rejoicing throughout the Confederacy, and Dowling and his men were recognized as heroes by the Confederate Congress.

Further Reading

Donald S. Frazier. *Cottonclads! The Battle of Galveston and the Defense of the Texas Coast* (Abilene, Tex.: McWhiney Foundation Press, McMurray University, 1998); Phillip R. Rutherford, "Six Guns against the Fleet." *Civil War Times Illustrated* 29, no. 5 (1990): 28–30, 32–34, 36, 38, 40–42, 44–45, 48–49; and Frank X. Tolbert. *Dick Dowling at Sabine Pass* (New York: McGraw-Hill, 1962).

✐ Sackets Harbor

New York (May 28–29, 1813) *War of 1812*

While Commodore Isaac Chauncey was occupied with the American capture of FORT GEORGE, the governor-general and British commander in chief of Canada, Sir George Prevost, decided to attack Chauncey's base at the Sackets Harbor shipyard.

Prevost assembled for the attack a force of approximately 800 regular soldiers, under the direct command of Col. Edward Baynes, and 450 Royal Navy officers and seamen commanded by Sir James Lucas Yeo. On the night of May 27, the combined force set off aboard Yeo's fleet, which included the *Wolfe, Moira, Prince George, Sir Sidney Smith,* and *Prince Regent.* Colonel Baynes planned to land his troops at the western cove of Horse Island, a small piece of land connected to the shipyard by a three-hundred-yard causeway, and then to cross for an attack on the American base.

From the beginning, the British faced obstacles. Unfavorable winds kept the landing party, including Prevost himself in a canoe, away from Horse Island for almost twenty-four hours, until the evening of May 28. In the meantime, the Americans at the shipyard prepared for attack. American general Henry Dearborn had left militia major general Jacob Brown in command of the shipyard, and Brown roused five hundred militiamen to supplement the four hundred regulars under Lt. Col. Electus Backus who occupied the two fortifications protecting Sackets Harbor.

When they were finally able to reach the intended landing beach on Horse Island, the British faced American defenses that included a fieldpiece in the forest and heavy cannon at the fortifications, so they disembarked instead at the north end of the island. Colonel Baynes organized his troops into lines and prepared to fight his way over the causeway, the only way off the island.

Baynes first faced opposition on the island. One company of American volunteers formed up on the right, and exposed militia forces in the front to a slowly advancing line of British bayonets. After firing just one round, most of the militia fled as the British pushed toward the western side of the island. The second line, regular troops that Major General Brown had placed behind the militia, held its ground, supported by steady fire from the volunteers on its right.

Backus's regulars held a blockhouse on the island, where they were aided by skillful fire from the American artillery. Winds prevented Yeo's ships from providing any covering fire for the British advance. The American fire became so dangerous that the captain of the *Prince Regent* had his schooner rowed into range of Fort Tomkins, the harbor's western fortification, to knock the artillerymen away from its guns. Lt. Woolcott Chauncey, the younger brother of Commodore Chauncey, had been told to prevent the capture by the British of American ships and stores in the harbor. Thinking (erroneously) that Fort Tomkins had surrendered and British victory was imminent, he set the naval warehouses afire.

While Prevost reorganized and resupplied his exhausted troops, Brown rallied many of the militiamen who had initially fled and advanced on the right in an attempt to isolate the British. The final British push toward the causeway ended when it came under heavy American fire, and Baynes had to fall back. Prevost decided he could not reach the forts and withdrew his troops to their boats.

Prevost lost 48 men killed and 211 wounded or missing, while among the British seamen only 1 was killed and 4 wounded. Twenty-three Americans were killed, 111 wounded, and 100 taken prisoner. Far more costly for the American side was the five hundred thousand dollars' worth of naval stores burned. Luckily for the younger Chauncey, the biggest ship under construction at Sackets Harbor, the *General Pike,* was only lightly damaged, and repairs were under way by the time his brother, the commodore, returned from Fort George.

Prevost's reputation was damaged by the loss, and his political enemies savaged him for not pursuing the attack more strenuously. Yeo went on to harass American forces up the lake, and his glimpse of the *General Pike* during the battle left him better prepared for future encounters and with a clear idea of the importance of shipbuilding for the Niagara campaign.

Further Reading

Richard A. Preston, "The First Battle of Sacket's Harbor." *Historic Kingston* 2 (1963): 3–7; and Patrick A. Wilder. *The Battle of Sacket's Harbour and the Struggle for Lake Ontario* (Baltimore: Nautical and Aviation, 1994).

Sacramento River

Mexico (February 28, 1847) *Mexican-American War*

Col. Alexander W. Doniphan was leading an American force from Santa Fe, New Mexico, to put down Indian revolts and to rendezvous with Brig. Gen. John E. Wool in Chihuahua, Mexico, when he met Mexicans under Brig. Gen. José A. Heredia at the Sacramento River, north of Chihuahua. Doniphan, commanding two regiments of mounted Missouri men who had volunteered in 1846 for Brig. Gen. Stephen W. Kearny's cross-country march to capture New Mexico and California, did not know that Wool was occupied elsewhere in the aftermath of the battle of BUENA VISTA, and he now became embroiled in his own pitched battle with the Mexicans.

Heredia and Angel Trías, the provincial governor of Chihuahua, had prepared the city for attack by heavily fortifying a position eighteen miles to the north on the Sacramento River. When Doniphan arrived on February 28 with his thousand men, he faced two to five thousand Mexican soldiers and volunteers, who covered every approach to the city along the El Paso road.

Doniphan carried off a tricky maneuver to bring his troops and four hundred wagons into position facing the Mexican fortifications. He marched his men in columns between four lines of wagons to the left of Mexican artillery positions and over a steep, fifty-foot hill until he met Heredia's force on a flat plain between the river and a dry stream bed called Arroyo Seco.

Heredia held off his attack until the Americans reached their final position, thus failing to take advantage of their difficulties with the terrain and misjudging the direction of their advance. Heredia finally ordered Brig. Gen. Pedro Garcia Condé's cavalry to attack, but they were driven back by Maj. Meriwether Clark Lewis's artillery fire.

After an hour of cannon exchanges, Capt. Richard H. Weightman and Maj. Samuel Owens led a disorganized attack against the southernmost Mexican earthworks, while the main American line advanced slowly within fifty yards of the Mexican fortifications. Trías, now in command, sent Condé's lancers against the southern attack, but they were again driven back by heavy fire. Meanwhile, Missouri volunteers took the upper Mexican redoubt after a hand-to-hand fight. Lewis's artillery stopped a final Mexican assault against the American wagons on the open plain.

Though the main action had ended, the Mexicans did not give up until after Captain Weightman's howitzers had blasted the last defenders out of the hills around the river. By nightfall, all that remained was an American victory celebration.

The only American killed was Major Owens, and only eight Americans were wounded. Doniphan estimated Mexican casualties at three hundred killed, three hundred wounded, and around forty captured.

Trías abandoned the city of Chihuahua to Doniphan, who took over the city of fourteen thousand unsympathetic residents to the sound of a band playing "Yankee Doodle" on March 2. As the Mexicans tried to regroup their resistance in the state of Chihuahua, Doniphan paused to resupply his men before being called farther south in April.

Further Reading

Kimball Clark, "The Epic March of Doniphan's Missourians." *Missouri Historical Review* 80, no. 2 (1986): 134–155.

➳ Sailor's Creek

See SAYLOR'S CREEK

➳ St. Augustine

Florida (November 8–December 29, 1702)
Queen Anne's War

The attempt in 1702 by a British expedition to take St. Augustine, the chief Spanish city on the eastern American coast, was part of a worldwide struggle known in Europe as the War of the Spanish Succession and in North America as Queen Anne's War.

The competition for colonies between Great Britain, France, and Spain heated up as an offshoot of a dispute over who should take over the Spanish throne. Britain wanted to keep the Bourbon dynasty, which controlled France, from extending its grasp to Spain. The rivalry was soon translated to the coast of America, where St. Augustine had been the major stronghold since its founding in 1565 by Pedro Menéndez de Avilés and his crushing defeat of the French at FORT CAROLINE. His successors had built a powerful fortress, the Castillo de San Marcos, which commanded the harbor and the town and seemed impregnable.

The closest British colony on the mainland was Carolina (still a single entity), founded in 1670 by British planters from Barbados on land that Spain claimed as its own. When war over the Spanish throne broke out in Europe in the fall of 1702, the colonial government of Carolina prepared an attack on St. Augustine, hoping to seize the city and wrest control of the seaways off Florida from Spain. Gov. James Moore led a force of between eight and twelve hundred men, including many Indian allies, onto ships and sailed southward.

St. Augustine was governed by Gov. Joseph de Zúñiga y Cerda, who commanded a small, inexperienced, and poorly equipped force of infantry. He ordered all the residents of the city and its outlying villages into the fort and prepared for a siege, herding cattle into the moat to assure a food supply.

On November 8, Governor Moore sailed into the harbor and took the town itself. He was joined by more troops under Col. Robert Daniels, who arrived two days later after marching overland. Moore laid siege to the fortress, but his men were held at some distance, since the Spanish had burned all the buildings for 750 yards around the fortress walls thus exposing attackers to gunfire from the fort. The Carolinians had only nine-pounder and twelve-pounder cannon, which made no impression at all on the thick shellstone walls of the Castillo. When heavier guns were brought from Jamaica, the bombardment fared little better. When the guns of the fortress returned fire, the Spanish artillery proved to be more effective.

On December 27, a squadron of four Spanish ships appeared but refused to engage the British ships in the harbor. The mere presence of the Spanish fleet, however, reinforced the futility of the British position, and two days later, the British abandoned the siege and withdrew, after setting the remaining buildings of the city on fire.

Spain retained its hold on the southeastern coast, but the raid by the Carolinians damaged the Spanish system of outlying missions.

Further Reading

Charles W. Arnade. *The Siege of St. Augustine in 1702* (Gainesville: University of Florida Presses, 1959); and Verner W. Crane. *The Southern Frontier, 1670–1732*. Reprint ed. (New York: W. W. Norton, 1981).

St. Augustine

Florida (May 31–July 20, 1740)
War of Jenkin's Ear

The second British attempt to take the Spanish capital of colonial Florida came in 1740, as part of an armed struggle between Spain and Great Britain over commerce, known as the War of Jenkin's Ear (for a British sea captain whose ear had been severed by a Spaniard). Britain wanted access to Spanish markets, especially in the New World, and Spain wanted to maintain economic control over her colonial possessions. On the southeastern coast of North America, the struggle focused on St. Augustine, which had been founded in 1565 to defend the sea route of the Spanish treasure fleets. The Spanish had subsequently constructed a strong fortress, the Castillo de San Marcos, which had withstood a colonial British siege in 1702 (*see also* ST. AUGUSTINE, 1702).

The new threat to St. Augustine came from the recently established British colony of Georgia, which had been founded specifically as a military buffer between the Spanish territories in Florida and the British colony of Carolina. The Spanish claimed the region in which British settlers and soldiers set up the new colony in 1732, but the British colonial governor, James Oglethorpe, who carried military as well as civilian rank, was expected to extend British influence and territory if he could. The outbreak of the war prompted him to attack St. Augustine. He established a post on the St. Johns River, captured a Spanish outpost at Fort Pupo, and recruited troops from Carolina to join his expedition. Supported by a small British fleet under Commodore Vincent Pease, Oglethorpe marched in early May on St. Augustine.

The Spanish governor, Manuel de Montiano, had been working hard to prepare for the inevitable attack from the

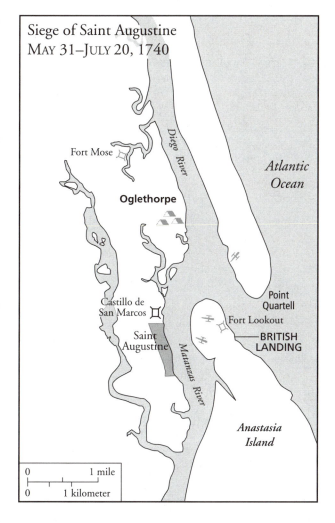

Siege of Saint Augustine
MAY 31–JULY 20, 1740

north, bringing in supplies and reinforcements from Cuba and putting the fortress into good order. Oglethorpe's slow movement southward aided the Spanish, who might have been easily overwhelmed earlier in the year. As it was, Oglethorpe did not get into position and begin his bombardment of the Castillo, into which all the Spanish troops and civilians of the city had retreated, until the last day of May. Since Commodore Pease made it clear he could not stay in hurricane waters past early July, time pressed for Oglethorpe. He failed, however, to cut off Spanish communications with the hinterland, so his siege was ineffective, and his light artillery had almost no effect on the thick fortress walls.

Montiano then took the initiative and sent a force of three hundred troops, made up of Spanish soldiers, black volunteers, and Indian allies, to attack the 135 British who had been left to garrison the nearby free black town of Fort Mose. On the night of June 15, the Spanish retook the post, further weakening Oglethorpe's position.

On July 20, Oglethorpe called off the siege and began a retreat back to Georgia. A year and a half later, he had to defend his own colony against a Spanish assault (*see* BLOODY SWAMP).

Further Reading

Ricardo Torres-Reyes. *The British Siege of St. Augustine in 1740* (Denver, Colo.: National Park Service, 1973).

⌘ St. Charles

Canada (November 25, 1837) *Papineau's Rebellion*

On November 23, 1837, Lt. Col. Francis Gore's detachment of the British army in Canada was defeated at ST. DENIS by a group of French-Canadian separatists loyal to rebel *Patriote* party leader Louis-Joseph Papineau. The British royal governor, Lord Gosford, was determined to prevent Papineau and his *Patriote* allies from declaring independence for the French-dominated province of Lower Canada. Another British officer, a Colonel Wetherell, led a second detachment of army forces to oust *Patriote* rebels in St. Charles who had captured the estate of wealthy landlord Pierre Debartzch. Wetherell marched into St. Charles on November 25 and delivered a blow to the rebel movement.

The *Patriote* rebels in St. Charles, led by Thomas Storrow Brown, had constructed fortifications at the Debartzch manor house to protect their hastily assembled irregular military force. As Wetherell's troops marched from Montreal to St. Charles, they were shot at by villagers friendly to the separatist movement. They anticipated strenuous resistance when they reached the rebel camp on November 25. Wetherell formed his men into lines across town from the manor house and ordered a frontal attack. Despite *Patriote* support in the countryside, there were only between sixty and eighty men inside the manor, and they soon gave way in the face of an onslaught of regular soldiers. The makeshift barricades and the manor house had to be deserted. No precise casualty figures exist, but several deaths occurred on both sides.

The army's victory at St. Charles effectively ended Papineau's resistance movement, though it took one more skirmish at ST. EUSTACHE on November 28 to crush his militant sympathizers completely.

Further Reading

The Canadian Encyclopedia. 2d ed. (Edmonton, Alberta: Hurtig, 1988).

⌘ St. Clair's Defeat

Indiana (November 4, 1791) *Little Turtle's War*

Following the disaster of HARMAR'S DEFEAT in 1790 at the hands of the Indian tribes of Ohio and Indiana, the U.S. government placed a new military commander on the frontier and ordered a renewed offensive. The result was even worse than the previous failure.

Pres. George Washington, himself no stranger to defeat on the frontier (*see also* FORT NECESSITY), blamed the earlier Indian victory on Brig. Gen. Josiah Harmar's tactical mistakes and the poor fighting qualities of the untrained and undisciplined militia that had made up the bulk of Harmar's forces. While this assessment had much truth to it, Washington and other officials, such as Sec. of War Henry Knox, underestimated the power and abilities of the victorious tribes, who were led in war by the estimable Little Turtle (Michikinikwa), an extremely talented soldier who fully exploited inherent American weaknesses and maximized Indian strengths.

Washington used Harmar's shame to win from a reluctant Congress, many members of which had a morbid fear of a standing army, the authority to appoint a new major general in the West and to expand the army with a second regiment of regulars. He also won approval to recruit two thousand "levies," who would be short-term enlistees—presumably a cut above state militia in quality but not a long-term threat to civilian control.

Arthur St. Clair, governor of the Northwest Territory and a veteran of the American Revolution, was Washington's choice for command. St. Clair was ordered to recruit new troops, train them, and march from Fort Washington (modern-day Cincinnati) to the head of the Maumee River at Kekionga (known as Miami Town to non-Indians), where Harmar had met disaster, building several forts along the way. By establishing a string of strong bases and then defeating the Indians, St. Clair hoped to take control of the region, thereby thwarting not only the allied tribes but also the British, who had remained in their trading posts around the Great Lakes and were rousing their former Indian allies against the upstart Americans.

St. Clair was only partially successful in raising a suitable army. Plagued by a painful illness, he discovered that many of the former regulars on the frontier had left the service at the end of their enlistments, and it was hard to replace them. Moreover, the hoped-for levies were also few in number, and those who did sign up were of poor quality. Adding to his difficulties was the near collapse of the army's logistical system, resulting in a shortage of food, equipment, and other supplies. Despite these problems, St. Clair set out in October with a force of twenty-three hundred soldiers—a few hundred regulars and more than fifteen hundred levies, the latter commanded by Maj. Gen. Richard Butler—and four hundred noncombatants, women and children. The column moved excruciatingly slowly through the dense forest, stopping each night to build hasty fortifications. The weather was terrible, and soon the expedition was miserable, with many of the levies threatening to desert.

After building a new post, called Fort Jefferson, St. Clair decided on October 24 to march on Kekionga. His column had advanced only a few miles when it bogged down, and the levies began to steal away. When St. Clair sent a detachment under a regular, Maj. John Hamtramck, after the deserters, the army was down to no more than fifteen hundred men fit for duty, the rest having run away, died, or taken sick. The column set out again, and on November 3—exhausted, miserable, and near starving—the army reached the Wabash River, where the men huddled around campfires, neglecting to erect breastworks or send out scouts.

Little Turtle was only a few miles away, with one thousand warriors from the Miami, Shawnee, Delaware (Lenni Lenape), Wyandot (Huron), Ottawa, Chippewa, Mingo, and Potawatomi tribes, and even a few Cherokee and members of the Iroquois Confederacy. The Indians, well fed and well equipped by the British, had been shadowing the American force for days. During the night they moved into position to encircle the American camp, and at first light they attacked, taking the sleepy soldiers completely by surprise.

The effect on the Americans was catastrophic. There was almost no organized resistance, as officers screamed in vain at the men to assemble in units. The terrified women and children added to the chaos. The Indians poured musket fire into the confused mass, and Americans began to die by the hundreds. St. Clair himself tried bravely to rally his men, but it was hopeless. Little Turtle's warriors met almost no resistance and took very few casualties, picking off the Americans almost at will. Lt. Col. William Darke organized a bayonet attack, but the Indians easily slipped aside and moved in behind it to kill the women and children exposed by the American sortie.

Hoping to escape total annihilation, St. Clair ordered a retreat, and those who were able abandoned the field, leaving the wounded behind to torture and death. As they streamed away from the killing field, members of Lieutenant Colonel Darke's command and a few regulars came on dozens of men who, scalped but alive, were wandering bleeding through the woods. Eventually, the remnants of the American army reached the safety of Fort Jefferson, while the Indian army staged a mass celebration at the site of the battle.

The Indians had killed around 650 American soldiers in addition to virtually all the four hundred women and children, while losing only a handful themselves, around twenty-one dead and forty wounded.

St. Clair's defeat on the Wabash was one of the worst ever suffered by an American army, and it was by far the most severe loss by an organized American force to Indian warriors, dwarfing the more famous LITTLE BIGHORN. For the second time in as many years, Little Turtle had thwarted the will and crushed the armed forces of the United States.

Further Reading

Harvey Carter. *The Life and Times of Little Turtle: First Sagamore of the Wabash Indians* (Urbana: University of Illinois Press, 1987); Douglas R. Hurt. *The Ohio Frontier: Crucible of the Old Northwest* (Bloomington: Indiana University Press, 1996); Dave R. Palmer. *1794: America, Its Army, and the Birth of a Nation* (Novato, Calif.: Presidio Press, 1994); and Wiley Sword. *President Washington's Indian War: The Struggle for the Old Northwest, 1790–1795* (Norman: University of Oklahoma Press, 1985).

St. Denis

Canada (November 23, 1837) *Papineau's Rebellion*

In the 1830s, a group of French-speaking inhabitants of Lower Canada rallied around Louis-Joseph Papineau, leader of the *Patriote* party in the region's assembly, in opposition to British rule. In 1837, the conflict between the French-controlled assembly and the British Colonial Office and the royal governor, Lord Gosford, came to a head when the assembly cut off all payments to British public servants, boycotted British goods, and threatened to declare independence. In November, when British officials sent an army detachment to arrest rebel *Patriote* leaders, several military clashes resulted.

Thomas Storrow Brown led *Patriote* rebels who seized the manor of landlord Pierre Debartzch in ST. CHARLES, while Dr. Wolfred Nelson organized another group at his distillery in the town of St. Denis. British lieutenant colonel Francis Gore led from Montreal one of two army detachments assigned to capture the rebels. On their way to St. Charles, Gore's troops marched north through St. Denis on November 23, and Nelson's men were waiting.

Nelson's rebels had entrenched themselves in the distillery and the walled estate of St. Germaine. Gore tried to blast them out with artillery fire, but the rebels held out, picking off Gore's men. By 3:00 P.M., fresh *Patriotes* were arriving from neighboring towns, and Nelson, afraid he would be unable to escape along his route to St. Charles, sounded a retreat.

Precise casualty figures for the battle at St. Denis are unknown, but some rebel leaders were eventually executed, and others deported to Australia in 1838 for the part they played.

The *Patriotes'* victory at St. Denis was short-lived; the British army crushed their rebellion swiftly in battles at St. Charles and ST. EUSTACHE. Another *Patriote* rebellion broke out one year later, but it was easily quashed, leaving a legacy of British-French conflict in Canada that survived even the nation's independence from Great Britain.

Further Reading

The Canadian Encyclopedia. 2d ed. (Edmonton, Alberta: Hurtig, 1988).

✍ St. Eustache

Canada (December 14, 1837) *Papineau's Rebellion*

After the British army in Canada defeated French-Canadian rebels supporting *Patriote* separatist Louis-Joseph Papineau in November 1837 (*see also* ST. DENIS and ST. CHARLES), it marched back toward Montreal and prepared to attack the only remaining rebel camps, in the villages of St. Eustache and St. Benoît. Though the French-Canadian separatist movement had little military strength left by December, Sir John Colbourne, commander of the British army in North America, was anxious to send a decisive message that no further political unrest would be tolerated by the British royal government. Colbourne personally led the army in an attack on the northern villages that sealed the fate of Papineau's rebel movement.

On December 14, Colbourne arrived in St. Eustache with twelve hundred regular soldiers, two hundred British volunteers from the village itself, and an artillery unit with twelve cannon. The military commitment of the rebels' rural allies had wavered since the defeat at St. Charles, and their local leader, William Henry Scott, argued that the *Patriote* rebels should surrender. Instead, Jean-Olivier

Chénier rallied the beleaguered troops to fortify their camp at a church in the village and to resist one more time. Colbourne's men attacked and easily ejected the rebels from the church, convent, and surrounding houses. They continued to St. Benoît the next day and burned the village to the ground.

No precise casualty figures are known, but nearly one hundred *Patriotes* were killed, including Chénier, and even more were taken prisoner.

Though Papineau's calls for independence for Lower Canada resurfaced in 1838, this time supported by American agitators, the *Patriote* movement was never again able to offer concerted military resistance to the British army.

Further Reading

The Canadian Encyclopedia. 2d ed. (Edmonton, Alberta: Hurtig, 1988).

✍ St. Jean's

See ST. JOHN'S

✍ St. John's

(St. Jean's)
Canada (May 17, 1775) *American Revolution*

After the capture of British-held FORT TICONDEROGA by a small American force from Connecticut and the Hampshire Grants (modern-day Vermont), the next logical step was to attack more British positions on the strategically important waterways leading toward Canada.

Benedict Arnold, a Connecticut merchant who had been commissioned as a colonel by the revolutionary Massachusetts Committee of Safety, had helped seize Ticonderoga on May 10, but he had been without troops of his own and had taken a back seat to Ethan Allen, leader of the Green Mountain Boys. However, when Arnold's own men arrived a week later with a small schooner, he organized an assault against the British post at St. John's.

The surprise attack overwhelmed the small British garrison, and Arnold and his men captured a sixteen-gun lake sloop along with supplies and a number of bateaux (small boats). Arnold commandeered the sloop and sailed back to Ticonderoga, passing Allen and his men on the way. Allen set up an ambush for a British relief column but was forced to withdraw under fire from light artillery.

Further Reading

Gustave Lanctot. *Canada and the American Revolution, 1774–1783* (Cambridge, Mass.: Harvard University Press, 1967).

✥ St. John's

(St. Jean's)

Canada (September 5–November 2, 1775)
American Revolution

In mid-1775, the Second Continental Congress decided that a successful invasion of Canada would win the war with the British, and it gave Maj. Gen. Philip Schuyler, a member of a wealthy and powerful New York family and a veteran of the French and Indian War, command of an army made up mostly of New Englanders. His extremely able second in command was Brig. Gen. Richard Montgomery, an Irishman by birth and a veteran of the British army who had been in the colonies only three years.

The plan was to advance up Lake Champlain, seize Montreal, and then take Quebec. To do so the Americans had to conquer the British at St. John's on the Richelieu River, only a few miles from Montreal. The British commander in chief, Gen. Guy Carleton, had built up the defenses of St. John's over the summer (it had been raided by Benedict Arnold in the spring) and garrisoned the fort with some of his best troops, mostly regulars of the Seventh Regiment (the Royal Fusiliers) and the Twenty-sixth (the Cameronians) under the command of Maj. Charles Preston. Preston was also building an armed gunboat, the *Royal Savage,* an asset that might become crucial in fighting on the waterways.

The Americans advanced toward St. John's, temporarily under Montgomery's command, and seized the Ile aux Noix, an island south of St. John's, as a base from which to attack and lay siege to the main British post. Montgomery had not only a large force, outnumbering the British garrison by more than three to one, but also a relatively powerful fleet of small armed vessels, as well as artillery. Unfortunately, the troops proved to be shaky. When Schuyler returned from a trip to Albany and resumed command on September 5, he ordered an attack, landing several hundred Americans near St. John's. They were ambushed by a very small number of Indians and were completely routed in panic after taking a handful of casualties. Schuyler broke off the attack and withdrew to Ile aux Noix, but on September 10 he sent another force of five hundred New Yorkers commanded by Rudolph

Ritzema and a large unit under Montgomery. The two columns collided by accident in the night, and the attack dissolved in confusion amid rumors of an impending sortie by the *Royal Savage.*

Six days later, Schuyler decided he was too sick to continue in the field and handed command of the Canadian expedition to Montgomery, who, although reinforced and strengthened by supplies captured from the British at CHAMBLY, found his New Englanders factious and constantly near mutiny. Nonetheless, he resolved to attack St. John's again. He positioned his artillery well and began a bombardment of the British, sinking their gunboat and battering their strong embankments. The garrison held out for several weeks, but with the failure of a rescue mission from Montreal and the arrival of more American guns to pound the fort's most vulnerable side, hope faded. Major Preston surrendered on November 2, with only three days' provisions left.

The British regulars were made prisoners of war, including Lt. John André, who was to become the most famous spy of the Revolution five years later, and their Canadian volunteer allies were sent home. Montgomery moved on to take Montreal without resistance, at which point he was free to march on Quebec.

Further Reading

Gustave Lanctot. *Canada and the American Revolution, 1774–1783* (Cambridge, Mass.: Harvard University Press, 1967); Hal T. Shelton. *General Richard Montgomery and the American Revolution: From Redcoat to Rebel* (New York: New York University Press, 1994); and *Papers Relating to the Surrender of Fort St. John and Fort Chambly* (Toronto: Canadiana House, 1971).

✥ St. Simon's Island

See BLOODY SWAMP

✥ San Gabriel

California (January 8, 1847)
Mexican-American War

The fighting during the Mexican-American War spread to the West Coast when Brig. Gen. Stephen W. Kearny led a small force in an invasion of California. Still recovering from wounds received at the battle of SAN PASCUAL, Kearny joined Commodore Robert F. Stockton in an attack against Capt. José María Flores at the San Gabriel River on January 8, 1847. Flores lost the engagement and only slightly delayed the American attack on Los Angeles that was designed to win California for the United States.

Stockton and Kearny could not agree who really commanded their combined force of 557 volunteers, dragoons, sailors, and marines, but it was Stockton who led the Americans toward Flores's Californians at the high Bartolo pass. As the Americans struggled through the fifty-yard defile they were slowed by patches of quicksand, and artillery was not unlimbered, as Kearny had ordered. Flores was able to position 350 men to meet them on the northern side of the San Gabriel, but the Californians' artillery was inaccurate and failed to halt the American advance.

Preceded by a mounted dragoon skirmishing party, Stockton's men forded the river in a square formation that protected their cattle and baggage. The dragoons drove the Californians off the northern riverbank and then returned to reinforce the American right. American artillery fire proved effective when Flores tried to push his right flank forward to halt the river crossing.

When his men and guns were finally across the river, Stockton ordered a charge. Yelling "New Orleans!" in honor of Andrew Jackson's victory on January 8, 1815, during the War of 1812, the Americans easily routed the Californians. Flores tried one more unsuccessful mounted attack on the American rear before withdrawing to Cañada de los Alisos, on the road to Los Angeles.

During the ninety-minute battle, both sides lost approximately two men killed and nine wounded.

Though occasioned by an ill-conceived advance, the battle at San Gabriel had strengthened the Americans' hand in California. They met Flores again the next day at MESA and pushed on toward Los Angeles.

Further Reading

K. Jack Bauer. *The Mexican War, 1846–1848* (New York: Macmillan, 1974).

San Jacinto

Texas (April 21, 1836) *Texas War of Independence*

After several months of small skirmishes and two crushing defeats of volunteer forces, at the ALAMO and GOLIAD, Gen. Sam Houston gathered an army of nine hundred Texans and prepared to attack Gen. Antonio López de Santa Anna's Mexican army. In the face of great odds, the Texans triumphed at San Jacinto, captured Santa Anna, and achieved their ultimate goal of Texas independence.

In April 1836, Santa Anna believed that he had Houston's troops hemmed in on the eastern side of the Brazos River. Santa Anna positioned his six hundred soldiers on a prairie between the San Jacinto River and Buffalo Bayou to await the arrival of his cousin, Martín Perfecto de Cós, with an additional twelve hundred troops. Meanwhile, Houston received a captured copy of Santa Anna's battle plans and, armed with this knowledge, decided to attack just after Cós arrived.

On April 21 Houston formed his infantry into line of battle, protected by artillery batteries and supported by a company of cavalry on the right flank. Moving quietly, Houston's troops managed to get within two hundred yards of the Mexican camp without being seen; their attack came as an almost complete surprise. Santa Anna had apparently failed to post sentries.

The Texans rushed the Mexican camp, shouting "Remember the Alamo!" and intent on revenge for the Texans killed in San Antonio in March. They destroyed the Mexican's hastily constructed breastworks and fired on the Mexican troops at point-blank range, using their cavalry to flush stragglers out of the woods that bordered the Mexican camp. After just eighteen minutes, the Mexicans surrendered.

The overwhelming impact of the Texans' surprise attack at San Jacinto showed in the imbalance of casualties. Houston's forces lost only nine killed and thirty wounded in the battle; Santa Anna's side suffered 630 killed, 208 wounded, and 730 captured. Santa Anna himself, who had tried to elude capture by dressing as a private, was taken prisoner on April 22 and forced to sign a treaty recognizing Texan independence (which the Mexican congress later tried to repudiate). Texas maintained its independence until it was annexed by the United States in 1845, but continued disputes over Texas territory would eventually lead to war between the United States and Mexico in 1846.

Further Reading

Stephen L. Hardin. *Texian Iliad: A Military History of the Texas Revolution* (Austin: University of Texas Press, 1997); Louis W. Kemp and Ed Kilman. *The Battle of San Jacinto and the San Jacinto Campaign* (Houston: n.p., 1947); James W. Pohl. *The Battle of San Jacinto* (Austin: Texas State Historical Association, 1989); and Frank X. Tolbert. *The Day of San Jacinto*. Reprint ed. (Austin: Pemberton Press, 1969).

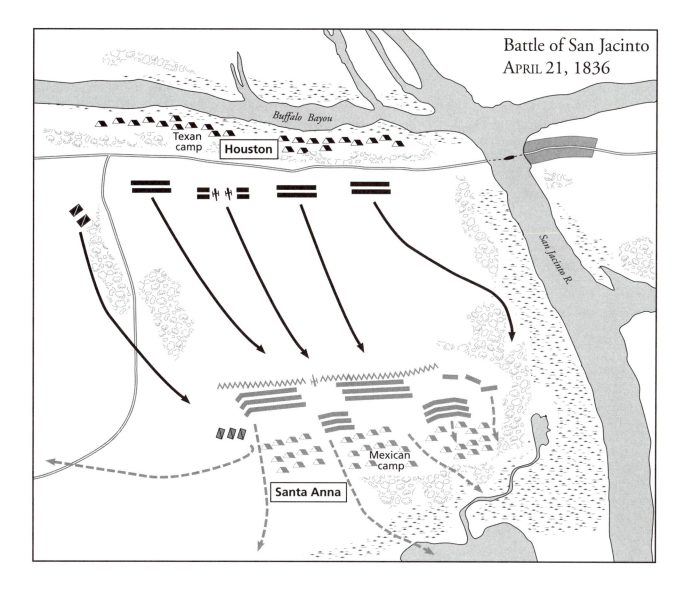

Battle of San Jacinto
APRIL 21, 1836

Buffalo Bayou

Texan camp

Houston

San Jacinto R.

Mexican camp

Santa Anna

San Pascual

California (December 6, 1846)
Mexican-American War

American brigadier general Stephen W. Kearny marched his U.S. Army regiment and a force of Missouri volunteers from Leavenworth, Kansas, across the Santa Fe Trail to California during the fall of 1846, seeking to carry out Pres. James K. Polk's plan to expand the war with Mexico into New Mexico and California. After setting up a provisional government in Santa Fe, Kearny moved into California, unaware that the American navy had already taken parts of the territory's Pacific coast. On December 6, as Kearny drove toward San Diego, he met his first resistance, at the Indian village of San Pascual.

Kearny's ill-conceived attack on San Pascual brought him up against Andres Pico, brother of the former territorial governor of California. Kearny's scout Kit Carson had wrongly informed him that Pico would not put up much of a fight. In fact, though Kearny commanded 150 men against Pico's force of 75, he did not unequivocally carry the day.

Kearny's men gathered to attack the town at 2:00 A.M. Capt. Abraham R. Johnston led a mounted dragoon charge on the Californians' camp, but he outran his infantry support and was forced to withdraw before Kearny's main force could come forward. Pico had formed his men carefully, and when Capt. Benjamin D. Moore led a second dragoon charge, Pico unleashed one of his own. During the ensuing half-hour-long fight at close quarters,

Mexican lances proved superior to American sabers. When the backup American force finally arrived with artillery, Pico withdrew his men, but he took with him a captured howitzer and mule team.

Kearny considered himself to have won the engagement, because Pico had withdrawn, but the Californians lost far less in the battle. Among the eighteen American dead were three officers, and Kearny himself was one of the twelve wounded. Pico's force suffered only twelve wounded and one captured.

The "victory" at San Pascual left Kearny's force battered and utterly exhausted after its long march. The men had to make camp and were unable to continue their march to San Diego for several days.

Further Reading

Charles B. Todd. *The Battle of San Pasqual* . . . (Pomona, Calif.: Progress, 1925); and Arthur Woodward. *Lances at San Pascual* (San Francisco: California Historical Society, 1948).

✌ Sand Creek

Colorado (November 29, 1864) *Colorado War*

The massacre of peaceful Cheyenne and Arapahoe at Sand Creek in 1864 by rabid, Indian-hating Colorado militia was one of the darkest episodes in the history of the American West, and it unfortunately typified an era when it seemed acceptable to many white westerners to kill Indians with no regard.

The victims of the attack were a mixed group of Cheyenne and Arapahoe led by Black Kettle (Moketavato), a chief who steadfastly refused the blandishments of the war faction of his tribe and had faith in his ability to live in peace with the steadily growing tide of white settlers. He had accepted what he understood to be a commitment by the governor of Colorado, John Evans, that any bands who chose to camp near military bases and report regularly would be protected from attack, and had set up a village of about six hundred men, women, and children at Sand Creek, near Fort Lyon. Evans, however, had subsequently bowed to pressure to open Indian lands to settlement and had relinquished his authority.

The man put in control of Indian affairs in Colorado was Col. John Chivington, a former minister and hero of the battle of GLORIETA PASS, who commanded the state militia. Chivington deeply hated Indians and openly advocated killing them all.

On the morning of November 29, Chivington positioned seven hundred men of the Colorado Third Volunteers and four field guns around Black Kettle's camp. The Cheyenne leader responded by hoisting an American flag and a white flag of peace on his lodge pole, assuming these would signal his peaceful intentions. Chivington, however, ordered a no-quarter attack, and his troops swept into the village in a frenzy of killing. They struck down, and often mutilated, any Indian they could reach, including pregnant women and little children. Black Kettle and a few others mounted a brief resistance but soon fled the scene. The Coloradans did not stop killing until more than two hundred Indians were dead.

The massacre was condemned in some quarters in the East, and Chivington was investigated by the U.S. Congress and discharged from the Colorado militia, but he escaped any other punishment. Black Kettle was later present at WASHITA, making his fate among the most lamentable of all Plains Indian leaders. The Sand Creek episode set off a series of conflicts known as the Colorado War (*see also* JULESBURG).

Further Reading

Stan Hoig. *The Sand Creek Massacre* (Norman: University of Oklahoma Press, 1963); Patrick M. Mendoza. *Song of Sorrow: Massacre at Sand Creek* (Denver, Colo.: Willow Wind, 1993); and Duane Schultz. *Month of the Freezing Moon: The Sand Creek Massacre, November 1864* (New York: St. Martin's Press, 1990).

✌ Sandusky

(Crawford's Defeat)

Ohio (June 4–5, 1782) *American Revolution*

In a disastrous defeat that presaged repeated American failures against the Indians of the upper Ohio River valley, veteran frontier fighter Col. William Crawford's force was repulsed by an army of mixed tribes and Loyalists, and Crawford himself was captured and tortured to death.

The fifty-year-old Crawford had been commissioned to head an expedition from Pennsylvania against the tribes of the upper Ohio and given command of 480 volunteers by vote of the troops. They set out in May for a 150-mile march into Indian territory. Crawford's son, son-in-law, and nephew were members of his force.

The Americans' route and intentions were well known by the British and the Indians, who prepared a trap near a village on the Upper Sandusky River. The Loyalist commander was Capt. William Caldwell, who had about one hundred of Butler's Rangers in addition to several hundred Indians, including warriors of the Delaware and Wyandot tribes.

The first day of fighting seemed to the Americans to be a draw—they killed several of their enemy and wounded more, including Caldwell—but they learned that reinforcements for the Loyalists were arriving, in the form of 140 Shawnee and a unit of loyalists with field artillery. In late evening the Americans decided to retreat, and they attempted to break through the ring of Indians. Some were cut off and killed, but others made it to a position five miles away on the Olentangy Creek, where the next day they fought another engagement, after which the bulk of the Americans managed to escape under the command of Maj. David Hamilton.

Colonel Crawford, however, lagged behind with a small group of officers, looking for his missing son. On June 7 they were captured by Delaware and taken to a nearby village, where Crawford was publicly tortured to death in front of several Loyalist officers. A member of his party survived to provide a grisly eyewitness account of Crawford's death.

Further Reading

Cosul Willshire Butterfield. *An Historical Account of the Expedition against Sandusky under Col. William Crawford in 1782 . . .* (Cincinnati: R. Clarke, 1873).

Santa Fe

New York (August 15–21, 1680) *Pueblo Revolt*

Following their subjugation in the late sixteenth century by the Spanish moving north from Mexico, the Pueblo Indians (a number of groups who shared a style of living in the north central region of what would become the state of New Mexico) had suffered massacres, mutilation, virtual enslavement, forced conversion to Christianity, and other extreme physical and cultural indignities at the hands of the conquerors. In 1680, they pooled their strength and pushed the Spanish completely out of the territory in an uprising in the pueblos (towns, often made of adobe brick buildings), culminating in a siege of the Spanish capital at Santa Fe.

The Pueblo Revolt was organized by a group of leaders from several tribes, chief among them Popé (Po'png), a Tewa religious leader from San Juan Pueblo. One of the sorest grievances of the Pueblo was the attempt of the Spanish to destroy their traditional kachina religion, and much of the revolt focused on killing or ejecting the Spanish missionaries, as well as the Spanish ranchers, who used forced Indian labor. The leaders of the revolt spread the word secretly among the people of the various pueblos that an uprising would begin in August 1680. When their plans were exposed, they pushed the date forward, catching the Spanish by surprise with attacks on ranches and missions that killed dozens and drove the remaining Spaniards onto the road as refugees.

Governor Antonio de Otermín in Santa Fe had only about fifty soldiers, but he was well equipped with brass cannon and protected by a central walled compound. He was somewhat short of supplies, however, since the Pueblo attack had been timed to catch the Spanish just before a supply train was to arrive from the south.

On August 15, after scouring the countryside, an army of around five hundred Indians approached Santa Fe and set up a siege from the rooftops of outlying buildings. They had no way to batter down the Spanish defenses, but they had their enemies hemmed in. The Spanish tried a series of sorties to dislodge the attackers but were unsuccessful. On the third day of fighting, the Indians took possession of the garrison's main water supply, but they still were too weak to overrun the Spanish. They disengaged the following day and withdrew to the surrounding hills.

Although undefeated, Otermín realized the hopelessness of his position and ordered a retreat from Santa Fe to El Paso, southward along the Rio Grande in what is today Mexico.

Popé and the other leaders of the revolt set up a new Indian government in Santa Fe and reestablished their own culture and political system, which held sway for nearly ten years.

Overall, about four hundred Spaniards were killed during the revolt, including many missionaries. About three hundred Indians were killed.

Further Reading

John L. Kessell. *Kiva, Cross, and Crown* (Albuquerque: University of New Mexico Press, 1990); and Andrew L. Knaut. *The Pueblo Revolt of 1680: Conquest and Resistance in Seventeenth Century New Mexico* (Norman: University of Oklahoma Press, 1995).

Saratoga, First

(Freeman's Farm)

New York (September 19, 1777)
American Revolution

The engagement at Freeman's farm, on the west bank of the Hudson River near Saratoga, New York, was the first

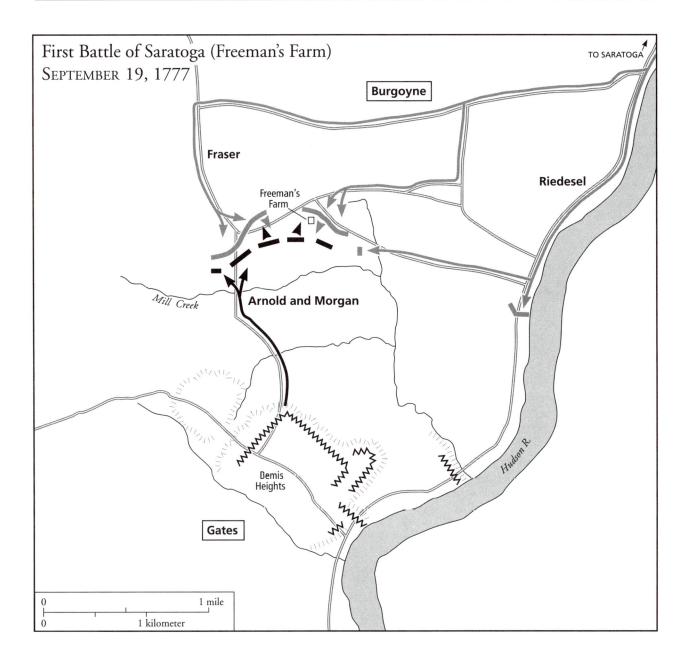

First Battle of Saratoga (Freeman's Farm)
SEPTEMBER 19, 1777

TO SARATOGA

Burgoyne

Fraser

Riedesel

Freeman's
Farm

Mill Creek

Arnold and Morgan

Demis
Heights

Hudson R.

Gates

0   1 mile

0   1 kilometer

of two battles that ended Maj. Gen. John Burgoyne's plan of invading from Canada and splitting the rebellious North American states. The draining battle grievously damaged British fortunes.

Burgoyne had left Canada in June 1777 with an army of nearly ten thousand, including British regulars, a large contingent of German mercenaries, Canadian militia and auxiliaries, American Loyalists, and hundreds of Indians. His progress across the heavily wooded stretches of upper New York State was painful and slow, with a check at HUBBARDTON and a serious loss at BENNINGTON. By September, Burgoyne had long since outrun his line of supply, and his army was melting away rapidly, in part from disease and malnourishment, in part from desertion and defeat. He pressed on, however, toward his goal of Albany, although his forces probably numbered no more than six thousand, and the odds against him increased daily.

In his path lay an American army, recently taken over by Maj. Gen. Horatio Gates, who had replaced the unpopular Philip Schuyler. Militia and regular reinforcements had swelled the size of Gates's forces until he probably had around between seven thousand and eight thousand men by the day of the battle. His principal lieutenant was the great combat general Benedict Arnold, although Arnold and Gates were on bad terms, and the Virginia colonel Daniel Morgan at the head of his riflemen was to prove a key figure in the fighting. Gates main force was entrenched strongly at Bemis Heights on high ground above the Hudson, waiting for Burgoyne to take the initiative.

On September 13, Burgoyne moved his army across to the west bank of the river. His Indian scouts had left, and he did not know exactly the size or the disposition of the American force in his path. He decided on a reconnaissance in force for September 19. Most of the field in front of Burgoyne (and for some distance from Gates's entrenchments) was heavily wooded, but on his right was an open area around a cabin known as Freeman's Farm. Burgoyne sent a column, about 1,100 men under Brig. Gen. Simon Fraser, toward this clearing. He sent Maj. Gen. Baron Friedrich von Riedesel, commander of the German troops, with another 1,100 to the left along a river road, and Burgoyne himself commanded the 1,100 men of the center column. By noon, the British had occupied Freeman's Farm and were waiting for all three columns to pull even with each other.

Gates, meanwhile, seemed content to stand pat—the commander himself had never smelled gunpowder and appears to have been dragged reluctantly into forcing a battle—until Major General Arnold persuaded him to send Morgan's riflemen, supported by light infantry, to probe the British right wing. Morgan's men opened the battle, picking off most of the British officers surrounding the main building at the farm, but they were themselves dispersed. Burgoyne then moved his center column to the farmstead, and a hot battle developed as American units came up to reinforce Morgan. A seesaw struggle for the clearing around the farm lasted for several hours, with first one side and then the other charging and retreating. (There is some controversy over the point, but apparently Arnold was on the field and directed the American effort.)

By late afternoon, Burgoyne called on Riedesel to reinforce his position at Freeman's Farm. The British commander had a dwindling force of three regiments, spearheaded by the Sixty-third, and he needed help. The Americans had been able to feed more and more troops into the fight, and at one stage they had nearly cut off and destroyed the Sixty-third. The arrival of Riedesel with five hundred men and several artillery pieces probably saved the British. The Germans attacked the American flank as soon as they reached the field and tipped the balance back toward a stalemate. The fighting ended for the day as the light failed and both sides gave up in exhaustion.

Burgoyne's men remained on the battlefield during the night, and the British general claimed victory since he occupied the disputed ground, but in fact his command had spent itself during the battle and he had taken casualties he could ill afford. Overall, the British and Germans lost about six hundred men, with some units, such as the Sixty-third, suffering severe damage (one estimate put the Sixty-third's losses at over 80 percent for the day).

The Americans losses were about half of those of Burgoyne, and they could be made up easily from new troops that were arriving. Moreover, only a portion of the main American force had been engaged at Freeman's Farm—nearly four thousand had remained on the heights. Unless Burgoyne could find a way to escape back across the Hudson, he was in a potentially disastrous situation.

Further Reading

Martha Byrd. *Saratoga: Turning Point in the American Revolution* (Philadelphia: Auerbach, 1973); Fred J. Cook. *Dawn over Saratoga: The Turning Point of the Revolutionary War* (Garden City, N.Y.: Doubleday, 1973); and Richard Ketchum. *Saratoga: Turning Point of America's Revolutionary War* (New York: Henry Holt, 1997).

Saratoga, Second

(Bemis Heights)
New York (October 7, 1777) *American Revolution*

After a depleting and indecisive battle at Freeman's farm on September 19, 1777 (*see also* SARATOGA, FIRST), British general John Burgoyne's army had been stuck in position. Burgoyne had fortified the battlefield and kept his force—now reduced to about five thousand men—in place, in difficult conditions, while he tried to decide what to do. A line of retreat across the Hudson River and back toward Canada was still open, but he was reluctant to admit defeat. He was encouraged by a letter from Sir Henry Clinton that spoke of a movement up the Hudson to relieve him, tempting him to try again to defeat the Americans. Burgoyne was hampered by a lack of scouts and intelligence, however, and he did not know the full extent of the American strength in their entrenchments on Bemis Heights.

In fact, the American army, commanded by Maj. Gen. Horatio Gates, grew considerably stronger while Burgoyne waited. Thousands of additional militia and regulars joined the army after the first battle, and by the first

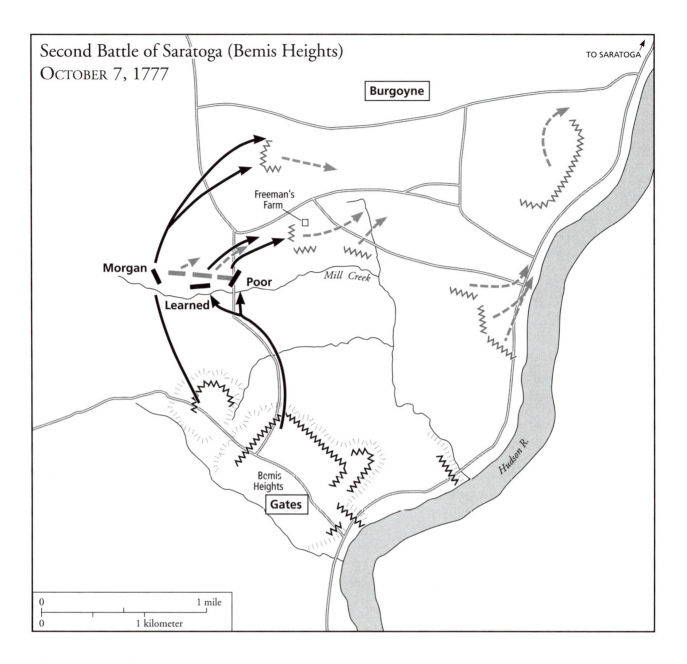

Second Battle of Saratoga (Bemis Heights)
OCTOBER 7, 1777

TO SARATOGA

Burgoyne

Freeman's Farm

Morgan

Poor

Mill Creek

Learned

Bemis Heights

Gates

Hudson R.

0   1 mile

0   1 kilometer

days of October the army may have totaled eleven thousand, most of them well supplied and well equipped, whereas the British were on their last legs and in some cases nearly starving. Moreover, the American fortifications had been significantly strengthened in the interval, and Gates's positions were now virtually unassailable by the forces available to Burgoyne.

The British commander decided finally on another reconnaissance in force, hoping it would lead to opportunities to attack the American fortifications. On October 7, sending a few light troops out to guard his right flank, Burgoyne marched his main forces into the open in front

of their entrenchments and formed a long line of battle. On the right wing was light infantry commanded by the earl of Balcarres, only a major but a tough fighter; the center was held by the ever-reliable Maj. Gen. Baron Friedrich von Riedesel, with the remnants of his German troops and one regiment of British regulars. On an entrenched hill on the left, Maj. John Acland commanded the assembled grenadier companies. Burgoyne also had ten cannon on the field.

The American commander, Gates, never left the safety and comfort of his headquarters behind the fortifications on Bemis Heights, and most historians doubt that he played more than a small role directing the battle, but he did begin the struggle by ordering Daniel Morgan to attack the British right wing and Brig. Gen. Enoch Poor to assault the enemy's elevated positions on their left.

Poor's regiments, from New Hampshire, New York, and Connecticut, moved out in midafternoon and attacked Acland's grenadiers with vigor. They overwhelmed the British, stopping a bayonet counterattack with a murderous volley, and overran the hilltop, wounding and capturing Acland in the process.

Morgan and his brigade of riflemen and light infantry were not far behind. Morgan's men swarmed to attack Balcarres and swept the British right wing back and out of the fight. British officers suffered especially at the hands of Morgan's riflemen, and Brig. Gen. Simon Fraser, one of Burgoyne's best commanders, was killed at long range by a rifleman.

Between the two American flank assaults advanced the brigade of Brig. Gen. Ebenezer Learned, which proceeded to push forward and drive the remaining British behind the entrenchments at their original starting points.

At this juncture, Maj. Gen. Benedict Arnold appeared on the scene. He was by a great margin the army's finest combat general and had been the hero of the battle the month before, but he had quarreled with Gates—Arnold had the knack of quarreling with almost everyone—and had been relieved of command. Disregarding orders, he rode out onto the field in front of the British, positions and dashed back and forth between the two American wings, directing attacks. Balcarres held a redoubt on the right flank of the British entrenchments and could not be broken, but the Germans under Lt. Col. Heinrich Breymann on the British left were overwhelmed by four American regiments, and Breymann was killed, according to some accounts by his own men.

As the fighting wore down at the end of the day, Burgoyne had clearly been defeated, although his men still held their defensive positions. They had lost at least six hundred men, killed, wounded, or captured. The Americans probably lost no more than 150 altogether, although Arnold was among the wounded, having taken a ball in the same leg as had been wounded at the gates of Quebec in 1775.

There was little left for Burgoyne to do but surrender, since it appeared that no help from Clinton would appear. The surrender of an entire British army was one of the most important events of the American Revolution and led directly to the intervention of France on behalf of the American rebels. It was, however, a clumsy business. Burgoyne twisted and turned for several days before conceding defeat, and Gates, finally emerged from his fortifications, botched the terms, granting a "convention" rather than a surrender and allowing Burgoyne and some of his officers parole to return to England, while the captive British and German troops were shunted around the states for the remainder of the war. Nevertheless, the proud professionals of the British army and their mercenary German allies had been humbled by the American amateurs.

Further Reading

Martha Byrd. *Saratoga: Turning Point in the American Revolution* (Philadelphia: Auerbach, 1973); Fred J. Cook. *Dawn over Saratoga: The Turning Point of the Revolutionary War* (Garden City, N.Y.: Doubleday, 1973); Richard Ketchum. *Saratoga: Turning Point of America's Revolutionary War* (New York: Henry Holt, 1997).

H.M.S. *Savage*

See U.S.S. *CONGRESS*

Savage's Station

(Allen's Farm, Peach Orchard)
Virginia (June 29, 1862) *American Civil War*

Union commander major general George B. McClellan's grand scheme to capture the Confederate capital at Richmond by means of an advance up the James River peninsula fell apart disastrously during the last days of June, when he virtually gave up and backed away from a smaller Confederate army commanded by Gen. Robert E. Lee. Even though his officers and men won (or at least tied) most of the series of engagements known as the Seven Days' Battles, McClellan became convinced he had to withdraw to Harrison's Landing and the protection of the guns of the U.S. Navy. McClellan's army was in full retreat through difficult, swampy, and confusing terrain when the Confederates attacked at Savage's Station.

Lee had a difficult time coordinating the movements of his principal subordinates, and he was unable to bring his full weight to bear. About 9:00 A.M., Maj. Gen. John B. Magruder attacked a retreating Union corps, commanded by Maj. Gen. Edwin Sumner, which held off the Confederates for two hours before withdrawing. Sumner's fellow corps commanders failed to move into covering positions, and Magruder was able to launch another attack later in the afternoon, although without the support of Maj. Gen. Thomas J. "Stonewall" Jackson's reinforced corps, which had been delayed in reaching the battlefield. The fighting was confusing, neither side holding the advantage, and it was ended by a severe thunderstorm and darkness.

The Confederates lost 626 casualties, and the Federals suffered 1,590.

McClellan continued his retreat the next day.

Further Reading

Clifford Dowdey. *The Seven Days: The Emergence of Lee*. Reprint ed. (Lincoln: University of Nebraska Press, 1993); James M. McPherson. *Battle Cry of Freedom: The Civil War Era* (New York: Oxford University Press, 1988); and Time-Life Staff. *Lee Takes Command: From Seven Days to Second Bull Run* (Alexandria, Va.: Time-Life Books, 1984).

⤚ Savannah

Georgia (December 29, 1778) *American Revolution*

The British began actively to shift the focus of the war south in late 1778, capturing the important port of Savannah as a way to stifle the southern rebels and maintain flexibility of movement by sea. The American forces proved unable to stand up to British professionalism and were easily brushed aside.

The expedition to capture Savannah sailed from New York City in late November, with about thirty-five hundred troops under Lt. Col. Archibald Campbell, with Commodore Hyde Parker in charge of the ships. The British reached the mouth of the Savannah River less than a month later and prepared to move on the city.

Savannah was defended by 900 Continentals and about 150 militia, commanded by Maj. Gen. Robert Howe, the congressionally appointed commander of the southern theater.

Campbell landed his troops below the city, and Lt. Col. John Maitland with men of his Seventy-first Highlanders secured the British position after a skirmish with a few Continentals under Capt. J. C. Smith. The terrain along the road leading to the city was one of swampland and marshes, making maneuvers difficult.

Howe had positioned his troops astride the road south of Savannah, and he had anchored his flanks on flooded rice fields and a swampy river. To his front was a stream and a ditch. It seemed like a strong defensive position, one that would force the British to make a costly frontal assault.

On December 29, the British marched to within a few hundred yards of the rebels, formed a line of battle, and appeared about to attack the American left wing, a movement that Howe was prepared to defend against. Unknown to the Americans, however, Campbell had discovered a little-known path through the swamps that Howe had neglected to guard, and he had sent a strong detachment of light infantry along this path to the American's rear. He was demonstrating before the defenses, feinting a frontal assault.

The British detachment struck the Americans from the rear with devastating effect, and Campbell began to cannonade the American position at the same time. Howe's resistance melted, and he ordered a retreat over a causeway. The majority of the Americans escaped, but a unit of Georgia militia became trapped in the swamp and took severe casualties, by drowning and from the British pursuit.

The Americans had 83 killed and 453 captured. The British suffered only three killed and ten wounded.

With little effort or loss, the British had secured an important seaport, which they held until the end of the war.

Further Reading

Christopher Ward. *The War of the Revolution*. Vol. 1 (New York: Macmillan, 1952).

⤚ Savannah

Georgia (October 9, 1779) *American Revolution*

A joint French-American venture to recapture Savannah from the British, who had seized the city in late 1778, turned into another disaster for the alliance: French admiral Comte Charles d'Estaing, for the second time (*see also* NEWPORT), performed poorly in working with Americans, whom he apparently despised.

Savannah occupied a potentially strong position on the south bank of the Savannah River, and it could be approached from only one direction, across swamps and difficult terrain. Earthworks, which the British repaired and improved, guarded the other approach. The British commander in the South, Maj. Gen. Augustine Prevost, was a skilled officer who consolidated the natural strengths of his situation with good fortifications and energetic reinforcement of his garrison.

Admiral d'Estaing seemed to hold the upper hand, however, since his powerful fleet comprised more than thirty ships and carried about four thousand soldiers, and it was a mobile force the like of which the Americans had lacked for the entire war. The British were mystified as to where d'Estaing would strike along the eastern seaboard, and the commander in chief, Sir Henry Clinton, in New York City, could do little except worry. D'Estaing's intentions finally became clear in September, when his ships appeared off the mouth of the Savannah River.

Prevost had about twenty-four hundred troops at his command, many of them Loyalist units, but also some German mercenary troops and British regulars, including most of the veteran Seventy-first Highlanders. Among the British officers was Sir James Wright, former royal governor of Georgia, now serving as a major of Loyalist volunteers.

The strongest point of defense for the British was on their right, where the Spring Hill redoubt anchored the fortified line. Even farther right, closer to the river, was the so-called Sailors' Battery, manned by gunners from the ships in waterway.

By mid-September d'Estaing had landed thirty-five hundred troops fourteen miles downriver and had them on the march into position. He was joined by fifteen hundred Americans under Maj. Gen. Benjamin Lincoln, including Carolinians under Brig. Gen. Lachlan McIntosh and the mounted legion of Brig. Gen. Count Casimir Pulaski, a volunteer Polish officer. On September 16, d'Estaing, on his own initiative, called on Prevost to surrender to the "arms of the King of France," apparently not regarding his American allies as worth mentioning. Prevost asked for time to consider, but in fact he used the interval to improve his fortifications and bring in more reinforcements.

The French and American forces set up for a siege of the city by hauling large-caliber guns from d'Estaing's ships and cutting a series of parallel and approaching trenches. In the late eighteenth century, if an attacker had sufficiently large cannon and enough troops, the success of such a siege was almost a given. With patience, the allies could force the British to surrender or to attempt flight. Unfortunately, d'Estaing had no patience at all. Despite the good progress of the siege work and the assurances of his engineers that only ten more days would be required for victory, d'Estaing demanded a full-scale frontal assault on the city.

The attack came during the early morning of October 9. While two columns spread out to assault the extreme British right and left (neither of these columns ever seriously engaged the enemy, one of them getting lost in the surrounding swamps), the main effort would be against the British strongpoint at Spring Hill redoubt. Three French columns and two American columns began to maneuver to positions from which they were to launch a coordinated attack at 5:00 A.M., but d'Estaing disregarded his own plan and sent in one of his French columns as soon as it was in position, without waiting for the others to close up.

The British defenders had plenty of time to prepare for each of the piecemeal French assaults, and they stopped all of them with accurate musket and artillery fire.

The American columns had better initial success. The South Carolina troops, led by Col. John Laurens and Col. Francis Marion, made it across the abatis and open ground and actually placed the state flag on the parapet. Five men were shot down trying to keep the flag flying, the last being Sgt. William Jasper, the hero of the defense of Fort Sullivan at CHARLESTON in 1776. A British counterattack, led by Maj. Beamsly Glazier, resulted in hot hand-to-hand fighting that finally drove the Americans back.

Meanwhile, to the left flank, Pulaski had foolishly ordered his mounted troopers to assault the British works—the cavalry was to have followed up an attack by infantry—and the result was carnage, horse soldiers standing no chance against entrenched artillery. Pulaski himself was hit by grapeshot and mortally wounded.

By midmorning the entire French-American assault force had been thrown back, and the British held their works unmolested. The allies had lost at least eight hundred, the majority of them among the French troops who made the initial assault. Probably between 175 and 200 were killed, and many of the wounded died later. The British losses were small by comparison: only sixteen killed and thirty-nine wounded, although this figure probably does not include all German or Loyalists losses.

D'Estaing had had enough, and despite the pleas of General Lincoln, the French commander loaded his infantry onto his ships and sailed away. Lincoln could do nothing but retreat to his base in Charleston.

Further Reading

Benjamin Kennedy, ed. *Muskets, Cannon Balls, and Bombs: Nine Narratives of the Siege of Savannah in 1779* (Savannah, Ga.: Beehive Press, 1974); and Alexander A. Lawrence. *Storm over Savannah: The Story of Count d'Estaing and the Siege of the Town in 1779.* Reprint ed. (Athens: University of Georgia Press, 1968).

Sayler's Creek

(Sailor's Creek)

Virginia (April 6, 1865) *American Civil War*

After the battle at FIVE FORKS, Virginia, which opened the month of April 1865 with a severe Confederate defeat, Gen. Robert E. Lee still hoped to hurry the remnants of his army southward to join Gen. Joseph E. Johnston and make a final stand in North Carolina. Lee's army left Amelia Court House on April 5 and marched toward Farmville, but on the way, his troops—led by Lt. Gens. James Longstreet, Richard Anderson, Richard Ewell, and John B. Gordon—became separated into three parts between Big Sayler's Creek (now spelled Sailor's) and Little Sayler's Creek (both tributaries of the Appomattox River twelve miles east of Farmville), when Anderson halted a long wagon train to engage Union cavalry but failed to notify Longstreet of the halt. Three Union officers, Brig. Gen. George Armstrong Custer, Maj. Gen. Horatio G. Wright, and Maj. Gen. Philip Sheridan, exploited the gaps in the Confederate lines and prepared to attack. Three separate fights broke out on April 6.

The first occurred when Major General Wright's ten thousand Federals confronted Ewell's thirty-six hundred men across Little Sayler's Creek. When Ewell established a defensive line on the creek's south side, Wright ordered twenty cannon unlimbered, and the Federal artillery opened up from a ridge to the north, near the Hillsman farm, around 5 P.M. The Northerners then forded the flooded creek and charged the Confederate line but were driven back by a sudden volley and a counterattack from Ewell's side. When Brig. Gen. George Washington Getty arrived with reinforcements, the Union troops managed a double envelopment of Ewell's line, where they took thirty-four hundred prisoners (including Ewell himself). Sheridan tried to take the opportunity to simultaneously hit Pickett's men, but the Southerner was able to get out of the way.

Lt. Gen. John B. Gordon expected to be attacked, as he was left between the two creeks at Double Bridge trying to protect a Confederate wagon train that had bogged down in the mud. While Ewell's men were under assault, Union major general Andrew A. Humphreys's 16,500-man Second Corps pushed toward Gordon's 7,000 troops, who had taken up a protective position at the Lockett farm behind their wagons. Slowly the Union attackers pushed the Confederates back to the creek, and when the Union troops flanked them to the north, Gordon's men retreated across the creek entirely. Darkness ended this second phase of the battle.

Meanwhile, Pickett, who had escaped from Ewell's section of the fight, met more Union resistance about one mile south of Little Sayler's Creek. Pickett and Maj. Gen. Bushrod Johnson, an Ohioan who had sided with the South, offered support in a cavalry duel that had broken out between Anderson and Union brigadier generals Custer and Thomas Devin. The Southern horsemen were simply overwhelmed: two Confederate generals were captured, and most of Anderson's men fled into the woods in disarray. As the men ran away in confusion, General Lee observed them from a high hill and exclaimed, "My God! Has the army been dissolved?" Lee was not far wrong, considering that Anderson's force lost 2,600 men, compared to a Federal loss of only 172.

In the three parts of the conflict at Sayler's Creek, Confederate casualties totaled 7,700, compared to just 1,148 Federals, of whom only 166 died. Union forces captured six southern generals during the engagements.

Severely damaged but not quite torn apart, remnants of Lee's force struggled on, to fight their last major battle the next day at FARMVILLE AND HIGHBRIDGE.

Further Reading

Jay Wertz and Edwin Bearss. *Smithsonian's Great Battles and Battlefields of the Civil War* (New York: William Morrow, 1997).

Seven Days

See GAINES'S MILL; GARNETT'S AND GOLDING'S FARM; MALVERN HILL; MECHANICSVILLE; OAK GROVE; SAVAGE'S STATION; WHITE OAK SWAMP

Seven Pines

See FAIR OAKS

H.M.S. *Shannon*

See U.S.S. *CHESAPEAKE*

Sharpsburg

See ANTIETAM

Shiloh

(Pittsburgh Landing)

Tennessee (April 6–7, 1862) *American Civil War*

The Union strategy in the West during the spring of 1862 was to pursue a vigorous campaign into Tennessee in order to disrupt the Confederacy's east-west rail connections. Maj. Gen. Ulysses S. Grant took command of a large Federal force and prepared to join his army with that of Maj. Gen. Don Carlos Buell and march on the rail center at Corinth. Before he could do so, however, Confederates under Gen. Albert Sidney Johnston, the second-ranking officer in the Confederate army and admired on both sides of the war, launched a surprise attack. The subsequent two-day battle produced the first of the huge casualty lists that came to characterize the Civil War.

Grant's army rode transports down the Tennessee River to Pittsburgh Landing, where it went into camp. Grant, with headquarters at nearby Crump's Landing, had orders to proceed against Corinth, but he was waiting for Buell to arrive from Nashville with his army of more than twenty thousand. Combined, the Union force would total more than sixty thousand men, with a full complement of artillery, cavalry, and transport. Neither Grant nor any of his subordinate commanders had any notion that a Confederate army was nearby, so the Union troops were allowed to bivouac at leisure. The outermost campsites, surrounding Shiloh Church, were occupied by troops under Brig. Gen. Benjamin Prentiss and Brig. Gen. William Tecumseh Sherman. The rest of the army was spread out toward the river, with a division under Brig. Gen. Lew Wallace a few miles away at Crump's Landing. Buell's troops were still on the march on the other side of the river.

Early on the morning of April 6, Confederate skirmishers stepped out of the woods and began an attack on the camps that caught the Union soldiers unawares. They were the lead units of a large Confederate army, numbering as many as forty-four thousand men, that Johnston had assembled to forestall the Union designs on Corinth. Johnston and his subordinates, second in command Gen. P. G. T. Beauregard and corps commanders Braxton Bragg, William Hardee, Leonidas Polk, and John C. Breckinridge, had positioned their troops overnight within a mile of the Union camp without arousing suspicion. They now intended to drive the Federal army into the river and destroy it.

Soon the Confederates were attacking in large numbers, hoping to overrun the untested units under Prentiss and Sherman, but despite their inexperience the Federals did not panic. Instead they put up a stiff fight, although forced by weight of numbers to retreat. The Federal lines constricted, and it appeared at several points during the morning that nothing could keep the Confederates from pushing them all the way back to the river's edge. However, at a key position, which came to be known as the Hornets' Nest, six thousand Federal troops under Prentiss and Brig. Gen. W. H. L. Wallace made a breathtaking stand. The greatly outnumbered defenders fought off attack after attack, and the Confederate troops under Bragg were unable to dislodge them, despite inflicting heavy casualties. After more than seven hours of fighting at the Hornets' Nest, the Confederates finally brought up sixty-two cannon—probably the largest concentration of artillery ever assembled in North America to that point—and blasted Prentiss's men into submission. Prentiss surrendered more than two thousand troops, and Wallace was fatally wounded.

Despite their hard-won achievements at the Hornets' Nest, the Confederates were short of a complete victory. The Union stand had allowed Grant to rally his demoralized troops (some of whom were found hiding in the shelter of the river bluffs) and organize a new line of defense, anchored to the river on one flank and to a creek on the other, with a strong battery of artillery. Gen. Lew Wallace arrived with his division from Crump's Landing, and one of Buell's divisions, commanded by Brig. Gen. William Nelson, made it across the river to join Grant's command. Two Union gunboats moved in behind the lines and added their firepower to the artillery barrage.

The Confederates suffered a serious loss in midafternoon when Johnston was hit by a minié ball in the knee and bled to death on the battlefield. Beauregard, who assumed command, was capable, but he could not sustain the initial success of early in the day. By nightfall, the Confederates occupied the former Union campsites, but the Federals were in a good position and Buell's troops were streaming across the river. Close to twenty thousand new infantrymen had come into the Union lines by morning, making good all of the losses of the previous day's fighting and giving Grant a decided edge in numbers. Moreover, Beauregard was apparently unaware of the change in the power of the army facing him.

Early in the morning of the next day, the Confederates began an attack that Beauregard believed would give him the final victory. Instead, he discovered that Grant had launched an attack of his own with fresh troops.

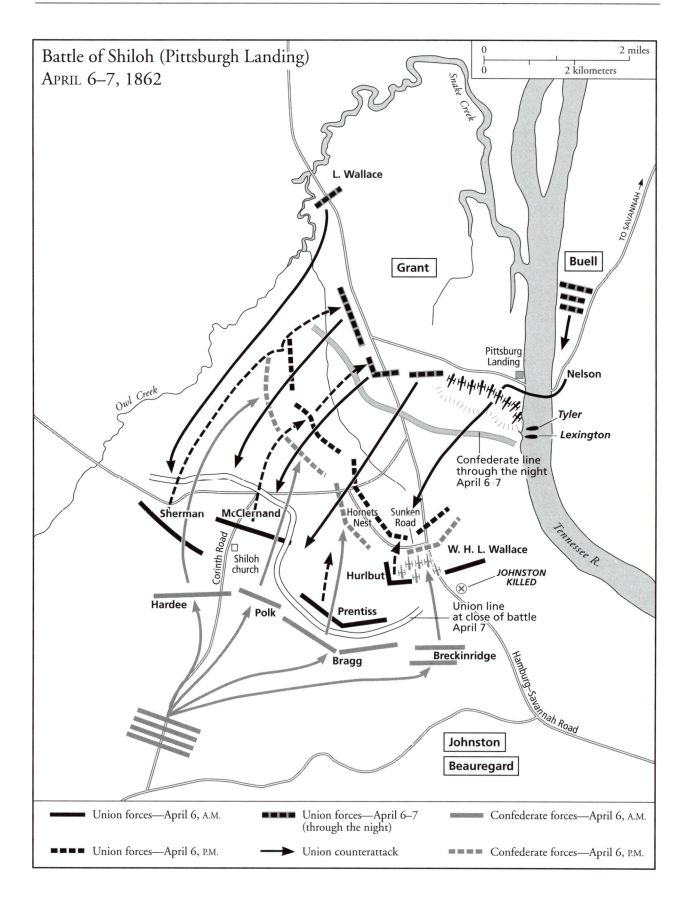

Battle of Shiloh (Pittsburgh Landing)
APRIL 6–7, 1862

Snake Creek

L. Wallace

Grant

Buell

TO SAVANNAH

Owl Creek

Pittsburg Landing

Nelson

Tyler

Lexington

Confederate line
through the night
April 6–7

Sherman

McClernand

Hornets
Nest

Sunken
Road

W. H. L. Wallace

Corinth Road

Shiloh
church

Hurlbut

JOHNSTON
KILLED

Hardee

Polk

Prentiss

Union line
at close of battle
April 7

Tennessee R.

Bragg

Breckinridge

Hamburg-Savannah Road

Johnston

Beauregard

	Union forces—April 6, A.M.		Union forces—April 6–7 (through the night)		Confederate forces—April 6, A.M.
	Union forces—April 6, P.M.	→	Union counterattack		Confederate forces—April 6, P.M.

All along the battle lines the Federals pushed forward, and the Confederates gave back ground they had won the day before. Despite a brief stand and a counterattack in midafternoon, by late in the day Beauregard concluded that he could no longer continue—hoped-for reinforcements had not arrived—so he ordered a retreat toward Corinth. Grant had recouped a victory from a near defeat.

The number of casualties was staggering, far surpassing anything before in American warfare. Nearly twenty-four thousand men were killed, wounded, or missing during the two days of fighting, more than had fallen during all the colonial wars and the Revolutionary War combined. More than seventeen hundred were killed on each side at Shiloh, a demonstration of the deadly efficiency of the new military technology, especially the effectiveness of Civil War era artillery.

Further Reading

Donald Bannister. *Long Day at Shiloh* (New York: Alfred A. Knopf, 1981); Larry J. Daniel. *Shiloh: The Battle That Changed the War* (New York: Simon & Schuster, 1997); Jay Luvass, Stephen Bowman, and Leonard Fullenkamp, eds. *Guide to the Battle of Shiloh* (Lawrence: University Press of Kansas, 1996); David Martin. *The Shiloh Campaign: March–April 1862* (Philadelphia: Combined Books, 1996); James L. McDonough. *Shiloh! In Hell before Night* (Knoxville: University of Tennessee Press, 1977); and Wiley Sword. *Shiloh: Bloody April* (New York: William Morrow, 1974).

Sitka

Alaska (October 1–7, 1804) *Russian-Indian War*

When minions of the Russian-American Company, a czarist imperial fur-trading concern, attempted to expand down the coast of Alaska during the last years of the eighteenth century, they came in conflict with the powerful Tlingit tribe. After several years of increasingly hostile contact—including a Tlingit attack on a Russian outpost in 1802—the conflict came to a head with a Russian attack on the village of Shee Atika (modern-day Sitka) in the fall of 1804.

The village was inhabited by the Kiksadi clan of the Tlingit, which had been trading with the Russians for several years. The Kiksadi realized, however, that the Russians would eventually demand more and more in return for less and less, and they had begun to resist Russian attempts to establish control over the clan. The Kiksadi built a strong log fort at the end of a headland where the Indian River entered Sitka Bay, and the entire clan—including women and children—moved into the stockade.

The Russians were led by Alexander Baranof, the general manager of the Russian-America Company. He was nominally in command of the expedition against Shee Atika, although he was a merchant, not a soldier. He had at his disposal a small force of armed Russian *promyshlenniki* (fur traders) and several hundred Aleut warriors (the Aleut had previously come under the control of the Russians and were more or less unwilling allies). The main source of Russian firepower was the *Neva,* a frigate commanded by an experienced naval officer, Yuri Lisiansky, who was in the midst of making the first Russian voyage around the world.

The Russians arrived at Shee Atika with the *Neva* and a flotilla of small boats in the last days of September. Lisiansky was unable to anchor close to the fort, due to hidden shoals just off shore, and the landward approaches were across long, open gravel beaches. On October 1, one of Lisiansky's junior officers, a Lieutenant Arboosoff, took a naval assault party ashore with a small, four-pounder cannon. Baranof landed shortly thereafter with a party of 150 men and several fieldpieces. The Russians moved boldly up to the fort and prepared to batter their way in.

The Kiksadi, however, under their war leader Katlian, were more than ready. They were well armed with muskets, and they allowed the Russians to come to close range before opening a withering fire. Several of the Russians and Aleut were killed, and more were wounded. The attackers turned and ran for their boats, pursued by the Kiksadi, who rushed out of the fort to chase their enemies down the beach. The Russians and their Aleut allies managed to escape under covering fire from the *Neva.* Baranof himself took a wound in the arm, and he turned over military command to Lisiansky.

For the next six days, the Russians bombarded the Kiksadi fort but apparently had little effect on the stout log structure. Nonetheless, on the seventh day of the siege, the Kiksadi, who were short of food and gunpowder, decided to withdraw. They slipped quietly away to begin a one-hundred-mile trek through the wilderness to escape Russian retaliation.

The Russians took possession of the fort and eventually established their Alaska fur-trading capital of Novo-Archangel nearby.

Further Reading

George P. Chaney, Robert C. Betts, and Dee Longenbaugh. *Physical and Cultural Landscapes of Sitka National Historical Park*

(Douglas, Alaska: Vanguard Research, 1995); and Yuri Lisiansky. *Voyage Round the World in the Years 1803, 1804, 1805 and 1806* (New York: DaCapo Press, 1968).

Six Mile House

See GLOBE TAVERN

Slim Buttes

South Dakota (September 9, 1876) *Black Hills War*

After the destruction of Lt. Col. George Armstrong Custer and a good share of his Seventh Cavalry at the LITTLE BIG HORN River in June 1876, large numbers of Teton Lakota dispersed and fled what they assumed would be a vigorous reaction from the U.S. Army. Sitting Bull (Tatanka Yotanka) led many of the Hunkpapa band of Teton Lakota, among others, back to South Dakota (and eventually into Canada).

Following some initial fumbling in the wake of Custer's defeat, the army finally organized a pursuit, in the form of a column under Brig. Gen. George Crook, which picked up the trail of the Lakota toward the Black Hills. The march was difficult, and soon food supplies began to run out. On September 7, Crook ordered Capt. Anson Mills to take 150 men on the best remaining horses (many had been eaten in desperation) and procure supplies from the mining settlement at Deadwood.

As Mills's troops approached the Black Hills, they discovered an Oglala Lakota village at Slim Buttes and attacked immediately. Although taken by surprise, the Lakota, led by American Horse, put up a stiff resistance, allowing most of the women and children to escape. Mills succeeded in trapping American Horse himself and a few followers in a cave. During the battle, Crook arrived with reinforcements, and shortly thereafter several hundred Lakota warriors—perhaps led by Crazy Horse (Tashunka Witco)—approached the scene, hoping to aid the Oglala, but the soldiers were too many.

American Horse was eventually fatally wounded and flushed from his hiding place to die, and the army seized or destroyed a large amount of supplies the Lakota needed for the coming winter months. This was one of the final large-scale armed encounters between the U.S. Army and the Lakota during the war over the Black Hills.

Further Reading

Jerome A. Greene. *Slim Buttes, 1876: An Episode of the Great Sioux War* (Norman: University of Oklahoma Press, 1982).

South Mountain

Maryland (September 14, 1862) *American Civil War*

In the fall of 1862, Confederate general Robert E. Lee invaded Union territory. He moved his army into Maryland, hoping to gain support from the population of that border state and to find an opportunity to attack parts of the Army of the Potomac, commanded by Maj. Gen. George B. McClellan. Though McClellan intercepted Lee's famous Order no. 191, which split the Confederate army into two wings under Maj. Gen. Thomas J. "Stonewall" Jackson and Maj. Gen. James Longstreet, the Union commander moved at his usual snail's pace trying to keep Lee's army from approaching Washington, D.C., too closely. As Jackson's men advanced on HARPERS FERRY, the other wing of Confederate forces met and engaged the Federals at South Mountain.

The first fighting on September 14 occurred at two mountain passes called Turner's Gap and Fox's Gap (additional action took place later in the day at CRAMPTON'S GAP). Early in the morning, Brig. Gen. Alfred Pleasanton's Federal cavalry attacked Confederate brigadier general D. H. Hill's division at Turner's Gap. Brig. Gen. Jacob D. Cox's Kanawha Division arrived at 9:00 A.M. to reinforce the Federal attack, which faced strong Confederate resistance. At noon, Federal major general Jesse L. Reno, a hero of the Mexican-American War, brought his Ninth Corps through Fox's Gap and was soon joined by Maj. Gen. Joseph Hooker's First Corps and Maj. Gen. Ambrose Burnside, who took command of the entire action.

Eventually the Union commanders had 28,480 men into action against the 17,852 Confederates at South Mountain, and fighting continued fiercely throughout the day as the Confederates sniped from behind trees and rocks. At 10 P.M. the Union troops managed to capture the heights above Turner's Gap, and within two hours Hill and Longstreet's Confederate troops began to withdraw.

Confederate casualties were estimated at 325 killed, 1,560 wounded, and 800 missing. Union forces lost 325 killed, 1,403 wounded, and 85 missing. Two general officers died at South Mountain: Confederate brigadier general Samuel Garland, Jr., and Union major general Jesse L. Reno. Reno was shot near sundown, and as he was carried from the field about to expire he said to his former West Point classmate Brig. Gen. Samuel S. Sturgis, "Hello, Sam–I'm dead."

The fierce battle at South Mountain provided a glimpse of the carnage to come in the next few days at Harpers Ferry and ANTIETAM.

Further Reading

John M. Priest. *Before Antietam: The Battle for South Mountain* (Shippensburg, Pa.: White Mane, 1992); and Edward J. Stackpole. *From Cedar Mountain to Antietam, August–September, 1862* (Harrisburg, Pa.: Stackpole, 1959).

≈ Spencer's Tavern

Virginia (June 26, 1781) *American Revolution*

During the spring and summer of 1781, the American army in Virginia under the marquis de Lafayette sparred with and maneuvered against a British army commanded after May by Lt. Gen. Lord Cornwallis, who sent out several raiding parties to seize or destroy rebel supplies. Maj. John Simcoe's Queen's Rangers, a veteran Loyalist unit, were given such an assignment in June, to raid along the Chickahominy River.

Lafayette dispatched a Pennsylvania regiment under Col. Richard Butler, along with the Virginia riflemen of Maj. William McCall and 150 mounted troopers under Maj. William McPherson, to find and stop Simcoe. McPherson pushed ahead of the infantry and pinned down Simcoe's force at Spencer's Tavern. He attacked and was soon supported by McCall's Virginians, but Simcoe counterattacked with his dragoons and got the upper hand.

Despite his immediate success, Simcoe feared that Lafayette and the rest of the main American army might be nearby. He disengaged and retreated toward the safety of Cornwallis's base in Williamsburg.

The Americans suffered nine killed and twenty-eight wounded or missing. The British reported a total of thirty-three casualties.

Further Reading

Mark M. Boatner. *The Encyclopedia of the American Revolution* (New York: David McKay, 1966).

≈ Spotsylvania

Virginia (May 12–18, 1864) *American Civil War*

After being given command of all Federal armies in the spring of 1864, Lt. Gen. Ulysses S. Grant devised a campaign against Gen. Robert E. Lee and the Army of Northern Virginia that he hoped would capture the Confederate capital at Richmond and end the war. Grant took the field to supervise the drive south by the Army of the Potomac, nominally commanded by Maj. Gen. George Meade. The campaign began with a horrendous two-day battle at the WILDERNESS on May 5 and 6. Despite taking heavy casualties, Grant pushed on southward, hoping to seize the crossroads of a crucial Confederate supply route at Spotsylvania, Virginia.

Unfortunately for Grant, Lee's cavalry reached the crossroads first, and the balance of his sixty-three-thousand-man army soon occupied the strategic position and began to dig in behind a long line of defenses built on the spot from logs and dirt. By the time Grant had his more numerous army—about 111,000 men—in position to attack, Lee was (as he had been so often during the war) in a nearly impregnable defensive position, ready to batter down a Union attack.

Despite the disadvantages, Grant ordered a frontal assault on the Southern field works. In the early morning hours of May 12, Maj. Gen. Winfield S. Hancock's Second Corps directly attacked a salient in the Confederate line, a salient that would come to be known as the "Bloody Angle." At first the Union attacks succeeded, capturing several thousand men of Lee's Second Corps, but the Federal assault was answered by vicious Confederate counterattacks that drove the Union troops back outside the trenches.

As the battle wore on, both commanders fed more and more troops into the narrow front at Bloody Angle until all semblance of an organized battle ceased, and the men on both sides were reduced to the most elemental forms of hand-to-hand combat, tearing at each other and killing at close range. The melee continued for hours, grinding up reinforcements. A heavy rainfall made conditions even worse as the day wore on, night fell, and the horrible killing continued until nearly midnight, when both sides fell back exhausted, leaving a scene of supreme horror at the Angle. Neither side had gained any advantage from the slaughter.

After six days, during which the rains continued, making the battlefield a quagmire strewn with wounded and corpses, Grant sent in another direct attack at the Bloody Angle, but it was again repulsed by the entrenched Confederates.

The Union losses at Spotsylvania were almost twice as high as the Confederates, eighteen thousand casualties

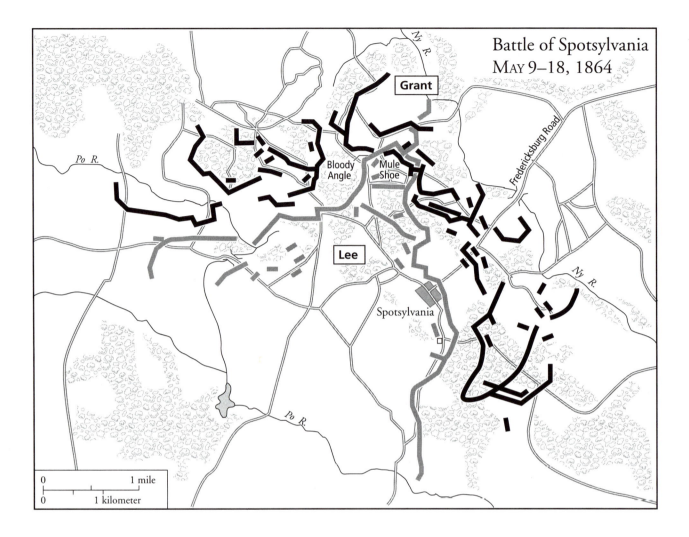

Battle of Spotsylvania
MAY 9–18, 1864

Grant

Bloody
Angle

Mule
Shoe

Fredericksburg Road

Po R.

Lee

Spotsylvania

Ny R.

Po R.

0   1 mile

0   1 kilometer

to around nine thousand. A Union corps commander, Maj. Gen. John Sedgwick, was among the dead.

After the battle, Grant once again demonstrated that he would not easily give up his intention of beating Lee, no matter the cost. Instead of licking his wounds, he ordered another crablike movement to the south and east, trying still to cut off and defeat the Army of Northern Virginia. The two sides would meet again at NORTH ANNA RIVER.

Further Reading

John Cannan. *The Spotsylvania Campaign: May 7–21, 1864* (Conshohocken, Pa.: Combined Books, 1997); Gary Gallagher, ed. *The Spotsylvania Campaign.* (Chapel Hill: University of North Carolina Press, 1998); William D. Matter. *If It Takes All Summer* (Chapel Hill: University of North Carolina Press, 1988); and Gordon C. Rhea. *The Battles for Spotsylvania Court House and the Road to Yellow Tavern, May 7–12, 1864* (Baton Rouge: Louisiana State University Press, 1997).

✒ Springfield

New Jersey (June 23, 1780) *American Revolution*

While the commander in chief, Sir Henry Clinton, campaigned in the South in 1780, the main British army based in New York City was commanded by Lt. Gen. Wilhelm Knyphausen, the highest-ranking German mercenary officer. Hearing rumors that elements of the American army at its winter quarters in Morristown had mutinied, Knyphausen decided on a heavy raid into New Jersey, hoping to encourage the mutineers and rally civilians back to the cause of the king.

The British crossed into New Jersey on June 7 with between four and five thousand troops and moved toward Morristown. Knyphausen's hopes of appealing to the civilians of the region ended almost at once, when local militia turned out to oppose his movements. A mere handful of patriot militiamen, backed by a few members of Col. Elias

Dayton's Third New Jersey Regiment, briefly stopped Knyphausen's column dead in its tracks by holding a bridge at Connecticut Farms. Since it was clear little could be done to achieve his original mission, Knyphausen simply went into camp and dug in, near Elizabethtown.

The American commander, Gen. George Washington, was indeed harassed by mutiny among some of his starving troops, but he ordered a strong force under Maj. Gen. Nathanael Greene to take up a position to cover Knyphausen's potential movements against the main American army. Meanwhile, Sir Henry Clinton arrived in New York and attempted to draw some advantage out of the strange position the German had gotten into. Clinton finally decided to withdraw Knyphausen when he learned that a French expeditionary force was approaching Newport, Rhode Island.

On June 23, Knyphausen began to move his men toward Springfield, New Jersey, but he found his way blocked at a bridge by Greene with about one thousand Continentals, plus militia under Brig. Gens. William Maxwell and Philemon Dickinson.

Knyphausen sent a column forward to engage Greene and, using the typical British tactic, tried to slip a second column around to the enemy's rear, sending it upstream to cross at a bridge and double back. Greene countered with mounted troops under Maj. Henry Lee, who slowed the flanking movement but were eventually driven back toward the main American position.

Greene's men—principally Rhode Islanders under Col. Israel Angell—blunted Knyphausen's main assault and then withdrew to a new position on high ground. The German had had enough. He disengaged, burned several houses in Springfield, and began a retreat toward New York City.

Overall, the Americans lost fifteen killed and forty nine wounded. The British did not report their losses.

Further Reading

Christopher Ward. *The War of the Revolution*. Vol. 2 (New York: Macmillan, 1952).

❧ Springfield Arsenal

Massachusetts (January 25, 1787) *Shays's Rebellion*

Throughout 1786, informal groups of armed American farmers, calling themselves Regulators, sought relief from prosecution for debt and failure to pay taxes by capturing and shutting down local courts. The most prominent group of Regulators was led by Daniel Shays, a charismatic former captain in the Continental army who had been hauled into court for debt. He organized his western Massachusetts neighbors to rebel against hardships brought on by high taxes, economic depression, and poor weather. During the summer of 1786, Shays's rebels tried to shut down courts and harassed lawyers, merchants, and government officials, whom they identified as their persecutors. In the winter of 1786 and 1787, Gov. James Bowdoin II and the Massachusetts state government grew increasingly worried about what became known as Shays's Rebellion, and Gen. Benjamin Lincoln called out the state militia to put it down.

The battle at the Springfield armory between a group of Shaysite rebels and local militia troops represented the climax of months of conflict between the farmers and government officials. The Shaysite farmers had organized themselves into regiments and planned to capture the armory as a first step toward taking over the state government. The Shaysites expected Lincoln to remain in Worcester, where he was gathering militia troops and preparing for a fight.

On January 21, three hundred Shaysites gathered from their homes all over the Berkshire region, surrounded the Springfield Armory, and captured the Chicopee Bridge just to the north. Another thousand farmers, including a few men from Vermont, took up a position at Palmer, east of the arsenal. The farmers effectively cut off the one thousand Hampshire County militiamen at the arsenal from Lincoln's forty-four hundred state militia in Worcester.

For several days, the Shaysites harassed local residents, stole food, and prepared to mount a three-part direct attack on the arsenal. On January 25, Gen. William Shepard, who commanded the militia troops inside the arsenal, intercepted a letter between regulators groups asking the farmers in Chicopee and Palmer to postpone the attack until reinforcements could be rounded up. At 4:00 P.M., however, fifteen hundred Shaysites marched against the arsenal without waiting for backup.

Shepard's aides, William Lyman and Samuel Buffington, rode out to warn the farmers they would be fired upon if they continued their progress toward the arsenal, but Daniel Shays responded by shouting, "March, God damn you, march!" at his men, who pressed forward. Shepard's militiamen, many of them Revolutionary War veterans like the Shaysite rebels, aimed their three cannon and one howitzer at the approaching farmers and fired two rounds over their heads, which failed to stop their advance.

Then the cannon fired around fifteen rounds of grapeshot directly into the advancing rebel line. The rebel farmers scattered, but they continued their plans to capture the government of Massachusetts until February 4, when three thousand men under Lincoln marched into their camp at Petersham and dispersed them once and for all.

Four Shaysite rebels were killed and twenty wounded during the January 25 attack on the Springfield Arsenal.

The most lasting consequence of the battle at the arsenal, and of Shays's entire rebellion, was not relief from economic hardship for indebted farmers. Rather, the rural uprising so frightened American elites and government officials that the rebellion helped to bolster support for the constitutional convention called in 1787 to devise a stronger American government than that of the Articles of Confederation. The U.S. Constitution was, in that sense, a response to the uprising of armed farmers.

Further Reading

David Szatmary. *Shays' Rebellion: The Making of an Agrarian Insurrection* (Amherst: University of Massachusetts Press, 1980).

☙ Stones River

(Murfreesboro)
Tennessee (December 31, 1862, and January 2, 1863) *American Civil War*

Two great armies fought an unusual and inconclusive battle near Murfreesboro that was among the bloodiest of the entire war, rivaling the better-known battles of the eastern theater for total casualties.

The Union Army of the Cumberland was commanded by Maj. Gen. William S. Rosecrans, a West Point graduate and former businessman, who had relieved Don Carlos Buell after the former commander had failed to follow up after PERRYVILLE in October. Rosecrans, with about forty-four thousand troops, many of them seasoned veterans, had orders to pursue the Confederate Army of Tennessee and take Chattanooga. Opposite him were between thirty-four and thirty-eight thousand Confederates commanded by Lt. Gen. Braxton Bragg, a West Pointer with a distinguished Mexican-American War record.

In December, the two armies arrived at facing positions astride the meandering Stones River. Neither side was dug in, although the Union army enjoyed the best ground for defense. Both commanding generals had reached the same tactical conclusion: they intended to mount massive attacks against the right side of their opponent's line. Had they been simultaneously successful, the battle would have resembled a rotating wheel. As it was, Bragg launched his attack first, at dawn, beating Rosecrans to the punch.

Moving forward at first light, troops under Lt. Gen. William Hardee surprised the Union soldiers over their morning campfires, and they folded the right side of the Federal line back on itself, inflicting heavy losses. The Union forces fought well, especially Maj. Gen. Philip H. Sheridan's men, who held their positions until the last moment to allow an orderly withdrawal of other Federals to new positions. However, Confederate cavalry under Brig. Gen. Joseph Wheeler had captured the Union ammunition trains, which left many Federal infantrymen with empty weapons.

Once alerted to the danger of a complete roll-up of his right, Rosecrans moved energetically, dashing about the field at great personal risk to establish new defensive positions.

The key to the first day's fight was a salient on the Union right where the line folded back. At the center was Maj. Gen. George Thomas, perhaps the most reliable of all Union generals in the West, and Rosecrans brought up artillery to support the salient. Bragg, intending to crush the Federals, sent in two massive attacks, but both failed. Near the end of the day, about 4:00 P.M., Bragg tried a third attack, which was repulsed with terrible losses.

Despite the failures, by usual standards Bragg would have been the victor, and so he believed himself to be during the following day, a break in the fighting. When his cavalry reported wagons moving behind enemy lines, Bragg assumed this meant a Federal withdrawal, and he telegraphed to Richmond news of a victory. Rosecrans, however, was determined to hold the field, and the wagons were merely part of an effort to strengthen his positions and reinforce vital river crossings that had been held during the first day. The suspension of fighting on January 1 allowed him to make good his lost ammunition.

On January 2, Bragg realized he still faced a Union army. Delaying until late afternoon, he finally ordered Maj. Gen. John C. Breckinridge, a former vice president of the United States whose Kentuckians held a position on the north side of the river, separate from the rest of the Confederate army, to assault the Union lines to his front, across an open field. Breckinridge protested furiously and at first refused the order, but Bragg insisted.

Charging into massed Federal artillery, Breckinridge's Kentuckians lost eighteen hundred men. When Union

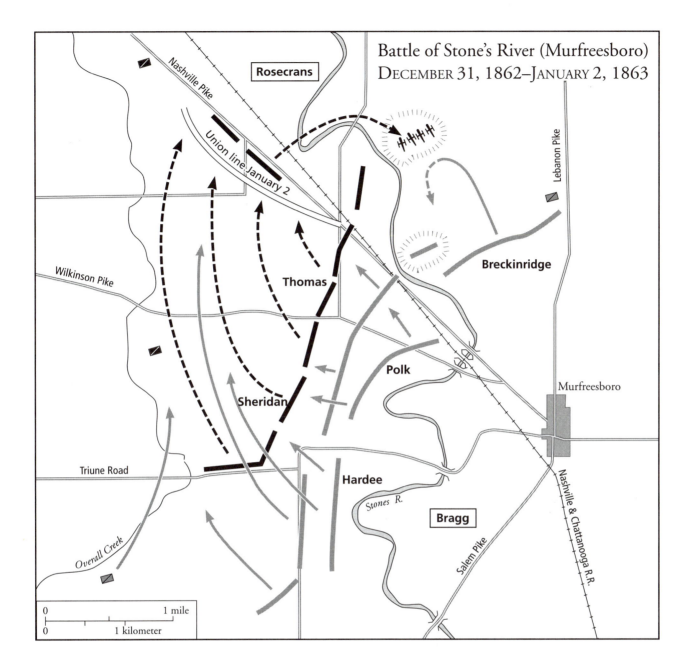

Battle of Stone's River (Murfreesboro)
DECEMBER 31, 1862–JANUARY 2, 1863

troops from Ohio and Illinois regiments splashed across the river and struck the Confederates in the flank, the battle was over.

The two days of fighting, separated by a one-day hiatus, produced some of the worst casualty figures of the entire war: the South lost nearly twelve thousand men killed or wounded, the Union lost thirteen thousand. Nearly one-third of the men engaged were dead or wounded at the end of the battle.

Though Rosecrans received the official thanks of Congress, however, neither side could claim a clear-cut

victory, and very little strategic advantage resulted from all the carnage. Bragg withdrew to winter quarters, and Rosecrans was content to occupy Murfreesboro quietly, without pursuing the Confederates.

Further Reading

Peter Couzens. *No Better Place to Die: The Battle of Stones River* (Urbana: University of Illinois Press, 1990); and James L. McDonough. *Stones River: Bloody Winter in Tennessee* (Knoxville: University of Tennessee Press, 1980).

Stono Ferry

South Carolina (June 20, 1779)
American Revolution

During the first five months of 1779, Maj. Gen. Augustine Prevost, the British commander in the South, ranged over Georgia and South Carolina, keeping the American patriot forces, under Maj. Gen. Benjamin Lincoln, off balance. In May, Prevost marched all the way up to Charleston but then withdrew by sea to his base in Savannah, leaving Lt. Col. John Maitland to secure his rear. Maitland fought a sharp battle with Lincoln's troops at Stono Ferry, just south of Charleston.

Maitland had about nine hundred men, most of them from his own Seventy-first Highlander Regiment, plus a German mercenary regiment and a few Loyalist militia. He held a strong fortification at the ferry point on James Island and a temporary bridge that gave him a means of withdrawal.

The Americans had concentrated sixty-five hundred troops in Charleston to fend off Prevost's feint. General Lincoln led twelve hundred of them out on a night march, intending to attack Maitland in the early morning of June 20. (There are conflicting accounts of the situation, and some say that Lincoln himself did not take the field but left the fighting to North Carolina brigadier general William Moultrie.)

The Americans divided into two columns, with a rear guard of mounted troops, and approached the British works in the predawn darkness. They emerged from a dense woods and opened fire at long range. The foremost British units were two companies of the Seventy-first, who formed up and fought a fierce battle with the advancing rebels, holding up the assault against the main British position. Finally overcoming the Highlanders' resistance, the Americans scattered a group of Germans and moved on to the abatis (a log-strewn obstacle) in front of the British works. Maitland countered by shifting his men, rallying the Germans, and calling for reserves from James Island.

Maitland's countermoves convinced the American officers to break off the engagement and withdraw, leaving the British once again in control of the ferry and the islands at the mouth of Charleston Harbor. Having no interest in holding the position for the time being, Maitland abandoned his works and withdrew toward Beaufort, South Carolina, three days later.

The Americans reported severe losses of 146 killed or wounded and another 155 missing. The British had 26 killed and 103 wounded.

Further Reading

Page Smith. *A New Age Now Begins: A People's History of the American Revolution* (New York: McGraw-Hill, 1976).

Stony Creek

(Stoney Creek)

Canada (June 6, 1813) *War of 1812*

After the American capture of FORT GEORGE, British brigadier general John Vincent withdrew to a position on Burlington Bay Heights in Upper Canada, where he hoped to protect Brig. Gen. Henry Proctor's force to his west. Maj. Gen. Henry Dearborn, the American commander on the Niagara frontier, decided to send Brig. Gen. William Winder to attack Vincent before he could organize a larger force.

Winder set out westward along Lake Ontario with fourteen hundred men but paused after twenty miles to wait for reinforcements under Brig. Gen. John Chandler, who took over command. Although both Winder and Chandler were officers in the regular army, they were political appointees, and their lack of military experience and strategic training quickly became evident.

The Americans established a disorganized camp at Stony Creek, about seven miles from the British position at Burlington Heights. Vincent considered withdrawing, but when careful reconnaissance revealed the weakness of the American camp, he decided to march with Lt. Col. John Harvey to lead a night attack.

The British force, totaling only seven hundred, reached the American position before dawn on June 6. The American sentries were quickly and silently dispatched, but surprise went by the board when the British soldiers let out a great cheer as they approached the edge of camp. At the last minute the Americans roused themselves to meet the attack, and a ferocious, disorganized, hand-to-hand fight through the dark forest began.

Both Winder and Chandler were captured, the latter as he tried to rally a group of men who turned out to be British. The American command fell to Col. James Burn, who decided to withdraw ten miles, to Forty Mile Creek, after daybreak. The greater American numbers had badly damaged Vincent's force, but Burn thought that both British naval and Indian reinforcements were close behind. Vincent, who had been wounded and lost in the forest, eventually made it back to the British camp and was able to claim that he had saved Burlington Heights.

During the battle of Stony Creek, the British lost 23 killed, 136 wounded, and 55 taken prisoner, while the Americans lost only 17 killed, 38 wounded, and fewer prisoners. Still, the retreat helped convince Dearborn to abandon all American positions on the Canadian side of the river, except Fort George. The British came away with a much stronger hand along the Niagara frontier.

Further Reading

George Stanley. *Battle in the Dark: Stoney Creek, 6 June 1813* (Toronto: Balmuir, 1991).

Stony Point

New York (July 16, 1779) *American Revolution*

In June 1779, the British commander in chief, Sir Henry Clinton, seized Stony Point and Verplank's Point across from each other on the Hudson River, only a dozen miles below West Point, and threatened American control of the Hudson River highlands and the routes east and west across the Hudson Valley. Gen. George Washington, the American commander in chief, ordered Maj. Gen. Anthony Wayne, one of the most dashing of his officers, to make a surprise attack on Stony Point, on the west side of the river.

Stony Point was a strong, fortified position, set on a high, rocky hill that thrust out into the river. It was protected by swampy approaches and by two timber-strewn abatis, separated by several hundred yards of cleared ground. The garrison was commanded by Lt. Col. Henry Johnson and his Seventeenth Regiment, along with the grenadiers of the Seventy-first Highlanders and a few Loyalists, numbering about 650 altogether.

Wayne had as his attacking force the twelve hundred troops of his light infantry brigade, with regimental commanders Col. Christian Febiger, Col. Richard Butler, and Col. Return Meigs. Col. Henry "Light-Horse Harry" Lee's mounted troopers were in reserve.

Wayne planned the attack meticulously. He would send his men forward in two columns, and no one would be allowed to fire a musket—the attack would be entirely by the bayonet. The most forward elements would be two suicide squads, called "forlorn hopes," who were expected to batter and chop their way through the abatis. The forlorn hopes were to be supported immediately by advance parties of 150 men each, followed eventually by the main body of troops. The idea was for the suicide squads to take the British defenders by surprise and for each succeeding

element to widen the breach. While the two columns were attacking, Maj. Hardy Murfee was to lead a diversionary movement against the center.

The Americans crossed the swamp land and approached the outer defenses by midnight, achieving the surprise they needed. When the two forlorn hopes ran forward and began to chop simultaneously at the first line of abatis, the British were finally roused and began to fire, but the Americans followed the plan and refused to return the fire, relying on speed and daring. The British soon wounded several men and officers (Wayne himself took a glancing head wound and was out of action for a few moments), but the attackers pressed on. At the head of the right-hand column, Lt. Col. François de Fleury (the marquis de Teissèdre de Fleury, a French volunteer officer using a more democratic form of his aristocratic name) pushed to the front and was the first to plunge into the British works. The squad on the left was not far behind, and soon there was hand-to-hand fighting inside the defenses.

Meanwhile, Col. Johnson had taken the bait and had led a detachment of half of his force out to attack Murfee's feint at the center. The British commander was cut off, surrounded, and forced to surrender. After fierce fighting at close quarters, the rest of his garrison finally gave up, and the Americans claimed possession of the fort.

Fifteen American attackers had been killed and eighty-three wounded. The British defenders lost twenty killed, seventy-four wounded, and fifty-eight missing. The Americans captured 472.

The brilliant operation boosted American spirits and won Wayne some revenge for his defeat at PAOLI, but it had little strategic significance. There were too few troops to hold the fort at Stony Point if the British counterattacked. After stripping the place of guns and supplies, Wayne and his men evacuated the fortification two days after taking it.

Further Reading

Edward H. Hall. *"Stony Point Battle-Field" A Sketch of Its Revolutionary History* (New York: American Scenic and Historic Preservation Society, 1902); I. W. Sklarsky. *The Revolution's Boldest Venture: The Story of General "Mad Anthony" Wayne's Assault on Stony Point* (Port Washington, N.Y.: Kennikat Press, 1965); Wilson Stradley, "Anthony Wayne on the Hudson River." *Valley Forge Journal 3*, no. 4 (1987): 288–307.

Stronghold

California (January 17, 1873) *Modoc War*

The Modoc, a small California tribe numbering only a few hundred, gave up their traditional home under a treaty signed in 1864, but when they were moved to Oregon by the federal government they quarreled with the Klamath tribe there and sought to return south of the state border to their former home. Several years of conflict between the federal government and the Modoc over where the tribe was to live came to a head in late 1872, when a dispute over the surrendering of arms led to gunfire and two deaths. A group of Modoc led by Captain Jack (Kintpuash) fled into a desolate region of lava beds, where they fortified themselves and awaited developments.

The government sent a group of mixed California and Oregon volunteers under Lt. Col. Frank Wheaton after the Modoc, but the men were untrained and unaccustomed to the strange landscape of the lava formations. Wheaton attempted to attack the Modoc camp, known as Stronghold, on the morning of January 17, but a heavy fog made movement impossible. The Americans tried to bombard the Modoc with artillery through the fog but hit nothing except their own advance party, and soon the skillful Modoc warriors began to pick off the soldiers from hiding places among the lava outcrops. With casualties rapidly mounting, Wheaton withdrew—none of his men had so much as seen their enemies.

Wheaton lost eleven dead and twenty-six wounded; the Modoc had no casualties.

The Modoc continued to hide in the lava beds until April, when Captain Jack and several other tribal representatives murdered Brig. Gen. Edward Canby and two other peace-mission members at a parley, after which the federal government hunted down the elusive Modoc. Captain Jack was arrested, tried, and hanged in October along with three other Modoc warriors.

Further Reading

Keith Murray. *The Modocs and Their War.* Reprint ed. (Norman: University of Oklahoma Press, 1984); Arthur Quinn. *Hell with the Fire Out: A History of the Modoc War* (Boston: Faber and Faber, 1997); Jeff Riddle. *The Indian History of the Modoc War and the Causes That Led to It* (Medford, Ore.: Pine Cone, 1973).

Summit Springs

Colorado (July 11, 1869) *Sheridan's Campaign*

Lt. Gen. Philip H. Sheridan's campaign to subdue the aggressive warriors of the Great Plains was only moderately successful during its first phases (*see also* BEECHER'S ISLAND and WASHITA), but the engagement at Summit Springs was a triumph for the army and seriously damaged the power of the Cheyenne Dog Soldier warrior society, which had gained power and influence among several tribes in the years immediately after the Civil War. In July 1869, the Fifth Cavalry, under Col. Eugene A. Carr, plus Maj. Frank North's fifty Pawnee scouts, marched out of Fort McPherson, Nebraska, into Colorado in search of Cheyenne Dog Soldiers. William Cody, who later became one of the nation's most famous showmen as "Buffalo Bill," accompanied the column. Near the site of the Beecher's Island fight, the scouts discovered a large camp of Cheyenne, led by Tall Bull (Hotoakhihoosis), including some Lakota and Arapaho and two captive white women.

Carr was able to surround the camp undetected, and he sprang a surprise dawn attack on July 11. The assault took the Indians completely unprepared, and they put up only a weak defense before scattering. About fifty Indians died, including Tall Bull, and the power of the Dog Soldier Society was broken.

Further Reading

George B. Grinnell. *The Fighting Cheyenne* (Norman: University of Oklahoma Press, 1956); James T. King. *War Eagle: A Life of General Eugene A. Carr* (Knoxville: University of Tennessee Press, 1963).

Talladega

Alabama (November 9, 1813) *Creek War*

The war that broke out in 1813 after the killing of several hundred white settlers by members of the large and powerful Creek Nation of Alabama pitted American regular and militia troops under Maj. Gen. Andrew Jackson against the pro-British Red Stick warrior faction of the tribe (which was responsible for the initial killing). There was also conflict between the prowar Red Sticks and the anti-war White Stick faction of Creek.

A few days after Brig. Gen. John Coffee destroyed several hundred Red Sticks at TALLASAHATCHEE, Jackson marched with two thousand soldiers to the aid of the White Stick village of Talladega, which was under attack from a force of a thousand Red Sticks, led by William Weatherford (Lamochattee, Red Eagle), an able warrior of mixed white-Creek parentage.

Jackson, whose force included large numbers of pro-American Indians, was cautious because of the fragility of his supply system. Two other American columns had gotten into serious trouble in the deep Alabama woods due to lack of food, and supplies Jackson had hoped would reach his base at Fort Strother had failed to materialize. Nonetheless, he pushed on to Talladega, hoping for a quick victory.

When the Americans approached the village, the besieged White Sticks called out greetings as Jackson started to deploy his troops to encircle the Red Sticks. Before the maneuvers were complete, however, the Red Stick warriors swarmed out of the woods and broke through the American lines. The fighting was fierce but brief. Jackson reported that his men had killed 299 of the enemy while suffering 95 casualties of their own.

Despite delivering a sharp blow to the Red Sticks, Jackson was forced after the battle to retreat all the way to his original base at Fort Deposit and wait for supplies and reinforcements.

Further Reading

Angie Debo. *Road to Disappearance: A History of the Creek Indians* (Norman: University of Oklahoma Press, 1941); David S. and

Jeanne T. Heidler. *Old Hickory's War: Andrew Jackson and the Quest for Empire* (Mechanicsburg, Pa.: Stackpole Books, 1996); Joel W. Martin. *Sacred Revolt: The Muskogees' Struggle for a New World* (Boston: Beacon Press, 1991); and Frank L. Owsley, Jr. *Struggle for the Gulf Borderlands* (Gainesville: University Presses of Florida, 1981).

Tallasahatchee

Alabama (November 3, 1813) *Creek War*

After an anti-American warrior faction of the Creek Nation of Alabama killed more than 450 white settlers at FORT MIMS in the summer of 1813, the government of Tennessee responded to intense pressure from aroused citizens to send an army to crush the Red Sticks, as the faction was known. Maj. Gen. Andrew Jackson was given command of thirty-five hundred militia, including many pro-American Creek (members of the White Stick faction of Creek), Cherokee, Chickasaw, and Choctaw, and marched south, where he established base camps near the Red Stick homeland.

Jackson ordered Brig. Gen. John Coffee forward to attack the nearest Red Stick village at Tallasahatchee, where there were approximately two hundred warriors and their families. Coffee divided his force of nine hundred into two main wings, one commanded by Col. John Allcorn and the second by Col. Newton Cannon, and surrounded the village. He sent a small third force to attack the village directly, in a feint.

The Red Sticks fell into the trap and rushed into the center of the encircling troops, where they were cut down by the American muskets. The soldiers then burned the cabins of the village, killing many women and children who had taken refuge in their homes.

The Creek lost around 186 warriors during the battle, with the likelihood that more were killed later outside the village. Eighty-four women and children were taken prisoner. The Americans lost only five dead and forty wounded.

Coffee's men regrouped under Jackson's command and moved toward another battle with the Red Sticks at TALLADEGA six days later.

Further Reading

Angie Debo. *Road to Disappearance: A History of the Creek Indians* (Norman: University of Oklahoma Press, 1941); David S. and Jeanne T. Heidler. *Old Hickory's War: Andrew Jackson and the Quest for Empire* (Mechanicsburg, Pa.: Stackpole Books, 1996); Joel W. Martin. *Sacred Revolt: the Muskogees' Struggle for a New World* (Boston: Beacon Press, 1991); and Frank L. Owsley, Jr. *Struggle for the Gulf Borderlands* (Gainesville: University Presses of Florida, 1981).

Tarrant's Tavern

North Carolina (February 1, 1781)
American Revolution

Hoping to recoup his losses after the defeat of his best striking force at the COWPENS, British southern commander Lt. Gen. Lord Cornwallis, set out to catch and defeat the American army under Maj. Gen. Nathanael Greene. On February 1, Cornwallis led a British force across the Catawba River at COWAN'S FORD and scattered the American militia rearguard. Later in the day, Lt. Col. Banastre Tarleton attacked militia as they attempted to regroup at Tarrant's Tavern, about ten miles from the river.

The details and numbers involved in the short fight are confused and contradictory, but Tarleton believed he had attacked a force of nearly five hundred Americans, with a much smaller detachment of his British Legion. The militia, however, scattered before a charge by Tarleton's troopers, and a number were killed.

The effect of the battle was to depress the recruitment of militia in the region for several weeks and to allow the British to move freely in pursuit of Greene's army. Greene himself was nearby, waiting for the militia, and he was nearly captured as he rode away alone.

Further Reading

Christopher Ward. *The War of the Revolution*. Vol. 2 (New York: Macmillan, 1952).

Taylor's Bridge

See NORTH ANNA RIVER

Tenochtitlán

Mexico (May 26–August 13, 1521)
Spanish Conquest

The largest and historically most significant battle (or, more properly, series of battles) ever fought in North America was the siege by Spanish conquistadores, led by Hernán Cortés, and their Indian allies against the people of the grand city of Tenochtitlán, resulting in the destruction of the empire of the Mexica (later known as the Aztec), a massive death toll, and the establishment of three centuries of Spanish colonial power.

The Mexica had originally migrated to the central Valley of Mexico from the north, and over several generations had conquered the local people, built a magnificent "floating" city on the valley's lake, and widely extended their empire through warfare and conquest. They had accumulated great wealth from the tribute they demanded from their conquered foes, and Tenochtitlán—a masterpiece of urban planning that far surpassed almost all European cities of the time—became the capital of a highly developed culture, with deep connections between political, military, and religious life. At the center of Mexican public life was the practice of human sacrifice, carried out regularly and sometimes on a huge scale by the Mexica. Military tactics were focused on an almost stylized form of combat that sought first and foremost to capture prisoners for sacrifice, rather than to kill on the battlefield. Along with their limited range of weapons—bows and arrows, spears and javelins, stone-throwing slings, and obsidian-bladed wooden swords—these tactics put the Mexica at a huge disadvantage when fighting the Spaniards.

The city itself (the site of modern-day Mexico City) was built on man-made landfill on top of the lake, connected to the shore by a series of causeways. There were thousands of masonry houses, connected to one another to form long streets laid out in a grid pattern. At the center of the city was a large temple square with a towering pyramid, where the human sacrifices took place. Estimates are approximate at best, but there were several hundred thousand inhabitants, representing all levels of Mexican society.

The stability of the life of the Mexica was disrupted forever by the arrival on the coastline in 1519 of several hundred Spanish soldiers, armed with Toledo-steel swords, crossbows, harquebuses (a primitive kind of shoulder firearm), and cannon, and accompanied by horses, an animal never before seen by the native population of North America. The conquistadores were led by the dynamic and intelligent Cortés, who had been commissioned by the Spanish governor of Cuba to explore the mainland, and they were fired with an overwhelming desire for gold and conquest. They soon discovered that a combination of their own skill and the Indians' faulty tactics and inferior weaponry allowed them to defeat huge numbers of Indian warriors at minimal loss to themselves. All the Indians of Mexico used the same tactics, and by a combination of vigorous swordplay, explosive weapons, and the over-

whelming intimidation of mounted men, the conquistadores won numerous skirmishes and defeated the army of TLAXCALA in open battle. They then moved on to Tenochtitlán itself, entering the city peacefully (and much in awe). Cortés hoped he could take control of the Mexica without a war, and he came close to doing so by kidnapping the indecisive emperor Montezuma and slowly beginning to enforce his will. Unfortunately, while Cortés was away from the city defeating a rival Spanish expedition (*see also* CEMPOALLAN), his second in command murdered several hundred Mexican leaders, precipitating a crisis in which Montezuma was killed by his people and the population of the city turned on the Spanish. The Europeans lost almost all the gold and booty they had confiscated, most of their cannon and horses, and about six hundred men in a disastrous retreat led by Cortés across the bridges and causeways of the city on July 1, 1520 (*see also* La NOCHE TRISTE). The wounded survivors fought off an attack of the pursuing Aztec at OTUMBA and straggled on to the safety of the city of Tlaxcala, where Indian allies allowed the Spanish to recover.

Shaking off his tremendous losses, Cortés resolved, immediately upon reaching safety, to renew the campaign against Tenochtitlán as soon as possible. He rebuilt his Spanish force upon the arrival of several ships with replenishments during the fall, and he assiduously cultivated Indian allies among the towns and cities that had long been subject to the Mexica. He also devised a brilliant strategy to take control of the lake surrounding the causeway to Tenochtitlán: he ordered the building of several small brigantine-rigged, flat-bottomed craft that could be either rowed or sailed and would give the Spanish superiority over the Mexican canoes. By dint of tremendous energy, Cortés's shipwright, Mártin de López, not only built the ships but had them carried in pieces by Indian auxiliaries over the mountains to the Lake of Mexico. There in late December 1520, Cortés assembled a force of about 550 Spanish infantry, 80 crossbowmen and harquebusiers, 9 or 10 cannon, and 40 horses.

He then set out on a campaign tour of the rim of the lake, reconnoitering the regions he had not previously visited, taking several Mexica or Mexica-allied towns, and winning new members to his anti-Mexica alliance. By May, fortified with more Spanish reinforcements that brought his numbers to about seventeen hundred infantry and ninety horses, he was ready to lay siege to Tenochtitlán in the European fashion, a style of warfare almost unknown in Mexico. He launched the brigantines onto the lake to destroy the Mexican canoes and take control of the causeways, thereby cutting off the city from its landward sources of food. On May 26, Cortés formally began the siege by capturing Chapultepec and destroying the aqueduct that supplied the city with drinking water.

Inside Tenochtitlán, the new emperor, Cuauhtémoc, a young nephew of Montezuma, led a population that probably numbered between 150,000 and 500,000 men, women, and children. They were implacably determined to resist the Spanish and their allies and, if possible, to defeat the alien invaders. Knowing that it would be impossible to fight the sort of open-field battles they were accustomed to, the Mexica prepared to attack the Spaniards on the causeways and through the city streets in the manner that had been so effective the previous year.

The Spanish brigantines began an offensive on June 1, attacking the Mexican canoe fleet with deadly use of small cannon mounted in the bows as well as crossbows and harquebuses fired from the decks. Within days, Cortés routed the canoes and took control of the waterways surrounding the city and the causeways. He divided his command to cover three of the four main causeways, intentionally leaving one open to allow the Mexican warriors to escape if they wished, since Cortés believed his men could always win an open battle.

Instead, however, a pattern of fighting developed in which the Spanish used their brigantines as floating bridges across gaps that the Mexica had hacked out of the causeways, filling them in with rubble as they advanced. The Spanish horses and cannon moved irresistably into the city during their attacks over the next several days, but Cortés, fearing his men would be cut off if they penetrated too far too soon, ordered them to withdraw to safe bases each night. During the hours of darkness, he Mexica would again break the causeways, and the Spanish would renew the attack the next day, relying on their Indian allies for the back-breaking labor of moving rubble. If the conquistadores were the least bit incautious, the Mexica would try to trap them in the narrow streets and rain stones and missiles down from the roof tops. Eventually Cortés realized that the Mexica were not inclined either to give up or leave their capital, so he sealed off the last causeway and began a long battle of destruction and attrition, similar to those of the twentieth century in which entire cities were to be destroyed street by street and the entire population—military and civilian alike—subjected to attack and death on a huge scale.

Throughout the first weeks of June, the Spanish continued the pattern of attack and withdrawal, pressing each time farther into the city and destroying more and more during their assaults. The Mexica resisted every step of the way but had only minimal success against Cortés's well-coordinated efforts. Despite occasional setbacks to the conquistadores, by the end of the month half of the city was in ruins, the Mexica were running low on food and water, and thousands more allies were flocking to the Spanish.

On June 30, however, the Spanish overreached, and the Aztec enjoyed their biggest victory since the expulsion of their enemies a year previous. Cortés had ordered a combined attack at the great marketplace in the suburb of Tlatelolco, where many of the Mexica had sought refuge. At first the Spanish penetrated deeply into the city, but the Mexica stole in behind and cut the causeway, trapping one column in a tangle of streets and swarming over it at close quarters, where the Spanish horses and artillery were of little use. The Mexica captured fifty-three conquistadores and killed twenty, and they captured a Spanish cannon and one brigantine. To their horror, the soldiers of Cortés's army watched from afar as their captured comrades were dragged naked to the top of the great temple pyramid and sacrificed: their hearts were ripped out of their living bodies with obsidian knives, their heads were cut off and flayed as trophies, their bodies were thrown down the pyramid steps to be butchered and cooked for ritual cannibalism.

The Spanish withdrew to the safety of their shoreline bases and gathered their strength, renewed in purpose by the fate of their captured companions. During the following weeks, it slowly became apparent that the victory of June 30 was the last gasp of serious Mexica resistance. Cuauhtémoc was running out of warriors and resources, and he was unable to devise tactics that would more than delay inevitable defeat. On July 22, the Spaniards lured thousands of Aztec into an ambush and slaughtered them. Five days later, Pedro de Alvarado, the second in command who had murdered the Mexica leaders in 1520, led a column that captured the central pyramid in the Mexican stronghold of Tlatelolco and raised Cortés's flag above the temple. The remaining Mexica refused for two more weeks to surrender, despite massacres and large-scale slaughter by the emboldened Indian allies of the Spanish.

Finally, on August 13, Cuauhtémoc tried to flee the city, but he was recognized, and his canoe was captured by a Spanish brigantine. The struggle was at an end, but not before thousands more were killed by the allies of the Spanish. The entire magnificent city that had been

Tenochtitlán lay in ruins, with the remaining remnant of her population begging for food.

While contemporary accounts of the casualties of the siege varied widely, a sober modern estimate puts the number of Spaniards killed at around a hundred and the deaths among the Mexica of the city—both military and civilian—at no less than a hundred thousand. It is impossible to calculate the numbers killed and wounded among the Spanish allies.

The rule of the Mexica and the independence of the native people of Mexico came to an end with the destruction of Tenochtitlán. For the next three hundred years, the Spaniards would rule.

Further Reading

Nigel Davies. *The Aztecs: A History* (Norman: University of Oklahoma Press, 1980); C. Harvey Gardiner. *Naval Power in the Conquest of Mexico* (Austin: University of Texas Press, 1956); Charles Gibson. *The Aztecs under Spanish Rule: A History of the Indians of the Valley of Mexico, 1519–1810* (Palo Alto, Calif.: Stanford University Press, 1964); Serge Gruzinski. *The Aztecs: Rise and Fall of an Empire* (New York: Harry N. Abrams, 1992); Salvador de Madariaga. *Hernán Cortés: Conqueror of Mexico.* Reprint ed. (Westport, Conn.: Greenwood Press, 1979); and Hugh Thomas. *Conquest: Montezuma, Cortés, and the Fall of Old Mexico* (New York: Simon & Schuster, 1993).

❧ Terry's Expedition

See FORT FISHER

❧ Thames

(Moraviantown)

Canada (October 5, 1813) *War of 1812*

Tecumseh, the charismatic Shawnee warrior and leader who had seen his campaign to halt American expansion ended by William Henry Harrison at the battle of TIPPECANOE in 1811, was killed fighting with the British against American forces at the Battle of the Thames. The loss of this important leader, and the disintegration of the confederacy of Indians he had organized, increased the significance of the brief encounter at the Thames, which also marked the end of British control of the Detroit frontier.

After Commodore Oliver Hazard Perry defeated the British at the battle of LAKE ERIE, British major general Henry Proctor was determined to retreat through Upper Canada before Major General Harrison could attack him.

Tecumseh, the leader of Proctor's Indian allies, opposed the withdrawal and publicly accused Proctor of abandoning the Indians, to whom the British had pledged to carry on the fight. Proctor prepared to retreat north toward Moraviantown, but he promised Tecumseh to make a stand somewhere on the River Thames along the way.

Meanwhile, Commodore Perry began ferrying Harrison's troops across Lake Erie and into Canada. He had gathered a large force that included over three thousand fresh Kentucky militia recruits, led personally by Gov. Isaac Shelby, and twelve hundred mounted riflemen under the command of a U.S. representative, Col. Richard Mentor Johnson. The forty-five hundred Americans who arrived on Canadian soil outnumbered Tecumseh's five hundred warriors and Proctor's force of around eight hundred British regulars.

Though Harrison was unsure he could catch up with Proctor's retreat, the British moved slowly (in part because they had so many families along with them) and did a poor job of destroying bridges in their wake. The American force captured British baggage and ammunition as they followed Proctor and prepared for a fight.

On October 5, Proctor took up position just west of Moraviantown. His regulars held a small forest on the left, while Tecumseh's force moved forward to the edges of a swamp by the river. Johnson assured Major General Harrison that their opponents' two thin lines were weak, and he requested permission to charge up the middle with his mounted force. Harrison, who had preferred to attack the British regulars, finally agreed.

Johnson's troops charged the Indian line, shouting "Remember the Raisin!" in reference to the Americans killed by Indians at FRENCHTOWN. The Indian warriors held the swamp and even advanced toward the American left during part of the fighting. After about thirty minutes, the Indians dispersed as American reinforcements arrived. The British line was dispatched even more quickly, and a column led by Colonel Johnson's brother, James Johnson, overran the lone British six-pounder, subjected the British to heavy crossfire, and forced their surrender.

Tecumseh was killed during the engagement. Richard Mentor Johnson always took credit for his death, although it could never be confirmed that it was he who struck down the Shawnee warrior. The boost in reputation Johnson gained from killing Tecumseh helped get him elected vice president in 1836. Despite the probability that Tecumseh's body was removed by the Indians, several American troops claimed to have cut pieces of skin from his body as souvenirs, in a grim confirmation of the Indian warrior's heroic reputation.

Other casualties in the battle included 33 dead Indian warriors and 477 British prisoners. The American force lost only fifteen killed and thirty wounded.

Proctor was convicted of misconduct and publicly reprimanded for his shoddy performance. American victory at the Thames crippled the British in the Old Northwest and shook Indian confidence in British power.

Further Reading

John Sugden. *Tecumseh's Last Stands* (Norman: University of Oklahoma Press, 1985); and Bennett H. Young. *The Battle of the Thames* (Louisville, Ky.: John P. Morton, 1903).

✎ Three Rivers

(Trois Rivières)
Canada (June 8, 1776) *American Revolution*

An American army of invasion had been decisively repelled when it had attempted to take QUEBEC in January 1776, but the British commander, Gen. Guy Carleton, had been too shorthanded to sortie and chase away the Americans. Six months later, they still held important posts on the St. Lawrence and Richelieu Rivers.

The Americans had a relatively large number of troops in the area, since reinforcements had trickled in from the colonies to the south, but they were poorly supplied, suffered bad morale, and had been ravaged by smallpox and other diseases. The new American commander, Brig. Gen. John Sullivan, ordered Brig. Gen. William Thompson to take the initiative again and attack the British at Three Rivers, a post midway between Quebec and Montreal. Sullivan thought the post was lightly defended, but in fact British major general John Burgoyne, who had arrived from Europe with eight regiments of British regulars and two thousand tough German mercenaries, had advanced downriver to shore up the British position.

Thompson had relatively fresh troops and a coterie of able lieutenants, but his attack on Three Rivers unraveled almost immediately, and all his plans went awry. The Americans advanced by boat to within a few miles of Three Rivers on the morning of June 8, but they were then led down the wrong road by a guide and blundered into a swamp. They floundered in the slime and muck for hours before getting back to the main road, now exhausted and

without the advantage of surprise. Worse, as the Americans approached Three Rivers they came under fire from British gunships and were forced from the road into another swamp.

The only bright spot came when a small detachment under Anthony Wayne boldly took on a much larger British force and sent it flying from the field. Thompson fared less well. As he finally came within sight of the town, he noted a line of entrenchments. He failed to realize, however, that several thousand of Burgoyne's men now manned the field fortifications. When Thompson's men attacked, they met a withering fire from the trenches and from the ships. They turned to flee, only to discover that another British force had landed from the river and cut them off. The American army disintegrated, and small groups fled through the swamps and woods, pursued by Canadians irregulars and their Indian allies. General Carleton allowed most to escape, since he had little food for prisoners.

The remnant of the American army was scarcely a fighting force any longer, and the way was open for Burgoyne to turn the tables and march south in an invasion of his own.

Further Reading

Christopher Ward. *The War of the Revolution.* Vol. 1 (New York: Macmillan, 1952).

✎ Throg's Neck

(Throg's Point)
New York (October 12, 1776) *American Revolution*

During the British campaign in 1776 to take New York City and destroy the rebel American army, the British commander in chief, Gen. Sir William Howe, moved very deliberately to corner George Washington on Manhattan Island. After a small battle, a stand-off, at HARLEM HEIGHTS in mid-September, Howe remained in camp for several weeks while Washington considered withdrawal northward to White Plains.

Howe had the Americans badly outnumbered, and he also had total superiority in the waters around New York. The Royal Navy had supplied a large fleet, including ten powerful ships of the line, and the Americans had no significant armed craft at all. The obvious tactic for Howe was to make a landing on the eastern shore of Manhattan, on Long Island Sound.

On the morning of October 18, Howe embarked four thousand troops from his base at KIP'S BAY for a landing at Throg's Neck. The men scrambled ashore from their boats unopposed, but they discovered that the site had been ill chosen: they were on a marshy, swampy island, connected to the mainland by a causeway-bridge combination. When they began to cross toward solid ground, the trouble began.

A group of thirty riflemen under Col. Edward Hand of the First Pennsylvania Rifles opened fire from behind a woodpile and stopped the British in their tracks. An effort to cross a nearby ford met similar opposition, and the entire British invasion force was stranded in the marsh. By the time it regrouped, the Americans had rushed in eighteen hundred men to reinforce the defense of Throg's Neck. The British were stymied.

Further Reading

Page Smith. *A New Age Now Begins: A People's History of the American Revolution.* Vol. 1 (New York: McGraw-Hill, 1976).

Tippecanoe

Indiana (November 7, 1811) *Indian Wars*

The inconclusive battle fought in 1811 near modern-day Lafayette, Indiana, was a significant chapter in the long story of violent conflict between white Americans and Native Americans, and, similar to many other such incidents, it was motivated by American desire for land and Indian desire to preserve their traditional way of life.

In the years following the American victory at FALLEN TIMBERS, the United States expanded into the region of the Old Northwest and negotiated or forced a combination of treaties that dispossessed the tribes that had traditionally lived there. The governor of Indiana Territory, William Henry Harrison, who had fought as a junior officer at Fallen Timbers under Maj. Gen. Anthony Wayne, was particularly aggressive in taking over tribal lands, and his efforts brought millions of acres at least nominally into ownership by the United States.

Harrison and the United States were opposed by perhaps America's most charismatic Indian leader and orator, Tecumseh (Tekamthi), the son of a Shawnee father and a Creek-Cherokee mother. Tecumseh was a skilled warrior, but his greatest talents lay in his remarkable abilities to rouse his audiences through oratory. He developed a vision of a grand confederation of American tribes that

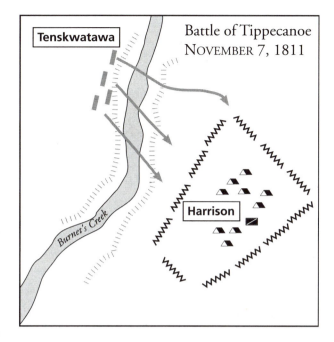

Battle of Tippecanoe
NOVEMBER 7, 1811

Tenskwatawa

Harrison

Burnet's Creek

would be strong enough to counter the expansion of the United States. He was closely associated in his activities with his brother, Tenskwatawa (the Shawnee Prophet), who had received a powerful spirit vision and acted as a spiritual leader and guide. The two established at the confluence of the Tippecanoe and Wabash Rivers a large village called Prophet's Town, where members of tribes from all over the region gathered. During the first decade of the nineteenth century, Tecumseh traveled widely among tribes all over the West and the South, spreading his message of unity and resistance.

In the fall of 1811, Tecumseh was away on one of his trips, and Harrison saw an opportunity to weaken the growing strength of the Shawnee-led confederation. Hoping to provoke an attack by the Indians, he marched toward Prophet's Town at the head of one thousand troops, most of them militia. Harrison camped near the village and waited for events to unfold.

Tecumseh had counseled Tenskwatawa to avoid conflict with Harrison, hoping eventually to persuade enough tribes to join his confederation to make their combined numbers too powerful for the Americans to overcome. Tenskwatawa, however, apparently influenced by other tribal leaders in the village, decided to attack Harrison, telling his warriors that his magic would protect them from the white soldiers' bullets.

At dawn on November 7 the Indians sprang their attack on Harrison's camp, where the soldiers had bivouacked in defensive formation. A sentry alerted the Americans before the Indian's advance reached the heart of the camp, and although his men were driven back by the first attack, Harrison managed to rally his troops and fight off several more assaults. The battle lasted for two hours, and despite heavy losses, the Americans held firm. The Indians eventually gave up the struggle and retreated.

The Americans lost 180 casualties; the Indians lost 30.

Harrison occupied Prophet's Town the next day and destroyed most of the village. The battle had short-circuited Tecumseh's grand design for a confederation, and he eventually allied himself with the British, dying at the Battle of the THAMES during the War of 1812. Harrison went on to a successful political career. He was elected president of the United States in 1840, campaigning in large part on the strength of his "victory" at Tippecanoe.

Further Reading

Gregory E. Dowd. *A Spirited Resistance: The North American Indian Struggle for Unity, 1745–1815* (Baltimore: Johns Hopkins University Press, 1992); R. David Edmunds. *The Shawnee Prophet* (Lincoln: University of Nebraska Press, 1983); and Bill Gilbert. *God Gave Us This Country: Tekamthi and the First American Civil War* (New York: Atheneum, 1989).

Tishomingo Creek

See BRICE'S CROSS ROADS

Tlaxcala

Mexico (August–September, 1519)
Spanish Conquest

In a series of skirmishes and battles during late August and early September 1519, a small group of Spanish conquistadores, led by Hernán Cortés, defeated the army of the Indian city of Tlaxcala, opening the way for Cortés's march on the Valley of Mexico.

The Spaniards, numbering about five hundred, had sailed from Cuba in February, and after encountering the Maya of the Yucatán Peninsula (*see also* POTONCHAN), had begun to march inland, where to their amazement they came upon large, sophisticated cities. Most of these were subject to the loose imperial rule of the dominate Mexica (referred to by later writers as the Aztec), who controlled most of the central region of what is now Mexico from their magnificent capital at Tenochtitlán (modern-day Mexico City). Tlaxcala was one of the most independent of the outlying cities, paying tribute to the Mexica but resisting incorporation into the Mexican Empire. The Tlaxcalans spoke the same language as the Mexica and shared most of their religious and cultural practices, including frequent human sacrifice and ritual cannibalism, practices that shocked the Spanish.

The city may have had as many as 150,000 inhabitants, comprising originally a coalition of four different but related tribes, including the Otomí, who formed the backbone of the Tlaxcalan army. The war leader was Xicotencatl the Younger, who advocated attacking and killing the alien white invaders without delay, although the older members of the ruling political council wanted to study the Spaniards first. The Tlaxcalans were confident in their power, having resisted absorption by the Mexica for several generations. Like all other Indian peoples of Old Mexico, they had developed battlefield tactics and weapons that aimed at wounding and capturing their enemies rather than killing, the object being to obtain as many prisoners as possible for sacrifice. This turned out to be a severe limitation when confronting the Spaniards on the battlefield. The Tlaxcalans were typically armed with bows and arrows, spears (often flung by throwing devices called *atlatls*), stone-throwing slings, and wooden swords edged with brittle obsidian blades.

Cortés's force was armed with fine steel-bladed swords, which the Spaniards used with deadly skill against the Indians, and it included crossbowmen and a handful of harquebusiers, whose weapons were primitive firearms. In addition to a number of vicious war dogs, trained to maim and kill in battle, the Spanish had with them sixteen horses, the first such animals ever seen in North America, which proved extremely effective in battle. They also had fourteen artillery pieces. When these weapons of advanced technology appeared on the battlefield, their physical and psychological impact was immense. Throughout the fighting with the Tlaxcalans, the Spaniards discovered that the combination of their superior weapons and tactics—the Indian warriors obligingly presented themselves for slaughter in attempts to capture the conquistadores—allowed them to defeat vastly larger numbers of their enemies.

The first battle took place in late August, when Cortés approached the city. The Tlaxcalans attempted to ambush the Spanish column. They succeeded in killing two horses whose riders had gotten ahead of the main body, but the rest of the riders scattered the Tlaxcalans. Several Spaniards were wounded, but none were killed. A few days later, the Tlaxcalans again ambushed the Spanish, capturing a mare and killing several of Cortés's men early in the battle, but crossbows, arquebuses, and artillery shattered the Indian attack, even though the Tlaxacalans may have numbered as many as forty thousand.

Cortés took possession of a hill called Tzompachtepetl outside the city and continued the fighting for nearly two weeks, personally leading into the countryside an expedition that brutally maimed and killed Indians in a deliberate attempt to intimidate the Tlaxcalans. The largest fight was against the full weight of the Tlaxcalan army, estimated by the Spanish at more than one hundred thousand, on the plain in front of the Spaniard's position. The sheer weight of numbers nearly overwhelmed the Spanish, but in the end the slaughter by the swordsmen and the effect of the Spanish horses and artillery beat off the masses of Indians. Two or three Spaniards were killed and about sixty wounded; large numbers of Tlaxcalans died. A second raid into the countryside was followed by yet another pitched battle, with much the same result. The final encounter was a night battle, during which the Spanish once again completely defeated the Tlaxcalans. After suffering massive casualties and observing that the Spaniards, though damaged, were little diminished after several battles, the Indians declared an end to the warfare.

Cortés and his men entered the city, and within a few days they forged an alliance with the Tlaxcalans, who became steadfast allies of the Spaniards in the conquest of the empire of the Mexica.

Further Reading

William H. Prescott. *History of the Conquest of Mexico . . .* (New York: Modern Library, 1936); Hugh Thomas. *Conquest: Montezuma, Cortés, and the Fall of Old Mexico* (New York: Simon & Schuster, 1993).

☙ Trenton

New Jersey (December 26, 1776)
American Revolution

Gen. George Washington's surprise raid against a large force of German mercenaries produced a crucial victory at one of the darkest hours of the Revolution and—along with a subsequent victory at PRINCETON—did much to revive flagging American fortunes.

Following the series of defeats on Long Island and Manhattan at the hands of a large professional British army under Maj. Gen. Sir William Howe, Washington's men had fled across New Jersey and had barely reached the safety of Pennsylvania ahead of the British pursuit, lead by Maj. Gen. Lord Cornwallis. The British, as was usual for an eighteenth-century European army, ceased operations for the year in December and settled in for the winter, with many units, including their German mercenary allies, dispersed throughout southern New Jersey.

Washington decided on a raid in force against the twelve hundred Germans at Trenton, commanded by Col. Johann Rall, a competent soldier but one given to careless contempt for his American opponents. Washington decided to hit the Germans on the day after Christmas by stealthily sending three divisions of his troops over the Delaware River in the dead of night. His plan may have been influenced in part by the fact that the enlistments of many of his men were due to expire at the end of the month.

Two of the American divisions, under Gen. James Ewing and John Cadwalader, failed completely in their missions. Ewing did not cross the river at all, and Cadwalader crossed over but returned immediately. This left only the division of about twenty-four hundred men commanded by Washington himself.

Washington's division embarked on Christmas night at McKonkey's Ferry aboard flat-bottomed Durham boats, designed for hauling grain and iron ore, which were handled skillfully in the foul weather by Col. John Glover's Marblehead Mariners. Washington crossed with the advance party and waited impatiently as the troops and eighteen pieces of field artillery were ferried over in the face of snow, sleet, and wind-driven chunks of floating ice that battered the boats.

By 3:00 A.M., his men and cannon were assembled on the New Jersey side, and they began the nineteen-mile march to Trenton. When it neared the town, the attacking force split into two corps. The first, under Maj. Gen. John Sullivan, marched directly along the river and entered Trenton from the south. Washington stayed with the second corps, commanded by Maj. Gen. Nathanael Greene, which looped around the town and entered from the north. The Germans had relaxed their discipline and precautions in order to celebrate the holiday, and many—including Rall himself—were drunk or asleep. The Americans met little resistance as they rolled into place, planting their cannon strategically at the town's main intersection and their infantry in blocking positions.

The attack surprised the Germans completely, and few were able to put up more than token resistance to the bayonets and musket fire of the Americans. Washington's men shot down many of the enemy as they ran through the streets in confusion, and artillery fire destroyed all German attempts to organize. Rall struggled out of his quarters and made it to a nearby orchard, where he tried to rally some of his troops, but he was mortally wounded by cannon fire, and all resistance collapsed. Within ninety minutes Washington had taken complete control of the town and captured nine hundred prisoners. In all, twenty-two Germans were killed and ninety-two wounded. The tactical surprise was so complete that no one in Washington's force was killed and only a few were wounded (including young Lt. James Monroe, a future president).

Washington knew that Cornwallis had a significant force not far away at Princeton, and he feared a response, which the exhausted Americans would find difficult to repel, since two-thirds of his force had failed to show up as planned. He ordered his troops, with their prisoners in tow, back to the river crossing and into the boats. Many suffered cruelly from exposure during the return across the Delaware, but the entire assault force and prisoners made it back to the safety of Pennsylvania.

The episode stunned the British and their German allies. Several outposts in other towns were evacuated immediately for fear of surprise attack, and the British command sought a way to strike back.

The success at Trenton was the only clear-cut victory personally commanded by Washington during the entire American Revolution, and it revived the will of the Americans to continue the war.

Further Reading

Alfred Hoyt Bill. *The Campaign of Princeton, 1776–1777* (Princeton, N.J.: Princeton University Press, 1948); William H. Dwyer. *The Day Is Ours! November 1776–January 1777: An Inside View of the Battles of Trenton and Princeton* (New York: Viking Press, 1983); Samuel S. Smith. *The Battle of Trenton* (Monmouth Beach, N.J.: Philip Freneau Press, 1965); Ray Thompson. *Washington along the Delaware: The Battles of Trenton and Princeton* (Fort Washington, Pa.: Bicentennial Press, 1970); and Kemble Widmer. *The Christmas Campaign: The Ten Days of Trenton and Princeton* (Trenton: New Jersey Historical Commission, 1975).

❧ Trevilian Station

Virginia (June 11–12, 1864) *American Civil War*

At the end of May 1864, Union major general Philip Sheridan's cavalry corps set out to destroy the railroad connection between Charlottesville and Richmond, Virginia, before a planned rendezvous with Maj. Gen. David Hunter's army at Charlottesville. Confederate general Robert E. Lee dispatched Maj. Gens. Wade Hampton and Fitzhugh Lee to foil Sheridan's plan. The two forces met at Trevilian Station (now Trevilians) on June 11 in one of the bloodiest cavalry engagements of the war.

On the morning of June 11, Major General Hampton split his force and hoped to envelop the Federals between Trevilian Station and the town of Louisa, but just as two of Hampton's brigades engaged Brig. Gen. Alfred Torbert's Union cavalrymen, Hampton realized that Federal brigades had almost encircled him. Brig. Gen. George Custer, who led one of Torbert's brigades, managed to get between Hampton and Lee's divisions and to seize eight hundred Confederate horses and vehicles.

Hampton had to break off his main engagement in order to recapture his horses and supplies. Though Hampton was able to accomplish this (with the help of Brig. Gen. Tom Rosser's Laurel Brigade) and even to capture some of Custer's wagons and several hundred Federal prisoners, Custer held on to Trevilian Station and prevented Fitzhugh Lee's division from rejoining Hampton's force.

The next day, Hampton changed his tactics and met with greater success. He entrenched his men along a defensive line between the railroad and the Gordonsville road. From this position, the Confederates were able to withstand several dismounted attacks by Sheridan's men. After destroying only six miles of railroad, Sheridan was forced to call off his assault.

Union casualties in the two-day battle at Trevilian Station totaled 735, and, though no sure figures are known, Confederate losses are estimated at more than 1,000.

Major General Hampton's victory at Trevilian Station thwarted the Union plan to reinforce Hunter's army in the Shenandoah Valley, and Sheridan had to withdraw to the James River instead.

Further Reading

Walbrook D. Swank. *The Battle of Trevilian Station: The Civil War's Greatest and Bloodiest All-Cavalry Battle . . .* (Shippensburg, Pa.: Burd Street Press, 1994).

❧ Trois Rivières

See THREE RIVERS

❧ U.S.S. *Trumbull* v. *Watt*

Off the Atlantic Coast (June 2, 1780)
American Revolution

Capt. James Nicholson, who had survived the threat of court-martial for surrendering the *Virginia* to the British in 1778, took command of the new thirty-gun frigate *Trumbull* in September 1779. After construction and recruiting delays, Nicholson sailed from New London, Connecticut, in May 1780 to patrol for illegal traders. When *Trumbull* engaged the British thirty-two-gun privateer *Watt* on June 2, Nicholson proved himself a worthy commander in what is considered one of the hottest single-ship encounters of the entire war.

By the time *Watt's* master, John Coulthard, brought his ship into pistol range of the Trumbull, Nicholson had ordered the decks sanded, the cannons prepared, and his gun captains to stand by with lighted slow matches. Nicholson hoisted the Continental colors and opened the battle with a broadside, which Coulthard returned. For the next two hours the ships exchanged fire, never more than eighty yards apart. Both ships were set afire at times as the crews fired at one another. Nicholson concentrated his fire at Watt's hull even as Coulthard shot at Trumbull's rigging, and both ships were severely damaged. After sustaining direct hits to his ship's hull, Coulthard disengaged and sailed away. Nicholson pursued for eight hours, but he was unable to catch up, because his sails were in tatters.

Nicholson reported six men killed and thirty-two wounded, while Coulthard acknowledged over ninety casualties.

After she lost two masts in a storm on June 3, Trumbull limped back toward Boston, where she arrived some twenty days later. Nicholson, who became a naval hero, was later captured in Trumbull by the British frigate *Iris* (*see also* U.S.S. TRUMBULL v. *IRIS*).

Further Reading

Gardner W. Allen. *A Naval History of the American Revolution.* Vol. 2 (New York: Russell & Russell, 1962); and William M. Fowler, Jr. *Rebels under Sail: The American Navy during the Revolution* (New York: Charles Scribner's Sons, 1976).

❧ U.S.S. *Trumbull* v. H.M.S. *Iris*

Off the Delaware Capes (August 8, 1781)
American Revolution

After the engagement between the U.S.S. *Trumbull* and the British privateer *Watt* in 1780, Capt. James Nicholson

took the *Trumbull* to Boston for repairs and then back to sea for a series of cruises off the Delaware Capes. In July 1781, Nicholson was ordered to deliver cargo to Havana, but he had barely left Delaware on August 8 when he was attacked and captured by H.M.S. *Iris.*

Iris had been one of the first American frigates ever constructed, as the *Hancock,* before being captured in 1777. When the thirty-two-gun *Iris,* accompanied by two other British ships, approached *Trumbull* during a heavy squall, Nicholson hoped to be able to escape, but bad luck and a disloyal crew conspired against him.

As *Trumbull* was trying to flee through the storm, two masts broke and severely damaged the rigging as they came crashing down. Nicholson ordered his crew to stand by their guns, but two-thirds of his men, the majority of whom were British prisoners of war, rushed below deck and refused to fight. Nicholson and his two lieutenants, Richard Dale and Alexander Murphy, tried to hold off *Iris* with only a few sailors, but when one of the other British ships, the *General Monk,* approached as well, Nicholson struck his colors in surrender.

Nicholson reported that eight of his men were wounded and five were killed. British casualties are unknown.

The British towed the crippled *Trumbull* into New York, where she was left to rot.

Further Reading

Gardner W. Allen. *A Naval History of the American Revolution.* Vol. 2 (New York: Russell & Russell, 1962); and William M. Fowler, Jr. *Rebels under Sail: The American Navy during the Revolution* (New York: Charles Scribner's Sons, 1976).

❧ Tupelo

(Harrisburg)
Mississippi (July 13–15, 1864) *American Civil War*

As one of the Confederacy's most feared generals, who seemed to his Federal counterparts in the western theater to bedevil their every move, Maj. Gen. Nathan Bedford Forrest had scored a success at OKOLONA in early 1864 and a brilliant victory at BRICE'S CROSS ROADS in June, defeating superior Union forces each time. But in July, he suffered a setback in a battle near his home base of Tupelo, Mississippi.

The western theater commander, Maj. Gen. William T. Sherman, was intent on his campaign into Georgia, but he feared that Forrest's hard-riding cavalry would cut the Union supply line from Nashville to Chattanooga by striking northward from Tupelo. Hoping to rid himself of the menace of Forrest and his growing mystique, Sherman ordered Maj. Gen. Andrew J. Smith to sweep toward Tupelo from near Memphis with fourteen thousand men, destroying everything in his path until he could engage and defeat Forrest. Smith set off on July 4, and his men, following orders, tore up the countryside along the line of march, reaching the vicinity of Tupelo on July 13.

Forrest and his commanding officer, Lt. Gen. Stephen D. Lee (a veteran of the eastern theater), decided to attack with the eight thousand men who were in camp at Okolona, a few miles away. They moved into position on the night of the 13th and were greeted the next morning by the sight of the Union army, strongly dug in on a long, low ridge. Uncharacteristically, Forrest made a serious tactical mistake, deciding that his Confederates could take the entrenched positions. He sent three headlong assaults against the Federals, but as was usual during the Civil War, valor and spirit could not overcome massed

musketry and cannon fire from the strong defensive position. Seeing the scale of the casualties produced by the futile charges, Forrest and Lee ordered a halt.

Smith, on the other hand, failed to perceive his victory and withdrew during the night from his position, leaving his wounded behind. The following morning, on July 15, Forrest led his cavalrymen in an attack on the rear guard of the retreating Union army, but the Confederates were repulsed, and Forrest himself was wounded.

Overall, the Confederates lost 1,326 casualties, the Federals only 674.

Although the engagement ended as a draw and Forrest was still free to make mischief, the Tennessee supply line was safe for the time being.

Further Reading

Edwin C. Bearss. *Protecting Sherman's Lifeline: The Battles of Brice's Creek and Tupelo, 1864* (Washington, D.C.: National Park Service, 1972).

Union Church

See CROSS KEYS

Valcour Island

New York (October 11–13, 1776)
American Revolution

Following their victory at the gates of QUEBEC on the first day of the year, the British were ready by mid-1776 to move into New York, push out the remnants of the American army, and launch a counterinvasion of their own. As part of this effort the British commander in chief, Gen. Guy Carleton, assembled a small fleet at the foot of Lake Champlain and set sail toward FORT TICONDEROGA, where the Americans were concentrating their forces.

Opposing him was a remarkable makeshift flotilla of American ships under the command of Brig. Gen. Benedict Arnold, the Americans' best field commander and also an experienced sailor. During the months following the withdrawal from Canada, Arnold had managed to build a number of gondolas (also called "gundalows")— small, flat-bottomed sailboats usually armed with a twelve-pounder and two nine-pounder cannon—and larger galleys, which had much heavier armament, including six-pounder broadsides in addition to bow and stern guns, and could maneuver against the wind by means of oar power. Arnold also commanded the schooners *Royal Savage,* captured from the British, and *Revenge,* as well as the sloop *Enterprise.* Altogether, the American naval force probably comprised about fifteen ships manned by as many as eight hundred men, although almost none of them were experienced sailors (Arnold was virtually the only man in the flotilla capable of aiming and firing a naval gun).

Carleton's British fleet was considerably stronger, with perhaps twice as much firepower, and it was well manned and equipped. He had a three-masted ship, the *Inflexible;* two schooners, *Carleton* and *Maria;* a huge, bargelike vessel called *Thunderer;* a gondola, and twenty small but heavily armed gunboats.

In early October, Carleton sailed south with his fleet while his land force marched overland. Arnold withdrew before the British ships and on October 10 hid his flotilla behind Valcour Island, a large, steep-hilled, wooded island near the eastern shore of the lake. He planned to sail out of his hiding place after the British had passed, seize the advantage of the strong prevailing wind, and attack Carleton. The next morning, the British failed to detect the American ships until well past Valcour Island, but they then turned into the wind and attempted to beat back toward the enemy. Arnold, commanding from the galley *Congress* in the middle of his line of ships, sent the *Royal Savage* and four galleys out to attack, but when he recognized the superior strength of Carleton's fleet, Arnold ordered a retreat. Unfortunately, the *Royal Savage* ran aground after coming under fire from the foremost British ships, and she was of little use for the rest of the engagement.

Two of Carleton's ships, *Inflexible* and *Maria*, beat to windward until they were within extreme range of the Americans, where they anchored and opened fire. The schooner *Carleton*, fighting the fickle winds swirling off the island cliffs, anchored directly opposite the middle of the American line. Her commander brought his guns to bear by means of a spring line, and began to pound away, supported by several of the British gunboats. A desperate battle continued for several hours until the *Carleton's* spring line was shot away and she swung helplessly around, exposed to raking fire and unable to escape. Finally, through the heroic efforts of Midshipman Edward Pellew (eventually to become an admiral), the *Carleton* managed to pass a line to the gunboats, who towed her away.

Meanwhile, the *Inflexible* had worked close to the American line and devastated several of Arnold's ships with broadside after broadside. In early evening, the British disengaged and withdrew to a blocking formation at the head of the island.

Arnold's flotilla was a shambles. Several of his ships were either aground or sinking fast, and he had lost around sixty men. If he waited for morning, the British would certainly be able to finish him off at their leisure; the American commander decided on a daring plan. Under cover of darkness and fog, the remaining American ships sailed silently toward the British line and slipped undetected through a narrow gap in the formation. Then began a race to escape.

Unfortunately for the Americans, the usual winds failed and they had to pull their craft by backbreaking oar power. They had advanced only a few miles by the next morning, by which time three more of the galleys had either run aground or sunk from battle damage. At midday the leading British ships caught up with the rearmost American galleys and destroyed them with cannon fire. Arnold, aboard his galley *Congress,* was left in a long running fight,

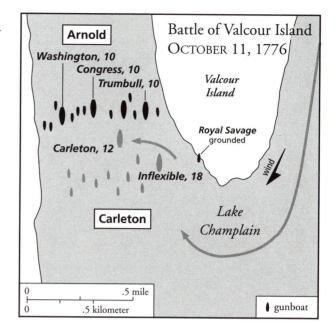

Battle of Valcour Island
OCTOBER 11, 1776

Arnold

Washington, 10
Congress, 10
Trumbull, 10

Valcour Island

Royal Savage grounded

Carleton, 12

Inflexible, 18

wind

Carleton

Lake Champlain

| 0 | | .5 mile |
| 0 | | .5 kilometer |

gunboat

his remaining vessels were severely damaged and could not sail much longer. He ordered his ships beached at Buttonmould Bay and set afire with flags flying. He and his remaining crews escaped overland toward Fort Ticonderoga.

Carleton and his fleet were completely victorious and left in command of the lake. They had destroyed eleven of the fifteen American ships and killed or wounded eighty of the enemy, while suffering only minor losses. However, Carleton's plan of invading New York and marching down the Hudson was disrupted by Arnold's stand at Valcour Island—it was too late in the year to press on with the campaign. The British commander ordered his ships and land forces back to their bases to the north and left the Americans undisturbed at Fort Ticonderoga for nearly another year.

Further Reading

Philip K. Lundeberg. *The Continental Gunboat Philadelphia and the Northern Campaign of 1776* (Washington, D.C.: Smithsonian Institution, 1966).

Veracruz

Mexico (March 22–29, 1847)
Mexican-American War

Though Brig. Gen. Zachary Taylor had won several battles in northern Mexico, by the spring of 1847 the Mexican government still showed no signs of capitulation in the war with the United States. The American president, James K. Polk, decided to send Maj. Gen. Winfield Scott, a hero of the War of 1812 and an excellent strategist, to capture the Mexican capital. Scott intended to land his army of thirteen thousand men at Veracruz, on Mexico's eastern coast, in March and then advance to the capital.

As Scott was gathering his forces off the coast of Mexico throughout early March, it became widely known across the country that he was planning to land at Veracruz. Acting president Valentin Gomez Farías ordered the National Guard to march to Veracruz and counter Scott's expected invasion, but the Guard, which opposed Farías's anticlerical policies, refused.

Meanwhile, Scott and Commodore David Conner planned their amphibious landing, a maneuver that Scott had first daringly executed during the War of 1812 at FORT GEORGE. On March 9, the complicated landing went off without a hitch. More than ten thousand men were first transferred from army vessels to navy ships, then ferried ashore at Collado in surfboats designed by Lt. George M. Totten in Philadelphia. When they reached the beach, the men waded ashore with their muskets held above the water, formed into lines, and charged up a row of sand dunes, led by Brig. Gen. William J. Worth. The Americans met no resistance, in part because the initial landing site was over two miles from the city, out of range of Mexican cannons.

The landing was only the first step toward conquering the city. Veracruz, situated across a harbor from the American landing site, was surrounded by nine forts and a fortified castle, all linked by thick walls. More than four thousand well-supplied Mexican troops were garrisoned in the city. Despite these imposing defenses, Scott's men faced only periodic cannon fire and a few Mexican skirmishing parties over the next several weeks as they extended their lines around the city. Maj. Gen. Robert Patterson urged Scott to assault the city before the yellow fever season set in, but Scott was determined to lay siege.

The navy landed supplies and heavy artillery, and the siege began on March 22 when the Mexican commander, Brig. Gen. Juan Morales, refused Scott's demand to surrender the city. Morales wished to avoid an open fight, but he was convinced the city could withstand a siege. The American artillery opened fire as Comdr. Josiah Tattnall pounded the southern fortifications of Veracruz from his small ships. Commodore Matthew C. Perry, who had taken command of the naval forces from Conner the day before, kept his ships out of range of Veracruz's heavy guns. Mexican cavalry tested weak points in the American

line and tried to break through to allow reinforcements and supplies into the city, but only a few attacks, like one led on March 12 by Col. Juan Aquayo, managed to push past the Americans, and heavy U.S. artillery fire cut off even these few opportunities.

A storm prevented any real activity on the twenty-third, but on the next day the three thirty-two-pounders and three eight-inch guns of the "Naval Battery," which the Americans had constructed on the beach, inflicted devastating blows on the city and breached the walls around the Santa Barbara Fort, where the Mexican flag was shot down, only to be nailed back up by two daring lieutenants, Sebastiàn Holzinger and Francisco Velez. Though the Mexicans had more and heavier guns, the American artillery continued to inflict heavy damage on March 25, when another battery swung into action, and Mexican defenders began to desert their positions in several of the forts on the city's outskirts. In the most important of several small skirmishes, Col. William S. Harney and Maj. Gen. Robert Patterson cleared a force of 150 Mexicans near the American center.

On the evening of March 25, fire was suspended after the French, British, Prussian, and Spanish consuls in Veracruz convinced Brig. Gen. José Juan Landero, now in command in place of an ailing Morales, to enter into negotiations with Scott to be allowed to evacuate the city in prelude to a surrender. Commissioners from both sides met at Punta de Hornos, agreed to terms on March 27, and reported to Scott and Landero on March 28. On March 29, the men of the Mexican garrison marched out of the city, surrendered their arms to Brigadier General Worth, and marched home on parole. The Americans promised to protect Veracruz's citizens and private property and preserve religious freedom. No cheers were heard as the American flag was raised over the city, and many observers commented on the stoicism displayed by both sides.

Winfield Scott's force suffered only nineteen men killed and approximately eighty-one wounded in the entire operation. The Mexicans lost an estimated eighty soldiers and one hundred civilians killed.

American artillery, which had fired 463,000 pounds of shot into the city, amplified by 1,800 rounds fired by the navy, had carried the day against a heavily fortified Mexican city. The capture of Veracruz marked a successful beginning to Scott's campaign, which would ultimately result in the capture of Mexico City and the end of the war.

Further Reading

K. Jack Bauer. *The Mexican War: 1846–1848* (New York: Macmillan, 1974); John D. Eisenhower. *Agent of Destiny: The Life and Times of General Winfield Scott* (New York: Free Press, 1997); and John E. Weems. *To Conquer a Peace: The War between the United States and Mexico* (Garden City, N.Y.: Doubleday, 1974).

⤫ Vicksburg

Mississippi (May 16–July 4, 1863)
American Civil War

Commanding an acute bend in the river from high bluffs, Vicksburg was the Confederacy's most important stronghold in the West, and its batteries and fortifications controlled traffic up and down the Mississippi River. The Union had possession of the river above Vicksburg and had easily taken New Orleans and almost all the towns below it, but without conquering the city itself, the Federals could not win the war in the West. The campaign against Vicksburg had taken nearly a year and cost thousands of casualties when Maj. Gen. Ulysses S. Grant, who was rapidly emerging as the North's most outstanding field commander, was finally able to bring an army of around seventy thousand troops to the outskirts of the city in mid-May 1863.

Vicksburg was defended by thirty thousand Confederates under Lt. Gen. John C. Pemberton, a West Point–trained northerner who had chosen to side with the South at the outbreak of the war. Pemberton had reluctantly allowed himself to be shut up in the city after battling Grant at CHAMPION'S HILL and BIG BLACK RIVER, and now he had no choice but to prolong his defense and hope for rescue from outside, perhaps by the nearby army commanded by Lt. Gen. Joe Johnston.

Confederate engineers had worked for the previous seven months to build and improve the city's landward fortifications, devising an immensely strong system of connected redoubts, redans, and lunettes (all types of earthen forts, of particular shapes) that took advantage of the deep ravines and gullies surrounding Vicksburg. The fortifications encircled the city, starting from the river to the north and extending all the way around the eastern side of the city and back to the river south of Vicksburg. These strong points were connected by a continuous system of trenches and rifle pits. Altogether, Vickburg's defenses seemed unbreachable.

Grant, however, knew he greatly outnumbered Pemberton, and he further believed that the defeats handed the Confederates on May 16 and 17 had left them shaken, perhaps shattered. He resolved to take Vicksburg by storm, expressing the idea that whatever the casualties from an assault, it would be less costly in the long run than a siege.

On May 19, Grant ordered Maj. Gen. William T. Sherman to attack the city's northern defenses at an area commanded by a strong point known as Stockade Redan, a triangular fortification at the top of a steep ravine. The assault was stopped in its tracks by determined musketry from the Confederate defenders, who hit the Union troops as they tried to cross strewn-log barriers and difficult terrain. One group of Federals reached the ditch directly in front of the Redan, but it was pinned down by heavy fire until nightfall, when it escaped back to the Union lines. Casualties among the Union troops were heavy, and at most the attack had only proved that the Confederates were ready to defend their city vigorously.

Three days later Grant tried again, mounting a massive frontal assault on the fortifications. In a style of attack that the world was to associate with the western front of World War I, Grant's artillery and river gunboats pounded a section of the fortifications with a huge, four-hour bombardment, after which a wave of infantry charged toward the defensive works, hitting several points at once in hopes of neutralizing the Confederate reserve forces. The Union attackers had to traverse timber-clogged ditches and ravines, while the Confederate defenders poured on an unimpeded musket fire and lobbed explosives. Despite great valor, almost all the Union attacks were destroyed before they could come close to the fortifications. Grant's troops reached the Confederate fortifications at only one spot, and Pemberton managed to rush in fresh troops and eject the attackers.

At the end of the day, the Union had lost around thirty-two hundred casualties and had nothing to show for the effort. Grant realized that only a prolonged siege could force Vickburg's surrender. Immediately, the Union troops began to dig entrenchments of their own, in a long line roughly parallel to the city's defensive fortifications. Grant stationed units to cut off all landward movement in and out of the city, and the Union riverboats stopped all water traffic. Within days, Vicksburg was sealed off from the outside world, and the Union army settled in to starve the Confederates into surrender. It dug angled siege trenches that brought sharpshooters into range, and it sited hundreds of cannon that fired incessantly into the city. Twice

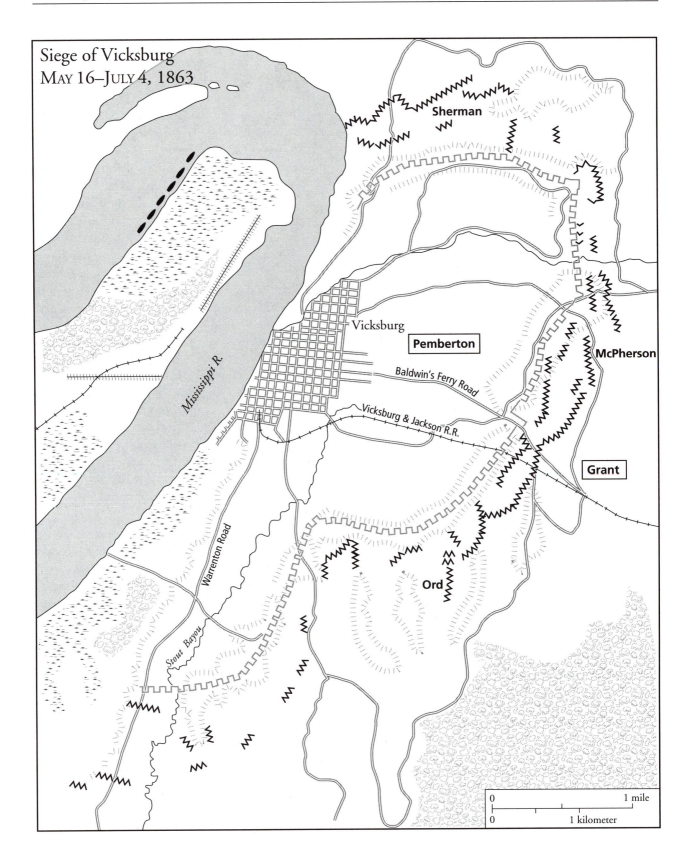

Siege of Vicksburg
MAY 16–JULY 4, 1863

Mississippi R.

Vicksburg

Pemberton

Sherman

Baldwin's Ferry Road

Vicksburg & Jackson R.R.

McPherson

Grant

Warrenton Road

Stout Bayou

Ord

| 0 | | 1 mile |
| 0 | | 1 kilometer |

Union engineers tunneled under the Confederate fortifications and set off huge blasts in attempts to break the defenses, but without success.

Where arms failed, patience eventually won. As the stifling hot days of June wore on, the city began to suffer more and more from lack of supplies—especially food—and from the constant din and danger of artillery shells. The Confederate soldiers could not relax their guard, so they spent long, hot days manning earthen forts and rifle pits. The citizens of Vicksburg, who on the whole suffered from the shortages more than did the soldiers, found life increasingly hard to bear. Many of them took refuge from the daily bombardments by burrowing into hillside caves.

By the end of the month, it was obvious to Pemberton that no Confederate relief force was coming to break the siege, and he polled his subordinate commanders about the chances of breaking out by an assault. They told him that his army was wasted, ill, and demoralized. He concluded that he had no other option than surrender, and on July 3 he rode out to meet Grant and discuss terms. Pemberton refused Grant's first demand for unconditional surrender, but the next day the Confederate commander agreed to modified terms, and the city was handed over to the Union on July 4, Independence Day.

Coming as it did simultaneously with the Union victory at Gettysburg, the surrender of Vicksburg marked one of the true turning points of the Civil War. The Union gained complete control of the Mississippi, and the Confederacy lost the power to impede the movement of Union forces up and down the river. The war in the West became a sideshow thereafter. Ulysses S. Grant had demonstrated his great abilities as a commander, and within the year he was commander in chief of all Union forces. Pemberton, on the other hand, fell precipitously. Accused of treason by virtue of his northern origins, he resigned his commission and volunteered as a private, although he was eventually recommissioned and finished the war as an artillery officer.

Further Reading

Jay Wertz and Edwin C. Bearss. *Smithsonian's Great Battles & Battlefields of the Civil War* (New York: William Morrow, 1997); and Editors of Civil War Times Illustrated. *Struggle for Vicksburg: The Battle and Siege That Decided the Civil War* (Harrisburg, Pa.: Stackpole Books, 1967).

Vincennes

Indiana (February 24–25, 1779)
American Revolution

During the first years of their rebellion, the United States had no military force in the remote but strategically important western region stretching from Kentucky to modern-day Illinois and Indiana. However, Britain had a strong base at Detroit, from which Lt. Gov. Henry Hamilton organized Indian raids into Kentucky, which was then still a county of Virginia. In late 1777, a twenty-six-year-old frontiersman, George Rogers Clark, convinced Virginia authorities to authorize an expedition under his command to capture western British outposts and stop the raiding. Clark's campaign in the Illinois and Indiana country culminated in his capture (or recapture) of the fort at Vincennes in early 1779.

Clark was commissioned as an officer in the Virginia militia and recruited about 150 frontiersmen as his army. They left the site of what is now Louisville in June 1778 and reached Kaskaskia, populated mostly by French-speaking inhabitants as were all the British outposts in early July. Clark took Kaskaskia without a shot, and one of his officers moved on to claim two other outposts. The more important was at Vincennes, where the French population changed allegiance and handed over the fort to Clark.

However, in December, lieutenant governor Hamilton arrived at Vincennes with a force of nearly five hundred men, mostly French-speaking militia and Indian auxiliaries, and reclaimed the post, when the few men left by Clark as a garrison quickly abandoned the place. Most of Hamilton's forces departed soon after, leaving him with only about thirty-five British regulars and a handful of Indians.

Clark, in Kaskaskia, was in not much better condition. Many of his men had returned to Kentucky when their enlistments had expired, and he was having trouble getting food and other supplies. Moreover, the prairies between Kaskaskia and Vincennes were either frozen sheets of ice or deep pools of frigid water. Nonetheless, Clark was determined to recapture Vincennes and eliminate Hamilton as a threat. He rallied his remaining men and set out. They traveled for days, wading at times up to their necks in icy waters with almost nothing to eat, but they made it to Vincennes on February 23, taking Hamilton by surprise.

Clark sent word to the French population that he would treat them well, as in fact he had previously, and prepared to intimidate Hamilton and his few troops.

Clark's men kept up a galling rifle fire at the fort's gun ports, killing several of the British defenders, and he scattered his men around the fort in an attempt to make their numbers appear to be much larger than they actually were. The next day Clark called on Hamilton to surrender, but the British commander refused. Clark then demonstrated the extremely brutal nature of frontier warfare: he paraded five Indian captives before the walls of the fort and had them tomahawked to death in cold blood as a warning to the garrison.

The next day, Hamilton surrendered and he was eventually sent to Virginia as a prisoner of war.

Further Reading

Lowell H. Harrison. *George Rogers Clark and the War in the West* (Lexington: University Press of Kentucky, 1976).

C.S.S. *Virginia*

See U.S.S. *MONITOR*

Wahab's Plantation

North Carolina (September 21, 1780)
American Revolution

In September 1780, Lt. Gen. Lord Cornwallis, who had been given command of the British effort in the South, decided on a campaign to move northward out of South Carolina toward Virginia. While he was organizing this campaign, however, his outposts and detached units repeatedly encountered Carolina partisans, as at the fight at Wahab's Plantation.

Cornwallis's best subordinate by far was Lt. Col. Banastre Tarleton, but the energetic Tarleton was ill and turned over temporary command of his Loyalist British Legion to Maj. George Hanger. Hanger and a contingent of about sixty troopers were surprised at Wahab's by eighty mounted Carolina militia and seventy riflemen under Col. William Davie.

Acting on information from a local partisan, Davie quietly maneuvered his men into position to trap the Loyalists, who had pulled in their sentries and were lounging casually near a cornfield. The patriot riflemen infiltrated through the corn, took possession of one of the plantation buildings, and began to fire on the Loyalists. Davie's mounted troops had meanwhile gone to the other end of a lane that ran through the plantation and, at the first shots, charged down on Hanger and his men, killing fifteen or twenty and wounding forty more.

The patriots had only one casualty—from friendly fire—and seized many of the legion's horses and equipment.

Further Reading

John Buchanan. *The Road to Guilford Courthouse: The American Revolution in the Carolinas* (New York: John Wiley & Sons, 1997).

Washita

Oklahoma (November 27, 1868)
Sheridan's Campaign

When Lt. Gen. Philip H. Sheridan became commander of the army in the West after the Civil War, he brought to the job the aggressive style he had demonstrated against the

Confederacy. During 1868 and 1869, he directed what became known as Sheridan's Campaign, which included new tactics (*see also* BEECHER'S ISLAND) and attacks on Indian villages during the winter months. Lt. Col. George Armstrong Custer, commanding the Seventh Cavalry, carried out one such attack on a large camp of unsuspecting Cheyenne on the Washita River, in modern-day Oklahoma. It was the ghastly fate of Cheyenne peace advocate Black Kettle (Moketavato), who had seen his band almost destroyed at the massacre at SAND CREEK, to be in his lodge on the Washita when Custer attacked.

The Seventh Cavalry fielded around eight hundred men, complete with a regimental band that played the unit's favorite tune, "Gary Owen," as it went into battle. Scouts had discovered the Cheyenne village under a blanket of snow the day before, and on the morning of November 27, Custer, who had demonstrated enthusiasm if not military acumen during the Civil War on a variety of battlefields, executed his usual tactic, sending troopers riding hard into the attack with little idea of the forces or situation they faced.

Luckily for Custer, his attack caught the Cheyenne almost completely by surprise. Black Kettle and his wife ran toward the approaching cavalry in an attempt to stop the charge, but they were shot dead and ridden over. The initial assault met little resistance, and the indiscriminate killing of men, women, and children was a massacre. After scattering the few defenders, Custer's men set fire to the Indian lodges and killed the entire Cheyenne pony herd.

Unknown to Custer, however, there were more villages farther along the river, and soon large numbers of Cheyenne warriors began to filter into the vicinity of Black Kettle's camp. By afternoon, they threatened to surround the Seventh. Custer finally took heed of the danger, and after a feint downstream he managed to withdraw his force, although he abandoned a detachment of fifteen men, leaving them to their fate.

Custer's overall losses were twenty-two dead and fourteen wounded. The troopers killed at least one hundred Cheyenne.

The blow badly damaged the Cheyenne, but it did little to end the conflict on the southern plains.

Further Reading

George B. Grinnell. *The Fighting Cheyennes* (Norman: University of Oklahoma Press, 1956); and Robert M. Utley. *Cavalier in Buckskin: George Armstrong Custer and the Western Military Frontier* (Norman: University of Oklahoma Press, 1988).

≫ Watt

See U.S.S. *TRUMBULL*

≫ Waxhaws

South Carolina (May 29, 1780)
American Revolution

With the capture of the entire southern American army at the fall of CHARLESTON to the British in mid-May 1780, only a small number of organized rebel troops remained: three hundred or so Continentals of Col. Abraham Buford's Third Virginia Regiment, plus a few cavalry survivors of MONCK'S CORNER and LENUD'S FERRY. The British commander in chief, Sir Henry Clinton, sent twenty-five hundred men under Lt. Gen. Lord Cornwallis to track these Americans down. Cornwallis's advance element, mounted units under the redoubtable Lt. Col. Banastre Tarleton, caught up with Buford at Waxhaws and wiped out the last American resistance to British control of the South.

Buford was fleeing rapidly after barely escaping at Lenud's Ferry on May 6, but Tarleton was fleeter still. Tarleton had about 250 men of his own largely Loyalist British Legion, consisting of dragoons and mounted infantry, plus 40 troopers from the Seventeenth Dragoons. He pushed ahead of Cornwallis's column on May 27, driving his men and their mounts cruelly in the stifling heat of an early South Carolina summer. Within two days Tarleton traveled more than one hundred miles and caught up with Buford's rear guard at Waxhaws.

Buford's column was strung out along the road, his artillery far ahead and out of reach. Tarleton hit Buford's rear guard in midafternoon, chopping it up and halting the column's flight. South Carolina governor John Rutledge, who had slipped out of Charleston ahead of the surrender, was with Buford but managed to escape before Tarleton struck. Buford turned down a chance to surrender to Tarleton and deployed his men on open ground to receive the British mounted attack.

Tarleton launched a three-pronged charge with his dragoons and infantry that managed to collapse the American line. Successful cavalry charges against solidly placed infantry are extremely rare in the history of warfare, despite the romantic notions of some writers; nonetheless, whatever the cause, the Americans went under almost at once, and Tarleton's men proceeded to saber and bayonet most of them without allowing surrender. The carnage was so thorough that the episode became famous in subsequent American anti-Loyalist and anti-British lore: "Tarleton's quarter" was henceforth an ironic comment on any battle carried to an ultimate conclusion.

Tarleton's men killed 113 Americans and wounded 203 more, most of them severely, with 53 others captured. Buford's force was almost completely destroyed, although he himself escaped. Tarleton reported only nineteen killed and wounded among his troops.

The destruction of Buford's Virginians extinguished the American presence in the South and set the stage for brutal partisan warfare in the Carolinas.

Further Reading

John Buchanan. *The Road to Guilford Courthouse: The American Revolution in the Carolinas* (New York: John Wiley & Sons, 1997); Jerome J. Nadelhaft. *The Disorders of War: The Revolution in South Carolina* (Orono: University of Maine at Orono Press, 1997); John S. Pancake. *This Destructive War: The British Campaign in the Carolinas* (Tuscaloosa: University of Alabama Press, 1985).

Waynesboro

Virginia (March 2, 1865) *American Civil War*

The final Civil War battle in the hotly contested Shenandoah Valley took place in the small eastern town of Waynesboro, just south of Winchester. Maj. Gen. Philip H. Sheridan's Union cavalry finally demolished the pugnacious Confederate force led by Lt. Gen. Jubal Early. After Sheridan's carefully executed campaign of destruction over the previous months, Early had fewer than two thousand men left and almost no artillery, and he finally succumbed to Sheridan's pressure.

Brig. Gen. George Armstrong Custer, who commanded one of Sheridan's cavalry divisions, found Early's troops gathered on a hill outside of Waynesboro on March 2, 1865, and ordered his 4,840 men to dismount and prepare to attack. Three of Custer's regiments enveloped the Confederate left side while two brigades attacked the middle. The Southerners resisted for a time but proved no match for the superior numbers of Union forces.

Though Early himself escaped, the Federal troops took sixteen hundred Southern prisoners—almost the entire Confederate force. Custer also claimed Early's wagons, cannons, and flags as Union prizes.

The final defeat of Jubal Early's force in the Shenandoah Valley ended four years of fighting in this highly contested region. Sheridan subsequently cut a destructive

path through eastern Virginia and joined Lt. Gen. Ulysses S. Grant outside of Richmond to conclude the war.

Further Reading

Jay Wertz and Edwin Bearss. *Smithsonian's Great Battles & Battlefields of the Civil War* (New York: William Morrow, 1997).

Wetzell's Ford

North Carolina (March 6, 1781)
American Revolution

After the southern American army under Maj. Gen. Nathanael Greene escaped into Virginia, British commander Lt. Gen. Lord Cornwallis began a long withdrawal toward his base in Hillsboro, North Carolina. Immediately, Greene sent detachments back across the Dan River to harass Cornwallis and to attack him in strength if possible.

Col. Otho Williams was directed to march against Cornwallis with a corps of light infantry, riflemen, and the dragoons of Lee and Washington, and he was shadowing the British army when Cornwallis detected him. Cornwallis dispatched a thousand light infantry under Lt. Col. James Webster and cavalry from the British Legion to snap up Williams's force. Williams crossed the Reedy Fork at Wetzell's Ford and retreated at speed, leaving a covering guard of Virginia riflemen under Col. William Prescott and the horsemen of Lee and Washington at the ford. Lt. Col. Henry Lee took command on the scene.

Webster, pushing ahead with a detachment of the Coldstream Guards, found Lee and Washington's dismounted troopers arranged in a defensive line on the other side of the ford, with riflemen in woods on the flank. Nonetheless, he ordered the Guards to cross and attack. Their first attempt was turned back by heavy fire, but Webster rode his horse back and forth in the water, exhorting his men forward, and the Guards got across, formed up, and drove the Americans into flight. Webster miraculously escaped the attention of the Virginia riflemen without so much as a scratch.

The British and Americans lost about twenty men each.

Further Reading

John S. Pancake. *This Destructive War: The British Campaign in the Carolinas* (Tuscaloosa: University of Alabama Press, 1985).

Wheldon Railroad

See GLOBE TAVERN

White Oak Swamp

(Glendale)

Virginia (June 30, 1862) *American Civil War*

Union commander Maj. Gen. George B. McClellan's attempt to take the Confederate capital came apart rapidly in the waning days of June 1862, when Confederate General Robert E. Lee pushed McClellan's huge Army of the Potomac out of its positions astride the Chickahominy River only a few miles from Richmond. In what have come to be called the Seven Days' Battles, Lee—despite poor organization and logistics—sent McClellan into retreat toward Harrison's Landing. The battle at White Oak Swamp was one of several confusing fights in this campaign, which took place in difficult terrain.

The Union army had crossed White Oak Swamp Creek and taken defensive positions on the other side after destroying the bridges. When the pursuing Confederates reached the creek they were stymied, and poor staff work frustrated Lee's attempts to coordinate a pursuit. Finally, at 4:30 P.M., the divisions under Maj. Gens. James Longstreet and A. P. Hill launched themselves against the left side of the Union defenses. In very heavy fighting the Confederates pushed back most of the Federal units facing them, inflicting high casualties but unable to gain completely the upper hand before darkness ended the battle.

The Union side lost 2,853, and the Confederates lost 3,615.

Despite the blow, McClellan was able to continue his movements toward Harrison's Landing the next day.

Further Reading

Cliford Dowdey. *The Seven Days: The Emergence of Lee.* Reprint ed. (Lincoln: University of Nebraska Press, 1993); James M. McPherson. *Battle Cry of Freedom: The Civil War Era* (New York: Oxford University Press, 1988); Time-Life Staff. *Lee Takes Command: From Seven Days to Second Bull Run* (Alexandria, Va.: Time-Life Books, 1984).

White Plains

New York (October 28, 1776) *American Revolution*

The small engagement at White Plains was part of a successful British campaign to seize New York City and the surrounding area. Once again the British claimed a victory and forced the rebels to retreat; however, the British commander, Gen. Sir William Howe, failed to destroy the American army.

In mid-October, when the American commander in chief, Gen. George Washington, realized that Howe's landings at THROG'S NECK and PELL'S POINT threatened to outflank the American positions at HARLEM HEIGHTS, he ordered a withdrawal toward the village of White Plains, north of Manhattan Island. Over the course of a week, Washington's fourteen thousand troops settled into new defensive lines.

Howe advanced toward White Plains with several British infantry regiments as well as artillery and mounted troops. In addition, Howe commanded more than four thousand German mercenaries and a powerful fleet. Altogether, the British and Germans probably numbered more than thirteen thousand highly trained, professionally led troops.

As the British force approached his lines, Washington decided to fortify Chatterton's Hill, a promontory to the right of the main American lines, with the narrow Bronx River running along its base. He sent about sixteen hundred men, comprising units from New York, Massachusetts, Connecticut, Maryland, and Delaware under Col. Joseph Reed, to build field fortifications on top of the hill. Col. Alexander McDougall took command from Reed and sent skirmishers out to make contact with the British advance units. By midmorning the Americans were entrenched atop the hill, and when the skirmishers were driven in, they knew that the British were approaching rapidly.

In one of those remarkable shows that eighteenth-century warfare sometimes provided, Howe marched eight regiments out into plain view and formed them up just across the Bronx River from the base of the hill. He planned a frontal assault, but he also sent three German regiments to take some nearby hills that would give them an enfilade fire, along the length of the American defenses.

When one of the German regiments was ordered to cross the river and attack up the hill, the men declined to get wet and halted to build a makeshift bridge, a delay that drew an attack from the New Yorkers and Marylanders. British general Alexander Leslie decided to cross with two regiments of British foot at a nearby ford, but he was repulsed and pinned to the bottom of the incline as the American defenders poured down fire from their protected positions. Finally, the British and Germans formed a column, marched to a better position, deployed into line, and attacked.

The right side of the American defenses collapsed when Massachusetts militiamen fled in the face of this determined bayonet charge, exposing the Maryland, Delaware, and New York Continentals. While mounted dragoons pursued the Massachusetts militia, the balance of the British and German attacking force pressed hard against the remaining Americans, who withdrew to their main defenses in White Plains. Howe called a halt and went into camp.

Reports of the battle were confused, but American casualties probably numbered less than two hundred, while the British and Germans had more than three hundred killed and wounded.

Howe paused several days before moving forward, and in the meanwhile Washington again pulled out of his defenses. The two armies would not face each other again in a similar fashion until the Pennsylvania campaign a year later.

Further Reading

Arthur A. Merrill. *The Battle of White Plains* (Chappaqua, N.Y.: Analysis Press, 1975).

Whitemarsh

Pennsylvania (December 5–8, 1777)
American Revolution

British commander in chief Sir William Howe's expedition to take the American capital had been successful when he occupied Philadelphia in September 1777 and defeated the American army under Gen. George Washington at both BRANDYWINE and GERMANTOWN. Washington had been forced to withdraw to Whitemarsh, although his army was still intact and therefore still a threat to the British in the long run. Howe wanted to catch and crush Washington.

In early December, Howe thought he detected a chance to catch Washington during a troop movement, and the British commander sent out a large portion of his troops toward Whitemarsh. Scouts commanded by Pennsylvania captain Allan McLane discovered the movement and informed Washington. McLane attacked and harassed the head of the British column and made its progress irksome.

On December 6, Howe came within sight of Washington's main defenses. While the British paused, Washington sent out six hundred Pennsylvania militia under Brig. Gen. James Irvin to attack their advance guard. The Pennsylvanians checked Howe's advance, although Irvin was wounded and captured.

The following day Howe tried again, with an encircling movement, led by Maj. Gen. Charles Grey, around Washington's left wing, but the probe was stopped. Howe decided at this point that further maneuver was pointless and withdrew his men. Washington eventually moved his army into winter quarters at Valley Forge.

Further Reading

Kay Thompson. *Washington at Whitemarsh: Prelude to Valley Forge.* Rev. ed. (Fort Washington, Pa.: Bicentennial Press, 1974).

The Wilderness

Virginia (May 5–6, 1864) *American Civil War*

In the spring of 1864, Ulysses S. Grant, the North's most consistently successful general in the western theater, was promoted to lieutenant general and given full command of all Union armies. He decided to attack the Confederacy from several directions at once, but he knew that the key to victory was to defeat Gen. Robert E. Lee and the Army of Northern Virginia. Grant attached himself to the Army of the Potomac, nominally commanded by Maj. Gen. George G. Meade, and personally supervised a great and bloody campaign to seize Richmond. The first large encounter of this campaign was a terrible battle in a region called the Wilderness.

Not far from the previous battlefield of CHANCELLORSVILLE, the Wilderness was a densely overgrown area that the Federal commander wished to avoid fighting in, but on May 5, the two great armies, 118,769 Union troops and 62,000 Confederates, stumbled into combat as advance units met and began hostilities. Lee was less reluctant to fight in the Wilderness, since he hoped the disadvantageous terrain would neutralize some of Grant's overwhelming superiority in numbers.

The battle shaped up as two nearly separate engagements, taking place along two parallel roads that ran more or less east and west through the Wilderness. The Federal army was moving in two columns, when the northernmost—led by elements of Maj. Gen. Gouverneur Morris's corps—encountered Confederates, the fighting began. Confederate lieutenant general A. P. Hill's corps was advancing parallel in the same direction a few miles to the south along the second road. While the bulk of Grant's army was closing in on the scene of combat, a major part of Lee's force, the entire corps commanded by Lt. Gen. James Longstreet, was still en route, and it was not in position when on the afternoon of May 5 the Union forces tried unsuccessfully to overrun the thin Confederate ranks. By the end of the day, Lee was holding firmly on the northernmost road (the Orange Turnpike) but feared that without Longstreet's men the southern position (along the Orange Plank Road) could not stand.

Early the next morning, the Federals attacked along the northern road, but the Confederates managed to hold their positions. To the south, a similar attack appeared to be on the brink of success—the Federals were about to turn Lee's right flank—when Longstreet's corps finally arrived. The fresh troops were fed into the battle immediately, and Lee himself attempted to lead a charge across open ground, until the Texans he was with demanded he go to the rear. The counterattack went ahead with the Southern commander safely in his proper place, smashed powerfully into the Union assault, and turned it back on itself. Toward nightfall, Lee tried simultaneous attacks on the Union flanks at the northern and southern roads, but they were turned back, if barely.

The day came to an end with neither army holding a clear advantage, but the fighting had been some of the most terrible of the war, due to the difficult conditions of the overgrown forest. Neither side could maneuver freely, and soldiers often could scarcely see their opponents through the dense foliage. Moreover, the abundance of dry forest detritus and undergrowth was set ablaze by the battle, and during the night hundreds of wounded were burned to death as they lay helpless on the forest floor. The fires added to the battle a hellish dimension that the survivors never forgot.

Lee lost 10,800 casualties during the two days; the Federal army suffered around 18,000.

Under any previous commander, the Army of the Potomac would have packed up and pulled out of the campaign, but instead Grant ordered the entire army on the march in a sliding movement to the left, hoping to flank and then attack Lee again. The Federals' southward march on May 6 marked a crucial turning point in the war.

Further Reading

John Cannan. *The Wilderness Campaign: May 1864.* (Conshohocken, Pa.: Combined Books, 1993); Gary W. Gallagher, ed. *The Wilderness Campaign* (Chapel Hill: University of North Carolina Press, 1997); Grady McWhiney. *Battle in the Wilderness: Grant Meets Lee* (Fort Worth, Tex.: Ryan Place, 1995); John M. Priest. *No Where to Run* (Shippensburg, Pa.: White Mane, 1995);———. *Victory without Triumph: The Wilderness* (Shippensburg, Pa.: White Mane, 1996); Gordon C. Rhea. *The Battle of the Wilderness, May 5–6, 1864* (Baton Rouge: Louisiana State University Press, 1994); Robert G. Scott. *Into the Wilderness with the Army of the Potomac* (Bloomington: Indiana University Press, 1985); and Edward Steele. *The Wilderness Campaign* (Harrisburg, Pa.: Stackpole Books, 1960).

Williamsburg

Virginia (May 4–5, 1862) *American Civil War*

During the first days of May 1862, Gen. Joseph E. Johnston, who was constantly feuding with Confederate president Jefferson Davis, decided to withdraw his forces from Yorktown and retreat north along the Virginia peninsula. Johnston sought to evade the attack that Maj. Gen. George B. McClellan seemed finally ready to deliver after pausing for a month before Yorktown. As Union troops chased Johnston's retreating force, the two sides engaged in a two-day battle at Williamsburg that caused heavy casualties but allowed most of the Confederate artillery and wagons to get away unscathed.

On May 3, Maj. Gen. John B. Magruder, who directly commanded the Confederate Department of Northern Virginia, began the withdrawal from Yorktown as Maj. Gen. J. E. B. "Jeb" Stuart provided artillery cover. The Federal cavalry commander, Maj. Gen. George Stoneman, pursued Magruder with four horse-drawn batteries and two infantry divisions commanded by Brig. Gens. Joseph Hooker and William F. "Baldy" Smith.

The two sides met just outside Williamsburg, Virginia's colonial capital, on May 4, but the Federal attack was slowed by heavy rains that turned dirt roads into quagmires. The main action did not get under way until the next day, after Maj. Gen. James Longstreet established a defensive line at a previously constructed Confederate fortification dubbed Fort Magruder. Longstreet held off attacks by Hooker, Smith, and Brig. Gen. Philip Kearny while awaiting reinforcements.

Brig. Gen. D. H. Hill's Confederate soldiers arrived to strengthen Longstreet's main line but were attacked almost immediately by Stoneman's cavalrymen. During the afternoon of May 5, Federal Brig. Gen. William S. Hancock's brigade managed to flank the Confederate left and capture several of the redoubts at Fort Magruder. Despite strong counterattacks led by Brig. Gen. Jubal Early's Virginians and North Carolinians, Hancock's men held their positions until the Confederates had to withdraw under cover of darkness.

Early's counterattacks increased the Confederate casualty count. In all, out of 31,823 troops at Williamsburg, the Southerners lost 1,603. Of the 40,768 Union soldiers engaged, 456 were killed, 373 went missing, and 1,410 were wounded. Several buildings at the College of William and Mary, which had been evacuated in May 1861, were used as hospitals.

After Longstreet withdrew his main force on the evening of May 5, the Confederate retreat up the peninsula continued. Heavy rains plagued their Federal pursuers for the next month.

Further Reading

Earl C. Hastings. *A Pitiless Rain: The Battle of Williamsburg, 1862* (Shippensburg, Pa.: White Mane, 1997).

Williamson's Plantation

South Carolina (July 12, 1780)
American Revolution

After the British took control of Georgia and South Carolina in early 1780 and eliminated all organized American forces, the warfare degenerated into a series of backcountry skirmishes and battles. In one such affair at Williamson's Plantation in July, South Carolina partisans defeated a detachment of Loyalists from Lt. Col. Banestre Tarleton's British Legion, led in this case by Capt. Christian Huck.

Huck, known even on his own side as a particularly vicious and foul-mouthed officer, was put at the head of around four hundred Loyalists who were usually part of Tarleton's Legion and was ordered to track down Col. Thomas Sumter, who the British feared was organizing partisan militia in the Catawba District. On July 11, Huck captured two patriot officers in their home and threatened to hang them. Their mother slipped away to warn Sumter, who was camped thirty miles away, while the Loyalists camped for the night at Williamson's Plantation.

Before dawn the following day, about ninety patriots under colonels William Hill and Thomas Neal sprang a surprise attack on the sleeping Loyalists, who had unwisely pitched their camp between two rail fences, which limited their mobility. The patriots caught their enemy in a deadly cross fire, and the fight was short-lived. Huck was killed on the spot, with thirty or forty others and fifty more wounded. The patriots lost only one casualty.

Further Reading

Mark M. Boatner. *The Encyclopedia of the American Revolution* (New York: David McKay, 1966).

Wilson's Creek

(Oak Hill)

Missouri (August 10, 1861) *American Civil War*

Missouri was a strategically important border state of which both sides desperately wanted to gain control during 1861. The battle at Wilson's Creek was the first major engagement of the Civil War in the West, and for a time it regained for the Confederacy some of the early advantage that had been seized by Federal authorities.

The leading Union figure in Missouri was Brig. Gen. Nathaniel Lyon, a West Point–trained regular officer and veteran of the Mexican-American War, who had commanded the Federal arsenal in St. Louis and had helped organize the army of ninety-day volunteers from Missouri and Iowa that he now led into the southwestern part of the state. Opposing him there was Maj. Gen. Sterling Price, an important prewar Missouri politician who now commanded the Confederate Missouri State Guard, backed by Arkansas, Texas, and Louisiana troops under Brig. Gen. Benjamin McCulloch.

The Confederates had a total strength of twelve to thirteen thousand men, and having decided on an offensive against Lyon, they were marching north when they paused and went into camp along Wilson's Creek to wait out a rainstorm. Lyon, who commanded only about seven thousand in all, prepared a surprise attack, detaching Col. Franz Sigel with twelve hundred men to march around the Confederates and hit their camp from the rear while Lyon—an aggressive officer—led the main Federal force in a direct assault from the north.

The Federals moved at dawn, and Lyon's first blow surprise the Confederates, driving their advance units off a hill (which came to be known as "Bloody Hill") until the advancing Union columns were brought to a halt by enfilading fire from a Confederate battery. General Price had just enough time to organize his men and form them into a battle line, stabilizing the main fight at Bloody Hill.

Meanwhile, Sigel had successfully reached the Confederate rear and launched his attack, having heard the sound of Lyon's assault. His men completely routed the Confederates and established a potentially strong position; however, when three regiments of Louisiana troops began to counterattack, Sigel mistook them for Iowans and allowed the Confederates to march to within close range. When the southerners fired a devastating volley, Sigel's formation dissolved and offered no further serious threat to the Confederate rear.

Price was then able to throw his weight of numbers into a series of powerful counterattacks at Bloody Hill, none of which could quite dislodge the Federals but that resulted in vicious, close-quarters fighting. During the second counterattack, Brig. Gen. Lyon was killed by a musket ball, becoming the first Union general of the war to die in combat. Shortly before noon, the remaining Federal troops began to withdraw from the hill, leaving Price the victory, but the Confederates were too exhausted to pursue.

The Confederates lost a total of 1,222 killed, wounded, or missing; the Federals suffered 1,317 losses during the six-hour battle.

General Price eventually followed up his success at Wilson's Creek by an advance northward into the state, but the gains in Missouri for the Confederate cause were temporary.

Further Reading

William R. Brooksher. *Bloody Hill: The Civil War Battle of Wilson's Creek* (Washington, D.C.: Brassey's, 1995).

Winchester, First

Virginia (May 25, 1862) *American Civil War*

Maj. Gen. Nathaniel Banks commanded an army of eighty-five hundred Federal soldiers stationed in the Shenandoah Valley in Virginia in May 1862. Banks was trying to maintain Union control over the valley, even as Confederate major general Thomas J. "Stonewall" Jackson made progress toward ejecting him. After Jackson's impressive victory over Col. J. R. Kenly's division at FRONT ROYAL on May 23, Banks moved his main force away from Jackson's next target at Strasburg and sought a safer position in Winchester. Jackson quickly pursued, and the two sides engaged.

Banks positioned Col. George Henry Gordon's brigade on the Federal right, with Col. Dudley Donnelly protecting his left. Major General Jackson rushed his battle-weary Confederates into position in the early hours of May 25. By pushing his men up the road, Jackson hoped to occupy the heights on the southwest side of Winchester before Banks could create a fortified position there. He also planned to rendezvous with Maj. Gen. Richard S. Ewell, whose division was approaching from the Front Royal road.

At dawn, Jackson ordered an attack on the Federal line. A small Confederate division encountered Federal pickets on the left and was turned back by artillery and

cavalry. Jackson then deployed Brig. Gen. Richard Taylor, the brother-in-law of Confederate president Jefferson Davis and son of former U.S. president Zachary Taylor, around the Federal right flank as Ewell simultaneously moved around the left flank.

At around 7:30 A.M., all the Confederates advanced under heavy fire. Banks's men were overpowered and retreated in disarray as soon as their opponents had advanced a few hundred yards. The Federal retreat continued in considerable disorder until the majority of Banks's division had crossed the Potomac. Jackson pursued them as far as Harpers Ferry, but, having no cavalry support, he doubled back into the Shenandoah Valley to savor his victory.

Jackson's force lost around 400 men in the battle, and Union casualties equalled 1,967.

Though Jackson had chased Banks from the Shenandoah Valley, he returned to fight other Union divisions at CROSS KEYS and PORT REPUBLIC, battles that would cement his reputation as the potential savior of the Confederacy.

Further Reading

Brandon H. Beck. *The First Battle of Winchester* (Lynchburg, Va.: H. E. Howard, 1992).

Winchester, Second

Virginia (June 13–15, 1863) *American Civil War*

Winchester, Virginia, traded hands seventy-two times during the Civil War, making it one of the most hotly contested points of the conflict (*see also* WINCHESTER, FIRST and WINCHESTER, THIRD). When Confederate general Robert E. Lee embarked on his second invasion of Union territory in mid-1863, Winchester again came under fire as Maj. Gen. Robert H. Milroy's Federals made a stand against the Confederate push. In mid-June, Milroy's outpost at Winchester was isolated from other Federal support, his troops were utterly defeated, and Winchester once again fell into Confederate hands.

Though badly outnumbered by an advancing Confederate corps under Lt. Gen. Richard S. Ewell, Milroy prepared to defend the Union fortifications at Winchester. Milroy's men constructed two earthen fortifications northwest of town, which complemented the Main (or Flag) Fort and Star Fort to the west. On June 13, Confederate major general Jubal Early's division advanced in front of Ewell's corps and cut off Milroy at Winchester.

One June 14, Ewell's main attack began in earnest, as he sent two brigades to skirmish with Federal troops south and east of Winchester. Covered by this initial movement, Ewell positioned the bulk of his infantry and artillery west of town and began to bombard the Federal fortifications at 6 P.M. After forty-five minutes, the Federal artillery was running out of steam, and the Louisiana brigade took the Star Fort. At dark, Milroy's troops took refuge in the Main Fort and tried to regroup.

Ewell, anticipating that the Union troops might try to withdraw under the cover of night, placed three brigades along the most likely escape route, the Martinsburg road. Milroy played right into Confederate hands when he ordered wagons and artillery destroyed and commanded his troops to leave the fort at 1 A.M. Around 3:30 A.M. the retreating Federals stumbled into Ewell's trap about four miles outside of town. A hot fight ensued between Milroy's men and Confederate brigades led by Maj. Gen. Edward Johnson and Brig. Gen. Francis Nicholls. Just as Milroy's men threatened to envelop their opponents, Confederate reinforcements arrived, a third brigade, and crushed Milroy's resistance. The Federals tried to escape, but 3,358 of them were captured.

In addition to those captured, the Union forces lost an additional 1,085 casualties. Confederate casualties totalled only 269.

The loss of Winchester and the capture of such a large number of soldiers was considered a disaster by Union commanders. Milroy was investigated by a court of inquiry, which cleared him of personal responsibility for the loss.

Further Reading

Charles S. Grunder. *The Second Battle of Winchester* (Lynchburg, Va.: H. E. Howard, 1989).

❧ Winchester, Third

(Opequon Creek)

Virginia (September 19, 1864) *American Civil War*

After Confederate lieutenant general Jubal Early defeated Brig. Gen. George Crook at Kernstown, Virginia, in July 1864, Lt. Gen. Ulysses S. Grant put Maj. Gen. Philip N. Sheridan in charge of a new Union offensive in the Shenandoah Valley (*see also* KERNSTOWN, SECOND). Grant felt that Sheridan, only thirty-three years old, would pursue Early with enough aggressiveness to end Confederate

control of the valley once and for all. Sheridan accepted the task, though it was September before he was able to coordinate an attack on Early's force, which had by then been reinforced by cavalry and infantry.

On September 16, Rebecca West, a Federal spy in Winchester, informed Sheridan that Early had lost some of his reinforcements, Maj. Gen. Joseph Kershaw's cavalry division and twelve heavy guns. Early believed that Sheridan was too timid to attack, but Sheridan quickly heeded Grant's simple instructions as to what to do, now that Early's force seemed to have been weakened: "Go in." Sheridan readied his 33,600 infantry and 6,400 cavalry troops, and reconnaissance on September 17 and 18 revealed Early's force to comprise only 8,500 infantry and 2,900 cavalry.

Sheridan planned a concentric attack for September 19: Brig. Gen. Alfred Torbert would lead Union cavalry against Maj. Gen. Lunsford Lomax's Southern horsemen on the left; Brig. Gen. James Wilson's cavalry would hit Maj. Gen. Fitzhugh Lee's position on the right; and twenty-five thousand infantry would drive against the Confederate center, in and around Winchester. The first Federal troops deployed at 2:00 A.M. on September 19, but Early quickly comprehended their movement and reinforced his main body to the east of town. Maj. Gen. Horatio Wright, countermanded direct orders from Sheridan, brought his entire wagon train up the Berryville Road as he made a bid to wipe out Maj. Gen. Stephen Ramseur's men, and in the process he blocked part of the Federal main body and created a gap in the line.

As heavy artillery fire rained down on both sides, Confederate major general Robert Rodes threw his men into the breach, but they made only slow progress after he was killed at the beginning of their assault. Early was able to coordinate two separate smaller counterattacks before Col. J. W. Keifer, who had helped to put down the New York draft riots a year earlier, filled the hole with his brigade.

Even in the face of vastly superior numbers, Early held his force together admirably and established a new defensive line near the Opequon Creek in the early afternoon. By evening, however, the Union numerical advantage was finally making itself felt, and Early was driven back. Two Federal divisions advanced toward Early's center and broke apart reinforcements under Maj. Gen. John C. Breckinridge. Confederate cavalry on the left finally gave way, and Federal troops streamed over the escape route along the Millwood Pike. Late in the day, Early finally admitted defeat and ordered a general withdrawal toward Strasburg.

Despite their victory, Federal troops suffered heavier casualties than their Southern counterparts. Sheridan's force counted 697 killed, 3,983 wounded, and 338 missing, while Early's losses totalled 276 killed, 1,827 wounded, and 1,818 missing. Several general officers on both sides were killed, including Brig. Gen. David Russell, a close friend of Sheridan's.

Sheridan had only begun to fill Grant's ambitious orders, and he engaged Early again three days later at FISHER'S HILL.

Further Reading

Roger U. Delauter. *The Third Battle of Winchester* (Lynchburg, Va.: H. E. Howard, 1997).

Wolf Mountain

Montana (January 8, 1877) *Black Hills War*

In the final large-scale engagement of the great war between the Lakota and U.S. Army over the Black Hills in 1876 and 1877 (*see also* ROSEBUD, LITTLE BIGHORN, and SLIM BUTTES), soldiers under Col. Nelson A. Miles achieved at least a draw with the Oglala Lakota, led by Crazy Horse (Tashunka Witco), which compelled the Indians eventually to surrender.

Miles, a Congressional Medal of Honor winner in the Civil War, was given command of the Fifth Infantry at Cantonment Keogh. Failing to entice the Lakota off the war trail following the bloody summer of 1876, he marched in late December to find them, with 350 men from the Fifth and Twenty-second Regiments.

Crazy Horse was waiting with about five hundred Oglala and Cheyenne warriors, but his opportunity to entice Miles into an ambush evaporated when a smaller group of Indians attacked the army column before the trap was ready. Miles, thus alerted, prepared to receive the main attack, which came in the middle of a snowstorm on January 8. The snow hampered the Indians, and Miles's two field cannon held the assault at bay. After a few hours the attack petered out, and Crazy Horse withdrew.

Casualties on both sides were light, but the battle had added to the stresses on the Oglala. Within a few months, Crazy Horse came in to surrender, along with many of the Oglala. In September, he was murdered by his captors.

Further Reading

Jerome A. Greene. *Yellowstone Command: Colonel Nelson A. Miles and the Great Sioux War, 1876–1877* (Norman: University of Oklahoma Press, 1991); and Donald E. Wooster. *Nelson A. Miles and the Twilight of the Frontier Army* (Lincoln: University of Nebraska Press, 1992).

Wood Lake

(Lone Tree Lake)

Minnesota (September 23, 1862) *Santee Uprising*

Disputes over food supplies due them by treaty, and the arrogance of the federal Indian agents assigned to them, provoked the Santee (Dakota) eastern branch of the Sioux Nation into a violent uprising that spread death along the Minnesota frontier in 1862. After killing many white settlers and unsuccessfully attacking FORT RIDGELY and NEW ULM in August, the Santee withdrew up the Minnesota River Valley.

In September, Col. Henry H. Sibley, a militia officer, gathered a motley force of more than sixteen hundred men, comprising civilians, militia, and volunteer units (many Minnesotans were away fighting for the Union cause), and marched in pursuit of the Santee bands. By the 22d, Sibley and his men had reached Lone Tree Lake (although they thought they were at Wood Lake). They set up camp for the night with little concern for security, unaware that there was a large concentration of Santee nearby under the leadership of Mankato of the Mdewkanton band of the Santee.

During the night, the Santee quietly approached the Minnesotans and encircled their camp, intending to attack early the next morning. Fortunately for Sibley, members of one of his ill-disciplined volunteer units decided to sneak off at dawn to forage for food, and they stumbled directly into the waiting Indian ambush. When this encounter set off firing on the camp's perimeter, Sibley's entire force was alerted. A brief battle followed, during which the Minnesotans' firepower and artillery were too powerful for the Santee, who broke off and fled before bringing the full weight of their numbers into play.

Sibley's command lost seven killed and thirty wounded. Thirty Santee were killed, including Mankato, who was struck with a cannonball, and about thirty more wounded.

Within a few days the Santee surrendered to Sibley, and the uprising came to an end. Subsequently, the federal government ordered the execution of thirty-eight Santee.

Further Reading

Kenneth Carley. *The Sioux Uprising of 1862* (St. Paul: Minnesota Historical Society, 1976).

Wounded Knee

South Dakota (December 29, 1890) *Sioux Wars*

Although it can scarcely be called a battle, the killing of a large number of Lakota (historically—together with the Dakota and Nakota—called Sioux) by the U.S. Army on the Pine Ridge Reservation in South Dakota was the final episode in the history of armed conflict between Indians and whites in the American West.

A majority of the Dakota, Lakota, and Nakota had finally bowed to the overwhelming power of the United States during the late 1870s, following a series of wars and battles that ranged across the plains, and had since refrained from violence. Most lived on reservations—including Pine Ridge, Rosebud, and Cheyenne River—and depended on the government for food and supplies. In 1889 and 1890, however, a mystical religious movement called the Ghost Dance spread among the various Dakota, Lakota, and Nakota—as well as other Plains tribes. One of these Lakota bands was the Miniconjou of the Cheyenne River Reservation, led by Big Foot (Si Tanka). The Ghost Dancers believed that the world would soon be transformed and that dead Indians would be reincarnated to inherit an earth cleansed of the whites. The Ghost Dance did not advocate war or killing, but white authorities saw it as a threat to the peace and moved to stamp out its gatherings.

Big Foot himself adhered to the Ghost Dance for only a short while, and by December 1890 he had given up on a miraculous solution to his people's problems. Nonetheless, when the great Hunkpapa Lakota leader Sitting Bull (Tatanka Yotanka) was killed in a dispute over the Ghost Dance, Big Foot decided to move his band of 350 (230 women and children and 120 men) to the Pine Ridge Reservation for protection. Brig. Gen. Nelson A. Miles ordered out troops to intercept and detain Big Foot's band, but the Miniconjou eluded the army until captured by Maj. Samuel Whitside and herded into a camp at Wounded Knee Creek. By that time, Big Foot himself was severely ill with pneumonia.

On December 28, Col. James Forsyth arrived with a contingent of the Seventh Cavalry and took command, surrounding the Lakota camp and placing four Hotchkiss field guns in position. The following morning, Forsyth sent soldiers into the camp to disarm the Indians, but the Lakota became alarmed during the process, and a scuffle broke out when a single shot was fired (probably by mistake). The soldiers opened fire at close range and killed several Lakota,

including Big Foot, before withdrawing to the edge of the camp. The Hotchkiss guns bombarded the remaining Lakota, only a few of whom put up any resistance. As a number of Lakota tried to flee down a shallow, dry ravine, troops pursued them, and the Hotchkiss guns fired on them.

About 150 of Big Foot's band were killed immediately in the attack, and 50 were wounded. Others died later—and elsewhere—of their wounds. The army suffered twenty-five dead and thirty-nine wounded, many reportedly by friendly fire, not by the Lakota.

General Miles removed Forsyth from command and called for an inquiry, which eventually cleared the colonel of charges and restored him to command. A large show of force prevented the remaining Lakota from turning the killing at Wounded Knee into a rallying point for renewed warfare, but it subsequently became a powerful symbol of Indian-white relations.

Further Reading

Dee A. Brown. *Bury My Heart at Wounded Knee* (New York: Holt Rinehart, 1970); Tom Streissguth. *Wounded Knee 1890: The End of the Plains Indian Wars* (New York: Facts On File, 1998). Robert M. Utley. *Last Days of the Sioux Nation* (New Haven, Conn.: Yale University Press, 1963).

Wyoming Valley

Pennsylvania (July 3–4, 1778) *American Revolution*

The fertile Wyoming River valley in present-day Pennsylvania had attracted hundreds of American settlers before the American Revolution, but it had been the scene of chronic political conflict between Pennsylvania and Connecticut over jurisdiction, a conflict that often turned violent. With the coming of the Revolution, the divisions between Loyalists and patriots deepened the existing disharmony among the settlers. Moreover, the settlements were isolated and prey for Indian raids. Several forts—generally small blockhouses—had been built to serve as gathering points for settlers and their families if attacked.

The patriots in the valley formed a unit of eighty regulars that had been authorized by Congress, and it could back up these troops with militia when needed, but many men had gone off to serve with the American armies in New Jersey and New York. Several members of Loyalist families had been arrested by their patriot neighbors and sent to confinement in Connecticut, which heightened tensions.

These conditions attracted the attention of Maj. John Butler, a Loyalist officer who helped manage Indian affairs for the British from a post at Niagara. Butler assembled a force of about four hundred Loyalists—comprising his own Rangers, Guy Johnson's Royal Greens, and volunteers—and four to five hundred Seneca and Cayuga, led by Gu Cinge, and set out in June to raid the Wyoming Valley. In the first days of July Butler and his men had reached Fort Wintermoot, a Wyoming Valley fort that had been built by a Loyalist family.

The patriots in the valley had assembled the small unit of regulars as well as about three hundred militia to oppose Butler's invasion. They were led by Col. Zebulon Butler, a resident of the valley and a Continental officer on leave. Convinced that no help could be expected from the American forces to the east, Col. Butler and his men marched on Fort Wintermoot, hoping to surprise the Loyalist-Indian force.

Major Butler was alerted, however, by Indian scouts and prepared to receive the patriot attack. The Americans deployed in a line of battle as they approached the fort, and the Loyalists and Indians did the same (or, they took positions behind cover—eyewitness accounts vary). In a brief battle, the Loyalists and Indians routed the Americans. Not only were the Americans outnumbered but their line collapsed, when Colonel Butler attempted to maneuver his right wing to avoid being flanked and the inexperienced militiamen thought he was ordering a retreat.

American losses were extremely high, especially since the Seneca and Cayuga gave no quarter on the battlefield. Probably close to three hundred Americans were killed, and many bodies were reported to have been mutilated. The Loyalists lost only three dead and eight wounded.

The loss sparked a panicked flight by most of the American families in the valley, and it turned into a terror and suffering-filled journey.

Perhaps because the Loyalist victory was so complete, and certainly because Indians were involved, the battle and its aftermath became known among Americans as a "massacre."

Further Reading

Ernest Gray. *The Sesqui-Centennial of the Battle of Wyoming.* (Wilkes-Barre, Pa.: Wyoming Historical and Genealogical Society, 1928).

Yellow Tavern

Virginia (May 11, 1864) *American Civil War*

While battle was raging at SPOTSYLVANIA in May 1864, Federal major general Philip H. Sheridan rode with his ten thousand cavalry south toward Richmond, Virginia, in order to draw Maj. Gen. J. E. B. "Jeb" Stuart's cavalry away from the action and into a separate conflict. Stuart took the bait, and the two sides met at Yellow Tavern on May 11. The battle demonstrated how far Union cavalry forces had progressed since the beginning of the war, as well as the extent of Confederate supply problems.

At 8 A.M. on May 11, Stuart's force took up a position at Yellow Tavern to stop Sheridan's progress toward Richmond, and by 11 A.M. the first Federal troops arrived. Col. Thomas Devin's Federal brigade established a line at a crossroads, and two Federal divisions proceeded with the first attacks of the day. Hand-to-hand fighting broke out all along the Confederate line, and at 4 P.M. a heavy mounted attack hit the Confederate right side.

The Confederate line held, though Stuart worried about his exposed left flank, where two heavy guns lay almost unprotected. As Stuart rode out to inspect the left, Brig. Gen. George Armstrong Custer and Lt. Col. Peter Stagg led the First Michigan Cavalry against the exposed position and captured the Confederate guns. The Fifth and Sixth Michigan simultaneously pushed back the whole left side of the Confederate line.

The Confederate troops, spurred on by Stuart, who fired his pistol at the advancing Michiganders, were able to halt the Federal advance at a ravine approximately four hundred yards behind their original line. As Virginia cavalry tried to push forward once more, Stuart was shot. The Confederates on the right side were then utterly routed, and the Southern cavalry force split up and withdrew.

No complete casualty statistics for the battle at Yellow Tavern exist, though the most important casualty was Stuart, who died from his wound on May 12. Stuart, a symbol of Confederate bravery and élan, was a severe loss to Southern command and morale.

Sheridan demonstrated at Yellow Tavern that Federal cavalry, now armed with repeating carbines, could best Confederate cavalry in open battle, something thought almost impossible in the first years of the war.

Further Reading

Rhea Gordon. *The Battle for Spotsylvania Courthouse and the Road to Yellow Tavern, May 7–12, 1864* (Baton Rouge: Louisiana State University Press, 1997).

✺ Yorktown

Virginia (September 28–October 18, 1781)
American Revolution

The Franco-American victory over the British army of Lt. Gen. Lord Cornwallis, following a three-week siege, was the crowning military event of the American Revolution, and for all practical purposes ended the war.

Cornwallis, the lieutenant general who exercised nearly independent command in the southern theater during 1780 and 1781, had backed his army into a dangerous position in August when he moved his entire force to the village of Yorktown, on a peninsula formed by the York and James Rivers and Chesapeake Bay. He previously had abandoned operations in North Carolina after the battle at GUILFORD COURTHOUSE, and he had moved into Virginia with the hope that the ever-victorious Royal Navy would resupply and reinforce him. He chose Yorktown principally for its good harbor. His forces numbered slightly fewer than seventy-five hundred, a combination of the seventeen hundred men of his army, plus the units that had been campaigning in Virginia under Maj. Gen. William Phillips and turncoat Brig. Gen. Benedict Arnold.

Included were several regiments of foot—some of them famous, such as the Twenty-third (also known as the Royal Welch Fusiliers) and the Seventy-first (Fraser's Highlanders)—the Brigade of Guards, several German mercenary regiments, a few veteran Loyalist units, artillerists, marines, and Lt. Col. Banastre Tarleton's infamous British Legion. This was a powerful, experienced army, one that had never been defeated by the Americans in open battle since the beginning of the southern campaign, but its strength was now bottled up in a small base, surrounded on three sides by water and fronted by hard-to-defend lowlands.

Opposing Cornwallis was a huge allied army commanded by Gen. George Washington, whose moment had finally come after six years of frustrating defeat by a succession of British generals. Washington had, in a sense, gambled the entire revolution on cornering and beating Cornwallis. He had been far to the north, conferring with Comte de Rochambeau, commander of the French forces in America, when word came that Cornwallis had moved to Yorktown. At almost the same time, Washington learned that a French naval squadron from the West Indies, commanded by Adm. Comte François de Grasse was on its way to the Chesapeake, bearing three thousand troops and able to keep the Royal Navy from rescuing Cornwallis. Washington immediately ordered the bulk of the American army and all the French troops on an all-out march to Virginia, leaving only a small covering force to contain the large British army in New York City. This concentration of allied forces against Cornwallis was a masterful and daring stroke—by the last days of September, Washington had surrounded Yorktown with a siege army of nearly sixteen thousand men, and following the naval and land battles of the CHESAPEAKE CAPES and GLOUCESTER, Cornwallis had no escape.

Washington had three grand divisions of American Continentals, commanded by Lafayette, Benjamin Lincoln, and von Steuben, as well as seven French regiments and numbers of artillerists and cavalry. The allied army also had siege guns, which had come on French ships, and highly skilled French engineers who could plan and execute a formal siege (a Frenchman had invented siege warfare as it was practiced in the eighteenth century). The allies thus commanded all the elements required for success: heavy artillery, numerous diggers, and experienced infantry. The siege proceeded toward its inevitable climax with the precision of a formal ballroom dance.

As soon as the allies arrived, Cornwallis drew in his lines and abandoned his outer works, except for three strong redoubts, since he had only enough troops to man his inner defenses. The French engineers staked out the first parallel trench at a distance of twelve hundred yards from the redoubts, and while French troops under Col. Claude Saint Simon Montblern delivered a diversionary attack during the night on the Fusiliers' Redoubt, fifteen hundred men began to dig. On October 9, the first batteries were in place, and the bombardment of the town began. Within days, the allied gunners were throwing thousands of cannon and mortar shells a day at the British, whose own artillery was soon silenced.

A second parallel trench was eventually started only three hundred yards from Redoubts 9 and 10, and during

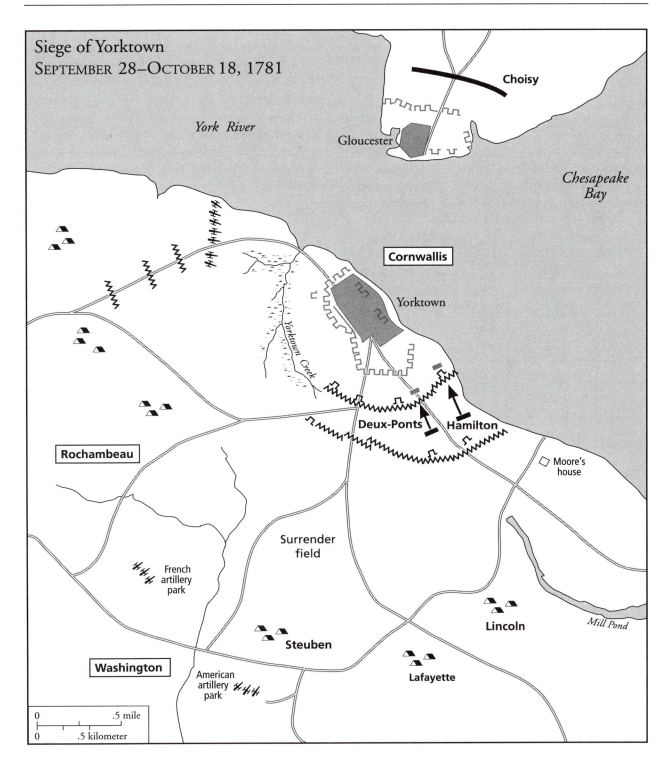

Siege of Yorktown
SEPTEMBER 28–OCTOBER 18, 1781

Choisy

York River

Gloucester

Chesapeake Bay

Cornwallis

Yorktown

Yorktown Creek

Deux-Ponts   Hamilton

Rochambeau

Moore's house

Surrender field

French artillery park

Lincoln

Mill Pond

Steuben

Washington

American artillery park

Lafayette

0   .5 mile

0   .5 kilometer

the night of October 14 the allies made simultaneous assaults on these two strong points. Lt. Col. Alexander Hamilton, subsequently the nation's first secretary of the treasury, led a force of mostly New York troops in an attack on Redoubt 10, spearheaded by a "forlorn hope" of Connecticut Continentals under Lt. John Mansfield. The assault overwhelmed the defenders of the redoubt within minutes. French troops under Col. Guillaume Deux-Ponts attacked Redoubt 10 but had a more difficult time getting through the obstacles and took more casualties than the Americans. In the end, however, the French battered their way into the stronghold and subdued the garrison.

The allied guns were then moved to almost point-blank range and began to pound the British inner defenses, so Cornwallis attempted the classic reply, a sortie to silence the closest batteries. During the early morning hours of October 16, Col. Robert Abercromby led 350 picked troops into an unused portion of the allied trenches and then, pretending to be Americans, they moved down the trench system and attacked a French battery, spiking four cannon. A French unit discovered the British party and drove it off with no further damage to the siege guns.

Down to his last resource, Cornwallis decided to try to slip away later the same night, and he ordered his troops to prepare to cross to Gloucester, from which he hoped to fight his way clear and escape overland. Unfortunately for the British, there were too few boats for the attempt, and a fierce storm blew up, eliminating any possibility of a crossing.

In midmorning on October 17, a redcoated British drummer boy mounted the top of the earthworks and beat the signal for a parley. Soon thereafter a British officer waving a white handkerchief crossed to the allied lines and delivered Cornwallis's offer of surrender. Two days later, the British and Germans sullenly marched out and laid down their arms. Cornwallis himself skulked in the town, claiming illness, but Gen. Charles O'Hara presented his sword to Gen. Benjamin Lincoln, who had been deputized by Washington to receive the surrender. Although the peace treaty was not completed for two more years, and British garrisons remained in New York City and Charleston, the Revolutionary War was over, and a new nation had been born.

Further Reading

Robert Arthur. *The End of the Revolution* (New York: Vantage Press, 1966); Burke Davis. *The Campaign That Won America: The Story of Yorktown* (New York: Dial Press, 1970); Thomas Fleming. *Beat the Last Drum: The Siege of Yorktown, 1781* (New York: St. Martin's Press, 1963); John O. Sands. *Yorktown's Captive Fleet* (Charlottesville: University of Virginia Press, 1983); J. F. Shafroth. *The Strategy of the Yorktown Campaign, 1781* (Annapolis, Md.: U.S. Naval Institute Press, 1931); and Theodore Thayer. *Yorktown: Campaign of Strategic Options* (Philadelphia: Lippincott, 1975).

GLOSSARY

abatis   A log-strewn obstacle guarding a fortification. Felled trees were piled at random (branches outward and sometimes sharpened) in a deep ditch, making a formidable obstruction for attackers to get through.

approaches   Zigzag or angled trenches dug by the attackers to connect the main parallel trenches during a siege. The approaches allowed troops and artillery to move closer to the fortifications under attack without exposure to enemy fire.

armistice   A formal cessation of armed hostilities between two opponents, usually agreed to by a signed document.

army   The term was used originally in a general sense to refer to any large military body or to the entire ground forces of a nation (e.g., the British army). By the time of the American Civil War, however, the numbers of troops involved and the widespread nature of the fighting demanded the formal organization of several large units, referred to as armies. The Union named armies, which were commanded by major generals, after rivers (e.g., the Army of the Potomac); the Confederate armies, commanded by full (four-star) generals, were named after regions (e.g., the Army of Northern Virginia). Units of Mexican armed forces were also usually designated as regional or personal armies.

artillery   A collective term for cannon or guns: large-bore weapons, ranging widely in size, mounted on wheeled frames called carriages. Artillery was used in almost every conceivable battle situation, in a wide variety of configurations, from broadsides aboard warships to highly mobile horse-drawn versions to powerful cannon installed in fortifications. In most armies fighting in North America, the guns and the men who operated them were regarded as one of the three main branches of an armed force, the others being infantry and cavalry (a combination known as "foot, horse, and gun" during the eighteenth century).

bastion   An angled projection from the walls of a fort, designed to give defenders an enfilading fire on attackers or to create a cross fire between two bastions. The term was also used in general to refer to strong fortifications.

bateau   Small, flat-bottomed boats with very shallow draft and easily built by unskilled labor. Bateaux were common military craft on the rivers and lakes in the wooded northern regions of the United States and in southern Canada, and they were used extensively during the colonial wars and the American Revolution. They could be rowed, poled, or sailed and were therefore a flexible and convenient mode of transportation.

battalion   The term, which changed in meaning over time, for a large military unit. During the American Revolution, "battalion" was virtually synonymous with "regiment" and referred to the largest common unit, 750 to 1,000 men. In Mexico during the first part of the nineteenth century, a battalion consisted of two regiments. By the time of the U.S. Civil War the term had fallen out of favor with most armies, only to return during the twentieth century.

battery   A collection of artillery pieces positioned to fire on the enemy. The term also came to mean the basic unit of organization within the artillery wing of an army, the equivalent of an infantry company.

blockade   A naval campaign to cut off the flow of shipping in or out of a port or coastal region.

breastwork   Temporary or improvised field fortifications, usually built by infantry to chest height, made out of whatever materials were at hand. Often existing structures, such as rail fences, formed the basis for breastworks, which could be formidable battlefield features.

brevet   An honorary and temporary rank awarded—usually during wartime—for bravery or merit. Brevet rank usually did not confer additional authority. Used by the British during the American Revolution and extensively by the Union army during the U.S. Civil War. The Confederate army did not have brevet ranks.

brigade   An organizational unit consisting of several regiments (typically four by the time of the American Civil War), commanded by a brigadier general.

broadside   The row of guns along one side of a warship, and their nearly simultaneous firing—the most effective fire tactic of the eighteenth century.

Buffalo Soldiers   Black troops who served in the U.S. Army in the West after the Civil War, supposedly so named by Indians. There were four black regiments: the Ninth Cavalry, Tenth Cavalry, Twenty-fourth Infantry, and Twenty-fifth Infantry.

canister   A deadly artillery weapon consisting of a cylindrical metal can filled with hundreds of musket-ball-sized shot. When fired from cannon at close range against infantry or cavalry, canister was devastating.

causeway   A roadway elevated over a body of water, usually as an approach to a city or a fortification, such as the causeways connecting the city of Tenochtitlán (now Mexico City) to the shore of its surrounding lake.

cavalry   Mounted troops, who originally fought with swords and lances from horseback, but who increasingly from the late eighteenth century on began to dismount to fight with firearms, which could not until the middle of the next century be used effectively from horseback. Cavalry was used extensively for reconnaissance and to screen (prevent detection of or interference with) the movements of infantry.

chevaux-de-frise   Moveable defensive obstacles made of logs or wooden beams, bristling with metal spikes. Commonly used during the late eighteenth and early nineteenth centuries as roadblocks or to fill in gaps in fortified lines. Underwater versions were used to block rivers or harbors.

citadel   A smaller fort built as a stronghold inside a larger fort.

column   A narrow but deep formation, only a few men wide but as many as several hundred long. Generally used to move troops, not as an attack formation. Also a general term meaning "a military force."

company   The smallest organizational infantry unit of an army, typically numbering around a hundred men and officers if at full strength; commanded by a captain, assisted by lieutenants and several noncommissioned officers.

Congreve rocket   The first practical rocket-powered weapon, invented by Lt. William Congreve and used by the British army during the War of 1812. They were notoriously inaccurate and were often used as much for show as for direct effect. When fired at night, they caused "rockets' red glare."

corps   A very large organizational unit, which did not come into use in North America until the creation of extremely large armies during the American Civil War. Consisting of two or three divisions, a Union army corps was usually commanded by a major general. Confederate army corps were commanded by lieutenant generals (the Confederacy had several lieutenant generals; the Union army lacked an equivalent rank until it was revived for U.S. Grant).

cottonclads   Wooden gunboats of the Confederate navy whose decks were heavily barricaded with cotton bales to absorb enemy fire.

demonstration   A fake assault made with maximum show, usually intended to divert the enemy's attention from a real attack elsewhere.

deployment   The manner in which military forces were arranged or positioned, or their movement into position.

division   A large organizational unit of an army. Seldom used during the eighteenth century, although the allied army at Yorktown was organized into "grand divisions." By the time of the American Civil War, the advent of extremely large armies called for new levels of organization, and it became a standard practice to designate divisions consisting of three or four brigades, under the command of a major general.

dragoons   Mounted units who traveled on horseback but who usually dismounted to fight as light infantry. Dragoons on both sides were among the most effective and mobile troops of the American Revolution. The regular U.S. Army had several dragoon units in the early nineteenth century.

earthworks   Fortifications made of dirt, gravel, or sand, sometimes temporary and improvised on the battlefield but in some cases massive, elaborate, and permanent structures.

enfilade   Fire from a flanking position that took defenders from the side, striking the long axis of a line formation. Enfilading fire was almost always effective, and when coupled with surprise, it could be devastating.

envelopment   A maneuver or attack wrapping around the enemy's flank and bringing force to bear from the front, side, and rear all at once. This was usually a decisive move, but it was very difficult to achieve. Amateur commanders often planned attacks based on double envelopment of both flanks simultaneously (modeled on a famous victory at Cannae of the Carthaginian general Hannibal), but this almost always failed.

field gun or field artillery   An artillery piece that was mounted on large wheels and light enough to be moved in the field to accompany infantry or cavalry.

firing step   A high ledge built into the wall of a fort that allowed defenders to stand and fire over the edge at attackers.

flank   The extreme ends of a defensive or attacking line, or the sides of a column. Typically vulnerable to attack.

flank companies   Common in the British Army during the eighteenth century, flank companies were special units comprising grenadiers and light infantry. They were usually stationed at the flanks of a line of infantry (hence the name). Flank companies from several regiments were often combined into a single elite striking force for special assignments, since the men of flank companies were assumed to be the best troops.

flying batteries   Highly mobile, horse-drawn field artillery, first used effectively by the U.S. Army in the Mexican War.

foot   In the eighteenth century, synonymous with "infantry." Infantry regiments were known as "foot" regiments.

forlorn hope   A small group of picked troops used as the leading attack force for an assault against fortifications. A forlorn hope relied on speed and surprise, but—as the name suggests—was regarded as almost a suicide squad. The term was used mostly during the late eighteenth and early nineteenth centuries.

fortifications   Any built-up defensive structure, ranging from the flimsiest improvised field defense to large, elaborate, interlocking series of forts, walls, and artillery batteries encompassing several miles from end to end.

frigate   A swift, medium-sized warship, varying greatly in size and armament over time and from navy to navy, used for scouting, escort duties, and against civilian shipping. The British navy had dozens of frigates in North American waters during the eighteenth and early nineteenth centuries, most of them relatively small with a limited number of medium-caliber guns. The United States built a new, larger class of heavy frigates, of stronger construction and with much greater firepower at the turn of the nineteenth century. Even the most powerful frigates could not engage ships of the line but rather fought ships of equal or inferior strength.

fusiliers Light infantry troops of the British army, sometimes organized into entire regiments (e.g., Royal Welch Fusiliers), named after soldiers of the seventeenth century who had been armed with an early form of firearm called a fusil.

galley A small warcraft resembling a long, narrow, oversized row boat, that carried troops and a small swivel gun or two. Galleys were used extensively during the colonial and revolutionary period on northern lakes and rivers. They were usually propelled by oars (and then referred to as "row galleys") but they also had masts and sails.

gondola or gundola A flat-bottomed boat, tapered to a point at each end, used on lakes and rivers during the colonial wars and the American Revolution as troop transports and warcraft. They could be either rowed or sailed.

grapeshot Small round shot fired in multiples from artillery against massed infantry, opposing batteries, light fortifications, or ships. The effect was similar to a massive shotgun blast.

grasshopper A small field cannon, mounted on legs, used by the British Army during the late eighteenth century. The cannon leaped about erratically when fired, hence the name.

grenadiers In the eighteenth century, elite troops formed into special companies or even regiments and employed for the most difficult or dangerous assignments. The term came originally from the seventeenth century, when grenadiers had been large, strong soldiers specially picked to throw the heavy hand grenades of the period.

guerrillas Irregular troops, who usually employed unconventional tactics. Often fought in small numbers by raiding and then retreating to secure havens.

gun Although in general the term could be applied to any weapon powered by gunpowder, in military usage it meant artillery and referred to individual cannon, groups of cannon, or the entire artillery branch of an army. Artillerymen, for example, were known as gunners. During the eighteenth century, armies were divided into three main parts: foot, horse, and gun.

gunboat Any armed small boat, but specifically the heavy boats that fought on the western rivers during the American Civil War.

horse Used as a special term to mean "cavalry," especially during the eighteenth century, when the three divisions of an army were foot, horse, and gun.

howitzer A specialized piece of field artillery designed to fire at long range with a high arc.

infantry Foot soldiers; the main branch of all armies.

ironclads Heavily armored warships constructed of wood with protective iron plate sheathing. Ironclads were much stronger than the traditional wooden ships and could withstand more punishment. They made their greatest impact during the American Civil War, especially on the western rivers.

jaegers Meaning "hunters" in German, jaegers were elite German mercenary units during the American Revolution. They were armed with short-barreled rifles and were trained to fight in wooded or rough terrain.

lancers Cavalry troops armed with long spears and trained in special techniques and tactics to make maximum use of the weapon. The Mexican army relied heavily on lancers during the Mexican-American War, although no amount of equestrian skill made lancers a match for massed musketry or artillery.

legion A name applied to a specialized force organized outside the usual army structure. During the American Revolution, both sides formed hybrid units called legions, combining mounted infantry (or dragoons) and light infantry, which were famous for their speed of movement and their effectiveness in combat. Later, during the military reorganization of the late 1790s, the revamped U.S. Army was called the Legion, although the name was short-lived. The most famous legion to fight in North America was probably the French Foreign Legion, which saw combat in Mexico.

light infantry An eighteenth-century term, referring to special troops with less equipment than the standard foot soldier and therefore presumably more mobile. Light infantry were usually thought of as elite fighters and were often given special assignments.

line   The most basic and commonly used battle formation, in which forces were arranged in a long line, often only one or two deep, facing the enemy. The formation was the same for infantry, cavalry, or ships at sea, and it was the starting point for either attack or defense.

loophole   Holes cut in a stockade or fortified wall to allow defenders to fire on attackers with muskets or rifles.

Loyalists   American colonists (sometimes called Tories) who remained loyal to the British king during the American Revolution. Thousands of Loyalists were organized into provincial military units and fought for the British during the war, and many irregular Loyalists units in the southern colonies fought locally against patriot irregulars.

magazine   A storage place inside a fort for gunpowder, ammunition, and arms.

Métis   With a lowercase *m* the term refers to any person of mixed French-Indian heritage. With a capital *M* it refers to a specific Canadian ethnic group, whose members identified themselves as a coherent political entity.

militia   Organized, officially recognized, part-time, amateur military units, called to active service by the central government during wartime or special emergencies. Militia were essentially civilians, organized locally on the company level, who trained in their spare time under their own elected officers. Although they were often well armed and equipped, militia were seldom effective in a formal battle situations, and their formations were almost always broken if attacked by disciplined regulars. American commanders were forced to rely on state or local militias to swell field armies during the American Revolution. Both the French and (later) the British recruited and employed militia units in Canada. In postrevolutionary Mexico, there were two formally recognized militias, active militia and civic militia. Both were nominally part of a national system, but in fact the militias were usually controlled by and represented regions or localities in struggles against the central government. At various points in the nineteenth century, Mexican militias formed the basis of revolutionary or counterrevolutionary armies and of armies that fought American and French invaders.

mine   Explosives placed next to or under fortifications in order to blow up defenders and create a breach for attackers.

Mines were often placed at the end of underground tunnels, which had been burrowed in secret.

minié ball   A large-caliber lead ball with a specially designed hollow base that expanded inside the barrel when fired to engage the rifling grooves, thus achieving accuracy from the spin. This special ammunition—which was simple for troops with little training to use—greatly increased the effectiveness and range of infantry firepower during the Civil War.

mortar   Specialized cannon, usually of large caliber with short barrels, designed to throw contact-exploding or fused shells in a high arc. Employed mainly against fortifications.

musket   The basic shoulder weapon of armies from the mid-eighteenth to the mid-nineteenth centuries, the musket was a smooth-bore, muzzle-loading gun of limited accuracy but extremely damaging and effective when fired in volleys at close range.

palisade   A fort built of hewn logs, usually sharpened at the top. Same as a stockade.

parallel trenches   The basic trenches built by attackers laying siege to a fortified place. The first parallel trench was dug just outside the range of the fort's cannon and was—as the name implies—parallel to the line of the fort's main wall. After battering the fort with artillery sited in the first parallel, attackers dug angled approach trenches to a new vantage point and started a new parallel trench line. Well-engineered parallel trenches made the defense of a fort or fortified city very difficult to sustain.

parapet   The walls of a fort.

partisans   Essentially the same as guerrillas: irregular troops, usually fighting in their own locality. There were many bands of partisans on each side in the southern colonies during the American Revolution, for example.

patriots   A term used specifically to identify rebellious American colonists during the American Revolution, those who were opposed to the British king and government, organized a new nation, and fought for its independence.

pioneers   Troops sent ahead of a main force to cut a trail or clear away obstacles, particularly in forests.

privateers   Private ships of war with official letters of "marque and reprisal" from a governing body allowing them to attack and capture ships of an opposing nation. Prizes were sold and profits split among the captain, owners, and crew. In effect, privateers were sanctioned pirates.

quarter   The granting of mercy to an enemy who has surrendered and is defenseless.

rake   A term of naval warfare, meaning to fire along the length of an opposing ship from directly ahead or behind; the maritime equivalent of enfilade fire and the most devastating form of gunfire attack.

rampart   A wide embankment raised as a fortification; bulwark.

reconnaissance or reconnoitering   Search for information about the enemy's strength and dispositions by sending out troops to scout and probe. A "reconnaissance in strength" might involve a probe by a large number of troops, but a simple reconnaissance was conducted by only a few infantry or cavalrymen.

redan   A two-sided, V-shaped projection from the wall of a fortification, often used to enclose an artillery battery.

redoubt   A self-contained, outlying fortification that formed part of the overall defensive system of a larger fortress. A redoubt was designed to function as a strong point of the defense, and it was manned and supplied to function almost independently. Attacks on redoubts were prominent events in many battles from the colonial period through the American Civil War.

regiment   The regiment was the fundamental organizational unit during the military history of North America, employed by all organized armies of all nations on the continent. It comprised from 750 to 1,000 men—at least on paper—and was usually the primary unit used to identify troops and organize their movements. Most regiments were commanded by a colonel, supported by several subordinate officers. Regiments were made up, in theory, of ten or so companies of around a hundred men each, but these numbers varied from place to place and over time. A regiment that saw heavy action was likely to be drastically

reduced in size—some U.S. Civil War regiments contained only a handful of men after fighting in several of the high-casualty battles of the war. The British army designated regiments by sequential number (supplemented in some cases by names). The French army generally used the name of the commander or a region to designate regiments. German mercenary regiments during the American Revolution were known by the name of their commanders. Units of the Mexican army, which was fluid in its organization, were usually known by the commanders' or sponsors' names. Volunteer U.S. Army regiments in general were designated by number and the name of the state where they were recruited. Regular U.S. Army regiments were known by numbers only. Confederate regiments were often named after commanders.

regulars   Full-time professional soldiers, who lived, trained, and fought as permanent parts of a nation's military establishment: in other words, members of the standing army. Regulars were long-enlistment soldiers and officers who held commissions from the central government (the king, Congress, etc.). Regulars were the backbone of armies fighting in North America and were usually the best trained, best equipped, and most experienced units on any battlefield. Regular regiments of the British army served in North America from the colonial era down to the advent of an independent Canada. The French, off and on, had regular units in North America—several during the American Revolution, for example. The regular U.S. Army was consistently small and inadequate to fight on more than a very minor scale. Even during frequent political changes in the nineteenth century, Mexican governments maintained a central core of regular officers and troops.

rifle   A shoulder weapon of considerable accuracy, especially in the hands of specialists, with interior barrel grooves that imparted a stabilizing spin to the bullet. Companies of riflemen were organized by both sides during the American Revolution. Later, the term was also applied to large-bore artillery with grooved ("rifled") barrels, which came into use during the American Civil War.

salient   A troop position or fortified structure that projected forward from a basic defensive or offensive line.

sally   An aggressive attack (also known as a sortie) by the defenders of a fortified place under siege, usually to capture or disable an artillery battery or destroy troop positions. Forts often had small gates, known as "sally ports," from which sallies could be launched.

ship of the line   The largest class of naval warship in the eighteenth and early nineteenth centuries, usually armed with a minimum of sixty-four heavy guns and manned by hundreds of sailors and marines. During fleet engagements, the standard formation was a long "line of battle," hence the designation—as ships powerful enough to take a place in the line. Both the British and French navies deployed ships of the line to North American waters during the American Revolution, but the United States had no vessels of this size and power until the early nineteenth century.

siege   A campaign against a heavily fortified and defended place, which might be a single fort or a huge complex of defenses around an entire city. Though it could end in a few days, a siege was usually a long-term affair, lasting up to a year or more, often eventually starving out or battering the defenders to submission. During the eighteenth century, siege warfare became almost an exact science, with moves and countermoves understood by both sides. If no outside force came to aid the defenders, the attackers were almost always successful. The outcome of a siege was less predictable by the time of the American Civil War, since the great increase in defensive firepower made assaults on fortifications difficult.

skirmish   A small battle; usually a limited action lasting only a short time with few casualties. Also a preliminary engagement by skirmishers, lightly armed troops, in a loose line ahead of a main body expecting combat, whose role was to detect and briefly delay (before withdrawing) the enemy, as it approached or was approached.

strike colors   The signal for surrender in naval warfare; to haul down the flag.

swivel gun   A small-bore cannon, mounted on a swivel so it could fire through a wide arc. Common armament for small boats and ships.

torpedo   An underwater explosive device, designed to detonate when struck by a ship; functionally the same as a twentieth-century naval mine, used to defend harbors or water passages.

troop   The cavalry unit equivalent to an infantry company; enlisted members were known as troopers.

volley   Massed, nearly simultaneous fire from infantry or artillery, concentrated on a narrow target. Disciplined volley fire was one of the most effective tactics on any battlefield.

volunteers   Untrained amateur soldiers who enlisted for a specific period of time in response to a war or national emergency. The U.S. Army during wartime has almost always consisted in the majority of volunteers. Almost all regiments on both sides of the Civil War, for example, were volunteers—not the same as militia, who were organized and trained in peacetime as units.

weather gage   During the age of sail, to hold the weather gage was to be in the all-important position upwind from the enemy from which one could control whether a battle took place or not. Sailing ships, especially square-rigged frigates and ships of the line, could not maneuver well into the wind; to have it blowing from astern was a huge advantage.

works   A general term for any kind of fortification.

ALPHABETICAL LIST OF BATTLES

* = battlefield site or park

Adobe Walls Texas (June 27, 1874) *Buffalo War*

Agua Prieta Mexico-Arizona Border (November 1, 1915) *Mexican Revolution*

Alamance North Carolina (May 16, 1771) *Regulator Uprising*

Alamo San Antonio, Texas (February 23–March 6, 1836) *Texas War of Independence**

U.S.S. Alfred v. H.M.S. Glasgow Off Block Island, Rhode Island (April 6, 1776) *American Revolution*

Allatoona Pass Georgia (October 5, 1864) *American Civil War*

Annapolis Royal (Port Royal) Canada (September 8–October 6, 1744) *King George's War*

Antietam (Sharpsburg) Maryland (September 17, 1862) *American Civil War**

Ash Hollow (Blue Lake) Nebraska (September 3, 1855) *Sioux Wars*

Atlanta Georgia (May 14–September 2, 1864) *American Civil War*

Augusta Georgia (September 14–18, 1780) *American Revolution*

Augusta Georgia (May 22–June 5, 1781) *American Revolution*

Bad Axe River Wisconsin (August 2, 1832) *Black Hawk War*

Ball's Bluff Virginia (October 21, 1861) *American Civil War*

Batoche Canada (May 9–12, 1885) *Second Riel Rebellion*

Baton Rouge Louisiana (August 5, 1862) *American Civil War*

Bear Paw Mountains Montana (September 30–October 5, 1877) *Nez Perce War*

Bear River Idaho (January 27, 1863) *Shoshone War*

Beaufort (Port Royal Island) South Carolina (February 3, 1779) *American Revolution*

Beaver Dams Canada (June 24, 1813) *War of 1812*

Beecher's Island Colorado (September 17–25, 1868) *Sheridan's Campaign*

Belmont Missouri (November 7, 1861) *American Civil War*

Bennington Vermont (August 16, 1777) *American Revolution**

Bentonville North Carolina (March 19, 1865) *American Civil War**

Big Bethel   Virginia (June 10, 1861) *American Civil War*

Big Black River   Mississippi (May 17, 1863) *American Civil War*

Big Hole Basin   Montana (August 8–11, 1877) *Nez Perce War*[*]

Big Meadows   Oregon (May 27, 1856) *Rogue River War*

Billingsport   New Jersey (October 2, 1777) *American Revolution*

Black Mingo Creek   South Carolina (September 29, 1780) *American Revolution*

Blackstocks   South Carolina (November 20, 1780) *American Revolution*

Bladensburg   Maryland (August 24, 1814) *War of 1812*

Bloody Brook (Pocumtuck, Deerfield)   Massachusetts (September 18, 1675) *King Philip's War*

Bloody Swamp (Bloody Marsh, St. Simon's Island)   Georgia (July 7, 1742) *War of Jenkin's Ear*

Blue Licks   Kentucky (August 19, 1782) *American Revolution*

Blue Savannah   South Carolina (September 4, 1780) *American Revolution*

Bound Brook   New Jersey (April 13, 1777) *American Revolution*

Brandy Station (Fleetwood Hill, Beverly's Ford)   Virginia (June 9, 1863) *American Civil War*

Brandywine   Pennsylvania (September 11, 1777) *American Revolution*[*]

Briar Creek   Georgia (March 3, 1779) *American Revolution*

Brice's Cross Roads (Brice's Creek Roads, Guntown, Tishomingo Creek)   Mississippi (June 10, 1864) *American Civil War*[*]

Bristoe Station   Virginia (October 14, 1863) *American Civil War*

Buena Vista   Mexico (February 22–23, 1847) *Mexican-American War*

Bull Run, First (Manassas)   Virginia (July 21, 1861) *American Civil War*[*]

Bull Run, Second (Manassas)   Virginia (August 29–30, 1862) *American Civil War*

Bull's Ferry   New Jersey (July 21, 1780) *American Revolution*

Bunker Hill (Breed's Hill)   Massachusetts (June 17, 1775) *American Revolution*[*]

Bushy Run (Edge Hill)   Pennsylvania (August 5–6, 1763) *Pontiac's Rebellion*[*]

Calderón Bridge (Puente de Calderón)   Mexico (January 17, 1811) *Hidalgo Revolt*

Camden   South Carolina (August 16, 1780) *American Revolution*[*]

Camerone   Mexico (April 30, 1863) *Mexican-French War*

Camp Texas (Fort Texas)   Texas (May 3–8, 1846) *Mexican-American War*

Cedar Creek   Virginia (October 19, 1864) *American Civil War*

Cedar Mountain   Virginia (August 9, 1862) *American Civil War*

Cedars   Canada (May 16, 1776) *American Revolution*

Celaya   Mexico (April 8–15, 1915) *Mexican Revolution*

Cempoallan   Mexico (May 28–29, 1520) *Spanish Conquest*

Cerro Gordo   Mexico (April 18, 1847) *Mexican-American War*

Chambly   Canada (October 18, 1775) *American Revolution*

Champion's Hill   Mississippi (May 16, 1863) *American Civil War*

Champoton   Mexico (March 1517) *Spanish Conquest*

Chancellorsville   Virginia (May 1–4, 1863) *American Civil War*

Chantilly (Ox Hill)   Virginia (September 1, 1862) *American Civil War*

Chapultepec   Mexico (September 13, 1847) *Mexican-American War*

Charleston (Sullivan's Island)   South Carolina (June 28, 1776) *American Revolution*

Charleston   South Carolina (April 1–May 12, 1780) *American Revolution*

Charlotte   North Carolina (September 26, 1780) *American Revolution*

Chateaugay (Châteauguay River)   Canada (October 25–26, 1813) *War of 1812*

Chattanooga (Lookout Mountain, Missionary Ridge)   Tennessee (November 23–25, 1863) *American Civil War*[*]

Cheat Mountain (Elkwater)   West Virginia (September 10–15, 1861) *American Civil War*

Cherry Valley   New York (November 11, 1778) *American Revolution*

U.S.S. *Chesapeake* v. H.M.S. *Shannon*   Off Boston, Massachusetts (June 1, 1813) *War of 1812*

Chesapeake Bay   Off the Maryland Coast (March 16, 1781) *American Revolution*

Chesapeake Capes   Off the Virginia–North Carolina Coast (September 5, 1781) *American Revolution*

Chickamauga Georgia (September 19–20, 1863) *American Civil War**

Chickasaw Bluffs (Chickasaw Bayou) Mississippi (December 27–29, 1862) *American Civil War*

Chippewa Canada (July 5, 1814) *War of 1812*

Chrysler's Farm Canada (November 11, 1813) *War of 1812*

Churubusco Mexico (August 20, 1847) *Mexican-American War*

Cloyd's Mountain Virginia (May 9, 1864) *American Civil War*

Cold Harbor Virginia (May 31–June 12, 1864) *American Civil War**

Columbus New Mexico (March 9, 1916) *Border Raids*

Combahee Ferry South Carolina (August 27, 1782) *American Revolution*

U.S.S. *Congress* v. H.M.S. *Savage* Off the South Carolina Coast (September 6, 1781) *American Revolution*

U.S.S. *Constitution* v. H.M.S. *Guerrière* Off Nova Scotia, Canada (August 19, 1812) *War of 1812*

Contreras (Padieras) Mexico (August 19–20, 1847) *Mexican-American War*

Cooch's Bridge (Iron Hill) Delaware (September 3, 1777) *American Revolution*

Corinth Mississippi (October 3–4, 1862) *American Civil War**

Cowan's Ford North Carolina (February 1, 1781) *American Revolution*

Cowpens South Carolina (January 17, 1781) *American Revolution**

Crampton's Gap Maryland (September 14, 1862) *American Civil War*

The Crater (Petersburg Mine Assault) Petersburg, Virginia (July 30, 1864) *American Civil War*

Cross Keys (Union Church) Virginia (June 8–9, 1862) *American Civil War*

Dade's Battle Florida (December 18, 1835) *Second Seminole War*

Danbury Raid Connecticut (April 23–28, 1777) *American Revolution*

Drewry's Bluff Virginia (May 16, 1864) *American Civil War*

Emuckfau Creek Alabama (January 22, 1814) *Creek War*

Enitachopco Creek Alabama (January 24, 1814) *Creek War**

Eutaw Springs South Carolina (September 8, 1781) *American Revolution*

Fair Oaks (Seven Pines) Virginia (May 31–June 2, 1862) *American Civil War*

Fallen Timbers Ohio (August 20, 1794) *Indian Wars**

Falling Waters West Virginia (July 14, 1864) *American Civil War*

Farmville and Highbridge Virginia (April 6–7, 1865) *American Civil War*

Fetterman Fight Wyoming (December 21, 1866) *Bozeman Trail War*

Fishdam Ford South Carolina (November 9, 1780) *American Revolution*

Fisher's Hill Virginia (September 22, 1864) *American Civil War*

Fishing Creek (Catawba Ford) North Carolina (August 18, 1780) *American Revolution*

Five Forks Virginia (March 30–April 1, 1865) *American Civil War*

Fort Anne New York (July 8, 1777) *American Revolution*

Fort Beauséjour Canada (June 4–17, 1755) *French and Indian War*

Fort Caroline Florida (September 20, 1565) *French-Spanish Colonial Wars**

Fort Clinton and Fort Montgomery New York (October 6, 1777) *American Revolution*

Fort Cumberland Canada (November 7–29, 1776) *American Revolution*

Fort Donelson Tennessee (February 13–15, 1862) *American Civil War**

Fort Erie, First Canada (August 15, 1814) *War of 1812*

Fort Erie, Second Canada (September 17, 1814) *War of 1812*

Fort Fisher (Terry's Expedition) North Carolina (January 12–15, 1865) *American Civil War**

Fort Frontenac Canada (August 25–27, 1758) *French and Indian War*

Fort George Canada (May 27, 1813) *War of 1812*

Fort Henry Tennessee (February 6, 1862) *American Civil War*

Fort Keyser New York (October 19, 1780) *American Revolution*

Fort Lee (Fort Constitution) New Jersey (November 20, 1776) *American Revolution*

Fort McHenry Baltimore, Maryland (September 12–14, 1814) *War of 1812**

Fort Mercer (Red Bank) New Jersey (October 22–November 21, 1777) *American Revolution*

Fort Mifflin Pennsylvania (October 10–November 15, 1777) *American Revolution*

Fort Mims Alabama (August 30, 1813) *Creek War*

Fort Motte South Carolina (May 12, 1781) *American Revolution*

Fort Necessity (Great Meadows) Pennsylvania (July 3, 1754) *French and Indian War**

Fort Niagara New York (July 6–25, 1759) *French and Indian War*

Fort Pillow Tennessee (April 12, 1864) *American Civil War*

Fort Pulaski Georgia (April 10–11, 1862) *American Civil War**

Fort Ridgely Minnesota (August 21 and 22, 1862) *Santee Uprising*

Fort Stanwix New York (August 3–23, 1777) *American Revolution**

Fort Stedman Virginia (March 25, 1865) *American Civil War*

Fort Stephenson Ohio (August 1–2, 1813) *War of 1812*

Fort Sumter Charleston, South Carolina (April 12–14, 1861) *American Civil War**

Fort Ticonderoga (Fort Carillon) New York (July 8, 1758) *French and Indian War**

Fort Ticonderoga (1775) New York (May 10, 1775) *American Revolution*

Fort Ticonderoga New York (July 2–5, 1777) *American Revolution*

Fort Ticonderoga New York (September 18, 1777) *American Revolution*

Fort Wagner (Battery Wagner) South Carolina (July 10 and 18, 1863) *American Civil War*

Fort Washington New York (November 16, 1776) *American Revolution*

Fort Watson South Carolina (April 15–23, 1781) *American Revolution*

Fort William Henry New York (August 3–9, 1757) *French and Indian War*

Franklin Tennessee (November 30, 1864) *American Civil War*

Franklin's Crossing (Deep Run) Virginia (June 5, 1863) *American Civil War*

Fredericksburg Virginia (December 13, 1862) *American Civil War**

Frenchtown (River Raisin) Ohio (January 18 and 22, 1813) *War of 1812*

Front Royal Virginia (May 23, 1862) *American Civil War*

Gaines's Mill Virginia (June 27, 1862) *American Civil War**

Galveston Texas (January 1, 1863) *American Civil War*

Garnett's and Golding's Farm Virginia (June 27–28, 1862) *American Civil War**

Germantown Pennsylvania (October 4, 1777) *American Revolution*

Gettysburg Pennsylvania (July 1–3, 1863) *American Civil War**

Globe Tavern (Wheldon Railroad, Six Mile House) Virginia (August 18–21, 1864) *American Civil War*

Glorieta Pass New Mexico (March 26 and 28, 1862) *American Civil War**

Gloucester Virginia (October 3, 1781) *American Revolution*

Goliad Texas (March 18–19, 1836) *Texas War of Independence*

Great Bridge Virginia (December 9, 1775) *American Revolution*

Great Savannah South Carolina (August 20, 1780) *American Revolution*

Great Swamp Rhode Island (December 19, 1675) *King Philip's War*

Green Spring Virginia (July 6, 1781) *American Revolution*

Guilford Courthouse North Carolina (March 15, 1781) *American Revolution**

Gwynn Island Virginia (July 8–10, 1776) *American Revolution*

Hanging Rock South Carolina (August 6, 1780) *American Revolution*

Hanover Courthouse Virginia (May 27, 1862) *American Civil War*

Harlem Heights New York (September 16, 1776) *American Revolution*

Harmar's Defeat Indiana (October 19 and 22, 1790) *Little Turtle's War*

Harpers Ferry West Virginia (September 12–15, 1862) *American Civil War**

Haw River (Pyle's Defeat) North Carolina (February 25, 1781) *American Revolution*

Helena Arkansas (July 4, 1863) *American Civil War*

Hillsborough Raid North Carolina (September 12, 1781) *American Revolution*

Hobkirk's Hill South Carolina (April 25, 1781) *American Revolution*

Holly Springs Mississippi (December 20, 1862) *American Civil War*

Horseshoe Bend Alabama (March 27, 1814) *Creek War*[*]

Hubbardton Vermont (July 7, 1777) *American Revolution*[*]

Irish Bend (Bayou Teche) Louisiana (April 12–14, 1863) *American Civil War*

Island Number 10 Tennessee (April 7, 1862) *American Civil War*

Iuka Mississippi (September 19, 1862) *American Civil War*

Jamestown Virginia (March 22, 1622) *Virginia-Indian Wars*

Jamestown Virginia (September 16, 1676) *Bacon's Rebellion*

Johnstown New York (October 25, 1781) *American Revolution*

Julesburg Colorado (January 7 and February 2, 1865) *Colorado War*

Kernstown, First Virginia (March 23, 1862) *American Civil War*

Kernstown, Second Virginia (July 23–24, 1864) *American Civil War*

Kettle Creek Georgia (February 14, 1779) *American Revolution*

Killdeer Mountain North Dakota (July 28, 1864) *Sioux Wars*

King's Mountain South Carolina (October 7, 1780) *American Revolution*[*]

Kip's Bay New York (September 15, 1776) *American Revolution*

Klock's Field New York (October 19, 1780) *American Revolution*

Knoxville (Fort Sanders) Tennessee (November 17–December 5, 1863) *American Civil War*

Lake Erie (Put-in-Bay) Ohio (September 10, 1813) *War of 1812*[*]

Lake George (Bloody Pond) New York (September 8, 1755) *French and Indian War*

Lake Okeechobee Florida (December 25, 1837) *Second Seminole War*

Lázaro Mexico (May 27, 1518) *Spanish Conquest*

Lenud's Ferry South Carolina (May 6, 1780) *American Revolution*

Lexington and Concord Massachusetts (April 19, 1775) *American Revolution*[*]

Lexington Missouri (September 18–20, 1861) *American Civil War*[*]

Little Bighorn (Custer's Last Stand, Greasy Grass) Montana (June 25, 1876) *Black Hills War*[*]

Lochry's Defeat Ohio (August 24 or 25, 1781) *American Revolution*

Long Island New York (August 27, 1776) *American Revolution*

Long Sault Canada (April 1659) *Indian Wars*

Louisbourg Canada (May 11–June 17, 1745) *King George's War*[*]

Louisbourg Canada (May 30–July 27, 1758) *French and Indian War*

Lundy's Lane Canada (July 25, 1814) *War of 1812*

Lynchburg Virginia (June 17–18, 1864) *American Civil War*

Mackinac Island (Fort Michilimackinac) Canada (August 4, 1814) *War of 1812*[*]

Malvern Hill Virginia (July 1, 1862) *American Civil War*[*]

McDowell Virginia (May 8, 1862) *American Civil War*[*]

Mechanicsville (Ellison's Mill) Virginia (June 26, 1862) *American Civil War*[*]

Memphis Tennessee (June 6, 1862) *American Civil War*

Mesa (La Mesa) California (January 9, 1847) *Mexican-American War*

Milk Creek Colorado (September 29–October 5, 1879) *Indian Wars*

Mill Springs (Logan Cross Road) Kentucky (January 19, 1862) *American Civil War*[*]

Minisink New York (July 22, 1779) *American Revolution*

Mobile Bay Alabama (August 5, 1864) *American Civil War*

Molino del Rey Mexico (September 8, 1847) *Mexican-American War*

Monck's Corner South Carolina (April 14, 1780) *American Revolution*

U.S.S. *Monitor* v. C.S.S. *Virginia* (*Monitor* v. *Merrimack*) Hampton Roads, Virginia (March 9, 1862) *American Civil War*

Monmouth New Jersey (June 28, 1778) *American Revolution*[*]

Monocacy Maryland (July 9, 1864) *American Civil War*[*]

Monongahela (Braddock's Defeat) Pennsylvania (July 9, 1755) *French and Indian War*

Monterrey Mexico (September 20–24, 1846) *Mexican-American War*

Montreal Canada (September 25, 1775) *American Revolution*

Moore's Creek Bridge North Carolina (February 27, 1776) *American Revolution*

Munfordville Kentucky (September 14–17, 1862) *American Civil War*

Mystic River Connecticut (May 26, 1637) *Pequot War*

Nashville Tennessee (December 15–16, 1864) *American Civil War*

New London Raid Connecticut (September 6, 1781) *American Revolution*

New Market Virginia (May 15, 1864) *American Civil War**

New Orleans Louisiana (January 8, 1815) *War of 1812**

New Orleans Louisiana (April 18–24, 1862) *American Civil War*

New Ulm Minnesota (August 23, 1862) *Santee Uprising*

Newport Rhode Island (July 29–August 31, 1778) *American Revolution*

Newtown New York (August 29, 1779) *American Revolution*

Ninety Six South Carolina (May 22–June 19, 1781) *American Revolution**

North Anna River (Hanover Junction, Jericho Mills, Taylor's Bridge) Virginia (May 23–27, 1864) *American Civil War*

Oak Grove (King's Schoolhouse) Virginia (June 25, 1862) *American Civil War**

Ocean Pond (Olustee) Florida (February 20, 1864) *American Civil War*

Okolona Mississippi (February 22,1864) *American Civil War*

Oriskany New York (August 6, 1777) *American Revolution**

Otumba Mexico (July 7, 1520) *Spanish Conquest*

Palo Alto Texas (May 8, 1846) *Mexican-American War*

Paoli Pennsylvania (September 21, 1777) *American Revolution*

Parker's Cross Roads Tennessee (December 31,1862) *American Civil War*

Parker's Ferry South Carolina (August 13, 1781) *American Revolution*

Parral Mexico (April 12, 1916) *Border Raids*

Paulus Hook New Jersey (August 19, 1779) *American Revolution*

Pea Ridge (Elkhorn Tavern) Arkansas (March 7–8, 1862) *American Civil War**

U.S.S. *Peacock* **v. H.M.S.** *Epervier* Off the Florida Coast (April 29, 1814) *War of 1812*

Pell's Point New York (October 18, 1776) *American Revolution*

Pensacola Florida (March–May 9, 1781) *American Revolution*

Perryville Kentucky (October 8, 1862) *American Civil War**

Petersburg Virginia (April 25, 1781) *American Revolution*

Petersburg Virginia (June 1864–April 1865) *American Civil War**

Philippi West Virginia (June 3, 1861) *American Civil War*

Pilot Knob (Fort Davidson) Missouri (September 27, 1864) *American Civil War*

Plattsburg Bay (Lake Champlain, Plattsburg) New York (September 11, 1814) *War of 1812**

Pleasant Hill Landing (Blair's Landing) Louisiana (April 9, 1864) *American Civil War*

Point Pleasant West Virginia (October 10, 1774) *Lord Dunmore's War*

Port Gibson Mississippi (May 1, 1863) *American Civil War**

Port Hudson Louisiana (May 22–July 9, 1963) *American Civil War**

Port Republic Virginia (June 9, 1862) *American Civil War**

Port Royal (Annapolis Royal) Canada (September 24–October 1, 1710) *Queen Anne's War*

Port Royal Sound (Forts Beauregard and Walker) South Carolina (November 7, 1861) *American Civil War*

Potonchan Mexico (March 25, 1519) *Spanish Conquest*

Prairie Grove Arkansas (December 7, 1862) *American Civil War**

Princeton New Jersey (January 3, 1777) *American Revolution*

Puebla Mexico (September 14–October 12, 1847) *Mexican-American War*

Puebla (Cinco de Mayo) Mexico (May 5, 1862) *Mexican-French War*

Quebec (Plains of Abraham) Canada (September 13, 1759) *French and Indian War*

Quebec Canada (December 31, 1775–January 1, 1776) *American Revolution*

Queenston   Canada (October 13, 1812) *War of 1812*

Quinby Bridge   South Carolina (July 17, 1781) *American Revolution*

Quintan's Bridge   New Jersey (March 18, 1778) *American Revolution*

Ramseur's Mill   North Carolina (June 20, 1780) *American Revolution*

Raymond   Mississippi (May 12, 1863) *American Civil War*

Resaca de la Palma (Resaca de Guerrero)   Texas (May 9, 1846) *Mexican-American War*

Rich Mountain   West Virginia (July 11, 1861) *American Civil War*

Richmond   Kentucky (August 29–30, 1862) *American Civil War*

Ridgeway   Canada (June 2, 1866) *Fenian Raid*

Roanoke Island   North Carolina (February 8, 1862) *American Civil War*

Rocky Mount   South Carolina (August 1, 1780) *American Revolution*

Rosebud Creek   Wyoming (June 17, 1876) *Black Hills War*

Rush Springs (Rush Creek)   Oklahoma (October 1, 1858) *Indian Wars*

Sabine Crossroads (Mansfield)   Louisiana (April 8, 1864) *American Civil War*

Sabine Pass (Fort Griffin)   Texas (September 8, 1863) *American Civil War*

Sackets Harbor   New York (May 28–29, 1813) *War of 1812**

Sacramento River   Mexico (February 28, 1847) *Mexican-American War*

St. Augustine   Forida (November 8–December 29, 1702) *Queen Anne's War**

St. Augustine   Florida (May 31–June 20, 1740) *War of Jenkin's Ear*

St. Charles   Canada (November 25, 1837) *Papineau's Rebellion*

St. Clair's Defeat   Indiana (November 4, 1791) *Little Turtle's War*

St. Denis   Canada (November 23, 1837) *Papineau's Rebellion*

St. Eustache   Canada (December 14, 1837) *Papineau's Rebellion*

St. John's (St. Jean's)   Canada (May 17, 1775) *American Revolution*

St. John's (St. Jean's)   Canada (September 5–November 2, 1775) *American Revolution*

San Gabriel   California (January 8, 1847) *Mexican-American War*

San Jacinto   Texas (April 21, 1836) *Texas War of Independence**

San Pascual   California (December 6, 1846) *Mexican-American War**

Sand Creek   Colorado (November 29, 1864) *Colorado War*

Sandusky (Crawford's Defeat)   Ohio (June 4–5, 1782) *American Revolution*

Santa Fe   New Mexico (August 15–21, 1680) *Pueblo Revolt*

Saratoga, First (Freeman's Farm)   New York (September 19, 1777) *American Revolution*

Saratoga, Second (Bemis Heights)   New York (October 7, 1777) *American Revolution*

Savage's Station (Allen's Farm, Peach Orchard)   Virginia (June 29, 1862) *American Civil War*

Savannah   Georgia (December 29, 1778) *American Revolution*

Savannah   Georgia (October 9, 1779) *American Revolution*

Sayler's Creek   Virginia (April 6, 1865) *American Civil War*

Shiloh (Pittsburgh Landing)   Tennessee (April 6–7, 1862) *American Civil War**

Sitka   Alaska (October 1–7, 1804) *Russian-Indian War**

Slim Buttes   South Dakota (September 9, 1876) *Black Hills War*

South Mountain   Maryland (September 14, 1862) *American Civil War*

Spencer's Tavern   Virginia (June 26, 1781) *American Revolution*

Spotsylvania   Virginia (May 12–18, 1864) *American Civil War**

Springfield   New Jersey (June 23, 1780) *American Revolution*

Springfield Arsenal   Massachusetts (January 25, 1787) *Shays's Rebellion*

Stones River (Murfreesboro)   Tennessee (December 31, 1862 and January 2, 1863) *American Civil War**

Stono Ferry   South Carolina (June 20, 1779) *American Revolution*

Stony Creek (Stoney Creek)   Canada (June 6, 1813) *War of 1812*

Stony Point   New York (July 16, 1779) *American Revolution**

Stronghold   California (January 17, 1873) *Modoc War**

Summit Springs   Colorado (July 11, 1869) *Sheridan's Campaign*

Talladega   Alabama (November 9, 1813) *Creek War*

Tallasahatchee   Alabama (November 3, 1813) *Creek War*

Tarrant's Tavern   North Carolina (February 1, 1781) *American Revolution*

Tenochtitlán   Mexico (May 26–August 13, 1521) *Spanish Conquest*

Thames (Moraviantown)   Canada (October 5, 1813) *War of 1812*

Three Rivers (Trois Rivières)   Canada (June 8, 1776) *American Revolution*

Throg's Neck (Throg's Point)   New York (October 12, 1776) *American Revolution*

Tippecanoe   Indiana (November 7, 1811) *Indian Wars*[*]

Tlaxcala   Mexico (August–September 1519) *Spanish Conquest*

Trenton   New Jersey (December 26, 1776) *American Revolution*[*]

Trevilian Station   Virginia (June 11–12, 1864) *American Civil War*

U.S.S. Trumbull v. Watt   Off the Atlantic Coast (June 2, 1780) *American Revolution*

U.S.S. Trumbull v. H.M.S. Iris   Off the Delaware Capes (August 8, 1781) *American Revolution*

Tupelo (Harrisburg)   Mississippi (July 13–15, 1864) *American Civil War*[*]

Valcour Island   New York (October 11–13, 1776) *American Revolution*

Veracruz   Mexico (March 22–29, 1847) *Mexican-American War*

Vicksburg   Mississippi (May 16–July 4, 1863) *American Civil War*[*]

Vincennes   Indiana (February 24–25, 1779) *American Revolution*[*]

Wahab's Plantation   North Carolina (September 21, 1780) *American Revolution*

Washita   Oklahoma (November 27, 1868) *Sheridan Campaign*[*]

Waxhaws   South Carolina (May 29, 1780) *American Revolution*

Waynesboro   Virginia (March 2, 1865) *American Civil War*

Wetzell's Ford   North Carolina (March 6, 1781) *American Revolution*

White Oak Swamp (Glendale)   Virginia (June 30, 1862) *American Civil War*[*]

White Plains   New York (October 28, 1776) *American Revolution*

Whitemarsh   Pennsylvania (December 5–8, 1777) *American Revolution*

The Wilderness   Virginia (May 5–6, 1864) *American Civil War*[*]

Williamsburg   Virginia (May 4–5, 1862) *American Civil War*

Williamson's Plantation   South Carolina (July 12, 1780) *American Revolution*

Wilson's Creek (Oak Hill)   Missouri (August 10, 1861) *American Civil War*[*]

Winchester, First   Virginia (May 25, 1862) *American Civil War*

Winchester, Second   Virginia (June 13–15, 1863) *American Civil War*

Winchester, Third (Opequon Creek)   Virginia (September 19, 1864) *American Civil War*

Wolf Mountain   Montana (January 8, 1877) *Black Hills War*

Wood Lake (Lone Tree Lake)   Minnesota (September 23, 1862) *Santee Uprising*

Wounded Knee   South Dakota (December 29, 1890) *Sioux Wars*[*]

Wyoming Valley   Pennsylvania (July 3–4, 1778) *American Revolution*

Yellow Tavern   Virginia (May 11, 1864) *American Civil War*

Yorktown   Virginia (September 28–October 18, 1781) *American Revolution*[*]

CHRONOLOGICAL LIST OF BATTLES

◆ **1517**

March—Champoton, Mexico

◆ **1518**

May 27—Lázaro, Mexico

◆ **1519**

March 25—Potonchan, Mexico

August–September—Tlaxcala

◆ **1520**

May 28–29—Cempoallan, Mexico

July 1—La Noche Triste, Mexico

July 7—Otumba, Mexico

◆ **1521**

May 26–August 13—Tenochtitlán, Mexico

◆ **1565**

September 20—Fort Caroline, Florida

◆ **1622**

March 22—Jamestown, Virginia

◆ **1637**

May 26—Mystic River, Connecticut

◆ **1659**

April—Long Sault, Canada

◆ **1675**

September 18—Bloody Brook, Massachussetts

December 19—Great Swamp, Rhode Island

◆ **1676**

September 16—Jamestown, Virginia

◆ **1680**

August 15–21—Santa Fe, New Mexico

◆ **1702**

November 8–December 29—St. Augustine, Florida

◆ **1710**

September 24–October 1—Port Royal, Canada

◆ **1740**

May 31–July 20—St. Augustine, Florida

◆ **1742**

July 7—Bloody Swamp, Georgia

◆ **1744**

September 8–October 6—Annapolis Royal, Canada

◆ **1745**

May 11–June 17—Louisbourg, Canada

◆ **1754**

July 3—Fort Necessity, Pennsylvania

◆ **1755**

June 4–17—Fort Beauséjour, Canada

July 9—Monongahela, Pennsylvania

September 8—Lake George, New York

◆ **1757**

August 3–9—Fort William Henry, New York

◆ **1758**

May 30–July 27—Louisbourg, Canada

July 8—Fort Ticonderoga, New York

August 25–27—Fort Frontenac, Canada

◆ **1759**

July 6–25—Fort Niagara, New York

September 13—Quebec, Canada

◆ **1763**

August 5–6—Bushy Run, Pennsylvania

◆ **1771**

May 16—Alamance, North Carolina

◆ **1774**

October 10—Point Pleasant, West Virginia

◆ **1775**

April 19—Lexington and Concord, Massachusetts

May 10—Fort Ticonderoga, New York

May 17—St. John's, Canada

June 17—Bunker Hill, Massachusetts

September 25—Montreal, Canada

October 18—Chambly, Canada

September 5–November 2—St. John's, Canada

December 9—Great Bridge, Virginia

December 31—Quebec, Canada

◆ **1776**

February 27—Moore's Creek Bridge, North Carolina
April 6—U.S.S. *Alfred* v. H.M.S. *Glasgow,* Off Block Island, Rhode Island
May 16—Cedars, Canada
June 8—Three Rivers, Canada
June 28—Charleston, South Carolina
July 8–10—Gwynn Island, Virginia
August 27—Long Island, New York
September 15—Kip's Bay, New York
September 16—Harlem Heights, New York
October 11–13—Valcour Island, New York
October 12—Throg's Neck, New York
October 18—Pell's Point, New York
October 28—White Plains, New York
November 7–29—Fort Cumberland, Canada
November 16—Fort Washington, New York
November 20—Fort Lee, New Jersey
December 26—Trenton, New Jersey

◆ **1777**

January 3—Princeton, New Jersey
April 13—Bound Brook, New Jersey
April 23–28—Danbury, Connecticut
July 2–5—Fort Ticonderoga, New York
July 7—Hubbardton, Vermont
July 8—Fort Anne, New York
August 3–23—Fort Stanwix, New York
August 6—Oriskany, New York
August 16—Bennington, Vermont
September 3—Cooch's Bridge, Delaware
September 11—Brandywine, Pennsylvania
September 18—Fort Ticonderoga, New York
September 19—Saratoga, First, New York
September 21—Paoli, Pennsylvania
October 2—Billingsport, New Jersey
October 4—Germantown, Pennsylvania
October 6—Fort Clinton, New York
October 6—Fort Montgomery, New York
October 7—Saratoga, Second, New York
October 10–November 15—Fort Mifflin, Pennsylvania
October 22–November 21—Fort Mercer, New Jersey
December 5–8—Whitemarsh, Pennsylvania

◆ **1778**

March 18—Quintan's Bridge, New Jersey
June 28—Monmouth, New Jersey
July 3–4—Wyoming Valley, Pennsylvania
July 29–August 31—Newport, Rhode Island
November 11—Cherry Valley, New York
December 29—Savannah, Georgia

◆ **1779**

February 3—Beaufort, South Carolina
February 14—Kettle Creek, Georgia
February 24–25—Vincennes, Indiana
March 3—Briar Creek, Georgia
June 20—Stono Ferry, South Carolina
July 16—Stony Point, New York
July 22—Minisink, New York
August 19—Paulus Hook, New Jersey
August 29—Newtown, New York
October 9—Savannah, Georgia

◆ **1780**

April 1–May 12—Charleston, South Carolina
April 14—Monck's Corner, South Carolina
May 6—Lenud's Ferry, South Carolina
May 29—Waxhaws, South Carolina
June 2—U.S.S. *Trumball* v. *Watt,* Off the Atlantic Coast
June 20—Ramseur's Mill, North Carolina
June 23—Springfield, New Jersey
July 12—Williamson's Plantation, South Carolina
July 21—Bull's Ferry, New Jersey
August 1—Rocky Mount, South Carolina
August 6—Hanging Rock, South Carolina
August 16—Camden, South Carolina
August 18—Fishing Creek, North Carolina
August 20—Great Savannah, South Carolina
September 4—Blue Savannah, South Carolina
September 14–18—Augusta, Georgia
September 21—Wahab's Plantation, North Carolina
September 26—Charlotte, North Carolina
September 29—Black Mingo Creek, South Carolina
October 7—King's Mountain, South Carolina

October 19—Fort Keyser, New York

October 19—Klock's Field, New York

November 9—Fishdam Ford, South Carolina

November 20—Blackstocks, South Carolina

◆ **1781**

January 17—Cowpens, South Carolina

February 1—Tarrant's Tavern, North Carolina

February 1—Cowan's Ford, North Carolina

February 25—Haw River, North Carolina

March 6—Wetzell's Ford, North Carolina

March–May 9—Pensacola, Florida

March 15—Guilford Courthouse, North Carolina

March 16—Chesapeake Bay, Maryland/Virginia

April 15–23—Fort Watson, South Carolina

April 25—Hobkirk's Hill, South Carolina

April 25—Petersburg, Virginia

May 12—Fort Motte, South Carolina

May 22–June 5—Augusta, Georgia

May 22–June 19—Ninety Six, South Carolina

June 26—Spencer's Tavern, Virginia

July 6—Green Spring, Virginia

July 17—Quinby Bridge, South Carolina

August 8—U.S.S. *Trumball* v. H.M.S. *Iris,*
    Off the Delaware Capes

August 13—Parker's Ferry, South Carolina

August 25—Lochry's Defeat, Ohio

September–October 18—Yorktown, Virginia

September 5—Chesapeake Capes, Off the
    Virginia/North Carolina Coast

September 6—U.S.S. *Congress* v. H.M.S. *Savage,*
    Off the South Carolina Coast

September 6—New London Raid, Connecticut

September 8—Eutaw Springs, South Carolina

September 12—Hillsborough Raid, North Carolina

September 28–October 18—Yorktown, Virginia

October 3—Gloucester, Virginia

October 25—Johnstown, New York

◆ **1782**

June 4–5—Sandusky, Ohio

August 19—Blue Licks, Kentucky

August 27—Combahee Ferry, South Carolina

◆ **1787**

January 25—Springfield Arsenal, Massachusetts

February 1—Cowan's Ford, North Carolina

◆ **1790**

October 19 and 22—Harmar's Defeat, Indiana

◆ **1791**

November 4—St. Clair's Defeat, Indiana

◆ **1794**

August 20—Fallen Timbers, Ohio

◆ **1804**

October 1–7—Sitka, Alaska

◆ **1811**

January 17—Calderón Bridge, Mexico

November 7—Tippecanoe, Indiana

◆ **1812**

August 19—U.S.S. *Constitution* v.
    H.M.S. *Guerrière,* Off Nova Scotia, Canada

October 13—Queenston, Canada

◆ **1813**

January 18 and 22—Frenchtown, Ohio

May 27—Fort George, Canada

May 28–29—Sackets Harbor, New York

June 1—U.S.S. *Chesapeake* v. H.M.S. *Shannon,*
    Off Boston, Massachusetts

June 6—Stony Creek, Canada

June 24—Beaver Dams, Canada

August 1–2—Fort Stephenson, Ohio

August 30—Fort Mims, Alabama

September 10—Lake Erie, Ohio

October 5—Thames, Canada
October 25–26—Chateaugay, Canada
November 3—Tallasahatchee, Alabama
November 9—Talladega, Alabama
November 11—Chrysler's Farm, Canada

◆ **1814**

January 22—Emuckfau Creek, Alabama
January 24—Enitachopco Creek, Alabama
March 27—Horseshoe Bend, Alabama
April 29—U.S.S. *Peacock* v. H.M.S. *Epervier*,
    Off the Florida Coast
July 5—Chippewa, Canada
July 25—Lundy's Lane, Canada
August 4—Mackinac Island, Canada
August 15—Fort Erie, First, Canada
August 24—Bladensburg, Maryland
September 7—Fort Erie, Second, Canada
September 11—Plattsburg Bay, New York
September 12–14—Fort McHenry, Maryland

◆ **1815**

January 8—New Orleans, Louisiana

◆ **1832**

August 2—Bad Axe River, Wisconsin

◆ **1835**

December 18—Dade's Battle, Florida

◆ **1836**

February 23–March 6—Alamo,
    San Antonio, Texas
March 18–19—Goliad, Texas
April 21—San Jacinto, Texas

◆ **1837**

November 23—St. Denis, Canada
November 25—St. Charles, Canada

December 14—St. Eustache, Canada
December 25—Lake Okeechobee, Florida

◆ **1846**

May 3–8—Camp Texas, Texas
May 8—Palo Alto, Texas
May 9—Resaca de la Palma, Texas
September 20–24—Monterrey, Mexico
December 6—San Pascual, California

◆ **1847**

January 8—San Gabriel, California
January 9—Mesa, California
February 22–23—Buena Vista, Mexico
February 28—Sacramento River, Mexico
March 22–29—Vera Cruz, Mexico
April 18—Cerro Gordo, Mexico
August 20—Contreras, Mexico
August 20—Churubusco, Mexico
September 8—Molino del Rey, Mexico
September 13—Chapultapec, Mexico
September 14–October 12—Puebla, Mexico

◆ **1855**

September 3—Ash Hollow, Nebraska

◆ **1856**

May 27—Big Meadows, Oregon

◆ **1858**

October 1—Rush Springs, Oklahoma

◆ **1859**

Spring—Crooked Creek, Texas

◆ **1861**

April 12–14—Fort Sumter, South Carolina
June 3—Philippi, West Virginia

June 10—Big Bethel, Virginia
July 11—Rich Mountain, West Virginia
July 21—Bull Run, First, Virginia
August 10—Wilson's Creek, Missouri
September 10–15—Cheat Mountain, West Virginia
September 18–20—Lexington, Missouri
October 21—Ball's Bluff, Virginia
November 7—Port Royal Sound, South Carolin
    November 7—Belmont, Missouri

◆ **1862**

January 19—Mill Springs, Kentucky
February 6—Fort Henry, Tennessee
February 8—Roanoke Island, North Carolina
February 13–15—Fort Donelson, Tennessee
March 7–8—Pea Ridge, Arkansas
March 9—U.S.S. *Monitor* v. C.S.S. *Virginia*
    (Merrimac), Hampton Roads, Virginia
March 23—Kernstown, Virginia
March 26 and 28—Glorieta Pass, New Mexico
April 6–7—Shiloh, Tennessee
April 7—Island No. 10, Tennessee
April 10–11—Fort Pulaski, Georgia
April 18–24—New Orleans, Louisiana
May 4–5—Williamsburg, Virginia
May 5—Puebla, Mexico
May 8—McDowell, Virginia
May 23—Front Royal, Virginia
May 25—Winchester, Virginia
May 27—Hanover Court House, Virginia
May 31–June 1—Fair Oaks, Virginia
June 6—Memphis, Tennessee
June 8–9—Cross Keys, Virginia
June 9—Port Republic, Virginia
June 25—Oak Grove, Virginia
June 26—Mechanicsville, Virginia
June 27—Gaines's Mill, Virginia
June 27–28—Garnett's and Golding's
    Farm, Virginia
June 29—Savage's Station, Virginia
June 30—White Oak Swamp, Virginia
July 1—Malvern Hill, Virginia
August 5—Baton Rouge, Louisiana
August 9—Cedar Mountain, Virginia
August 21–22—Fort Ridgely, Minnesota
August 23—New Ulm, Minnesota

August 29–30—Bull Run, Second, Virginia
August 29–30—Richmond, Kentucky
September 1—Chantilly, Virginia
September 12–15—Harpers Ferry, West Virginia
September 14—South Mountain, Maryland
September 14—Crampton's Gap, Maryland
September 14–17—Munfordville, Kentucky
September 17—Antietam, Maryland
September 19—Iuka, Mississippi
September 23—Wood Lake, Minnesota
October 3–4—Corinth, Mississippi
October 8—Perryville, Kentucky
December 7—Prairie Grove, Arkansas
December 13—Fredericksburg, Virginia
December 20—Holly Springs, Mississippi
December 27–29—Chickasaw Bluffs, Mississippi
December 31—Parker's Cross Roads, Tennessee
December 31 and January 2, 1863—Stone's River,
    Tennessee

◆ **1863**

January 1—Galveston, Texas
January 27—Bear River, Idaho
February 17—Camerone, Mexico
April 12–14—Irish Bend, Louisiana
April 30—Camerone, Mexico
May 1—Port Gibson, Mississippi
May 1–4—Chancellorsville, Virginia
May 12—Raymond, Mississippi
May 16—Champion's Hill, Mississippi
May 16–July 4—Vicksburg, Mississippi
May 17—Big Black River, Mississippi
May 22–July 9—Port Hudson, Louisiana
June 5—Franklin's Crossing, Virginia
June 9—Brandy Station, Virginia
June 13–15—Winchester, Virginia
July 1–3—Gettysburg, Pennsylvania
July 4—Helena, Arkansas
July 10–11 and 18—Fort Wagner, South Carolina
July 14—Falling Waters, West Virginia
September 8—Sabine Pass, Texas
September 19–20—Chickamauga, Georgia
October 14—Bristoe Station, Virginia
November 17–December 5—Knoxville, Tennessee
November 23–25—Chattanooga, Tennessee

◆ 1864

February 20—Ocean Pond, Florida
February 22—Okolona, Mississippi
April 8—Sabine Crossroads, Louisiana
April 9—Pleasant Hill Landing, Louisiana
April 12—Fort Pillow, Tennessee
May 16—Drewry's Bluff, Virginia
May 5–6—The Wilderness, Virginia
May 9—Cloyd's Mountain, Virginia
May 11—Yellow Tavern, Virginia
May 12–18—Spotsylvania, Virginia
May 14–September 2—Atlanta, Georgia
May 15—New Market, Virginia
May 16—Drewry's Bluff, Virginia
May 23–27—North Anna River, Virginia
June 1864–April 1865—Petersburg, Virginia
June 3—Cold Harbor, Virginia
June 6—Memphis, Tennessee
June 10—Brice's Cross Roads, Mississippi
June 11–12—Trevilian Station, Virginia
June 17–18—Lynchburg, Virginia
July 9—Monocacy, Maryland
July 13–15—Tupelo, Mississippi
July 14—Falling Waters, West Virginia
July 23–24—Kernstown, Virginia
July 28—Killdeer Mountain, North Dakota
July 30—The Crater, Petersburg, Virginia
August 5—Mobile Bay, Alabama
August 18–21—Globe Tavern, Virginia
September 19—Winchester, Virginia
September 22—Fisher's Hill, Virginia
September 27—Pilot Knob, Missouri
October 5—Allatoona Pass, Georgia
October 19—Cedar Creek, Virginia
November 29—Sand Creek, Colorado
November 30—Franklin, Tennessee
December 15–16—Nashville, Tennessee

◆ 1865

January 7 and February 2—Julesburg, Colorado
January 12–15—Fort Fisher, North Carolina
March 2—Waynesboro, Virginia
March 19—Bentonville, North Carolina
March 25—Fort Stedman, Virginia
March 30–April 1—Five Forks, Virginia

April 6—Sayler's Creek, Virginia
April 6–7—Farmville and Highbridge, Virginia

◆ 1866

June 2—Ridgeway, Canada
December 21—Fetterman Fight, Wyoming

◆ 1868

September 17–25—Beecher's Island, Colorado
November 27—Washita, Oklahoma

◆ 1869

July 11—Summit Springs, Colorado

◆ 1873

January 17—Stronghold, California

◆ 1874

June 27—Adobe Walls, Texas

◆ 1876

June 17—Rosebud Creek, Wyoming
June 25—Little Bighorn, Montana
September 9—Slim Buttes, South Dakota

◆ 1877

January 8—Wolf Mountain, Montana
August 8–11—Big Hole Basin, Montana
September 30–October 5—Bear Paw Mountains,
   Montana

◆ 1879

September 29–October 5—Mill Creek, Colorado

◆ **1885**

May 9–12—Batoche, Canada

◆ **1890**

December 29—Wounded Knee, South Dakota

◆ **1915**

April 8–15—Celaya, Mexico

November 1—Agua Prieta, Mexico-Arizona border

◆ **1916**

March 9—Columbus, New Mexico

April 12—Parral, Mexico

LIST OF BATTLES BY WAR

THE COLONIAL WARS

Annapolis Royal   Canada (September 8–October 6, 1744) *King George's War*

Bloody Swamp   Georgia (July 7, 1742) *War of Jenkin's Ear*

Cempoallan   Mexico (May 28–29, 1520) *Spanish Conquest*

Fort Beauséjour   Canada (June 4–17, 1755) *French and Indian War*

Fort Caroline   Florida (September 20, 1565) *French-Spanish Colonial Wars*

Fort Frontenac   Canada (August 25–27, 1758) *French and Indian War*

Fort Necessity   Pennsylvania (July 3, 1754) *French and Indian War*

Fort Niagara   New York (July 6–July 25, 1759) *French and Indian War*

Fort Ticonderoga   New York (July 8, 1758) *French and Indian War*

Fort William Henry   New York (August 3–9, 1757) *French and Indian War*

Lake George   New York (September 8, 1755) *French and Indian War*

Louisbourg   Canada (May 11–June 17, 1745) *King George's War*

Louisbourg   Canada (May 30–July 27, 1758) *French and Indian War*

Monongahela   Pennsylvania (July 9, 1755) *French and Indian War*

Port Royal   Canada (September 24–October 1, 1710) *Queen Anne's War*

Quebec   Canada (September 13, 1759) *French and Indian War*

St. Augustine   Florida (November 8–December 29, 1702) *Queen Anne's War*

St. Augustine   Florida (May 31–July 20, 1740) *War of Jenkin's Ear*

THE INDIAN WARS

Adobe Walls   Texas (June 27, 1874) *Buffalo War*

Ash Hollow   Nebraska (September 3, 1855) *Sioux Wars*

Bad Axe River   Wisconsin (August 2, 1832) *Black Hawk War*

Bear Paw Mountain   Idaho (September 30–October 5, 1877) *Nez Perce War*

Bear River   Idaho (January 27, 1863) *Shoshone War*

Beecher's Island   Colorado (September 17, 1868) *Sheridan Campaign*

Big Hole Basin   Montana (August 8–11, 1877) *Nez Perce War*

Big Meadows   Oregon (May 27, 1856) *Rogue River War*

Bloody Brook   Massachusetts (September 18, 1675) *King Philip's War*

Bushy Run   Pennsylvania (August 4–6, 1763) *Pontiac's Rebellion*

Champoton   Mexico (February 1517) *Spanish Conquest*

Dade's Battle   Florida (December 18, 1835) *Second Seminole War*

Emuckfau Creek   Alabama (January 22, 1814) *Creek War*

Enitachopco Creek   Alabama (January 24, 1814) *Creek War*

Fallen Timbers   Ohio (August 20, 1794) *Indian Wars*

Fetterman Fight   Wyoming (December 21, 1866) *Bozeman Trail War*

Fort Mims   Alabama (August 30, 1813) *Creek War*

Fort Ridgely   Minnesota (August 21 and 22, 1862) *Santee Uprising*

Great Swamp   Rhode Island (December 19, 1675) *King Philip's War*

Harmar's Defeat   Indiana (October 19 and 22, 1790) *Little Turtle's War*

Horseshoe Bend   Alabama (March 27, 1814) *Creek War*

Jamestown   Virginia (March 22, 1622) *Virginia-Indian Wars*

Julesburg   Colorado (January 2 and February 2, 1865) *Colorado War*

Killdeer Mountain   North Dakota (July 28, 1864) *Sioux Wars*

Lake Okeechobee   Florida (December 25, 1837) *Second Seminole War*

Lázaro   Mexico (May 27, 1518) *Spanish Conquest*

Little Bighorn   Montana (June 25, 1876) *Black Hills War*

Long Sault   Canada (April 1659) *Indian Wars*

Milk Creek   Colorado (September 29–October 5, 1879) *Ute War*

Mystic River   Connecticut (May 26, 1637) *Pequot War*

New Ulm   Minnesota (August 23, 1862) *Santee Uprising*

La Noche Triste   Mexico (July 1, 1520) *Spanish Conquest*

Otumba   Mexico (July 7, 1520) *Spanish Conquest*

Point Pleasant   West Virginia (October 10, 1774) *Lord Dunmore's War*

Potonchan   Mexico (March 25, 1519) *Spanish Conquest*

Rosebud Creek   Wyoming (June 17, 1876) *Black Hills War*

Rush Springs   Oklahoma (October 1, 1858) *Indian Wars*

St. Clair's Defeat   Indiana (November 4, 1791) *Little Turtle's War*

Sand Creek   Colorado (November 29, 1864) *Colorado War*

Santa Fe   New Mexico (August 15–21, 1680) *Pueblo Revolt*

Sitka   Alaska (October 1–7, 1804) *Russian-Indian War*

Slim Buttes   South Dakota (September 9, 1876) *Black Hills War*

Stronghold   California (January 17, 1873) *Modoc War*

Summit Springs   Colorado (July 11, 1869) *Sheridan's Campaign*

Talladega   Alabama (November 9, 1813) *Creek War*

Tallasahatchee   Alabama (November 3, 1813) *Creek War*

Tenochtitlán   Mexico (May 26–August 13, 1521) *Spanish Conquest*

Tippecanoe   Indiana (November 7, 1811) *Indian Wars*

Tlaxcala   Mexico (August–September 1519) *Spanish Conquest*

Washita   Oklahoma (November 27, 1868) *Sheridan's Campaign*

Wolf Mountain   Montana (January 8, 1877) *Black Hills War*

Wood Lake   Minnesota (September 23, 1862) *Santee Uprising*

Wounded Knee   South Dakota (December 29, 1890) *Sioux Wars*

THE AMERICAN REVOLUTION

U.S.S. *Alfred* **v. H.M.S.** *Glasgow*   Off Block Island, Rhode Island (April 16, 1776)

Augusta   Georgia (September 14–18, 1780)

Augusta   Georgia (May 22–June 5, 1781)

Beaufort   South Carolina (February 3, 1779)

Bennington   Vermont (August 16, 1777)

Billingsport   New Jersey (October 2 and 9, 1777)

Black Mingo Creek   South Carolina (September 29, 1780)

Blackstocks   South Carolina (November 20, 1780)

Blue Licks   Kentucky (August 19, 1782)

Blue Savannah   South Carolina (September 4, 1780)

Bound Brook   New Jersey (April 13, 1777)

Brandywine   Pennsylvania (September 11, 1777)

Briar Creek   Georgia (March 3, 1779)

Bull's Ferry   New Jersey (July 21, 1780)

Bunker Hill   Massachusetts (June 17, 1775)

Camden   South Carolina (August 16, 1780)

Cedars   Canada (May 16, 1776)

Chambly   Canada (October 18, 1775)

Charleston   South Carolina (June 28, 1776)

Charleston   South Carolina (April 1–May 12, 1780)

Charlotte   North Carolina (September 26, 1780)

Cherry Valley   New York (November 11, 1778)

Chesapeake Bay   Maryland/Virginia (March 16, 1781)

Chesapeake Capes   Off the Virginia–North Carolina Coast (September 5, 1781)

Combahee Ferry   South Carolina (August 27, 1782)

U.S.S. *Congress* **v. H.M.S.** *Savage*   Off the South Carolina Coast (September 6, 1781)

Cooch's Bridge   Delaware (September 3, 1777)

Cowan's Ford   North Carolina (February 1, 1781)

Cowpens   South Carolina (January 17, 1781)

Danbury Raid   Connecticut (April 23–28, 1777)

Eutaw Springs   South Carolina (September 8, 1781)

Fishdam Ford   South Carolina (November 9, 1780)

Fishing Creek   North Carolina (August 18, 1780)

Fort Anne   New York (July 8, 1777)

Fort Clinton and Fort Montgomery   New York (October 6, 1777)

Fort Cumberland   Canada (November 7–29, 1776)

Fort Keyser   New York (October 19, 1780)

Fort Lee   New Jersey (November 20, 1776)

Fort Mercer   New Jersey (October 22–November 21, 1777)

Fort Mifflin   Pennsylvania (October 10–November 15, 1777)

Fort Motte   South Carolina (May 12, 1781)

Fort Stanwix   New York (August 3–23, 1777)

Fort Ticonderoga   New York (May 10, 1775)

Fort Ticonderoga   New York (July 2–5, 1777)

Fort Ticonderoga   New York (September 18, 1777)

Fort Washington   New York (November 16, 1776)

Fort Watson   South Carolina (April 15–23, 1781)

Germantown   Pennsylvania (October 4, 1777)

Gloucester   Virginia (October 3, 1781)

Great Bridge   Virginia (December 9, 1775)

Great Savannah   South Carolina (August 20, 1780)

Green Spring   Virginia (July 6, 1781)

Guilford Courthouse   North Carolina (March 15, 1781)

Gwynn Island   Virginia (July 8–10, 1776)

Hanging Rock   South Carolina (August 6, 1780)

Harlem Heights   New York (September 16, 1776)

Haw River   North Carolina (February 25, 1781)

Hillsborough Raid   North Carolina (September 12, 1781)

Hobkirk's Hill   South Carolina (April 25, 1781)

Hubbardton   Vermont (July 7, 1777)

Johnstown   New York (October 25, 1781)

Kettle Creek   Georgia (February 14, 1779)

King's Mountain   South Carolina (October 7, 1780)

Kip's Bay   New York (September 15, 1776)

Klock's Field   New York (October 19, 1780)

Lenud's Ferry   South Carolina (May 6, 1780)

Lexington and Concord   Massachusetts (April 19, 1775)

Lochry's Defeat   Ohio (August 24 or 25, 1781)

Long Island   New York (August 27, 1776)

Minisink   New York (July 22, 1779)

Monck's Corner   South Carolina (April 14, 1780)

Monmouth   New Jersey (June 28, 1778)

Montreal   Canada (September 25, 1775)

Moore's Creek Bridge   North Carolina (February 27, 1776)

New London Raid   Connecticut (September 6, 1781)

Newport   Rhode Island (July 29–August 31, 1778)

Newtown   New York (August 29, 1779)

Ninety Six   South Carolina (May 22–June 19, 1781)

Oriskany   New York (August 6, 1777)

Paoli   Pennsylvania (September 21, 1777)

Parker's Ferry   South Carolina (August 13, 1781)

Paulus Hook   New Jersey (August 19, 1779)

Pell's Point   New York (October 18, 1776)

Pensacola   Florida (March–May 9, 1781)

Petersburg   Virginia (April 25, 1781)

Princeton   New Jersey (January 3, 1777)

Quebec   Canada (December 31, 1775–January 1, 1776)

Quinby Bridge   South Carolina (July 17, 1781)

Quintan's Bridge   New Jersey (March 18, 1778)

Ramseur's Mill   North Carolina (June 20, 1780)

Rocky Mount   South Carolina (August 1, 1780)

St. John's   Canada (May 17, 1775)

St. John's   Canada (September 5–November 2, 1775)

Sandusky   Ohio (June 4–5, 1782)

Saratoga, First   New York (September 19, 1777)

Saratoga, Second   New York (October 7, 1777)

Savannah   Georgia (December 29, 1778)

Savannah   Georgia (October 9, 1779)

Spencer's Tavern   Virginia (June 26, 1781)

Springfield   New Jersey (June 23, 1780)

Stono Ferry   South Carolina (June 20, 1779)

Stony Point   New York (July 16, 1779)

Tarrant's Tavern   North Carolina (February 1, 1781)

Three Rivers   Canada (June 8, 1776)

Throg's Neck   New York (October 12, 1776)

Trenton   New Jersey (December 26, 1776)

U.S.S. *Trumbull* v. *Watt*   Off the Atlantic Coast (June 2, 1780)

U.S.S. *Trumbull* v. H.M.S. *Iris*   Off the Delaware Capes (August 8, 1781)

Valcour Island   New York (October 11–13, 1776)

Vincennes   Indiana (February 24–25, 1779)

Wahab's Plantation   North Carolina (September 21, 1780)

Waxhaws   South Carolina (May 29, 1780)

Wetzell's Ford   North Carolina (March 6, 1781)

White Plains   New York (October 28, 1776)

Whitemarsh   Pennsylvania (December 5–8, 1777)

Williamson's Plantation   South Carolina (July 12, 1780)

Wyoming Valley   Pennsylvania (July 3–4, 1778)

Yorktown   Virginia (September 28–October 18, 1781)

THE WAR OF 1812

Beaver Dams   Canada (June 24, 1813)

Bladensburg   Maryland (August 24, 1814)

Chateaugay   Canada (October 25–26, 1813)

U.S.S. *Chesapeake* v. H.M.S. *Shannon*   Off Boston, Massachusetts (June 1, 1813)

Chippewa   Canada (July 5, 1814)

Chrysler's Farm   Canada (November 11, 1813)

U.S.S. *Constitution* v. H.M.S. *Guerrière*   Off Nova Scotia, Canada (August 19, 1812)

Fort Erie, First   Canada (August 15, 1814)

Fort Erie, Second   Canada (September 7, 1814)

Fort George   Canada (May 27, 1813)

Fort McHenry   Baltimore, Maryland (September 12–14, 1814)

Fort Stephenson   Ohio (August 1–2, 1813)

Frenchtown   Ohio (January 18 and 22, 1813)

Lake Champlain   New York (September 11, 1814)

Lake Erie   Ohio (September 10, 1813)

Lundy's Lane   Canada (July 25, 1814)

Mackinac Island   Canada (August 4, 1814)

New Orleans   Louisiana (January 8, 1815)

U.S.S. *Peacock* v. H.M.S. *Epervier*   Off the Florida Coast (April 29, 1814)

Pensacola   Florida (November 7, 1814)

Plattsburg Bay   New York (September 11, 1814)

Queenston   Canada (October 13, 1812)

Sackets Harbor   New York (May 28–29, 1813)

Stony Creek   Canada (June 6, 1813)

Thames   Canada (October 5, 1813)

THE MEXICAN-AMERICAN WAR

Buena Vista   Mexico (February 22–23, 1847)

Camp Texas   Texas (May 3–8, 1846)

Cerro Gordo   Mexico (April 18, 1847)

Chapultepec   Mexico (September 13, 1847)

Churubusco   Mexico (August 20, 1847)

Contreras   Mexico (August 20, 1847)

Mesa   California (January 9, 1847)

Molino del Rey   Mexico (September 8, 1847)

Monterrey   Mexico (September 20–24, 1846)

Palo Alto   Texas (May 8, 1846)

Puebla   Mexico (September 14–October 12, 1847)

Resaca de la Palma   Texas (May 9, 1846)

Sacramento River   Mexico (February 28, 1847)

San Gabriel   California (January 8, 1847)

San Pascual   California (December 6, 1846)

Veracruz   Mexico (March 22–29, 1847)

THE AMERICAN CIVIL WAR

Antietam   Maryland (September 17, 1862)

Atlanta   Georgia (May 14–September 2, 1864)

Ball's Bluff   Virginia (October 21, 1961)

Baton Rouge   Louisiana (August 5, 1862)

Belmont   Missouri (November 7, 1861)

Bentonville   North Carolina (March 19, 1865)

Big Bethel   Virginia (June 10, 1861)

Big Black River   Mississippi (May 17, 1863)

Brandy Station   Virginia (June 9, 1863)

Brice's Cross Roads   Mississippi (June 10, 1864)

Bristoe Station   Virginia (October 14, 1863)

Bull Run, First   Virginia (July 21, 1861)

Bull Run, Second   Virginia (August 29–30, 1862)

Cedar Creek   Virginia (October 19, 1864)

Cedar Mountain   Virginia (August 9, 1862)

Champion's Hill   Mississippi (May 16, 1863)

Chancellorsville   Virginia (May 1–4, 1863)

Chantilly   Virginia (September 2, 1862)

Chattanooga   Tennessee (November 23–25, 1863)

Cheat Mountain   West Virginia (September 10–15, 1861)

Chickamauga   Georgia (September 19–20, 1863)

Chickasaw Bluffs   Mississippi (December 27–29, 1862)

Cloyd's Mountain   Virginia (May 6, 1864)

Cold Harbor   Virginia (May 31–June 12, 1864)

Corinth   Mississippi (October 3–4, 1862)

Crampton's Gap   Maryland (September 14, 1862)

The Crater   Petersburg, Virginia (July 30, 1864)

Cross Keys   Virginia (June 8–9, 1862)

Drewry's Bluff   Virginia (May 16, 1864)

Fair Oaks and Seven Pines   Virginia (May 1–June 2, 1862)

Falling Waters   West Virginia (July 14, 1864)

Farmville and Highbridge   Virginia (April 7, 1865)

Fisher's Hill   Virginia (September 22, 1864)

Five Forks   Virginia (March 30–April 1, 1865)

Fort Donelson   Tennessee (February 15, 1862)

Fort Fisher   North Carolina (January 6–15, 1865)

Fort Henry   Tennessee (February 6, 1862)

Fort Pillow   Tennessee (April 12, 1864)

Fort Pulaski   Georgia (April 10–11, 1862)

Fort Stedman   Virginia (March 25, 1865)

Fort Sumter   Charleston, South Carolina (April 12–14, 1861)

Franklin   Tennessee (November 30, 1864)

Franklin's Crossing   Virginia (June 5, 1863)

Fredericksburg   Virginia (December 13, 1862)

Front Royal   Virginia (May 23, 1862)

Gaines Mill   Virginia (June 27, 1862)

Galveston   Texas (August 3, 1861)

Garnett's and Golding's Farm   Virginia (June 27–28, 1862)

Gettysburg   Pennsylvania (July 1–3, 1863)

Globe Tavern   Virginia (August 18–21, 1864)

Glorieta Pass   New Mexico (March 28, 1862)

Hanover Courthouse   Virginia (May 27, 1862)

Harpers Ferry   West Virginia (September 12–15, 1862)

Helena   Arkansas (July 4, 1863)

Holly Springs   Mississippi (December 20, 1862)

Irish Bend   Louisiana (April 12–14, 1863)

Island No. 10   Tennessee (April 7, 1862)

Iuka   Mississippi (September 19, 1862)

Kernstown   Virginia (March 23, 1862)

Kernstown   Virginia (July 23–24, 1864)

Knoxville   Tennessee (November 29, 1863)

Lexington   Missouri (September 18–20, 1861)

Lynchburg   Virginia (June 17–18, 1864)

Malvern Hill   Virginia (July 1, 1862)

McDowell   Virginia (May 8, 1862)

Mechanicsville   Virginia (June 26, 1862)

Memphis   Tennessee (June 6, 1862)

Mill Springs   Kentucky (January 19, 1862)

Mobile Bay   Alabama (August 5, 1864)

U.S.S. *Monitor* v. C.S.S. *Virginia* (*Merrimack*)   Hampton Roads, Virginia (March 9, 1862)

Monocacy   Maryland (July 9, 1864)

Munfordville   Kentucky (September 14–17, 1862)

Nashville   Tennessee (December 15–16, 1864)

New Market   Virginia (May 15, 1864)

New Orleans   Louisiana (April 18–24, 1962)

North Anna River   Virginia (May 23–27, 1864)

Oak Grove   Virginia (June 25, 1862)

Ocean Pond   Florida (February 20, 1864)

Okolona   Mississippi (February 22, 1864)

Parker's Cross Roads   Tennessee (December 31, 1862)

Pea Ridge   Arkansas (March 7–8, 1862)

Perryville   Kentucky (October 8, 1862)

Petersburg   Virginia (June 1864–April 1865)

Philippi   West Virginia (June 3, 1861)

Pilot Knob   Missouri (September 27, 1864)

Pleasant Hill Landing   Louisiana (April 12, 1864)

Port Gibson   Mississippi (May 1, 1863)

Port Hudson   Louisiana (May 22–July 9, 1863)

Port Republic   Virginia (June 9, 1862)

Port Royal Sound   South Carolina (November 7, 1861)
Prairie Grove   Arkansas (December 7, 1862)
Raymond   Mississippi (May 12, 1863)
Rich Mountain   West Virginia (July 11, 1861)
Richmond   Kentucky (August 29–30, 1862)
Roanoke Island   North Carolina (February 8, 1862)
Sabine Crossroads   Louisiana (April 8, 1864)
Sabine Pass   Texas (September 8, 1863)
Savage's Station   Virginia (June 29, 1862)
Sayler's Creek   Virginia (April 6, 1865)
Shiloh   Tennessee (April 6–7, 1862)
South Mountain   Maryland (September 14, 1862)
Spotsylvania   Virginia (May 12–18, 1864)
Stones River   Tennessee (December 31, 1862 and January 2, 1863)
Trevilian Station   Virginia (June 11–12, 1864)
Tupelo   Mississippi (July 13–15, 1864)
Vicksburg   Mississippi (May 16–July 4, 1863)
Waynesboro   Virginia (March 2, 1865)
Westport   Missouri (October 23, 1864)
White Oak Swamp   Virginia (June 30, 1862)
The Wilderness   Virginia (May 5–6, 1864)
Williamsburg   Virginia (May 4–5, 1862)
Wilson's Creek   Missouri (August 10, 1861)
Winchester, First   Virginia (May 25, 1862)
Winchester, Second   Virginia (June 13–15, 1863)
Winchester, Third   Virginia (September 19, 1864)
Yellow Tavern   Virginia (May 11, 1864)

Batoche   Canada (May 9–12, 1885) *Second Riel Rebellion*
Calderón Bridge   Mexico (January 17, 1811) *Hidalgo Revolt*
Camerone   Mexico (February 17, 1863) *Mexican-French War*
Celaya   Mexico (April 15, 1915) *Mexican Revolution*
Columbus   New Mexico (March 9, 1916) *Border Raids*
Goliad   Texas (March 18–19, 1836) *Texas War of Independence*
Jamestown   Virginia (September 16, 1676) *Bacon's Rebellion*
Parral   Mexico (April 12, 1916) *Border Raids*
Puebla (Cinco de Mayo)   Mexico (May 5, 1862) *Mexican-French War*
Ridgeway   Canada (June 2, 1866) *Fenian Raid*
St. Charles   Canada (November 25, 1837) *Papineau's Rebellion*
St. Denis   Canada (November 23, 1837) *Papineau's Rebellion*
St. Eustache   Canada (December 14, 1837) *Papineau's Rebellion*
San Jacinto   Texas (April 21, 1836) *Texas War of Independence*
Springfield Arsenal   Massachusetts (January 25, 1787) *Shays's Rebellion*

OTHER WARS

Agua Prieta   Mexico-Arizona Border (November 1, 1915) *Mexican Revolution*
Alamance   North Carolina (May 16, 1771) *Regulator Uprising*
Alamo   San Antonio, Texas (February 23–March 6, 1836) *Texas War of Independence*

BATTLEFIELD SITES IN ALPHABETICAL ORDER

Following is a partial list in alphabetical order of battlefield sites that are open to visitors. Addresses and phone numbers appear in the regional listing of the sites in Appendix 5.

Alamance
Alamo
Antietam
Bennington
Bentonville
Big Hole
Brandywine
Brice's Cross Roads
Bull Run *See* Manassas
Bunker Hill
Bushy Run
Camden
Canyon Creek
Champion Hill
Chancellorsville
Charleston
Chattanooga

Chickamauga
Cold Harbor
Corinth
Cowpens
Cross Keys
Fallen Timbers
Fort Caroline
Fort Donelson
Fort Fisher
Fort McHenry
Fort Meigs
Fort Necessity
Fort Niagara
Fort Pulaski
Fort Stanwix
Fort Sumter
Fort Ticonderoga
Fort William Henry
Fredericksburg
Gaines's Mill
Gannett's and Golding's Farms
Gettysburg
Glorieta Pass

Guilford Courthouse
Harpers Ferry
Horseshoe Bend
Hubbardton
Kennesaw Mountain
King's Mountain
Lake Erie
Lexington, Missouri
Lexington and Concord
Little Big Horn
Lookout Mountain
Malvern Hill
Manassas
McDowell
Mechanicsville
Mill Springs
Missionary Ridge
Monmouth
Monocacy
Moore's Creek Bridge
New Market
New Orleans
Ninety Six
Oak Grove
Oriskany
Pea Ridge
Perryville
Petersburg
Port Gibson

Port Hudson
Port Republic
Prairie Grove
Sackets Harbor
San Jacinto
San Pasqual
Saratoga
Savage's Station
Sayler's Creek
Shiloh
Sitka
Spotsylvania
Stones River
Stony Point
Stronghold
Tippecanoe
Trenton
Tupelo
Vicksburg
Vincennes
Washita
White Oak Swamp
The Wilderness
Wilson's Creek
Wounded Knee
Yorktown

BATTLEFIELD SITES LISTED BY REGION

The following battlefield sites are open to visitors. For information, write or call the addresses and phone numbers listed. The address for information may be different than the actual location of the site. In some cases, a single office administers several sites.

NORTHEAST

MASSACHUSETTS

Bunker Hill
Bunker Hill Monument
Boston National Historical Park
Charlestown Navy Yard
Boston, MA 02129
617/242-5641

Lexington and Concord
Minute Man National Historic Park

174 Liberty Street
P.O. Box 160
Concord, MA 01742
617/369-6993

NEW JERSEY

Monmouth
Monmouth Battlefield State Park
347 Freehold-Englishtown Road
Freehold, NJ 07728
908/462-9616

Trenton *See* **Pennsylvania**

NEW YORK

Bennington
Bennington Battlefield State Park
P.O. Box 11W
Hoosick Falls, NY 12090
516/686-7109

Fort Niagara

Old Niagara Association, Inc.

P.O. Box 169

Youngstown, NY 14174

716/745-7611

Fort Stanwix

Fort Stanwix National Monument

122 East Park Street

Rome, NY 13440

315/336-2090

Fort Ticonderoga

Fort Road

P.O. Box 390

Ticonderoga, NY 12883

518/585-2821

Fort William Henry

Route 87

Lake George, NY

518/668-5471

Oriskany

Oriskany Battlefield State Historic Site

P.O. Box 275, RD 1

Oriskany, NY 13424

315/768-7224

Sackets Harbor

Sackets Harbor State Historic Site

P.O. Box 27

505 W. Washington Street

Sacket's Harbor, NY 13685

Saratoga

Saratoga National Historical Park

R.D. 2, P.O. Box 33

Stillwater, NY 12170

518/669-9821

Stony Point

Stony Point Battlefield State Historic Site

P.O. Box 182

Stony Point, NY 10980

914/786-2521

PENNSYLVANIA

Brandywine

Brandywine Battlefield Park

P.O. Box 202

Chadd's Ford, PA 19317

215/459-3342

Bushy Run

Bushy Run Battlefield

Bushy Run Road

Jeanette, PA 15644

412/527-5584

Fort Necessity

Fort Necessity National Battlefield

One Washington Parkway

Farmington, PA 15437

724/329-5512

Gettysburg

Gettysburg National Military Park

P.O. Box 1050

Gettysburg, PA 17325

717/334-1124

Trenton

Washington Crossing Historic Park

P.O. Box 103

1112 River Road

Washington Crossing, PA 18977

215/493-4076

VERMONT

Bennington *See* **New York**

Hubbardton

Vermont Division for Historic Preservation

Montpelier, VT 05602

802/828-3226

SOUTHEAST

FLORIDA

Fort Caroline

Fort Caroline National Memorial
12713 Fort Caroline Road
Jacksonville, FL 32225
904/641-7155

GEORGIA

Fort Pulaski

Fort Pulaski National Monument
P.O. Box 30757
Savannah, Georgia 31418
912/786-5787

Kennesaw Mountain

Kennesaw Mountain National Battlefield Park
P.O. Box 1610
Marietta, GA 30061
404/427-4686

MARYLAND

Antietam

Antietam National Battlefield and Cemetery
P.O. Box 158
Sharpsburg, MD 21782
301/432-5124

Fort McHenry

Fort McHenry National Monument
    and Historic Shrine
East Fort Avenue
Baltimore, MD 21230
301/962-4280

Monocacy

Monocacy National Battlefield
4801 Urbana Road
Frederick, MD 21701
301/662-3514

NORTH CAROLINA

Alamance

Alamance Battleground
Route 1, P.O. Box 108
Burlington, NC 27265
919/227-4785

Bentonville

Bentonville Battleground State Historic Site
P.O. Box 27, Route 1
Four Oaks
Newton Grove, NC 28366
919/594-0789

Fort Fisher

Fort Fisher State Historic Site
P.O. Box 169
Kure Beach, NC 28449
910/459-5538

Guilford Courthouse

Guilford Courthouse National Military Park
P.O. Box 9806
Greensboro, NC 27408
919/288-1776

King's Mountain

King's Mountain Military Park
P.O. Box 40
King's Mountain, NC 28986
864/936-7921

Moore's Creek Bridge

Moore's Creek National Battlefield
P.O. Box 69
Currie, NC 28435
919/283-5591

SOUTH CAROLINA

Camden

Camden District Heritage Foundation
Historic Camden
P.O. Box 710
South Broadway Street
Camden, SC 29020
803/432-9841

Charleston

Fort Moultrie
1214 Middle Street
Sullivan's Island, SC 29482
803/883-3123

Cowpens

Cowpens National Battlefield
P.O. Box 308
Chesnee, SC 29323
803/461-2828

Fort Sumter

Fort Sumter National Monument
1214 Middle Street
Sullivan's Island, SC
803/883-3123

Ninety Six

Ninety Six National Historic Site
P.O. Box 496
Ninety Six, SC 29666
803/543-4068

VIRGINIA

Bull Run

Manassas National Battlefield Park
P.O. Box 1830
Manassas, VA 22110
703/361-1339

Chancellorsville *See* **Fredericksburg and Spotsylvania**

Cold Harbor *See* **Richmond**

Cross Keys

Lee Jackson Foundation
P.O. Box 8121
Charlottesville, VA 22906
804/977-1861

Fredericksburg

Fredericksburg and Spotsylvania National
Military Park
120 Chatham Lane
Fredericksburg, VA 22405
540/371-0802

Gaines's Mill *See* **Richmond**

Gannett's and Golding's Farms *See* **Richmond**

Malvern Hill *See* **Richmond**

McDowell

(split private ownership)
Lee Jackson Foundation
P.O. Box 8121
Charlottesville, VA 22906
804/977-1861
Association for the Preservation of Civil War Sites
11 Public Square
Suite 200
Hagerstown, MD 21740

Mechanicsville *See* **Richmond**

New Market

New Market Battlefield Park
P.O. Box 1864
New Market, VA 22844
703/740-3101

Oak Grove *See* **Richmond**

Petersburg

Petersburg National Battlefield
Box 549
Petersburg, VA 23803
804/732-3531

Port Republic

Association for the Preservation of Civil War Sites
11 Public Square
Suite 200
Hagerstown, MD 21740

Richmond National Battlefield Park

3215 E. Broad Street
Richmond, VA 23223
804/226-1981

Richmond NBP

administers sites for Cold Harbor, plus the Seven
Days' Battles: Gaines's Mill; Garnett's and Golding's
Farms; Malvern Hill; Mechanicsville; Oak Grove;
Savage's Station; and White Oak Swamp.

Savage's Station *See* **Richmond**

Sayler's Creek
Sayler's Creek Battlefield State Park
Route 2, Box 70
Green Bay, VA 23942
804/392-3435

Spotsylvania *See* **Fredericksburg**

White Oak Swamp *See* **Richmond**

The Wilderness *See* **Fredericksburg**

Yorktown
Yorktown Battlefield
Colonial National Historical Park
P.O. Box 210
Yorktown, VA 23690
804/898-3400

WEST VIRGINIA

Harpers Ferry
Harpers Ferry National Historical Park
Box 65
Harpers Ferry, WV 24425
304/535-6223

SOUTH

ALABAMA

Horseshoe Bend
Horseshoe Bend National Military Park
Box 103
Daviston, AL 36256
205/234-7111

ARKANSAS

Pea Ridge
Pea Ridge National Military Park
Highway 62 East
Pea Ridge, AR 72751
501/451-8122

Prairie Grove
Prairie Grove Battlefield State Park
P.O. Box 306
Prairie Grove, AR 72753
501/846-2990

KENTUCKY

Mill Springs
Mill Springs Battlefield Association
P.O. Box 814
Somerset, KY 42502
606/679-1859

Perryville
Perryville Battlefield State Historic Site
P.O. Box 296
1825 Battlefield Road
Perryville, KY 40468
606/332-8631

LOUISIANA

New Orleans
New Orleans
Chalmette Unit
Jean Lafitte National Historical Park and Reserve
8606 West Street
Bernard Highway
Chalmette, LA 70043
504/589-4430

Port Hudson
Port Hudson State Commemorative Area
756 West Plains Port Hudson Road
Zachary, LA 70791
504/654-3775

Brice's Cross Roads *See* **Tupelo**

Champion Hill *See* **Vicksburg**

Corinth
Siege and Battle of Corinth Commission
Corinth, MS
601/287-9501

Port Gibson

Grand Gulf Military Monument
P.O. Box 389
Port Gibson, MS 39158
601/437-5911

Tupelo

National Battlefield Site
c/o Natchez Trace Parkway
RR1, NT-143
Tupelo, MS 38801
601/680-4025

Vicksburg

Vicksburg National Military Park
3201 Clay Street
Vicksburg, MS 39180
601/636-0583

MISSOURI

Lexington

Battle of Lexington Historic Site
North 13th Street
Lexington, MO 64067
816/259-2112

Wilson's Creek

Wilson's Creek National Battlefield Route 2, P.O.
Box 75
Republic, MO 65738
417/732-2662

TENNESSEE

Chatanooga *See* **Chickamauga**

Chickamauga

Chickamauga and Chattanooga National Military Park
P.O. Box 2126
Fort Oglethorpe, GA 30742
404/866-9241

Fort Donelson

Fort Donelson National Battlefield
P.O. Box 434
Dover, TN 37058
615/931-5706

Shiloh

Shiloh National Military Park
P.O. Box 67
Shiloh, TN 38376
901/689-5275

Stones River

Stones River National Battlefield
3501 Old Nashville Highway
Murfreesboro, TN 37129
615/893-3501

TEXAS

Alamo

Daughters of the Republic Museum
P.O. Box 2599
San Antonio, TX 78199
201/225-1391

San Jacinto

San Jacinto Battleground State Historic Park
3523 Battleground Road
La Porte, TX 77571
713/479-2431

MIDWEST

INDIANA

Tippecanoe

Tippecanoe Battlefield State Memorial
909 South Street
Lafayette, IN 47901
317/742-8411

Vincennes

George Rogers Clark National Historical Park
401 South Second Street
Vincennes, IN 47591
812/882-1776

OHIO

Fallen Timbers

Toledo Metro Parks
5100 West Central Avenue
Toledo, OH 43615
614/466-1500

Lake Erie

Perry's Victory and International Peace Memorial
P.O. Box 549
Put-in-Bay, OH 43456

WEST

ALASKA

Sitka

Sitka National Historical Park
P.O. Box 738
Sitka, AK 99835
907/747-6281

CALIFORNIA

Stronghold

Lava Beds National Monument
P.O. Box 867
Tule Lake, CA 96134
916/607-2282

MONTANA

Big Hole

Big Hole National Battlefield
P.O. Box 237
Wisdom, MT 59761
406/689-3155

Little Bighorn

Little Bighorn Battlefield National Monument
P.O. Box 39
Crow Agency, MT 59022
406/638-2622

NEW MEXICO

Glorieta Pass

Glorieta Unit
Pecos National Historical Park
P.O. Box 418
Pecos, NM 87552
505/757-6032

OKLAHOMA

Washita

Black Kettle Museum
P.O. Box 252
Cheyenne, OK 73628
405/497-3929

SOUTH DAKOTA

Wounded Knee

Wounded Knee Monument
Pine Ridge Reservation
Wounded Knee, SD 57770

BIBLIOGRAPHY

GENERAL

Alexander, Joseph H. *A Fellowship of Valor: The Battle History of the United States Marines.* New York: HarperCollins, 1997.

Deaderick, John Barron. *Campaigns and Battles of America, 1755–1865: Fort Duquesne to Appomattox.* Boston: Christopher, 1959.

Dupuy, R. Ernest, and Trevor N. Dupuy. *The Encyclopedia of Military History.* 2d ed. New York: Harper & Row, 1986.

Esposito, Vincent J., ed. *The West Point Atlas of American Wars.* Rev. ed. Vol. 1. New York: Henry Holt, 1995.

Fuller, J. F. C. *Decisive Battles of the U.S.A.* New York: Beechurst Press, 1953.

Heitman, Francis G. *Historical Register and Dictionary of the United States Army . . .* 2 vols. Washington, D.C.: U.S. Government Printing Office, 1914.

Perrett, Bryan. *The Battle Book: Crucial Conflicts in History from 1469 to the Present.* New York: Arms and Armour, 1992.

Stevens, Joseph E. *America's Battlefield Parks: A Guide.* Norman: University of Oklahoma Press, 1990.

THE COLONIAL WARS

Alberts, Robert C. *A Charming Field for an Encounter: The Story of George Washington's Fort Necessity.* Washington, D.C.: National Park Service, 1975.

Arnade, Charles, W. *The Siege of St. Augustine in 1702.* Gainesville: University of Florida Presses, 1959.

Baker, Raymond F. *A Campaign of Amateurs: The Siege of Louisbourg, 1745.* Ottawa: Parks Canada, 1995.

Bennet, Charles E. *Laudonniere and Fort Caroline: History and Documents.* Gainesville: University of Florida Presses, 1964.

Brebner, John B. *New England's Outpost: Acadia before the Conquest of Canada.* Reprint ed. New York: B. Franklin, 1973.

Cowan, John P. "George Washington at Fort Necessity." *Western Pennsylvania Historical Magazine* 37, nos. 3 and 4 (1955): 12–14, 92–111.

Crane, Verner W. *The Southern Frontier, 1670–1732.* Reprint ed. New York: W. W. Norton, 1981.

Donaldson, Gordon. *Battle for a Continent: Quebec, 1759.* Garden City, N.Y.: Doubleday, 1973.

Dunigan, Brian Leigh. *Siege—1759: The Campaign against Niagara.* Youngstown, N.Y.: Old Fort Niagara Association, 1986.

———. "Vauban in the Wilderness: The Siege of Fort Niagara, 1759." *Niagara Frontier* 21 (1974): 37–52.

Eccles, W. J. "The Battle of Quebec: A Reappraisal."

French Colonial Historical Society Proceedings 3, no. 1 (1978): 70–81.

Ferling, John. *Struggle for a Continent: The Wars of the Colonial Age.* Arlington Heights, Ill.: Harlan Davidson, 1993.

Fiedmont, Jacau de. *The Siege of Beausejour in 1755: A Journal of the Attack on Beausejour.* Saint John, Canada: n.p., 1936.

Gallay, Alan. *Colonial Wars of North America, 1512–1763: An Encyclopedia.* New York: Garland, 1996.

Georgia Historical Society. *The Spanish Official Account of the Attack on the Colony of Georgia, in America, and of Its Defeat on St. Simons Island by James Oglethorpe.* Savannah, Ga.: Savannah Morning News, 1913.

Godfrey, William G. *Pursuit of Profit and Preferment in Colonial North America: John Bradstreet's Quest.* Waterloo, Canada: Wilfred Laurier University Press, 1982.

Graham, Dominick. "The Planning of the Beauséjour Operation and the Approaches to War in 1755." *New England Quarterly* 41 (1968): 551–566.

Grinnell-Milne, Duncan William. *Mad, Is He? The Character and Achievement of James Wolfe.* London: Bodley Head, 1963.

Hamilton, Edward P. *Fort Ticonderoga, Key to a Continent.* Boston: Little, Brown, 1964.

———. *The French and Indian Wars: The Story of Battles and Forts in the Wilderness.* Garden City, N.Y.: Doubleday, 1962.

Hindman, William B. *The Great Meadows Campaign and the Climactic Battle of Fort Necessity.* Leesburg, Va.: Potomac Press, 1967.

Hitsman, J. Mackay, and C. C. J. Bond. "The Assault Landing at Louisbourg, 1758." *Canadian Historical Review* 35, no. 4 (December 1954): 314–330.

Kopperman, Paul E. *Braddock at the Monongahela.* Pittsburgh: University of Pittsburgh Press, 1977.

Lacock, John K. *Washington's Military Expedition of 1754.* Farmington, Pa.: Fort Necessity Battlefield Site, 1940.

Lloyd, Christopher. *The Capture of Quebec.* London: Batsford, 1959.

Lyon, Eugene. *The Enterprise of Florida: Pedro Menéndez de Avilés and the Spanish Conquest of 1565–1568.* Gainesville: University of Florida Presses, 1976.

———, ed. *Pedro Menéndez de Avilés.* New York: Garland, 1995.

Martin, Ronald D. "Confrontation at the Monongahela: Climax of the French Drive into the Upper Ohio Region." *Pennsylvania History* 37 (1946): 133–150.

Mathieu, Jacques, Eugen Kedl, and Kathe Roth, trans. *The Plains of Abraham: The Search for the Ideal.* Sillery, Quebec: Septentrion, 1993.

McLennan, John Stewart. *Louisbourg from Its Foundation to Its Fall, 1713–1758.* 4th ed. Halifax, Canada: Book Room, 1979.

O'Meara, Walter. *Guns at the Forks.* Englewoods Cliffs, N.J.: Prentice-Hall, 1965.

Parkman, Francis. *Montcalm and Wolfe.* Reprint ed. New York: F. Ungar, 1965.

Paterson, T. W. "Siege at the Long Sault." *Canadian West* 6, no. 3 (1990): 114–118.

Peckham, Howard. *The Colonial Wars.* Chicago: University of Chicago Press, 1964.

Preston, R. A., ed. *Royal Fort Frontenac.* Toronto: Champlain Society, 1958.

Pother, Bernard. "The Siege of Annapolis Royal." *Nova Scotia Historical Review* 5, no. 1 (1985): 59–71.

Pouchot, Pierre. *Memoirs on the Late War in North America between France and England.* Michael Cardy, trans. Youngstown, N.Y.: Old Fort Niagara Association, 1994.

Rahmer, Frederick A. *Dash to Frontenac: An Account of Lt. Col. John Bradstreet's Expedition to and Capture of Fort Frontenac.* Rome, N.Y.: n.p., 1973.

Rawlyk, George A. *Yankees at Louisbourg.* Orono: University of Maine Press, 1967.

Reid, W. Max. *Lake George and Lake Champlain: The War Trail of the Mohawk and the Battle-Ground of France and England in their Contest for the Control of North America.* New York: G.P. Putnam's Sons, 1910.

Smith Henry M. "Fort Necessity." *Virginia Magazine of History and Biography* 41 (1933): 204–214.

Steele, Ian K. *Betrayals: Fort William Henry and the Massacre.* New York: Oxford University Press, 1990.

Tilberg, Frederick. *Fort Necessity National Battlefield Site, Pennsylvania.* Rev. ed. Washington, D.C.: National Parks Service, 1956.

Torres-Reyes, Ricardo. *The British Siege of St. Augustine in 1740.* Denver: National Park Service, 1973.

Webster, John Clarence. *The Forts of Chignecto: A Study of the Eighteenth Century Conflict between France and Great Britain in Acadia.* n.p.: author, 1930.

———. *Journals of Beausejour.* Sackville, Canada: Tribune Press, 1937.

THE INDIAN WARS

Anderson, Niles. *The Battle of Bushy Run.* Harrisburg: Pennsylvania Historical and Museum Commission, 1966.

Baker, T. Lindsay, and Billy R. Harrison. *Adobe Walls: The History and Archaeology of the 1874 Trading Post.* College Station: Texas A&M University Press, 1986.

Ball, E. "Cibicu—An Apache Interpretation" in Ray Brandes, ed. *Troopers West: Military and Indian Affairs on the American Frontier.* San Diego: Frontier Heritage Press, 1970.

The Battles of Adobe Walls and Lyman's Wagon Train, 1874. Canyon, Tex.: Panhandle-Plains Historical Society, 1964.

Beal, Merrill D. *"I Will Fight No More Forever": Chief Joseph and the Nez Perce War.* Seattle: University of Washington Press, 1963.

Bourne, Russell. *The Red King's Rebellion: Racial Politics in New England, 1675–1678.* New York: Atheneum, 1990.

Brown, Dee A. *Bury My Heart at Wounded Knee.* New York: Holt Rinehart, 1970.

———. *The Fetterman Massacre: An American Saga.* Lincoln: University of Nebraska Press, 1984.

Brown, Mark H. *The Flight of the Nez Perce: A History of the Nez Perce War.* New York: G. P. Putnam, 1967; Lincoln: University of Nebraska Press, 1982.

Carley, Kenneth. *The Sioux Uprising of 1862.* St. Paul: Minnesota Historical Society Press, 1976.

Carrington, Henry Beebe. *The Indian Question: Including a Report by the Secretary of the Interior on the Massacre of Troops near Fort Kearney, December 1866.* New York: Lewis, 1973.

Carter, Harvey. *The Life and Times of Little Turtle: First Sagamore of the Wabash.* Urbana: University of Illinois Press, 1987.

Chaney, George P., Robert C. Betts, and Dee Longenbaugh. *Physical and Cultural Landscapes of Sitka National Historical Park.* Douglas, Alaska: Vanguard Research, 1995.

Cleaves, Freeman. *Old Tippecanoe: William Henry Harrison and His Times.* New York: Charles Scribner's Sons, 1939.

Cook, David C. *Fighting Indians of America.* New York: Dodd, Mead, 1966.

Davies, Nigel. *The Aztecs: A History.* Norman: University of Oklahoma Press, 1980.

Debo, Angie. *Road to Disappearance: A History of the Creek Indians.* Norman: University of Oklahoma Press, 1941.

Dowd, Gregory Evans. *A Spirited Resistance: The North American Indian Struggle for Unity, 1745–1815.* Baltimore: Johns Hopkins University Press, 1992.

Dowd, James. *Custer Lives!* Fairfield, Wash.: Ye Galleon Press, 1982.

Drake, James D. *King Philip's War: Civil War in New England, 1675–1676.* Amherst, Mass: University of Massachusetts Press, 2000.

Dunn, William R. *I Stand by Sand Creek: A Defense of Colonel John M. Chivington and the Third Colorado Cavalry.* Lincoln: University of Nebraska Press, 1985.

Eby, Cecil. *"That Disgraceful Affair," The Black Hawk War.* New York: W. W. Norton, 1973.

Edmunds, R. David. *The Shawnee Prophet.* Lincoln: University of Nebraska Press, 1983.

Finerty, John. *War-Path and Bivouac or the Conquest of the Sioux.* Norman: University of Oklahoma Press, 1961.

Forsyth, George A. *Thrilling Days in Army Life.* Reprint ed. Lincoln: University of Nebraska Press, 1994.

Fox, Richard Allan Jr. *Archaeology, History, and Custer's Last Battle.* Norman: University of Oklahoma Press, 1993.

Gardiner, C. Harvey. *Naval Power in the Conquest of Mexico.* Austin: University of Texas Press, 1956.

Gibson, Charles. *The Aztecs under Spanish Rule: A History of the Indians of the Valley of Mexico, 1519–1810.* Palo Alto, Calif.: Stanford University Press, 1964.

Gilbert, Bill. *God Gave Us This Country: Tekamthi and the First American Civil War.* New York: Atheneum, 1989.

Glassley, Ray Hoard. *Pacific Northwest Indian Wars.* Portland, Ore.: Binfords & Mort, 1953.

Goodrich, Thomas. *Scalp Dance: Indian Warfare on the High Plains, 1865–1879.* Mechanicsburg, Pa.: Stackpole, 1997.

Gray, John S. *Centennial Campaign: The Sioux War of 1876.* Fort Collins, Colo.: Old Army Press, 1976.

———. *Custer's Last Campaign: Mitch Boyer and the Little Bighorn Reconstructed.* Lincoln: University of Nebraska Press, 1991.

Greene, Jerome. *Slim Buttes, 1876: An Episode of the Great Sioux War.* Norman: University of Oklahoma Press, 1982.

———. *Yellowstone Command: Colonel Nelson A. Miles,*

and the Great Sioux War, 1876–1877. Norman: University of Oklahoma Press, 1991.

Grinnell, George Bird. *The Fighting Cheyennes.* Norman: University of Oklahoma Press, 1956.

Gruzinski, Serge. *The Aztecs: Rise and Fall of an Empire.* New York: Harry N. Abrams, 1992.

Haines, Aubrey L. *An Elusive Victory: The Battle of Big Hole.* West Glacier, Mont.: Glacier Natural History Association, 1991.

Haley, James L. *Apaches: A History and Culture Portrait.* Norman: University of Oklahoma Press, 1997.

Hampton, Bruce. *Children of Grace: The Nez Perce War of 1877.* New York: Henry Holt, 1994.

Hardorff, Richard G. *Cheyenne Memories of the Custer Fight: A Source Book.* Spokane, Wash.: Arthur H. Clark, 1995.

Hart, Newell. *The Bear River Massacre: Being a Complete Sourcebook and Storybook of the Genocidal Action against the Shoshones in 1863.* 2d ed. Preston, Idaho: Cache Valley Newsletter, 1982.

Hauptman, Lawrence M., and James D. Wherry. *The Pequots in Southern New England: The Rise and Fall of an American Indian Nation.* Norman: University of Oklahoma Press, 1990.

Heidler, David S., and Jeanne T. *Old Hickory's War: Andrew Jackson and the Quest for Empire.* Mechanicsburg, Pa.: Stackpole Books, 1996.

Hoig, Stan. *The Sand Creek Massacre.* Norman: University of Oklahoma Press, 1963.

Horowitz, David. *The First Frontier: The Indian Wars and America's Origins, 1607–1776.* New York: Simon and Schuster, 1978.

Hurt, Douglas R. *The Ohio Frontier: Crucible of the Old Northwest, 1720–1830.* Bloomington: Indiana University Press, 1996.

Jackson, Donald, ed. *Black Hawk: An Autobiography.* Urbana: University of Illinois Press, 1964.

Jennings, Francis. *The Founders of America.* New York: W. W. Norton, 1993.

———. *The Invasion of America: Indians, Colonialism, and the Cant of Conquest.* Chapel Hill.: University of North Carolina Press, 1975.

Keenan, Jerry. *Encyclopedia of American Indian Wars, 1492–1890.* Santa Barbara, Calif.: ABC Clio, 1997.

Keim, DeB. Randolph. *Sheridan's Troopers on the Border: A Winter Campaign on the Plains.* Lincoln: University of Nebraska Press, 1985.

Kelly, Luther S. *Yellowstone Kelly: The Memoirs of Luther S.*

Kelly. Lincoln: University of Nebraska Press, 1973.

Kessell, John L. *Kiva, Cross, and Crown: The Pecos Indians and New Mexico, 1540–1840.* Albuquerque: University of New Mexico, 1990.

Kip, Lawrence. *Army Life on the Pacific: A Journal.* Reprint ed. Fairfield, Wash.: Ye Galleon Press, 1986.

Knaut, Andrew L. *The Pueblo Revolt of 1680: Conquest and Resistance in Seventeenth-Century New Mexico.* Norman: University of Oklahoma Press, 1995.

Laumer, Frank. *Dade's Last Command.* Gainesville: University Press of Florida, 1995.

———. *Massacre!* Gainesville: University of Florida Press, 1968.

Leach, Douglas Edward. *Arms for Empire: A Military History of the British Colonies in North America, 1607–1763.* New York: Macmillan, 1973.

———. *Flintlock and Tomahawk: New England in King Philip's War.* New York: Macmillan, 1958.

Lewis, Virgil Anson. *History of the Battle of Point Pleasant.* Charleston, W. Va.: Tribune Printing, 1909.

Libby, Orin Grant. *The Arikara Narrative of the Campaign against the Hostile Dakotas, June, 1876.* Glorieta, N. Mex.: Rio Grande Press, 1976.

Longstreet, Stephen. *Indian Wars of the Great Plains.* New York: Indian Head Books, 1970.

Madariaga, Salvador de. *Hernan Cortés, Conqueror of Mexico.* Reprint ed. Westport, Conn.: Greenwood Press, 1978.

Madsen, Brigham D. *The Shoshoni Frontier and the Bear River Massacre.* Salt Lake City: University of Utah Press, 1985.

Mangum, Neil C. *The Battle of the Rosebud: Prelude to the Little Bighorn.* El Segundo, Calif.: Upton and Sons, 1987.

Mahon, John K. *History of the Second Seminole War, 1835–1842.* Gainesville: University of Florida Presses, 1967.

Marshall, S. L. A. *Crimsoned Prairie: The Indian Wars of the Great Plains.* New York: Charles Scribner's Sons, 1972.

Martin, Joel W. *Sacred Revolt: The Muskogees' Struggle for a New World.* Boston: Beacon Press, 1991.

McDermott, John D. *Forlorn Hope: The Battle of White Bird Canyon and the Beginning of the Nez Perce War.* Boise, Idaho: State Historical Society, 1978.

———. "We Had a Terribly Hard Time Letting Them Go." *Nebraska History* 77, no. 2 (1996): 78–88.

Melvoin, Richard I. *New England Outpost: War and Society*

in Colonial Deerfield. New York: W. W. Norton, 1989.

Mendoza, Patrick M. *Song of Sorrow: Massacre at Sand Creek*. Denver: Willow Wind, 1993.

Monnett, John H. *The Battle of Beecher Island and the Indian War of 1867–1869*. Boulder: University Press of Colorado, 1992.

Murphy, John A. *Harmar's Defeat: Letters, Journals, and Narratives*. Pataskala, Ohio: Brockston, 1990.

Murray, Keith. *The Modocs and Their War*, 1959. Reprint ed. Norman: University of Oklahoma Press, 1984.

Owsley, Frank Lawrence, Jr. *Struggle for the Gulf Borderlands: The Creek War and the Battle of New Orleans, 1812–1815*. Gainesville: University Presses of Florida, 1981.

Palmer, Dave R. *1794: America, Its Army, and the Birth of the Nation*. Novato, Calif.: Presidio Press, 1994.

Patterson, T. W. "Siege at the Long Sault." *Canada West* 6, no. 3 (1990): 114–118.

Paul, R. Eli, ed. "Battle of Ash Hollow: The 1909–1910 Recollections of General N. A. M. Dudley." *Nebraska History* 62, no. 3 (1981): 373–399.

Peckham, Howard H. *Pontiac and the Indian Uprising*. Detroit: Wayne State University Press, 1994.

Pfaler, Louis. "The Sully Expedition of 1864." *North Dakota History* 31 (1964): 1–54.

Powell, William S. "The Aftermath of the Massacre." *Virginia Magazine of History and Biography* 66 (1958): 44–75.

Prescott, William H. *History of the Conquest of Mexico, and The History of the Conquest of Peru*. New York: Modern Library, 1936.

Price, George F. *Across the Continent with the Fifth Cavalry*. New York: Antiquarian Press, 1959.

Prucha, Paul. *The Sword of the Republic: The United States Army on the Frontier, 1783–1846*. Lincoln: University of Nebraska Press, 1969.

Putnam, Charles. "Incidents of the Modoc War." *Journal of the Shaw Historical Library* 1, no. 2 (1987): 1–12.

Quinn, Arthur. *Hell with the Fire Out: A History of the Modoc War*. Boston: Faber & Faber, 1997.

Reber, Bruce, comp. *The United States Army and the Indian Wars in the Trans-Mississippi West: 1860–1898*. Carlisle Barrack, Pa.: U.S. Army Military Institute, 1978.

Riddle, Jeff. *The Indian History of the Modoc War and the Causes That Led to It*. Medford, Ore.: Pine Cone, 1973.

Roundtree, Helen C. *The Powhatan Indians of Virginia*.

Norman: University of Oklahoma Press, 1989.

Russell, Don. *The Lives and Legends of Buffalo Bill*. Norman: University of Oklahoma Press, 1960.

Sandoz, Mari. *The Battle of Little Bighorn*. Philadelphia: Lippincott, 1966.

Schultz, Duane. *Month of the Freezing Moon: The Sand Creek Massacre, November 1864*. New York: St. Martin's Press, 1990.

Scott, Robert A. *Chief Joseph and the Nez Percés*. New York: Facts On File, 1993.

Sprague, Marshall. *Massacre: The Tragedy at White River*. Boston: Little Brown, 1957.

Steele, Ian K. *Warpaths: Invasions of North America*. New York: Oxford University Press, 1994.

Stewart, Edgar. *Custer's Luck*. Norman: University of Oklahoma Press, 1956.

Stuart, John. *Memoir of the Indian Wars, and Other Occurrences*. Reprint ed. New York: New York Times, 1971.

Sully, Langdon. *No Tears for the General: The Life of Alfred Sully, 1821–1879*. Palo Alto, Calif.: American West, 1974.

Sword, Wiley. *President Washington's Indian War: The Struggle for the Old Northwest, 1790–1895*. Norman: University of Oklahoma Press, 1985.

Tebbel, John W., and Keith Jennison. *American Indian Wars*. New York: Harper, 1960.

Thomas, Hugh. *Conquest: Montezuma, Cortés, and the Fall of Old Mexico*. New York: Simon and Schuster, 1993.

Thompson, Erwin. *Modoc War: Its Military History and Topography*. Sacramento, Calif.: Argus Books, 1971.

Utley, Robert M. *Cavalier in Buckskin: George Armstrong Custer and the Western Military Frontier*. Norman: University of Oklahoma Press, 1988.

———. *Custer and the Great Controversy: The Origin and Development of a Legend*. Lincoln: University of Nebraska Press, 1988.

———. *Custer Battlefield: A History and Guide to the Battle of the Little Bighorn*. Washington, D.C.: U.S. Dept. of the Interior, 1988.

———. *Frontier Regulars: The United States Army and the Indian, 1866–1891*. New York: Macmillan, 1974.

———. *Frontiersmen in Blue: The United States Army and the Indian, 1848–1865*. New York: Macmillan, 1962.

———. *Last Days of the Sioux Nation*. New Haven, Conn.: Yale University Press, 1963.

Utley, Robert M., and Wilcomb E. Washburn. *The*

American Heritage History of the Indian Wars. New York: Barnes & Noble Books, 1977.

Ware, Eugene F. *The Indian War of 1864.* Lincoln: University of Nebraska Press, 1994.

Welch, James, and Paul Stekler. *Killing Custer: The Little Big Horn and the Fate of the Native Americans.* New York: W. W. Norton, 1995.

White, Lonnie J., ed. *Hostiles and Horse Soldiers: Indian Battles and Campaigns in the West.* Boulder, Colo.: Pruett, 1972.

Wooster, Donald E. *Nelson A. Miles and the Twilight of the Frontier Army.* Lincoln: University of Nebraska Press, 1992.

THE AMERICAN REVOLUTION

Abbatt, William. *The Battle of Pell's Point (or Pelham) October 18, 1776.* New York: W. Abbatt, 1901.

Allen, Gardiner W. *A Naval History of the American Revolution.* 2 vols. New York: Russell and Russell, 1962.

Arthur, Robert. *The End of a Revolution.* New York: Vantage Press, 1966.

Baker, Thomas E. *Another Such Victory: The Story of the American Defeat at Guilford Courthouse That Helped Win the War for Independence.* New York: Eastern Acorn Press, 1981.

Bayley, John. *In Another Country.* Reprint ed. Oxford: Oxford University Press, 1986.

Berg, Richard H. "The Southern Campaigns: The British Effort to Retake the South, 1778–1781." *Strategy and Tactics,* no. 104 (1985): 14–23.

Bill, Alfred Hoyt. *The Campaign of Princeton, 1776–1777.* Princeton, N.J.: Princeton University Press, 1948.

Bird, Harrison. *Attack on Quebec: The American Invasion of Canada, 1775.* New York: Oxford University Press, 1968.

Boatner, Mark Mayo, III. *The Encyclopedia of the American Revolution.* New York: David McKay, 1966.

Brownlow, Donald G. *A Documentary History of the Paoli "Massacre,"* 1952. 2d ed. West Chester, Pa.: Horace F. Temple, 1977.

Buchanan, John. *The Road to Guilford Courthouse: The*

American Revolution in the Carolinas. New York: John Wiley & Sons, 1997.

Butterfield, Consul Willshire. *An Historical Account of the Expedition against Sandusky under Col. William Crawford in 1782.* Cincinnati: R. Clarke, 1873.

Byrd, Martha. *Saratoga: Turning Point in the American Revolution.* Philadelphia: Auerbach, 1973.

Campbell, William V. *Annals of Tyron County, or, The Border Warfare of New York, during the Revolution.* 4th ed. New York: Dodd, Mead, 1924.

Canby, Henry Seidel. *The Brandywine.* Reprint ed. New York: Farrar & Rinehart, 1941.

Clarke, Ernest. *The Siege of Fort Cumberland, 1776: An Episode in the American Revolution.* Buffalo, N.Y.: McGill-Queen's University Press, 1995.

Coburn, Frank Warren. *The Centennial History of the Battle of Bennington.* Boston: G. E. Littlefield, 1877.

Cooch, Edward W. *The Battle of Cooch's Bridge, Delaware, September 3, 1777.* Wilmington, Del.: W. N. Cann, 1940.

Cook, Fred J. *Dawn over Saratoga: The Turning Point of the Revolutionary War.* Garden City, N.Y.: Doubleday, 1973.

Davis, Burke. *The Campaign That Won America: The Story of Yorktown.* New York: Dial Press, 1970.

———. *The Cowpens-Guilford Courthouse Campaign.* Philadelphia: Lippincott, 1962.

Davis, Robert S. *Georgians in the Revolution: at Kettle Creek (Wilkes Co.) and Burke County.* Easley, S.C.: Southern Historical Press, 1986.

Davis, Robert S., and Kenneth H. Thomas. *Kettle Creek: The Battle of the Cane Brakes.* Atlanta: Department of Natural Resources, 1975.

Davis, T. E. *The Battle of Bound Brook, 1895.* Reprint ed. Bound Brook, N.J.: Washington Camp Ground Association, 1981.

DeCosta, B. F. *Notes on the History of Fort George during the Colonial and Revolutionary Periods.* New York: J. Sabin & Sons, 1871.

Dorwart, Jeffrey, M. *Fort Mifflin of Philadelphia: An Illustrated History.* Philadelphia: University of Pennsylvania Press, 1998.

Draper, Lyman C. *King's Mountain and Its Heroes: History of the Battle of King's Mountain, October 7th, 1780, and the Events Which Led to It.* Reprint ed. Spartansburg, S.C.: Reprint, 1967.

Dupuy, Trevor N., and Gay M. Hammerman. *The*

Military History of Revolutionary War Land Battles. New York: Watts, 1970.

Dwyer, William H. *The Day Is Ours! November 1776–January 1777: An Inside View of the Battles of Trenton and Princeton.* New York: Viking Press, 1983.

Edgar, Gregory T. *Reluctant Break with Britain: From Stamp Act to Bunker Hill.* Bowie, Md.: Heritage Books, 1997.

Elting, John R. *The Battle of Bunker's Hill.* Monmouth Beach, N.J.: Philip Freneau Press, 1975.

Fisher, David Hackett. *Paul Revere's Ride.* New York: Oxford University Press, 1994.

Fleming, Thomas. *The Battle of Springfield.* Trenton: New Jersey Historical Society, 1975.

———. *Beat the Last Drum: The Siege of Yorktown, 1781.* New York: St. Martin's Press, 1963.

———. *Cowpens: "Downright Fighting": The Story of Cowpens.* Washington, D.C.: National Parks Service, 1988.

———. *The First Stroke: Lexington, Concord, and the Beginning of the American Revolution.* Washington, D.C.: National Parks Service, 1978.

———. *Now We Are Enemies: The Story of Bunker Hill.* New York: St. Martin's Press, 1960.

Fletcher, Ebenezer. *The Narrative of Ebenezer Fletcher, a Soldier of the Revolution, Written by Himself.* 4th ed. Freeport, N.Y.: Books for Libraries Press, 1970.

Fowler, William M., Jr. *Rebels under Sail: The American Navy during the Revolution.* New York: Charles Scribner's Sons, 1976.

Flood, Charles B. *Rise, and Fight Again: Perilous Times along the Road to Independence.* New York: Dodd, Mead, 1976.

Futhey, J. Smith. *The Massacre of Paoli,* 1877. Philadelphia: J. Carbutt, 1990.

Galvez, Bernardo de. *Yo Solo: The Battle Journal of Bernardo de Galvez during the American Revolution.* Eric Beerman, trans. New Orleans: Polyanthos, 1978.

Galvin, John R. *The Minute Men: The First Fight: Myths and Realities of the American Revolution.* 2d ed. Washington, D.C.: Pergamon-Brassey's International Defense, 1989.

Hall, Edward H. *Stoney Point Battle-Field: A Sketch of Its Revolutionary History.* New York: American Scenic and Historic Preservation Society, 1902.

Hamilton, Edward Pierce. *Fort Ticonderoga, Key to a Continent.* Boston: Little, Brown, 1964.

Harrison, Lowell. *George Rogers Clark and the War in the West.* Lexington: University Press of Kentucky, 1976.

Hatch, Robert McConnell. *Thrust for Canada: The American Attempt on Quebec in 1775–1776.* Boston: Houghton Mifflin, 1979.

Heidler, David S. "The American Defeat at Briar Creek." *Georgia Historical Quarterly* 66, no. 3 (1982): 317–331.

Henry, Robert. *Narrative of the Battle of Cowan's Ford, February 1st, 1781.* Greensboro, N.C.: Reece & Elam, 1891.

Hough, Franklin Benjamin. *The Siege of Charleston, by the British Fleet and Army under the Command of Admiral Arbuthnot and Sir Henry Clinton, which terminated with the surrender of that place on the 12th of May, 1780.* Spartanburg, S.C.: Reprint, 1975.

Jackson, John W. *With the British Army in Philadelphia, 1777–1778.* San Rafael, Calif.: Presidio Press, 1979.

Johnston, Henry Phelps. *The Battle of Harlem Heights, September 16, 1776.* New York: Macmillan for Columbia University Press, 1897.

Judd, Jacob. *Fort Lee on the Palisades: The Battle for the Hudson.* Tarrytown, N.Y.: Sleepy Hollow Restorations, 1963.

Kennedy, Benjamin, ed. *Musket, Cannon Balls and Bombs: Nine Narratives of the Siege of Savannah in 1779.* Savannah, Ga.: Beehive Press, 1974.

Ketchum, Richard M. *Decisive Day: The Battle for Bunker Hill.* Garden City, N.Y.: Doubleday, 1974.

———. *Saratoga: Turning Point of America's Revolutionary War.* New York: Henry Holt, 1997.

Killion, Ronald G., and Charles T. Waller. *Georgia and the Revolution.* Atlanta: Cherokee, 1975.

Lanctot, Gustave. *Canada and the American Revolution, 1774–1783.* Cambridge, Mass.: Harvard University Press, 1967.

Lawrence, Alexander A. *Storm over Savannah: The Story of Count d'Estaing and the Siege of the Town in 1779.* Athens: University of Georgia Press, 1951.

Leslie, Vernon E. *The Battle of Minisink: A Revolutionary War Engagement in the Upper Delaware Valley.* 2d ed. Middletown, N. Y.: T. E. Henderson, 1976.

Lumpkin, Henry. "The Battle off the Capes." *Virginia Cavalcade* 31, no. 2 (1981): 68–77.

Lundberg, Philip K. *The Continental Gunboat Philadelphia and the Northern Campaign of 1776.* Washington, D.C.: Smithsonian Institution, 1966.

Lundin, Leonard. *Cockpit of the Revolution: The War for*

Independence in New Jersey. Princeton, N.J.: Princeton University Press, 1940.

Macaltioner, George B. *150th Anniversary of the Skirmish at Quinton's Bridge and the Massacre at Hancock's Bridge.* Salem, N.J.: Sunbeam, 1928.

MacWethy, Lou D. *The Battle of Klock's Field, October 19, 1780.* St. Johnsville, N.Y.: Enterprise and News, 1930.

Manders, Eric I. *The Battle of Long Island.* Monmouth Beach, N.J.: Philip Freneau Press, 1978.

McCusker, John J. *Alfred: The First Continental Flagship, 1775–1778.* Washington, D.C.: Smithsonian Studies in History and Technology, no. 20, 1973.

McDevitt, Robert F. *Connecticut Attacked, a British Viewpoint: Tryon's Raid on Danbury.* Chester, Conn.: Pequot Press, 1974.

McGuire, Thomas J. *The Surprise of Germantown, or, The Battle of Cliveden: October 4th, 1777.* Gettysburg, Pa.: Thomas Publications, 1994.

Merrill, Arthur A. *The Battle of White Plains.* Chappaqua, N.Y.: Analysis Press, 1995.

Messick, Hank. *King's Mountain: The Epic of the Blue Ridge "Mountain Men" in the American Revolution.* Boston: Little, Brown, 1976.

Morrill, Dan L. *Southern Campaigns of the American Revolution.* Baltimore: Nautical and Aviation, 1993.

Morrison, James F. *The Battle of Johnstown, October 25th, 1781.* n.p.: Third Battalion of Tryon County, 1991.

Nadelhaft, Jerome J. *The Disorders of War: The Revolution in South Carolina.* Orono: University of Maine at Orono Press, 1981.

O'Brien, Michael Joseph. *The Irish at Bunker Hill.* Shannon, Ireland: Irish University Press, 1968.

Pancake, John S. *This Destructive War: The British Campaign in the Carolinas.* Tuscaloosa: University of Alabama Press, 1985.

Papers Relating to the Surrender of Fort St. Johns and Fort Chambly. Toronto: Canadiana House, 1971.

Pickens, Andrew Lee. *Skyagunsta: The Border Wizard Owl, Major-General Andrew Pickens.* Greenville, S.C.: Observer, 1934.

Purcell, L. Edward. *Who Was Who in the American Revolution.* New York: Facts On File, 1993.

Rankin, Hugh F. *Francis Marion: The Swamp Fox.* New York: Thomas Crowell, 1973.

———. *Greene and Cornwallis: The Campaign in the Carolinas.* Raleigh, N.C.: Dept. of Cultural Resources, Division of Archives and History, 1976.

———. *The Moore's Creek Bridge Campaign, 1776.*

Conshohocken, Pa.: Eastern Parks and Monuments Association, 1986.

Rathbun, Jonathan. *The Narrative of Jonathan Rathbun, of the Capture of Fort Griswold, the Massacre That Followed, and the Burning of New London, Conn.* Reprint ed. New York: W. Abbatt, 1911.

Richardson, William H. *Washington and "The Enterprise against Powles Hook." A New Study of the Surprise and Capture of the Fort, Thursday, August 19, 1779.* Jersey City: New Jersey Title Guarantee and Trust, 1929.

Roberts, Kenneth. *The Battle of Cowpens: The Great Morale-Builder.* Garden City, N.Y.: Doubleday, 1958.

Roberts, Robert B. *New York's Forts in the Revolution.* Cranbury, N.J.: Associated University Press, 1980.

Rush, Nixon Orwin. *The Battle of Pensacola, March 9 to May 8, 1781: Spain's Final Triumph over Great Britain in the Gulf of Mexico.* Tallahassee: Florida State University Press, 1966.

Sands, John O. *Yorktown's Captive Fleet.* Charlottesville: University Press of Virginia, 1983.

Scott, John Albert. *Fort Stanwix (Fort Schuyler) and Oriskany: The Romantic Story of the Repulse of St. Leger's British Invasion of 1777.* Rome, N.Y.: Rome Sentinel, 1927.

Servies, James A., ed. *The Log of H.M.S. Mentor, 1780–1781: A New Account of the British Navy at Pensacola.* Pensacola: University Presses of Florida, 1982.

Shafroth, J. F. *The Strategy of the Yorktown Campaign, 1781.* Annapolis, Md.: United States Naval Institute, 1931.

Shelton, Hal T. *General Richard Montgomery and the American Revolution: From Redcoat to Rebel.* New York: New York University Press, 1994.

Shepherd, William R. *The Battle of Harlem Heights.* New York: G. P. Putnam, 1898.

Sklarsky, I. W. *The Revolution's Boldest Venture: The Story of General "Mad Anthony" Wayne's Assault on Stony Point.* Port Washington, N.Y.: Kennikat Press, 1965.

Smith, Ernest G. *The Sesqui-Centennial of the Battle of Wyoming.* Wilkes-Barre, Pa.: Wyoming Historical and Geological Society, 1928.

Smith, Page. *A New Age Now Begins: A People's History of the American Revolution.* 2 vols. New York: McGraw Hill, 1976.

Smith, Samuel Stelle. *The Battle of Brandywine.*

Monmouth Beach, N.J.: Philip Freneau Press, 1976.

———. *The Battle of Monmouth.* Trenton: New Jersey Historical Commission, 1975.

———. *The Battle of Princeton.* Monmouth Beach, N.J.: Philip Freneau Press, 1967.

———. *The Battle of Trenton.* Monmouth Beach, N.J.: Philip Freneau Press, 1965.

Spargo, John. *The Bennington Battle Monument: Its Story and Its Meaning.* Rutland, Vt.: Tuttle, 1925.

Standard, Janet H. *The Battle of Kettle Creek: A Turning Point of the American Revolution in the South.* Washington, Ga.: Wilkes, 1973.

Stanley, George. *Canada Invaded, 1775–1776.* Toronto: Hakkert, 1973.

Stokely, Jim. *Fort Moultrie: Constant Defender.* Washington, D.C.: National Park Service, 1985.

Stone, William Leete. *The Campaign of Lieut. Gen. John Burgoyne, and the Expedition of Lieut. Col. Barry St. Leger.* New York: Da Capo Press, 1970.

Stradley, Wilson. "Antony Wayne on the Hudson River." *Valley Forge Journal* 3, no. 4 (1987): 288–307.

Thayer, Theodore. *The Making of a Scapegoat: Washington and Lee at Monmouth.* Port Washington, N.Y.: Kennikat Press, 1976.

———. *Yorktown: Campaign of Strategic Options.* Philadelphia: Lippincott, 1975.

Thompson, Ray. *Washington along the Delaware: The Battles of Trenton and Princeton as Told by the Men Who Were There and through Washington's Own Official Dispatches.* Fort Washington, Pa.: Bicentennial Press, 1970.

———. *Washington at Germantown.* Fort Washington, Pa.: Bicentennial Press, 1971.

———. *Washington at Whitemarsh: Prelude to Valley Forge.* Rev. ed. Fort Washington, Pa.: Bicentennial Press, 1974.

Tourtellot, Arthur Bernon. *William Diamond's Drum: The Beginning of the War of the American Revolution.* Garden City, N.Y.: Doubleday, 1959.

U.S. Army War College. *The Battle of Camden, South Carolina, August 16, 1780.* Washington, D.C.: U.S. Government Printing Office, 1929.

Valliant, Joseph N., Jr. *Revolution's Fate Sealed at Sea.* Herndon, Va.: Empire Press, 1995.

Wallace, Willard M. *Appeal to Arms: A Military History of the American Revolution.* New York: Harper & Bros., 1951.

Ward, Christopher. *The War of the Revolution.* 2 vols. New York: Macmillan, 1952.

White, Katherine Keogh. *The Kings Mountain Men: The Story of the Battle, with Sketches of the American Soldiers Who Took Part.* Baltimore: Genealogical Publishing, 1966.

Widmer, Kemble. *The Christmas Campaign: The Ten Days of Trenton and Princeton.* Trenton: New Jersey Historical Commission, 1975.

Williams, John Andrew. *The Battle for Hubbardton: The American Rebels Stem the Tide.* Montpelier: Vermont Division for Historic Preservation, 1988.

Wilson, Samuel M. *Battle of Blue Licks, August 19, 1782.* Lexington, Ky.: n.p., 1927.

Winfield, Charles H. *The Block-House by Bull's Ferry.* New York: W. Abbatt, 1904.

Wingo, Elizabeth B. *The Battle of Great Bridge.* Chesapeake, Va.: Norfolk County Historical Society, 1964.

Wrike, Peter J. *The Governors' Island: Gwynn Island during the Revolution.* Gwynn, Va.: Gwynn Island Museum, 1993.

Young, Bennet Henderson. *History of the Battle of Blue Licks.* Louisville, Ky.: Morton, 1897.

THE WAR OF 1812

Albright, Harry. *New Orleans: Battle of the Bayous.* New York: Hippocrene Books, 1990.

Allen, Robert S. "A History of Fort George, Upper Canada." *Canadian Historic Sites* 11 (1974): 61–93.

Berton, Pierre. *Flames across the Border: The Canadian-American Tragedy, 1813–1814.* Boston: Little, Brown, 1981.

Bilow, John A. *Chateaugay, N.Y. and the War of 1812.* Plattsburgh, N.Y.: Payette & Simms, 1984.

Bowlus, Bruce. "A 'Signal Victory': The Battle for Fort Stephenson, August 1–2, 1813." *Northwest Ohio Quarterly* 63 (1991): 43–57.

Burdick, Virginia Mason. *Captain Thomas Macdonough: Delaware Born Hero of the Battle of Lake Champlain.* Wilmington: Delaware Heritage Press, 1991.

Carter, Samuel. *Blaze of Glory: The Fight for New Orleans, 1814–1815.* New York: St. Martin's Press, 1971.

Carter-Edwards, Dennis. "The War of 1812 along the

Detroit Frontier: A Canadian Perspective." *Michigan Historical Review* 13 (1987): 18–26.

Chidsey, Donald Barr. *The Battle of New Orleans, An Informal History of the War That Nobody Wanted: 1812.* New York: Crown, 1961.

Coleman, Margaret. *The American Capture of Fort George, Ontario.* Ottawa: Department of Northern and Indian Affairs, 1977.

Coles, Harry L. *The War of 1812.* Chicago: University of Chicago Press, 1965.

Compton, Smith C. *The Battle of Queenston Heights, U.C.* Toronto: McGraw-Hill, 1968.

Cross, Charles. *The Chesapeake: A Biography of a Ship.* Chesapeake, Va.: Norfolk County Historical Society, 1968.

Cruikshank, Ernest A. *The Battle of Fort George.* Niagara Falls, Ontario, Canada: Niagara Historical Society, 1904.

———. "The Defense of Mackinac." *Canadian History* 1 (1900): 195–201.

Dillon, Richard. *We Have Met the Enemy: Oliver Hazard Perry, Wilderness Commodore.* New York: McGraw-Hill, 1978.

Ellison, David. "David Wingfield and Sacket's Harbor." *Dalhousie Review* 52 (1972): 407–413.

Everest, Allan S. *The War of 1812 in the Champlain Valley.* Syracuse, N.Y.: Syracuse University Press, 1981.

Graves, Donald E. *The Battle of Lundy's Lane: On the Niagara in 1814.* Baltimore: Nautical and Aviation, 1993.

———. *Red Coats & Grey Jackets: The Battle of Chippewa, 5 July, 1814.* Niagara Falls, N.Y.: Dundurn Press, 1994.

Green, Ernest. *Lincoln at Bay. A Sketch of 1814.* Welland, Canada: Tribune-Telegraph Press, 1923.

Havinghurst, Walter. *Three Flags at the Straits: The Forts of Mackinac.* Englewood Cliffs, N.J.: Prentice-Hall, 1966.

Heidler, David S., and Jeanne T. Heidler, eds. *Encyclopedia of the War of 1812.* Santa Barbara, Calif.: ABC Clio, 1997.

Heidler, David S., and Jeanne T. Heidler. *Old Hickory's War: Andrew Jackson and the Quest for Empire.* Mechanicsburg, Pa.: Stackpole Books, 1996.

Hollis, Ira N. *The Frigate Constitution: The Central Figure of the Navy under Sail.* Boston: Houghton Mifflin, 1931.

Horgan, Thomas P. *Old Ironsides: An Illustrated History of USS Constitution.* Dublin, N.H.: Yankee, 1980.

Keefer, Frank H. *Beaver Dams.* Thorold, Canada: Thorold Post, 1914.

Lewis, Dennis M. *British Naval Activity on Lake Champlain during the War of 1812.* Plattsburg, N.Y., and Elizabethtown, N.Y.: Clinton County Historical Association and Essex County Historical Association, 1994.

Lord, Walter, *The Dawn's Early Light.* New York: W. W. Norton, 1972.

Mahan, Alfred Thayer. *Seapower in Its Relation to the War of 1812.* 2 vols. Boston: Little, Brown, 1919.

Malcomson, Robert, and Thomas Malcomson. *HMS Detroit: The Battle for Lake Erie.* Annapolis, Md.: Naval Institute Press, 1990.

Marine, William Matthew. *The British Invasion of Maryland, 1812–1815.* Baltimore: Society for the War of 1812 in Maryland, 1913.

Martin, Tyrone G. *A Most Fortunate Ship: A Narrative History of Old Ironsides.* Rev. ed. Annapolis: Naval Institute Press, 1997.

Montross, Lynn. "An Amphibious Doubleheader." *Marine Corps Gazette* 42 (1957): 131–140.

Muller, Charles G. *The Darkest Day: The Washington-Baltimore Campaign.* Philadelphia: Lippincott, 1963.

———. *The Proudest Day: Macdonough on Lake Champlain.* New York: Curtis Books, 1960.

Owen, David A. *Fort Erie: An Historical Guide.* n.p.: Niagara Parks Commission, 1986.

Padfield, Peter. *Brooke and the Shannon.* London: Hodder & Stoughton, 1968.

Preston, Richard A. "The First Battle of Sacket's Harbor." *Historic Kingston* 2 (1963): 3–7.

Pullen, H. F. *The Shannon and the Chesapeake.* Toronto: McClelland and Stewart, 1970.

Ramsay, Jack C. *Jean Laffite: Prince of Pirates.* Austin, Tex.: Eakin Press, 1996.

Reilly, Robin. *The British at the Gates: The New Orleans Campaign.* New York: G. P. Putnam, 1974.

Quimby, Robert S. *The U.S. Army in the War of 1812: An Operational and Command Study.* 2 vols. East Lansing: Michigan State University Press, 1997.

Richardson, John. *Richardson's War of 1812.* Toronto: Historical Publishing, 1902.

Rimini, Robert V. *The Battle of New Orleans.* New York: Viking, 1999.

Roosevelt, Theodore. *The Naval War of 1812.* Reprint ed. St. Clair Shores, Mich.: Scholarly Press, 1970.

Sellar, Robert. *The U.S. Campaign of 1813 to Capture Montreal.* 2d ed. Huntingdon, Quebec: Gleaner Office, 1914.

Shomette, Donald. *Flotilla Battle for the Patuxent.* Solomons, Md.: Calvert Marine Museum Press, 1981.

Skaggs, David Curtis, and Gerard T. Altoff. *A Signal*

Victory: The Lake Erie Campaign, 1812–1813. Annapolis, Md.: Naval Institute Press, 1997.

Stanley, George F. G. *Battle in the Dark: Stoney Creek, 6 June, 1813.* Toronto: Balmuir, 1991.

Sugden, John. *Tecumseh's Last Stand.* Norman: University of Oklahoma Press, 1985.

Swanson, Neil H. *The Perilous Fight.* New York: Farrar and Rinehart, 1945.

Welsh, William J., and David C. Skaggs. *War on the Great Lakes: Essays Commemorating the 175th Anniversary of the Battle of Lake Erie.* Kent, Ohio: Kent State University Press, 1991.

Whitehorne, Joseph. *While Washington Burned: The Battle for Fort Erie.* Baltimore: Nautical and Aviation, 1992.

Whitfield, Carol. "The Battle of Queenston Heights." *Canadian Historic Sites* 11 (1974): 9–59.

Wilder, Patrick A. *The Battle of Sackett's Harbour and the Struggle for Lake Ontario.* Baltimore: Nautical and Aviation, 1994.

Young, Bennett H. *The Battle of the Thames.* Louisville, Ky.: John P. Morton, 1903.

Zaslow, Morris, ed. *The Defended Border: Upper Canada and the War of 1812.* Toronto: Macmillan, 1964.

THE MEXICAN-AMERICAN WAR

Battalla de la Mesa: The Battle of the Mesa, 1847. Los Angeles: East Side, 1926.

Bauer, Jack K. *The Mexican War, 1846–1848.* New York: Macmillan, 1974.

Benham, Henry Washington. *Recollections of Mexico and the Battle of Buena Vista Feb. 22 and 23, 1847.* Boston: n.p., 1871.

Carleton, James Henry. *The Battle of Buena Vista.* New York: Harper, 1848.

Clark, Kimball. "The Epic March of Doniphan's Missourians." *Missouri Historical Review* 80, no. 2 (1986): 134–155.

Dufour, Charles L. *The Mexican War: A Compact History.* New York: Hawthorn Books, 1968.

Haecker, Charles M. *On the Prairie of Palo Alto: Historical Archaeology of the U.S.-Mexican War Battlefield.* College Station: Texas A&M University Press, 1997.

Henry, Robert S. *The Story of the Mexican War.* Reprint ed.

New York: Frederick Ungar, 1961.

Lavender, David S. *Climax at Buena Vista: The American Campaign in Northeastern Mexico, 1846–47.* Philadelphia: Lippincott, 1966.

Stevens, Peter F. "The Proving Ground." *American History Illustrated* 23, no. 3 (1988): 38–44.

Todd, Charles Burr. *The Battles of San Pasqual: A Study: With Map, Itinerary and Guide to the Battlefields.* Pomona, Calif.: Progress, 1925.

Weems, John Edward. *To Conquer a Peace: The War between the United States and Mexico.* Garden City, N.Y.: Doubleday, 1974.

Winders, Richard Bruce. *The Boys for Mexico: Mr. Polk's Army.* College Station: Texas A&M University Press, 1997.

Woodward, Arthur. *Lances at San Pascual.* San Francisco, Calif.: California Historical Society, 1948.

Wynn, Dennis. *The San Patricio Soldiers: Mexico's Foreign Legion.* El Paso: Texas Western Press, University of Texas at El Paso, 1984.

THE CIVIL WAR

Alberts, Don E. *The Battle of Glorieta: Union Victory in the West.* College Station: Texas A&M Press, 1998.

Aman, William. *Personnel of the Civil War.* New York: Thomas Yoseloff, 1961.

Armour, Robert. *The Attack upon and the Defense of Fort Sanders, Knoxville, Tennessee, November 29, 1863: An Eyewitness Account.* Knoxville, Tenn.: Fine Arts Press, 1991.

Armstrong, Richard L. *Jackson's Valley Campaign: The Battle of McDowell, March 11–May 18, 1862.* Lynchburg, Va.: H. E. Howard, 1990.

Bailey, Ronald H. *Battles for Atlanta: Sherman Moves East.* Alexandria, Va.: Time-Life Books, 1985.

Bannister, Donald. *Long Day at Shiloh.* New York: Alfred A. Knopf, 1981.

Baltz, Louis J. *The Battle of Cold Harbor, May 27–June 13, 1864.* Lynchburg, Va.: H. E. Howard, 1994.

Baumgartner, Richard, and Larry M. Strayer, eds. *Echoes of Battle: The Struggle for Chattanooga.* Huntington, W. Va.: Blue Acorn Press, 1996.

Bearss, Edwin C. *Battle of Five Forks.* 2d ed. Lynchburg,

Va.: H. E. Howard, 1985.

———. *Protecting Sherman's Lifeline: The Battles of Brice's Creek Roads and Tupelo, 1864.* Washington, D.C.: National Parks Service, 1972.

Beck, Brandon H. *The First Battle of Winchester: May 25, 1862.* Lynchburg, Va.: H. E. Howard, 1992.

Blackford, Charles Minor: *Campaign and Battle of Lynchburg, Virginia:* Lynchburg, Va.: Warwick House, 1994.

Boatner, Mark M., III. *The Civil War Dictionary.* Rev. ed. New York: David McKay, 1988.

Bowman, John, ed. *The Civil War Almanac.* New York: World Almanac, 1983.

Bradley, Mark L. *Last Stand in the Carolinas: The Battle of Bentonville.* Campbell, Calif.: Savas Publishing, 1996.

Brocke, Heros von. *The Great Cavalry Battle of Brandy Station, 9 June 1863.* Winston-Salem, N.C.: Palaemon Press, 1976.

Brooksher, William R. *Bloody Hill: The Civil War Battle of Wilson's Creek.* Washington, D.C.: Brassey's, 1995.

Burchard, Peter, *"We'll Stand by the Union": Robert Gould Shaw and the Massachusetts Regiment.* New York: Facts on File, 1993.

The Campaign for Atlanta and Sherman's March to the Sea: Essays on the Civil War in Georgia. 2 vols. Campbell, Calif.: Savas, 1994.

Cannan, John. *The Atlanta Campaign: May–November 1864.* Conshohocken, Pa.: Combined Books, 1991.

———. *Spotsylvania Campaign: May 7–21, 1864.* Conshohocken, Pa.: Combined Books, 1997.

———. *The Wilderness Campaign: May 1864.* Conshohocken, Pa.: Combined Books, 1993.

Carter, Samuel. *The Seige of Atlanta, 1864.* New York: St. Martin's Press, 1973.

Castel, Albert E. *Decision in the West: The Atlanta Campaign of 1864.* Lawrence: University Press of Kansas, 1992.

Catton, Bruce. *The Army of the Potomac.* 3 vols. Garden City, N.Y.: Doubleday, 1962.

———. *The Centennial History of the Civil War.* 3 vols. Garden City, N.Y.: Doubleday, 1961–1965.

———. *The Civil War.* New York: American Heritage Press, 1985.

———. *Gettysburg: The Final Fury.* Garden City, N.Y.: Doubleday, 1974.

Coles, R. T. *From Huntsville to Appomattox.* Knoxville: University of Tennessee Press, 1996.

Colling, B. Franklin. *Monocacy: The Battle That Saved Washington.* Shippensburg, Pa.: White Mane, 1997.

Collins, Darrell L. *The Battles of Cross Keys and Port Republic.* Lynchburg, Va.: H. E. Howard, 1993.

Cooling, B. Franklin. *Fort Donelson's Legacy: War and Society in Kentucky and Tennessee, 1862–1863.* Knoxville: University of Tennessee Press, 1997.

———. *Fort Henry and Donelson: The Key to the Confederate Heartland.* Knoxville: University of Tennessee Press, 1987.

Cottom, Robert I., Jr., and Mary Ellen Hayward. *Maryland in the Civil War: A House Divided.* Baltimore: Johns Hopkins University Press, 1994.

Cozzens, Peter. *The Darkest Days of the War: The Battles of Iuka and Corinth.* Chapel Hill: University of North Carolina Press, 1997.

———. *No Better Place to Die: The Battle of Stones River.* Urbana: University of Illinois Press, 1990.

Cunningham, Edward. *The Battle of Baton Rouge, 1862.* Baton Rouge, La.: Committee for the Preservation of the Port Hudson Battlefield, 1962.

Current, Richard N. *Lincoln and the First Shot.* Philadelphia: J. B. Lippincott, 1963.

Daly, Robert W. *How the Merrimac Won: The Strategic Story of the C.S.S. Virginia.* New York: Thomas Y. Crowell, 1957.

Daniel, Larry J. *Island No. 10: Struggle for the Mississippi Valley.* Tuscaloosa, Ala.: University of Alabama Press, 1996.

———. *Shiloh: The Battle That Changed the Civil War.* New York: Simon and Schuster, 1997.

Davis, John (William Adams, ed.). "Up the Beach and into Battle." *Civil War Times Illustrated* 25, no. 6 (1986): 332–342, 343.

Davis, William C. *Battle at Bull Run: A History of the First Major Campaign of the Civil War.* Garden City, N.J.: Doubleday, 1977.

———. *The Battle of New Market.* 2d ed. Harrisburg, Pa.: Stackpole Books, 1993.

DeKay, James Tertius. Monitor: *The Story of the Legendary Civil War Ironclad and the Man Whose Invention Changed the Course of History.* New York: Walker, 1997.

Delauter, Roger U. *The Third Battle of Winchester.* Lynchburg, Va.: H. E. Howard, 1997.

Dowdey, Clifford. *The Seven Days: The Emergence of Lee.* Reprint ed. Lincoln: University of Nebraska Press, 1993.

Downey, Fairfax Davis. *Clash of Cavalry: The Battle of*

Brandy Station, June 9 1863. New York: David McKay, 1959.

Dudley, G. W. *The Lost Account of the Battle of Corinth, and Court-Martial of Gen. Van Dorn.* Wilmington, N.C.: Broadfoot, 1991.

Dufour, Charles L. *The Night the War Was Lost.* Garden City, N.Y.: Doubleday, 1960.

Du Pont, Henry. *The Campaign of 1864 in the Valley of Virginia: And the Expedition to Lynchburg.* New York: National Americana Society, 1925.

Dyer, Frederick. *Compendium of the War of the Rebellion.* 3 vols. Dayton, Ohio: National Historical Society, 1979.

Ecelbarger, Gary L. *We Are In for It!: The First Battle of Kernstown, March 23, 1862.* Shippensburg, Pa.: White Mane, 1997.

Editors of *Civil War Times Illustrated. Struggle for Vicksburg: The Battles and Siege That Decided the Civil War.* Harrisburg, Pa.: Stackpole Books, 1967.

Edrington, Thomas S. *The Battle of Glorieta Pass: A Gettysburg in the West, March 26–28, 1862.* Albuquerque: University of New Mexico Press, 1997.

Eicher, David J. *The Civil War in Books: An Analytical Bibliography.* Champaign: University of Illinois Press, 1996.

Emilio, Luis F. *A Brave Black Regiment: History of the Fifty-fourth Regiment of Massachusetts Volunteer Infantry, 1863–1865.* 3d ed. Salem, N.H.: Ayer, 1990.

Engerud, Hal. *The Battle of Munfordville, September 14th–17th, 1862.* Munfordville, Ky.: Hart County Historical Society, 1984.

Evans, Clemet, ed. *Confederate Military History.* 13 vols. Atlanta: Confederate Publishing, 1899.

Evans, David. *Sherman's Horsemen: Union Cavalry Operations in the Atlanta Campaign.* Bloomington: Indiana University Press, 1996.

Farwell, Byron. *Balls Bluff: A Small Battle and Its Long Shadow.* McLean, Va.: EPM, 1990.

Fassinito, William A. *Antietam: The Photographic Legacy of America's Bloodiest Day.* New York: Charles Scribner's Sons, 1978.

Finfrock, Bradley. *Across the Rappahannock: From Fredericksburg to the Mud March.* Bowie, Md.: Heritage Books, 1994.

Fitzgerald, W. Norman, Jr. *President Lincoln's Blockade and the Defense of Mobile.* Madison: Lincoln Fellowship of Wisconsin, 1954.

Fonielle, Chris E. *The Wilmington Campaign: Last Rays of Departing Hope.* Campbell, Calif.: Savas, 1997.

Foote, Shelby. *The Civil War: A Narrative.* 3 vols. New York: Random House, 1974.

Franklin, Robert Morris. *Battle of Galveston, January 1, 1863.* Galveston, Tex.: San Luis Press, 1975.

Frazier, Donald S. *Cottonclads! The Battle of Galveston and the Defense of the Texas Coast.* Abilene, Tex.: McWhiney Foundation Press, McMurray University, 1998.

Fuchs, Richard L. *An Unerring Fire: The Massacre at Fort Pillow.* Rutherford, N.J.: Fairleigh Dickinson University Press, 1994.

Furgurson, Ernest B. *Chancellorsville, 1863: The Souls of the Brave.* New York: Alfred A. Knopf, 1992.

Gaff, Alan D. *Brave Men's Tears: The Iron Brigade at Brawner Farm.* Rev. ed. Dayton, Ohio: Morningside, 1988.

Gallagher, Gary W., ed. *Chancellorsville: The Battle and Its Aftermath.* Chapel Hill: University of North Carolina Press, 1996.

———. *The Confederate War.* Cambridge, Mass.: Harvard University Press, 1997.

———, ed. *The First Day at Gettysburg: Essays on Confederate and Union Leadership.* Kent, Ohio: Kent State University Press, 1992.

———, ed. *The Second Day at Gettysburg: Essays on Confederate and Union Leadership.* Kent, Ohio: Kent State University Press, 1993.

———, ed. *The Third Day at Gettysburg and Beyond.* Chapel Hill: University of North Carolina Press, 1994.

———, ed. *The Spotsylvania Campaign.* Chapel Hill: University of North Carolina Press, 1998.

———, ed. *Three Days at Gettysburg.* Kent, Ohio: Kent State University Press, 1999.

———, ed. *The Wilderness Campaign.* Chapel Hill: University of North Carolina Press, 1997.

Garrison, Webb B. *Atlanta and the War.* Nashville, Tenn.: Rutledge Hill Press, 1995.

———. *Lincoln's Little War.* Nashville, Tenn.: Rutledge Hill Press, 1997.

Gindlesperger, James. *Seed Corn of the Confederacy: The Story of the Cadets of the Virginia Military Institute at the Battle of New Market.* Shippensburg, Pa.: Burd Street Press, 1997.

Gragg, Rod. *Confederate Goliath: The Battle of Fort Fisher.* New York: HarperCollins, 1991.

Greene, A. Wilson, and Gary. W. Gallagher. *National*

Geographic Guide to the Civil War National Battlefield Parks. Washington, D.C.: National Geographic Society, 1992.

Groom, Winston. *Shrouds of Glory: From Atlanta to Nashville: The Last Great Campaign of the Civil War.* New York: Atlantic Monthly Press, 1995.

Grunder, Charles S. *The Second Battle of Winchester, June 12–15, 1863.* Lynchburg, Va.: H. E. Howard, 1989.

Hafendorfer, Kenneth A. *Perryville: Battle for Kentucky.* Louisville, Ky.: KH Press, 1991.

Hamilton, James J. *The Battle of Fort Donelson.* South Brunswick, N.J.: T. Yoseloff, 1968.

Hamlin, Augustus C. *The Attack of Stonewall Jackson at Chancellorsville.* Fredericksburg, Va.: Sergeant Kirkland's, 1997.

Hankinson, Alan. *First Bull Run, 1861: The South's First Victory.* London: Osprey, 1991.

Harrison, Noel Garraux. *Chancellorsville Battlefield Sites.* Lynchburg, Va.: H. E. Howard, 1990.

Hartwig, D. Scott, ed. *The Battle of Antietam and the Maryland Campaign of 1862: A Bibliography.* Westport, Conn.: Meckler, 1990.

Hassler, Warren W. *Crisis at the Crossroads: The First Day at Gettysburg.* Tuscaloosa, Ala.: University of Alabama Press, 1970.

Hastings, Earl C. *A Pitiless Rain: The Battle of Williamsburg, 1862.* Shippensburg, Pa.: White Mane, 1997.

Hearn, Chester G. *The Capture of New Orleans, 1862.* Baton Rouge: Louisiana State University Press, 1995.

———. *Mobile Bay and the Mobile Campaign: The Last Great Battles of the Civil War.* Jefferson, N.C.: McFarland, 1993.

Henderson, William D. *The Road to Bristoe Station: Campaigning with Lee and Meade, August 1–October 20, 1863.* 2d ed. Lynchburg, Va.: H. E. Howard, 1987.

Hendrickson, Robert. *Sumter, The First Day of the Civil War.* Chelsea, Mich.: Scarborough House, 1990.

Hennessy, John. *The First Battle of Manassas: An End to Innocence July 18–21, 1861.* Lynchburg, Va.: H. E. Howard, 1989.

Hodgkins, William Henry. *The Battle of Fort Stedman (Petersburg, Virginia) March 25, 1865.* Boston: author, 1889.

Hoffmann, John. *The Confederate Collapse at the Battle of Missionary Ridge. The Reports of James Patton Anderson and His Brigade Commanders . . .* Dayton,

Ohio: Morningside, 1985.

Hopkins, Garland Evans. *The First Battle of Modern Naval History.* Richmond, Va.: House of Dietz, 1943.

Horn, John. *The Destruction of the Weldon Railroad, Deep Bottom, Globe Tavern, and Reams Station, August 14–25, 1864.* Lynchburg, Va.: H. E. Howard, Inc., 1991.

———. *The Petersburg Campaign: June 1864–April 1865.* Conshohocken, Pa.: Combined Books, 1993.

Horn, Stanley Fitzgerald. *The Decisive Battle of Nashville.* Baton Rouge: Louisiana State University Press, 1956.

Howe, Barbara J. "The Civil War at Bulltown." *West Virginia History* 44, no. 1 (1982): 1–40.

Howell, H. Grady. *Hills of Death: The Battle of Champion Hill.* Madison, Miss.: Chickasaw Bayou Press, 1993.

Hughes, Nathaniel Cheairs, Jr. *The Battle of Belmont: Grant Strikes South.* Chapel Hill: University of North Carolina Press, 1991.

———. *Bentonville: The Final Battle of Sherman and Johnston.* Chapel Hill: University of North Carolina Press, 1996.

Huske, Benjamin R. (Walter Brown, Jr., ed.). "More Terrible than Victory." *Civil War Times Illustrated* 20, no. 6 (1981): 28–31.

Jaynes, Gregory. *The Killing Ground: Wilderness to Cold Harbor.* Alexandria, Va.: Time-Life Books, 1986.

Johnson, Curt, and Mark McLaughlin. *Civil War Battles.* New York: Fairfax Press, 1977.

Johnson, Ludwell H. *The Red River Campaign: Politics and Cotton in the Civil War.* Kent, Ohio: Kent State University Press, 1993.

Johnson, Robert Underwood, and Clarence Clough, eds. *Battles and Leaders of the Civil War.* 4 vols. New York: Century, 1887.

Johnson, R. M. *Bull Run: Its Strategy and Tactics.* Boston: Houghton Mifflin, 1913.

Josephy, Alvin M., Jr. *The Civil War in the American West.* New York: Alfred A. Knopf, 1992.

Kelly, Dennis. *Kennesaw Mountain and the Atlanta Campaign: A Tour Guide.* Marietta, Ga.: Kennesaw Mountain Historical Association, 1990.

Kennedy, Francis H., ed. *The Civil War Battlefield Guide.* Boston: Houghton Mifflin, 1990.

Kennerly, Dan. *Forrest at Parker's Crossroads.* 6th ed. Houston, Tex.: D. Kennerly, 1993.

Kennett, Lee B. *Marching through Georgia: The Story of Soldiers and Civilians during Sherman's Campaign.* New York: HarperPerennial, 1996.

Key, William. *The Battle of Atlanta and the Georgia*

Campaign. New York: Twayne, 1958.

Kinard, Jeff. *The Battle of the Crater.* Fort Worth, Tex.: Ryan Place, 1995.

Kitchens, Ben Earl. *Rosecrans Meets Price: The Battle of Iuka, Mississippi.* Florence, Ala.: Thornwood Books, 1982.

Klein, Maury. *Days of Defiance: Sumter, Secession, and the Coming of the Civil War.* New York: Alfred A. Knopf, 1997.

Krick, Robert K. *Stonewall Jackson at Cedar Mountain.* Chapel Hill: University of North Carolina Press, 1990.

Lambert, D. Warren. *When the Ripe Pears Fell: The Battle of Richmond, Kentucky.* Richmond, Ky.: Madison County Historical Society, 1997.

Lewis, Thomas. *The Guns of Cedar Creek.* New York: Harper & Row, 1988.

Longacre, Edward G. "The First of Seven: A Battle at Oak Grove." *Civil War Times Illustrated* 25, no. 9 (1987): 10–19.

Luvaas, Jay, Stephen Bowman, and Leonard Fullenkamp, eds. *Guide to the Battle of Shiloh.* Lawrence: University Press of Kansas, 1996.

Lykes, Richard Wayne. *Campaign for Petersburg.* Washington, D.C.: U.S. National Parks Service, 1970.

Mahr, Theodore. *The Battle of Cedar Creek: Showdown in the Shenandoah, October 1–30, 1864.* 2d ed. Lynchburg, Va.: H. E. Howard, 1992.

Maney, R. Wayne. *Marching to Cold Harbor: Victory and Failure, 1864.* Shippensburg, Pa.: White Mane, 1995.

Martin, David G. *The Chancellorsville Campaign: March–May 1863.* Conshohocken, Pa.: Combined Books, 1991.

———. *The Second Bull Run Campaign, July–August 1862.* Conshohocken, Pa.: Combined Books, 1997.

———. *The Shiloh Campaign, March–April, 1862.* Conshohocken, Pa.: Combined Books, 1996.

Matloff, Maurice, ed. *The Civil War: A Concise Military History of the War between the States, 1861–1865.* Washington, D.C.: Office of the Chief of Military History, U.S. Army, 1978.

Matter, William D. *If It Takes All Summer: The Battle of Spotsylvania.* Chapel Hill: University of North Carolina Press, 1988.

McCartney, Martha. *The Battle of Drewry's Bluff in Chesterfield County, Virginia: The Historical Background.* Harrisonburg, Va.: James Madison University Archaeological Research Center, 1988.

McDonald, JoAnna M. *The World Will Long Remember: A Guide to the Battle of Gettysburg.* Shippensburg, Pa.: White Mane, 1996.

McDonough, James L. *Shiloh: In Hell before Night.* Knoxville: University of Tennessee Press, 1977.

———. *Stones River: Bloody Winter in Tennessee.* Knoxville: University of Tennessee Press, 1990.

McDonough, James L., and Thomas L. Connelly. *Five Tragic Hours: The Battle of Franklin.* Knoxville: University of Tennessee Press, 1983.

McPherson, James M., ed. *The Atlas of the Civil War.* New York: Macmillan, 1994.

———. *Battle Cry of Freedom: The Civil War Era.* New York: Oxford University Press, 1988.

———. *Ordeal by Fire: The Civil War and Reconstruction.* 2d ed. New York: McGraw-Hill, 1992.

McWhiney, Grady. *Battle in the Wilderness: Grant Meets Lee.* Fort Worth, Tex.: Ryan Place, 1995.

Meredith, Roy. *Storm over Sumter: The Opening Engagement of the Civil War.* New York: Simon & Schuster, 1957.

Miles, Jim. *Fields of Glory: A History and Tour Guide of the Atlanta Campaign.* Nashville, Tenn.: Rutledge Hill Press, 1989.

Miller, J. Michael. *The North Anna Campaign: "Even to Hell Itself," May 21–26, 1864.* 2d ed. Lynchburg, Va.: H. E. Howard, 1989.

Mitchell, Joseph B. *Decisive Battles of the Civil War.* New York: G. P. Putnam, 1955.

Mokin, Arthur. *Ironclad: The Monitor and the Merrimack.* Novato, Calif.: Presidio, 1991.

Morris, George S. *Lynchburg in the Civil War: The City—the People—the Battle.* 2d ed. Lynchburg, Va.: H. E. Howard, 1984.

Murfin, James V. *The Gleam of Bayonets: The Battle of Antietam and Robert E. Lee's Maryland Campaign, September 1862.* Baton Rouge: Louisiana State University Press, 1965.

Musicant, Ivan. "Hot Pursuit Up the Sounds." *Proceedings* 122, no. 10 (1996): 68–72.

———. *The Naval History of the Civil War.* New York: HarperCollins, 1997.

Myers, Raymond E. *The Zollie Tree.* Louisville, Ky.: Filson Club Press, 1964.

Newton, Steven Harvey. *The Battle of Seven Pines, May 31–June 1, 1862.* Lynchburg, Va.: H. E. Howard, 1993.

Nulty, William H. *Confederate Florida: The Road to*

Olustee. Tuscaloosa: University of Alabama Press, 1990.

O'Reilly, Frank A. *"Stonewall" Jackson at Fredericksburg.* 2d ed. Lynchburg, Va.: H. E. Howard, 1993.

Panzer, Mary. *Matthew Brady and the Image of History.* Washington, D.C.: Smithsonian Institution Press, 1997.

Park, Hugh, ed. *Pea Ridge: The Place Where the South Lost the Civil War.* Van Buren, Ark.: Press-Argus, 1961.

Parker, Foxhall A. *The Battle of Mobile Bay: And the Capture of Forts Powell, Gaines, and Morgan.* Boston: A. Williams, 1878.

Patch, Joseph Dorst. *The Battle of Ball's Bluff.* Leesburg, Va.: Potomac Press, 1958.

Patterson, Gerard A. *Debris of Battle: The Wounded of Gettysburg.* Mechanicsburg, Pa.: Stackpole Books, 1997.

Peterson, Cyrus Asbury, and Joseph Mills Hanson. *Pilot Knob, the Thermopylae of the West.* Reprint ed. Cape Girardeau, Mo.: Ramfire Press, 1964.

Pfanz, Harry W. *Gettysburg: Culp's Hill and Cemetery Hill.* Chapel Hill: University of North Carolina Press, 1993.

———. *Gettysburg: The Second Day.* Chapel Hill: University of North Carolina Press, 1987.

Phillips, Herb. *Champion Hill!* Edwards, Miss.: Champion Hill Battlefield Foundation, 1984.

Plummer, Alonzo H. *Confederate Victory at Mansfield.* Mansfield, La.: United Daughters of the Confederacy, 1969.

Priest, John M. *Before Antietam: The Battle for South Mountain.* Shippensburg, Pa.: White Mane, 1992.

———. *Nowhere to Run.* Shippensburg, Pa.: White Mane, 1995.

———. *Victory without Triumph: The Wilderness, May 6th & 7th, 1864.* Shippensburg, Pa.: White Mane, 1996.

Reardon, Carol. *Pickett's Charge in History and Memory.* Chapel Hill: University of North Carolina Press, 1997.

Reese, Timothy J. "Gapland Turnpike: Ribbon of History." *Maryland Historical Magazine* 85, no. 1 (1990): 77–84.

Rhea, Gordon C. *The Battle of the Wilderness, May 5–6, 1864.* Baton Rouge: Louisiana State University Press, 1994.

———. *The Battles for Spotsylvania Court House and the Road to Yellow Tavern, May 7–12, 1864.* Baton

Rouge: Louisiana State University Press, 1997.

Roe, Alfred S. *Recollections of Monocacy.* Providence, R.I.: Society, 1885.

Rutherford, Phillip R. "Six Guns against the Fleet." *Civil War Times Illustrated* 29, no. 5 (1990): 28–30, 32–34, 36, 38, 40–42, 44–45, 48–49.

Scaife, William R. *Allatoona Pass: A Needless Effusion of Blood.* Atlanta: Etowah Valley Historical Society, 1995.

Schiller, Herbert H. *Sumter Is Avenged: The Siege and Reduction of Fort Pulaski.* Shippensburg, Pa.: White Mane, 1995.

Scott, Robert. *Glory, Glory, Gloryieta: The Gettysburg of the West.* Boulder, Colo.: Johnson Books, 1992.

Scott, Robert G. *Into the Wilderness with the Army of the Potomac.* Bloomington: Indiana University Press, 1985.

Sears, Stephen W. *Chancellorsville.* Boston: Houghton-Mifflin, 1996.

———. *Landscape Turned Red: The Battle of Antietam.* New Haven, Conn.: Ticknor & Fields, 1983.

Seaton, John. *The Battle of Belmont, November 7, 1861.* Leavenworth, Kans.: Military Order of the Loyal Legion of the United State, 1902.

Shea, William L. *Pea Ridge: Civil War Campaign in the West.* Chapel Hill: University of North Carolina Press, 1992.

———. *War in the West: Pea Ridge and Prairie Grove.* Fort Worth, Tex.: Ryan Place, 1996.

Sifakis, Stewart. *Who Was Who in the Civil War.* New York: Facts On File, 1988.

Smith, Gene A. *Iron and Heavy Guns: Duel between the Monitor and the Merrimac.* Fort Worth, Tex.: Ryan Place, 1996.

Sommers, Richard J. *Richmond Redeemed: The Siege at Petersburg.* Garden City, N.Y.: Doubleday, 1981.

Spedale, William A. *The Battle of Baton Rouge, 1862.* Baton Rouge, La.: Land and Land, 1985.

Stackpole, Edward J. *Chancellorsville: Lee's Greatest Battle.* 2d ed. Harrisburg, Pa.: Stackpole Books, 1988.

———. *Drama on the Rappahannock: The Fredericksburg Campaign.* 2d ed. Harrisburg, Pa.: Stackpole Books, 1962.

———. *From Cedar Mountain to Antietam, August–September, 1862.* Harrisburg, Pa.: Stackpole Books, 1959.

Stackpole, Edward J., and Wilbur Nye. *The Battle of Gettysburg: A Guided Tour.* Rev. ed. Mechanicsburg,

Pa.: Stackpole Books, 1988.

Steere, Edward. *The Wilderness Campaign.* Harrisburg, Pa.: Stackpole Books, 1960.

Still, William N., Jr. *The Confederate Navy: The Ships, Men and Organization, 1861–1865.* Annapolis, Md.: Naval Institute Press, 1997.

Stockdale, Paul H. *The Death of an Army: The Battle of Nashville and Hood's Retreat.* Murfreesboro, Tenn.: Southern Heritage Press, 1992.

Stutler, Boyd B. "The Civil War in West Virginia." *West Virginia History* 47 (1988): 29–38.

Sutherland, Daniel E. *The Emergence of Total War.* Fort Worth, Tex.: Ryan Place, 1996.

Swanburg, W. A. *First Blood: The Story of Fort Sumter.* New York: Charles Scribner's Sons, 1957.

Swank, Walbrook D. *The Battle of Trevilian Station: The Civil War's Greatest and Bloodiest All Cavalry Battle, with Eyewitness Memoirs.* Shippensburg, Pa.: Burd Street Press, 1994.

Sword, Wiley. *Embrace an Angry Wind: The Confederacy's Last Hurrah: Spring Hill, Franklin, and Nashville.* New York: HarperCollins, 1991.

———. *Shiloh: Bloody April.* New York: William Morrow, 1974.

Symonds, Craig L. *Stonewall of the West: Patrick Cleburne and the Civil War.* Lawrence: University Press of Kansas, 1997.

Symonds, Craig L., and William J. Clipson. *Gettysburg: A Battlefield Atlas.* Baltimore: Nautical and Aviation, 1992.

———. *A Battlefield Atlas of the Civil War.* 3d ed. Baltimore: Nautical and Aviation, 1994.

Tapp, Hamilton. *The Confederate Invasion of Kentucky, 1862, and the Battle of Perryville, October 8, 1862.* Lexington, Ky.: n.p., 1962.

Time-Life Staff. *Lee Takes Command: From Seven Days to Second Bull Run.* Alexandria, Va.: Time-Life Books, 1984.

Tolbert, Frank X. *Dick Dowling at Sabine Pass.* New York: McGraw-Hill, 1962.

Toomey, Daniel Carroll. *The Civil War in Maryland.* Baltimore: Toomey Press, 1983.

Trudeau, Noah Andre. *Bloody Roads South: The Wilderness to Cold Harbor, May–June 1864.* Boston: Little, Brown, 1989.

———. *The Last Citadel: Petersburg, Virginia, June 1864–April 1865.* Boston: Little, Brown, 1991.

Tsouras, Peter G. *Gettysburg: An Alternate History.* Mechanicsburg, Pa.: Stackpole Books, 1997.

Tucker, Glenn. *The Battle of Chickamauga.* New York: Eastern Acorn Press, 1969.

Tucker, Phillip T. "Disaster at Big Black River" *Journal of America's Military Past* 19, no. 1 (1992): 85–95.

Warner, Ezra. *Generals in Blue: Lives of the Union Commanders.* Baton Rouge: Louisiana State University Press, 1964.

———. *Generals in Gray: Lives of the Confederate Commanders.* Baton Rouge: Louisiana State University, 1959.

Wert, Jeffrey. "The Old Killing Ground: The Second Battle of Kernstown, 1864." *Civil War Times Illustrated* 23, no. 6 (1984): 40–47.

Wertz, Jay, and Edwin C. Bearss. *Smithsonian's Great Battles & Battlefields of the Civil War.* New York: William Morrow, 1997.

Whan, Vorin E. *Fiasco at Fredericksburg.* University Park: Pennsylvania State University Press, 1961.

Wheeler, Richard. *Lee's Terrible Swift Sword: From Antietam to Chancellorsville: An Eyewitness History.* New York: HarperCollins, 1992.

———. *A Rising Thunder: From Lincoln's Election to the Battle of Bull Run: An Eyewitness History.* New York: HarperCollins, 1994.

White, William Chapman, and Ruth White. *Tin Can on a Shingle.* New York: E. P. Dutton, 1957.

Whitehorne, Joseph W. A. *The Battle of New Market: Self-Guided Tour.* Washington, D.C.: U.S. Army Center of Military History, 1988.

———. *The Battle of Cedar Creek: Self-Guided Tour.* Washington, D.C.: U.S. Army Center of Military History, 1992.

———. *The Battle of Second Manassas: Self-Guided Tour.* Washington, D.C.: U.S. Army Center of Military History, 1990.

Wilkerson, JoAnn B. *400 Days to Perryville.* Perryville, Ky.: Perryville Battlefield Development Association, 1970.

Wise, Stephen R. *Gate of Hell: Campaign for Charleston Harbor, 1863.* Columbia: University of South Carolina Press, 1994.

Worthington, Glenn H. *Fighting for Time: The Battle That Saved Washington.* Rev. ed. Shippensburg, Pa.: White Mane, 1988.

Wright, Howard C. *Port Hudson: Its History from an Interior Point of View,* 1862. Baton Rouge, La.: Eagle Press, 1978.

Zinn, Jack. *R. E. Lee's Cheat Mountain Campaign.* Parsons, W. Va.: McClain, 1974.

OTHER WARS

Cabello-Argandoña, Roberto. *Cinco de Mayo: A Symbol of Mexican National Resistance.* Encino, Calif.: Floricanto Press, 1997.

The Canadian Encyclopedia. 2d ed. Edmonton: Hurtig, 1988.

Caruso, John Anthony. *The Liberators of Mexico.* Gloucester, Mass.: Peter Smith, 1967.

Clark, William. "In Search of Pancho Villa." *Palacio* 97, no. 3 (1992): 20–23, 47–54.

Cumberland, Charles C. *Mexican Revolution: The Constitutionalist Years.* Austin: University of Texas Press, 1972.

Davis, William C. *Three Roads to the Alamo: The Lives and Fortunes of David Crockett, James Bowie, and William Barret Travis.* New York: HarperCollins, 1998.

Denison, George T. *History of the Fenian Raid on Fort Erie; With an Account of the Battle of Ridgeway.* Toronto: Rollo & Adam, 1866.

Eisenhower, John D. *Intervention! The United States and the Mexican Revolution, 1913–1917.* New York: W. W. Norton, 1993.

Fitch, William Edward. *The Battle of Alamance.* Burlington, N.C.: Alamance Battle Ground Commission, 1939.

Hamill, Hugh M., Jr. *The Hidalgo Revolt: Prelude to Mexican Independence.* Gainesville: University of Florida Press, 1966.

Hardin, Stephen L. *Texian Iliad: A Military History of the Texas Revolution.* Austin: University of Texas Press, 1997.

Haultain, Arnold. *A History of Riel's Second Rebellion and How It Was Quelled.* Toronto: Grip, 1885.

Hildebrandt, Walter. *The Battle of Batoche: British Small Warfare and the Entrenched Métis.* Rev. ed. Ottawa: National Historic Parks and Sites, 1986.

Huffines, Alan C. *The Alamo: An Illustrated Micro History of the Siege and Battle as Told by the Participants and Eye-Witnesses February 23–March 6, 1836.* Austin, Tex.: Eakin Press, 1997.

Huneycutt, C. D. *The Alamo: An In-Depth Study of the Battle.* New London, N.C.: Gold Star Press, 1986.

Kemp, Louis Wiltz, and Ed Kilman. *The Battle of San Jacinto and the San Jacinto Campaign.* Houston, Tex.: n.p. 1947.

Lisiansky, Yuri. *Voyage around the World in the Years 1804,* *1805, and 1806.* New York: DaCapo Press, 1968.

MacDonald, John A. *Turbulous Times in Canada: A History of the Fenian Raids of 1866 and 1870.* Toronto: W. S. Johnston, 1910.

Middlekauff, Robert, ed. *Bacon's Rebellion.* Chicago: Rand McNally, 1964.

Nelson, Paul David. *William Tryon and the Course of Empire: A Life in British Imperial Service.* Chapel Hill: University of North Carolina Press, 1990.

Pohl, James W. *The Battle of San Jacinto.* Austin: Texas State Historical Association, 1989.

Powell, William, James K. Huhta, and Thomas J. Farnham, eds. *The Regulators in North Carolina: A Documentary History, 1759–1776.* Raleigh, N.C.: State Dept. of Archives and History, 1971.

Pruett, Jakie L. *Goliad Massacre: A Tragedy of the Texas Revolution.* Austin, Tex.: Eakin Press, 1985.

Roell, Craig H. *Remember Goliad! A History of La Bahia.* Austin: Texas State Historical Association, 1994.

Ryan, James W. *Camerone: The French Foreign Legion's Greatest Battle.* Westport, Conn.: Praeger, 1996.

Senior, Hereward. *The Fenians and Canada.* Toronto: Macmillan, 1978.

Smyser, Craig. "The Columbus Raid." *Southwest Review* 68. no. 1 (1983): 78–84.

Stanley, George. *The Birth of Western Canada: A History of the Riel Rebellion.* London: Longmans Green, 1936.

Steele, Rollin M. *The Lost Battle of the Alamance, also Known as the Battle of Clapp's Mill.* n.p.: n.p., 1993.

Szatmary, David. *Shays's Rebellion: The Making of an Agrarian Insurrection.* Amherst: University of Massachusetts Press, 1980.

Tolbert, Frank X. *The Day of San Jacinto.* Reprint ed. Austin, Tex.: Pemberton Press, 1969.

Viramontes de Marin, Maria C. *Cinco de Mayo: A Review of the Battle of Puebla.* 2d ed. San Diego, Calif.: Marin, 1994.

Webb, Stephen Saunders. *1676, The End of American Independence.* Reprint ed. Syracuse, N.Y.: Syracuse University Press, 1995.

Wertenbaker, Thomas Jefferson. *Torchbearer of the Revolution: The Story of Bacon's Rebellion and Its Leader.* Princeton, N.J.: Princeton University Press, 1940

INDEX

Page numbers in **boldface** indicate main articles. Page numbers followed by *m* indicate maps. Page numbers followed by *g* indicate glossary entries.

A

abatis 305*g*
Abercromby, James
　Fort Frontenac 100
　Fort Ticonderoga 112
Abercromby, Robert
　Petersburg 212
　Yorktown 304
Aburto, Juan 223
Acadia 6–7, 94, 95, 96, 220
Acland, John 252, 253
acoustic shadow 149, 212
Actaeon 58
Active 58
Adobe Walls **3–4**
African-American soldiers 80
　Fort Pillow 107–8
　Fort Wagner 115, 116
　New Orleans 194
　Port Hudson 219
Agua Prieta, 4
Alabama
　Emuckfau Creek 85–86
　Enitachopco Creek 86
　Fort Mims 85, 86, 105, 270
　Horseshoe Bend 146–47, 146m
　Mobile Bay 178–79
　Talladega 269–70
　Tallasahatchee 269, 270
Alamance, **4–5**
Alamo, **5**, 133, 246

Alaska, Battle of Sitka in 259–60
Albany 94
Alden, Ichabod 63–64
Aleut 259
Alexander, William (Lord Stirling)
　Brandywine 30
　Long Island 168
　Monmouth 183
　Paulus Hook 209
Alfred, U.S.S., H.M.S. *Glasgow* v. **6**
Algonkin 169
Algonzanas, Tomas 45, 46
Allalimya Takanin (Looking Glass) 17, 23
Allatoona Pass, **6**, 11
Allcorn, John 270
Allen, Ethan 113, 186, 244
Allen, John 96
　Frenchtown 121
Allende, Ignacio de 42–43
Allen's Farm (Savage's Station), **253–54**
Alligator (Halpatter Tustenuggee) 82, 162
Alvarado, Pedro de 50
　La Noche Triste 198–99
　Tenochtitlán 272
Álvarez, Juan 179, 180
ambush 142, 152, 178, 197
American Horse 260

American Indians *See specific tribes*
Amherst, Jeffrey, Lord 41
　Louisbourg 170, 171
Ampudia, Pedro de 33, 46, 205
　Cerro Gordo 50
　Monterrey 185, 186
Anahotaha 169
Anaya, Pedro María 70
Anderson, George T. 126
Anderson, Richard H.
　North Anna River 200
　Sayler's Creek 256
Anderson, Robert 111, 112
Anderson, Samuel R. 63
André, John 245
Andres, Patrick 56
Andrews, T. P. 180
Angell, Israel 263
La Angostura 33
Annapolis Royal (Port Royal [King George's War]) **6–7**
Annapolis Royal (Port Royal [Queen Anne's War]) **220**
Antietam (Sharpsburg), **7–9**, 8*m*, 143
Appomattox Courthouse 90, 91, 213
Appomattox River 91
approaches 305*g*
Aquayo, Juan 284
Arapahoe 248
Arboosoff, Lieutenant 259

Arbuthnot, Marriot 59, 65
Arista, Ariano 46
　Palo Alto 205–6
　Resaca de la Palma 232, 233
Arizona 4
Arkansas
　Helena 144
　Pea Ridge 209–10
　Prairie Grove 221–22
Arkansas 16
Armistead, George 103
Armistead, Lewis
　Gettysburg 130
　Malvern Hill 174
armistice 305*g*
Armstrong, John 30, 69, 214
　Chateaugay 60–61
　Harmar's Defeat 142
Armstrong, William 25
army 305g
　reorganization of 89
Army of Georgia 21
Army of Mississippi 211
　Atlanta 10
Army of Northern Virginia 71, 83, 175, 213
　Antietam 7–9
　Gaines's Mill 124–25
　Gettysburg 128, 130
　Malvern Hill 174
　Oak Grove 201
　Spotsylvania 261–62
　Wilderness 293–94

Army of Tennessee 66
    Atlanta 10–11
    Bentonville 21
    Nashville 190
    Stones River 264–65
Army of the Cumberland 66
    Atlanta 10–11
    Chattanooga 61, 63
    Stones River 264–65
Army of the James 83, 84
Army of the North 70, 75
Army of the Ohio 212
    Atlanta 10–11
Army of the Potomac 15, 37, 47, 79, 83, 88, 119, 125, 158, 175, 260
    Antietam 7–9
    Chattanooga 61
    Cold Harbor 71
    Fredericksburg 121
    Gaines's Mill 124–25
    Gettysburg 128
    Malvern Hill 174
    Oak Grove 201
    Spotsylvania 261–62
    White Oak Swamp 292
    Wilderness 293–94
Army of the Valley 183
Army of Virginia 47
Arnold, Benedict 52, 65, 83, 113, 302
    Cedars 48
    Fort Stanwix 110
    New London Raid 191
    Petersburg 212
    Quebec 48, 226–28, 227m, 245, 274
    St. John's 244, 245
    Saratoga, First 251
    Saratoga, Second 253
    Valcour Island 282
Arpeika 162
Ashby, Turner 122
    Kernstown, First 153
Ashe, John 31
Ash Hollow (Blue Lake) 10
Atalaya 51
Atkinson, Henry 14
Atlanta 10–11
Atlanta, Ga. 66
Auger de Subercase, Daniel d' 220
Augur, Christopher C. 24
    Cedar Mountain 48
Augusta 104
Augusta, (September 14–18, 1780) 12
Augusta (May 22–June 5,

1781) 12–13
Ayers, Romeyn Beck 131
Aztec (Mexica) 49, 198, 204, 276, 277
    Tenochtitlán 270–73

B

Back Creek 71
Backus, Electus 185, 239
Bacon, Nathaniel 151
Bad Axe River 14–15
Bahamas 6
Baker, Edward 15
Balcarres, earl of 252, 253
Ball, John 25
Ball's Bluff 15
Baltimore, Md. 102–3
Baltimore & Ohio Railroad 143, 213
Banks, Nathaniel P. 47, 48, 122
    First Winchester 80
    Galveston 125
    Irish Bend 148
    Kernstown, First 153, 154
    Pleasant Hill Landing 216–17
    Port Hudson 218–19
    Sabine Crossroads 216, 237–38
    Winchester, First 296
Baranof, Alexander 259
Baratarians 192
Barclay, Robert H 159–60
Barnard, Moses 57
Barney, Joshua 26
Barrett, James 164
Barth Walback, John de 69
Bartow, Francis 35
bastion 305g
bateau 305g
Batoche 15–16
Baton Rouge 16
battalion 306g
battery 306g
Battery Wagner (Fort Wagner) 115–16
Baum, Friedrich 20–21
Baxter, Colonel 116, 117
Baynes, Edward 238, 239
Bayou Teche (Irish Bend) 148
Bear Hunter (Wirasuap) 17, 18
Bear Paw Mountains 17
Bear River 17–18
Beasley, Daniel 105

Beaufort 181
Beaufort (Port Royal Island) 18
Beaujeau, Daniel Hyacinthe-Marie Liénard de 184, 185
Beauregard, P. G. T.
    Bull Run, First 35, 36, 37
    Contreras 75
    Drewry's Bluff 83, 84
    Fort Sumter 111
    Petersburg 213
    Shiloh 257, 259
Beaver Dams 18–19
Bedel, Timothy 52
Bee, Bernard 35
Beecher, Frederick H. 19
Beecher's Island 19
Belknap, W. W. 167
Belmont 19–20
Bemis Heights (Second Battle of Saratoga) 251–53, 252m
Bennington 20–21, 20m
Benteen, Frederick W. 165, 167
Benton 176
Bentonville 21–22
Berkeley, William 151
Berra, Francisco de 186
Beverly's Ford (Brandy Station) 29
Big Bear 15
Big Bethel 22
Big Black River 22–23, 285
Big Foot (Si Tanka) 299
Big Hole Basin 23, 23m
Big Meadows 24
Big Sayler's Creek 256
Billingsport 24
Black Hawk (Ma-ka-ta-i-me-she-kia-kiak) 14–15
Black Hills 167, 235, 298
Black Kettle (Moketavato) 248, 290
Black Mingo Creek 24–25
black soldiers 80
    Fort Pillow 107–8
    Fort Wagner 115, 116
    New Orleans 194
    Port Hudson 219
Blackstocks 25
Black Watch (Forty-second Highlanders) 117, 141
Bladensburg 25–26
Blair's Landing (Pleasant Hill Landing) 216–17
blockade 306g

Block Island, U.S.S. Alfred v. H.M.S. Glasgow engagement at 6
Bloody Act 4
Bloody Angle 261
Bloody Brook (Pocumtuck, Deerfield) 26–27
Bloody Hill 295
Bloody Lane 9
Bloody Marsh (Bloody Swamp) 27
Bloody Pond (Lake George) 160–61
Bloody Swamp (Bloody Marsh, St. Simon's Island) 27
Blue Jacket (Weypapiersenwah) 89
Blue Lake (Ash Hollow) 10
Blue Licks 28
Blue Savannah 28
Blunt, James G. 222
Boerstler, Charles G. 18–19
Bohlen, Henry 81
Bolivar Heights 143
Bonham, Milledge 35
Booker, Alfred 234
Boone, Daniel 28
Booth, Lionel F. 107
Boscawen, Edward 170
Boston, Mass. 64
Boston Army 39
Bound Brook 28
Bouquet, Henry 41
Bowdoin, James, II 263
Bowen, John S. 23
    Port Gibson 218
Bowie, James 5
Boyd, Belle 122, 123
Boyd, Colonel 154–55
Boyd, John P. 18
    Chrysler's Farm 69
Bozeman Trail 91, 235
Brackett, Alfred E. 155
Braddock, Edward 106
    Monongahela 184–85
Braddock, James 161
Braddock's Defeat (Monongahela), 184–85
Bradford, William F. 107
Bradstreet, John 100–101
Bragg, Braxton 22, 76, 157
    Buena Vista 33, 34
    Chattanooga 61, 62, 63
    Chickamauga 66
    Fort Fisher 99, 100
    Monterrey 185
    Munfordville 187–88
    Perryville 211–12

Shiloh 257
Stones River 264–65
Branch, Lawrence O. 140
Brandy Station (Fleetwood Hill, Beverly's Ford) **29**
Brandywine **30–31**, 30*m*, 126, 293
Brant, Joseph (Thayendanegea) 167
Cherry Valley 63, 64
Minisink 178
Newtown 197
Oriskany 203
Queenston 229
Bravo, Nicholás 56, 70
breastwork 306*g*
Breckinridge, John C. 16
Kernstown, Second 154
Lynchburg 172
New Market 191–92
Shiloh 257
Stones River 264
Winchester, Third 297
Breed's Hill (Bunker Hill) **39–41**, 39*m*
Breese, K. R. 100
brevet 306*g*
Breymann, Heinrich 21
Saratoga, Second 253
Briar Creek **31**
Brice's Cross Roads (Brice's Creek Roads, Guntown, Tishomingo Creek) **31–32**, 32*m*
brigade 306*g*
Brigade of Guards 302
Bristoe Station 32–33
Bristol 58
British Legion 78
Blackstocks 25
Camden 44
Fishdam Ford 91
Gloucester 132
Green Spring 135
Hanging Rock 139, 140
Haw River 144
Monck's Corner 180
Waxhaws 290
Wetzell's Ford 291
Williamson's Plantation 295
Yorktown 302
broadside 306*g*
Brock, Isaac 229
Broke, Philip 64
Bronx River 292
Brooke, Arthur 103
Brooklyn Heights 168
Brower, Charles B. 57

Brown, Frederick H. 91
Brown, Jacob 46, 99
Chippewa 67–68, 69
Chrysler's Farm 69
Lundy's Lane 171, 172
Sackets Harbor 239
Brown, John 52, 186
Fort Keyser 102
Fort Ticonderoga 115
Brown, Thomas Storrow 242, 243
Brown, William F. 122
Browne, Thomas
Augusta 12–13
Hanging Rock 139
Brownstown 122
Bryan, Morgan 140
Bryan's Station 28
Buchanan, Franklin
Mobile Bay 178, 179
U.S.S. *Monitor* v. C.S.S. *Virginia* 181
Buchanan, James 111
Buckner, Simon Bolivar 98
Munfordville 188
Buell, Don Carlos 257
Perryville 212, 264
Buena Vista **33–35**, 34*m*
Buffalo Hump (Pochanaw-quoip) 236
Buffalo Soldiers 19, 177, 306*g*
Buffington, Samuel 263
Buford, Abraham
Lenud's Ferry 162, 163
Waxhaws 290–91
Buford, John
Brandy Station 29
Falling Waters 90
Gettysburg 128
Bull Bear 19
Bull Run 55
Bull Run, First (First Manassas) **35–37**, 36*m*, 38
Bull Run, Second (Second Manassas) **37–38**, 38*m*, 55, 56
Bull's Ferry **38–39**
Bunker Hill (Breed's Hill) **39–41**, 39*m*
Burgoyne, John 20, 21, 48, 94, 203
Bunker Hill 39, 40
Fort Clinton and Fort Montgomery 95–96
Fort Stanwix 109–10
Fort Ticonderoga 113, 115, 147

Saratoga, First 96, 250–51
Saratoga, Second 251–53
Three Rivers 274
Burke, Thomas 144
Burlington Heights 266
Burn, James 266
Burning, the 46–47, 92
Burnside, Ambrose 54
Antietam 9
Crater 80
Fredericksburg 119–21
Knoxville 157–58
North Anna River 200
Roanoke Island 234–35
South Mountain 260
Burrell, I. S. 125
Bushy Run (Edge Hill), Battle of **41**
Butler, Benjamin F.
Big Bethel 22
Drewry's Bluff 83–84
Fort Fisher 99
New Orleans 194, 195
Butler, John 63
Guilford Courthouse 136
Hillsborough Raid 144
Newtown 197
Wyoming Valley 299–300
Butler, Richard
St. Clair's Defeat 243
Spencer's Tavern 261
Stony Point 267
Butler, Walter
Cherry Valley 63, 64
Newtown 197
Butler, Zebulon 300
Butler's Rangers 249
Butterfield, Isaac 48
Buttrick, John 164

C

Cadwalader, George 70
Contreras 75
Molino del Rey 179
Cadwalader, John
Princeton 222
Trenton 277
Cadwalader, Lambert 116, 117
Cairo 176
Cajuns 6
Calderón Bridge (Puente de Calderón) **42–43**
Caldwell, John 32
Caldwell, William 248–49

California 57
Mesa 176
San Gabriel 245–46
San Pascual 247–48
Stronghold 267–68
Calleja del Rey, Félix María 42–43
Callender, Franklin D. 75
Calles, Plutarco 4
Camden **43–46**, 43*m*, 134, 139
Camden, South Carolina 235
Cameron, Robert A. 238
Camerone **45–46**
Campbell, Archibald 254
Campbell, Arthur 156
Campbell, John
Fort Clinton and Fort Montgomery 96
Moore's Creek Bridge 187
Pensacola 211
Campbell, Richard 198
Campbell, William 58
King's Mountain 156
Campbell's Station 158
Camp Texas (Fort Texas) **46**, 205
Canada
Annapolis Royal 6–7
Batoche 15–16
Beaver Dams 18–19
Cedars 48
Chambly 52
Chateaugay 60–61, 69
Chippewa 67–69, 68*m*
Chrysler's Farm 61, 69–70
U.S.S. *Constitution* v. H.M.S. *Guerrière* 74, 74*m*
Fort Beauséjour 94–95, 96
Fort Cumberland 96–97
Fort Erie 67, 98–99
Fort Frontenac 100–101
Fort George 101, 238
Long Sault 169
Louisbourg 169–71
Lundy's Lane 171–72, 171*m*
Mackinac Island 173
Montreal 60, 61, 69, 169, 286, 245, 274
Port Royal 220
Quebec 48, 226–28, 227*m*
Queenston 228–29

Ridgeway 234
St. Charles 242, 243, 244
St. Denis 242, 243–44
St. Eustache 242, 244
St. John's 52, 186, 244–45
Stony Creek 101, 266–67
Thames 273–74
Three Rivers 274
Canby, Edward 268
Cane Hill 222
canister 306g
Cannon, Newton 270
Canonchet 135
Cape Breton Island 169
Captain Jack (Kintpuash) 268
Carden, John 139, 140
Carleton 282, 283
Carleton, Guy 48, 186, 274
Quebec 228
St. John's 245
Valcour Island 282–83
Carney, William H. 116
Carolina 12, 240–41
Caroline 192
Carondelet 149, 176
Carothers, George 4
Carpenter, Louis 19
Carr, Eugene A. 268
Carranza, Venustiano 4, 48, 49, 208
Columbus 72, 73
Carrick's Ford 233
Carrington, Henry B. 91
Carson, Kit 247
Casa Mata 179, 180
Casey, Silas 56–57
Castillo de San Marcos 240, 241
Caswell, Richard 187
Catawba 184
Catawba Ford (Fishing Creek) 92–93, 134
Catawba River 270
Caughnawaga 18
causeway 306g
cavalry 301, 302, 306g
Cayuga *See also* Iroquoi 300
Cedar Creek 46–47
Cedar Mountain 47–48
Cedars 48
Celaya 48–49, 72
Cemetery Hill 128, 130
Cemetery Ridge 128, 130

Cempoallan 49–50
Cerro Gordo 50–52, 51m
Cetan Wakan Mani (Little Crow) 109, 195
Chadd's Ford 30, 31
Chalmers, James R.
Fort Pillow 107
Munfordville 187
Chamberlain, Joshua 130
Chambly 52
Champion's Hill 52–53, 285
Champoton 53
Chancellorsville 54–55, 54m
Chandler, John 266
Chantilly (Ox Hill) 38, 55–56, 55m
Chapultepec 179, 272
Chapultepec 56–57, 223
Charleston (Sullivan's Island; June 28, 1776) 57–59
Charleston (April 1–May 12, 1780) 59–60, 290
Charleston, S.C. 73, 115, 162, 180, 266
Charleston Bay 111
Charlestown, Mass. 39–41
Charlotte 60
Charlottesville 278
Chateaugay (Châteauguay River) 60–61, 69
Chattanooga (Lookout Mountain, Missionary Ridge) 61–63, 66
Chattanooga, Tenn. 264, 279
Chatterton's Hill 292
Chauncey, Isaac 171
Fort George 101, 238
Lake Erie 159
Chauncey, Woolcott 239
Cheat Mountain (Elkwater), 63
Cheatam, Benjamin 212
Chénier, Jean-Olivier 244
Cherokee 184, 209, 243, 270
Cherry Valley 63–64
Chesapeake, U.S.S., H.M.S. *Shannon* v 64
Chesapeake Bay 25
Chesapeake Bay 64–65
Chesapeake Capes 65
Chesapeake & Ohio Canal 143
chevaux-de-frise 306g
Chew, Benjamin 126–27
Cheyenne

Dog Soldiers 19, 268
Fetterman Fight 91
Julesburg 152
Little Bighorn 165–67
Sand Creek 152, 248, 290
Washita 290
Wolf Mountain 298
Cheyenne River Reservation 299
Chickahominy River 88, 124, 261, 292
Chickamauga 62, 66–67
Chickasaw 89, 270
Chickasaw 178, 179
Chickasaw Bluffs (Chickasaw Bayou) 67
Chignecto Isthmus 95
Chihuahua 239, 240
Childs, Thomas 223
Chippewa 15, 243
Chippewa 67–69, 68m
Chivington, John 132
Sand Creek 248
Choctaw 89, 270
Choisy, marquis de 132
Christianity 249
Chrysler's Farm 61, 69–70
Chrystie, John 229
Chub 216
Churchill, Thomas J. 217
Churubusco 70–71, 74, 75
Cincinnati, Ohio 233
Cinco de Mayo (Puebla) 224–25
citadel 306g
Clark, George Rogers 167
Vincennes 287–88
Clark, Jonathan 208
Clarke, Elijah 25
Augusta 12
Clarke, N. S. 70
Clarke, Newman 57
Cleburne, Patrick 11
Richmond 233
Cleveland, Benjamin 156
Clinch, Duncan 82
Clinton, George 96
Clinton, Henry 44, 162, 180, 182, 183
Bunker Hill 39, 40
Charleston 57–58, 59, 60
Fort Clinton and Fort Montgomery 95–96
Long Island 168
Newport 196
Saratoga, Second 251, 253

Savannah 255
Springfield 262, 263
Stony Point 267
Waxhaws 290
Clinton, James 96
Cloyd's Mountain 71
Cluseret, Gustave P. 81
Coachoochee (Wild Cat) 162
Coates, John 230
Cochrane, Alexander 25
Fort McHenry 102, 103
New Orleans 192, 193
Cockrell, Francis M. 52
Port Gibson 218
Cockspur Island 108
Cody, William "Buffalo Bill" 268
Coffee, John
Emuckfau Creek 85–86
Horseshoe Bend 146
Tallasahatchee 269, 270
Coffin, John 87
Colbourne, John 244
Cold Harbor 71–72, 72m, 213
Coldstream Guards 77
College of William and Mary 295
Colorado
Beecher's Island 19
Julesburg 152
Milk Creek 176–77
Sand Creek 152, 248, 290
Summit Springs 268
Colorado Third Volunteers 248
Colquitt, Alfred 202
Columbus (N.Mex.) 49, 72–73, 208
Columbus, Ky. 19
column 306g
Comanche 3, 236
Combahee Ferry 73
Commisary Hill 218
company 306g
Compos, Sabastian I. 46
Concord and Lexington 113, 163–64, 163m
Condé, Pedro Garcia 240
Confederate Trans-Mississippi Department 237
Confiance 216
Congress 181, 283
Congress, U.S. 89
Congress, U.S.S., H.M.S. *Savage* v. 73

Congreve rockets 26, 306*g*
Connecticut 299
  Danbury Raid 82–83
  Mystic River 188–89
  New London Raid 191
Conner, David 284
Connor, Patrick E. 17–18
Conquering Bear
  (Mahtoiowa) 10
Conrad's Mill 63
Constitution, U.S. 264
Constitution, U.S.S., H.M.S.
  Guerrière v. **74**, 74*m*
Constitutionalists 48, 49
Contreras (Padierna) 70,
  74–75
Conventionists 48, 49
Conway, Thomas 126
Cooch's Bridge (Iron Hill),
  75–76
Cooke, John Rogers 32
Cooper River 180
Corinth **76**
Corinth, Miss. 149, 257,
  259
Cornstalk (Wynepuechsika)
  217
Cornwallis, Charles, Lord
  25, 59, 77, 92, 143–44,
  144, 231, 261, 277, 278,
  291
  Bound Brook 28
  Brandywine 30, 31
  Camden 44, 45
  Charlotte 60
  Cooch's Bridge 76
  Cowan's Ford 76–77,
    270
  Fishdam Ford 91, 92
  Fort Lee 102
  Fort Washington 117
  Germantown 126, 128
  Green Spring 135–36
  Guilford Courthouse
    136–37
  Hobkirk's Hill 145
  King's Mountain 155,
    156
  Monmouth 182
  New London Raid 191
  Princeton 222–23
  Tarrant's Tavern 270
  Wahab's Plantation 289
  Waxhaws 290
  Yorktown 65, 73, 132,
    302–4
corps 306*g*
Corse, John M. 6
Corse, Montgomery 93

Cortés, Hernán
  Cempoallan 49–50
  La Noche Triste 198–99
  Otumba 203–4
  Potonchan 221
  Tenochtitlán 270–73
  Tlaxcala 276–77
Cós, Martin Perfecto de 5
Cotaxtla Squadron 45
cottonclads 125, 307*g*
Coulon de Villiers, Joseph,
  sieur de Jumonville 106
Coulon de Villiers, Louis
  106
Coulthard, John 279
Cowan's Ford **76–77**, 270
Cowpens **77–78**, 77*m*, 136
Cox, Jacob D. 260
Crampton's Gap **79**, 79*m*
Crater (Petersburg Mine
  Assault) **79–80**
Craven, Tunis A. M. 179
Crawford, Samuel W.
  Cedar Mountain 48
  Globe Tavern 131
Crawford, William 248–49
Crawford's Defeat
  (Sandusky) **248–49**
Crazy Horse (Ta-sunko-
  witko; Tashunka Witco)
  165, 167
  Fetterman Fight 91
  Rosebud Creek 235–36
  Slim Buttes 260
  Wolf Mountain 298
Cree 15
Creek 12
  Emuckfau Creek 85–86
  Fort Mims 85, 86, 105
  Horseshoe Bend 146
  Talladega 269
  Tallasahatchee 270
Crittenden, George 177,
  178
Crittenden, Thomas L. 66
  Perryville 212
Crittenden Lane 48
Crocker, Frederick 238
Crocker, Marcellus 53
Crockett, Davy 5
Croghan, George 173
Crook, George A.
  Little Bighorn 165
  Rosebud Creek 235
  Slim Buttes 260
Crook, George R. 47, 71
  Farmville and
    Highbridge 91
  Fisher's Hill 92

Kernstown, Second 154,
  297
Cross Keys (Union Church),
  Battle of **80–81**, 219
Crow 17, 235
Crown Point (Fort Frédéric)
  160–61
Cruft, Charles 233–34
Cruger, John 197, 198
Crump's Landing 257
Cuauhtémoc 272
Cuba 49
Cuitláhuac 204
Culpeper County, Va. 29,
  47–48
Cumberland 181
Cumberland Church 91
Cumberland Gap 177, 178
Cumberland River 97
Curtis, Newton 99–100
Curtis, Samuel 209, 210
Custer, George Armstrong
  Cedar Creek 47
  Five Forks 93
  Little Bighorn 165–67,
    236, 260
  Sayler's Creek 256
  Trevilian Station 278
  Washita 290
  Waynesboro 291
  Yellow Tavern 301
Custer's Last Stand
  (Little Bighorn)
  165–67, 166*m*, 236,
  260

D

Dacres, James 74
Dade, Francis 82
Dade's Battle **82**
Dakota 91, 109, 152, 235,
  299 *see also* Sioux
  New Ulm 195
  Wood Lake 298
Dale, Richard 279
Dalton, Ga. 11
Dan River 291
Danbury Raid **82–83**
Daniels, Robert 240
Danjou, Jean 45, 46
Darke, William 243
Davidson, William 76, 77
Davie, William
  Charlotte 60
  Hanging Rock 139
  Wahab's Plantation 289
Davis, Benjamin F.
  "Grimes" 29
  Harpers Ferry 143

Davis, Charles H. 176
Davis, Jefferson 11, 14, 33,
  61, 63, 110, 294
  Monterrey 186
Dawes, William 163
Dayton, Elias 262–63
Dearborn, Henry 19
  Fort George 101
  Sackets Harbor 239
  Stony Creek 266, 267
Debartzch, Pierre 242, 243
Deep Run (Franklin's
  Crossing) **119**
Deerfield (Bloody Brook)
  26–27
"Defence of Fort M'Henry"
  (Key) 103
Degataga (Stand Watie)
  209
De Kalb, Johann 43, 44
De la Place, William 113
Delaware
  Cooch's Bridge 75–76
  U.S.S. *Trumbull* v.
    H.M.S. *Iris* 279
Delaware Continentals 145
Delaware Indians *see* Lenni
  Lenape
Delaware Prophet (Neolin)
  41
Delaware River 24, 103,
  104, 277, 278
demonstration 307*g*
Dennis, Elias 232
Dennis, James 229
deployment 307*g*
Destouches, Charles,
  chevalier 65
Detroit 159, 160
Detroit, Mich. 121, 122,
  228, 273, 287
Deux-Ponts, Guillaume
  304
Devin, Thomas
  Sayler's Creek 256
  Yellow Tavern 301
Díaz, Porfirio 224
Dickinson, Philemon 263
Dieskau, Jean-Armand de
  161
Dimick, Justin 75
Dinwiddie, Robert 106
division 307*g*
Dodge, Francis 177
Dodge, Henry 15
Dollard, Adam, sieur des
  Ormeaux 169
Domeco Jaruta, Calendonio
  223

Doniphan, Alexander W. 239, 240
Donnelly, Dudley 296
Doubleday, Abner 112
Douglas, William 157
Douty, Jacob 80
Dowling, Richard 238
Downie, George 216
Dragoon Redoubt 21
dragoons 307g
Dragoons of Spain 43
Drewry's Bluff **83–84**
Drum, Simon H. 179
Drummond, Gordon
    Fort Erie, First 98, 99
    Lundy's Lane 171, 172
Drummond, William 99
Duchambon de Vergor, Louis Dupont, sieur 94, 170
Ducharme, Dominique 18
Duffié, Alfred 29
Dumont, Gabriel 16
Dunbar, Thomas 185
Duncan, James
    Churubusco 70
    Molino del Rey 180
    Palo Alto 205, 206
Dundas, Thomas 132
Dunham, Cyrus 207
Dunmore 138
Dunmore, John Murray, Lord 133–34
    Gwynn Island 137–38
    Point Pleasant 217
Du Plessis, Thomas 103, 104
du Pont, Henry A. 154, 192
Du Pont, Samuel Francis 220–21
Duquesnel, Jean-Baptiste-Louis 7
Duvivier, François Du Pont 7

E

Eagle 216
Early, Jubal 55
    Cedar Creek 47
    Cedar Mountain 48
    Fisher's Hill 92
    Kernstown, Second 154, 297
    Lynchburg 172
    Monocacy 183–84
    Waynesboro 291
    Williamsburg 294–95
    Winchester, Second 296

Winchester, Third 297–98
earthen forts 285
earthworks 307g
Eaton, Pinketham 12
    Guilford Courthouse 136
Echeagaray, Miguel María 179–80
Eddy, Jonathan 96
Edge Hill (Bushy Run) **41**
Eighteenth Corps 213
Eighth Corps 92
Eighth U.S. Colored Regiment 202
Elbert, Samuel 31
Eleventh Corps 55
Eleventh Infantry 75, 180
Eleventh Massachusetts 147
Elkhorn Tavern (Pea Ridge) **209–10**
Elkwater (Cheat Mountain) **63**
Ellet, Charles 176
Elliot, L. Jesse Duncan 160
Elliott's Salient 80
Ellison's Mill (Mechanicsville) **175–76**
Emancipation Proclamation 9
Emory, William H. 238
Emparán, Colonel 43
Emuckfau Creek **85–86**
enfilade 307g
Enitachopco Creek **86**
Enterprise 282
envelopment 307g
Epervier, H.M.S., U.S.S. *Peacock* v. **210**
Ericsson, John 181
Erskine, William 83
Estaing, Charles, comte d' 195–96, 254–55
Euryalus 103
Eutaw Springs **86–87**, 87*m*
Evans, John 248
Evans, Nathan G. "Shanks" 15
    Bull Run, First 35
Ewell, Richard S. 29, 122
    Cross Keys 80–81, 219
    Gettysburg 128
    North Anna River 200
    Port Republic 219, 220
    Sayler's Creek 256
    Winchester, First 296
    Winchester, Second 296–97
Ewing, James 277

Ewing, Thomas 214
Eyre, Edmund 191

F

Fair Oaks (Seven Pines) **88–89**
Fallen Timbers **89–90**
Falling Waters **90**
Fannin, James Walker 133
Fanning, David 144–45
Farías, Valentin Gomez 284
Farmville and Highbridge **90–91**
Farragut, David G.
    Mobile Bay 178, 179
    New Orleans 194, 195
Febiger, Christian 267
Federal West Virginia Brigade 71
Feltham, Jocelyn 113
Fenians 234
Fenwick, John R. 229
Ferguson, Patrick
    Charleston 60
    King's Mountain 155–56
    Monck's Corner 180
Ferrero, Edward 80
Fetterman, William J. 91
Fetterman Fight **91**
Few, James 4
field gun, field artillery 307g
Fifteenth Alabama Volunteers 81
Fifth Cavalry 125, 268
Fifth Corps 124, 140, 175, 199, 201
Fifth Infantry 70, 298
Fifty-fourth Massachusetts 202
Fifty-second Regiment 96
Finch 216
Finegan, Joseph 202
firing step 307g
First Brigade 67
First California Cavalry 17
First Colorado Volunteers 131–32
First Corps 260
First Corps d'Afrique 219
First Louisiana Native Guards 219
First Maryland Continentals 145
First New Hampshire 197
First North Carolina Regiment of Continentals 187

First Pennsylvania Rifles 275
First Rhode Island Cavalry 123
First Winchester 80
Fishdam Ford **91–92**
Fisher, Victor 98
Fisher's Hill 47, **92**
Fishing Creek (Catawba Ford) **92–93**, 134
Fitzgibbon, James 18
Five Forks **93**
Flandrau, Charles 195
flank 307g
flank companies 307g
Fleetwood Hills (Brandy Station) **29**
Fleury, François de 267
Flon, Francisco 43
Flores, José María
    Mesa 176
    San Gabriel 245–46
Florida
    Dade's Battle 82
    Fort Caroline 95
    Lake Okeechobee 161–62
    Ocean Pond 202
    U.S.S. *Peacock* v. H.M.S. *Epervier* 210
    Pensacola 211
    St. Augustine 240–42, 241*m*
Flournoy, Thomas 122
Floyd, John B. 98
flying batteries 205, 206, 232, 307g
foot 307g
Foote, Andrew
    Fort Donelson 97, 98
    Fort Henry 101
    Island Number 10 149
Fordyce, Captain 134
Foreign Legion 45–46
Forey, Elie-Frédéric 45, 224
forlone hopes (suicide squads) 198, 209, 235, 267, 304, 307g
Forrest, Nathan Bedford 61, 202
    Brice's Cross Roads 31–32
    Fort Pillow 107–8
    Parker's Cross Roads 207
    Tupelo 279–80
Forsyth, George A. 19
Forsyth, James 299

Fort Abraham Lincoln 165
Fort Anne, Battle of **94**
Fort Beauregard (Port Royal Sound) **220–21**
Fort Beauséjour **94–95**, 96
Fort Brooke 82
Fort Carillon (Fort Ticonderoga; July 8, 1758) 100, **112–13**
Fort Caroline **95**
Fort Clinton and Fort Montgomery **95–96**
Fort Constitution (Fort Lee) **102**
Fort Cornwallis 12
Fort Cumberland **96–97**
Fort Darling 84
Fort Delegal 27
Fort Deposit 269
Fort Desperate 218
Fort Donelson **97–98**, 97m, 101
Fort Douglas 17
Fort Duquesne 106, 184–85
Fort Ellis 165
Fort Erie 67 172, 234
Fort Erie **98–99**
Fort Erie, Second Battle of **99**
Fort Fetterman 165
Fort Fisher (Terry's Expedition) **99–100**
Fort Frédéric (Crown Point) 160–61
Fort Frederica 27
Fort Frontenac **100–101**
Fort George **101**, 238, 267
Fort Grierson 12
Fort Griffin (Sabine Pass) **238**
Fort Griswold 191
Fort Haskell 110
Fort Henry 97, **101–2**
Fort Holmes 197, 198
fortifications 307g
Fort Jackson 194, 195
Fort Jefferson 243
Fort Keogh 17
Fort Keyser **102**
Fort King 82
Fort Lane 24
Fort Lawrence 94
Fort Lee 116
Fort Lee (Fort Constitution) **102**
Fort Libertad 186
Fort Magruder 294
Fort McHenry **102–3**

Fort McPherson 268
Fort Mercer (Red Bank) **103–4**
Fort Michilimackinac (Mackinac Island) **173**
Fort Mifflin 103, **104**
Fort Mims 85, 86, **105**, 270
Fort Montgomery and Fort Clinton **95–96**
Fort Mose 241
Fort Motte **105**
Fort Moultrie (Fort Sullivan) 58, 59, 111
Fort Necessity (Great Meadows) **106**
Fort Niagara **106–7**
Fort Paris 102
Fort Phil Kearney 91
Fort Pillow **107–8**
Fort Pulaski **108–9**, 108m
Fort Pupo 241
Fort Rankin 152
Fort Recovery 89
Fort Ridgely **109**, 195
Fort St. Philip 194, 195
Fort St. Simon 27
Fort Saybrook 188
Fort Stanwix **109–10**
Fort Stanwix, Treaty of 217
Fort Stedman **110**, 213
Fort Strother 269
Fort Sullivan (Fort Moultrie) 58, 59
Fort Sumter 22, **111–12**
Fort Texas (Camp Texas) 46, 205
Fort Ticonderoga, N.Y. 282, 283
Fort Ticonderoga (Fort Carillon; July 8, 1758) 100, **112–13**
Fort Ticonderoga (May 10, 1775) **113**
Fort Ticonderoga (July 2–5, 1777) **113–15**, 114m, 147
Fort Ticonderoga (September 18, 1777) **115**
Fort Tomkins 239
Fort Trumbull 191
Fort Wagner (Battery Wagner) **115–16**
Fort Walker (Port Royal Sound) **220–21**
Fort Washington 60, 89, 102, **116–17**
Fort Watson **117**
Fort William Henry

117–18
forts, earthen 285
Fort Wintermoot 300
Forty-fifth Regiment of Foot 183
Forty Mile Creek 266
Forty-second Highlanders (BlackWatch) 117, 141
Forty-second Regiment 24, 41
Foster, John G. 234, 235
Fourth Corps 88
Fourth Missouri Cavalry 202
Fox (Mesquakie) 14
Fox's Gap 79, 260
Francis, Turbott 147
Franklin **118–19**
Franklin, Benjamin 184
Franklin, William B.
    Crampton's Gap 79
    Fredericksburg 121
    Harpers Ferry 143
    Sabine Pass 238
Franklin's Crossing (Deep Run) **119**
Fraser, Simon
    Hubbardton 147
    Saratoga, First 251
    Saratoga, Second 253
Fraser, Thomas 208
Fredericksburg 54, **119–21**, 120m
Fredericksburg, Va. 55
Freeman's Farm (First Battle of Saratoga) 96, **249–51**, 250m
Frémont, John C. 47
    Cross Keys 80–81, 219
    McDowell 175
    Port Republic 219, 220
French, Samuel G. 6
French Foreign Legion 45–46
Frenchtown (The River Raisin) **121–22**, 273
frigate 307g
Front Royal **122–23**, 296
Fry, Joshua 106
Fry, Speed 177
Fulkerson, Samuel 219
Fuller, John W. 207
Funston, Frederick 4
fur trade 259
fusiliers 308g

G

Gadsden, Christopher 59, 60

Gage, Thomas
    Bunker Hill 39, 40
    Lexington and Concord 163, 164
Gaines 178, 179
Gaines, Edmund P. 98
Gaines's Mill **124–25**
Galbraith, Thomas J. 109
galley 308g
Galveston **125**
Gálvez, Bernardo de 211
Ganey, Micajah 28
Gansevoort, Peter 110
García Conde, José María 186
Gardiner, William 18
Gardner, Frank 51
Gardner, Franklin 218, 219
Garland, John 57, 70
    Monterrey 185, 186
Garland, Samuel, Jr. 260
Garnett, Richard 153
Garnett, Robert S.
    Philippi 213
    Rich Mountain 233
Garnett's and Golding's Farm **125–26**
Gates, Horatio
    Camden 43–45, 134
    Saratoga, First 250–51
    Saratoga, Second 251–53
Geddes, George 73
General Monk 279
General Pike 239
Georgetown Road 184
Georgia 27, 59, 63, 241, 279, 295
    Allatoona Pass 6, 11
    Atlanta 10–11
    Augusta 12–13
    Bloody Swamp 27
    Briar Creek 31
    Chickamauga 62, **66–67**
    Fort Pulaski 108–9, 108m
    Kettle Creek 154–55
    Savannah 59, 254–55
Gere, Thomas P. 109
Germantown **126–28**, 127m, 293
Getty, George Washington 47
    Sayler's Creek 256
Gettysburg 90, **128–30**, 129m
Ghent, Treaty of 192
Ghost Dance 299

Gibbon, John 23
    Bull Run, Second 37
    Little Bighorn 165
Gibbs, Samuel 194
Gilbert, Charles 212
Gillmore, Quincy Adams
    83, 84, 109, 202
Girty, Simon 28
Gist, Mordecai 44, 73
Glasgow, H.M.S., U.S.S.
    Alfred v. **6**
Glazier, Beamsly 255
Glendale (White Oak
    Swamp) **292**
Globe Tavern (Weldon
    Railroad; Six Mile House)
    131
Glorieta Pass **131–32**,
    132*m*
Gloucester **132–33**
Glover, John
    Newport 196
    Pell's Point 211
    Trenton 277
gold 24, 162, 235
Golding's and Garnett's
    Farm **125–26**
Goldsboro 234
Goldsborough, Louis M.
    234
Goliad **133**
gondolas 282, 308*g*
González Garza, Roque
    49
Gordon, Henry 296
Gordon, John B. 90–91
    Cedar Creek 47
    Fort Stedman 110
    Kernstown, Second 154
    Sayler's Creek 256
Gore, Francis 242, 243–44
Goreham, Joseph 96, 97
Gorham, John 7
Gosford, Lord 242, 243
Grafton 214
Grant, Ulysses S. 67, 71,
    79, 80, 83, 110, 154, 192,
    207, 291
    Atlanta 10, 11
    Belmont 19–20
    Big Black River 22–23,
        285
    Champion's Hill 52–53,
        285
    Chapultepec 57
    Chattanooga 61–62, 63
    Cold Harbor 71–72,
        213
    Farmville 91

Fort Donelson 97–98
Fort Fisher 99
Fort Henry 97, 101
Iuka 149
North Anna River
    199–200
Petersburg 131, 213
Port Gibson 217–18
Ridgeway 234
Shiloh 257–59
Spotsylvania 261–62
Vicksburg 145, 232,
    285–87
Wilderness 293–94
Winchester, Third 297,
    298
grapeshot 308*g*
Grasse, François, comte de
    65, 302
grasshopper 308*g*
Grattan, John L. 10
Graves, Thomas 65
Greasy Grass (Little
    Bighorn) **165–67**, 166*m*,
    236, 260
Great Basin 17, 18
Great Bridge **133–34**
Great Lakes 100, 106, 242
Great Meadows (Fort
    Necessity) **106**
Great Plains 19
Great Salt Lake 17
Great Savannah **134**
Great Swamp **134–35**
Green, Martin E. 52
    Port Gibson 218
Green, Thomas 237
Greene, Christopher 103,
    104
Greene, Dana 181
Greene, Nathanael 28, 45,
    73, 76, 77, 143, 291
    Augusta 12
    Brandywine 30
    Eutaw Springs 86, 87
    Fort Lee 102
    Fort Motte 105
    Fort Watson 117
    Germantown 126, 127
    Guilford Courthouse
        136–37
    Harlem Heights 140
    Hobkirk's Hill 145
    Long Island 168
    Monmouth 182, 183
    Newport 196
    Ninety Six 197–98
    Parker's Ferry 207, 208
    Quinby Bridge 230

Springfield 263
Tarrant's Tavern 270
Trenton 277
Green Mountain Boys 113,
    186, 244
Green Spring **135–36**
Gregg, David M. 29
Gregg, John I.
    Farmville and
        Highbridge 91
    Raymond 232
Gregg, Maxcy 124
grenadiers 308*g*
Grey, Charles
    Germantown 127
    Paoli 207
    Whitemarsh 293
Gridley, Samuel 40
Grierson, Benjamin 32
Grierson, Colonel 12
Griffin, Charles 131
Grijalva, Juan de 162, 221
Groton, Conn. 191
Grover, Cuvier 148
Grummond, George W. 91
Guadalajara 42, 43
Guadalupe Hidalgo, Treaty
    of 223
Gu Cinge 300
guerrillas 308*g*
Guerrero, José María 5
Guerrière, H.M.S., U.S.S.
    Constitution v. **74**, 74*m*
Guilford Courthouse
    136–37, 136*m*
Gulf of St. Lawrence 170
gun 308*g*
gunboat 308*g*
Gunby, John 145
Guntown (Brice's Cross
    Roads) **31–32**, 32*m*
Gutiérrez, Eulalio 49
Gwynn Island **137–38**

H

Hale, Nathan 147
Halpatter Tustenuggee
    (Alligator) 82, 162
Hamilton 101
Hamilton, Alexander
    Princeton 223
    Yorktown 304
Hamilton, David 249
Hamilton, Henry 287–88
Hamilton, John 154
Hampton, Wade 22, 29
    Chateaugay 61, 69
    Trevilian Station 278
Hampton Roads, U.S.S.

Monitor v. C.S.S. *Virginia*
    at **180–81**
Hamtramck, John 243
Hancock 279
Hancock, William S. 294
Hancock, Winfield S.
    North Anna River 199
    Spotsylvania 261
Hand, Edward 275
Hanger, George
    Charlotte 60
    Wahab's Plantation 289
Hanging Rock **139–40**,
    235
Hanover Courthouse **140**
Hanover Junction (North
    Anna River) **199–200**
Hardee, William J. 22
    Atlanta 10
    Perryville 212
    Shiloh 257
    Stones River 264
Hardin, John 141, 142
Hardin, William 207–8
Harlem Heights **140–41**,
    211, 274, 292
Harmar, Josiah 141–42,
    242
Harmar's Defeat **141–42**,
    242
Harney, William S. 10
    Cerro Gordo 51
    Veracruz 284
Harpers Ferry 7, 79,
    142–43
Harpers Ferry, Va. 214
Harrisburg (Tupelo)
    279–80
Harrison, William Henry
    160
    Frenchtown 121, 122
    Tippecanoe 273,
        275–76
Harrison's Landing 253,
    292
Hartford 178, 179
Hartranft, John F. 110
Harvey, John 266
Haslet, John 223
Hathorn, John 178
Hawkins, Edgar S. 46
Haw River (Pyle's Defeat)
    143–44
Hayes, Rutherford B. 71
    Kernstown, Second 154
Hayne, Arthur P. 192
Heath, Richard 103
Hébert, Louis 210
Heckman, Charles A. 84

Heinmot Tooyalaket (Chief Joseph) 17, 23
Heintzelman, Samuel 35
  Malvern Hill 174
Heister, Leopold von 168
Helena **144**
Hendrick, Chief (Tiyanoga) 161
Henry, Judith 35
Henry House Hill 35–36, 37–38
Heredia, José A. 239–40
Herkimer, Nicholas 203
Hernández de Córdoba, Francisco 53, 162
Herron, Francis 222
Herron, John 224
Hessians 168
Heth, Henry
  Falling Waters 90
  Globe Tavern 131
Hidalgo y Costilla, Don Miguel 42–43
Highlanders 24, 41, 187
  Forty-second 117
  Seventy-first 31, 44, 78, 254, 255, 266, 267, 302
Hill, A. P. 110
  Antietam 9
  Bristoe Station 32–33
  Bull Run, Second 37
  Cedar Mountain 48
  Gaines's Mill 124, 125
  Gettysburg 128
  Globe Tavern 131
  Harpers Ferry 143
  Mechanicsville 175
  North Anna River 200
  White Oak Swamp 292
  Wilderness 293
Hill, D. H.
  Antietam 9
  Big Bethel 22
  Fair Oaks 88
  Harpers Ferry 143
  Malvern Hill 174
  South Mountain 260
  Williamsburg 294
Hill, John 94
Hill, William 295
Hillsborough Raid **144–45**
Hilton Head Island 221
Hindman, Thomas 221–22
Hobkirk's Hill **145**
Hoke, Robert F. 22
  Fort Fisher 99, 100
Holly Springs 67, **145–46**
Holmes, Asher 230

Holmes, Theophilius H. 144
Holzinger, Sebastiàn 284
Hood, John Bell
  Allatoona Pass 6
  Antietam 9
  Atlanta 10, 11
  Franklin 118–19
  Gaines's Mill 125
  Gettysburg 130
  Nashville 190–91
Hooker, Joseph "Fighting Joe" 29, 128
  Antietam 9
  Chancellorsville 54–55
  Chattanooga 61–62
  Franklin's Crossing 119
  Fredericksburg 119–21
  Oak Grove 201
  South Mountain 260
  Williamsburg 294
Hopkins, Esek 6
Hornets' Nest 257
Horry, Hugh 134
Horse Island 238–39
horses 271, 276, 308g
Horseshoe Bend **146–47**, 146m
Horton, Albert C. 133
Hotchkiss, Jedediah 47
Hotoakhihoosis (Tall Bull) 19, 268
Hough, Daniel 112
Houston, Sam 5
  Goliad 133
  San Jacinto 246
Hovey, Alvin 52
Howard, John 77, 78
Howard, Oliver O.
  Bentonville 21, 22
  Chancellorsville 55
Howe, Robert 254
Howe, Trylingham 6
Howe, William 24, 95, 103, 157, 182, 207, 230, 277
  Brandywine 30, 31, 293
  Bunker Hill 39, 40
  Cooch's Bridge 75–76
  Fort Washington 102, 116–17
  Germantown 126, 128, 293
  Harlem Heights 140, 274
  Long Island 168
  Pell's Point 210–11
  Philadelphia 104
  Throg's Neck 274–75

Whitemarsh 293
White Plains 292–93
howitzer 308g
Huamantla 223, 224
Hubbardton **147**
Huck, Christian 295
Hudson River 102, 116, 267
Huerta, Victoriano 48
Huger, Benjamin 56
  Fair Oaks 88
  Malvern Hill 174
  Molino del Rey 179
Huger, Isaac 136
  Hobkirk's Hill 145
  Monck's Corner 180
Hull, Isaac 74
Humphreys, Andrew A.
  Farmville and Highbridge 91
  Sayler's Creek 256
Hunkpapa 165, 235, 260, 299
Hunt, Henry J. 57
Hunter, David 35, 278
  Kernstown, Second 154
  Lynchburg 172
Huron 141, 169, 217, 243

I
Idaho 17–18
Île aux Noix 245
Imboden, John D. 191
Indiana
  Harmar's Defeat 141–42, 242
  St. Clair's Defeat 242–43
  Tippecanoe 273, 275–76, 275m
  Vincennes 287–88
Indian Territory 161, 162
infantry 308g
Inflexible 282, 283
Inglis, George 160
Inkpaduta 155
In-mut-too-yah-lat-lat (Chief Joseph) 17, 23
Ireland 234
Iris, H.M.S., U.S.S. *Trumbull* v. **279**
Irish Bend (Bayou Teche) **148**
Iron Brigade 37
ironclads 176, 178–79, 308g
  U.S.S. *Monitor* v. C.S.S. *Virginia* **180–81**
Iron Hill (Cooch's Bridge) **75–76**

Iroquois 63, 161, 196–97, 243
  Long Sault 169
Irvin, James 293
Isatai 3
Island Number 10 **149**
Iuka **149**
Izard, George 214

J
Jackson, Andrew 246
  Horseshoe Bend 146
  New Orleans 192–94
  Talladega 269–70
  Tallasahatchee 270
Jackson, Thomas J. "Stonewall" 37, 81, 254, 260
  Bull Run, First 35
  Cedar Mountain 47–48
  Chancellorsville 54, 55
  Chantilly 56
  Chapultepec 56
  death of 55, 128
  Emuckfau Creek 85, 86
  Enitachopco Creek 86
  First Winchester 80
  Fredericksburg 119, 121
  Front Royal 122–23, 296
  Gaines's Mill 125
  Harpers Ferry 7, 79, 143
  Kernstown, First 153–54
  Malvern Hill 174
  McDowell 122, 174–75
  Mechanicsville 175
  Port Republic 219–20
  Winchester, First 296
Jacksonville, Fla. 202
jaegers 308g
Jalapa 50
Jamaica Pass 168
James Island 59, 266
James River 83, 88, 135, 253
Jamestown (Bacon's Rebellion) **151**
Jamestown (Virginia-Indian Wars) **150–51**
Jamestown Ford (Green Spring) **135–36**
Jasper, William
  Charleston 58
  Savannah 255
Jeanningros, Pierre 45
Jefferson, Thomas Garland 192
Jenkins, Albert G. 71
Jericho Mills (North Anna River) **199–200**

Jesup, Thomas S. 161
  Lundy's Lane 171
John (Old John) 24
Johnson, Andrew 234
Johnson, Bushrod
  Five Forks 93
  Sayler's Creek 256
Johnson, Edward "Allegheny
  Ed"
  McDowell 175
  Winchester, Second 297
Johnson, Guy 300
Johnson, Henry 267
Johnson, James 273
Johnson, John
  Fort Keyser 102
  Klock's Field 157
Johnson, Richard Mentor
  273
Johnson, William 107, 161
Johnston, Abraham R. 247
Johnston, Albert Sidney 98
  Shiloh 257
Johnston, Joseph E. 93,
  256, 285, 294
  Atlanta 10, 11
  Bentonville 21–22
  Bull Run, First 35, 36,
    37
  Cerro Gordo 51
  Chapultepec 56
  Fair Oaks 88
Johnstown **152**
Joint Committee on the
  Conduct of the War 15
Jones, William E. 29
Jonesboro 11
Joseph, Chief (Heinmot
  Tooyalaket) 17, 23
Juárez, Benito 45, 224
Julesburg **152**
Jumper (Ote Ematha) 82

K

Kanawha Division 260
Kaskaskia 287
Katlian 259
Keane, John 193
Kearny, Philip
  Bull Run, Second 37
  Chantilly 55–56
  Churubusco 70–71
  Contreras 75
  Williamsburg 294
Kearny, Stephen W.
  Sacramento River 239
  San Gabriel 245–46
  San Pascual 247–48
Keifer, J. W. 297

Kekionga (Miami Town)
  141–42, 242, 243
Kenly, J. R. 122, 296
Kennesaw Mountain 11
Kentucky 97, 101, 287
  Blue Licks 28
  Mill Springs 177–78
  Munfordville 187–88
  Perryville 211–12, 264
  Richmond 233–34
Kernstown First **153–54**
Kernstown Second **154**,
  297
Kershaw, Joseph B. 47
  Winchester, Third 297
Kettle Creek **154–55**
Key, Francis Scott 103
Keyes, Erasmus 88
Kiksadi 259
Killdeer Mountain **155**
Kilpatrick, Judson "Kill
  Cavalry" 90
Kimball, Nathan 63
  Front Royal 122
  Kernstown, First 153
King's American Rangers
  155
King's Mountain **155–57**,
  156m
King's Rangers 12
King's Schoolhouse (Oak
  Grove) **201**
Kintpuash (Captain Jack)
  268
Kip's Bay 141, 157
Kirkland, William W. 32
Klamath 268
Klock's Field 102, **157**
Knowlton, Thomas 40
  Harlem Heights 141
Knox, Henry 242
  Harmar's Defeat 141
Knoxville (Fort Sanders)
  157–58
Knyphausen, Wilhelm von
  Brandywine 30, 31
  Fort Washington 117
  Monmouth 182, 183
  Springfield 262–63
Kosciuszko, Tadeusz 197
Koslowski's Ranch 132
Kwahadie 3
Kwanah (Quanah Parker) 3

L

Lackawanna 178
Lafayette, Ind. 275
Lafayette, Marie-Joseph-
  Paul-Yves-Roch-Gilbert du

Motier, marquis de 65,
  261
  Brandywine 30–31
  Green Spring 135–36
  Monmouth 182
  Newport 196
  Yorktown 302
Laffite, Jean 192
Laine, Ramon 46
Lake Champlain 61, 216,
  245
Lake Erie (Put-in-Bay)
  159–60, 160m
Lake George (Bloody Pond)
  160–61
Lake of Mexico 271
Lake Okeechobee **161–62**
Lake Ontario 100, 101
Lakota 10, 15, 19, 91, 152,
  167, 235 *see also* Sioux
  Ash Hollow 10
  Little Bighorn 165–67,
    236
  Slim Buttes 260
  Wolf Mountain 298
  Wounded Knee 299
Lamb, William 99, 100
Lambert, John 194
Lamochatte (William
  Weatherford) 105, 146,
  269
lancers 308g
Landero, José Juan 284
Lane, Joseph 223, 224
Lathrop, Thomas 27
Latrille, Charles 45, 224
Laudonnière, René de 95
Laurel Brigade 278
Laurel Mountain 233
Laurens, John 73
  Savannah 255
Laurie, Walter 164
Lauzun, duc de 132
Lawrence 159, 160, 173
Lawrence, Charles 94
  Louisbourg 170
Lawrence, James 64, 159
Lawson, Robert 136
Lázaro **162**
Learned, Ebenezer 253
Ledlie, James 80
Ledyard, William 191
Lee, Albert L. 238
Lee, Charles
  Charleston 58
  Monmouth 182–83
Lee, Fitzhugh
  Farmville and
    Highbridge 90, 91

Five Forks 93
Trevilian Station 278
Winchester, Third 297
Lee, Henry "Light-Horse
  Harry," Jr.
  Augusta 12–13
  Fort Motte 105
  Fort Watson 117
  Guilford Courthouse
    136
  Haw River 143–44
  Ninety Six 197, 198
  Paulus Hook 208–9
  Quinby Bridge 230
  Springfield 263
  Stony Point 267
  Wetzell's Ford 291
Lee, Robert E. 10, 21, 32,
  33, 47, 70, 71, 79, 83, 89,
  110, 119, 125, 143, 192,
  221, 253, 256, 260
  Antietam 7–9, 143
  Brandy Station 29
  Bull Run, Second 37,
    38
  Cerro Gordo 51
  Chancellorsville 54–55
  Chantilly 55, 56
  Cheat Mountain 63
  Cold Harbor 71–72,
    213
  Contreras 75
  Falling Waters 90
  Farmville and
    Highbridge 91
  Five Forks 93
  Fredericksburg 119–21
  Gaines's Mill 124–25
  Gettysburg 128–30
  Globe Tavern 131
  Harpers Ferry 143
  Lynchburg 172
  Malvern Hill 174
  Mechanicsville 175
  North Anna River
    199–200
  Oak Grove 201
  Petersburg 131, 213
  Sayler's Creek 90
  Spotsylvania 261–62
  surrender of 90, 91, 213
  Trevilian Station 278
  White Oak Swamp 292
  Wilderness 293–94
  Winchester, Second 296
Lee, Stephen D. 52
  Tupelo 280
Lee, W. H. Rooney 29
legion 308g

Le Loutre, Jean-Louise 7
Lenni Lenape (Delaware) 41, 141,142, 217, 243, 249
Lenud's Ferry 60, **162–63**
León, Antonio 179
Leslie, Alexander 73
  Guilford Courthouse 137
  Harlem Heights 141
  White Plains 292
levies 242
Lewis, Andrew 138
  Point Pleasant 217
Lewis, Meriwether Clark 240
Lewis, Morgan
  Fort George 101
  Klock's Field 157
Lewis, William 121
Lexington (September 18–20, 1861) **164–65**
Lexington and Concord (April 19, 1775) 113, **163–64**, 163*m*
light infantry 308*g*
Lillington, John 187
Limpy 24
Lincoln, Abraham 14, 15, 47, 61, 63, 119
  Antietam 9
  Fort Pillow 108
  Fort Sumter 111
Lincoln, Benjamin 18, 162, 304
  Bound Brook 28
  Charleston 59–60
  Savannah 255
  Springfield Arsenal 263–64
  Stono Ferry 266
  Yorktown 302
Lindley's Mill 144
line 309*g*
Linnet 216
Lisiansky, Yuri 259
Little, Lewis Henry 149
Little Bighorn (Custer's Last Stand, Greasy Grass), Battle of **165–67**, 166*m*, 236, 260
Little Crow (Cetan Wakan Mani) 109, 195
Little Sayler's Creek 256
Little Turtle (Michikinikwa) 89, 90, 141, 142
  St. Clair's Defeat 242, 243
Lochry, Archibald 167

Lochry's Defeat **167**
Locke, Francis 231
Lockyer, Nicholas 192
Logan, John A. 52
Lomax, Lunsford
  Fisher's Hill 92
  Winchester, Third 297
Lombardini, María 33
Lone Tree Lake (Wood Lake) **298**
Long, Pierce 94
Long Island **168**
Long Island, N.Y. 58
Long Sault **169**
Longstreet, James 7, 29, 35, 54, 57, 61, 66, 90, 260
  Bull Run, Second 37–38
  Fair Oaks 88, 89
  Fredericksburg 119, 121
  Gettysburg 128, 130
  Knoxville 157–58
  Malvern Hill 174
  Mechanicsville 175
  Sayler's Creek 256
  White Oak Swamp 292
  Wilderness 293–94
  Williamsburg 294, 295
Looking Glass (Allalimya Takanin) 17, 23
loophole 309*g*
López, Mártin de 271
Lorencez, Charles Latrille, comte de 45, 224
Loring, William 53
Los Angeles, Calif. 176
Loudon Heights 143
Louisbourg (French and Indian War) **170–71**
Louisbourg (King George's War) **169–70**
Louisiana 6, 94, 95
  Baton Rouge 16
  Irish Bend 148
  New Orleans 192–95, 193m
  Pleasant Hill Landing 216–17
  Port Hudson 148, 218–19
  Sabine Crossroads 216, 237–38
Louisiana 192, 193
Louisiana, U.S.S. 99
Louisville 176
Lovell, Mansfield 76
  New Orleans 194
Loyalists 78, 309*g see also* British Legion

Augusta 12–13
Black Mingo Creek 24–25
Blue Savannah 28
Bull's Ferry 39
Camden 44
Charleston 57–58, 59
Charlotte 60
Cherry Valley 63–64
Combahee Ferry 73
Eutaw Springs 87
Fort Watson 117
Hanging Rock 139–40, 235
Haw River 144
Hillsborough Raid 144–45
Johnstown 152
Kettle Creek 154–55
King's Mountain 155–56
Klock's Field 157
Minisink 178
Moore's Creek Bridge 58, 187
Newtown 197
Ninety Six 197–98
Oriskany 203
Parker's Ferry 207–8
Quinby Bridge 230
Ramseur's Hill 231
Rocky Mount 235
Sandusky 248–49
Spencer's Tavern 261
Waxhaws 290
Williamson's Plantation 295
Wyoming Valley 299–300
Lundy's Lane, Battle of **171–72**, 171*m*
Lyman, William 263
Lynchburg **172**
Lyon, Nathaniel 295, 296

M

MacDonell, John 229
Macdonough, Thomas 216
machine guns 49
Mackenzie, Samuel 56
Mackinac Island (Fort Michilimackinac) **173**
Macomb, Alexander 214–16
Madison, James 25, 26, 74
magazine 309*g*
Magruder, John B.
  Big Bethel 22
  Contreras 75

Galveston 125
  Malvern Hill 174
  Savage's Station 253–54
  Williamsburg 294
Maham, Hezekiah 117
Maham Towers 12, 13, 117, 198
Mahone, William "Little Billy" 90–91
Mahtoiowa (Conquering Bear) 10
Maine, Phillipe 46
Maisonneuve, Simon de 169
Maitland, John
  Savannah 254
  Stono Ferry 266
Majoribanks, John 86, 87
Ma-ka-ta-i-me-she-kia-kiak (Black Hawk) 14–15
Malecite 6, 7
Malvern Hill **174**
Manassas 32, 33, 153
Manassas, First (First Bull Run) **35–37**, 36*m*, 38
Manassas, Second (Second Bull Run) **37–38**, 38*m*, 55, 56
Manhattan 178
Manhattan Island 102, 116, 140, 141, 157, 168, 274, 292
Manitoba 15
Mankato 298
Mansfield (Sabine Crossroads), 216, **237–38**
Mansfield, John 304
Mansfield, Joseph 9
Manson, Mahlon 233–34
Marblehead Mariners 277
Maria 282, 283
Marion, Francis "Swamp Fox"
  Black Mingo Creek 24–25
  Blue Savannah 28
  Fort Motte 105
  Fort Watson 117
  Great Savannah 134
  Ninety Six 197
  Parker's Ferry 207–8
  Quinby Bridge 230
  Savannah 255
Marsh, John S. 109
Marshall, Humphrey 33
Marshall, James 107
Martin, George 220
Martin, Josiah 187
Marye's Heights 121

Maryland
  Antietam 7–9, 143
  Bladensburg 25–26
  Chesapeake Bay 64–65
  Crampton's Gap 79, 79m
  Fort McHenry 102–3
  Monocacy 183–84
  South Mountain 79, 260–61
Maryland Continentals 136
Maryland Heights 143
Mascarene, Paul 6, 7
Mason, James 70
Mason, John 188
Massachusetts
  Bloody Brook 26–27
  Bunker Hill 39–41, 39m
  U.S.S. Chesapeake v. H.M.S. Shannon 64
  Lexington and Concord 113, 163–64, 163m
  Springfield Arsenal 263–64
Massachusetts Committee of Safety
Massachusetts Fifty-fourth 115, 116
Massachusetts Provincial Congress 163
Matthews, George 127, 128
Maumee River 121
Mawhood, Charles
  Princeton 222
  Quintan's Bridge 230
Maximillian Ferdinand Joseph 46, 224
Maxwell, William 30
  Cooch's Bridge 76
  Springfield 263
May, Charles
  Palo Alto 206
  Resaca de la Palma 233
Maya 53, 162, 221, 276
McAllister, Archibald 209
McArthur, John 190
McCall, George A. 232
McCall, James 12
McCall, William 261
McCausland, John 184
McClellan, George B. 15, 47, 63, 79, 119, 125, 140, 153, 154, 220, 253, 254, 260, 294
  Antietam 7–9, 143
  Bull Run, Second 37, 38

Fair Oaks 88–89
Gaines's Mill 124–25
Harpers Ferry 143
Malvern Hill 174
Mechanicsville 175–76
Oak Grove 201
Philippi 214
Rich Mountain 233
White Oak Swamp 292
McClernan, John 52
McClernand, John A.
  Fort Donelson 98
  Port Gibson 218
McCook, Alexander 66
  Perryville 212
McCown, John 149
McCulloch, Benjamin
  Pea Ridge 209, 210
  Wilson's Creek 295
McDonald, Allan 187
McDonald, Donald 187
McDouall, Robert 173
McDougall, Alexander 292
McDowell 122, **174–75**
McDowell, Charles 156
McDowell, Irvin P. 47
  Bull Run, First 35–36, 37
  Kernstown, First 154
McDowell, Joseph 156
McGary, Hugh 28
McGaw, Robert 116
McIntosh, James S.
  Molino del Rey 180
  Palo Alto 205
  Pea Ridge 210
McIntosh, Lachlan 255
McKay, Lieutenant 117
McKean, Robert 157
McKinley, William 47
McLane, Allen 73, 208
  Whitemarsh 293
McLaws, Lafayette
  Crampton's Gap 79
  Harpers Ferry 143
McLean, Nathaniel 175
McLeod, Donald 187
McMillen, William L. 32
McPherson, James B.
  Atlanta 10, 11
  Port Gibson 218
  Raymond 232
McPherson, Lieutenant 105
McPherson, William 261
Mdewkanton 298
Meade, George Gordon 32, 33, 199, 293
  Cold Harbor 71
  Crater 80

Fredericksburg 121
Gettysburg 128, 130
Ridgeway 234
Spotsylvania 261
Mechanicsville (Ellison's Mill) **175–76**
Mechanicsville, Va. 124
Meeker, Nathan 177
Meigs, Return 267
Mejía, Francisco 185
Memphis **176**
Menéndez de Avilés, Pedro 95, 240
Mercer, Hugh 222, 223
Mercer, John 133
Merlin 104
Merritt, Wesley
  Five Forks 93
  Milk Creek 177
Mesa (La Mesa) **176**
Mesquakie (Fox) Tribes 14
Metacomet 178, 179
Metacomet (King Philip) 26
  Great Swamp 134–35
Métis 309g
  Batoche 15–16
Mexica (Aztec) 49, 198, 204, 276, 277
  Tenochtitlán 270–73
Mexican Military College 56
Mexico 5, 176, 247
  Agua Prieta 4
  Buena Vista 33–35, 34m
  Calderón Bridge 42–43
  Camerone 45–46
  Celaya 48–49, 72
  Cempoallan 49–50
  Cerro Gordo 50–52, 51m
  Champoton 53
  Chapultepec 56–57, 223
  Churubusco 70–71, 74, 75
  Contreras 70, 74–75
  Lázaro 162
  Molino Del Rey 56, 179–80
  Monterrey 185–86
  La Noche Triste 198–99
  Otumba 203–4
  Parral 208
  Potonchan 221
  Puebla 45, 46, 57, 223–25

Sacramento River 239–40
Tenochtitlán 49, 50, 203, 270–73, 276
Tlaxcala 276–77
Veracruz 45, 50, 224, 283–85
Mexico City 45, 49, 56, 57, 71, 74, 75, 179, 180, 223, 224, 271, 276, 284
Mexico City National Guard 70
Miami 141, 142, 243
Miami Town (Kekionga) 141–42, 242, 243
Micanopy 82
Michigan 121, 173
Michigan, U.S.S. 234
Michikinikwa (Little Turtle) 89, 90, 141, 142
  St. Clair's Defeat 242, 243
Micmac 6, 7
Middleton, Frederick 15–16
Miles, Dixon S. 143
Miles, Nelson A. 17
  Wolf Mountain 298
  Wounded Knee 299
Milford Station 199
militia 309g
Milk Creek **176–77**
Miller, James
  Fort Erie, Second 99
  Lundy's Lane 171
Mills, Anson 260
Mill Springs (Logan Cross Road) **177–78**
Milroy, Robert H. 81
  McDowell 175
  Winchester, Second 296–97
Mims, Samuel 105
mines 309g
  underwater (torpedoes) 178, 179, 311g
Mingo 41, 243
Mingo John (Tah-gah-jute) 217
Miniconjou 299
minié ball 309g
Minisink **178**
Minnesota
  Fort Ridgely 109
  New Ulm 195
  Wood Lake 298
Minnesota 181
Minutemen 39, 163
missionaries 249

Mississippi
   Big Black River 22–23,
     285
   Brice's Cross Roads
     31–32, 32m
   Champion's Hill 52–53,
     285
   Chickasaw Bluffs 67
   Corinth 76, 149
   Holly Springs 67,
     145–46
   Iuka 149
   Okolona 202
   Port Gibson 217–18
   Raymond 232
   Tupelo 279–80
   Vicksburg 22–23, 52,
     53, 66, 67, 144, 145,
     202, 207, 217–19, 222,
     232, 285–87, 286m
Mississippi River 19, 66,
   67, 148, 149, 176, 219,
   287
Missouri
   Belmont 19–20
   Lexington 164–65
   Pilot Knob 214
   Wilson's Creek 295–96
Mitchell, Alexander M. 185
Mitiwemeg 169
Mobile Bay **178–79**
Mochcouoh 53
Modoc 267–68
Mohawk 18, 161, 188, 203
   see also Iroquois
   Cherry Valley 63–64
   Minisink 178
   Queenston 229
Mohawk River 63, 157
Mohegan 135, 188, 189
Moira 238
Moketavato (Black Kettle)
   248, 290
Molino Del Rey 56,
   179–80
Monck's Corner 60, **180**
Monckton, Henry 183
Monckton, Robert 94–95
Monitor, U.S.S., C.S.S.
   Virginia v. (*Monitor v.*
   Merrimack) **180–81**
Monmouth 59, **181–83**,
   182m
Monocacy **183–84**
Monongahela 178
Monongahela (Braddock's
   Defeat) **184–85**
Monro, George 118
Monroe, James 26, 278

Montana
   Bear Paw Mountains 17
   Big Hole Basin 23, 23m
   Little Bighorn 165–67,
     166m, 236, 260
   Wolf Mountain 298
Montcalm-Gozon de Saint-
   Véran, Louis-Joseph, mar-
   quis de 112
   Fort William Henry 118
   Quebec 226–27
Monterrey **185–86**
Montezuma 49, 50, 198,
   199, 271, 272
Montgomery, Richard
   Quebec 227–28
   St. John's 245
Montiano, Manuel de 27,
   241
Montreal **186**
Montreal, Canada 60, 61,
   69, 169, 245, 274
Moore, Benjamin D. 247
Moore, James 187, 240
Moore, John 231
Moore's Creek Bridge 58,
   187
Morales, Francisco 186
Morales, Juan 284
Moraviantown (Thames)
   273–74
Moreno, Francisco Rosenda
   70
Morgan 178, 179
Morgan, Daniel
   Cowpens 77–78, 136
   Newtown 197
   Quebec 228
   Saratoga, First 251
   Saratoga, Second 253
Morgan, David 194
Morris, Gouverneur 293
Morrison, Joseph 69
mortar 309g
Motte, Rebecca 105
Moultrie, William 18
   Charleston 58
   Stono Ferry 266
Mount Defiance 115
Mount Hope 115
Mouton, Jean Jacques
   Pleasant Hill Landing
     217
   Sabine Crossroads 237,
     238
Muhlenberg, John Peter
   127
   Petersburg 212
Mulligan, James A.

Kernstown, Second 154
Lexington 164
Munfordville **187–88**
Murfee, Hardy 267
Murfreesboro (Stones River)
   264–65, 265m
Murphy, Alexander 279
Murphy, Robert 145, 146
Murray, John (Lord
   Dunmore) 133–34
   Gwynn Island 137–38
   Point Pleasant 217
Musgrave, Thomas
   Germantown 126
   Paoli 207
musket 309g
Myrick, Andrew J. 109
Mystic River **188–89**

N

Nakota 91, 152, 235, 299
   see also Sioux
Napier, Charles 103
Napoleon III, emperor of
   the French 45, 46, 224
Narraganset 26, 188, 189
   Great Swamp 134, 135
Narragansett Bay 196
Narváez, Pánfilo de 49–50
Nashville **190–91**
Nashville, Tenn. 279
Nassau 6
Natera, Pánfilo 48
National Road 184
Neal, Thomas
   Rocky Mount 235
   Williamson's Plantation
     295
Nebraska 10
Nelson, William
   Richmond 233, 234
   Shiloh 257
Nelson, Wolfred 243, 244
Nemattanew 150
Neolin (Delaware Prophet)
   41
Neva 259
New Era, U.S.S. 107
New Hope Church 11
New Jersey
   Billingsport 24
   Bound Brook 28
   Bull's Ferry 38–39
   Fort Lee 102, 116
   Fort Mercer 103–4
   Monmouth 59, 181–83,
     182m
   Paulus Hook 208–9
   Princeton 222–23

Quintan's Bridge 230
Springfield 262–63
Trenton 222, 277–78
New London Raid **191**
New Market **191–92**
New Market Bridge 22
New Market Road 92
New Mexico
   Columbus 49, 72–73,
     208
   Glorieta Pass 131–32,
     132m
   Santa Fe 249
New Orleans (American
   Civil War) **194–95**
New Orleans (War of 1812)
   192–94, 193m
New Orleans, La. 285
Newport **195–96**
Newtown **196–97**
New Ulm **195**
New York 102
   Cherry Valley 63–64
   Fort Anne 94
   Fort Clinton and Fort
     Montgomery 95–96
   Fort Keyser 102
   Fort Niagara 106–7
   Fort Stanwix 109–10
   Fort Ticonderoga 100,
     112–15, 114m
   Fort Washington 60, 89,
     102, 116–17
   Fort William Henry
     117–18
   Harlem Heights
     140–41, 211, 274, 292
   Johnstown 152
   Kip's Bay 157
   Klock's Field 102, 157
   Lake George 160–61
   Long Island 58, 168
   Minisink 178
   Newtown 196–97
   Oriskany 203
   Pell's Point 210–11
   Plattsburg Bay 214–16,
     215m
   Sackets Harbor 238–39
   Saratoga 96, 249–53,
     250m, 252m
   Stony Point 267
   Throg's Neck 211,
     274–75
   Valcour Island 282–83,
     283m
   White Plains 292–93
New York City 262, 263,
   274, 292, 302

Nez Perce 17, 23
Niagara 160, 173
Niagara Falls 171
Niagara River 101, 106, 267
Niantic 188, 189
Nicholls, Francis 297
Nicholson, Francis 220
Nicholson, James 279
Nineteenth Regiment 230
Ninety Six **197–98**
Niños Heroicos 56
Ninth Corps 200, 260
Ninth Infantry 180
Ninth Regiment 94
Ninth Virginia 127
Nipmuc 26, 134
La Noche Triste (Tenochtitlán) **198–99**
Norfolk, Va. 134
North, Frank 268
North Anna River (Hanover Junction, Jericho Mills, Taylor's Bridge) **199–200**
North Carolina 302
  Alamance 4–5
  Bentonville 21–22
  Charlotte 60
  Chesapeake Capes 65
  Cowan's Ford 76–77, 270
  Fishing Creek 92–93, 134
  Fort Fisher 99–100
  Guilford Courthouse 136–37, 136m
  Haw River 143–44
  Hillsborough Raid 144–45
  Moore's Creek Bridge 58, 187
  Ramseur's Hill 231–32
  Roanoke Island 234–35
  Tarrant's Tavern 270
  Wahab's Plantation 289
  Wetzell's Ford 291
Northcote 16
North Dakota 155
Nova Scotia 6, 96, 169
  U.S.S. *Constitution* v. H.M.S. *Guerrière* 74, 74m
  Fort Beauséjour 94–95
Noyan et de Chavoy, Pierre Payen de 100

O

Oak Grove (King's Schoolhouse) **201**
Oaxaco Brigade 179
Obispado 186
Obregón, Alvaro 49, 72
O'Brien, John Paul Jones 33, 34
O'Brien, Nicolas J. 152
Ocaneechi 151
Ocean Pond (Olustee) **202**
Oglala Lakota 19
  Slim Buttes 260
  Wolf Mountain 298
Oglethorpe, James 27
  St. Augustine 241–42
O'Hara, Charles 77, 304
Ohio 141
  Fallen Timbers 89–90
  Frenchtown 121–22, 273
  Lake Erie 159–60, 160m
  Lochry's Defeat 167
  Sandusky 248–49
Ohio River 106, 167
Ohio Valley 184, 185
Ojibway 15
Oklahoma
  Rush Springs 236
  Washita 289–90
Okolona **202**
Old John 24
Old Northwest 141, 274, 275
Ollikut 17, 23
Olmstead, Charles 108–9
Olustee (Ocean Pond) **202**
O'Neill, John 234
Opdyke, Emerson 119
Openchancanough 150–51
Opequon Creek (Third Winchester) **297–98**
Orchard Knob 62
Ord, Edward 90
  Iuka 149
Order No. 191 260
Oregon 24
Oriskany **203**
Ortega, José María 186
Osceola 161
Osterhaus, Peter 218
Ote Ematha (Jumper) 82
Otermín, Antonio de 249
Otomí 276
Ottawa 217, 243
Otumba **203–4**
Owens, Samuel 240

Ox Hill 200
Ox Hill (Chantilly) 38, **55–56**, 55m

P

Pacheco, Francisco 33
Padierna (Contreras) 70, **74–75**
Paine, Halbert E. 219
Pakenham, Edward 192, 193, 194
palisade 309g
Palo Alto 46, **205–6**, 206m, 232
Pamunkey 151
Paoli **207**
Papineau, Louis-Joseph 242, 243, 244
parallel trenches 309g
parapet 309g
Parke, John G. 234
Parker, Cynthia Ann 3
Parker, Hyde 254
Parker, John 163
Parker, Peter 58
Parker, Quanah 3
Parker's Cross Roads **207**
Parker's Ferry **207–8**
Parral **208**
Parsons, Samuel 157
partisans 309g
Patriotes 242, 243
patriots 309g
Patterson, Robert 35
  Cerro Gordo 50, 51
  Veracruz 284
Patton, John M. 81
Paula-Milan, Francisco de 45, 46
Paulus Hook **208–9**
Pawnee 268
Pawnee Killer 19
Payne, J. Scott 177
Pea Ridge (Elkhorn Tavern) **209–10**
Peach Orchard (Savage's Station) **253–54**
Peachtree Creek 11
Peacock, U.S.S., H.M.S. *Epervier* v. **210**
Peacocke, George 234
Pearson, Thomas 67
Pease, Vincent 241
Pegram, John 47
Pegram, Willie 93
Pelham, John B. 121
Pellew, Edward 283
Pell's Point **210–11**
Pemberton, John C.

Big Black River 22–23
  Champion's Hill 52, 53
  Raymond 232
  Vicksburg 285, 287
Peña y Barragán, Matías 57, 180
Pennsylvania 103
  Brandywine 30–31, 30m, 126, 293
  Bushy Run 41
  Fort Mifflin 103, 104
  Fort Necessity 106
  Germantown 126–28, 127m, 293
  Gettysburg 90, 128–30, 129m
  Monongahela 184–85
  Paoli 207
  Whitemarsh 293
  Wyoming Valley 64, 299–300
Pennypacker, Galusha 100
Penpenhihi (White Bird) 17
Pensacola **211**
Pepperill, William, Jr. 170
Pequot 188–89
Percy, Earl 117, 168
  Lexington and Concord 164
Pérez, Francisco 34
  Molino del Rey 179, 180
Perfecto de Cós, Martín 246
Perry, Matthew C. 284
Perry, Oliver Hazard
  Fort George 101
  Lake Erie 159–60
  Thames 273
Perryville **211–12**, 264
Pershing, John J. 73, 208
Petersburg (American Civil War) 131, **213**
Petersburg (American Revolution) **212–13**
Petersburg, Va. 93, 110, 131
Petersburg Mine Assault (The Crater) **79–80**
Pettigrew, James J. 90
Pettigrew, Johnston 130
Philadelphia, Pa. 30, 31, 75–76, 103, 126, 128, 181–82, 207, 293
Philip, King (Metacomet) 26
  Great Swamp 134–35
Philippi 22, **213–14**

Phillips, William 302
　Petersburg 212
Pickens, Andrew 12
　Cowpens 77, 78
　Haw River 144
　Kettle Creek 154–55
Pickens, Francis 111
Pickett, George E. 57
　Five Forks 93
　Gettysburg 130
　Sayler's Creek 256
Pickett's Charge 90, 130
Pickett's Mill 11
Pico, Andres 247–48
Pierce, Franklin 70
　Contreras 75
Pigeon's Ranch 132
Pigot, Robert 40
　Newport 196
Pike, Albert 209, 210
Pillow, Gideon J. 19, 70
　Cerro Gordo 51
　Chapultepec 56
　Contreras 75
　Fort Donelson 98
Pilot Knob (Fort Davidson)
　214
Pine Ridge Reservation 299
pioneers 310*g*
Pitcairn, John 163, 164
Pitt, William 226
Pittsburg 149
Pittsburgh Landing (Shiloh)
　257–59, 258*m*
Plains of Abraham (Quebec)
　226–27, 227*m*
Plattsburg Bay (Lake
　Champlain, Plattsburg)
　214–16, 215*m*
Pleasant, Henry 79–80
Pleasant Hill Landing
　(Blair's Landing) **216–17**
Pleasonton, Alfred
　Brandy Station 29
　South Mountain 260
Pochanaw-quoip (Buffalo
　Hump) 236
Pocumtuck (Bloody Brook)
　26–27
Point Pleasant **217**
Poker Joe (Wahwookya
　Wasaaw) 17, 23
Polk, James K. 35, 57, 176,
　233, 247, 283
Polk, Leonidas 11, 61
　Atlanta 10
　Belmont 19–20
　Perryville 212
　Shiloh 257

Pontiac (Ponteach) 41
Poor, Enoch 197
　Saratoga, Second 253
Popé (Po'pnug) 249
Pope, John 37, 38, 55
　Cedar Mountain 47, 48
　Island Number 10 149
Porter, David D.
　Fort Fisher 99
　New Orleans 195
　Sabine Crossroads 237
Porter, Fitz-John 140
　Bull Run, Second 37
　Gaines's Mill 124, 125
　Malvern Hill 174
　Mechanicsville 175, 176
　Oak Grove 201
Porter, Peter B. 68
　Fort Erie, Second 99
Porterfield, George
　Alexander 213
Port Gibson **217–18**
Port Hudson **218–19**
Port Hudson, La. 148
Port Republic **219–20**
Port Royal (Annapolis Royal
　[King George's War]) **6–7**
Port Royal (Annapolis Royal
　[Queen Anne's War]) **220**
Port Royal Island (Beaufort)
　18
Port Royal Sound (Forts
　Beauregard and Walker)
　220–21
Potawatomi 243
Potomac River 15, 26, 37,
　80, 90
Potonchan **221**
Pouchot de Maupas, Pierre
　107
Poundmaker 15
Powell, Samuel 212
Powell, William 115
Powhatan (Wahunsonacock)
　150–51
Powhatan Indians 150–51
Prairie Grove **221–22**
Preble 216
Prentiss, Benjamin
　Helena 144
　Shiloh 257
Prescott, William
　Bunker Hill 39, 40
　Wetzell's Ford 291
Preston, Charles 245
Prevost, Augustine 18
　Briar Creek 31
　Savannah 254, 255
　Stono Ferry 266

Prevost, George
　Plattsburg Bay 214–16
Sackets Harbor 238, 239
Prevost, Mark 31
Price, Sterling 76, 209
　Helena 144
　Iuka 149
　Lexington 164–65
　Pilot Knob 214
　Wilson's Creek 295–96
Price, William 90
Prideaux, John 107
Priest Cap 218, 219
Prince George 238
Prince Regent 238, 239
Prince of Wales Loyal
　American Volunteers 139,
　140
Prince of Wales Regiment 134
Princeton **222–23**
privateers 73, 310*g*
Proctor, Henry 266
　Frenchtown 121, 122
　Thames 273, 274
Prophet's Town 275–76
Providence, R.I. 196
Province Island 104
Puebla 45, 46
Puebla 57, **223–24**
Puebla (Cinco de Mayo)
　224–25
Pueblo 249
Puente de Calderón
　(Calderon Bridge) **42–43**
Pulaski, Casimir 255
Pulaski Legion 44
Punta de Hornos 284
Purdy, Robert 61
Puritans 27
Put-in-Bay (Lake Erie)
　159–60, 160*m*
Putnam, Israel 39, 40
　Harlem Heights 140
　Long Island 168
Pyle, John 144
Pyle's Defeat (Haw River)
　143–44
Pyron, Charles 131

Q

Quanah (Quanah Parker) 3
quarter 310*g*
Quebec **227–28**
Quebec (Plains of Abraham)
　226–27, 227*m*
Quebec, Canada 48, 245,
　274
Queen Charlotte, H.M.S.
　160

Queen of the West 176
Queen's Rangers 261
Queenston **228–29**
Queenston, Canada 18
Quinby Bridge **230**
Quintan's Bridge **230**
Quitman, John A. 56, 57
　Monterrey 185, 186

R

railroads 35
　Baltimore & Ohio 143,
　213
　Southside 90, 93
　Virginia and Tennessee
　71
　Wheldon 131
Raisin River 121, 122, 273
Raisin River (Frenchtown)
　121–22, 273
rake 310*g*
Raleigh 181
Rall, Jacob 117
Rall, Johann 277, 278
ram ships 176, 179
Ramírez, Simeon 179
rampart 310*g*
Ramseur, Stephen 47
　Monocacy 184
　Winchester, Third 297
Ramseur's Hill **231–32**
Rangel, Joaquín 57
　Molino del Rey 179
Ransom, Robert, Jr. 84
Ransom, Thomas E. G. 238
Ransom, Trueman B. 56
　Contreras 75
Rapidan River 32, 37, 48,
　54
Rappahannock River 37,
　54, 55, 119
Rawdon, Lord (Francis
　Rawdon-Hastings) 86
　Camden 44
　Fort Motte 105
　Hobkirk's Hill 145
　Ninety Six 197, 198
Rawlings, Moses 116
Raymond **232**
Rea, Joaquín 223–24
reconnaissance, reconnoiter-
　ing 310*g*
redan 310*g*
Red Bank (Fort Mercer)
　103–4
Red Eagle (William
　Weatherford) 105, 146,
　269
redoubt 310*g*

Red Sticks 85–86, 105, 146, 269, 270
Reed, Joseph 292
Reese, Harry 80
regiment 310*g*
regulars 310*g*
Regulators 4, 263
Reno, Jesse L. 51, 56
  Churubusco 70
  Contreras 75
  Roanoke Island 234, 235
  South Mountain 260
Reno, Marcus A. 165–67
Renshaw, W. B. 125
Renville Rangers 109
Resaca, Ga. 11
Resaca de la Palma (Resaca de Guerrero) **232–33**
reservations 299
Revenge 282
Revere, Paul 163
Reynolds, John F. 128
Reynolds, John G. 56
Reynolds, Joseph J. 63
Rhode Island 65
  U.S.S. *Alfred* v. H.M.S. *Glasgow* 6
  Great Swamp 134–35
  Newport 195–96
Riall, Phineas
  Chippewa 67, 68–69
  Lundy's Lane 171
Ribault, Jean 95
Richardson, Israel B. "Fighting Dick" 9
Richelieu River 274
Richmond **233–34**
Richmond, Va. 35, 71, 83, 88, 93, 125, 140, 174, 175, 199, 200, 213, 220, 253, 261, 278, 293
Rich Mountain **233**
Ricketts, James B.
  Fisher's Hill 92
  Monocacy 184
Ridgeley, Randolph
  Monterrey 185
  Resaca de la Palma 232, 233
Ridgeway **234**
Riedesel, Friedrich von
  Fort Ticonderoga 115
  Hubbardton 147
  Saratoga, First 251
  Saratoga, Second 252
Riel, Louis 15–16
rifle 310*g*
rifled cannon 109

Riley, Bennett
  Cerro Gordo 51
  Contreras 75
Rincón, Manuel 70
Ringgold, Samuel 232
  Palo Alto 205, 206
Rio Grande 233
Ripley, Eleazar 172
Ritzema, Rudolph 245
River Raisin 121, 122, 273
River Raisin (Frenchtown) **121–22**, 273
Roanoke Island **234–35**
Roberts, William 234
Robertson, James 216
Robinson, Frederick 216
Rochambeau, Jean de Vimeur, comte de 65, 302
Rocky Mount 139, **235**
Rodes, Robert E.
  Monocacy 184
  Winchester, Third 297
Rogue River 24
Roman Nose (Woquini) 19
Rosebud Creek 165, **235–36**
Rosebud Reservation 299
Rosecrans, William S. 61
  Chickamauga 66
  Corinth 76
  Iuka 149
  Rich Mountain 233
  Stones River 264–65
Ross, John 152
Ross, Robert 25, 26
  Fort McHenry 102, 103
Rosser, Tom 278
Roundhead 122
Rowley, Aaron 152
Royal Americans 41
Royal Navy 6
Royal Savage 245, 282, 283
Royal Welch Fusiliers 44, 77, 133, 302
Rush Springs (Rush Creek) **236**
Russell, David 298
Russian-American Company 259
Rust, Albert 63
Rutherford, Griffith 231
Rutledge, John 59, 60
  Waxhaws 290

S

Sabine Crossroads (Mansfield) 216, **237–38**

Sabine Pass (Fort Griffin) **238**
Sac (Sauk) 14–15
Sackets Harbor **238–39**
Sacramento River **239–40**
Sailor's Creek (Saylor's Creek) 90, **256**
St. Augustine (Queen Anne's War) **240–41**
St. Augustine (War of Jenkin's Ear) **241–42**, 241*m*
St. Augustine, Fla. 27, 95
St. Benoît 244
St. Charles **242**, 243, 244
St. Clair, Arthur 89
  Fort Ticonderoga 113–15, 147
St. Clair's Defeat **242–43**
St. Denis 242, **243–44**
St. Eustache 242, **244**
St. John's (St. Jean's; May 17, 1775) 52, **244–45**
St. John's (St. Jean's; September 5–November 2, 1775) 186, **245**
St. John's River 95
St. Lawrence, Gulf of 170
St. Lawrence River 61, 69, 100, 274
St. Leger, Barry
  Fort Stanwix 110
  Oriskany 203
St. Louis 176
St. Simon's Island (Bloody Swamp) **27**
Sakonnet River 196
Salaberry, Charles de 61
salient 310*g*
sally 310*g*
San Antonio, Tex. 70
  Alamo 5, 133, 246
San Blas Battalion 56
Sand Creek 152, **248**, 290
Sandoval, Gonzalo de 50
Sandusky (Crawford's Defeat) **248–49**
San Gabriel **245–46**
San Jacinto 33, 133, **246**, 247*m*
San Pascual **247–48**
San Patricio Brigade 70
Santa Anna, Antonio López de 5, 179, 224
  Buena Vista 33, 34, 35
  Cerro Gordo 50, 51, 52
  Chapultepec 56, 57
  Churubusco 70, 71
  Contreras 74–75

Goliad 133
Puebla 223, 224
San Jacinto 246
Santa Barbara Fort 284
Santa Fe, **249**
Santa Isabel 72
Santee 109, 155
  New Ulm 195
  Wood Lake 298
Santee River 162
Saratoga 216
Saratoga First (Freeman's Farm) 96, **249–51**, 250*m*
Saratoga, Second (Bemis Heights) **251–53**, 252*m*
Saskatchewan River 16
Sassacus 188
Sauk (Sac) 14–15
Saukenuk 14
Saunders, Charles 226
Savage, H.M.S., U.S.S. *Congress* v. 73
Savage's Station (Allen's Farm, Peach Orchard) **253–54**
Savannah (December 29, 1778) **254**
Savannah (October 9, 1779) **254–55**
Savannah, Ga. 59
Savannah River 254, 255
Sayler's Creek (Sailor's Creek) 90, **256**
Schenck, Robert C. 81
  McDowell 175
Schoepf, Albin 177
Schofield, John M.
  Atlanta 10
  Franklin 118–19
School House Ridge 143
Schuyler, Philip 52, 227
  Fort Stanwix 110
  St. John's 186, 245
  Saratoga, First 250
Scots Glengarries 101
Scott, Charles 89
Scott, Hercules 98, 99
  Lundy's Lane 172
Scott, William Henry 244
Scott, Winfield 35, 67, 70, 71, 179, 180
  Bad Axe River 14–15
  Cerro Gordo 50, 51
  Chapultepec 56, 57, 223
  Chippewa 68, 69
  Contreras 74–75
  Fort George 101
  Fort Sumter 111

Lundy's Lane 171, 172
Queenston 229
Veracruz 283–84
Scurry, William 132
Second Battalion 31
Second Carolina Regiment 58
Second Cavalry 125
Second Continental Congress 39, 245
Second Corps 172, 183, 199, 261
Second Country Regiment 17
Second Division 50
Second Indiana 33
Second New Hampshire 147, 197
Secord, Laura 18, 19
Sedgwick, John
    Chancellorsville 55
    Franklin's Crossing 119
    Spotsylvania 261
Seguín, Juan Nepomuceno 5
Selma 178, 179
Seminole 82
    Lake Okeechobee 161–62
Semmes, Raphael 57
Seneca 300 *see also* Iroquois
Seven Days Battles 47, 124, 125, 253, 292
    Gaines's Mill 124–25
    Garnett's and Golding's Farm 125–26
    Malvern Hill 174
    Mechanicsville 175–76
    Oak Grove 201
    Savage's Station 253–54
    White Oak Swamp 292
Seven Pines (Fair Oaks) **88–89**
Seventeenth Dragoons 78, 290
Seventeenth Regiment 230, 267
Seventh Cavalry
    Little Bighorn 165–67, 236, 260
    Washita 290
    Wounded Knee 299
Seventh Country Regiment 17
Seventh Infantry 23
Seventh Iowa Cavalry 152
Seventh Regiment of Foot 52
Seventy-first Highlanders 31, 44, 78, 254, 255, 266, 267, 302

Seventy-seventh Highlanders 41
Sevier, John 156
Seymour, Truman 202
Shannon, H.M.S., U.S.S. *Chesapeake* v. **64**
Sharpsburg (Antietam) **7–9**, 8*m*, 143
Sharpsburg, Md. 79, 143
Shaw, Robert Gould 116
Shawnee 41, 141, 142, 243
    Point Pleasant 217
Shawnee Prophet (Tenskwatawa) 275
Shays, Daniel 263–64
Shays's Rebellion 263, 264
Sheaffe, Roger H. 229
Shee Atika 259
Shelby, Isaac
    King's Mountain 155–56
    Thames 273
Shenandoah Valley 46–47, 80, 92, 122, 154, 172, 174, 191, 192, 219, 220, 291, 296, 297
Shepard, William 263
Sherburne, Henry 48
Sheridan, Philip H. 19, 46–47, 93, 154, 172, 291
    Cedar Creek 46–47
    Cold Harbor 72
    Fisher's Hill 92
    Perryville 212
    Petersburg 213
    Sayler's Creek 256
    Stones River 264
    Summit Springs 268
    Trevilian Station 278
    Washita 289–90
    Winchester, Third 297–98
    Yellow Tavern 301–2
Sheridan's Campaign 290
Sheridan's Ride 47
Sherman, Thomas W. 34, 220
Sherman, William Tecumseh 6, 32, 53, 110, 118, 202
    Atlanta 10, 11
    Bentonville 21, 22
    Chattanooga 61, 62
    Chickasaw Bluffs 67
    Shiloh 257
    Tupelo 279–80
    Vicksburg 285
Shields, James 57, 80
    Cerro Gordo 51
    Churubusco 70

Kernstown, First 153
    Port Republic 219, 220
Shiloh (Pittsburgh Landing) **257–59**, 258*m*
ship of the line 311*g*
Shirley, William 94
    Louisbourg 169–70
Shoshone 17–18, 235
Shreveport, La. 216
Sibley, Henry H.
    Glorieta Pass 131
    Killdeer Mountain 155
    Wood Lake 298
Sickles, Daniel 130
siege 59, 118, 219, 255, 285, 302, 311*g*
Sigel, Franz
    New Market 191–92
    Pea Ridge 209
    Wilson's Creek 295
Silliman, Gold Selleck 83
Simcoe, John
    Petersburg 212
    Quintan's Bridge 230
    Spencer's Tavern 261
Sinclair, Arthur 173
Sioux 10, 91, 109, 235
    Julesburg 152
    Killdeer Mountain 155
    Wood Lake 298
    Wounded Knee 299
Sir Sidney Smith 238
Si Tanka (Big Foot) 299
Sitka **259–60**
Sitting Bull (Tatanka Yotanka) 17, 23, 165, 167, 235–36, 260, 299
Six Mile House (Globe Tavern), Battle of **131**
Sixth Corps 92, 119
Sixth Pennsylvania Cavalry 29
Sixty-fourth Regiment 208
Sixty-third Regiment 25, 91, 134
skirmish 311*g*
Slack, James R. 218
Slaughter's Field 218
slavery 9
Slim Buttes **260**
Slocum, Henry 21, 22
Slocum, Herbert J. 72, 73
Slough, John P. 131, 132
Small, William F. 223–24
Smith, Alexander 229
Smith, Andrew Jackson 24
    Nashville 190
    Tupelo 280

Smith, Charles F.
    Fort Donelson 98
    Resaca de la Palma 232
Smith, Edmund Kirby 233, 234
Smith, Francis 163, 164
Smith, G. W. 88
Smith, J. C. 254
Smith, James M. 70
Smith, John E. 232
Smith, Kirby 211
Smith, Martin 67
Smith, Persifor 57, 70
    Contreras 75
Smith, Samuel
    Fort McHenry 102, 103
    Fort Mifflin 104
Smith, William F. "Baldy"
    Drewry's Bluff 83, 84
    Petersburg 213
    Williamsburg 294
Smith, William "Sooey" 202
Soleby 58
South Carolina 12
    Beaufort 18
    Black Mingo Creek 24–25
    Blackstocks 25
    Blue Savannah 28
    Camden 43–45, 43*m*, 139
    Charleston 57–60, 290
    Combahee Ferry 73
    U.S.S. *Congress* v. H.M.S. *Savage* 73
    Cowpens 77–78, 77*m*, 136
    Eutaw Springs 86–87, 87*m*
    Fishdam Ford 91–92
    Fort Motte 105
    Fort Sumter 22, 111–12
    Fort Wagner 115–16
    Fort Watson 117
    Great Savannah 134
    Hanging Rock 139–40, 235
    Hobkirk's Hill 145
    King's Mountain 155–57, 156*m*
    Lenud's Ferry 60, 162–63
    Monck's Corner 60, 180
    Ninety Six 197–98
    Parker's Ferry 207–8
    Port Royal Sound 220–21
    Quinby Bridge 230

Rocky Mount 139, 235
Stono Ferry 266
Waxhaws 156, 290–91
Williamson's Plantation 295
South Carolina Rangers 139
South Dakota 235
Slim Buttes 260
Wounded Knee 299
South Mountain 143
South Mountain 79, **260–61**
Southside Railroad 90, 93
Spencer, Joseph 140
Spencer's Tavern **261**
Spotsylvania **261–62**, 262*m*
Springfield **262–63**
Springfield Arsenal **263–64**
Spring Hill 255
Stagg, Peter 301
Stahel, Julius 81
Stamp Act 4
Stand Watie (Degataga) 209
Stansbury, Tobias 26
Stanton, Edwin M. 47
Stark, John
Bennington 20–21
Bunker Hill 40
Star of the West 111
"Star-Spangled Banner, The" (Key) 103
Steedman, James B. 190
Stephen, Adam 30
Germantown 127
Stephens, Alexander 100
Sterling, Thomas
Billingsport 24
Fort Washington 117
Steuart, George H. 80, 81
Steuben, Friedrich von
Monmouth 182, 183
Yorktown 302
Stevens, Edward 136
Stevens, Isaac 55–56
Stewart, A. P. 22
Stewart, Alexander 86, 87
Stirling, Charles 73
Stirling, William Alexander, Lord
Brandywine 30
Long Island 168
Monmouth 183
Paulus Hook 209
Stockade Redan 285
Stockton, Robert F.
Mesa 176
San Gabriel 245–46
Stone, Charles P. 15

Stone Bridge 35
Stoneman, George 294
Stones River (Murfreesboro) **264–65**, 265*m*
Stono Ferry **266**
Stony Creek 101, **266–67**
Stony Point **267**
Stony Ridge 37
Stopford, Major 52
Strasburg, Va. 80, 92, 122, 296
Stricker, John 102–3
strike colors 311*g*
Strong, George C. 115, 116
Stonghold **267–68**
Stuart, J. E. B. "Jeb" 128
Brandy Station 29
Williamsburg 294
Yellow Tavern 301–2
Sturgis, Samuel S.
Brice's Cross Roads 32
South Mountain 260
Sudley Springs 35
Suffren, Pierre de 196
suicide squads (forlone hopes) 198, 209, 235, 267, 304, 307*g*
Sullivan, John
Brandywine 30
Germantown 126
Long Island 168
Newport 196
Newtown 197
Three Rivers 274
Trenton 277
Sully, Alfred 155
Summit Springs **268**
Sumner, Edwin V. "Bull"
Antietam 9
Fair Oaks 88
Fredericksburg 119, 121
Malvern Hill 174
Molino del Rey 179
Savage's Station 253
Sumter, Thomas 25
Fishdam Ford 91–92
Fishing Creek 92, 134
Hanging Rock 139–40, 235
Quinby Bridge 230
Rocky Mount 235
Williamson's Plantation 295
Susquehannok 151
Sutherland, William 208, 209
swivel gun 311*g*
Syren 58

T
Tah-gah-jute (Mingo John) 217
Takelma 24
Taliaferro, William B.
Fort Wagner 115–16
McDowell 175
Talladega **269–70**
Tallasahatchee 269, **270**
Tall Bull (Hotoakhihoosis) 19, 268
Tampa Bay 82
Tampico 49
Tarleton, Banastre
Blackstocks 25
Charleston 59–60
Cowpens 77, 78
Fishing Creek 92
Gloucester 132–33
Green Spring 135
Guilford Courthouse 137
Hanging Rock 139
Haw River 144
Lenud's Ferry 162–63
Monck's Corner 180
Tarrant's Tavern 270
Wahab's Plantation 289
Waxhaws 156, 290–91
Williamson's Plantation 295
Yorktown 302
Tarrant's Tavern **270**
Ta-sunko-witko (Tashunka Witco; Crazy Horse) 165, 167
Fetterman Fight 91
Rosebud Creek 235–36
Slim Buttes 260
Wolf Mountain 298
Tatanka Yotanka (Sitting Bull) 17, 23, 165, 167, 235–36, 260, 299
Tattnall, Josiah 220, 284
Taylor, Richard 81
Front Royal 122
Irish Bend 148
Pleasant Hill Landing 216, 217
Port Republic 219–20
Sabine Crossroads 237
Winchester, First 296
Taylor, Thomas 230
Taylor, Zachary 14, 46, 216, 283
Buena Vista 33, 34
Lake Okeechobee 161–62
Monterrey 185, 186

Palo Alto 205–6, 232
Resaca de la Palma 232, 233
Taylor's Bridge (North Anna River), Battle of **199–200**
Tecumseh (Tekamthi) 14, 105
Thames 273–74
Tippecanoe 275, 276
Tecumseh 178–79
Tennessee 6, 31–32, 177, 202
Chattanooga 61–63, 62*m*, 66
Fort Donelson 97–98, 97*m*, 101
Fort Henry 97, 101–2
Fort Pillow 107–8
Franklin 118–19
Island Number 10 149
Knoxville 157–58
Memphis 176
Nashville 190–91
Parker's Cross Roads 207
Shiloh 257–59, 258*m*
Stones River 264–65, 265*m*
Tennessee 178, 179
Tennessee River 97
Tenochtitlán **270–73**
Tenochtitlán, Mexico 49, 50, 203, 276
Tenskwatawa (Shawnee Prophet) 275
Tenth Cavalry 19
Tenth Indiana 177
Tenth Military District 25
Tenth Ohio 177
Ternay, Charles, chevalier de 65
Terrés, Andrés 57
Terret, George H. 57
Terrible 65
Terry, Alfred H.
Fort Fisher 99
Little Bighorn 165
Terry's Expedition (Fort Fisher) **99–100**
Teton Lakota 235, 260
Ash Hollow 10
Killdeer Mountain 155
Little Bighorn 165–67, 236
Texas
Adobe Walls 3–4
Alamo 5, 133, 246
Camp Texas 46, 205
Galveston 125
Goliad 133

Palo Alto 46, 205–6, 206*m*, 232
Resaca de la Palma 232–33
Sabine Pass 238
San Jacinto 33, 133, 246, 247*m*
Thames (Moraviantown) **273–74**
Thayendanegea (Joseph Brant) 167
Cherry Valley 63, 64
Minisink 178
Newtown 197
Oriskany 203
Queenston 229
Thayer, Simeon 104
Third Brigade 67–68
Third Corps 32
Third Infantry 70
Third Louisiana Native Guard 219
Third New Jersey Regiment 263
Third New York Regiment 110
Third Virginia Regiment 290
Thirteenth Cavalry 72, 208
Thirteenth Infantry 229
Thirty-ninth Infantry Regiment 146
Thomas, George H. 34, 66
Atlanta 10
Chattanooga 61, 62
Mill Springs 177, 178
Nashville 190–91
Perryville 212
Stones River 264
Thompson, William 274
Thornburg, Thomas 177
Thornton, William 194
Three Rivers (Trois Rivières) **274**
Throg's Neck (Throg's Point) **274–75**
Throg's Neck, N.Y. 211
Thunderer 58, 282
Ticonderoga 216
Tilghman, Lloyd 101
Tippecanoe 273, **275–76**, 275*m*
Tishomingo Creek (Brice's Cross Roads) **31–32**, 32*m*
Tiverton 196
Tiyanoga (Chief Hendrick) 161
Tlatelolco 272

Tlaxcala **276–77**
Tlingit 259
tobacco 150
Tohopeka 146
Tompkins, Frank 72–73, 208
Toohoolhoolzote 17, 23
Toombs, Robert 126
Torbert, Alfred
Trevilian Station 278
Winchester, Third 297
torpedoes 178, 179, 311*g*
Torrejón, Anastasio 57
Palo Alto 205, 206
Resaca de la Palma 232
Tory Redoubt 21
Totten, George M. 284
Totten, Joseph G. 229
Tourtelotte, John F. 6
Townshend Acts 4
Tracy, Edward D. 218
Travis, Lieutenant 134
Travis, William B. 5
Treaty of Fort Stanwix 217
Treaty of Guadelupe Hidalgo 223
Treaty of Ghent 192
Trenton 222, **277–78**
Trevilian Station **278**
Trías, Angel 239, 240
Trimble, Isaac R.
Cross Keys 80
Gettysburg 130
La Trinidad 45–46
Trois Rivières (Three Rivers) **274**
troop 311*g*
Trotter, James 141
Trousdale, William B. 56
Truby, Christopher 141
Trumbull, U.S.S., H.M.S. *Iris* v. **279**
Trumbull, U.S.S., *Watt* v. **279**
Tryon, William 4, 5, 83
Tryon County, N.Y. 178
Tupelo (Harrisburg) **279–80**
Turnbull, George 235
Turner, Zephaniah 122, 123
Turner's Gap 79, 260
Tusten, Benjamin 178
Tututni 24
Twelfth Georgia 122, 175
Twentieth Maine 130
Twiggs, David E. 56, 70
Contreras 75
Twiggs, Levi 50, 51
Chapultepec 56–57

Tyler, Bezaleel 178
Tyler, Daniel 35
Tyler, Erastus B.
Monocacy 184
Port Republic 219
Tyler, U.S.S. 144
Tzompachtepetl 277

U

Uncas 188
Underhill, John 188
Union Church (Cross Keys) **80–81**, 219
Urrea, José 133
Ute 176–77

V

Valcour Island **282–83**, 283*m*
Valencia, Gabriel 70
Contreras 74–75
Van Buskirk, Abraham 191
Paulus Hook 208, 209
Van Dorn, Earl
Corinth 76
Holly Springs 145–46
Pea Ridge 209–10
Rush Springs 236
Van Rensselaer, Henry 94
Van Rensselaer, Robert
Fort Keyser 102
Klock's Field 157
Van Rensselaer, Solomon 229
Van Rensselaer, Stephen 228–29
Van Shaick's Mill 21
Varnum, William 196
Vásquez, Ciriaco 50, 51
Velázquez, Diego 49, 162, 221
Velez, Francisco 284
Veracruz 45, 50, 224, **283–85**
Vermont
Bennington 20–21, 20*m*
Hubbardton 147
Verplank's Point 267
Vicksburg 66, 67, 144, 202, 222, **285–87**, 286*m*
Vicksburg, Miss. 22–23, 52, 53, 145, 207, 217–18, 219, 232
Villa, Francisco "Pancho" 48, 73
Agua Prieta 4
Celaya 49, 72
Columbus 72–73, 208

Vincennes **287–88**
Vincent, John
Fort George 101
Stony Creek 266
Virginia 128, 136, 213, 287
Ball's Bluff 15
Big Bethel 22
Brandy Station 29
Bristoe Station 32–33
Bull Run, First 35–37, 36*m*, 38
Bull Run, Second 37–38, 38*m*, 55, 56
Cedar Creek 46–47
Cedar Mountain 47–48
Chancellorsville 54–55, 54*m*
Chantilly 38, 55–56, 55*m*
Chesapeake Capes 65
Cloyd's Mountain 71
Cold Harbor 71–72, 72*m*, 213
The Crater 79–80
Cross Keys 80–81, 219
Drewry's Bluff 83–84
Fair Oaks 88–89
Farmville and Highbridge 90–91
Fisher's Hill 47, 92
Five Forks 93
Fort Stedman 110, 213
Franklin's Crossing 119
Fredericksburg 54, 55, 119–21, 120*m*
Front Royal 122–23, 296
Gaines's Mill 124–25
Garnett's and Golding's Farm 125–26
Globe Tavern 131
Gloucester 132–33
Great Bridge 133–34
Green Spring 135–36
Gwynn Island 137–38
Hanover Courthouse 140
Harpers Ferry 7, 79, 142–43
Jamestown 150–51
Kernstown 153–54, 297
Lynchburg 172
Malvern Hill 174
McDowell 122, 174–75
Mechanicsville 124, 175–76
U.S.S. *Monitor* v. C.S.S. *Virginia* 180–81

New Market 191–92
North Anna River
  199–200
Oak Grove 201
Petersburg 131, 212–13
Port Republic 219–20
Savage's Station 253–54
Sayler's Creek 90, 256
Spencer's Tavern 261
Spotsylvania 261–62,
  262m
Trevilian Station 278
Waynesboro 291
White Oak Swamp 292
Wilderness 55, 261,
  293–94
Williamsburg 294–95
Winchester, First 296
Winchester, Second
  296–97
Winchester, Third
  297–98
Yellow Tavern 301–2
Yorktown 65, 73, 132,
  302–4, 303m
Virginia, C.S.S., U.S.S.
  Monitor v. (*Monitor* v.
  Merrimack) **180–81**
Virginia and Tennessee
  Railroad 71
Virginia Cavalry 122
Virginia Continentals 136,
  145
Virginia Military Institute
  (VMI) 192
volley 311*g*
Voltigeur Regiment 180
volunteers 311*g*
Volunteers of Ireland 44
Von Donop, Carl Emil
  103, 104

W

Wadsworth, James 157
Wadsworth, William 229
Wahab's Plantation, Battle
  of **289**
Wahunsonacock (Powhatan)
  150–51
Wahwookya Wasaaw (Poker
  Joe) 17, 23
Wales, Richard H. 210
Walke, Henry 149
Walker, John G.
  Harpers Ferry 143
  Pleasant Hill Landing
    217
  Sabine Crossroads 237
Walker, Samuel H. 46

Wallace, Lew
  Fort Donelson 98
  Monocacy 183–84
  Shiloh 257
Wallace, W.H.L. 257
Walloomsac River 21
Wampanoag 26, 134
Ward, Artemus 39, 40
Ward, Thomas 39
Warner, Seth 21
  Hubbardton 147
War of Reform 224
Warren, Gouverneur K.
  Five Forks 93
  Gaines's Mill 124
  Gettysburg 130
  Globe Tavern 131
  North Anna River 199
Warren, Joseph 39, 40
Warrington, Lewis 210
Warrior 15
Washington, D.C. 25, 26,
  32, 55, 153, 154, 172,
  183, 184, 194, 260
Washington, George 28,
  39, 59, 65, 73, 75–76,
  102, 103, 113, 116, 117,
  144, 145, 157, 196–97,
  207, 230, 274
  army reorganization and
    89
  Brandywine 30–31
  Fort Necessity 106
  Germantown 126, 128
  Harlem Heights
    140–41, 210–11, 292
  Harmar's Defeat 141,
    242
  Long Island 168
  Monmouth 181–83
  Monongahela 184–85
  Paulus Hook 208
  Princeton 222–23
  Quebec 228
  Springfield 263
  Stony Point 267
  Trenton 222, 277–78
  Whitemarsh 293
  White Plains 292, 293
  Yorktown 302
Washington, J. A. 63
Washington, John M. 34
Washington, William
  Cowpens 77, 78
  Eutaw Springs 86, 87
  Guilford Courthouse
    136, 137
  Hobkirk's Hill 145
  Lenud's Ferry 162, 163

Washita **289–90**
Wateree River 92
Watt, U.S.S. *Trumbull* v.
  279
Waxhaws 156, **290–91**
Wayne, Anthony 275
  Brandywine 30
  Bull's Ferry 39
  Fallen Timbers 89–90
  Germantown 126, 127
  Green Spring 135–36
  Monmouth 183
  Paoli 207
  Stony Point 267
  Three Rivers 274
Waynesboro **291**
Weatherford, William
  (Lamochatte; Red Eagle)
  105, 146, 269
weather gage 311*g*
Webster, James 44
  Charlotte 60
  Guilford Courthouse
    137
  Monck's Corner 180
  Wetzell's Ford 291
Weedon, George 132
Weightman, Richard H.
  240
Wemyss, James 91–92
West, Rebecca 297
West Virginia
  Cheat Mountain 63
  Falling Waters 90
  Philippi 22, 213–14
  Point Pleasant 217
  Rich Mountain 233
Wetherell, Colonel 242
Wethersfield 188
Wetzell's Ford **291**
Weypapiersenwah (Blue
  Jacket) 89
Wharton, Gabriel C. 154
Wheaton, Frank 268
Wheeler, Joseph 264
Wheldon Railroad (Globe
  Tavern) **131**
White, Anthony 162, 163
White Bird (Penpenhihi)
  17
White Horse 19
White House 194
White Marsh **293**
White Oak Swamp
  (Glendale) **292**
White Plains **292–93**
White River Agency 177
White Sticks 85, 86, 105,
  146, 269, 270

Whiting, William H. C.
  100
Whitmore, Edward 170
Whitside, Samuel 299
Wichita expedition 236
Wild Cat (Coachoochee)
  162
Wilder, John T. 187–88
Wilderness 55, 261,
  293–94
Wilkinson, James 69
  Chateaugay 60–61
Willet, Marinus
  Fort Stanwix 110
  Johnstown 152
Williams, A. T. H. 16
Williams, Ephraim 161
Williams, James 156
Williams, Otho
  Camden 44
  Guilford Courthouse
    136
  Hobkirk's Hill 145
  Wetzell's Ford 291
Williams, Thomas 16
Williamsburg **294–95**
Williamson's Plantation **295**
Williamsport, Md. 90
Wilmington, N.C. 99, 100,
  131
Wilson, James 297
Wilson, Lewis D. 223
Wilson, Woodrow 4, 73,
  208
Wilson's Creek (Oak Hill)
  295–96
Winchester First **296**
Winchester, James 121–22
Winchester Second **296–97**
Winchester Third (Opequon
  Creek) **297–98**
Winchester, Va. 92, 122,
  153, 154
Winder, Charles 219, 220
Winder, William 25, 26
  Stony Creek 266
Winnebago 178
Winslow, John 94
Winslow, Josiah 135
Winston, Joseph 156
Winthrop, Theodore 22
Wirasuap (Bear Hunter)
  17, 18
Wisconsin 14–15
Wise, Henry 234, 235
Wolfe 238
Wolfe, James
  Louisbourg 170
  Quebec 226–27, 228

Wolf Mountain **298**
Wood, Thomas J. 190
Woodford, William 134
Wood Lake (Lone Tree
Lake) **298**
Woods, Thomas 66
Wool, John 229
Wool, John E. 24, 33, 239
Wooster, David 83
Woquini (Roman Nose)
19
Worden, John Lorimer
181
works 311g
World War I 49, 285

Worth, William J. 56, 70
Cerro Gordo 51
Chapultepec 57
Molino del Rey 179
Monterrey 185, 186
Veracruz 284
Wounded Knee **299**
Wright, Horatio G. 47
Kernstown, Second 154
Sayler's Creek 256
Winchester, Third 297
Wright, James 255
Wyandot 41, 141, 142,
169, 217, 243, 249
Wyllys, John 142

Wyndham, Percy 29
Wynepuechsika (Cornstalk)
217
Wyoming
Fetterman Fight 91
Rosebud Creek 165,
235–36
Wyoming Valley 64, **299–300**

X
Xicotencatl the Younger 276

Y
Yakama 24
Yazoo River 67

Yell, Archibald 33
Yellow Tavern **301–2**
Yeo, James Lucas 238, 239
Yorktown 65, 73, **302–4**,
303m
Yorktown, Va. 132
Yucatán 53, 162, 221, 276

Z
Zapata, Emiliano 48, 49
Zaragoza, Ignacio 224
Zollicoffer, Felix 177
Zouaves 22, 124
Zúñiga y Cerda, Joseph de
240